BEFORE JUTLAND

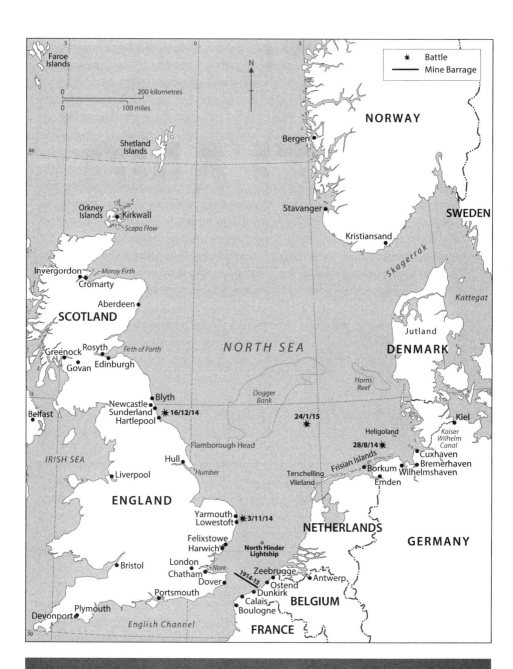

FRONTISPIECE. **North Sea**

BEFORE JUTLAND

THE NAVAL WAR IN NORTHERN EUROPEAN WATERS, AUGUST 1914–FEBRUARY 1915

JAMES GOLDRICK

Naval Institute Press
Annapolis, Maryland

This book has been brought to publication with
the generous assistance of Marguerite and Gerry Lenfest.

Naval Institute Press
291 Wood Road
Annapolis, MD 21402

Library of Congress Cataloging-in-Publication Data

Goldrick, James.

Before Jutland : the naval war in Northern European waters, August 1914–February 1915 / James Goldrick.

pages cm

Includes bibliographical references and index.

ISBN 978-1-59114-349-9 (alk. paper) — ISBN 978-1-61251-881-7 (ebook) 1. World War, 1914–1918—Naval operations. 2. World War, 1914–1918—Campaigns—North Sea. I. Title.

D581.G629 2015

940.4'54—dc23

2015000477

♾ Print editions meet the requirements of ANSI/NISO z39.48-1992 (Permanence of Paper). Printed in the United States of America.

23 22 21 20 19 18 17 16 15   9 8 7 6 5 4 3 2 1
First printing

All maps are provided by the author.

CONTENTS

PHOTOS AND MAPS

Photos

MAPS

TABLE OF EQUIVALENTS

GUNS

METRIC	BRITISH
75-mm	3-inch
88-mm	3.4-inch
10.5-cm	4.1-inch
15-cm	5.9-inch
21-cm	8.2-inch
28-cm	11-inch
30.5-cm	12-inch
38-cm	15-inch

TORPEDOES

METRIC	BRITISH
45-cm	17.7-inch
45.7-cm	18-inch
50-cm	19.7-inch
53.3-cm	21-inch

DISTANCES

All distances in this book are given in nautical miles giving the old Admiralty mile as the reference for the nautical mile. This is one minute of arc subtended along a great circle. It is some 4 feet or 1.248 meters longer than the current nautical mile:

1 nautical mile = 1,853.2 meters = 6,080 feet

1 knot = 1 nautical mile per hour

COMPASS

360 degrees in a circle

32 points in a circle

1 point = 11 1/4 degrees

8 points = 90 degrees

16 points = 180 degrees (reversal of course)

ACKNOWLEDGMENTS

I AM VERY GRATEFUL TO DAVID STEVENS—NOT ONLY FOR HIS CONSTANT friendship, but also for all the help and advice he has given me, including the benefit of his own extensive research into the navies of the Great War. I am also grateful to my friends on the staff of the Sea Power Centre–Australia and to Chris Dawkins and the splendid staff of the library of the Australian Defence Force Academy for all their assistance with my research. Similar thanks go to Stephen Prince and the equally splendid staff of the Royal Navy's Historical Branch at Portsmouth, as well as the helpful staffs of Churchill College Archives, the Royal Naval Museum Library, the Liddell Hart Centre, the Liddle Archive at the University of Leeds, the UK National Archives, the National Maritime Museum, and the Imperial War Museum.

Although I listed acknowledgments to many old friends in the first edition of this study, I want to recognize a continuing debt to Vice Admiral Peter Jones, Professors Jon Sumida and Jack Sweetman, and to the late Captain Stephen Roskill and the late Lieutenant Commander Patrick Beesly, all of whom gave me much help and counsel. Valuable advice for the new edition as well as the old has come from Commander George Nekrasov (and Christine Nekrasov's original translations of German material have again proved vital) and Commander James McCoy. Dr. Nicholas Rodger, to whom I also owe much, read parts of the manuscript and gave me good advice, as did Dr. Norman Friedman. Dr. Michael Epkenhans assisted me with my inquiries about certain aspects of German operations and very kindly consented to my use of quotations from some of his own scholarly—and extremely important—work on the Imperial German Navy. Keith Mitchell kindly drew new charts of the North Sea and the Baltic. Dr. Nicholas Lambert gave me the benefit of his reflections on many issues. Steven Firth, as ever, contributed many insights.

Grateful acknowledgment is made to the following authors, literary estates, and publishers for permission to quote from the following works in the first edition of this book and that remain in the text: the literary estate of Admiral Sir Henry Pelly and Chatto & Windus Ltd. for *300,000 Sea Miles*; the literary estate of Brigadier C. F. Aspinall-Oglander and The Hogarth Press for *Roger Keyes*; the late Misses King-Hall and Faber & Faber Ltd. for *My Naval Life 1906–1929*; the late Misses King-Hall and Methuen & Co Ltd. for *A Naval Lieutenant 1914–1918*; Mr. Winston Churchill, the Hamlyn Publishing Group Ltd., and Charles Scribner & Sons for *The World Crisis;* the Hutchinson Publishing Group for *Admiral von Hipper;* the late Mrs. A. J. Marder and Jonathan Cape for *Portrait of an Admiral* and *Fear God and Dread Nought*; the late Vice Admiral Sir Peter Gretton and Cassell Ltd. for *Former Naval Person*; Cassell Ltd. for *With the Battle Cruisers* and *Germany's High Sea Fleet in the World War*; the literary estate of Rear Admiral W. S. Chalmers and Hodder & Stoughton Ltd. for *Max Horton and the Western Approaches*; the literary estate of Rear Admiral W. S. Chalmers and A. P. Watt Ltd. for *The Life and Letters of David Earl Beatty*; the literary estate of Captain Taprell Dorling and A. P. Watt Ltd. for *Swept Channels* and *Endless Story*; MacDonald & Co. for *The Kaiser and His Court*; Sir Reginald Tyrwhitt; the late Professor A. Temple Patterson and MacDonald & Co. for *Tyrwhitt of the Harwich Force*; the late second Lord Chatfield for *The Navy and Defence*; and the literary estate of Admiral Sir Lewis Bayly and Harrap Ltd. for *Pull Together*.

Among quoted works in copyright in the new edition, I am grateful to the Lieutenant Commanders Phillip and Mark Bush (sons of the late Captain Eric Bush) and Allen & Unwin for *Bless Our Ship*; and to Conway Maritime Press for *Scrimgeour's Small Scribbling Diary*. For those whose literary heirs and original publishers I have been unable to trace, may I here record my acknowledgments.

I am grateful to the literary executors of the estates concerned for permission to quote from the papers of William Clarke and Shane Leslie, Lieutenant Commander G. C. Harper, Commanders Colin Buist and Fraser MacLiesh; Captain John Creswell; Rear Admirals Tufton Beamish and Horace Hood; Vice Admiral Sir Lennon Goldsmith; Admirals Sir Charles Daniel, John Godfrey, and Sir Reginald Plunkett-Ernle-Erle-Drax; and Admiral of the Fleet Sir Doveton Sturdee, housed in Churchill College Archives.

I am grateful to the literary estates concerned for permission to quote from the papers of Vice Admirals H. T. Baillie-Grohman and K. G. B. Dewar, Admirals Sir Barry Domvile, Sir Alexander Duff, Sir Bertram Ramsay, Sir Herbert Richmond, and Sir William Tennant, and Admirals of the Fleet Earl Beatty and Sir Henry Oliver, housed in the National Maritime Museum; to the Trustees of the Imperial War Museum and the literary estates concerned for the papers of Erskine Childers, Midshipman H. W. Williams, Commanders C. H. Drage and B. W. L. Owen, Captains Sir Philip Bowyer-Smyth and C. J. Wintour, Rear Admiral H. E. C. Blagrove, Vice Admiral Sir Cecil Talbot, Admirals Trevylyan Napier and Philip Dumas, and Admiral of the Fleet Sir Dudley Pound; to the Archivist of the National Museum of the Royal Navy for the papers of Able Seaman Chesterton, Lieutenant T. A. Voysey, Commander A. B. Downes, and Paymaster Captain Guy Ward-Smith; and to the Liddell Hart Centre at King's College London for the papers of Admiral Bernard Currey. The late Mrs. Oswald Frewen kindly gave me permission to quote from the diaries of Captain Oswald Frewen. Where I have been unable to trace the literary estates concerned, I here record my acknowledgments.

My particular thanks go to the present editor of the *Naval Review*, Vice Admiral Sir Jeremy Blackham, for the permission to cite additional articles from the *Naval Review*, as well as to his predecessors, the late Rear Admiral J. R. D. Nunn and Rear Admiral Richard Hill, for permissions in the first edition. To all of them, as well as the late Vice Admiral Sir Ian McGeoch, go my thanks for their advice as well as for their friendship over many years.

Notwithstanding my debt to so many, I emphasize that the judgments and interpretations in the text are mine alone, as is the responsibility for any errors.

.

ABBREVIATIONS

BEF	British Expeditionary Force
CAPTAIN (D)	captain commanding a destroyer flotilla
C-IN-C	commander-in-chief
COMMODORE (S)	commodore commanding submarines
COMMODORE (T)	commodore commanding torpedo craft
GHQ	General Headquarters (German army)
HMAS	His Majesty's Australian Ship
HMS	His Majesty's Ship
HVB	*Handelsverkehrbuch*
NID	Naval Intelligence Division
SKM	*Signalbuch der Kaiserlichen Marine*
SMS	His Majesty's Ship (German)
VB	*Verkehrsbuch*

INTRODUCTION

THIS BOOK STARTED IN 1971 WHEN MY FATHER NOTICED A COLLECTION of elderly Admiralty books at HMAS *Encounter* in Port Adelaide. They proved to be the *Naval Staff Monographs (Historical),* the Royal Navy's (RN's) internal history of the First World War. The last volume, covering British home waters from May to July 1917, was issued in August 1939. How they got into the office of the Naval Officer in Charge South Australia was not clear. Presumably they were landed early in the Second World War, but from which ship is unknown. The books were on no one's charge and in danger of unthinking disposal. Knowing my fascination for naval history, my father gave them to me. I soon realized that the *Monographs* were a comprehensive narrative of the war at sea. Although I was old enough to realize that much was left unsaid, with facts left to speak for themselves, I was also old enough to realize why this would be. They have never had a wide audience and, unlike some of the equivalent *Staff Histories* of the Second World War, have not been published.[1]

In 1978 the last year of my undergraduate degree lay ahead and I had very little to do, having overloaded credits in my first two years. During a visit to Britain I met Stephen Roskill who suggested strongly that, since I would be at sea and fully occupied for many years afterward, I do something more than a few hours of lectures and tutorials each week. The idea of studying the opening of the Great War in the North Sea came from that conversation. Stephen believed that the operations of the First World War were not well understood and that it was time that they were reexamined.

The *Monographs* became a fundamental source. Stephen shared my opinion of them, although he confirmed that any criticism tended to be indirect, with the notable exception of the *Naval Staff Appreciation* of Jutland, a volume not in my collection, for reasons that explained why the *Monographs* were so restrained in their commentary. Written after the official history *Naval Operations,* they had the benefit of all the material collated for Julian Corbett and Henry Newbolt, plus other Admiralty files (some of which have since been weeded), as well as *Der Krieg zur See* and increasing numbers of first-hand accounts in both English and

German. Throughout 1978 I worked on early drafts. I went to sea in 1979. The end of that year offered an unexpected opportunity to qualify as a bridge watch-keeper on loan to the Royal Navy on fishery protection duties in the North Sea, based on Rosyth. Before joining my first British ship, I was able to take leave and conduct research in British archives. I also benefitted from the perspectives that Stephen Roskill could bring, as well as his criticism of parts of my draft. Operating in northern British waters soon began to open my eyes to the difficulty of what ships were trying to do in 1914: hard enough from the comfort of an enclosed bridge, with radar and (usually) radio navigation aids. As a result, I rewrote much of the original text. At the suggestion of Professor Jack Sweetman of the U.S. Naval Academy, I added more in the way of analysis and reflection.

After the 1984 publication of *The King's Ships Were at Sea: The War in the North Sea August 1914–February 1915*, three things happened. The first was that the products of an increasingly sophisticated approach to the history of the period before 1914 appeared—the work of trained historians, as well as experts in naval technology such as Norman Friedman. They tackled subjects critical to under-standing the operational record. Their works were based on much more compre-hensive and rigorous use of the archives than had before been possible. They were also marked by recognition of the complexity of the problems that navies faced in an era of extraordinary change.

Second, although I was deeply impressed by the quality of this new work, I began to develop an uncomfortable feeling that our operational knowledge of the war was being eroded over time. With the passing of the last veterans of that conflict we moved, in some ways, further away from understanding the opera-tional record than we were when I first started writing. There have been areas of illumination, such as Andrew Gordon's remarkable study of the Royal Navy's command culture, *The Rules of the Game,* as well as Nicholas Lambert's work on communications, command, and control, and Jon Sumida's on naval gunnery. Yet we no longer comprehend the way in which ships were worked and fought in 1914–18. Indeed, the public interest in the Nelsonic era and the combination of extensive research, historically informed fiction, and the operation of replicas, as well as continuing square-rigged sail training have meant that our knowledge of what was happening on board *Victory* and her sisters in 1805 is greater than it is for *Iron Duke* and the Grand Fleet in 1914.[2] The deficiency becomes even more apparent comparing naval operational history with that of land forces, particu-larly on the Western Front. While debates continue, there is now a body of work that has profoundly changed our view of the land war, dispelled the legends of "lions led by donkeys," and above all conveyed both the complexity of the military environment and the learning curve that all concerned needed to follow. For the war at sea, understanding of the conflict remains incomplete—and what there is, is "too much Jutland."

The third thing that happened after publication of my book in 1984 was that I grew up. The insights that I had gained around British waters were deepened by service around the world and increasingly responsible appointments. This included more time with the Royal Navy—ironically again based in Rosyth—which included deployments to the Falklands and the Baltic, as well as further operations in the North Sea, the Norwegian Sea, and the Atlantic. Later I commanded a patrol boat on surveillance work around the Australian coast and on deployments to Southeast Asia and the Southwest Pacific, as well as twice commanding the guided missile frigate *Sydney*. In 2002 I led an Australian task group in the Persian Gulf, which included tactical command of the multinational force enforcing UN sanctions on Iraq. From 2006 to 2008 I was Australia's Border Protection Commander, in operational control of the units responsible for national maritime security surveillance and enforcement.

These were parallel, but not entirely separate, developments. The more I listened to the historians and the more that I reflected on their analysis, the more I found that they were influencing my own approach to contemporary problem solving. The greater my sea command experience, the more I realized that effective doctrine and equally effective command and control arrangements were central to effective naval operations. I also came to understand that success in exploiting an emerging situation, however ambiguous it may appear at first, has a direct relationship with the effort that has been expended on considering the operational context beforehand. If there were a clear parallel between my experience and the events of a century ago, it was in the way in which communications and thus command and control systems were evolving at breakneck pace, in ways difficult enough to manage in their immediate effects, but that had unexpected (and yet to be understood) second- and third-order consequences for the conduct of operations at sea.

One insight in particular caused me to look at 1914 with different eyes. I am old enough not only to have been taught to navigate out of sight of land without artificial aids such as radio beacons and satellites, but also have had to do so for real, and for extended periods. I am also old enough to have had to operate computerized combat systems and data links between ships and aircraft so equipped before the era of the Global Positioning System (GPS). The difference that GPS makes in maintaining oneself in a shared frame of reference with other units is so profound that, when people talk of the revolution in military affairs in maritime warfare, I think first and primarily of GPS. It was comprehending just how important is this new shared certainty of position that made me realize not only how difficult must have been the problems that the navigators and commanders of 1914 faced in knowing where they were—and where others were in relation to them—but also how vital their solution was in determining operational success or failure.

All this changed my own outlook on the First World War, particularly its beginning when so much was new and unknown. We are inclined to consider what is known as the Fisher Era as a continuum from Admiral Fisher's accession as First Sea Lord in 1904. In reality, the pace of operational development not only accelerated, but also became truly multilane only after about 1909, just before the great reformer went into his first retirement. The pressures at all levels within navies were therefore intensifying in the years immediately before the outbreak of the war in ways that were not understood, nor necessarily recognized. In short, those involved were struggling to learn a new language of naval operations and warfare with an incomplete dictionary and very little grammar. As I came to understand what this really meant, what had seemed important to me no longer appeared so significant, but elements that I had barely recognized in my original analysis now looked fundamental to understanding what happened in 1914–15. I became less critical of some errors and more critical of others. I realized the truth of the comment in the *Narrative of the Battle of Jutland,* that the problem of determining just what did happen and why "is more of the nature of a complicated mosaic or puzzle picture whose composition requires a great deal of knowledge, skill and patience—how much can only be known by those who have tried it."[3]

This new edition is my effort to cast light on what happened in 1914–15. My focus on the first six months of the war is because very important events occurred during that time. Despite the loose ends that inevitably remain, important things can thus be said. As with its predecessor, this is an operational history that tries to balance coverage of the major incidents with treatment of the continuum of activity. It also seeks to provide the context within which the protagonists were actually working, without the application of excessive hindsight, because in 1914 so much was new and experimental. My focus, as will be clear, is primarily on the British, but both the Germans and the Russians are integral to the study. Indeed, my inclusion of the Baltic in this edition comes from a recognition that neither the British nor the Germans' North Sea activities can be fairly assessed without giving due weight to this theater of operations. My intent within the scene-setting chapters is not to attempt a complete survey of the events of the previous decade, but rather to situate each navy within the environment of 1914. In all, I try to show not only what happened, but also how the services evolved to meet the challenges that they faced, and then whether or not that evolution was successful.

Now read on.

The Beginning

THE WEATHER OF EARLY SUMMER 1914 WAS BRILLIANT, AS THOUGH IT mirrored the hope for peace in Europe. For the first time in many years the Balkans were quiet, while the armaments race that had gripped the world seemed to be slowing. In Germany it was Kiel Week, celebration of the young empire's maritime success. The annual festivities at Kiel had become ever more splendid as Germany's prosperity and its merchant and naval fleets grew apace. This year there was a special reason for rejoicing: the formal reopening of the Kiel Canal. It had been dredged and widened to be capable of taking the largest battleships directly between the Baltic and North Seas without the potentially dangerous passage around Denmark. At 1300 on 24 June the imperial yacht *Hohenzollern* cut the ribbon suspended across the entrance to the main locks. Laid out in review were the ships of the magnificent German High Sea Fleet. Alongside, present in a gesture of friendship, were four British battleships and three light cruisers.

King George V, Ajax, Audacious, and *Centurion* were among the most powerful dreadnoughts Britain possessed. The cruisers *Southampton, Birmingham,* and *Nottingham* were also the most modern of their type. They, like the German ships around them, were products of the sixteen-year-old naval race between Great Britain and Germany. Much had changed since the original canal opening in 1895, when a British squadron, also composed of the largest and most modern capital ships and cruisers, dominated a small German fleet, only just receiving its first ocean-going battleships. The concern then was not the Anglo-German relationship, but rather the latter's long rivalry with France, and the occasion a chance for the young Kaiser Wilhelm II to make gestures of peace to Germany's old enemy.[1] This 1914 rendezvous might help ease the dangerous rivalry with Britain.

The ships were *en fête.* Paintwork gleamed and brass shone. *Southampton's* carpenter's crew had even planed her teak decks to remove any spots. Many commented on the yacht-like appearance of the German warships' light grey hulls and upper works, compared to which the dark grey of the British looked somber indeed. Ironically, the lighter shade was much more suitable for North Sea conditions and the Royal Navy's ships would soon lose their peacetime livery. While sporting activities and visits were organized for the sailors, life for their officers was a constant dash between duty, official functions, and private fun "until about 6 a.m., when one returned . . . in a dilapidated condition and prepared for the next official function," as young Lieutenant Stephen King-Hall reported.[2] Despite this hectic round and fraternization, there were tensions. The officers attempted to see as much as they could of the other's navy. The Germans were disappointed that the British had covered all their gunnery instruments, and for their part could not help noticing British interest in the widened Kiel Canal and new submarines.[3]

There was another cause for comment. There was a second British squadron in the Baltic at the end of June. Four battle cruisers and two light cruisers under Rear Admiral Sir David Beatty visited Russian Reval (modern Tallinn) before moving on to Kronstadt, and, for the smaller ships, Saint Petersburg itself. There they were entertained by the local community and received by the tsar. The festivities culminated in a ball on board the rafted-together battle cruisers *Lion* and *New Zealand*, the latter chosen because her quarterdeck was "better for dancing on," while *Lion* functioned as the supper hall.[4] The significance of British squadron's visit was not missed in Germany. Newspapers remarked on its "ostentation" and the implicit message that the Royal Navy did not regard the Baltic as a "closed sea."[5]

The event was also important for the Imperial Russian Navy, emerging from the disaster of the war with Japan a decade before. The four battleships and five of the six armored cruisers that were the core of the Russian Baltic Fleet anchored alongside the British squadron at Reval. Several were elderly, and all were obsolescent, but they provided the foundation of the new force emerging in the eastern Baltic. The shape of things to come was *Novik,* which made a high-speed pass of the British ships at sea, first of a new class of fast and powerful destroyers. By the end of 1914 the Russian fleet would be joined by four new dreadnoughts. For many years the Germans had not had to consider the Russians as a serious naval threat on their eastern flank; this was about to change.

On 28 June festivities at Kiel ended abruptly. While on a tour of Bosnia, the heir to the Austro-Hungarian throne, Archduke Franz Ferdinand, and his wife were assassinated. The murders cast a pall of gloom over Kiel as the German court went into mourning. Few realized the political ramifications. It was another incident in the Balkans that might end in a minor local war, but could not possibly involve Britain or Germany. Grand Admiral Alfred von Tirpitz, the moving spirit behind Germany's naval expansion, suggested that the British cruisers return home through the Kiel Canal, an offer immediately accepted by their commodore, William Goodenough.[6] The parting was amicable. When on 30 June the British ships left Kiel, Sir George Warrender, the vice admiral commanding, signaled to the Imperial German Navy, "Friends in the past, friends forever."[7]

The assassinations were having their effect on the rigid European alliances. Austria-Hungary, with its own ethnic problems, felt threatened by the emergent

Slavic states in the Balkans and increasing Russian interest in the area. The Austro-Hungarians were especially suspicious of Serbia, from which they had been estranged since the Austro-Hungarian annexation of Bosnia-Herzegovina in 1908. Because of their Serb population, these provinces were a source of concern for Serbia, many of whose people wanted to wrest the provinces from Austria-Hungary. The assassin was a Bosnian Serb. Quick to see a conspiracy involving the Serbian government, for several weeks Austria-Hungary considered its move. The danger was that Russia, self-styled protector of the Slavs, might enter the ring. On 5 July the Austro-Hungarian chargé d'affaires in Berlin asked what Germany's position would be in the event of an Austro-Serbian war with the threat of Russian intervention. Kaiser Wilhelm II did not believe that Russia would attack, since Serbia had so compromised its own position. He instructed his chancellor to inform the Austro-Hungarians that Germany would stand by them whatever their decision. This blank check convinced the Austro-Hungarians that they had freedom of action.

The High Sea Fleet was preparing for a cruise to Norway in mid-July. The German naval staff, the Admiralstab, held that it would run a considerable risk in leaving German waters at a time of international tension.[8] During the cruise the fleet would be split into squadrons to visit various Norwegian ports. This scattering of forces could leave them vulnerable to a surprise attack. The Admiralstab never forgot that "Copenhagening" the High Sea Fleet by an unexpected assault at German ships in their anchorages had been publicly advocated in Britain. While the High Sea Fleet was in Norway, the Royal Navy would be unusually prepared for war as the result of a long-planned test mobilization. On 5 July Admiral Hugo von Pohl, Chief of the Admiralstab, remarked that the kaiser's decision to let the cruise proceed was wise only if the international situation had calmed down.[9]

Yet cancellation could be construed by the British as preparation for hostilities. Germany's alliance with Austria-Hungary would come into effect only in the event of war with Russia. That prospect seemed remote enough, the possibility of conflict with Britain even more distant. On 10 July the High Sea Fleet sailed to begin exercises in the Skagerrak before continuing north to Norway. The situation appeared calmer, so quiet that most of the navy's senior officers went on summer leave. Perhaps the only formal precaution was made on 7 July, when the gunboat *Eber*, refitting in the British base at Cape Town in South Africa, was instructed not to commit to a dry-docking.[10]

Across the North Sea the Royal Navy was more focused on Ireland. The Liberal government's decision to give home rule to that country had brought the nation close to civil war. Rival factions were arming and Conservative Unionist circles in both Ireland and Britain had declared they would fight to prevent implementation of home rule, particularly in the Protestant majority counties of Ulster. The government's efforts earlier in 1914 to prepare for military intervention had misfired. The sympathies of at least the commissioned ranks of the armed forces were strongly Unionist. The prospect of using force against them had caused army officers to resign en masse. The navy was not brought to this pass, but senior officers worked hard to limit deployments of major units into Irish waters. Some were content that "we might have to bombard Belfast and that would be that," but many more were doubtful that they could support any operations to enforce home rule.[11] In one of the ships sent to Ireland, the flotilla leader *Blanche,* both the captain and the executive officer made it clear to their wardroom that they would resign rather than coerce Ulster.[12] The most thoughtful, however, were conscious that dissension among the officers at a time of increasing industrial and social unrest could undermine service discipline. A letter from his army brother to the battleship *Benbow*'s captain summed up the dilemma: If "discipline is allowed to become dependent on personal considerations, what is there between the country and revolution?"[13]

The Royal Navy's major activity for 1914 was intended to be a test mobilization of the reserve fleets and the accompanying royal review at Spithead. In previous years, Grand Maneuvers were conducted in July, but economy now prevailed. The First Lord, Winston Churchill, was under great pressure to reduce the naval estimates and saving "nearly 200,000 pounds" was not to be missed. As Churchill noted, the 1912 and 1913 maneuvers had given the Admiralty "a great deal of valuable data which requires to be studied."[14] A mobilization, even when accompanied by a few days of exercises, would be much cheaper and test the system of activating the ships from reserve. It would also be a useful demonstration of Britain's naval strength.

The operation began on 12 July. Junior flag officers were sent to the major ports to identify any defects, but found little to report. Since no state of emergency had been proclaimed, the reserves could not be called up and the Admiralty had to offer bonuses to those who came forward. This proved to be an effective strategy, and 20,000 volunteered, which enabled every ship in the war plan to be put into service. The drawback was that few sailed with their assigned war complement. Much work was needed, since many of the Third Fleet had been laid up with only small care and maintenance parties with their machinery concealed under layers of preservatives. Not all of the elderly battleships and cruisers were in good condition and they were "commonly, and disrespectfully, known as the 'Baltic Fleet' after the unfortunate Russian fleet defeated so decisively at Tsushima."[15] Nevertheless, it took only five days for the last ships to depart their home ports.

The assembly at Spithead was the largest and most powerful ever seen: twenty-four dreadnought battleships and battle cruisers, thirty-five pre-dreadnoughts, and 123 smaller ships lay together under the White Ensign. The three fleets—the First, composed of the most modern ships; the Second, whose units had reduced permanent complements and served as an operational reserve; and the Third, the oldest vessels—made up almost the entire Royal Navy. Only four battle cruisers, three pre-dreadnoughts, and a few armored cruisers were absent on foreign stations or refitting. For the first time (and the last) the assembly included mooring spots for seaplanes from the newly established Royal Naval Air Service. In spite of "grave reservations as to the watertightness of their floats, all survived the ordeal."[16] Overflown by the seaplanes and aircraft from the naval air station at Eastchurch, the fleets sailed on 20 July, passing the royal yacht *Victoria and Albert*. Other dignitaries watched from the second royal yacht *Alexandra* and the Admiralty yacht *Enchantress*.

The situation in Europe still appeared relatively calm, but that same day the Austro-Hungarian government warned Germany of its intention to issue a brutal ultimatum to Serbia, one setting such terms it was unlikely Serbia would ever accept it. Kaiser Wilhelm still believed that Russia would not act, but ordered that commanders on overseas stations be informed and the German merchant marine warned to take precautions with its ships abroad. The kaiser also directed that the High Sea Fleet not disperse around the ports but remain concentrated when in Norway.[17] The remaining German preparations were disjointed. There was a division between the German foreign ministry and the navy as to what Britain would do if war broke out between Russia and France and the Triple Alliance. The foreign ministry believed that Britain would remain neutral at least for a time, but the Admiralstab still feared a preemptive attack. What made the situation doubly confusing was that not all senior personnel in either department knew of the Austrian ultimatum's contents. Only the day after its dispatch did Admiral Friedrich von Ingenohl, commander in chief (C-in-C) of the High Sea Fleet, learn of the demand, while the Admiralstab did not issue an update to the East Asiatic Squadron until 25 July and to other units abroad on 26 July.[18]

The decision to send the fleet to Norway hung in the balance, but the foreign ministry's protests that its recall would aggravate the situation won the day. The Germans were aware that the British fleets were due to disperse on 27 July and, until then, would be at much higher readiness for war than was the German navy; nothing should be done to prevent that dispersal. Late on 23 July the Admiralstab ordered von Ingenohl to take the battle squadrons into Sogne Fjord. The gesture was wasted, for events now moved quickly. No mobilizations had yet occurred, but war with Russia loomed large. On 25 July the kaiser, in Sogne Fjord on board *Hohenzollern*, directed von Ingenohl to take the fleet to the Baltic to prepare against Russia. The C-in-C was more pessimistic, predicting that war between the Triple Alliance and Russia would inevitably drag in France and eventually Britain. He noted,

> I urged with great seriousness the obvious probability of England
> taking part in the war, and said that this was the greatest danger
> to be considered and that the major part of the fleet, in any case

all the heavy ships ought therefore to go to the North Sea. The Kaiser replied with great decision that Great Britain's participation in the war was out of the question. After repeated objections I only succeeded in getting permission to send various units to their home ports and this only on the ground that it would facilitate and hasten [the] process of mobilization considerably. This at least gave the greater number of heavy ships and scouting forces the possibility of proceeding to the North Sea.[19]

The High Sea Fleet started south. For their part, the Russians were also moving. On 25 July Admiral Nikolai von Essen, the Baltic Fleet commander, cancelled all exercises and initiated patrols at the entrance of the Gulf of Finland. The fleet's minelaying force was also brought to immediate readiness. The Russians had few illusions as to the defensibility of their western bases and preparations began to withdraw from Libau (modern Liepaja).

For seventy-two hours the British fleets took part in daily "P. Z." tactical exercises, many ships anchoring each night. They finally parted on 23 July, the same day the Austro-Hungarian ultimatum was issued. The C-in-C, Admiral Sir George Callaghan, brought the First Fleet into Portland and Weymouth Bay, while the Second and Third Fleets headed for their home ports. On 24 July the Admiralty signaled to Callaghan, "First Fleet Squadrons all disperse on Monday 27th in accordance with your approved programme."[20] The dreadnought *Bellerophon* was detached to refit at Gibraltar, but the rest of the fleet remained together to conduct a boat regatta and refuel before the squadrons began gunnery exercises. The Admiralty therefore had three days before any decision had to be made on its disposition. The formation was key to Britain's naval readiness for war. The First Fleet was the most powerful naval force in the world, superior to the entire Imperial German Navy. Although the British Cabinet was apprised of the ultimatum to Serbia at a meeting on 24 July, Churchill decided to let matters ride rather than taking precautions that might only inflame the situation further.

Meanwhile, the auxiliary branches of the Royal Navy, which had been on a war footing for the test mobilization, were disbanding. The Third Fleet ships returned to care and maintenance and the Second Fleet prepared to give four days' leave to each watch. The First and Second Destroyer Flotillas were sent into Portsmouth, while the Third Flotilla went to Harwich and the Fourth remained in Irish ports. Were the situation to deteriorate further, these ships would have to be recalled to the fleet or sent to their war stations. By the evening of 24 July many personnel were already on leave—a holiday shortly curtailed, but one the watch off were to be thankful they had enjoyed.[21]

The German naval attaché reported the lack of warlike activity to Germany, where the news was greeted with relief. As if to emphasize Britain's desire for peace, on Saturday 25 July the First Lord went to the seaside to be with his family. The First Sea Lord, Admiral Prince Louis of Battenberg, remained at the Admiralty to keep watch, somewhat indignant at the politicians' regard for "their week-end holidays."[22] By noon that day the increasing tension between Russia and Austria-Hungary, accompanied by threats of mobilization, had caused the situation to deteriorate to such an extent that Churchill decided to return to London. At 1600, on his own initiative, Battenberg telegraphed Callaghan, "No ships of the First Fleet or Flotillas are to leave Portland until further orders." By the time Churchill returned to the Admiralty, the first restrictions on naval leave had been applied and the First Fleet had begun coaling.

The Russians, in the midst of reorganizing their armies, did not want war. On Russia's advice Serbia sent a conciliatory reply to the ultimatum—so conciliatory, in fact, that the kaiser declared that Austria-Hungary had been given everything it wanted. He ordered Chancellor von Bethmann-Hollweg to dispatch a congratulatory telegram to Austria-Hungary. Unfortunately, it was transmitted incomplete and the Austro-Hungarians did not receive the section that declared Germany could see no reason for hostilities. The Germans did not realize how determined the Austro-Hungarians were.

While the Admiralstab and the German foreign ministry continued their soul-searching over the High Sea Fleet's return, the British Admiralty took a more realistic view. The silence of Austria-Hungary was ominous, the risk of war increasingly high. As 27 July dawned, further measures were applied. A press statement was issued: "[I]t has been decided not to re-open the Schools after the manoeuvres for the present; consequently the balance crews of the Second Fleet ships and vessels will remain in their ships."

Orders were issued to bring the Second Fleet to full complement, complete with coal, ammunition, and stores. The remaining destroyers and torpedo boats were ordered out of reserve. The Admiralty directed that these actions were to be carried out as unobtrusively as possible, although word was soon around Weymouth that the First Fleet might be sailing for the North Sea. Late on the evening of 28 July, "a couple of steamers came round the fleet . . . full up of shore going people who cheered like anything as they passed each ship."[23] The machinery of mobilization was beginning to turn as orders were issued for patrols around the major ports, Scottish coast, and anchorages. A warning was sent out to the overseas stations that war was an increasing possibility: "[B]e prepared to shadow possible men-of-war, and consider dispositions of HM Ships under your command from this point of view. Measure is purely precautionary." The Admiralty wanted to ensure that the Royal Navy was ready well before it appeared inevitable that Britain would enter a conflict with Germany.

On 28 July Austria-Hungary rejected the Serbian note and declared war. The Russian General Staff was urging the tsar to mobilize. In an attempt to keep hostilities confined to the Balkans, Tsar Nicholas ordered that the mobilization be restricted to the units allocated against Austria-Hungary. The Russian fleet, however, continued its own preparations in the Baltic. Mines were laid around Kronstadt the same day. The kaiser was thrown into a fury by the news that Russia would act. The German naval attaché in London informed the Admiralstab of what he knew of the Royal Navy's preparations. For their part, the British had only a general idea of the whereabouts of the High Sea Fleet. With Portland considered vulnerable to torpedo attack, the Admiralty determined to move the First Fleet to safety and telegraphed the C-in-C, "The First Fleet is to leave Portland tomorrow, Wednesday, for Scapa Flow. Destination is to be kept secret."

Callaghan was called to the Admiralty for consultations, and the Grand Fleet, as it was henceforth known, was placed under the temporary command of Vice Admiral Warrender. The first line destroyer flotillas were summoned, the Fourth hastening back from the Irish coast and the First and Second Flotillas recalling their men from leave as they prepared to depart Portsmouth. The Third was ordered to remain at Harwich, its war station. Even as Callaghan boarded his train to London, the ships of the Grand Fleet were moving out of the anchorage.

Their destination was kept secret. The fourteen-mile long formation first headed west, reversing course for the Dover Strait when out of sight of land. As they moved into the Channel, the squadrons passed the French battleships *Jean Bart* and *France,* hurrying home with their president after a state visit to Russia.[24] Operational security was tight; one officer's guests for a tea party in *Dreadnought* on 30 July discovered only on their arrival in Portsmouth that the ship was not there.[25] A formation the size of the Grand Fleet could not go unnoticed by other mariners, however, and the German merchant ship *König Friedrich August* observed the British after they had turned east. To the chagrin of the German navy, she did not report the sighting until her arrival in Cuxhaven on 31 July.[26]

The Admiralty conference made key changes to the plans for the fleet. Scapa Flow had been intended as a preliminary anchorage, for use only in the period that war threatened, with Rosyth as the principal fleet base. Because neither had any antisubmarine defenses, and because Scapa was the better anchorage—less prone to fog and largely protected from submarine penetration (so it was thought) by strong tides and navigational hazards—the meeting decided that the Grand Fleet would use the Flow. The second alteration was caused by a change of plans for the army. The Imperial General Staff proposed that the British expeditionary force to France begin crossing within hours of a declaration of war, but the government had not yet agreed that any troops were to go. The political situation was complex and this matter would not be resolved until war had broken out.

While the Grand Fleet steamed north, the Admiralty continued to put its affairs in order. By now Germany had given Russia an ultimatum to end its mobilization against Austria-Hungary. Even at this stage, many in the German naval leadership remained sanguine about British intentions, von Tirpitz remarking that he thought that the British foreign secretary, Sir Edward Grey, "was bluff-ing."[27] All British naval leave was cancelled on 29 July and the Warning Telegram issued. This provided for most preparations short of actual war. The examination service for merchant ships was complete, awaiting only the Admiralty's final direction to start. The war signal stations and naval centers were connected to the general telegraphic network, putting the communications system on to a war footing. One small but significant order was the lifting of restrictions on the use of oil in mixed oil/coal fired ships.[28] Peacetime economy was giving way to the reality of conflict.

Meanwhile, the German concern was with the Russians, whose full mobiliza-tion was ordered on 30 July. Deployment began the next day of Russia's defensive minefields in the Gulf of Finland, although only after von Essen had threatened to begin the work on his own initiative. He was determined that there would be no German coup de main against his fleet like the Japanese attack at Port Arthur in 1904. The navy minister, Vice Admiral Grigorovich, gave von Essen approval on his own authority.[29]

On 30 July the kaiser ordered that precautionary measures be taken. Reports came in of the disappearance of the British fleet. Although Sir Edward Grey informed the German ambassador that the fleet's "movements were wholly free from any offensive nature and that it would not approach German waters," the Germans were certain that the Grand Fleet had gone to its war station—wherever that might be.[30] The navy's priority was now the British threat. On 31 July all the most modern units of the High Sea Fleet were ordered to move to the North Sea through the Kiel Canal. This was not a straightforward operation, since the new battleships had to discharge coal to reduce their draft for the transit.[31] The kaiser's confidence in the strength of the German position in the Baltic was demonstrated by his decision to name his brother, Prince Heinrich, as commander there, despite the doubts of other senior officers. At this stage, efforts in the North Sea focused on the defense of ports and anchorages, with patrols organized around the Heli-goland Bight. The Germans began to activate their own port defenses and exam-ination service.

The Russians had effectively achieved full naval mobilization, but the German assessment of the situation in the Baltic was accurate. Although the Russian fleet commander favored an aggressive approach, Russian doubts as to the position of Sweden and the ability of the Germans to deploy overwhelming strength meant that defending the Gulf of Finland would occupy all the Baltic Fleet's energies. Meanwhile, the Germans still hoped that Britain could be kept out of the conflict, and the C-in-C of the High Sea Fleet was ordered to keep all warship movements as covert as possible. Not until 1 August was a general naval mobilization ordered, and still the foreign ministry insisted no measures be taken that would risk war between Germany and Britain. The result was that none of the merchant ships allocated as commerce raiders was allowed to begin its conversion, let alone sail, disrupting a significant component of the navy's war plans.[32]

On 1 August, as war broke out between Russia and Germany, British Third Fleet ships began to receive their assigned war complements, the examination service went into operation, and chartering trawlers for minesweeping began. The supply ships, particularly colliers, needed to serve the fleet at its distant bases were being called up. The order "Mobilize Naval Reserves" went out—the final stage in the preparations. Merchant ships had already been forbidden to use wireless inside British waters and the local flotillas began nighttime patrols. Even in the short darkness of summer, inexperience and nerves converted some of these into near farce. The Royal Navy was as prepared as it could be, but there was much to learn. In the destroyer *Stour*,

> We took up positions a mile apart on a line parallel to the coast about 2 miles from the Tyne Breakwater and tooled up and down this patrol line, turning 16 points every 1/2 hour by deck watch time. Some of the boats didn't get the W/T [wireless telegraphy] signal to [zero deck watches] and we were soon in a pretty good mess, altho' I know the old *Stour* was up to time. . . . As a consequence we kept on meeting each other, and as some boats were awfully slack in replying to the "challenge" it was a miracle that none of us fired at each other, especially, as being the first night out, so to speak, we were all more or less jumpy. . . . It was a pitch dark night and the knowledge that if we got inside 4000 yards of the entrance, the leathernecks up at the forts had orders to biff off at us did not add to our sense of security. I stayed on the bridge all the blessed night, & was pretty well in a state of coma when we got back to harbour in the morning about 7 am. . . . [A]t 9.30 am we were out again.[33]

Matters were no better around Scapa Flow. The night before there had been "a dense fog and two of the patrolling destroyers went ashore. *Victor* touched on Stanger Head—but escaped with a twisted forefoot. *Porpoise* went stern first on to Brimsness and damaged both propellers."[34]

That day, Germany declared war on France and the position of Britain hung in the balance. The Germans seemed ready to agree not to attack the French northern coasts, which Britain had agreed to protect. On 2 August Sir Edward Grey confirmed to Cambon, the French ambassador, that he was "authorised to give an assurance that, if the German Fleet comes into the Channel or through the North Sea to undertake hostile operations against French coasts or shipping, the British Fleet will give all the protection in its power."[35] That night the Admiralty informed its ships in the Channel of this declaration, instructing them to "be prepared for surprise attack."[36] The warning to the Germans might have been enough. Their plan of action against France, however, depended on moving armies across Belgian territory. This would be a clear violation of that country's neutrality, something Britain had long promised by treaty to protect. As early as 31 July the Germans were informed that Britain would not countenance such a violation. The hope of peace lessened as the German government failed to make any reply. On 1 August Sir Edward Grey repeated the warning to the German ambassador. War between Britain and Germany could not be long delayed.

Churchill saw the writing on the wall. The navy's dispositions made, he turned to the warships completing in Britain for foreign powers. The Royal Navy was not so powerful that the addition of further units would not be of immense value. There was also the possibility that some might eventually come under the control of hostile powers. While Britain would not receive such a windfall as Germany from the ships the latter was building for Russia, there were several vessels very near commissioning. The most important were battleships being completed for Turkey. *Reshadieh* and *Sultan Osman V* were powerful ships, the former modelled on the *Iron Duke* class and the latter a design originally conceived for Brazil, carrying no fewer than fourteen 12-inch guns. The First Lord was determined that the Turks, whose loyalties in the coming conflict were doubtful, would not be permitted to take them. On 2 August both battleships were occupied by local troops, with the promise that the British would pay the Turkish government compensation, and return the ships after the emergency. In Turkish eyes this was not much recompense. A number of smaller units being built for other countries were also requisitioned, including three Chilean flotilla leaders, four Greek destroyers, and three Brazilian monitors. Nevertheless, not all the foreign ships under construction were immediately taken over. The Admiralty delayed some months before moving in on two 14-inch gunned dreadnoughts for Chile, and did not take over two light cruisers for Greece until 1915.

Churchill has since been accused of sacrificing Turkey remaining neutral, or even becoming an ally, in exchange for the addition of these two battleships to the Royal Navy. In hindsight, Turkey's ancient fear of Russia, strong German political and economic influence, and the later arrival in Turkish waters of Rear Admiral Wilhelm Souchon's squadron, *Goeben* and *Breslau*, would all have combined to tip the balance in favor of the Central Powers. Perhaps, too, the decision was of value because it indicated the firmness with which Britain intended to deal with the European crisis.

As the last hours of peace passed, the dominant feeling was one of uncertainty: uncertainty as to the outcome and uncertainty as to the capabilities of ships and men. The Royal Navy had not fought a major war at sea since 1815; the Germans, never. It had yet to be seen how the new weapons and systems would perform and whether all the theorizing and exercising would provide a basis for effective operations.

2

THE BRITISH

THE ROYAL NAVY OF 1914 WAS THE MOST POWERFUL AND IN MANY RESPECTS the most advanced in the world, but it was also experiencing the effects of very rapid changes in technology and society. The strain was exacerbated by continuing expansion and the need to manage an ever-greater diversity of capabilities. The system that ran the navy struggled to meet the challenge. Control was vested in the Lords Commissioners for executing the Office of the Lord High Admiral, jointly known as the Board of Admiralty. At the Board's head sat the First Lord, the minister responsible to Cabinet and Parliament. Two Civil Lords, one of whom was a member of Parliament, handled matters such as contracts and public works. The professional side was represented by four Sea Lords. The First was responsible for the navy's operations and fighting efficiency; the Second for personnel; the Third, or Controller, for warship design and construction; and the Fourth Sea Lord for stores, supply, and transport. The two other senior Admiralty officials were the permanent secretary, a nonvoting member of the Board in charge of the department's administration; and the parliamentary and financial secretary, a junior member of Parliament who assisted the First Lord.

The politician serving as First Lord possessed ultimate authority, but could not act alone. Supported by an officer who served as his naval secretary, he could appoint and dismiss the naval Lords, but the Admiralty had to function as a board. The permanent secretary provided continuity and advice to both politicians and sailors. For their part, the Sea Lords accepted the First Lord's overall authority. They would object, however, if the latter acted without consulting them or disrupted the formal chain of command between the Admiralty, the various C-in-Cs, and their subordinates. The Sea Lords possessed a powerful, though drastic, weapon in resignation. Were a First Lord to exceed his competence, he might find himself without naval colleagues or anyone willing to take their place.

The difficulty, and it was getting worse, was that the administration was undermanned.[1] The various divisions were expanding, but not quickly enough and not necessarily in the right areas. The Treasury played a part here. Its refusal to approve funding often forced the Admiralty to employ devices such as appointments to shore establishments or requisitioning officers ostensibly serving in seagoing ships.[2] This accentuated tendencies to overcentralization, to senior officers and public servants doing their own donkey work (in 1912 the naval secretary, a rear admiral, "had no staff whatever, not even a typist"), and to individuals having too much scope to set policy with insufficient preparation.[3]

These problems particularly affected the supervision of operations. Although a War Staff was formed in January 1912, partly manned by abolishing the old Naval Intelligence Division (NID), it was very small (some twenty-seven officers formally assigned at its start, together with eighteen civil personnel) and overextended.[4] The War Staff and its

PHOTO 2.1
Winston Churchill
Imperial War Museum

division into Operations, Mobilization, and Intelligence elements had been advertised as reform, with implicitly a greater capacity for planning than the old NID, but the uniformed manning was much the same as its predecessor.[5] Despite the navy's strategic interest in blockade and economic warfare, there had been no Trade Division since 1909; a new section was still forming as war broke out.

In such circumstances, the First Lord, Winston Churchill (photo 2.1), was in many ways the most difficult character conceivable for the job. At forty-one he had already served in government for nearly a decade, coming to the Admiralty after the Agadir crisis of 1911, which revealed a lack of coordination between the war plans of the army and the navy, and the apparent absence of an effective staff organization within the Admiralty. Churchill had been charged with the necessary changes. The War Staff of 1912 was the result, although its organization reflected expert professional opinion as much as any of the new First Lord's ideas.

Coming intent upon change and with a reputation for championing social reform at the expense of the services' budgets, Churchill had been regarded with apprehension. His reputation did not improve over time. Although soon persuaded of the need to strengthen the navy against the German menace, he was hard to work with. Churchill was slightly contemptuous of senior officers, an attitude probably engendered by his experiences as a war correspondent and frequent combatant in the Sudan and South Africa. Extraordinarily fluent on paper and in speech (a particular challenge for many naval officers), with a passionate interest in every aspect of the navy, it was inevitable that Churchill should come into conflict with the admirals and, indeed, with the staff as a whole. A shrewd biographer of one of the key military leaders of the Second World War noted, "Churchill's most provoking weakness in his direction of the war was his passion for detail."[6] This was equally true in the armed peace before 1914 and it was a greater problem

PHOTO 2.2
**Admiral Prince Louis
of Battenberg**
*(pictured as a
vice admiral)*
Imperial War Museum

because the Admiralty was so short of the capacity to channel, block, or develop Churchill's ideas.[7] The situation was made worse by the fact that the War Staff acted in only an advisory capacity. In theory, this advice was provided to the First Sea Lord, but there was sufficient ambiguity in the status of the separate Chief of the War Staff to allow an overactive minister to work independently with him. This suited Churchill very well.

After failing with Sir Arthur Wilson and Sir Francis Bridgeman, Churchill found a more amenable colleague as First Sea Lord in Prince Louis of Battenberg (photo 2.2). The latter's acceptance of the First Lord's tremendous desire to be up and doing smoothed over several dangerous conflicts. Nevertheless, Churchill's relations with the Sea Lords were never comfortable. Sir John Jellicoe, Second Sea Lord and prospective C-in-C of the Home Fleets, complained that he "sat on a volcano here and may fall out so seriously with the First Lord any day that even if he did at one time intend offering me the command he might change his mind."[8] Churchill was occasionally bested, particularly when he forgot that he possessed no military authority unless two members of the Board were assembled. At sea, a ship carrying this collective flew the flag of the Lord High Admiral. During the 1913 maneuvers, when Winston Churchill "proceeded to sea in a destroyer of exceptional speed called the *Swift* . . . Churchill began to send signals to the C-in-C [Sir George Callaghan] telling the latter what he thought his movements should be. The C-in-C . . . seizing a telescope examined the *Swift*. Then with a satisfied smile on his face he sent a signal: 'C-in-C to *Swift*: What are those signals from the Board of Admiralty? I do not see Admiralty Flag.' The *Swift* disappeared over the horizon at thirty knots."[9]

Rear Admiral Horace Hood was Churchill's naval secretary. A few months older than the battle cruisers' commander, David Beatty, Hood's war record was equally distinguished and his promotion nearly as meteoric, having become a rear admiral at forty-two. The intelligent but unassuming Hood found Churchill very difficult to handle, much more than had Beatty as naval secretary in 1911–12. While the latter operated as a "personal Staff Officer," Hood was largely confined to his formal role of arranging the appointments of senior officers.[10] This was significant, because the naval secretary worked within the private office and could give quiet advice, acting "as the keeper of his conscience" and restraining some of Churchill's enthusiasms.[11]

Admiral Prince Louis of Battenberg had a reputation as one of the more able officers of his generation. He had both benefitted and suffered from his royal connections, particularly as a junior officer, but by 1914 Prince Louis had extensive Admiralty experience, particularly within the old NID, as well as much service as a flag officer at sea. He was also alert to new technologies and an early supporter of the emerging air arm.[12] Unfortunately, Battenberg was regarded with suspicion by some for his German birth. That he should have to fight Germany was a source of anguish for Prince Louis, but he was intensely loyal to the United Kingdom. There was little love lost between the House of Hohenzollern and the Battenbergs, and, in any case, as Prince Louis once tartly responded to the kaiser's jibe, he had joined the Royal Navy before a united Germany existed.[13] The problem, should there be any naval reverses in the coming war, was that Prince Louis would soon be singled out by the popular press. The First Sea Lord was also not well. He was overweight and suffered from gout, particularly when tired and run down. The duties of the First Sea Lord were monumental in both peace and war, and required enormous energy. There must be at least an impression that Prince Louis' powers were fading under this pressure. Battenberg later admitted that the strain affected his health.[14] He appears to have spent much of his time reacting to Churchill and the War Staff rather than giving direction.

Matters were not helped by Churchill's decision to form a War Group. This informal body included the First Lord, the First Sea Lord, the Chief of the War Staff, and, for the first few weeks, the Second Sea Lord and the permanent secretary. The arrangement recognized the preeminent interest of the senior personnel directly involved in operations, but ignored the other Sea Lords and did not fully utilize the available talent. The junior Sea Lords—Vice Admiral Sir Frederick Hamilton, Rear Admiral Frederick Tudor, and Captain Cecil Lambert—might have been distinguished more by general competence than any special brilliance, although Lambert was an early enthusiast for naval aviation, but Hamilton in particular had extensive command experience at sea.[15] Although in theory they had to be consulted over Board decisions, all were largely sidelined. Furthermore, too often the Group acted as its own staff, immersed in details better left to junior officers.

Coordination of the Admiralty's operational responsibilities was further complicated by the fact that the Chief of the War Staff, Vice Admiral Sir Doveton Sturdee, and the Director of the Operations Division, Rear Admiral Arthur Leveson, were new to the Admiralty—Sturdee had been formally in office only five days when mobilization began (photo 2.3). Sturdee's predecessor, Sir Henry Jackson, in a generous, but short-sighted, gesture, had stood aside a month early to give the new chief a clear run. Jackson himself remained at the Admiralty on special service, but his focus became the global conflict rather than the war in home waters. Neither of the new leaders of the staff was entirely suited to his post, although things might have been worse. As the chief, Churchill originally proposed

PHOTO 2.3
Vice Admiral Sir Doveton Sturdee
(pictured as a full admiral)
and Commodore Roger Keyes
(pictured as a rear admiral)
Imperial War Museum

Admiral Sir Reginald Custance, a retired officer greatly senior to and no friend of the First Sea Lord, with very different (and strongly held) views on many issues. Battenberg immediately recognized that this would be unworkable, even if the chief were merely an adviser, and very rightly refused to agree. This once, Battenberg's preference prevailed.[16]

Sturdee was a capable tactician—of surface forces—fresh from cruiser squadron command. He had served as assistant Director of Naval Intelligence and as head of the 1911 Admiralty Submarine Committee. He was also a protégé of Admiral Lord Charles Beresford, Fisher's bitter rival, having served as his chief of staff in the old Channel Fleet. Sturdee had a reputation as a student of naval history. He gave an early and sensible priority to the management of trade and shipping problems, but, despite the quality of his curriculum vitae, did not provide the mix of firm direction and wide consultation inherent to his role, nor possess much facility for responding to the new technology at sea.[17] Rear Admiral Henry Oliver, Director of Naval Intelligence, later described him as "a pompous man who would never listen to anyone else's opinion."[18] Captain Herbert Richmond, assistant Director of the Operations Division, complained in August 1914, "Sturdee goes about looking very important & mysterious, & none of the naval assistants—not even Admiral Duff [Director of the Mobilization Division] is allowed to know what great issues are in contemplation. The result is that no one can help."[19] Despite these failings, Sturdee was a formidable presence. Together, the First Lord and the Chief of the War Staff dominated the Admiralty's operational effort in the early months of the war.

Leveson, although he had Admiralty experience, did not enjoy staff duties. He was irritated by his juniors' (particularly Richmond's) unsolicited proposals and was unlikely to question directives from the First Sea Lord or the Chief of the War Staff. Leveson was perhaps typical of his generation, convinced that a subordinate's primary duty was obedience. One of his officers commented in later years, "He puts his head down and charges like the Bull of Bashan—Don't get out in front."[20] Oliver, Director of Naval Intelligence since 1913, was another key personality. He was shrewd and reserved, with a talent for getting his own way. Having an immense capacity for hard work and confidence in his own judgment, however, Oliver's background as a specialist navigator meant he was even more prone to overcentralize than most. As Fisher later observed, Oliver too often "so overburdens himself he is 24 hours behind with his basket of papers."[21]

Matters within the War Staff and the War Rooms that managed the operational picture were not improved by the decision to bring in unemployed and retired officers to fill out staff and watch-keeping positions. This supplement would have been necessary in any case (there was a second tranche in October), but neglected the Admiralty civil service personnel who had been trained during prewar exercises. Having the War Room manned by naval officers was under consideration before the outbreak, but the new supernumeraries' lack of familiarity caused great confusion.[22] Information was lost or not directed to the appropriate authority. Furthermore, the naval officers would have been much better employed on planning, rather than keeping the War Room's operational picture up to date. Sturdee himself later admitted that he "often went in to correct the enlarged charts," curious employment for a man in his position.[23]

The Admiralty as a whole faced formidable challenges and almost every element of the navy had profoundly changed during the past decade in the attempt to meet them. It now mustered some twenty dreadnought battleships and eight battle cruisers. None had been afloat in 1904. Two battleships and a battle cruiser were approaching completion and there were even bigger and more powerful units under construction. They were supplemented by thirty-eight older pre-dreadnoughts. Yet, apart from the three battle cruisers in the Mediterranean, the Australian navy's *Australia* in the Pacific, and single pre-dreadnoughts in the East Indies and China, there were no capital ships outside British waters. Their concentration was one indication of the way in which strategic, financial, and human problems had been managed since 1904. At 146,000 officers and ratings, active manpower had increased in the decade by nearly 12 percent, but there were far fewer people overseas—some ten thousand had left the Mediterranean, where battleships had been replaced by a handful of battle cruisers and armored cruisers, while 2,500 had returned from the China Station.[24] Others were lent to the newly formed Royal Australian and Canadian navies, which were important parts of the long-term solution for maintaining the British Empire's maritime security, but this was only until the Dominions trained their own people. There were also many more in the rapidly increasing destroyer and submarine forces and the new Royal Naval Air Service.

Solutions such as the Dominion services were necessary, for the navy was under financial pressure. Churchill was being urged by his colleagues in government to reduce spending. This was not easy. While the navy's budget increased by more than 55 percent between 1900 and 1914, demands had multiplied.[25] This was reflected in expenditure on equipment relative to shipbuilding and in the constantly increasing cost of individual units, recently aggravated by the First Lord's plunge for 15-inch guns and oil firing in the newest battleships. It was also shown in the amounts devoted to vessels other than battleships and cruisers. In 1900–1901, torpedo craft constituted less than 8.5 percent of the appropriations for new construction. By 1913–14 these vessels were more than a fifth, with submarines alone representing more than 5 percent of the total build.[26] The highly qualified personnel necessary to man the new ships and equipment did not come cheap. Pension costs alone jumped by more than a third by 1913, with more rises in store.[27] Potential manpower savings in the adoption of oil fuel were an important reason for accepting the other expenses of the new venture.[28]

The challenge in adapting to emergent technology—in particular, in making the necessary changes in organization and administration—was further complicated by the British Treasury's ability to veto spending on individual new proposals, even for very small amounts of money. Although the allocations were never as unbalanced as those in Germany, new construction often came at the expense of infrastructure and other needs. To pay for the new 15-inch gunned ships, Churchill made economies in acquiring war stocks of mines and torpedoes, as well as reserve ammunition and other supplies.[29] This had serious consequences when war broke out.

The officer corps itself was in a state of flux, and this also had important implications for the war at sea. The Royal Navy had substantially professionalized much of its officer education and training since the mid-nineteenth century, but did not adopt the unrestricted line of the United States Navy. The idea was implicit in the officer entry and training scheme started in 1902, and designation of the Engineers in 1903 as a "military" branch with the associated status, uniform, and authority helped in stilling their discontent. Yet the concept of interchange between the executive and marine engineering branches never really took within the Royal Navy, despite Fisher's efforts to make it happen.[30]

Such separation from the executive branch, however, related at this time effectively only to propulsion and hull engineering. The emerging disciplines of weapon and electrical and communications engineering were retained in the form of the gunnery, torpedo, and signals subspecializations, all of which possessed their own schools and pyramids of instructional courses. In particular, the torpedo branch was responsible for electrical systems. The maintenance and operation of electrical equipment represented a constantly increasing part of the workload for the officers and ratings concerned. In addition, the more recently created subspecialization of signals was incorporating progressively more material on wireless communications into its training syllabus.

The development of subspecialist officers was frequently criticized, but it produced men who were immersed in their profession. The lengthy training courses were a mixture of higher mathematics, particularly for the gunnery officers, and theoretical science with extensive hands-on work. Even among the less academic, these were officers generally at ease with new technology, with a strongly practical bent, and ready to innovate further. Furthermore, in the age of the motor car and the dawn of powered flight, many young men were fascinated by the new machinery and (more or less) adept at its use and repair. There was a readiness to experiment and make do—and there needed to be.

Yet this was not quite enough. There were scientists enlisted in the navy of 1914, but the navy had yet to enlist science. Despite the presence of men such as Vice Admiral Sir Henry Jackson, a pioneer of wireless, the system tended to produce mathematicians and mechanics. Among the evidence for this are the many instruments invented by naval officers, including Prince Louis of Battenberg himself, whose circular slide rule for calculating courses and speeds to steer remains in use a hundred years later.[31] The fixation on mechanics was apparent in the strenuous efforts before 1914 to produce antisubmarine devices. From 1910 on the Submarine Committee experimented with an array of antisubmarine sweeps, explosive devices, and nets, but did not systematically explore the issue of detection within the medium that the submarines operated.[32] Ironically, separate experiments were being conducted at the same time with underwater sound signaling.[33]

The problem of an unscientific outlook was accentuated by three factors. The first was that personnel in the operational units, with their necessarily utilitarian approach, were too closely involved in experiments and trials, some of which necessarily had a distant timeframe for perfection of the systems concerned. The second factor was that the navy was adjusting to the fact that hulls, propulsion machinery, and guns were giving room to computers, sensors, and communications equipment as both cost drivers and the deciding elements of fighting advantage. In neither case did organizations exist that were capable of managing all the backroom elements involved.

The third was that the Royal Navy was still trying to develop a concept of staff work and the role of the staff officer in supporting higher command. The navy's requirements were not those of the army; much of what the latter considered as legitimate staff duties were managed in ships by navigators and engineers, when not the concern of other subspecialists. The provision of fresh water, for example, is generally a problem of transport for an army, but as much one of engineering for a navy. Yet there was a clear requirement for planners in the fleet and at the Admiralty capable of managing strategic and operational matters in an increasingly complex environment. Army officers were rightly critical of the deficiencies in the way that naval operational orders and signals were structured and written, something clearly apparent to observers during the 1913 maneuvers.[34] Procedures had yet to catch up with the inherent requirements for clarity and flexibility when communicating and operating remotely. Only in 1912 was a War Staff course for junior officers established; both the concept and the product had yet to be accepted in the service at large. This acceptance was made more difficult by a pervasive anti-intellectualism that was another aspect of the preoccupation with the practical. Thus, while there were some very impressive individuals in the early War Staff courses and on the teaching staff (including several founders of the *Naval Review*), the officers qualified for staff duties were not necessarily an elite, nor were they regarded in such a light.

There were other problems. The Royal Navy's officer corps suffered from having an inadequate base for the expansion that had occurred, which made promotion nearly automatic. The July 1881 cadet entry to the training ship *Britannia* that included "Scott of the Antarctic" represented the peak of this effect. Of the twenty-five officers who became lieutenants, twenty-three were promoted commander and all of these were promoted captain. The failure of a clean sweep was because two died as lieutenants.[35] This result was extreme, but the January 1885 term, which included Richmond, had thirty-six lieutenants, of whom six died or were invalided. Of the remaining thirty, twenty-seven became commanders and twenty later became captains.[36] The Autumn 1889 term had forty-three lieutenants, of whom nine died or were invalided, twenty-five became commanders, and eighteen went on to become captains.[37] These remain historically unmatched statistics. Shortages were also apparent in the junior officer ranks, and the Admiralty was repeatedly forced to recruit merchant service officers with reserve experience to provide additional watch-keeping lieutenants, as well as a special entry that took in cadets after completing secondary school, rather than at twelve years old, the standard entry through the Naval College at Osborne.

The relationship between quality and competition for promotion was, however, complex. The evidence of the war to come suggests that there was an improvement in the average officer around the vintage of the 1881 entry. This was earlier than the establishment of a more competitive entry selection process in 1886,[38] but was perhaps an early sign of increasing enthusiasm for the navy in the upper middle classes and thus a higher quality of applicants. It may also have been the result of what, however flawed it may appear, was a steadily increasing effort in formal training and education, one that provided even those who avoided specialization with a much better professional grounding than before.

There were some talented officers in command at sea or in junior positions at the Admiralty in 1914. Apart from Commodores William Goodenough in the First Light Cruiser Squadron, Roger Keyes of the submarines, and Reginald Tyrwhitt (photo 2.4) leading the destroyer flotillas, they included Reginald Hall, the brilliant captain of *Queen Mary*, who was to make his name as Director of Naval Intelligence; Ernle Chatfield of *Lion*, future First Sea Lord and minister of Defence; and William Wordsworth Fisher of *St. Vincent*, a formidable all-rounder and one of the youngest captains on the list. There were more, of equal talent, at the rank of commander, including Reginald Plunkett, flag commander in *Lion*; Roger Backhouse, flag commander in *Iron Duke*; and Charles Forbes at the Admiralty. Perhaps the Royal Navy's misfortune was that these officers were not ten years more senior in 1914.

Two key issues would emerge in war for the navy's officers. The first derived most from the culture of command. Even if it had not been involved in a major European conflict since the Crimean War, the Royal Navy saw itself as a fighting service in which demonstrated physical courage was important. A majority of the flag officers at sea in 1914 had seen active service; several (including Jellicoe and

PHOTO 2.4
**Commodore Reginald Tyrwhitt
and Mrs. Tyrwhitt**
(pictured later in the war)
Imperial War Museum

Beatty) had been wounded, and many possessed awards for saving life. A number had distinguished themselves as operational leaders, including Stanley Colville, senior naval officer on the Nile in 1896; and Doveton Sturdee, in the international crisis over Samoa in 1899; or, more recently, Vice Admiral Sir Cecil Burney in the Balkans. But there were two critical elements to such service. First, it was usually ashore (or inshore). Second, the sustained demonstrations of initiative were in detached command, well away from authority. The presence of a senior officer created different behaviors, a syndrome most pronounced in those who remained in the big ships. Nevertheless, even the young commanders of torpedo craft with their need for instant decision making and self-reliance were not immune. A senior officer's authority was almost absolute and following the senior ship's movements and routines was obligatory, while there was an unhealthy emphasis on choreographed close order maneuvering. This problem and some of its origins have been dealt with by Andrew Gordon, but the effect of the highly centralized control of fleets and squadrons was to create a mindset of speedy response to direction rather than initiative in ambiguity.[39] It was not so much a cult of the senior officer as it was one of "the senior officer present." Furthermore, the use of wireless was moving this syndrome into virtual reality, with units on maneuvers failing to exercise initiative because of their assumption that the remote authority knew better.[40]

The second issue would soon be a source of frustration for the officers who were in no way technocrats and often came from a hunting, shooting, and fishing background in county aristocracy, sometimes from the Anglo-Irish ascendancy. The frustration would be shared by the more historically aware. This was a tendency on the part of officers with specialist training to make tactical decisions on the basis of essentially arithmetical comparisons of relative strength, perhaps the result of becoming too immersed in their material. The reverse assumption, that fighting spirit would prevail, could certainly be taken too far, as in the blindness that Sturdee, in particular, displayed to the inefficiency of hastily mobilized reserve units. Too often in the war's opening months, however, the Royal Navy would refuse action for the wrong reasons. The service had moved a long way from Nelson's "something must be left to chance."[41]

The lower deck was also changing as growing complexity forced the creation of new specializations. The engineering branch was steadily expanding, with an increasing demand for expert artificers to manage sophisticated machinery. Another new requirement was for ratings expert in wireless, needing not only operator skills, but also understanding of the physics of radio propagation and (even if other technical ratings were meant to do the work) the ability to repair and tune the gear. A separate telegraphist branch came into being in 1907. There were some lateral solutions to the challenges of other new equipment. The number of bands multiplied rapidly after 1900—not through the desire for more ceremonies, but because musicians were believed to possess the aptitude to operate complex gunnery fire control instruments.[42]

Diversification was occurring not only within ships, but also through the development of new branches within the navy. These elements were creating new subcultures that carried within them the seeds of further change. Destroyers represented one such group, but submarines demonstrated most clearly the distinction between the old navy and the emerging capabilities. The number of personnel in submarines was always small in relation to the total navy, but all were expected to possess significant specialist and boat skills; they quickly came to regard themselves as an elite, with their own nickname as "the Trade." The newly created Royal Naval Air Service was rapidly becoming another such center of activity. Richard Bell Davies, first lieutenant at Eastchurch in 1914, commented later, "[T]he general atmosphere was so happy. The main reason was that everyone, ratings as well as officers, was intensely interested in his job. There were literally no defaulters."[43]

The core of the Royal Navy's lower deck was formed by the boys and very young men who entered, after basic training, on a twelve-year engagement in one of the seaman branches. Many remained for further engagements to qualify for pension. From these sailors, after their service as petty officers and chief petty officers, came the more than 2,600 warrant officers who were the backbone of their ships, working closely with the specialist officers to maintain and operate equipment and supervise training. There were no conscripts. Because ships normally did a two- or three-year commission with the same crew (although this was starting to change in 1914), levels of expertise and efficiency were high.[44] They were to remain high for the duration of the war, despite a considerable leavening by reservists.

The navy, however, had been slow to respond to the workforce's changing demography. It was not immune to the social and industrial tensions of the period, and the engineering ratings in particular, joining as adults, brought different attitudes than those engendered by the training ships in the boy seamen. In some ways, the increasing diversity of ships' companies, viewed as creating real challenges for teamwork by more old-fashioned officers, actually limited these new influences. The expert, highly educated artificers had an outlook that derived from the guilds of master craftsmen, even after the navy began to recruit and train its own in the same way as the seamen. The stokers, entered on short engagements, frequently from the industrial and mining regions and often with limited schooling, had a much more modern trade unionist approach, but often did not see their interests as aligning with the artificers or with deck personnel, while both the latter groups tended to regard the stokers as a culture apart. As did the stokers themselves.

Causes of discontent varied. To his credit, Winston Churchill made improving lower-deck conditions a priority from the time he joined the Admiralty, and he had the support of many of the more thoughtful senior officers, including Prince Louis himself. Pay was one issue, although it had recently been improved for many; others included the difficulty of advancing to commissioned rank and unnecessary restrictions on leave. The requirement to purchase uniforms rankled, particularly as the new Australian and Canadian navies were providing free issues to their sailors. There was a well-founded belief that the disciplinary system was capricious and gave too much power to individual commanding officers. The ease with which a sailor could be disrated was a particular disincentive to seeking promotion. The Admiralty had been forced to intervene on more than one occasion as a result of public pressure, one of the most notorious recent incidents being collective disobedience in the battleship *Zealandia* in early 1914, largely caused by a harsh and overdemanding captain, Walter Cowan. Ships' disciplinary staff were also viewed as liable to corruption and favoritism. The conditions in which junior ratings lived were barely acceptable, and probably only so because of the primitive nature of contemporary British industrial conditions. Captain Reginald Hall did something to improve the situation in 1913 with the new battle cruiser *Queen Mary* by installing proper washing facilities—vital in a coal-burning ship—and introducing a host of other welcome amenities (photo 2.5). Hall also tried to make greater use of the warrant and petty officers. Except in the smallest ships, officers were inclined to oversupervise evolutions, and senior ratings tended

PHOTO 2.5   HMS *Queen Mary*   *Imperial War Museum*

to leave the enforcement of discipline to the unpopular ship's police, with whom Hall dispensed in *Queen Mary*.[45] It was some time before the rest of the navy followed suit. Hall had the reputation of being "an enthusiast [who] has in other places instituted reforms which, as soon as he has left, have been abandoned as impractical," although his subordinates considered him a man who "would take any amount of trouble to remove any possible cause of legitimate grievance or avoidable discomfort."[46]

The separation between officers and ratings was greater than it should have been, even in destroyers, and the better living conditions of the wardroom, particularly their access to bathrooms and hot water, a source of resentment. However, the fact that the officers lived on board in harbor and were clearly imbued with an ethos that put duty first eased the pressure somewhat. What also helped was the collective misery of coaling, a long, dirty, and dangerous evolution that involved practically every member of the crew in manual work. If the ship's executive officer did not like music, even the usually privileged band had to coal.[47] Fancy dress was the order of the day and a curiously rank-free atmosphere prevailed in the bunkers and coal holds. As a junior officer commented many years after, "This all-out, communal effort fostered a fine ship spirit, an esprit-de-corps."[48] A rating later noted, "That was the only time that everybody could swear at each other. . . . [Y]ou could say what you like. . . . The idea was that the officer was working just as hard as you were on the same job, so you were all equals there."[49]

In all, however, as one observer declared, "the men today are convinced that the bulk of their officers are out of touch with them, and content to be so."[50] Yet in August 1914 none of this affected the intense pride in the Royal Navy and its tradition of victory shared by all its members. This collective confidence was one of the great psychological advantages that the British enjoyed at the start of the conflict. It remained to be seen what they would do with it.

THE GERMANS

3

THE IMPERIAL GERMAN NAVY OF 1914 WAS A PRODUCT OF THE AMBITION of Grand Admiral Alfred von Tirpitz and the vanity of Kaiser Wilhelm II. This combination and its flaws were reflected not only in the fleet's vast expansion since 1898, but also in the navy's command. Their deficiencies contained the seeds of Germany's naval failures. Divided authority was at the root of many difficulties to come. No fewer than eight naval officials had direct access to the kaiser. The first was the Chief of the Naval Cabinet (Marine Kabinett), Admiral Georg Alexander von Müller, responsible for senior promotions and appointments, and managing the kaiser's naval correspondence and orders to the navy. Serving in the post since 1906, but associated with the court long before, propinquity made von Müller highly influential. His influence was accentuated by the mercurial Wilhelm's unfortunate tendency to make decisions on the basis of what he had been told by the last person to speak with him. Von Tirpitz later complained that von Müller "became more and more a court politician, and less and less a sailor."[1] He had a point, but it was made as justification for von Tirpitz's own failures.

The grand admiral was the most powerful figure in the navy and real leader of the peacetime service, as state secretary of the Imperial Naval Office (Reichs Marine Amt) since 1897 (photo 3.1). His subordinate departments were responsible for ship construction and design, stores and supply, and personnel training and education. Apart from matters handled by the Naval Cabinet, the only element outside his jurisdiction was operational command, something he had accepted when the kaiser abolished the High Command of the navy at von Tirpitz's suggestion in 1899.[2] The Imperial Naval Office prepared the annual budgets, managed their passage through the imperial parliament, and determined not only the size of the fleet, but also the specifications of all designs. Every element of the navy bore the mark of von Tirpitz: Its ships were built according to his personal determination of the strategic situation. The leadership also carried his stamp, since the Imperial Naval Office's staff was carefully selected by him. Officers adept at meeting his requirements and the complex politics involved in expanding Germany's naval capability went on to higher rank. The very best alternated between

PHOTO 3.1
**Grand Admiral
Alfred von Tirpitz**
Bibliothek fur Zeitgeschichte

the Naval Office and sea appointments. It was a matter of notoriety that the torpedo specialization, of which von Tirpitz had been one, became "the object of the ambition of every efficient officer."[3]

Nevertheless, von Tirpitz possessed no direct operational authority. The Inspector-General of the Navy, the Chief of the Baltic Station, the Chief of the North Sea Station, the commander of the East Asiatic Squadron, and the commander of the High Sea Fleet, as well as the Chief of the Admiralstab, had rights of audience with the kaiser. Von Tirpitz accepted these peacetime arrangements because he knew no other officer could develop a power base sufficient to match his influence as state secretary. He had not hesitated to intrigue against any fleet commander or Chief of the Admiralstab who disagreed with him, and he did so from a position of advantage. All but the Admiralstab were to some degree isolated by geography and by the needs of their commands. As the British naval attaché noted drily in 1910, "[I]t seems that if they differ from Tirpitz, it generally ends in their losing their appointments."[4] Von Tirpitz failed to recognize, however, that forcing the removal of would-be rivals built up a legacy of distrust among the navy's senior officers, even his protégés, as well as a growing suspicion that he was out of touch with technological development.[5] Furthermore, apart from his rivalry with von Müller and the kaiser's determination to remain in personal control, however fitful, the state secretary had reckoned without one most important body.

PHOTO 3.2
Admiral Hugo von Pohl
Bibliothek fur Zeitgeschichte

The Admiralstab, led by Admiral Hugo von Pohl, was created in 1899 to supervise naval operations, partially replacing the old Naval High Command. In peace, the Admiralstab's role was largely advisory, concerned with the preparation of war plans and analyzing intelligence. With the war, the situation changed dramatically. The Admiralstab was the only organization with the machinery to manage the naval conflict and the kaiser was likely to make the greatest possible use of it. Von Pohl himself was a dour officer who had distinguished himself during the Boxer Rebellion (photo 3.2). His professional reputation was high but, despite his recent ennoblement, von Pohl suffered in a class-obsessed officer corps because his father was only a paymaster. The admiral's difficulties would be increased by the requirement to remain with the kaiser at German army General Headquarters (GHQ), well away from the navy and, most critically, separated from the main body of the Admiralstab.

Rear Admiral Paul Behncke was von Pohl's deputy. He had been in the Admiralstab since late 1911 and was closely involved in the debates over war plans. Running affairs in Berlin when his chief was absent, Behncke was also the point man for explaining the navy's operational actions to politicians and to other interests in the capital. Although he was a trusted colleague of von Pohl's and did much to consolidate the Admiralstab's position, the fact that Behncke remained in Berlin and von Pohl at GHQ would encourage divergent views and the Berlin-based staff's evolution into an agency somewhat independent of its de jure chief.

He had not been preferred for the appointment at sea, but von Pohl was better regarded by many than Admiral Friedrich von Ingenohl, C-in-C since 1913. Ennobled that year, von Ingenohl served under von Tirpitz and later commanded the East Asiatic Squadron, as well as the Second Squadron, before taking over as C-in-C. He was a cautious officer of some intelligence, but had not impressed his personality on the fleet, and proved ill prepared for the ambiguities of his situation.[6] Von Ingenohl's relationship with von Pohl was to be particularly important. The Chief of the Admiralstab was even more concerned about the potential risks from submarines and light craft than was the C-in-C, and would block many of the latter's initiatives. A shrewd observer later made the point that von Ingenohl lacked "the characteristics of a great leader because he doesn't have the necessary willingness to take responsibility and initiative."[7] There was truth to this, particularly since the army command did not hesitate to ignore the kaiser's directives when they did not align with its requirements. Despite its own internal tensions, however, the German General Staff was institutionally united in a way that the navy was not, as well as being much more powerful in its own right. To make matters worse, neither von Pohl nor von Ingenohl's relations with von Tirpitz had been happy before the war.[8]

There was one senior appointment that surprised the naval leadership.[9] The kaiser installed his brother, Prince Heinrich, as commander in the Baltic. A former C-in-C of the High Sea Fleet, Heinrich was no fool and a much more stable personality than Wilhelm, as well as being the first qualified pilot in the navy, but the Baltic's secondary priority rather than his professional reputation made the selection acceptable. Germany had a tradition of royal command of military formations supported by a first class staff. This was what Wilhelm had in mind, and von Müller hurried to assemble an effective team.[10]

Von Tirpitz did his best to take charge, proposing on 29 July that the Admiralstab come under his direction. This the kaiser would not permit, but he issued a directive that gave von Tirpitz advisory rights on any recommendations from the Admiralstab. Furthermore, von Tirpitz was ordered to join GHQ. This complicated the chaotic naval command organization even further, and von Pohl had no illusions what it meant.[11] As one of von Tirpitz's staff noted later, the decision reflected a "half-heartedness" that typified much of the German naval effort in 1914.[12]

There was a concentration of talent among the commanding officers of the battle cruisers that included Magnus von Levetzow of *Moltke*, Ludwig von Reuter of *Derfflinger*, and Mathias von Egidy of *Seydlitz*. These officers were veterans of the expansion that followed the 1898 Navy Law. Enormously confident of the quality of their service and their own abilities, and experienced in both line and staff duties, they constituted an alternative and highly critical naval staff. Although not all were products of von Tirpitz's departments, most were well connected and highly skilled in employing their networks.[13] They shared two primary faults. First, if German naval officers felt more at ease with the big picture than did some of their British contemporaries, it was within a flawed context. Their inability to integrate naval strategy with national requirements, particularly economic realities, would prove fatal, as would their lack of sensitivity to neutral opinion. Second, they also too often proved oblivious to the demands of leadership that the coming conflict brought. Despite their expertise and eagerness to do the best for their service, they had a certain lack of sympathy with their crews, creating a gap between wardroom and lower deck even wider than that in the Royal Navy.

Germany's officer corps had expanded even more rapidly than Britain's. Its constitution was largely from the upper middle class but, although the origins of many were in academia, business, or industry, their ethos aped the exclusive attitudes of the military aristocracy and sought recognition as its naval equivalent. The technological and social demands of the navy made this ethos difficult to sustain. Engineers were treated as an inferior caste, more so than in Britain, and bitterly resented the executive branch's superior status. Despite repeated efforts, they made little progress, which did not help redress a chronic shortage of engineers in the fleet. *Deckoffizieres* were also treated with less respect than were warrant officers in the Royal Navy. It was a natural consequence that they were neither as useful nor as reliable as their British equivalents.[14]

There were strengths to the system. German naval officers received excellent basic training, including a foreign cruise as cadets, followed by comprehensive specialist courses. Wisely (although von Tirpitz's self-interest played a key part), the navy had not followed the German army in creating a specialist corps that undertook only staff duties. The brightest junior officers were selected for the two-year naval staff course, but rotated between staff appointments and operational command. Royal Navy officers were once inclined to think that their German equivalents were more comfortable in office work than at sea, but the assessment was never wholly fair and was rapidly changing, particularly with regard to officers experienced in torpedo craft.[15] Any continuing truth in the judgment probably resulted from the operational environment that was more restricted than that of the British. The navy was still very much a coastal defense force in outlook as well as organization. Many senior officers were concerned by the confinement of such a high proportion of the fleet to German waters and worried about its effects on junior personnel.[16] The Germans also operated directly from their home ports much more than did the British, who frequently deployed to remote anchorages. This meant, among other things, that they spent more time with their families and expected to do so. Even bachelor officers maintained apartments ashore, something virtually unheard of for unmarried British officers in a seagoing ship. This deepened the gulf between officers and the lower deck and disguised the tensions inherent in the wardroom's privileged existence. It was true that the communities of torpedo craft, submarines, and aviation had much less rigid divisions between officers and men and a shared enthusiasm for their work. These were still relatively small parts of the total establishment, but they were already beginning to drain the big ships of some of their best young talent.

The judgment of the British lower deck that the German sailors were more regimented and restricted was much more valid. The German navy relied largely on a three-year program of conscription. It also actively sought volunteers, sourced where possible from maritime regions, and maintained a number of avenues to make entry as attractive as possible. In addition, there were increasing efforts to recruit and train boys as a nursery of future petty officers. The triennium for conscripts required that ships turn over a third of their complement every autumn, marking the start of a new annual training cycle. Although this had the benefit of predictability, there were problems of operational readiness. The High Sea Fleet's increasing size suggested a new solution—that each year one of the three battle squadrons and a third of the units in other formations turn over all their conscripts and work up on that basis. Implementation of this scheme provoked a lively debate, but it also focused attention on the reality that a major war would not necessarily happen after the harvest had been taken in and that a rigid annual cycle of training with related levels of readiness was not the best answer.

There was a developing view among the younger officers of the fleet, who were termed "the front," that naval funding was unbalanced and light forces and new technologies underresourced. They largely attributed this situation to von Tirpitz. The argument was not new. The essentially political purpose of the fleet created by von Tirpitz's Navy Laws, the grand admiral's own mindset, and the limits of funding were significant restraints on innovation. Von Tirpitz had seen off a number of critics in earlier years who had wanted a greater priority for torpedo craft and development of submersibles to pursue what was termed the *Kleinkrieg* (little war).[17] Von Tirpitz himself viewed the battleship as the defining unit of power, sufficient numbers of which would force Britain to acknowledge Germany as a naval near equal, too strong to be attacked without the risk of losses on a scale that would undermine Britain's historic maritime supremacy. This was the Risk Fleet theory. His priority was thus the big ships and his political arguments for funding centered on them. Von Tirpitz's difficulty was that the increasing demands from "the front" for a more flexible distribution of funds came when the whole basis of the Navy Laws was under question. The political complexion of the national parliament had changed and the unsympathetic Social Democrats were dominant. Furthermore, the threat from the resurgent French and Russian armies greatly strengthened the army's arguments for a higher priority than the navy, whose only achievement by 1912, in many eyes, had been to alienate the British. Although von Tirpitz himself never admitted it, that year saw the foundations of his policy destroyed. These factors combined with the realities of Germany's finances to slow, if not halt, the High Sea Fleet's expansion. There was little prospect of any increase and, in such circumstances, neither von Tirpitz nor the Imperial German Navy could ever really be ready for war with the British—something of which the younger von Moltke, Chief of the German General Staff, had accused the grand admiral in December 1912.[18]

The dead hand of economy lay on many elements. Since the Navy Laws, the fleet had expanded from a force that included only four battleships that could match the Royal Navy's first line units, to one that mustered thirteen dreadnought battleships and four battle cruisers, of which only the battle cruiser *Goeben* was not in German waters. Four more battleships and a battle cruiser were nearing completion. The German capital ships were designed for the North Sea and the Baltic. Their internal subdivisioning was excellent and they were well armored, but their main armament was lighter than that of their British contemporaries, and the 28-cm gun in the older ships was probably too small for the job against the British battle line. Against the more lightly protected British battle cruisers it would be a different matter, although the 30.5-cm gun of the newest units was a much more powerful weapon. The restraint on gun size had been largely a matter of money and von Tirpitz's judgment; the Germans finally moved to 38-cm in battleships laid down in 1913, but the first would not complete until 1916. The other deficiency was the ships' machinery. Apart from the problems with coal that would soon emerge, propulsion plants had rarely been subjected to extended high-speed running and the other demands that war would bring. The navy later admitted that it "took too optimistic a view of the probable performance of our ships with regard to speed, particularly the battle cruisers."[19]

The near parity of the battle lines was not wholly reflected in the other arms. Von Tirpitz later justified his approach by acknowledging in part that the available funding left "less room than ever for subsidiary matters."[20] Such restrictions had their effects. German mines were better designed and considerably more reliable than British mines, but stocks were limited and the need to conserve them was to be a significant constraint in the deployment of defensive and offensive fields. Von

Tirpitz also asserted that he was the first to make submarines a priority "as soon as sea-going boats were built," but the Germans were not the leaders in submersible construction or operations in 1914—and, despite the work on rigid airships, not in naval aviation, about which von Tirpitz was equally cautious.[21] The submarine force was still learning its trade. Although there had been some startling successes in the 1913 maneuvers, the airships had yet to prove themselves. Furthermore, neither the numbers of light cruisers nor the size and endurance of the torpedo boats were adequate to meet emerging operational requirements, a point repeatedly made by the fleet commander and his subordinates in the Scouting Groups.[22]

The High Sea Fleet had been evolving its own conception of a Grand Fleet of Battle, but the light forces were not yet up to the task of operating for extended periods well into the North Sea, and many of the coordinated operations conducted with the battle squadrons had been in the context of coastal defense, not extended offshore sorties. There had been fleet deployments into the Atlantic in earlier years, but after 1911 they fell victim to financial restraint. Individual cruises by battle cruisers across the Atlantic and that of two *Kaiser*-class battleships to West Africa and South America early in 1914 were very much the exception, and the latter had only a single light cruiser in company. The dangers of the big ships operating without torpedo craft support were clear, and so was the fact that a fleet action had to be in the southeastern North Sea to allow their participation. Here and in many other areas the Germans had difficult problems to solve, since even the most modern units had deficiencies. A misguided effort to reduce the cost of torpedo boats in the *V1* class of 1912 resulted in their being poor sea-keepers and with such limited endurance that they received the derisive sobriquet of *Lans-Krüppel* (Lans cripples).[23] In this case, Vice Admiral Wilhelm von Lans took the blame as Inspector of Torpedo Forces, but the attempt to save money was inspired by von Tirpitz. The grand admiral had much to answer for.

4

THE RUSSIANS

HOSTILITIES CAME TOO SOON FOR THE IMPERIAL RUSSIAN NAVY, WHICH had a target of 1917 to achieve a fully operational state. The nine years that followed the end of the disastrous war with Japan had been a long haul for the Baltic Fleet. Dispatched as reinforcements to the Far East, its most modern ships had been sunk or captured at Tsushima. While it did not experience violence on the scale of the mutiny in the battleship *Potemkin* and other Black Sea units in 1905, the rump of the Baltic Fleet was wracked by the popular upheavals of the day. Rebuilding was slow. Many of the units interned in Far Eastern ports during the war made their way back to the Baltic by 1906, but Russia's financial situation and the disruption following the aborted revolution of 1905 practically paralyzed the shipyards for years. The battleship *Slava*, completed too late in 1905 to deploy, was the only modern capital ship in the Baltic until the return of *Tsesarevich* the following year and the completion of *Imperator Pavel* and *Andrei Pervozvanny* at the end of 1910. These ships had been modified in the light of war experience, but their pre-dreadnought design meant that they were no match for the first line of the High Sea Fleet. The cruiser force was in similar shape. Although completed in France and Russia between 1908 and 1911, *Admiral Makarov* and her two sisters were obsolete by the time of their commissioning. The only really useful heavy unit was the powerful armored cruiser *Rurik*, commissioned in Britain in 1908, but she was outclassed by the German battle cruisers, which possessed not only much more powerful broadsides, but also several knots' speed advantage.

There was a building program under way, but its shape and size had taken years to settle. Even when funds became available as the economy expanded rapidly after 1906, the naval effort was divided between the Baltic Sea (map 4.1) and the Black Sea, since Russia had to consider both theaters. Indeed, the Turkish threat became progressively more serious after 1910 as the Turks embarked on their own effort to acquire dreadnoughts. The first four battleships, which were to be the core of the future Baltic Fleet, were not laid down until 1909. Two, *Sevastopol* and *Poltava,* were complete but not yet fully operational. The second pair was not far behind, but all would require several months' work before they were ready

MAP 4.1   Baltic Sea

for combat. Four battle cruisers were at a less advanced stage of construction and the first could not be available until at least 1915. She would never be completed.

Russia's limited ability to produce modern warships had been recognized by the order of two light cruisers from German yards, but these were now lost to the Imperial Russian Navy and would soon enter German service. None of the four light cruisers under construction in the Russian Baltic shipyards would be finished before the end of the war. The submarine force consisted of only eight obsolescent and unreliable boats in the frontline brigade and three even more elderly craft as training units. The *Bars* class were building, but their completion would be delayed because much of their machinery had been ordered from Germany.[1] In fact, the only product of the new fleet plan already in service was the fast destroyer *Novik*, forerunner of what was intended to be a large class of the fastest and most heavily armed destroyers in the world.

The deficiencies reflected the difficulties of reforming the navy. Despite the starkness with which the service's inadequacies had been demonstrated during the Russo-Japanese War, its reorganization was protracted and too dependent on individual personalities. While many, particularly in the junior ranks, were

determined not to repeat the mistakes of 1904–5, there remained highly conservative vested interests, both within the navy and in the civil bureaucracy and a
system dominated by committees whose accountability was, at best, ambiguous.[2]
Soon after the end of the Russo-Japanese conflict, the younger officers set up
"study groups" to agitate for reform, paralleling a similar Young Turks movement
in the army. They gained an important ally in the tsar himself. Nicholas II had
received some naval training, including a period at sea, and his understanding
of naval matters was more sophisticated than many of his advisers. The antique
office of General-Admiral, usually occupied by a member of the royal family, was
replaced by a minister of the navy shortly after the battle of Tsushima. With the
tsar's approval, a Naval General Staff was formed in 1906 to conduct long-range
planning.[3] The Naval General Staff's numbers rapidly expanded from fifteen to
forty. Its activities eventually subsumed much of the efforts of the study groups,
probably because it involved the same officers.[4]

At the same time, political developments following the establishment of the
Russian parliament, the Duma, in 1906 put a spotlight on naval and military
reform. From 1907 liberal elements within the Duma became increasingly vocal,
but it was not until 1911 as a result of their pressure that the energetic Vice Admiral Ivan Grigorovich took over the navy portfolio and momentum developed for
real reform elsewhere in the naval administration. In that year the Naval General
Staff was placed under the minister, which meant that the navy's planning and
administrative elements were under one authority. Similarly, although he was a
key figure within the Baltic Fleet as a junior flag officer from 1906 onward, it took
the accession of Vice Admiral Nikolai von Essen to the post of commander in
the Baltic in 1908 to bring about really substantial improvements within the fleet
itself. One of the relatively few senior officers to distinguish himself in the war
with Japan, von Essen's dynamism put new life into his people and ships.

There were other factors. Apart from the tsar's continuing strong personal
support, the Duma found the navy's officials much more cooperative than those
of the War Ministry and was thus more inclined to provide them money.[5] Grigorovich himself proved particularly adept at working with the Duma's financial
committees. By 1911 the navy was receiving more funding for new ships than was
the army for its reequipment. The funding was not only official: in this more hopeful environment, popular support also grew. A National Committee was formed
that raised enough subscriptions to pay for a substantial number of extra destroyers and submarines.[6]

The Russian navy and its design elements were not unsophisticated. It is arguable that the technical and innovative capacities of its expert personnel were considerably greater than the ability of Russian industry to support their intent. This
forced the Russians to purchase much of their equipment overseas, which allowed
them to acquire emergent technology, such as the new fire control systems being
developed in Britain, and combine it with their own devices, but left them hostage

to situations in which a supplier such as Germany became an enemy.[7] The effect in 1914 on the shipbuilding program would be devastating. It was also awkward for torpedoes, since substantial Russian purchases were made from the Whitehead factory at Fiume (modern Rijeka) in Austria-Hungary, and much of the Russian local effort to that point had been the licensed assembly of components.[8] Nevertheless, Russian torpedo and gunnery standards were not behind those of their adversaries and some of their thinking, such as automatic torpedo salvo firing and triple torpedo tubes, the provision of higher gun elevation to extend the range, triple turrets, and the quality of weapon design were in the forefront of development. The Russians were also acutely aware of their industrial vulnerability and had made substantial efforts to establish local armament works, including a cooperative venture with the British firm of Vickers, as well as improving their shipyards.[9] This work had consumed almost as much money as the shipbuilding programs themselves.

The Baltic Fleet had its own difficulties. There were formidable challenges for training in the eastern part of the sea. The key challenge was environmental. As the Baltic iced up from December—and sometimes earlier—navigation became impossible and remained so until at least April. This meant that the ships had to remain at their bases, with limited opportunities for practical training, a situation exacerbated by the cold and hours of darkness. Admiral von Essen did his best to train all year round, operating in ice-free waters to the west for as long into winter as he could, but it was no easy matter.[10] The problem was partly solved, particularly for basic training, by the dispatch of squadrons to cruise in southern European waters over the winter months, but this alternative was not available to the torpedo craft and submarines, which were lucky to experience a seven-month window of operations annually. Even the long daylight hours of summer caused problems, since they limited the ability of the torpedo forces and the offensive minelayers to practice in tactically realistic settings. Climate had another effect, since the more temperate Black Sea was a better location for experiments. This meant, among other things, that the bulk of the early aviation effort was not available to the Baltic Fleet, although an aviation element was formally established in the Baltic in 1912.[11]

Many of the ratings had limited education and this, combined with the lack of modern equipment in the fleet, created difficulties in developing collective expertise. There were too many conscripts and the annual turnover of ratings represented another challenge for the maintenance of unit efficiency. Efforts to encourage junior sailors to reengage and to recruit boy seamen as future long-service petty officers helped, but were not enough. There also remained great gulfs between officers and sailors, and there is evidence that the gap widened in the decade after the 1905 disturbances, perhaps because of mutual uncertainty and suspicion.[12] The events of 1905 had highlighted the potential of the navy as a seed-bed of dissidence to the revolutionary forces in Russia and there was constant concern as to the possibility of internal subversion. Although many of the younger officers possessed a much more professional outlook than their predecessors and their training curriculum had greatly improved since 1905, the system of discipline remained harsh and the disparity between the living conditions of the wardroom and the lower deck was extreme—the sailors appearing to exist on "bowls of soup and black bread."[13] Just as in the other navies, relationships in the small ship and submarine forces were much closer than in the battleships and cruisers, but a British submarine officer in 1914 was horrified to see "the [Russian] officer of the watch spit in a rating's face when he was brought up as a defaulter."[14]

The key Russian advantage was in mine warfare. Russian mines caused the majority of Japanese losses in 1904–5. Von Essen had been appointed to command the Baltic mine and torpedo craft force in 1906 and continued to oversee its improvement after he assumed leadership of the whole Baltic Fleet. Systematic development of new and increasingly effective mine types continued until the outbreak of war, together with regular purchases of additional war stocks—5,000 in 1912 and 4,200 in 1914, of which 1,800 were intended for the Baltic. By the outbreak of war, there were some 7,000 mines available in theater.[15] Von Essen was not satisfied with a purely defensive role and agitated for years for minelaying raids into the southern part of the sea to be an integral component of the fleet's operational concept. This had yet to be formally incorporated into the war plans, but high hopes were held for the offensive capabilities of the new large destroyers, such as *Novik,* that combined the capacity to lay mines with a formidable gun and torpedo armament, as well as the new submarines.

There was another strength. The Russians had already developed relatively sophisticated techniques in signals intelligence, with ships' radio personnel being trained in interception and simple analysis. Basic direction finding and interception had been practiced during the prewar maneuvers.[16] Realizing its vulnerability, the Russians, like the British but unlike the Germans, were relatively circumspect in their own employment of wireless. Organizational capacity for higher-level work came in the form of the Observation and Communications Service established by Captain A. I. Nepenin, who was to be one of the key figures in the Baltic conflict. This was intended as a control and observation system to link the coastal defenses at the entrance to the Gulf of Finland with the seagoing units, particularly the minesweepers, but it also included a signals intelligence element to support the higher command. This would prove extremely useful when the major German code books passed into Russian hands after the grounding and capture of the light cruiser *Magdeburg.*

Much would depend for the Russians on the success of their land campaigns. The defensive mindset of the Russian high command in the theater could be overcome only if there was reasonable confidence as to the security of Saint Petersburg. This had yet to be achieved and the absence of that security would restrict fleet operations for months to come.

Operational Challenges

5

T HE OPERATIONAL CHALLENGES OF 1914 ARE NOT EASY TO UNDERSTAND A century later. The breakneck development of technology at the time makes them difficult to define, all the more because many of the ways in which things actually worked are no longer known to us. The experience of sea combat during the war creates filters that distort our view, while the absence, destruction, or corruption of records blurs analysis. Hindsight plays a part, as does the tendency to minimize (or highlight) what were later seen as mistakes.

Yet an attempt can be made and historians have done much in the past few decades. Managing technical advances was a work in progress in August 1914. Each service labored under its own institutional and strategic constraints, but the need to bring together complex systems had become increasingly apparent and was being addressed, however imperfectly. Given the "perfect collision" that had arisen from the sudden emergence of so many new technologies—such as wireless, aviation, and submarines, as well as analog computers and gyroscopes— arguably the biggest problem was that the protagonists ran out of time. There were difficulties at every level, since nothing stood still and there was never enough money. Furthermore, there was constant tension between the achieved capabilities of the emergent technology and those promised but yet to be realized. The added complication was that integration of the new had to include the old. A similar discipline applied in trying to decide just what the potential adversary could and would do—as well as what he could not do.

Matters were not helped by the fact that there were many prophets of the new technology, whose predictions were revolutionary—and often prescient—but did not reflect the realities of the day. The necessary preoccupation of commanders at sea with the practical issues of operations was different from the debates that went on over future force structures and new construction. There was, of course, a dynamic relationship between planners and practitioners and the achievement of operational status by new technology could be remarkably fast, but the acceptance of proposals for new force structures with their associated operational concepts did not equate to immediate adoption within contemporary doctrine. Many of the statements of those responsible for capability development as they spoke of "airy navies grappling in the central blue"—Admiral of the Fleet Lord Fisher is a key example—had to be understood in the future tense, even when the rate of change of technology was so rapid.[1] On the other hand, operational commanders and staffs had always to keep in mind what was achievable with the tools at hand.

The battle fleet itself epitomized many of the factors at play. Moves had begun more than a decade before in all the major navies toward what the British came to call the Grand Fleet of Battle. This was an attempt to create a force capable of matching any kind of gun or torpedo threat by bringing together battleships, battle cruisers, and other scouting units and light forces into one tactical formation. The combination was intended to ensure the destruction of an opposing force, while the battleships on which the construct was centered were adequately protected. This would now be termed a combined arms approach, one whose logic in retrospect is obvious, particularly as it represented the conceptual basis for the battle groups or task forces that dominated maritime warfare for the remainder of the twentieth century.

But there were extraordinarily complicated problems in making the idea work. The new tactical formation had four to five times more ships than the customary battle fleets of the previous era. Even though wireless helped make its command and control feasible, there were great difficulties to be overcome in managing so many ships at much greater distances (and speeds) than in the past, and the communications organization as a whole was under enormous stress. The formation also had to employ units not designed to meet the operational conditions involved. This included pre-dreadnoughts, still significant in every battle line; as well as armored cruisers, which were too weak to face the new battle cruisers but too slow to run away; and torpedo craft, which lacked the endurance to operate with a fleet for more than a couple of days, even if weather conditions did not force them to run for cover. There were many other factors to consider, the submarine and aircraft being only two, but the difficulties encountered in making the fleet work as a whole were such that some senior British commanders were having increasing doubts as to its practicability.[2] The coming conflict was to demonstrate that there was little alternative, but that such an assessment could be made by expert authority indicates just how complex the problems of naval warfare were in 1914.

Geography, oceanography, and climate combined to present formidable problems for the would-be operators of the new technology at sea. First, there were tyrannies of both distance and proximity. That the British Isles lay between Germany and the open ocean and that Russia was largely confined within the Baltic were strategic realities within which the conflict in northern European waters would be fought. The British were in a position to close the English Channel in the south to surface traffic and, with greater difficulty, the passages between the

Scottish islands, Norway, Iceland, and Greenland. Yet there was much more to the matter than this. The Germans were disadvantaged in their access to the open ocean, but had the benefit of a short and well-defended North Sea coast with the outpost of Heligoland as a base for light craft. The British east coast, on the other hand was long and sparsely protected. It was less than twenty hours steaming at eighteen knots from the principal anchorages of the High Sea Fleet to the north-eastern ports of England, but some fourteen hours from the Grand Fleet's base at Scapa Flow. If the Germans were to strike for the Thames estuary, the problem was even worse, since the Grand Fleet had nearly twice the distance to travel to support the much weaker British forces in the south. Without warning, it would be very difficult to achieve an interception even of a retreating German formation by the main fleet.

The entrance to the Baltic represented a complication for both sides. The Germans feared that the British would send a fleet through the Kattegat, while the British were concerned that the Germans, particularly their battle cruisers, would deploy unexpectedly into the North Sea by the same route. For both, the attitude of Denmark would be critical and that, although the subject of much debate within both naval staffs in previous years, was yet to be determined. Even if the British did not attempt an entry, the problem of warning time also existed in the Baltic, in which the transit distances were much the same as in the North Sea. While the Russians could close off the eastern Gulf of Finland, their western coasts were open to attack. Similarly, although the major German bases were well defended, there were long stretches of German coast and shipping routes that would be vulnerable.

A second problem was the climate, an enemy in itself. The North Sea was not an easy place in which to operate. Conditions were grim in the Scottish winter, with little more than six hours of daylight at Scapa Flow in late December. Gale-force winds prevailed in that season for nearly half the time, at temperatures only a few degrees above freezing. Cloud cover was almost constant, while rain, snow, or fog frequently reduced visibility to a few yards. The summer months were even more subject to fog than were the winter months, negating some of the benefits of extended daylight and lighter winds. The prevalence of mist increased farther away from the coast. There were also strong tidal streams around the northern islands, whose effects could be felt well out to sea. Matters were not much better in the south. There were not as many gales, but fog was a perennial problem. It was rare to have fewer than five fogbound days a month, and there were periods and regions in which visibility was restricted for up to a third of the time. Ironically, the foggiest place in the North Sea was some one hundred miles to seaward of Heligoland, perhaps the most likely location for a fleet encounter. Many areas of the sea had tidal streams and currents of two knots or more, while their strength and direction were subject to weather, making prediction very difficult.[3]

The Baltic was just as confronting and shared with the North Sea the characteristic that there could be intense weather in one locality, while totally different conditions prevailed only a short distance away. Large parts of the sea became icebound from November onward, with some coastal areas in the northeast not free of ice until May in a severe season. The closure of the inner regions of the Gulf of Finland was expected, but a bitter winter could see even the channels between Denmark and Sweden shut to shipping without the assistance of ice breakers. In these circumstances, practically every port in the Baltic would be more or less icebound in the absence of such help. Fog was even more frequent than it was in the North Sea, although the effects of the landmass surrounding the Baltic and the interaction of ice and water made it more likely in winter than in summer. Gales were also common, particularly in southern waters, while currents around the sea were strong. Predictable in calm weather, they were susceptible to the influence of wind in ways that the British Admiralty's guide for local navigation, the *Baltic Pilot,* declared called for "constant watchfulness and forethought" on the part of the mariner.[4] Both Germans and Russians would soon be painfully reminded of this reality.

Fog had potential to combine with another challenge—funnel smoke.[5] The bigger the coal-burning fleet, the greater was the volume of smoke. Apart from the direct effect of such pollution on visibility, there was often the formation of smog when particulates combined with moisture in the atmosphere. While rarely the impenetrable yellow-grey of a London pea-souper, the resulting mixture could reduce local visibility to within a few hundred yards, making visual signaling, scouting, and fire control very difficult.

Navigation affected many operational issues in 1914. The North Sea and Baltic were ringed by lights, fog signals, and buoys, but the onset of war would see the dousing or removal of many devices. Ships would have to rely largely on their own ability to calculate their positions. This was as much art as science. Gyroscopic compasses had only just come into service. The Germans were the first to move, in 1908 (the first British sea trial was in 1910), but the new compasses were not trusted,[6] and for good reason, particularly in rough weather.[7] Associated with fire control systems, gyros were also largely confined at this time to capital ships—in the Royal Navy at the outbreak of war only the 13.5-inch gun units were fitted. The exception was submarines, for which the gyro compass represented almost as important a development as the periscope, since there were problems with magnetic compasses inside a submerged metal hull, but even here the British fit was just beginning.

The great majority of ships still relied on magnetic units. Unlike the gyro, there was a vast body of knowledge—seventy-eight pages were devoted to the subject in the Admiralty's first *Manual of Navigation.*[8] Such expertise was vital as the influence of the metal in a ship's structure (deviation) and local magnetic changes (variation) could be significant. Furthermore, these effects were not completely predictable. Gunfire could unsettle a magnetic compass, as could rotating turrets, and there were increasing concerns about interference from wireless installations and other electrical systems.[9] In some battleships, in which the compass was positioned near the forward funnel, deviation could vary between 2 and 5 degrees depending on the wind's direction and its cooling effect on the mass of metal in the funnel. Variation could change by up to 5 degrees during a four-hundred-mile passage around the English coast.[10] There were also local magnetic anomalies, not all of which were known. Although compass cards had been marked with 360 degrees in the Royal Navy from 1910, the imprecision of magnetic compasses meant that courses were normally ordered in no smaller units than half points (5.625 degrees).

Measurement of speed through the water was achieved by a patent log fitted in the larger and more modern units, but this had its own inaccuracies. Some of the smaller ships were yet to carry such equipment and used engine revolutions to estimate distance run. This became very hit and miss in rough weather. Even if a compass were accepted as accurate within half a degree and the calculation of speed to 5 percent either way, the resulting pool of errors when steaming at ten knots for just one hour created an area of more than 350 yards in breadth and 1,000 yards in length. In ten hours, in the absence of other navigational information, the pool could be nearly two nautical miles in one direction and five in the other.

It was true the ability of expert navigators—and experienced seamen generally—to estimate their position could be uncanny. One legendary example was Henry Oliver's achievement, as navigator of the British Channel Fleet in 1901, in bringing it in formation from Islay to an anchorage off the Scilly Islands in thick fog—some 470 miles.[11] Yet even in peacetime things could easily go wrong, particularly in poor visibility. It took the war for a magnetic compass to be fitted to the bridge of the older British destroyers, which hitherto had only a unit in the wheelhouse below. In its absence, a destroyer captain, in dense fog "turned a complete circle and did not realize it until I found myself cutting through the line and nearly having a collision."[12] Uncertain of his own navigational skills, the captain of a torpedo boat accompanying a submarine flotilla on a coastal passage to Newcastle had his faith severely shaken in the expertise of the depot ship. His guide "mistook *Blyth* [emphasis in original] for Newcastle, and was leading us up to the front door of that seaport before the error was discovered!"[13] The formation had steamed nearly ten miles straight past its intended destination. In November 1914 a German block ship nearly entered the Russian port of Libau in mistake for the German port of Memel (Klaipeda), some fifty nautical miles farther south.[14] Of wartime conditions, one experienced navigator noted, "I never expected to be within five miles [of my estimated position] after eight hours steaming."[15]

There were other sources of information, but they had their limits. Astronomical navigation was one, but the requirement for the right combination of clear skies and a definite horizon—possible only just before or just after sunrise—meant that stars could rarely be relied on. Matters were not much better for measuring the sun's altitude, even in clear weather, since the calculations were largely dependent for accuracy on ships maintaining a steady course and speed between sights. This would rarely be operationally practicable. On the other hand, depth measurements and the type of seabed were very important. So were accurate data about tidal streams and currents and the British did much to improve their knowledge. Surveying was conducted around the northern islands as early as 1895 and in the Firth of Forth the year after. This was followed by work on the west coast of Scotland and, from 1906, around Scapa Flow. After 1907 there were efforts to improve tidal stream and magnetic variation data in the North Sea itself.

The British emphasis on depth soundings increased further in 1910, partly because the development of sounding machines to replace the traditional hand-held lead line allowed more systematic exploitation of bottom topography. The significance of accurate soundings for those who "have to act on the offensive on a low-lying, stormy coast, without lights, beacons or buoys" had been recognized years before.[16] So important did improved knowledge of the southern North Sea's depth contours become that four cruisers were assigned to assist the surveying ships. Two trawlers were specially fitted out for North Sea surveying in 1912, while in 1913 tidal measurement was undertaken southward from the Dogger Bank.[17] Yet in mid-1914 many small ships had yet to be fitted with a sounding machine, despite the recognition that "the hand lead . . . as a general rule is thoroughly unreliable."[18] The Germans were generally no better off, notwithstanding gyro compasses. Despite a rapidly increasing potential for long-range operations, none of their U-boats carried a chronometer, essential in providing accurate time for astro-navigation calculations.[19] This meant, in effect, that they were not intended to operate out of sight of land for extended periods.

Navigational concerns were recognized within the Royal Navy. Efforts were made from 1903 to increase the expertise of the specialist navigators, as well as the skills of all seamen officers, since many ships were too small to carry an officer qualified "N." In addition to a comprehensive suite of training courses, a *Pilotage Handbook* for general use was produced in 1906 and superseded in 1914 by the first *Manual of Navigation*.[20] Nevertheless, the very basic tools available and the working environment of a wind-, rain-, and sometimes sea-swept open bridge, with a canvas dodger often all there was to protect the chart table, meant that many ships were hard pushed to maintain an accurate navigational solution, even at the best of times. In battle, with the competing requirements of armament, signaling, station keeping, and maneuvering, navigation would often be more guesswork than calculation.

This difficulty of each unit knowing where it was created problems of coordination that in 1914 had still to be fully worked through. Unless vessels were in sight of each other, a commander receiving a report could not be sure of the relative error in a stated position. There was always the risk that the combined errors would be cumulative. Depending on the visibility, a small difference in reckoning could result in failure to make contact with the enemy. There were also implications for friendly forces. Accumulating navigational errors made rendezvous or return to the main body in the open sea a chancy business.

This was a well-recognized problem and one reason why the British viewed night fighting as risky. It may have been at the root of the difference between attitudes to night warfare, in that the Royal Navy had to assume it would be working in or from the open sea, with an uncertain sense of position, while the High Sea Fleet expected to be operating defensively, close to its own coasts and with more confidence in its collective navigational reckoning. As the British C-in-C of the Home Fleets reported of the 1913 maneuvers, "[N]ight attacks by destroyers were practically non-existent, the reason being doubtless the same as it would be in war time, namely, that no one knew where to send them to attack either the enemy fleet or enemy torpedo craft."[21]

New issues came with wireless. Before its introduction, because the admiral was always in sight of the scouting unit or its relay, it was enough to pass a simple bearing when reporting the enemy. This was not the case with radio, since the units concerned could be many miles apart, but there was no servicewide message format in the Royal Navy for reporting an enemy contact. This reflected a collective lack of understanding. The 1913 maneuvers showed that many units left out vital information, failing to indicate either their own position or that of the enemy, as well as omitting other details such as courses and speeds, but the problem had yet to be faced in full. For example, March 1913 instructions to "Ships Watching the Enemy" did not refer to position among the required elements ("class, number, order, course and speed"), even of a first sighting report.[22] The Germans were further ahead than the British through their creation of a square system that provided reference positions much simpler to transmit than latitude and longitude. Although this had been experimented with during maneuvers, the Royal Navy did not introduce an equivalent until the end of 1914.[23]

One reason for progress being slow was that the concept did not yet exist of a tactical plot—that is, a plan on which the movements of own and enemy forces were systematically set down in what would now be described as near real time on charts and used for tactical decision making. Ships already maintained charts to record and predict their own navigation, and flagships that of their formations, but they did not extend the practice to reckoning the position and likely movements of the enemy in battle in the same way. That aspect was still managed within the heads of the opposing commanders, or at best with a Mooring Board or a Battenberg that gave a relative velocity solution in relation to just *one* other unit. Curiously, this was despite the fact that tactical war games, which involved plotting and prediction, were frequently conducted within contemporary navies.[24]

Until the creation of a fleet that possessed multiple types, the basic tactical problem was one of two opposed battle lines, but more was needed when other formations had to be coordinated as well. Early efforts to develop what were thought of as tactical plots focused on achieving what was fundamentally a fire control solution on a single unit or formation, rather than plotting the movements of multiple forces on both sides with the aim of coordinating the movements of one's own *entire* fleet with regard to *all* the enemy forces.[25] The 1914 proposals had the same limitation to one "target," even when providing for the movement of separate divisions of battleships against the enemy.[26] The first efforts to improve accuracy were focused on the flagship's own movements, as in the clockwork Chalmers Dead Reckoning Calculator, rather than the mechanized plotting table eventually produced that could keep multiple tracks up to date. The idea existed in part in 1914 in the intelligence offices set up in major units as part of their preparations for war, but not enough to help in real time. They recorded the general positions of friendly, neutral, and enemy ships, but initially worked at intervals of hours (or even days) and on small-scale charts (such as one of the entire North Sea, as in *Lion*).[27] The intelligence offices were also usually somewhat removed from the bridge and conning tower and difficult to access in a fast-moving situation.

The Admiralty worked hard to create a system of controlling dispersed forces based on its fusion of sighting reports and intelligence within the War Room, which was eventually divided into two to cover home waters and the rest of the globe. These plots were a solid foundation for the conduct of naval operations at the strategic level and were maintained in peacetime to provide a picture of global warship movements as well as merchant traffic. The home waters War Room (No. 1) was brought into full operation for the prewar Grand Maneuvers, but proved a mixed success for operational control, notwithstanding the 1910 experiment in which the First Sea Lord in Whitehall maneuvered a battle squadron off Spain.[28] Although Admiralty radio direction of the movements of major formations was central to the concept and further experimented with during fleet exercises, its limitations were such that the division of authority between the C-in-C of the Home Fleets and the Admiralty had yet to be fully defined. This would cause significant problems in the early months of the war.[29]

There proved to be no alternative to controlling widely dispersed formations at sea by such means. The War Room was never subject to radio silence and was inherently much better equipped for operational decision making than even a fleet flagship. Yet it would not be quite enough in 1914–18. The position errors were too great using the technology of the era to achieve consistent success in allowing reports to be translated consistently into information sufficiently precise for tactical use. In the absence of sensors other than the human eye, the limits of visibility determined the range at which units could make contact with the enemy. As was to be confirmed during the war—and had already been demonstrated during maneuvers—that range was sometimes close to zero. Given that the combined pool of errors was potentially greater than the visual horizon, even when conditions were good, achieving contact would always be an uncertain business. It was no coincidence that the major surface actions of the North Sea war—Dogger Bank and Jutland—both started on mornings of exceptional visibility.

Both the Grand Fleet of Battle and the use of the War Rooms by the Admiralty depended on the extended range communications that wireless made possible. But this technology had significant drawbacks. Radio performance depended directly on the available power, as well as the wavelength, which itself depended on the antenna size. Thus, larger ships generally had longer-range outfits, which operated on different frequencies to those of the small ships. The operating ranges for the latter were severely limited, with sixty miles being the accepted range for destroyer installations in 1914. Radios were expensive and trained personnel in short supply; even the most modern big ships did not have enough installations to cover all the frequencies in use in a fleet. This required arrangements by which particular big ships were designated to guard the small ship frequencies, passing back and forth any information to their flagship. The reliability of such practices depended directly on the serviceability of the gear and the expertise of those involved. Both could vary significantly.[30]

In all navies, shortages of trained personnel created problems of maintenance and operation, exacerbated by the fit of radios to ever more ships. The effects of atmospherics on wireless performance were still to be fully comprehended, even by the most expert. The fact that wireless quickly became clogged by excessive signaling was, however, well understood. Guidance was developed to overcome this, including direction that only the senior officer of a group should make reports to higher authority. When in doubt, a unit was to transmit only if there had been no signal from the senior ship.[31] In the congested radio environment of multiship encounters, this was not easy to confirm.

Congestion, as well as timeliness, also complicated wireless' use for maneuvering, even when conducted via separate, low-power radio sets. Timeliness could be purchased at the expense of security, since the simplest coding procedures lengthened the process inordinately, but congestion was difficult to avoid, particularly when the tactical situation became complicated. Given that visual signals could often not span the complex new formations being organized, radio was essential, but the balance of radio and visual signaling to order maneuvers had yet to be settled. This was one of the biggest problems for operations on the scale of one hundred ships or more as it became apparent that the difficulties became overwhelming during the critical encounter phase. The British C-in-C himself had realized that a point was reached when control by one commander became impossible. The only alternative seemed to be delegation. Callaghan explained to his admirals that, from this point in an action, "vessels . . . should expect neither signals nor instructions as to what is required of them. . . . *[N]one should remain inactive if they are able to make effective use of their force.*"[32] The difficulty, as Andrew Gordon has explained, was that such ideas went against much of the Royal Navy's tactical culture.[33] They were also in conflict with commanders such as Jellicoe, who came to believe that close control of the fleet provided surety that maneuvers neither be at the expense of accurate fire control, nor expose isolated subformations to concentrated enemy torpedo and gunfire.

Other aspects to radios needed consideration. Signals intelligence was in its infancy and communications security still an open frontier. With their hard-won combat experience, the Russians were further ahead than others, but every navy was slowly becoming aware of the possibilities of exploiting wireless.[34] The Germans began monitoring British wireless traffic as early as 1907, but, although they gained much useful information, they focused more on British radio technology and procedures than operational intelligence. They were first alerted by the Austro-Hungarian navy to the potential of this aspect of signals intelligence in 1912, but did not advance beyond the basic monitoring of traffic already occurring.[35] Formal British efforts began in 1908. Overall, the Royal Navy had much the same approach to the Germans, monitoring wireless traffic during the 1913 High Sea Fleet maneuvers to study their methods.[36] The major Admiralty stations occasionally took in and recorded high-power German wireless transmissions, but this was not systematic.[37] Activity from 1911 centered on a small-scale analysis effort, led by Fleet Paymaster C. J. E. Rotter in the NID, with at least one attempt made to purchase German codes from a spy in country.[38]

There was much more grassroots activity, even including enthusiastic amateur civilians, although the term "amateur" does not convey a wholly fair impression of who were the real experts, since the culture within the radio rooms was similar to that of present-day computer hackers. Ships frequently did their own traffic analysis and decryption, as well as experimenting with jamming and deception. Ships with linguists in their crews paid close attention to transmissions in other languages. Estimates of distance based on signal strength were very hit-and-miss, but the identity of particular stations and even individual operators could often be established with near certainty. This was more useful information in the less-crowded environment of overseas stations than it was in northern Europe, but it sometimes proved valuable during exercises. Instructions for the British 1913 maneuvers declared, "[T]here is no objection to attempts being made to discover codes and cyphers, and to use information obtained from intercepted signals, whether made *en clair* or otherwise."[39] The mathematical skills available at sea were enough to deal with some of the early, very simple cyphers.[40] It was assessed in 1913 that the British transposition cypher took only an hour to break.[41] Nevertheless, although many were well aware of the potential for wireless' exploitation by an adversary, a systematic approach to achieving the right balance between security, particularly radio silence, and communication had yet to develop in any navy. Just listening in would prove much more valuable than it should have.

Problems of movement affected every aspect of operations in the coming conflict. Steam ships' requirements for fuel had needed careful consideration from their first entry into service. If a leeward shore and unfavorable winds were no longer the primary concerns of commanders, coal consumption certainly was. As the nineteenth century had drawn on, improved machinery efficiency reduced but never removed this problem. For a fleet deployed away from its own coasts, matters were managed by rigorous fuel economy and the establishment of forward operating bases at which colliers were stationed. This remained so even after the development of torpedo craft, since, with quick-firing guns, ships could defend themselves by day and, if not surprised, by night. The limitations of torpedo boats in finding and attacking an enemy were much less if the target was located in a known position. In the North Sea, with its shallow water and multitude of sand- and mud-banks, temporary secret anchorages could be organized between the banks, even if sheltered and protectable harbors were not available. The Baltic offered similar opportunities in the lee of its many islands. An early attraction of oil firing was that oil could be much more easily provided in such circumstances than coal. British attempts before 1908 to transfer coal between big ships and destroyers in a seaway did not go well.[42]

The submarine changed the situation completely, creating the constant possibility of surprise attack during daylight hours. This was bad enough for surface ships when close to the enemy's coast, but the submersible's rapid development made it much more than an asset for local defense. The submarine was evolving into an offensive weapon for the high sea. Indeed, as a former commander of the Royal Navy's submarine force noted in 1913, the operational endurance of submarines had become "greater . . . than [ever was] possible in steamships."[43] This not only created the need for much more comprehensive protection of bases, but also meant that any warship at sea was at risk practically all the time. An early victim was the use of anchorages among the North Sea banks, which would be extremely vulnerable to submarine attack if located. The Royal Navy abandoned the idea in 1910, although the Germans continued with the technique in the Baltic well into 1915.[44] While work went on to develop active defenses against submarines, it was becoming apparent to the more thoughtful—although admittedly, not to all—that the only safety lay in high speed and frequent course changes.

The implications were profound. Before 1914, high speed in surface ships was fundamentally a requirement only for the encounter, chase, and engagement phases of a battle. There had been efforts for well over a decade to improve the speeds of capital ship formations, starting with John Fisher's success in advancing the Mediterranean Fleet of 1902 from twelve knots with breakdowns to fifteen without, while the turbine created the potential for sustained high-speed runs such as the seven-thousand-mile passage of the battleship *Dreadnought* at seventeen knots.[45] In reality, however, the customary speed of a big ship formation in 1914 was closer to ten knots (and often less). This was to save fuel: even at ten knots, big ships consumed significantly more coal than they did at seven, while full power represented between a fourfold and eightfold increase.

The need for economy made slow speed understandable in peacetime. In the presubmarine era there were also good reasons for slow speed in war. Largely because most still underestimated the ranges at which submarines could operate, it remained the practice at the start of the conflict.[46] The rate of fuel use affected both the ability to remain at sea and readiness for battle. Low consumption allowed the progressive transfer of coal from remote bunkers to those for ready use (or, as was the German practice, use of the remote bunkers first), which meant that the capacity to achieve full speed was maintained almost to the limit of endurance.[47] How easily this could be managed depended largely on well-designed internal arrangements, but, at high speed, at least 25 percent of the coal storages were effectively inaccessible—fuel could simply not be moved quickly enough.[48] In British battle cruisers this started as early as 60 percent of capacity.[49] German units had the same problem. In some ships, poor bunker layout created difficulties in remaining with their formations at sea after significant amounts of coal had been consumed.[50]

Even with good bunker design, the operational endurance of the majority of ships at speeds of fourteen knots (the effective minimum for antisubmarine defense) or more was limited to a few days. Despite the short distances in the North Sea and the Baltic, naval operations, although submarines were the exception, would have to be considered in terms of sorties and sweeps, not sustained presence. A British dreadnought typically had a stated range of over four thousand miles at a sustained speed of eighteen knots; in practice it was well under three thousand miles. This might have been enough, but most British destroyers were limited to fifteen hundred miles at fifteen knots, while German torpedo craft were even worse, some having a range of little more than a thousand miles at seventeen knots.[51] The latter equated to an effective radius (which included a margin of high-speed and high-fuel consumption for battle) of only 250 miles, barely halfway across the North Sea.[52] The Russians were no better off, although their new destroyers were intended to have much longer range at high speed to fulfill their intended offensive roles. Given that composite tactical formations only had the range of the shortest-legged units within them—usually the torpedo craft that formed the vital protective screens for the big ships—it is unsurprising that, for every navy, operational endurance would be a "nagging tooth" in the conflict to come.[53]

The vulnerability of a fleet low on fuel had long been recognized. Efforts to improve the speed of coaling started with Admiral Beresford in the Mediterranean Fleet in 1905. It rapidly became a highly competitive evolution and the Germans soon followed. In the Royal Navy the rate moved in two years from an hourly average in which 162 tons by a battleship was cited as exceptional, to one in which the record average per hour stood at 289.2 tons for a total loading of 1,180 tons.[54] During the 1908 naval maneuvers the High Sea Fleet conducted a tactical coaling in which the maximum hourly rates achieved ranged from 328 tons for the battleship *Elsass* to 435 for the armored cruiser *Yorck*.[55] Such efforts, however, might reduce the time that ships and formations were unavailable, but could not deal with the matter of endurance as such—particularly the time out for transiting to and from coaling.

Some of the difficulties were already understood. Manpower was the first issue. Even with the best Welsh "Admiralty" steam coal, maintaining fires in multiple boilers for long periods, keeping them clean, and transferring fuel from the depths of steadily emptying bunkers created intense demands on personnel. At the same time, the constant threat of submarines, as well as torpedo craft by night, required that the secondary armament be at high readiness, which meant supplementing the stokers with seamen (customary for extended high-speed steaming) could not work.[56] The C-in-C of the Home Fleets pointed out to the Admiralty in 1912 that a crisis had been averted only by the conclusion of the annual maneuvers as there were not enough stokers to do the work, but personnel could be made available only by denuding gun crews and lookouts. The Admiralty responded by raising the big ships' complement of seamen, but this did not solve the whole problem.[57] For the Germans' part, embarkation of additional stokers (some 10 percent above peacetime establishment) was a key element in bringing their big ships, particularly the battle cruisers, to a war state.[58]

For this reason Churchill's decision in August 1914 to use what he regarded as surplus reservist personnel to form the Royal Naval Division was particularly unwise.[59] The big ships were already finding that every additional man (especially stokers) was useful.[60] The scheme created immediate concern in the Admiralty and would be deeply resented by the commanders at sea, who complained bitterly about undermanning, as well as by long-serving reservists.[61] Ironically, the Germans went through the same exercise shortly afterward with the formation of the Marinekorps Flandern (Flanders Naval Marine Corps)—with much the same results.[62]

The quality of coal was also critical. Not only did this relate to combustive efficiency and the power generated through steam production, but unsuitable coal sooner or later choked the boilers. The more boilers in use at high capacity, the more that accumulating waste and the need to clean furnaces affected performance. With their control of the Welsh coal fields, this was less of a difficulty for the British, but it was a challenge for the Germans, who had purchased high-quality steaming coal for their torpedo craft from Wales until the outbreak and may have conducted their big ship speed trials with it.[63] They were to find their own coal was not up to the task. This caused particular problems for their battle cruisers, and it is arguable that no German heavy unit *ever* achieved more than twenty-four knots during war operations.[64] There was a partial, but only partial, solution in which oil was sprayed over the coal fires. A precursor to all-oil firing, the British had adopted this a decade earlier. As the reality of their coal supply situation dawned, the Germans made its fit a priority. There were oil-propelled capital ships on the way for the British, with the majority of the destroyers and an increasing number of light cruisers already so equipped, but even in 1918 major oil-burning units represented just a third of the Grand Fleet's battle line. For the Germans, although oil supplies were to prove more reliable than expected, only the very latest major units had mixed firing and only the newest torpedo craft were oil fired alone.

Responding to developments in the range, reliability, and hitting power of the heavy gun and the torpedo were key drivers behind the change in fleets into national versions of the Grand Fleet of Battle. This change directly reflected the competition between the two weapons, as well as the presence of the submarine. As the effective ranges of the new torpedo types with their improved propulsion and internal gyroscopes moved rapidly from two thousand or three thousand yards to eight thousand and then to ten thousand yards and more, they threatened the dominance of the big gun in several ways, even though the latter's range had itself increased markedly. The problem was intensified by the development of the submarine.

Torpedo boats and destroyers had to become organic to the main fleet, both to protect it against other light craft and submarines and to attack the enemy's heavy ships. The screening effort that the protective role involved was becoming more demanding as formation speeds increased. Older and smaller light craft could not maintain the speeds required for extended periods, even if the sea state was low. The need for scouting cruisers had also become greater, since the larger fleets needed as much warning time as possible to allow deployment into the most favorable formation. This was a key reason for German interest in the zeppelin airship, especially as the German navy was so short of light cruisers. Controlling an entire fleet was a formidable proposition in both the North Sea and the Baltic, since daytime visibility was so often less than the potential ranges of both guns and torpedoes.[65]

Furthermore, for gunnery, different ranges required different systems and techniques. In limited visibility, medium-caliber guns could be very effective in a way that they were not when ships were able to fight at extreme ranges, but it was increasingly clear that there were circumstances of visibility in which no big ship gunnery barrage of any caliber could be effective quickly enough to prevent the launch of a massed torpedo attack—hence the importance of light forces as protection (and their potential for attack). Even in good visibility, the effective gun range was no longer necessarily enough to ensure destruction of the torpedo carriers before launch. The threat of torpedoes could also be used to force an adversary into maneuvers that disrupted gunnery fire control solutions and thus the ability to engage the enemy battle line, although the British in particular were working hard to develop tactics to deal with this. The difficulty of maintaining such solutions during or immediately after a change of course remained one of the greatest challenges for accurate shooting, particularly, but not only, at long range.[66] All these factors contributed to the doubts among the Home Fleets' commanders as to the viability of the Grand Fleet of Battle despite strenuous efforts to devise practical solutions to the gun/torpedo dilemma.[67]

The undersea element complicated matters still further. The Royal Navy was more advanced in this arm than either the German or Russian navies, but had much to do before either the technology or the doctrine for its employment was mature. For the British, the submarine was not really a long-range, sea-going weapon until the *D*-class submarines of 1908. The first submarine wireless set was not trialed until 1910, and a systematic installation program started only in 1912.[68] As late as 1913 the C-in-C of the Home Fleets was pointing out that the submarines with radios had yet to have soundproof cabinets installed and that operators found it very difficult to hear signals when the diesels were running.[69] When wireless was fitted, its effective range was often no more than thirty miles, the original 1911 staff requirement.[70] Very few of the earlier boats were yet equipped; some that were had no ability to transmit and anything sent to them had to be en clair.[71]

Even in the coast defense role, submarines had to remain in close contact with the shore or a surface ship to have any chance of getting warning of an approaching enemy. In the offensive role, limited radio ranges meant that submarines had either to be pre-positioned or that surface ships had to provide them with support to receive their reports or direct them into station. The alternative method of underwater sound signals by explosive charge was useful only up to twenty miles and probably less.[72] This meant that, like the destroyers, they needed their own leaders if they were to operate with the fleet. If submarines were to operate independently, their role was more akin to being a minefield of limited mobility than anything else, and their positioning required careful planning. There were ideas that submarines could become forward reporting units close to an enemy's coast, but this would need significant improvement of their wireless installations.

Progress was being made, but not necessarily in the right direction. The Royal Navy was preoccupied with using submarines as an integral element of the battle fleet, not simply in cooperation with it. The C-in-C of the Home Fleets noted in 1913, after the first major fleet encounter exercise to test submarines in direct support of the fleet in the open sea, that the submersibles, "given opportunity, might well inflict severe losses on the enemy before a general action takes place." Rear Admiral William Pakenham had witnessed the submarine attacks and commented, "For a first attempt these results must be considered very good."[73] Commodore Keyes later made the point that Callaghan "perhaps above all other flag officers, appreciated the powers and limitations of submarines," but this was in the context of fleet cooperation.[74] That they might be better suited to a much more independent offensive function and that full integration was a dead end had still to be learned.

The Imperial German Navy was no further ahead. The early antiship practices of the U-boats had not been remarkable, but 1913 showed promise and the exercises of May 1914 were even more successful, both in coastal areas and in the open water environment north of Heligoland. The C-in-C High Sea Fleet, von Ingenohl, was deeply impressed by the high percentage of assessed hits achieved in whatever situation the submarines were placed. This was to limit significantly his willingness to accept the risk of underwater attack on his heavy ships, but it did not mean that he had come to grips with the possibilities of using submarines in an offensive role.[75] The U-boats were still very much conceived and operated as local defense units, as their navigating equipment demonstrated. Their radios were also no better than those of the British.

The gap between technical promise and actual delivery was even greater in the air. The Germans were struggling to determine the capabilities of the new airships. Zeppelins had been available only to support the High Sea Fleet as scouts since completion of the first naval unit in 1912. Their potential to detect dispersed surface ships and direct superior forces toward them was a reason the British feared this new capability so much.[76] The performance (with suitable weather) of that first zeppelin in the September 1913 maneuvers was extremely encouraging, but L1 crashed in a North Sea thunderstorm later that month with fourteen dead. In October 1913 L2 burnt up in the air, killing all its crew after a hydrogen explosion during a test flight. Although the Germans hired a commercial unit to allow basic training to continue, the naval zeppelin force in August 1914 was a single airship, L3, which had been complete for less than three months. The most basic techniques of scouting, reporting, and navigation over the sea were still being learned, as were the effects of weather. Five more zeppelins were due to commission before the end of the year, but it had taken much persuasion to get von Tirpitz to allocate the funds for them.[77] There were only a few other airships and fixed wing aircraft. In the first days of the war, just six serviceable aircraft were available for the North Sea and eight for the Baltic, although the Germans were rushing to establish new naval air bases at Borkum and Norderney.[78] None had radios and their operational range was barely thirty nautical miles.

The Royal Naval Air Service had a few small airships, but was more advanced with fixed wing aircraft, some 140 of which were in service in May 1914.[79] The

Germans themselves expected the British to employ embarked aircraft at sea from the start of the conflict.[80] However, there had been only one sustained British attempt at ship-borne operations in a tactical environment, with the old cruiser *Hermes* carrying two seaplanes as part of "Red" fleet for the 1913 maneuvers. Significantly, the exercise rules were designed specifically to have the aircraft simulate the assessed eight hundred nautical mile–range of a zeppelin, indicating British concern over the German development.[81] For its part, the "Blue" opposition in 1913 had only two shore stations, each with two or three operational seaplanes.[82] In August 1914 the British had their own hasty arrangements to make to allow their air arm to operate usefully in war, with three ferries being requisitioned for conversion and *Hermes* brought out of reserve. Ironically, it was the small airships that were initially most useful with patrols over the Channel.[83]

Life for active people had its dangers. Lieutenant Oswald Frewen, although better off than some financially, was probably typical, spending nearly a hundred pounds on two motor-bikes during 1909 and suffering eight major breakdowns or accidents as he coursed between dockyard ports, London, and his family's home in Kent.[84] However, despite a general acceptance of incidents (one destroyer commodore, tongue in cheek, informed the First Lord of the day in 1908 that he "did not expect to lose more than one [destroyer] every six months"), safety inevitably limited the pace of development.[85] Directions for the 1913 British exercises were explicit in reminding torpedo craft commanders that they were "not justified in incurring war risks in peace maneuvers."[86] For their part, the Germans did not allow heavy ships to turn toward torpedo boats during a simulated attack.[87] There was good reason for this caution. Between 1900 and 1914 the British lost eight destroyers, four to collision, while the Germans also suffered eight sinkings of torpedo boats, with an even higher proportion by collision.[88] The year 1912 was a particularly bad year for the High Sea Fleet, with two serious collisions between big ships and torpedo boats. The numbers of minor collisions and near misses were much greater. Lieutenant Lionel Dawson, holding small ship commands between 1908 and 1912, "bent" them in berthing or ship-handling accidents on five occasions, as well as going aground (which he did not report) at least once. Some of the incidents were the result of misjudgment, but others were due to poor design or material defects.[89] Safety concerns extended to all units at night or in restricted visibility, and with reason. The majority of the nine major collisions between British capital ships in the previous decade were largely due to fog, and there were many more with merchant ships.[90] Among the early naval aviators, Lieutenant Richard Bell Davies had four crashes or forced landings before the war and got off lightly by comparison with some. He had earlier survived a sinking and a grounding in small ships.[91]

Submarines were considered to be even more at hazard—most operator navies having lost boats (five by the British)—and had their own operational restrictions.

Mistakes could be made even in the most favorable conditions. *C32* ran straight into the battleship *Prince of Wales* in June 1913 while conducting a daylight practice attack—in good visibility, with the battleship steering a steady course.[92] Lieutenant C. G. Brodie, one of the earliest submariners, received the Admiralty's "severe displeasure" for a procedural error that resulted in the destruction of His Majesty's Submarine *A11*'s petrol (gasoline) engine. He grounded *C11* in 1908 and then nearly sank with the boat when she was run down by a merchant ship in July 1909.[93] Safety limitations could result in conservatism descending into denial, as it frequently did in the early exercise encounters between submariners and surface ships. Lieutenant Max Horton did not succeed in persuading Arthur Leveson, captain of the battle cruiser *Indefatigable,* that he was "sunk" during the 1912 Grand Maneuvers, and the British C-in-C had to admit the difficulties of determining submarines' "*actual* capabilities."[94] Such constraints could also work in the other direction, as the Russians were to discover. Before the war, their surface ships acting as targets always had to steer known courses to pass through predetermined positions. Thus, "the submarine commanders needed no special skill to approach the ships they were attacking."[95] This would limit their success rate under the much more arduous conditions of conflict.

Other restrictions could be more subtle in their effects. To derive the maximum benefit from the fuel and ammunition available, fleets tended to schedule their most challenging exercises in periods of good weather, or went in search of it—the British operated off the Spanish coast during the northern winter. This was understandable, but it helped disguise many deficiencies of design and practice that would emerge when ships were forced to endure heavy weather and extremes of temperature.

So did the limits imposed by money. Both British and Germans were under intense financial pressure, forcing economies. Fuel expenditure was a concern of both navies.[96] At two pounds sterling a ton, the combined British fleets in home waters could use well over 16,000 tons of coal and spend some 32,000 pounds in a single day steaming at their maximum sustained speeds. Oil, although it had a higher calorific value, was even more expensive at four pounds a ton. Its introduction contributed to the Royal Navy's fuel bill increasing by more than 23 percent in 1911–12, which resulted in tight restrictions on its use—mixed coal/oil firing was not permitted except for basic familiarization.[97]

As a result, very high speeds were extremely rare. Exercises were usually conducted at scaled-down speeds, which provided for realism in relative movement, but did not highlight the intense difficulties that higher speeds created for command and for weapons—smoke and structural vibration being only two. A typical German tactical exercise in 1914 allowed battleships only twelve or fifteen knots, battle cruisers sixteen, and light craft nineteen.[98] British battle cruisers exercised forming order of battle "while working up to full power" in June 1913, but this was exceptional and the achieved speeds were just "22 to 23 knots," equating to only three fifths of full power.[99] The realities of fighting at full speed would come as a shock.

Fuel restrictions also limited the time ships spent at sea. The average annual distance steamed by a British capital unit before 1914 was around ten thousand miles.[100] At ten knots this equated to one thousand hours under way, or just under forty-two full days out of 365. Day running, with the ships returning to harbor overnight, was frequently employed to make the best use of the steaming time to complete practice programs and conduct tactical exercises, but the problem would always be fitting everything in. One result was that not all personnel gained the first-hand experience of operating with the new technology, notably submarines, which would prove vital in responding when a real threat developed.

There were limits other than fuel. Ammunition was expensive (a 12-inch armor-piercing shell cost forty-six pounds in 1912), and gun barrels had limited lives.[101] The latter was why many practice firings were conducted with reduced charges. Gunnery was a dynamic domain and all navies were struggling to resolve the problem of finding—and maintaining—firing solutions under likely battle conditions, but this had to be balanced against unit efficiency and the priority generally went to the latter. This affected gunnery practices, which were choreographed and did not fully reproduce realistic battle conditions. German firings in 1912–13 were conducted at the same speeds for each ship type as the tactical evolutions, with one or two course alterations at the most.[102] British dreadnought firings in 1914 were conducted at fourteen knots by day and fifteen by night.[103] British battleships in full commission in the First Fleet averaged four day main armament shoots and one night practice in the year before July 1914, as well as two day and two night secondary armament practices.[104] The Germans did somewhat more, particularly at night. Their First Squadron of dreadnoughts conducted five day tactical and one test firing of their main and secondary armaments in 1912–13, together with five night firings, with two more for the tertiary (88-mm) antitorpedo craft weapons.[105] There were many subcaliber practices, as well as range-finding exercises that did not involve the expense of full caliber firings. These were useful in training gunnery teams, but could not deal with more than individual elements of the problem.

Torpedoes were another difficulty. A British 21-inch weapon cost over a thousand pounds, an 18-inch not much less. The loss of one was the cause of searching inquiry.[106] Even when their firing was permitted at night, which was rare, Royal Navy guidance was that only a single weapon could be launched by each ship and that it had to be found and recovered before another firing was permitted.[107] Multiple firings, the tactically most realistic use of the torpedo, were allowed only in daylight. While weapon reliability was steadily improving, the accompanying increases in range also increased the difficulties of relocating torpedoes at the end of their runs. This stymied one early experiment with smoke screens, a tactic possible with oil firing (coal was more hit-and-miss) to disguise an attack by torpedo craft for at least part of the time that they would be within range of the enemy's guns. The British Second Destroyer Flotilla followed up on a preliminary trial in 1912 with a series of mass attacks so screened. They were "fairly successful but unfortunately we lost, during an attack, one of the precious new torpedoes and everything had to give way to finding it."[108] Submarines had similar problems. They had little experience in firing the heavier warshot torpedoes and not enough in penetrating screens of light craft to make their attack. In the early months of the war these would be factors behind frequent loss of depth control when attacking, a problem experienced in all navies, which contributed to the loss of at least one boat.

Lack of money could exacerbate other institutional problems. The Royal Navy's approach to mine warfare had not been consistent in the previous decade, reflecting changing approaches to blockade policy, and it did not receive a high priority in funding.[109] After 1911 mining effectively fell off the back of the truck. The financial constraints immediately before 1914 and the redirection of money to new construction strangled what had been a modest, but progressive, development program. Known defects in the mines, notably their mooring wires, sinkers, and pistols, were not fixed, experiments were terminated, and even exercise mine-laying reduced sharply, while there was no one in the Admiralty solely employed to staff mine matters.[110] So short were funds that the handful of elderly minelayers were used as additional patrol vessels during the 1913 maneuvers, rather than laying exercise fields. They were instructed to "go through the motions" of mining the enemy into a harbor, if the opportunity offered.[111] The reason was that "owing to the scarcity of practice mines and sinkers, they will be unable to undertake their proper work."[112]

It was the accumulation of such challenges that made Sir George Callaghan comment ruefully in 1913 of the role of destroyers, "That better results were not obtained by the destroyers is accountable directly to the fact that it is only recently that a systematic start has been made to train them to work with a battlefleet, and it is evident that they require much more practice."[113] A year later, this was still as true for the Royal Navy's torpedo craft and for its other types of warship as it was for the Germans. But time had run out and all would now have to learn as they went.

WAR PLANS

6

B RITAIN HAD STRUGGLED FOR YEARS TO DEVELOP AN EFFECTIVE NAVAL WAR
plan against Germany.[1] By August 1914 a degree of coherency had been
achieved, although there were still unresolved arguments about the conduct of a maritime campaign, inside and outside the Admiralty. The problems
associated with both close and intermediate blockades were manifest. Even if
either could have been conducted for any time with the forces available, the risks
of defeat in detail and the exposure to attrition were such that either approach
would play into the Germans' hands, weakening the British to a point where the
High Sea Fleet could have a real chance of victory. The Admiralty had not completely abandoned ideas of investing the German coast, but the tools to do so did
not yet exist.

Nevertheless, the aim was to cut Germany off from the maritime world. The
navy's economic focus had tightened greatly as the vulnerabilities of "just in time"
became apparent and understanding of the global trade system more sophisticated. Significantly, the Senior Officers' War Course included lectures by leading
experts on the maritime economy.[2] The Royal Navy intended to shut off Germany
by closing all exits to the open ocean, keeping the patrol lines as far away as possible, and cutting its global telegraph cables. German shipping would be captured
or confined to port, and British vessels would not carry materials to Germany.
While neutral merchantmen were an unknown, the tonnage available would be
insufficient to make up the difference, even if they could not be controlled by other
means. The idea was not simply to eat away progressively at the German economy,
but rather to attack it directly, creating financial disruption, massive unemployment, and shortages that would undermine the German nation's capacity to function, let alone wage war. One of the key elements was food, in recognition not only
of Britain's reliance on imported supplies, but also of Germany's.

Much planning had gone into the concept. Nevertheless, although government assent had been apparently secured, several factors meant that implementation would be incomplete. The first was the complexity and scale of global trade
by sea, sufficient to overwhelm the limited capacity of the Admiralty (and other

government departments in 1914), even after the re-creation of the Trade Division, to track cargo movements, let alone control them. Just as complicated and sensitive were the financial networks. They needed to be carefully managed if Germany was to be attacked this way, since there were huge collateral implications for Britain. Second, Britain was a liberal, mercantile state based on free trade. It had the previous Great Wars of 1793–1815 to justify the importance of encouraging national commerce, even with the enemy, to sustain the war effort by maintaining a strong economy. In this, much of the business community was at one with elements of the British administration, particularly the Board of Trade, and there were many who feared for Britain the social disruption intended for Germany. Third were the neutral countries that not only had to protect their own economies, but also, in the case of Denmark and the Netherlands, wanted to avoid antagonizing the Germans, or, like Sweden, were sympathetic to them. The attitude of the Americans would also prove critical, since Britain could not afford conflict with the United States. Fourth, closely tied to the position of the neutrals was the state of international law, which dictated that the only valid commercial blockade was one that involved constant investment of the enemy's ports and coasts. Arguably, Britain had weakened its position by initial acceptance of the 1909 Declaration of London, which substantially restricted attacks on commerce. The Admiralty, however, took a realistic, indeed cynical, view about such limits.[3] The British Parliament's failure to ratify the measure had created room for maneuver, particularly if the Germans did not adhere to the Declaration.

The strategy had operational problems as well, many of which turned on the key weakness: uncertainty as to how long it would take to work. The British east coast lay open to attack and even, some believed, invasion. Although the Admiral of Patrols' organization was intended to provide flotilla units for port defense, it was increasingly clear that such elderly light craft, unsupported by capital units, would not be enough, even when submarines were also available, while coordination and warning time were unresolved issues. Furthermore, there was the question of where to base the main fleet. The slow development of the new dockyard at Rosyth and lack of investment elsewhere in the north meant that there were no first class naval bases or repair facilities in the northeast and no properly prepared anchorages. The logistic problems of supplying coal and oil to the north were being addressed, but only just.

The longer the conflict continued, the greater would be the pressure for supposedly more decisive actions. Churchill, never to be cured of applying cavalry sentiments to naval operations, hungered for what he considered to be a more offensive approach. He had once advocated covering the passage of the army to France at the outbreak of a war with Germany by getting the entire fleet to "sweep [the Germans] in a jumble back into the Elbe . . . and then picket the Elbe with the full strength of our flotillas."[4] He also sought to revive projects for the capture of forward operating bases. These had been rejected because of their prospect of heavy losses for little return—not only in the assault, but also in any attempt to protect and supply such outposts, as well as the potential for defeat in detail of forward-based units. Many required substantial land forces, which the British army, focused on its potential campaign in France, was unwilling to provide. Even if the limited resources of the Royal Marines were enough, such ideas were viewed with little enthusiasm by the War Staff. Churchill nevertheless continued the effort by coopting like-minded officers, such as Vice Admiral Sir Lewis Bayly, to prepare new plans. Despite the lack of support within the Admiralty, Churchill tried to revive the concept even as war started, evoking "marvelous" language from the War Office's Director of Military Operations when a scheme was presented to him.[5] Sturdee regarded resistance to such proposals as "one of my principal duties, and it meant endless controversies."[6]

To be fair, Churchill's preference for the offensive was shared by many within the naval leadership who understood the strategic problem. For officers such as Beatty, British forces needed to operate in ways that forced the enemy's fleet to give battle. In their view, this could not be accomplished by what they saw as a passive strategy totally reliant on the distant blockade, but by sorties into German waters and harassment of any German units that ventured to sea. They could not believe that the High Sea Fleet would remain quiescent in the face of the existential threat created by the assault on the German economy, and it was vital that the British be positioned to achieve decisive results. The Grand Fleet of Battle itself was intended to allow the main fleet to operate offensively despite the threat of submarines and torpedo craft. The problems with this operational/tactical construct were such, however, that the details of just how that fleet could work remained uncertain. There were proposals to return to a much closer investment of the German coast, which the Admiralty had ideas of introducing in the future, but these depended on technologies and ships that were only just entering service, such as wireless-equipped long-range submarines, and the new fast light cruisers.

The Baltic was another facet to the debate over an active strategy. The leading proponent of a Baltic campaign would be Lord Fisher, still active as an adviser to Churchill. German control of the sea represented a fundamental weakness in any British blockade strategy, given the access that it provided to Scandinavia, as well as to the North Sea. Forcing an entry was a recurrent element in British naval thought, although proposals varied widely, ranging from amphibious assaults employing either the British or the Russian army, to largely naval ventures that might include the capture of advanced bases but that were focused on investing the German Baltic ports and cutting off trade with Sweden. The practical objections to any Baltic scheme were legion, but the fundamental naval problem was that a precondition had to be confinement of the Germans within their North Sea anchorages, something that Fisher well understood. Powerful as they were, the

PHOTO 6.1

**Admiral Sir George
Callaghan** *(pictured as
a vice admiral)*

Imperial War Museum

British could not risk the defeat in detail possible if the High Sea Fleet were able to emerge into the North Sea and attack a Baltic venture from the rear. Perhaps the central questions in the "endless controversies" during the coming months were whether confinement was preferable to enticing the Germans into battle, and, if it were, just how it could be achieved. Underlying the debate was the conundrum that if the blockade was not effective enough to create an existential challenge, the Germans had little reason to move.

Command of the Grand Fleet was one of the first matters tackled by the First Lord in the crisis. Callaghan had been C-in-C of the Home Fleets since 1911 (photo 6.1) and Jellicoe was nominated to succeed him at the end of 1914. At the Admiralty conference on 29 July, Churchill told the C-in-C that Jellicoe would join immediately as his second in command. Caught by surprise, Callaghan nevertheless welcomed the idea.[7] What he did not realize was that the First Lord had decided to relieve him in the event of war. Churchill later claimed, with limited evidence, that Callaghan's health would not stand the strain.[8] Before his departure, Jellicoe was handed a sealed envelope. Churchill warned Jellicoe, who knew perfectly well what its contents were, that he would be instructed to open the envelope should war become imminent.[9]

Jellicoe left London on 31 July. By the time he arrived at the Scottish port of Wick, to be taken to Scapa Flow by the light cruiser *Boadicea*, Jellicoe had serious doubts. He telegraphed to Churchill and Battenberg, "[T]he step you mentioned to me is fraught with gravest danger." Jellicoe was well aware that the sudden change of command could have a marked effect on the fleet's morale and, on 2 August repeated his warning. But Churchill was determined to carry the thing through. "I can give you 48 hours after joining Fleet. You must be ready then." The same night, Jellicoe replied, "[S]tep contemplated is most dangerous. . . . Am perfectly willing to act onboard Fleet Flagship as assistant. . . . Hard to believe it is realised what grave difficulties change Commander-in-Chief involves at this moment."[10]

Throughout 3 August Jellicoe sent further messages, but the die was cast. The First Lord signaled, "I am telegraphing to the Commander-in-Chief directing him to transfer command to you at the earliest moment suitable to the interests of the Service. I rely on him and you to effect this change quickly and smoothly, personal feeling cannot count now, only what is best for us all."[11]

Callaghan was roused early on the morning of 4 August with the bald message that he was to hand over command that day to Jellicoe. He had been given no intimation of the proposed change. The breakfast that the admirals shared was, as Jellicoe's secretary remarked, "a meal not to be forgotten."[12] To the credit of both, they accomplished the transfer without delay, their friendship unimpaired. Years later Callaghan stood godfather to Jellicoe's son.

The fleet was shocked. Callaghan was much admired and it was thought grossly unfair that he should be dismissed in such a cavalier fashion. Captain C. J. Wintour, commanding the Fourth Destroyer Flotilla, noted that the super-session would "cause widespread indignation."[13] Lieutenant Bertram Ramsay in *Dreadnought* commented, "This was a regular bolt from the blue & everyone was horrified at the C-in-C being turned out at the last moment."[14] Warrender, Bayly, and Beatty sent messages of protest. In the event, the fleet's indignation was short-lived. The two concerned had behaved with such propriety that there was nothing to be said. The Admiralty for its part did no more than gently reprove the senior officers for making their complaints and Churchill was sensible enough to ensure that Callaghan went as C-in-C of the Nore when that appointment became vacant in late 1914.[15]

The change may not have been as wise as it seemed to Churchill and others at the time. At sixty-one Callaghan was older than Jellicoe, but in good health—perhaps better than the tired Jellicoe, who was plagued with piles in the coming months.[16] Although Jellicoe had married money and did not suffer the financial anxieties that half-pay meant for many, he was rarely given the break between appointments customary for senior officers and certainly desirable after service in an undermanned and overworked Admiralty.[17] Moved from one demanding post to another, Jellicoe was feeling the strain.

Callaghan's relationship with the Admiralty was robust (perhaps too robust for Churchill), and he had identified many of the problems that the Royal Navy faced in dealing with Germany. Providing strong leadership, he advanced the tactics of the Grand Fleet of Battle considerably, giving space to his subordinates (who included Jellicoe in the Second Division in 1911–12) to experiment. He knew the deficiencies and the changes that needed to be made. If the correspondence between flag officers, their staffs, and other interested officers is any indication, there was a culture of tactical innovation in the Home Fleets of 1913–14.[18] Roger Keyes, the commodore commanding submarines (hereafter Commodore [S]), acknowledged as much in his memoirs.[19]

Nevertheless, when Acting Admiral Sir John Jellicoe assumed the appointment of C-in-C, it was the culmination of a career that seemed devoted to preparing for this task (photo 6.2). Jellicoe was born in 1859, the son of a merchant captain, and joined HMS *Britannia* in 1871. He rapidly distinguished himself as an unusually clever, able, and hardworking officer, ambitious but unassuming, and very much a leader. Jellicoe came early to the attention of John Fisher, for he made gunnery his specialization and did splendid work. By the time Fisher

PHOTO 6.2
Admiral Sir John Jellicoe
(on board HMS Iron Duke)
Imperial War Museum

was First Sea Lord, he had begun to think of Jellicoe as Britain's "future Nelson."[20] Unlike some of Fisher's favorites, the choice of Jellicoe was not faulted by other factions in the service, despite his intimate involvement with many of Fisher's innovations, including *Dreadnought* herself. Alternating between sea commands and successively more important Admiralty appointments, Jellicoe built a reputation for quiet brilliance. He was probably one of the most popular senior officers in the navy. That Jellicoe was a chronic overcentralizer was not at this time remarkable in a navy of overcentralizers. He was a very easy man for whom to work, since he possessed an extraordinarily even temper, great courtesy, and was above all consistent in decision. Indeed, Jellicoe never underestimated the complexity of the task he faced in the Grand Fleet and progressively expanded his own staff. Jellicoe's problem was not so much that he interfered with his juniors' work, although he did so on occasion, as it was his determination to make himself aware of every detail, robbing himself of time to consider the big picture.

The origins of the flaws in Jellicoe's approach to the training and operation of the Grand Fleet may have been in his sea time. The new C-in-C had not served in a small ship on detached service since he was a midshipman. Practically all his appointments were in the main fleets—and flagships at that. This was no way to develop an understanding of the need for individual initiative in commanders. He also may have known too much. Responsible for many of the material aspects of the Royal Navy and having himself had to accept many compromises to remain within budget, Jellicoe was well aware of the weaknesses of his fleet, an awareness reinforced by his command of the Second Division and of the Red Fleet of the 1913 Grand Maneuvers. He had been directly involved in much of the early tactical development required by the Grand Fleet of Battle and thus was conscious of its limitations, although, critically, he did not have the experience of the work of the previous twelve months. His prewar time at sea had displayed flair and readiness to innovate (as well as a willingness to cheat when the opportunity offered during maneuvers), but Jellicoe was to prove himself much more cautious with the Grand Fleet. He may have been right, but the result was not the tactical aggression on which the Royal Navy had long prided itself and that was still needed.

Apart from bringing his own secretary, Hamnet Share (it was the practice to retain the same officer as secretary in successive flag appointments), Jellicoe kept Callaghan's staff. This included Commodore First Class Alan Everett, captain of the fleet, who was to be instrumental in developing the systems necessary to maintain such a large force in remote anchorages. Churchill arranged for Rear Admiral Charles Madden to join as Jellicoe's chief of staff. Their wives were sisters and the two officers were old friends. Madden was an austere officer with a formidable capacity for hard work. Not without a sense of humor, he was an amenable second to Jellicoe and was an important, although perhaps not sufficiently questioning, support in the years ahead.

Lewis Bayly commanded the First Battle Squadron, which included the older 12-inch gun dreadnoughts. Aggressive and energetic, Bayly had extensive experience, having successively commanded the Home Fleets' destroyers, the First Battle Cruiser Squadron, and the Third Battle Squadron, appointments broken only by command of the War College. Bayly's relationship with Jellicoe was uncomfortable, which was unfortunate as Bayly's eagerness to be at the enemy's throat might otherwise have acted as a counterweight to his new C-in-C's prudence. He was a leading advocate of an active policy. Unfortunately, Bayly had failed to grasp the implications of the new technology, despite graphic demonstrations by submarines against his ships in the 1913 maneuvers.[21] Jellicoe was more realistic and Bayly's ideas were dismissed by the C-in-C, as well as most of the Grand Fleet's leadership, as impractical.

The deputy in the First Battle Squadron was Rear Admiral Hugh Evan-Thomas, a quiet officer more to Jellicoe's taste. The Second was led by Sir George Warrender and consisted of the most modern 13.5-inch gun battleships. Warrender had a high reputation but was suffering deafness and increasing ill health. His second in command was the redoubtable Rear Admiral Sir Robert Arbuthnot, a formidable disciplinarian with a single-minded belief in the merits of physical fitness. He as much as any officer embodied the culture of the senior officer present. He led from the front, but permitted no deviation from regulations and would not question an order.

Vice Admiral Edward Bradford and Rear Admiral Montague Browning led the *King Edward VII*–class pre-dreadnoughts of the Third Battle Squadron. Bradford had been afloat almost continuously since being promoted rear admiral in 1908. Shortly after the outbreak, the squadron was supplemented by three *Duncan*-class pre-dreadnoughts, under Rear Admiral Stuart Nicholson. The Fourth, smallest of the battle squadrons, had as its commander Vice Admiral Sir Douglas Gamble, flying his flag in *Dreadnought*. Gamble had headed the naval mission to Turkey in 1909 and done much good work there. He was experienced in staff duties, having served in the Intelligence Division and as a naval attaché.

The Grand Fleet had eight relatively modern and ten elderly armored cruisers on its strength, as well as six large and five small light cruisers. Directly attached to the fleet were two squadrons of armored cruisers: the Second under Rear Admiral the Honorable Somerset Gough-Calthorpe and the Third under Rear Admiral William Pakenham. Gough-Calthorpe was a reserved man, but with an acute mind, having rendered distinguished service as a torpedo specialist, as captain of the fleet to Admiral Sir William May, and as the Admiralty's representative at the *Titanic* enquiry. Both admirals had been closely involved in the Russo-Japanese conflict—Gough-Calthorpe as naval attaché in Saint Petersburg, and Pakenham, with distinction, as observer in the Japanese fleet. The latter had impressed even the Japanese by his imperturbability under fire.

The six large light cruisers were formed into the First Light Cruiser Squadron, commanded by Commodore Second Class William Goodenough, with smaller and older units distributed around the battle squadrons as local scouts and signal relays (photo 6.3). Goodenough was a sea officer in the finest sense. Apart from a lapse in the early months of the war, he was to handle his squadron with great skill. Two other cruiser squadrons—the Sixth, consisting only of the armored cruisers *Drake* and *King Alfred* under Rear Admiral William Grant, and the Tenth, under Rear Admiral Dudley de Chair—were allocated to the northern patrols against German shipping. De Chair's eight *Edgar*-class cruisers were among the oldest

in service and could be considered only a stopgap. De Chair himself was a careful officer with a strict sense of duty. A friend of Jellicoe, he served for a time as Churchill's naval secretary, but the relationship was not warm.[22] De Chair became operational commander of the northern blockade and proved well suited to this thankless task. Two destroyer flotillas were directly assigned to the Grand Fleet. These were the Second, under Captain J. R. P. Hawksley in the light cruiser *Active*, with twenty *H*-class destroyers; and the Fourth, under Wintour in the destroyer leader *Swift*, with twenty *K*-class destroyers.

The four battle cruisers of the First Battle Cruiser Squadron under Sir David Beatty formed the Grand Fleet's primary scouting force (photo 6.4). The youngest flag officer since Nelson and darling of the popular press, David Beatty had a meteoric career after he distinguished himself in gunboats on the Nile from 1896 to 1898. Award of the Distinguished Service

PHOTO 6.3
Commodore William Goodenough *(pictured later in the war)*
Imperial War Museum

Order and promotion to commander at the age of
twenty-seven resulted. During the Boxer Rebellion
in China, Beatty again displayed great gallantry and
was promoted captain well before his time. Marriage
to Ethel Tree, divorced daughter of the American
millionaire Marshall Field, earned him a certain
notoriety, but he flourished in successive cruiser
commands and as naval liaison officer to the Army
Council. Command of the pre-dreadnought *Queen*
in the Atlantic Fleet followed.

By 1909 Beatty was at the top of the Captains'
List. Because of service ashore and periods spent
recovering from wounds, he did not have the necessary sea time for promotion to flag rank. An exception
was made and a special Order-in-Council promulgated, allowing his promotion to rear admiral—
at thirty-nine. In 1910 Beatty was offered the appointment of Second in Command of the Atlantic Fleet.
He refused it. Whatever his reasons, this decision caused a great deal of comment
among his seniors and contemporaries. Beatty, rumor went, would not be offered
another job and would be forced to retire under the unemployment clauses. But
Beatty was introduced to Winston Churchill shortly after the latter became First
Lord. The young politician and the young admiral appealed to each other and
Beatty soon became Churchill's naval secretary. Beatty had the presence, wit, and
confidence to work effectively with his political master. Although far junior to
most members of the Admiralty Board, propinquity alone ensured that his influence was great. The naval secretary was also the man responsible for arranging
flag officers' appointments. Unless he crossed Churchill, Beatty could pick his
next post.

As he did. In 1913 Beatty was appointed to the First Battle Cruiser Squadron,
the finest post available. Carping comments as to it being a "job" were stilled by
Beatty's undoubted competence at handling his ships.[23] With the outbreak of war,
he received yet another advance. It had been the intention that the battle cruisers'
commander should be the senior cruiser admiral, responsible to the C-in-C for
tactical employment of all the scouting forces. This logical arrangement was upset
(much to Beatty's indignation) by the appointment of Rear Admiral Grant, next
above Beatty on the flag list, to the Sixth Cruiser Squadron.[24] To remedy this,
Beatty was appointed an acting vice admiral on 2 August 1914, at least a year
before he could expect promotion to that rank.

As soon as the battle cruiser *Invincible* completed refitting and rejoined the
fleet, Rear Admiral Sir Archibald Gordon Moore was to hoist his flag in her as

PHOTO 6.5
**Vice Admiral
Sir Cecil Burney
(pictured as
a full admiral)**
Imperial War Museum

Beatty's deputy. Moore had achieved Churchill's respect through his willingness to champion introduction of the 15-inch gun, but he did not get on at all well with Beatty, a situation that was to have unfortunate results.

The forces in the south were more loosely organized. Twenty-one pre-dreadnoughts under Vice Admiral Sir Cecil Burney constituted the Channel Fleet (photo 6.5). Burney had distinguished himself in the Mediterranean supervising international naval operations at the end of the Second Balkan War. The navy had a more cynical view of his success: "[T]he only English word the Montenegrins [*sic*] knew was 'Damn' and . . . they understood the admiral perfectly."[25] Although not particularly dynamic, Burney was an old friend of Jellicoe, who had great confidence in the Channel Fleet's commander. His flag flew in *Lord Nelson* of the Fifth Battle Squadron, whose divisional commanders were Rear Admirals Bernard Currey and Cecil Thursby. After reorganization on 8 August, Vice Admiral Sir Alexander Bethell commanded the Eighth Battle Squadron in *Prince George*, with Rear Admiral Henry Tottenham in *Albion*. By a narrow margin, Bethell was the oldest officer in command afloat in home waters. In the Admiralty and as commandant of the War College in 1913, he had done much to develop the War Staff and the training of officers in staff work. The progressive detachment of ships from his squadron for harbor defense and overseas duties would soon force Bethell ashore temporarily, but this would not be his last service in the Channel Fleet. The only light forces directly attached were four light cruisers, one of which would soon be removed. The intention was that the destroyer flotillas based on Harwich would support the pre-dreadnoughts if they deployed into the North Sea. If the fleet should head south, destroyers from Dover or the home ports could do the job.

Between Jellicoe and Burney was interposed a collection of units that the Admiralty came to designate the Southern Force. Rear Admiral Arthur Christian was named in command on 16 August in *Euryalus*. The major units consisted of *Euryalus* and four other old armored cruisers, designated Cruiser Force C, under Rear Admiral Henry Campbell in *Bacchante*. Despite their age and inevitable inefficiency after activation, these ships were intended as the heavy support for the light forces that operated out of Harwich. Commodore Second Class Reginald Tyrwhitt, flying his broad pendant in the light cruiser *Amethyst* as commodore commanding torpedo craft (hereafter Commodore [T]), commanded the destroyers that were to become famous as the Harwich Force.

While the southern naval ports had their own flotillas under the command of the local C-in-Cs, the east coast was under the protection of older destroyers and submarines distributed among the ports under the command of the Admiral of Patrols, Commodore First Class George Ballard. He had been one of the key strategic planners within both the old NID and in the War Staff, serving as Director of the Operations Division before his appointment to the Patrols command.

The kaiser's decision as to whether the North Sea or the Baltic would be the "Principal Theatre of War" was the most straightforward element in the Imperial German Navy's strategy.[26] Once the British entered the fray, the Admiralstab and the Fleet Command believed priority had to go to the North Sea. The conflict in the Baltic depended, in their view, much more on the conduct of the land campaign.

The uncertainty that was apparent in so many other areas reflected the fundamental problems that existed within the navy's entire strategic and operational construct. There was a robust tradition of wargaming both in the naval staff and in the fleet and commands down to the unit level. Within, in retrospect, overly restricted limits, German tactical training was realistic and innovative. The Germans were further ahead than the British in some aspects of communications and maneuvering, with more-flexible single flag orders and better use of low-powered wireless, as well as a willingness to engage in tactics, such as the battle turn, in which the ships in the battle line turned almost simultaneously, a tactic the British considered too risky.[27] They also devoted more resources to night fighting. On the other hand, they were well behind in the integration of light forces with the capital ships, as well as the employment of submarines. Perhaps most important, German experience of fleet operations at any distance from the German coast was limited and had not extended to exercising the battle squadrons or even the First Scouting Group in close cooperation with flotilla craft in such circumstances. The fleet existed very much within a coastal defense mindset.

The Germans had always monitored British maneuvers and doctrinal development with great care, through open and clandestine means, to determine what strategy the Royal Navy would adopt and how best to prepare for it. Those involved identified many of the problems that would come with the war. However, the work went largely on parallel tracks, since the Admiralstab lacked the authority to distill the results into a credible and approved plan. The prewar years were marked by a series of increasingly bitter disputes among von Tirpitz, the Admiralstab, and the Fleet Command over strategic and operational concepts, with von Tirpitz in particular maintaining a divide-and-rule approach that was successful for him personally but did little for effective planning.

All assessment of a war with the British was based on the assumption that the High Sea Fleet would be weaker than its opponent.[28] The key questions were how the British would employ their superiority and what vulnerabilities this would create for German exploitation. For the first decade of the century, their judgment was generally that the British would either seek to attack the High Sea Fleet in its anchorages, or that they would seize a forward operating base to allow the imposition of a close blockade. This made a defensive posture logical, since the British would be vulnerable to attrition by torpedo craft and to surprise sorties by heavy units, even if they did not tangle directly with coastal defenses or minefields. A British naval assault on the Baltic was also feared, and the navy more than once considered—and discussed with the army—preemptive occupation of Denmark to close the passages from the Kattegat.

This problem of two fronts always had to be borne in mind, with respect not only to the Russians, but also to the British if the latter attacked in the Baltic. Even after its enlargement, the Kiel Canal was not a panacea for transferring forces between the two seas. The big ships' draft had to be reduced to twenty-eight feet to permit transit.[29] For the most modern battleships and the battle cruisers, this required the discharge of up to 1,700 tons of coal and ammunition. Transfer of the First and Third Squadrons and the First Scouting Group required four to five days to complete.[30] It was the security that the canal provided that was important, not timeliness, since a passage around Denmark would take the same force only two and a half days. Switching substantial formations between theaters had to be planned carefully; it could not be an instant response to a short-notice threat.

As early as 1906 a distant, or what the Germans termed a wide blockade, was mentioned as a reasonable possibility—the idea had been dismissed outright in 1903 and 1905. There was increasing evidence in the years that followed that the British lacked the strength to maintain a close blockade. Successive exercises produced evidence that both the close positioning of light forces with distant cover provided by a battle fleet, or the offshore deployment of patrol lines, similarly covered, made the British open to substantial attrition if German forces were handled effectively. The Germans were initially encouraged by the Declaration of London, which confirmed the requirement for a commercial blockade to be close and continuous if it were to have legal status, but the British failure to ratify the Declaration and their own realism as to likely British ruthlessness soon dispersed any comfort. The prospect of a wide blockade became a matter of public discussion in 1912, with analysts who wrote for the public assessing the issues very accurately.[31] The Germans also had their own proponents of economic warfare who urged a greater priority for oceanic commerce raiding. Even von Tirpitz had begun to look sympathetically on increased cruiser construction as a way of strengthening the navy, but there were too few ships available in 1914 to increase numbers beyond the handful already overseas.

The implications of the idea that the British would not attempt a major surface presence close to German waters were not fully worked through. Here the navy suffered from its institutional history, given the limitations that von Tirpitz's essentially political approach had forced on the fleet and its planning. Both the Admiralstab and the Fleet Command at various times examined alternative concepts, including use of the Kattegat and ventures toward the British coast, but got nowhere. The Admiralstab's analyses in late 1913 and May 1914 of the British maneuvers the previous summer and of their planned dispositions in northern waters were generally accurate, although the potential role of Scapa Flow as a fleet base rather than an outpost anchorage was not recognized. There was some discussion of the possibility of raiding the British coast, but there was no enthusiasm in the army, preoccupied with planning campaigns against France and Russia, for joint operations. Any attacks would have to be purely naval. The army's focus on the speedy defeat of France also meant that there was no desire to divert resources to occupying Denmark. This meant that Denmark's neutrality would have to be accepted and the open passages from the Kattegat managed. It also effectively stymied any ideas about using the Kattegat as an avenue of German attack, something proposed in earlier years by Admiral Henning von Holtzendorff when C-in-C of the fleet.

The new British strategy remained a conundrum. If they did not come, what should the Germans do? In May 1914, in a rare moment of candor, Grand Admiral von Tirpitz himself asked von Ingenohl and his staff what their plans were "if the English did not appear in the German Bight." He received no answer.[32] If the British would not attack, then much more thought had to be given to how an offensive campaign could be mounted. Raids undertaken against the British coast in any strength would need cover and this meant that the High Sea Fleet would have to operate well into the North Sea. Several factors militated against this. The first was the kaiser, loath to risk the battleships with which he was so closely associated against the enemy he both envied and feared. The second was the desire to maintain the fleet as a bargaining counter. At this point, the commitment of the British to their alliance was not seen as total. The Germans saw prospects of a settlement in the wake of a rapid French defeat, a settlement that would be more favorable if the British still had the High Sea Fleet to consider. There was also fear of the unknown, confirmed by the unsatisfactory results of war games based on offensive operations by the main fleet. After a 1912 war game that examined the problem of the British remaining at a distance, one staff officer commented, "[T]he role of our beautiful fleet will be a sad one. The submarines will have to do the job."[33] Finally, because long-range operations had not been exercised by the High Sea Fleet, there were many unanswered questions as to their practicality.

The confusion was reflected in Operation Order No. 1 for the North Sea. Admiral Gustav Bachmann, not involved in its drafting, later acknowledged that it was a "vague and oracular" document.[34] The Order declared,

1. Our object is to damage the British fleet by means of offensive advances against the forces watching or blockading the

German Bight, and also by means of a ruthless mining, and if possible, submarine offensive, carried as far as the British coast.

2. When an equalization of forces has been achieved by these measures, all our forces are to be got ready and concentrated, and an endeavor will be made to bring our Fleet into action under favorable conditions. If a favorable opportunity for an action occurs before this, advantage is to be taken of it.[35]

The let-out was in the last sentence, but how a "favorable opportunity" was to be created was not stated. Later, von Ingenohl was severely criticized for failing to exploit this "advantage" clause, but he was in no doubt at this point that he lacked authority to lead the High Sea Fleet into the North Sea.[36] That there was wishful thinking in the hope that the British would risk their fleet close enough to German shores to be worn down is clear, but it was wishful thinking shared by the majority at the end of July 1914. The collective view of the naval leadership was that the High Sea Fleet should remain on the defensive. This approach was not confined to the major units; the light craft and submarines required for the Kleinkrieg would be kept on a tight rein from the start—indeed, they had practically no experience of the long-range operations needed to mount an offensive. If there were misgivings, they had yet to be openly expressed, even if von Tirpitz's realization of the implications of the fleet's relative inactivity for the navy's political position—and his own—meant his change of heart took only a few days. By 6 August he was stressing, although not to every audience, the importance of seeking a fleet engagement.[37]

In stark contrast, the German operational concept for the Baltic was to finesse the Russian Fleet into maintaining a defensive posture. It accepted that the Germans would have to adopt an aggressive approach that took the war as close to the Russians as possible. The priority given the North Sea Theater inevitably left the Baltic with weaker forces than the Russians. This was particularly true in the opening weeks, since the older battleships and armored cruisers needed time to mobilize. The Germans had not committed to withdrawal from their most vulnerable bases in the east, such as Danzig, but they were resigned to the likelihood of Russian domination of the eastern Baltic. However, they hoped that the Russians could be intimidated into inactivity and plans were already in train to achieve this.

Von Ingenohl's second in command in the High Sea Fleet was Vice Admiral Wilhelm von Lans, who also commanded the First Squadron of the eight oldest dreadnoughts. Like von Pohl, von Lans had distinguished himself in China, commanding a ship at the taking of the Taku Forts where he was badly wounded.

His divisional commander was Rear Admiral Friedrich Gadeke. The Second Squadron, which contained the most modern pre-dreadnoughts, was led by Vice Admiral Reinhard Scheer (photo 6.6). Widely regarded as one of the most talented officers in the service, he was long associated with von Tirpitz and most recently had served in charge of the General Naval Department within the Naval Office. Despite extensive shore time, he proved himself a highly capable sea commander, and it was this that brought about an invitation by the then C-in-C of the High Sea Fleet to serve as his chief of staff in 1909.[38] Notably, the admiral concerned, von Holtzendorff, had significant differences with von Tirpitz, but Scheer was able to navigate between the rivals. His divisional commander in the Second Squadron was Rear Admiral Franz Mauve.

PHOTO 6.6
**Vice Admiral
Reinhard Scheer**
(pictured as an admiral)
Bibliothek fur Zeitgeschichte

The new *König*-class battleships, the first two of which would commission on 30 July and 9 August, were being collected into the newly formed Third Squadron under Rear Admirals Felix Funke and Carl Schaumann, along with the *Kaiser* class. The Fourth Squadron was composed of the remaining useful pre-dreadnoughts under Vice Admiral Ehrhardt Schmidt and Rear Admiral Hermann Alberts. The still older armored ships, only of utility as coast defense units, were in the process of recommissioning into the Fifth Squadron (Vice Admiral Max von Grapow, from the Hydrographic Office on mobilization, and Commodore Alfred Begas) and Sixth Squadron (Rear Admiral Richard Eckermann, although he was soon to become von Ingenohl's chief of staff). The oldest squadrons were not yet operational, since all their units had been in refit, reserve, or on training duties before mobilization.

Rear Admiral Franz Hipper, commanding the battle cruisers and senior officer of the Scouting Groups, seemed more cast in the British mold than the German (photo 6.7). A fine seaman with extensive torpedo boat experience, he loathed paperwork and was practically unique in that he had spent no time whatsoever in staff or shore appointments. Reticent in the extreme, he disdained intrigue but was politic enough to have enjoyed a successful appointment in the imperial yacht *Hohenzollern,* and sufficiently shrewd to employ an extremely competent staff. That staff included Commander Erich Raeder (later C-in-C of the German navy), who was one of von Tirpitz's circle but also enjoyed a close connection with Admiral von Müller.[39] Raeder could do all the politicking that Hipper required.

Although Hipper was senior officer, the Scouting Groups were divided into five—the battle cruisers in the First, the light cruisers in the Second and Fourth,

PHOTO 6.7
**Rear Admiral Franz Hipper with his staff
(including Commander Erich Raeder
on the right)**
U.S. Naval Institute Photo Archive

and the armored cruisers in the Third and Fifth Scouting Groups. The oldest armored cruisers were intended primarily for coast defense, while the more modern units would operate with the High Sea Fleet. Rear Admiral Leberecht Maass commanded the Second Scouting Group and also served as senior officer of the torpedo boats, assisted by Captain Johannes Hartog of *Rostock*. Rear Admiral Arthur Tapken acted as Hipper's deputy in the battle cruisers, commanding a division consisting of *Derfflinger* (although she would not commission until October) and *Von der Tann*, with his flag in the latter. Rear Admiral Hubert von Rebeur-Paschwitz commanded the Third Scouting Group from *Roon*. Captain Karl von Restorff commanded the older light cruisers in the Fourth. Like the old pre-dreadnought squadrons, none of the Fourth's ships would be fully operational until mid-August, for all either had been laid up or were in use as training vessels. The Fifth Scouting Group, also being brought forward from reserve or training, was commanded by Rear Admiral Gisbert Jasper in *Hansa*.

Since the North Sea would be the principal theater of war, all the dreadnoughts and modern pre-dreadnoughts were based there, together with the Scouting Groups. Eight torpedo boat flotillas, with a total of ninety vessels, were at the High Sea Fleet's disposal, together with twenty older and smaller units deployed around Heligoland and the various anchorages for local patrols. The flotillas with the main fleet were of a more workable size than the British units, consisting as they did of eleven vessels made up of a leader and ten torpedo boats, frequently operated as half-flotillas.

Two U-boat flotillas, the First under Commander Hermann Bauer and the Second under Commander Otto Feldmann, were attached to the High Sea Fleet. Their strength totaled nineteen submarines, the cruisers *Hamburg* and *Stettin*, and four torpedo boats. Six more submarines were completing, but could not be expected to join until at least the beginning of September. Lacking experience of long-range operations, this was a pitifully small force on which to base a significant part of the *Kleinkrieg*. Neither the minelaying nor the commerce raid-ing forces were much better. At this point, all the purpose-built minelayers were occupied in the Baltic and the only unit immediately available was the auxiliary *Königin Luise*. *Kaiser Wilhelm der Grosse* was the lone auxiliary cruiser preparing to sail for commerce operations. Two other former merchant vessels, *Berlin* and *Viktoria Luise*, were fitting out, *Berlin* as a minelayer as well. The handful of other ships intended as raiders had been caught in foreign waters, which forced hasty extemporizing on the overseas stations.

Apart from minesweepers and the smallest patrol vessels, the North Sea forces were completed by the older light cruisers allocated for the defense of the Ems and Elbe Rivers, and the Jade and Weser Estuary anchorages. The tiny aviation ele-ment was distributed evenly between the North Sea and Baltic. The zeppelin L3 and a handful of aircraft were in the west, while two small requisitioned airships and eight other machines were allocated to the Baltic. There were more airships on the way, and further requisitioning of civil aircraft would bring the fixed wing numbers up in both theaters before war emergency programs could be instituted. Nevertheless, aviation would remain makeshift for some time.

So would the North Sea command arrangements. The defensive mindset was reflected in Admiral Hipper's role controlling the Heligoland Bight patrols. The arrangements were necessarily complex, given the geography involved, and required extensive planning and management. The difficulty was that this drew the admiral and his small staff away from planning offensive operations and strained the communications facilities of his flagship. It was hardly logical employment for the commander of the Scouting Groups.

In the Baltic, Grand Admiral Prince Heinrich could call on seven cruisers of varying age. These included the modern *Augsburg* and *Magdeburg*. In addi-tion, fourteen torpedo boats, four U-boats, and four minelayers were eventually permanently assigned to the Baltic Command. The latter ships were laying defen-sive minefields off the German coast and they had been joined temporarily by the High Sea Fleet's *Nautilus, Albatross,* and *Pelikan*. As all in the Baltic were aware, this was a tiny force compared with what the Russians could assemble. Whether it was enough would depend on whether the Russians were willing to go on the offensive at sea.

Perhaps fortunately for the Germans, they were not. The fundamental aim of the Baltic Fleet was to defend the Gulf of Finland to protect Saint Petersburg and its industries.[40] This limited ambition reflected recognition of Russia's weaknesses at sea, but also the experience of the 1904–5 war and subsequent war gaming. The loss of Port Arthur had demonstrated the vulnerability of an isolated base, how-ever well-fortified, and it was felt that the western ports in Russian territory were exposed to a German advance. Russia had also to consider Sweden. If the latter were to enter the conflict on the side of the Germans, there would be even more pressure. The priority for funding therefore went to the Gulf of Finland and the local bases, notably Reval.

The defensive line designated as the Central Position was intended to consist of a series of minefields laid north-south well inside the Gulf of Finland, with extensive gun batteries placed on either shore to protect the extremities, while heavy units patrolled to the east to support the middle of the barrier. Working out of Reval and the island of Uto off the Finnish coast, destroyers and submarines would provide another line of defense outside the Gulf. The idea was a relatively simple one: even if they were able to fight off the small craft, the Germans could not strike at the protecting big ships until the mines were cleared, and they would not be able to clear the mines while the latter were covered by the big ships.

There were problems with the concept. It protected Saint Petersburg, but left much of Russia's western coasts undefended. Although this had been accepted and Libau would be largely emptied of naval units, the Gulf of Riga was vulnerable to a flanking attack by a seaborne force, which would then permit the landing of troops and the isolation of Reval. Furthermore, time and finances had not allowed Reval's full development. Major work could be undertaken only at Kronstadt, which was completely iced in for the majority of the winter and early spring. There would thus be periods in which the Germans could still attack the Gulf while the Russian fleet had no access to the immediate repair of heavy battle damage.

The Fleet labored under the specter of Tsushima—the fear that the Russian navy would suffer another devastating defeat at the hands of a superior opponent. Von Essen himself had confidence in his forces, properly employed, and foreign observers were struck by the extent to which the Russians had consciously sought to implement the lessons of 1904–5 in areas such as damage control.[41] The tsar and many in the army high command, however, were less sanguine and there would be tight restrictions on the deployment of the capital ships, particularly the new dreadnoughts. Furthermore, the fleet was placed under the operational control of the Sixth Army, charged with the defense of Saint Petersburg. That army's succession of commanders had little understanding of the potential of their maritime forces and less enthusiasm for hazardous ventures.[42]

Sweden also needed to be watched carefully. Von Essen had long considered a preemptive attack on the Swedish fleet as being preferable to leaving the initiative to a potential enemy and even set about arranging it, but wiser counsels prevailed. Increasing confidence as to Sweden's continuing neutrality would be one factor in allowing the Baltic Fleet greater operational freedom; the other would be a more favorable outlook on the security of Saint Petersburg. Until these were achieved, the possibility of making the Baltic unusable for the Germans could not be realized.

There was another theater of operations to consider: the Arctic. The Imperial Russian Navy was represented there by a single fishery protection vessel. The

Russians did not expect that the Germans could undertake substantial operations against their Arctic coast, given the British strength, but it was vital that the local ports remain open as long as the ice permitted. For the Russian navy, the principal requirement was for Welsh steam coal. Russian sources were of variable quality, a key factor for high-speed steaming, and subject to seasonable availability as well as the vagaries of the primitive national transport system. However, the closure of the Black Sea would soon make the Arctic ports, despite their limitations, vital supports for the Russian war economy as a whole.

The Baltic Fleet itself was built around a battleship squadron of four ships, under the command of Vice Admiral Baron Vasili Fersen. One of the few officers to emerge with some credit from Tsushima, he had refused to obey the order to surrender his cruiser, *Izumrud,* and escaped the Japanese cordon, only to lose the ship by grounding. There were two older battleships, effectively just coast defense units, in a training division under Captain E. N. Odintzov, while none of the quartet of new dreadnoughts would be available for several months. Of the cruisers, *Rurik* was Admiral von Essen's flagship, while the remaining eight units were divided into two squadrons under Rear Admiral N. N. Kolomeitsov and Commodore P. N. Lysekov. *Novik* and thirty-seven other destroyers were in the First Flotilla under Rear Admiral I. A. Shtorre, with eighteen more destroyers and eight smaller torpedo boats in the Second Flotilla under Rear Admiral Alexander Kurosh. The large Russian destroyer flotillas were broken down into divisions of nine or ten units, which constituted the basic tactical formation. There were eight elderly submarines under Rear Admiral Levitzki, with three more boats for training, and a six-ship squadron of minelayers, most of which were converted old cruisers, commanded by Rear Admiral Vasili Kanin. How such a mixed bag of units performed would depend critically on the quality of its leadership. For the moment, this was in good hands—but von Essen was only one man.

7

FIRST BLOOD IN THE NORTH SEA

T HE GRAND FLEET ARRIVED AT SCAPA FLOW ON 31 JULY AND REMAINED in the desolate anchorage for the next few days, deploying torpedo nets and manning searchlights and secondary armament at night. The fleet's colliers appeared soon after and most ships coaled on 2 August. Internal preparations continued. What to land in readiness for battle was a vexed question and enthusiasm often outran judgment. Many boats were sent away, while interiors were stripped of paneling and furniture. This often went too far, ranging from wooden flag-lockers, which created angst for the signalmen, to desks and library cupboards.[1] William Tennant in *Lizard* at Harwich noted, "[T]he harbour presented the most comic sight imaginable. Everything from straw hats to wardroom chairs were floating about, so one may imagine what had sunk."[2] The boats soon returned; ships could not manage harbor routines without them, and they were vital for life-saving.

Common sense occasionally prevailed. *Southampton*'s executive officer, Commander Edward Astley Rushton, had studied the observers' reports from the Japanese fleet during the 1904–5 war. *Southampton* kept the furniture.[3] Some ships took the unsanctioned opportunity to remove unwanted structural items, the pre-dreadnought *Prince of Wales* in the Channel Fleet disposing of her entire after-bridge.[4] Many units fashioned antiaircraft mountings for the machine guns carried for landing parties.[5] Most useful was removal of paint, particularly the enamel used to beautify ceremonial areas. This could be inches thick. In the oldest ships, even though "Officers joined in . . . it was an impossible task and was never finished."[6] Weird external paint schemes intended to confuse enemy spotters also flourished, ranging from red, white, and blue striped masts and funnels and lurid camouflage, to HMS *Monarch*'s black and white checkerboard "B" and "X" turrets. This eventually proved too much for the C-in-C, who called a halt to artistic efforts. The battleships reverted to grey. The Germans were better off than the British, but the older ships did not have the same fireproof materials as the most modern and removal became a dockyard job.[7] Admiral Scheer complained ruefully of "those weeks of the war in which the tapping of hammers and the scraping of chisels never ceased . . . and mountains of wood and superfluous paint vanished from the ship."[8]

The two sides settled down to await events. The first loss occurred on 3 August when the British oil tanker *San Wilfrido* struck three mines and sank in shallow water off Cuxhaven. Instructed to call there before departing German waters, the master attempted to enter without a pilot and ran foul of the newly laid defensive minefield. There were no casualties, but her crew was interned. War came at 1830 on 4 August. Britain waited on expiry of its ultimatum, but Germany had determined to declare war first. The Grand Fleet itself was already at sea. The previous day the Admiralty received reports that three German transports had left the Baltic. The British feared that the Germans would occupy the sparsely inhabited Shetland Islands and Callaghan had sent ships to patrol the area two days earlier. On hearing of the German movement, the new C-in-C ordered out the Third Cruiser Squadron, as well as *Achilles* and *Cochrane* of the Second, with the battle cruisers as a covering force.

There was nothing there. An encounter between the battle cruisers and "2 enemy cruisers" was resolved when it was realized that "it was old Packs pottering off to coal."[9] Apart from the understandable first night nerves involved (Beatty was unsurprised that the report came from the highly strung "Blinker" Hall's *Queen Mary*), this demonstrated the problem dispersed forces faced in maintaining awareness of each other's location.[10] "Pottering" was also an apt description. The cruisers were usually steaming at between only eight and ten knots, while the battle cruisers' overnight speeds were no higher.

The Admiralty was not satisfied that the Shetlands were clear of enemy forces and ordered out the entire Grand Fleet. Reports were also coming in of German raiders being sent into the Atlantic. Jellicoe headed east toward Norway, while the cruiser squadrons separated to sweep south into the North Sea and west around the coast of Scotland. At 2300 on 4 August the Admiralty issued the War Telegram. Reactions varied. Ramsay in *Dreadnought* commented, "[I]t created no excitement whatever."[11] Commander Edward Evans of Antarctic fame, captain of the destroyer *Mohawk* at Dover, later claimed that his ratings greeted the news with "a howl of joy," but an exhausted Basil Owen in *Stour* recorded, "[A]t midnight a signalman woke me up to report; 'Admiralty to All Ships. Commence hostilities against Germany.' I said, 'Oh Damn!' & went to sleep again at once as I was dog tired."[12]

Farther south, Britain's first move at sea was already under way. In accordance with plans made in 1911, the cable ship *Alert* sailed from Dover immediately after the declaration and by 0330 on 5 August was grappling with the first of five trans-Atlantic cables to be cut. Her job was complete by 1000, largely severing German high-data rate communications with the western hemisphere. As a follow-up, six Britain-Germany cables were cut by another cable layer later that day. The war of information had begun.[13]

The Grand Fleet's sweep had little result, being too far west. A lone commerce raider, *Kaiser Wilhelm der Grosse*, designated Cruiser D, sailed from Bremen on 4 August. Her track took her within thirty miles of the British. *Kaiser Wilhelm* carefully monitored British wireless traffic, some en clair, to help herself keep clear of them. The basic radio disciplines had yet to be learned. Cruisers did steam along the Norwegian coast, but they were nearly a day too late to intercept the raider. This movement was to investigate whether the Germans had a secret base in Norway. Again, the intelligence proved false. Reports nevertheless continued to flow in that the Germans were collecting merchant ships off the Lofoten Islands to convert into raiders. This seemed credible enough; the British suspected that certain German merchant ships not only were strengthened to mount medium-caliber guns, but also, as was recent British practice, carried armament in peacetime.[14] The desperate attempts made to arm liners cut off from Germany, such as *Cap Trafalgar,* prove this to be untrue, and in fact the number of commerce raiders intended under prewar plans was not large. It would be some time before the British could rid themselves of the belief. On 7 August the Third Cruiser Squadron and the Third Destroyer Flotilla were sent into Norwegian territorial waters but found nothing. Formal protests were made about the breach of neutrality involved, but the Norwegian government, perhaps relieved to have got off lightly so far from both belligerents, did not seem unduly disturbed.

It was manifest to Jellicoe that the northern blockade would be insecure until the cruisers assigned to it arrived on station. Even to examine the few trawlers and merchantmen met during the sweep involved stopping the entire Grand Fleet. Furthermore, irregular sweeps could not substitute for systematic patrols by ships within visual contact of each other. Apart from a couple of trawlers, which had been unaware of the war, not one German had been seen, but Jellicoe could not believe they were making no attempt to send out commerce raiders.

The *Edgars* were on their way. De Chair, hoisting his flag in *Crescent* at Portsmouth, managed to get her and two other cruisers to sea on 3 August. This had been achieved only by working around the clock with a very mixed bag of newly joined personnel. A fourth cruiser had to be left behind, while in *Crescent* herself frantic efforts were made to fix the ship's primitive gunnery equipment and extemporize "an efficient fire control system."[15] The three cruisers, and three that left Devonport the same day, were delayed by the need to intercept various merchant ships, but arrived at Scapa Flow on 6 August and began coaling immediately. Next day de Chair took his ships into the Orkney-Shetland Passage. Not until the Grand Fleet moved clear on 8 August did the cruisers divide and *Edgar, Theseus,* and *Gibraltar* begin patrolling off the Norwegian coast.

Although the squadron was soon at full strength with the arrival of *Hawke* and *Royal Arthur,* the *Edgars* could be only a stopgap. They were old and ill-suited to the northern weather. Conditions were likely to remain favorable for about a month, but then the equinoctial gales would begin. Their numbers were also only just sufficient. Even in the finest visibility, four ships—the maximum available for each passage—would be just enough to watch the entire 150-mile span of the Shetlands-Norwegian gap, and this did not allow for coaling every six to eight days. For the moment, they were better than nothing. German orders to their merchant fleet to shelter in neutral ports meant that the shipping lanes were almost clear. Even Scandinavian ships were keeping away, for in the days leading up to the declarations many sailings had been cancelled while shipping companies awaited the outcome. What strained the Tenth Cruiser Squadron was following up repeated reports of German bases on the Norwegian coast and among the islands. High-speed steaming bore hard on the aged ships.

In the south the British finally decided to send troops to France. The Imperial General Staff's plans provided for the one cavalry division and all six infantry divisions in the regular field army to be dispatched, but Cabinet would not immediately allow this. The government was concerned both by the possibility of internal disorder—an increase in unemployment being one factor—and by the fact that the Germans might land an invasion force in the weeks that would elapse between the dispatch of the British Expeditionary Force (BEF) and full mobilization of the reserve Territorial Army. Two infantry divisions were therefore held back.

The movement was still a huge undertaking and much effort had gone into its planning. The list of the 240 merchant vessels to be requisitioned had been prepared years before and the Admiralty kept watch on the movements and cargo state of each vessel, as part of its overall monitoring of the tonnage required for use in conflict. Many needed conversion, notably the horse carriers and ambulance ships, but all the work was completed on time. The troops were to move from Southampton to Le Havre, and the majority of stores from Newhaven to Boulogne. Because the numbers were so large and the reserve transport capacity small, it was decided not to convoy the transports but rather to sail each one as soon as it was ready. Preliminary movements began on 6 August, and embarkation was scheduled for the ninth, while the disembarkation of the main body and stores was to finish on the nineteenth, with the entire operation complete by the twenty-third. The process was complicated by Cabinet's decision to send another infantry division, but this was included with little disruption. The operation was conducted without loss and was regarded, with justification, as the most efficient dispatch of an army by sea in British history.

Protection of the transport routes involved almost every unit in home waters. The Admiralty was relieved of the need to provide additional ships at the western entrances to the Channel as the French were willing to employ their Atlantic squadrons. Consequently, only Cruiser Force G, with its four old *Talbot* class, was allocated to the area. The French provided ten armored and four light cruisers under the command of Rear Admiral Rouyer. The force patrolled along a line from Land's End to Ushant, with four French armored cruisers as a covering group. The Admiralty did not think that a major German thrust was likely from this direction, but feared that a fast raider or minelayer might slip in from the Atlantic. Consequently, Admiral Wemyss was directed to send all merchant ships into Falmouth for examination. As events turned out, the cruisers spent their time almost entirely on trade control.

The Channel Fleet was also at sea. Burney took the Fifth Battle Squadron to protect the Newhaven-Boulogne route from an attack from the North Sea, while Bethell went with his battleships to cover the Southampton–Le Havre line and be in a position to support both Burney's units and the Allied forces to the south. The battleships had no destroyer escort, since the Admiralty did not believe there was much risk of submarine attack. For the moment, that assessment was correct. Although neither Burney nor Bethell was entirely happy, their reservations did not prevent either admiral ordering his ships to stop for protracted periods in broad daylight.

The French had every vessel out they could muster, the situation on land making them anxious to get the British across the Channel. By day, at least half a flotilla of British destroyers was in the Strait of Dover. By night, with the increased potential for German units to slip through, every available ship was sent out. At this early stage, when morale was at its peak, fatigue had not set in, and machinery was not worn out by overuse, it was easy to muster full availability. For nights on end, every destroyer, scout, and gunboat from Dover was at sea. By 11 August additional patrols of drifters and trawlers had been organized. At this point in the war, undetected passage of the Channel by any German craft was unlikely. Farther north, around the area off the Dutch coast known as the Broad Fourteens, patrolled the old armored cruisers of Force C. They remained here by day, as cover for the destroyers, but at night moved south and joined the Fifth Battle Squadron.

To the Harwich Force went the first blood. Tyrwhitt went to sea at first light on 5 August. He had long planned a sweep toward Terschelling for the war's first day. Tyrwhitt and Keyes agreed that it would be useful to combine this with a submarine reconnaissance of Heligoland Bight. When the force sailed, the cruiser *Amethyst* had *E6* in tow, while the destroyer *Ariel* was allocated *E8*. The submarines were quite capable of making the distance themselves, but Keyes considered that the more help, the better. The submarines could be towed at up to fifteen knots, while Keyes thought they would be a useful backstop if the slow and weak *Amethyst* encountered heavier metal.[16] The flotillas sailed separately, Tyrwhitt in *Amethyst* leading out *Fearless* and the First Flotilla. The two forces were to operate out of visual range of one another, but within supporting distance. Commodore (T) intended to stay at sea as long as he could, with the Third Flotilla returning to Harwich on 6 August to refuel, while the First Flotilla patrolled off the Dutch coast. On 7 August they would exchange duties.

At 1015 *Amphion* and the Third Flotilla sighted a steamer ten miles distant, heading east. Captain Cecil Fox sent *Lance* and *Landrail* to investigate, but, as the ship "had every appearance of being one of the Hook of Holland steamers," which ran the Great Eastern Railway's ferry service between Britain and the Netherlands, was not much concerned.[17] Then *Laurel*, on the western flank, signaled, "Trawler reports that liner has been seen dropping things overboard presumably mines." *Amphion* increased speed and headed after the destroyers. The latter soon observed that their quarry was deploying mines even as she fled. This was no British ferry. At 1045, at a range of 4,400 yards, *Lance* opened fire with her forward 4-inch, the first shot of the war in the North Sea.

Königin Luise was a Hamburg-Amerika line excursion steamer completed in 1912. With a good turn of speed, she ran from Hamburg to Heligoland and was long marked down as an auxiliary minelayer. When the war orders went out, she was immediately requisitioned. The conversion was hasty, however, and all the time allowed was to load 180 mines and their launching gear and repaint the ship in the colors of the Great Eastern Railway Company. *Königin Luise* was intended to mount two 88-mm guns, but these were not installed and she carried only two light pom-poms and some rifles. The crew was a scratch one, made up largely by *Königin Luise*'s old crew, with a stiffening of regular personnel and reservists. Still on board were most of her merchant fittings, including the promenade deck windows. Late on 4 August *Königin Luise* slipped out of Emden. Her orders were somewhat vague: "Proceed at utmost speed in the direction of the Thames. Lay your mines as near as possible to the English coast. Do not lay mines off neutral coasts, or further north than 53 north."[18]

The 180 mines that *Königin Luise* carried were paltry in comparison with the numbers some British observers had expected would be laid at the start of the war. The Germans had to husband their mine stocks, and the Admiralstab was not yet willing to utilize cruisers or torpedo boats for such a dangerous mission as offensive minelaying. Because the few purpose-built minelayers were occupied in the Baltic with defensive fields and the conversion of other auxiliaries would not be complete for some time, *Königin Luise* was all that was available for the North Sea.

The Fleet Command's decision to dispatch the converted (and untrained) minelayer suggested a desire to do something offensive, rather than thinking through the implications, operational and strategic, of being the first to initiate open-sea mine warfare. The Admiralstab's assessment of the risks was more accurate and the conditions in early August, with good weather, extended daylight, and a full moon, were particularly unfavorable. *Königin Luise,* however, enjoyed early luck in that squalls concealed her passage. When she began minelaying at dawn, her captain had reason to hope the ship could complete the field and escape unscathed. But for the trawler's report to *Laurel*, he might have been right.

Amphion followed the chase north, but Fox did not think he was within effective range for half an hour (photo 7.1). *Lance* and *Landrail* had been firing with

PHOTO 7.1   HMS *Amphion*   *Imperial War Museum*

little result. Only after *Amphion* (which won the light cruisers' gunnery trophy in 1913) began to score hits at seven thousand yards did the destroyers also find their target. To the surprise of *Amphion*'s gunnery officer, the excitement was too much for the crews of the three 4-inch in action: "They started off firing as fast as they could, and it was a good minute before by dint of throwing things at them that I could stop them."[19]

Königin Luise had not long to live. Her pom-poms were completely ineffective, despite the weapon crews' bravery. She was soon on fire, listing badly after a 4-inch shell burst on the waterline and blew a hole in her side. Some of the ex–merchant service sailors began to panic and abandoned ship without orders.[20] By noon, with *Königin Luise* on her beam-ends, the action was over. Fox ordered his ships to close and pick up survivors. The three British units rescued five officers and seventy men. In *Amphion* the only available spaces were the captain's day cabin and a compartment in the bows. The prisoners were placed in the latter with the idea that, "if we did go up on a mine they might just as well go first." As Fox later remarked, "It was little thought at the time how true these words would be."[21]

The rescue complete, the ships turned to rejoin the remainder of the flotilla, although *Lance* was sent back into Harwich with a defective 4-inch gun. Teething troubles in the newest ships were to be commonplace. The sweep continued until 2100 that night when the flotilla neared Terschelling. With nothing significant detected, Fox turned for home. He took care to avoid the area in which *Königin Luise*'s mines were thought to lie, as well as to keep clear of the British submarine patrol off the Outer Gabbard. At the same time, Tyrwhitt's *Amethyst,* with *Fearless* and the destroyers of the First Flotilla, came to the planned eastern limit of their sweep as they approached Borkum. From here they would alter southwest and patrol along the Dutch coast before relief by the Third Flotilla. As they turned away, *Amethyst* and *Ariel* cast off *E6* and *E8* to begin the first offensive war patrols of the British submarine service.

Meanwhile, although Fox's ships attempted to keep clear of the German minefield, their planning went awry. They applied a margin of seven miles west to their very uncertain idea of the danger area's location, but this was in the wrong direction—the line of lay was east.[22] The Third Flotilla ran over the field near the local time of low tide. At 0635 on 6 August a mine exploded under *Amphion*'s bridge. The entire forecastle was immediately aflame and there were heavy casualties among the seamen, whose mess decks were forward, as well as among the German prisoners housed there. *Linnet* took *Amphion* in tow, but it seemed to Fox that the ship's back had broken. She was badly hogged, a deep crack running across the upper deck. With a fire raging in the forecastle there was the danger that the forward magazine would explode. Fox ordered *Amphion* abandoned and it was well he did. As he later wrote,

> [S]carcely had I left the ship and being about 50 yards away . . . the
> foremost half of the ship seemed to rise up out of the water and
> break into a mass of flames and smoke, causing . . . a terrific roar
> resembling a volcano; masses of material were thrown into the
> air to a great height, and I personally saw one of the 4-inch guns
> and a man turning head over heels about 150 feet up; this gun
> just missed falling on the *Linnet*, much to the relief of her C.O.,
> who saw it coming and thought his number was up.[23]

Fox thought that the explosion was caused by another mine. The ship must have travelled forward a considerable distance, and the green glow surrounding *Amphion* suggested that the lyddite filling in the high-explosive shells had gone up, not propellant. This would have been the case with a mine, since the shell rooms were below the magazines. Despite *Linnet*'s escape from the plunging 4-inch gun, she was showered with splinters, while a bunker-lid struck her amidships and pierced a boiler room. Fortunately, *Linnet* suffered no casualties, but a shell exploded on board *Lark* and killed the sole German to escape *Amphion*, as well as two wounded stokers from the ship. Total British casualties were one officer and 131 men killed. The water was so shallow that *Amphion*'s stern was in the air when her bow was on the bottom, but, within fifteen minutes of the second explosion, the light cruiser disappeared. After ensuring no survivors were still in the water, the much chastened British resumed the passage to Harwich.

Fifteen miles out another suspicious steamer was sighted. Since she was also in the colors of the Great Eastern Railway Company and even flying a large German flag, it was too much for the destroyers sent to investigate and they opened fire. At this, the remainder of the flotilla "automatically opened out into a fan and went full speed for her, opening fire at the same time." The steamer quickly replaced the German flag with a British Red Ensign, but this made no difference. Captain Fox, now in *Llewellyn*, realizing that the flotilla was "seeing red," had to take the ship and foul their range before they would cease fire, neither radio nor flag signals having worked.[24] It was soon clear why *Saint Petersburg* had been flying a German flag: she was conveying the former German ambassador and his staff to the neutral Netherlands and was indicating her immunity to any German forces. Fortunately she went unscathed in the hail of shells.

Neither *E6* nor *E8* saw or did anything of real importance. Both had been ordered to stay in the Bight only three days, "and unless . . . very well placed for offensive operations they were to return after two."[25] The outer Bight was empty and neither went close enough to Heligoland to see the Germans' patrols. They reported, however, that they had been sighted by large numbers of fishing vessels. Keyes concluded that these boats were radio-equipped pickets and proposed an operation by Tyrwhitt's destroyers against them. This idea had to be laid aside in the face of other priorities. Given that the Germans would have sent out torpedo craft had they news of the submarines' presence, it is difficult to see on what Keyes based his conclusion. The trawlers did report their sightings, but only on return to port.

After the *Königin Luise* incident, the Admiralty took the sensible measure of creating a war channel with marked buoys north from the southern side of the Thames Estuary to the Humber. At this time the patrolled channel and its associated charts were secret and intended only for military use. It was, however, a first step toward achieving control of all shipping movements around Britain. Ominously, suggesting just how poor were the information processes around the Admiralty, the Admiral of Patrols discovered the channel's existence only by accident, several days after it was activated.[26]

By now it was apparent to the Germans that the British would not attempt a close blockade, and even the prospect of incursions into Heligoland Bight was doubtful. Although the kaiser, the Admiralstab, and von Ingenohl were not prepared to allow a sortie by surface ships, pressure to do something was increasing. Disappointment at its inactivity was already being felt within the High Sea Fleet and there was an obvious dichotomy between its efforts and the bloody war on land.[27] On 6 August ten submarines of the First Flotilla were ordered north to find the Grand Fleet and the British blockade line. They were to proceed, spread at seven-mile intervals, up the North Sea until they reached a line between Scapa Flow and Hardanger, before turning south to a line between Scapa Flow and Stavanger. Here they were to patrol before returning to Heligoland.

The estimate as to the Grand Fleet's position was fairly accurate, but the operation failed. The First Flotilla was sent only because it had the most experienced captains, thought to stand a better chance than the raw commanders of the brand new Second Flotilla. The First's submarines were the oldest U-boats in frontline service, with unreliable machinery, renowned for the pall of yellow smoke their petrol engines emitted on the surface by day and the sheets of flame that issued forth at night. Most had never operated so far out to sea, or at such length. The boats were also not handy under water, having poor depth control.[28] This was to prove critical.

With acceptance that the British were mounting a distant blockade came assessment that the British observation line lay between Buchan Ness and Egersund. This was a fair guess, since the line struck the Norwegian coast where there were few islands or fjords to provide shelter for blockade runners. What the Admiralstab and U-boat staff failed to appreciate was that the British would never use the line because it was vulnerable to attack from the Kattegat, as well as too near Germany's North Sea bases.

The first indication of submarines came at 1145 on 8 August. The battleships *Monarch* and *Ajax* had been detached to conduct a practice shoot at a target towed by *Orion*. The latter was streaming the target when *Monarch* reported being attacked by a torpedo. A reliable witness declared that he saw a submarine break surface launching a weapon, which missed.[29] Although there were other claimants to the sighting, the position was so far west of the U-boats' tracks it is likely this was a false alarm. The battleships nevertheless fired a hail of 4-inch while *Orion* hastily hauled the target under her stern. All departed the area at fourteen knots, but only thirty minutes later *Orion* stopped again to recover the target.

The day was punctuated by further submarine scares. The Grand Fleet had a right to be frightened because its movements were taking it back and forth across the U-boats' line. However, there were many more reports than submarines. Many alleged sightings were made by older personnel, particularly warrant officers and senior ratings. Commander Dudley Pound of *Colossus* commented on the fleet's "severe attack of 'Submarinitis' . . . half the officers and men have never seen a periscope coming towards them. If they had been given some opportunities in peacetime to see it I fancy there would be fewer false alarms."[30] This syndrome was to continue. Despite the threat, the fleet's speed was reduced shortly after any submarine warning was cancelled. After one from *Orion* at 1830, which was followed by periscope sightings by *Iron Duke* and *Dreadnought*, the formation "eased to 8 knots and proceeded on our course."[31] Both battleships had attempted to ram their supposed periscopes. They felt no shock and nothing more was seen (photo 7.2).

At 0535 *Orion* and other ships "passed a patch of oil fuel on the water, with bubbles rising."[32] Some assessed this as a sunken trawler, but (although south of the patrol line) the position was close to the planned track of Count Arthur von Schweinitz's *U13*, which disappeared without trace. The battle squadrons had turned west only ninety minutes before and were retracing their course, so it is possible that the submarine had been struck by a big ship while attempting an attack. It was not unknown for a surface unit to be oblivious to such an encounter.

PHOTO 7.2   **HMS *Iron Duke***   *Imperial War Museum*

Somewhat later, the cruiser *Achilles* reported that there had been a strong smell of petrol in her vicinity at 0240—which matched the submarines' general locality.[33]

A more certain success came when the light cruiser *Birmingham*, screening thirty miles ahead of the main body, sighted a periscope at 0340 on 9 August. She immediately turned to ram and struck the submarine a glancing blow, forcing her to the surface. *Birmingham* circled back and hit the hapless *U15* amidships, cutting her in half. The wreckage disappeared in seconds, taking Lieutenant Commander Richard Pohle and his crew of twenty-two men with it. The stoutly built *Birmingham* suffered no more than superficial damage and remained with the fleet.

It was now clear that the Germans could operate submarines well offshore. Believing that the area was no longer safe for heavy ships, an alarmed Jellicoe proposed to withdraw northwest of the Orkneys. He had already ordered every available cruiser and destroyer to clear the North Sea of submarines, although how this was to be achieved was a moot point. Only the need to cover the passage of the BEF restrained Jellicoe from departing on his own authority, and the Admiralty's prompt approval came as a considerable relief. By 10 August the battleships were out of the North Sea.

U5 had turned back early with engine trouble. The remaining German submarines returned on 11 August, having learned little. The Admiralstab still did not know where the Grand Fleet was operating or where the blockade line lay. Valuable experience had been gained, along with greater confidence in the submarines' ability to conduct long-range operations, but to balance this, two boats and, more important, their trained crews had been lost. *U13* remained a mystery, although later German assessments attributed its destruction to the battleships.[34]

British announcements of *Birmingham's* success confirmed at least one sinking, but that it was *U15* was not known until after the war.

Jellicoe still believed the U-boats were either operating from secret bases or else had parent ships at sea. Wireless intercepts ostensibly supported the latter idea, but there was not a grain of truth, although it was a theory "very generally . . . held in naval circles."[35] Over the next few days, searches were conducted around the Norwegian coast, while the cruiser *Drake* examined the Faroe Islands. Again, nothing was found, although the scouts returned with the welcome news that the Norwegians were keeping careful watch and would not permit the use of their waters for any belligerent purpose. While off Norway the Fourth Destroyer Flotilla had the embarrassing experience of mistaking a school of jellyfish for a minefield. The error was discovered only after the leader *Swift* "bumped" one while attempting to extricate herself.[36]

Jellicoe ordered that Loch Ewe, on the west coast of Scotland, be prepared as a secondary base. This would involve much disruption, since the number of colliers was only just sufficient to keep Scapa Flow supplied. The C-in-C also had to change his handling of the fleet. Its speed needed to increase. Unless there was surety the area was clear of submarines, formations would have to maintain at least twelve knots during the day. Night speeds could vary depending on visibility—the darker the night, the slower the speed—but battleships could never again operate in the North Sea without considering the underwater threat. The fuel consumption involved would be yet another cause for anxiety. Renewed effort went into developing screening instructions and the prewar judgment that, in such a threat environment, battleships must be accompanied by cruisers and light craft was confirmed. This marked the beginning of Jellicoe's demands for ever more destroyers.

Meanwhile, despite the Grand Fleet's wanderings, the passage of the expeditionary force proceeded unmolested. The Germans were surprised by the speed of the BEF's dispatch. It was a combined shock to the Admiralstab that, first, the British dared transport almost their entire regular army to France while the High Sea Fleet remained intact and Germany capable of launching a seaborne invasion, and, second, the British had not sent ships into the Bight during the BEF's passage. This, combined with continuing uncertainty as to the form of the distant blockade, meant that the atmosphere was one of confusion. Though many in the navy wanted to raid the transports, the army was eager to "settle accounts" on land.[37] Furthermore, the German General Staff believed that defeat of her troops in the field would be more likely to convince Britain of the futility of the struggle than even wholesale losses at sea. The chancellor still nursed hopes of a rapprochement, and his pleas for restraint complicated the situation further.

Matters were not helped by disagreements among the senior leaders. The kaiser was prepared to authorize the use of torpedo craft, submarines, and minelayers, but still would not risk the heavy ships. Von Tirpitz, on the other hand, was increasingly anxious about the political dangers of the fleet's continuing inactivity and urged its deployment. In view of the kaiser's restrictions, neither von Pohl nor von Ingenohl believed anything practicable could be done on the large scale. With the First Submarine Flotilla out on its sweep and the bulk of the remaining U-boat force required for defensive patrols, there were only four submarines available. This was not enough to have much chance of substantial success.

Von Ingenohl examined the idea of a massed torpedo boat attack, but the predicted position of the Grand Fleet was at least 150 miles farther from Heligoland than the operational radius of the light craft. Furthermore, the torpedo boats would have to go without heavy cover, since providing it would breach the kaiser's order. This would probably result in the German force being cut to pieces by the Grand Fleet's cruisers and powerful destroyers. Similarly, minelaying would be suicidal in summer. The Germans were beginning to realize the folly of relying on Britain enforcing a close blockade, and restricting so many of the High Sea Fleet's capabilities to this construct. The Admiralstab in particular needed time for reflection.

On 8 August, however, *U19, U21, U22,* and *U24* were sent to investigate past a line drawn between the Terschelling lightship and the Swarte Bank, where the British forward patrols were thought to operate. It was hoped that the submarines would encounter heavy ships to the southwest, but they were given strict instructions to proceed in that direction only if they could withdraw to safety submerged. Since their underwater endurance was seventy miles at best, and effectively much less, this was a considerable limitation. The U-boats saw nothing but patrolling destroyers, several of which they only narrowly avoided. When they returned empty-handed on 11 August, all the intelligence they could give was that there appeared to a continuous destroyer patrol off the Dutch coast. To add to its uncertainty about the Grand Fleet, the Admiralstab now had to admit that it did not know from what positions the pre-dreadnoughts were covering the passage of the BEF—and was unsure whether they were in southern waters at all. Though the Admiralstab still believed that the operation was heavily guarded, the Fleet Command suspected that the pre-dreadnoughts had gone north to join the Grand Fleet. Knowing almost nothing, closely restricted, and with few offensive weapons to hand, the Germans could do little.

But this very inactivity, as well as the apparent failure to move against the BEF transports, was creating suspicions in Britain that the Germans might attempt invasion or, more likely, raids on the east coast with the small number of troops they were thought to have available. It was known that the High Sea Fleet was concentrated in the North Sea and the Admiralty could not persuade itself that the German offensive would be confined to one auxiliary minelayer and a handful of submarines. By 12 August the Admiralty wanted the Grand Fleet back in the North Sea, despite the risk of U-boats. Jellicoe acquiesced, but insisted that the operation be simply a sweep to ensure that the area was clear of German surface forces. He did not wish to linger. He was careful, too, to ensure that Cruiser Force C and Tyrwhitt's flotillas were available to reinforce him. The operation began as soon as the battle squadrons had coaled and completed essential maintenance, the Grand Fleet leaving Scapa late on the night of 13 August.

Before the sweep started, Jellicoe asked the Admiralty to assume operational control of the flotillas at Harwich. He did not think it practicable to exercise command of them from *Iron Duke*, whether at Scapa or at sea. The distances were too great and wireless too unreliable. The Admiralty immediately consented to the change, which in any case aligned with the concept under which the War Room was meant to operate. Despite the First Lord's pleasure at being able to direct the frontline forces of the naval war, it was decided to amalgamate all the units from Harwich under one command to ensure that Tyrwhitt's destroyers and Keyes' submarines had heavy cover in the form of the armored cruisers. Rear Admiral Arthur Christian, with his flag in *Euryalus,* was assigned to lead this new Southern Force. He was in a difficult position but did not prove himself decisive enough for the role. Tyrwhitt and Keyes continued their operations uninterrupted and had direct liaison with the Admiralty in their planning of offensive sweeps. Keyes was taking advantage of his many hats in the submarine arm, but Tyrwhitt had also made a good impression in Whitehall. Churchill was greatly taken with him and Commodore (T) was able to return triumphant to Harwich with a promise of the first available of the new light cruisers. Oil-burning and with a designed speed of nearly thirty knots, *Arethusa* would be an enormous improvement on Tyrwhitt's slow and weakly armed *Amethyst*.

While the Grand Fleet came south, Tyrwhitt's destroyers, Force C in support, were ordered to sweep near to Terschelling Light. Keyes was directed to have submarines watch for the Germans as they emerged and sent *D2* and *D3* to the Ems and *E5* and *E7* to the Weser. Although the Grand Fleet's scouts moved as far south as the Horns Reef, which marked the northern limit of the Heligoland Bight, there was only one warning of a U-boat, a report by *New Zealand* that proved to be false. No enemy surface ships were sighted. It would have been a chance for a massed German torpedo boat attack, but the British cruisers swept just too far to the north to be seen by the U-boat patrols. They had no inkling of the close presence of the British fleet. At 0930 on 16 August the Grand Fleet turned north. Tyrwhitt found the cupboard equally bare. His destroyers and the armored cruisers remained around Terschelling until noon on 17 August, but by then it was obvious the Germans were not at sea. Accordingly, while Cruiser Force C moved to the Downs, Commodore (T) took the Third Flotilla into Harwich, leaving the First Flotilla to reestablish the patrol line on the Broad Fourteens, which the Admiralty had ordered for the duration of the BEF's passage.

The submarines were also unsuccessful. The approaches to the German rivers were heavily patrolled. Although *D2* repeatedly tried to approach an armored cruiser moored off the western entrance to the Ems, the shoals proved too much. *E5* and *D2* both attacked torpedo boats, but these maneuverable shallow-draft targets were difficult to hit, and their efforts came to nothing. All *E7* could do was stay out of the way of the patrols, and it was with relief that the four withdrew late on 17 August. Like their U-boat equivalents, the British submariners had much to learn. The Germans had been considerably alarmed by the British presence. Many of the units that plagued the four boats were sent to hunt for them, and it was not surprising that they returned to Harwich with an exaggerated idea of the strength of routine surveillance. From their reports, however, Keyes deduced that it would be worthwhile to place submarines on rotation permanently inside the Bight. To simplify their problem, Keyes suggested that a surface operation should be mounted against the torpedo boats and numerous suspected trawler-scouts.

For their part, the Germans embarked on a second attempt to find the British blockade, this time by sending three units of the Second U-Boat Flotilla to reconnoiter along the Norwegian coast and investigate the British east coast ports suspected of being used as fleet bases. Still inclined to favor the Firth of Forth and the Humber, which were indeed the anchorages the Admiralty had selected before the war, the Germans had no idea that the Grand Fleet was operating out of Scapa Flow, or that Loch Ewe was just about to come into use.

U20 and *U21* set out for Norway on 15 August and passed through the screen of cruisers ahead of the Grand Fleet. Only *U20* saw anything, however, and the cruiser and destroyer that she observed were too far away to attack. She did notice the Grand Fleet's smoke to the west, but her engines and compass developed defects that forced her to turn back. *U20* returned to Heligoland on 19 August, having spent thirty-four hours submerged during her patrol, considered a great feat. *U21* passed very close to both the First Battle Cruiser Squadron and the Second Cruiser Squadron without observing them. Her reconnaissance of Moray Firth, at the head of which was Invergordon, came to nothing. Although few were in naval service, there were so many fishing vessels that the submarine had to submerge repeatedly. It was not long before *U21*'s captain decided it was impossible to penetrate the Firth in such conditions. Turning south, the *U21* sighted four destroyers near the entrance to the Firth of Forth, but night descended before she could get into position to attack. Eventually she had to return empty handed. The third boat, *U22*, had more luck in her reconnaissance of the Humber. Although she found no targets and was several times detected and chased, *U22* brought back valuable information about local patrols, as well as the assessment that no mines had been laid. This was significant, for it suggested that they had not been laid around any of the other east coast ports.

The submarines' reports convinced the staffs that the blockade line was much farther north than they had thought. In the circumstances, the Germans decided to halt long-range submarine operations. They had already lost two U-boats, and machinery defects put several more out of action. Instead, cruiser operations would be mounted against the east coast and Channel. The Admiralstab was now almost certain that all the modern British capital ships were in the north and that light cruisers could be sent out without heavy support at little risk. The first operation would be to attack the patrols over the Broad Fourteens. The Admiralstab had no idea of the presence of the armored cruisers, but estimated that not more than one destroyer flotilla could be at sea at a time.

Two of the newest light cruisers, *Stralsund* and *Strassburg*, were selected, along with *U19* and *U24*. The two cruisers would move southwest and penetrate the British patrol lines unobserved during the dark hours of the morning of 18 August. They were then to turn back at dawn and drive the British destroyers before them. The two U-boats were to intercept any heavier British ships that might attempt to follow the cruisers. Some measure of support was to be provided by the cruiser *Kolberg*, stationed off Terschelling, while Hipper was instructed to have the First Scouting Group ready to sail from the Schillig Roads.

Under the command of Captain Victor Harder, the two cruisers sailed from Heligoland at 0700 on 17 August. Despite a report of British light cruisers in the area, the operation continued. The first encounter occurred west of Smith's Knoll Light at dawn the next day. *E5* and *E7*, returning on the surface from their patrols off the Weser, were astonished to see a cruiser approaching them. Her four funnels suggested the *Cressy* class, but the two submarines were quickly disabused when *Strassburg* replied to their challenge by opening fire. Considerably shaken, *E5* and *E7* submerged in what they later claimed was "the record time for the Navy up to date, with mast, signals [*sic*] and all up!"[38] The fast-moving German was no target at all, and the submarines were forced to remain under water until the area was clear.

At 0540 *Stralsund* was sighted bearing due east by the destroyer *Lizard*. The First Flotilla was farther to the west than the Germans had hoped and their plans to roll up the British were set at naught. Nevertheless, *Stralsund* turned to engage and within a few minutes the four destroyers of the Fifth Division were under heavy fire. William Tennant, asleep in *Lizard,* was roused by an excited call, "Exercise Action, Sir!" As he noted, "after all these years of peace it is hard to stop the 'Exercise' part of it."[39] On receiving *Lizard*'s sighting report, with the elaboration that the enemy appeared to be a *Karlsruhe*-class light cruiser, Captain Blunt in *Fearless* ordered his flotilla to chase. A little after 0600 *Fearless* came in sight of the German vessel, but Blunt was alarmed to hear from his lookouts aloft that she appeared to be an armored cruiser such as *Yorck*.

Near identical silhouettes made the mistake understandable, but it had serious consequences. Against a light cruiser with 10.5-cm guns, Blunt could be confident that the 4-inch guns and torpedoes of *Fearless* and his numerous destroyers gave him the advantage. *Yorck,* however, was armed with 21-cm and 15-cm weapons. Such heavier and longer-range metal, with the advantage of a steadier gun platform, convinced Blunt that he should turn away and call for help. At 0610 *Fearless* ordered the destroyers to turn southwest, while Blunt attempted to make contact with the remainder of the Southern Force. This produced a tirade of signals from the closest (and bitterly disappointed) destroyers, asserting that the enemy was not an armored cruiser, but they failed to change their Captain (D)'s mind.[40]

The effect of Blunt's message was galvanic. Cruiser Force C was coaling in the Downs, but Campbell had the colliers cast off and his squadron moving within twenty minutes—something of a tribute to the engineers. Christian was at the Nore in *Sapphire*, but he too was soon at sea, having shifted to *Euryalus*. Tyrwhitt was just leaving Harwich with the Third Flotilla. Hearing the news, his ships immediately worked up to full speed, joyful at the first real prospect of action since *Königin Luise*.

Though Harder turned to follow the British, he was unhappy. The only reason he could find for the enemy's action was that they were trying to lure *Stralsund* toward something heavier; he could not guess at the mistake that had been made. The British transmitting en clair (still a practical necessity for timely transmission) heightened his suspicions that he was being led into a trap. In this state of mind, it was natural that the German captain would expect any further contacts to be British warships hunting for *Stralsund*. At 0645 another sighting was indeed made, a ship identified as a light cruiser. Where such a vessel was, more destroyers were likely to be. Reasoning thus, Harder turned away. There were no other British light cruisers in the vicinity, but it is possible that this was the old torpedo gunboat *Halcyon*, minesweeping in the area. She was just large enough to be converted into a cruiser by fevered imagination.

Seeing *Stralsund* turn away, Blunt was inclined to follow. An aggrieved *Goshawk* and *Lizard*, the ships that had been closest to the German, were continuing to submit in the strongest terms that she was a *Karlsruhe*-class ship. Blunt was inclined to credit their judgment, for not only had the "armored cruiser" turned away, but also there had been no heavy gunfire, despite his force being well within the effective range of such weapons. After he had collected the destroyers around *Fearless*, Blunt turned to follow *Stralsund*. By then it was too late. Despite later efforts by Tyrwhitt to cut off their retreat at Terschelling, both cruisers got clear away. They were soon followed home by the U-boats, neither of which saw anything. It had been a dispiriting episode for the British. All concerned were certain that the German ship had been only a light cruiser, and it was difficult to avoid the conclusion that the flotilla might have defeated *Stralsund* had it been better handled. Tyrwhitt, too, was bitterly disappointed, but he and the Admiralty avoided censuring Blunt, although it was decided to station three submarines around Smith's Knoll to deal with any further excursions.

Operational conditions proved a challenge in other ways. On patrol in *Lookout* on 19 August, her navigator, Oswald Frewen, mistook the Ymuiden light for that of Terschelling, some sixty miles northeast. Misled by their similar characteristics, he could not account for the huge set that would have put him fifty miles out from his reckoning and failed to realize that he had been set nine miles in the opposite direction. As Frewen remarked, "I suppose one cannot help being a B. F. [bloody fool]." Only an accidental meeting with Force C put him right.[41]

The Germans were not long in launching another operation. Sharing the British preoccupation with the idea of wireless equipped trawlers as scouts, the Admiralstab decided to attack the British fishing fleet on the Dogger Bank. It was an informal convention that civilian fishing vessels should be left to their trade by belligerents. Even though this immunity had been respected by neither side, the Germans were convinced that the British were taking advantage of it. A raid involving two cruisers and a torpedo boat flotilla was to take place as soon as a reconnaissance north of the Heligoland Bight could be completed. A report of British submarines, however, caused the C-in-C to cancel the reconnaissance and go ahead with the raid anyway. Commodore Keyes had sent *D5, E4,* and *E9* into the Bight on 20 August, and their discovery caused the Fleet Command concern that they might be the forerunners of a destroyer sweep. However, extensive searches on 21 August failed to uncover any sign of the submarines or of British surface forces.

Thus reassured, von Ingenohl ordered the Dogger Bank operation to begin. *Strassburg, Rostock,* and Sixth Torpedo Boat Flotilla were allocated, but there was dispute over the decision to send only the light cruiser *Mainz* in support. Hipper considered that a movement so far into the North Sea should have heavy cover, at the least by the First Scouting Group. Von Ingenohl, with the kaiser's dictum in mind, refused to allow the battle cruisers to do anything more than wait in the Schillig Roads. This was dangerous practice, for the Dogger Bank was 150 miles away. If the light cruisers made contact with a stronger and potentially faster force, notably the First Battle Cruiser Squadron, they would have little hope of escape.

This "somewhat inglorious venture" resulted in the destruction of eight British trawlers.[42] No wireless installations were found, but the exercise in total war continued nevertheless. The British submarine *D5* attacked the force seventy-five miles from Heligoland but botched the job, although she was in a good position, six hundred yards off *Rostock*'s bow. Her two torpedo salvo missed. *D5*'s captain was heavily criticized on his return, for Keyes had specifically directed that only one torpedo be launched at a time, supposedly to give the chance to fire a second if the first had missed. *D5* might have had another opportunity, but it is equally likely that the range would have been opening by the time the failure was realized. It is also possible that the torpedoes ran beneath *Rostock,* given that warshot torpedoes were running deeper than their setting.[43]

The next operation that the Admiralstab proposed was the real beginning of the German North Sea mining campaign. Two minelayers, the purpose-built

Nautilus and *Albatross*, were now available. Each accompanied by a light cruiser and a half-flotilla of torpedo boats, they were ordered to lay fields off the Humber and the Tyne. The intention behind the Humber field was to close the main shipping channel along the east coast, while the Tyne was selected because the Admiralstab believed it to be a major base. Yet again, no heavy support was permitted, Hipper's strong objections being ignored. Intended for 23 August, the operation had to be delayed for twenty-four hours because *Mainz,* the cruiser allocated to accompany *Nautilus,* ran aground. At 2000 on 24 August, *Albatross, Stuttgart,* and the six boats of the Eleventh Half-Flotilla left Heligoland for the Tyne. *Nautilus, Mainz,* and Third Half-Flotilla, with less distance to go, departed at 0500 the following morning. Both groups had been instructed to take off the crews and sink every British trawler they encountered, wireless equipped or not.

The minefields went down in the first hours of 26 August. Each layer carried two hundred mines and deployed them in a little under an hour. *Albatross'* single field was eleven miles in length, while *Nautilus* set two, each of five miles. Both had great trouble fixing their positions in the foggy conditions, which resulted in *Albatross* setting her field well northwest of the planned location. Both groups returned to Germany late on 26 August. Even as they were entering the Bight, their mines claimed a first victim. At 2200 the Danish fishing vessel *Skuli Fogett* sank on the Tyne field, with the loss of four men. Early the next morning, the trawler *City of Belfast* came into the Humber with the news that she had exploded two mines in her nets. The Tyne field would claim several victims in the months ahead, the majority neutral ships.

This was arguably a false step by Germany. Britain was finding it difficult to impose a blockade anywhere near as absolute as prewar plans had proposed. Neutral pressure was increasing, but so was domestic concern, with the City and many elements of government urging relaxations in order to maintain British industry and employment and support the balance of payments. That Germany had been the first to resort to mine warfare in the vicinity of major shipping lanes did not breach international law, but it lowered her credit considerably. The resultant ill feeling gave the British more freedom to move when the time came to tighten the blockade and impose controls on shipping around the British Isles.

The Humber field came close to claiming two very important victims. Unknown to the Germans, the Humber had just become the base of the new Cruiser Force K. The commanders at Harwich had informed the Admiralty that there was little protection for the Southern Force. Were the Germans to sortie with the First Scouting Group against the patrols on the Downs and the Broad Fourteens they could decimate the destroyer flotillas and annihilate the antiquated *Cressys*. Furthermore, it was likely that the Germans would be back at their bases before the Grand Fleet or the British battle cruisers had even reentered the North Sea. The argument was incontrovertible.

A force of battle cruisers was allocated and Rear Admiral Moore appointed in command. *Invincible* had only just returned to service, with her turret power converted to hydraulics after an experimental electrical system had proved unsatisfactory. Beatty was expecting that she would join his command; he not only had to do without, but also suffer the loss of *New Zealand* to Cruiser Force K. He was partly mollified by the assurance that *Inflexible* and *Indomitable* would join him as soon as they returned from the Mediterranean. Moore was promised three of the new light cruisers when they were completed. On 12 August he hoisted his flag at Queenstown (modern Cobh) where *Invincible* had been calibrating her armament. A week later, the two battle cruisers were in the Humber.

At all events, when Force K sailed at 1100 on 27 August for the sortie that resulted in the Battle of the Heligoland Bight, the ships passed within two miles of *Nautilus'* first field. The Admiralty sent minesweepers, but it was not until the battle cruisers had passed clear of the area that it was understood how small had been the margin of safety. The discovery spurred efforts to organize a more comprehensive minesweeping service along the entire east coast. Additional trawlers were requisitioned, converted, and allocated to each major port. It was soon realized that, as long as the limits of the German fields were known and fixed, it was not necessary to sweep all the mines. This was another step toward a cleared War Channel along the coast that would have other benefits in providing a mechanism for effective British control of all shipping, Allied or neutral.

A heated debate was in progress as to the German methods of minelaying. The Admiralty and many of the coastal patrols were in the throes of "trawler phobia" and thought that fishing vessels had crept into the coast and deployed the mines. The fact that the Germans were willing to conduct mine warfare near a shipping lane lent some credence to the idea, but the Inspecting Captain of Minesweepers, T. P. Bonham, correctly asserted that these operations were impractical on such a scale. Despite his views, on 31 August the Admiralty issued a statement denying that any British mines had yet been laid and declaring, "The mines off the Tyne were laid 30 miles to seaward, not as part of any definite military operation, nor by German ships of war, but by German trawlers, of which a considerable number appear to have been engaged in this work."[44]

The accusation was wishful thinking, despite the claim that "*A.E.24*" of Emden had actually been seen at work, but it was an early blow in the propaganda war being waged alongside the conflict at sea.

8

THE BALTIC BEGINS

THE FIRST PROBLEM THE GERMANS FACED IN THE BALTIC WAS DEFINING HOW the new command organization would work. Prince Heinrich's appointment came out of the blue for the commander of the Baltic Naval Station, Vice Admiral Gustav Bachmann. Eventually, it was agreed that Bachmann would retain responsibility for the defense of Kiel and its immediate approaches, including the local exercise areas, while Prince Heinrich, as C-in-C of the Baltic Forces, watched over the passages into the Baltic from the Kattegat, as well as operations against the Russians. Heinrich's Baltic Coast Defence Division under Rear Admiral Robert Mischke was formally assigned to the defense of the western Baltic on 2 August. An additional complication came with the potential use of the High Sea Fleet in the theater. In such circumstances, all forces would come under the command of the fleet's C-in-C.

Key to the Baltic plans were the light cruisers *Augsburg* and *Magdeburg*, the only modern German surface units in the Baltic and certainly the only ones that could be employed offensively at the start of the war—and even then *Magdeburg* had a defective turbine. The Germans were aware that Libau was no longer intended as the main Russian naval base, but they feared its potential for destroyers and submarines to use against the flank of forces advancing on the Gulf of Finland. The first operation was thus planned as a bombardment of the port and deployment of mines off its approaches. Admiral Bachmann had issued orders for this sortie before Prince Heinrich assumed control, but the two cruisers were not allowed to sail until there was certainty that Russians had started hostilities. Only on 2 August was the leash slipped, and by this time intelligence of the withdrawal in progress at Libau caused their orders to be modified, with *Augsburg*'s minelaying split between Libau and the approaches to the Gulf of Riga.

The operation suffered from a bad case of nerves. Continuing Russian demolitions at Libau were mistaken for gunfire, while the cruisers initially thought that enemy warships were emerging from the harbor to attack them. *Augsburg*, contrary to instructions, laid all her mines off Libau without precisely recording their position, something that was to cause the Germans difficulties in later weeks.

To be fair, *Augsburg* had not been given detailed direction by the C-in-C as to the required locations. For fear of Russian mines, the bombardment was conducted at long range and this, combined with the small weight of the 10.5-cm shells, limited its effects. The two cruisers also did little to achieve the follow-on task of interfering with Russian shipping, although this was probably because most merchantmen had sheltered in the nearest safe port, while those still at sea were using territorial waters.

Meanwhile, the prospect of war with Britain loomed, and the passages from the Kattegat were of much greater concern to the Germans than was the enemy in the east. Prince Heinrich's orders stressed the need to protect Kiel Bay. This reflected the key role of its installations and the local exercise areas in supporting the High Sea Fleet, given the threat that the Germans believed the British also posed to the North Sea bases. Prince Heinrich was warned by the Admiralstab on 2 August that there were indications that the British were preparing an attack through the Kattegat. Although this intelligence was untrue, the nearest channel, the Great Belt, was barely twenty miles northeast of Kiel Fjord, and the Little Belt was not much farther away. Of the three major passages, the westernmost, the Little Belt, ran through German territorial waters and could be quickly closed by a minefield. The other two, which included the Great Belt's deep-water channel, represented a much more complicated problem, since the central Great Belt ran through waters of Denmark, and the Sound to the east went through those of Denmark and Sweden.

Heinrich's concerns were well based, particularly in relation to warning time. Although patrol vessels were posted at the passage entrances, their wireless installations were so underpowered that it was unlikely that a report would reach Kiel. Additional minelayers were being commissioned, but the number of mines ready for use was limited. Furthermore, the C-in-C Baltic's total strength in theater was so weak that reinforcement from the North Sea would be vital, requiring some form of defense in depth to buy the necessary time for the transfers through the Kiel Canal.

Denmark's attitude was critical and a diplomatic note was dispatched to determine whether she intended to close the passages. Prince Heinrich, however, decided that he had to ignore Danish neutrality, whatever her answer. Two minefields were therefore laid on 5 August—one in German waters in the Little Belt and the other, of 243 mines, at the southern entrance to the Great Belt. With the possibility of a German invasion always in mind, the Danes accepted the fait accompli. They had already set mines in their part of the Sound and now declared that they would not permit warlike operations by any belligerent in Danish waters. Danish minelaying followed farther north in both the Little Belt and the Great Belt.

Sweden, generally pro-German in outlook, did not have to be so careful to placate Germany. The Sound was not completely blocked, although precautions were taken to protect Swedish harbors and contingency measures set in place to allow the dousing of lights and the removal of markers if a belligerent attempted to pass through Swedish waters. All this the Germans had to accept, although they warned the Swedes that they reserved the right to act if Swedish waters were used to allow the passage of enemy units. The Germans had to accept something else. The ability of their own ships to enter the North Sea through the Kattegat was not completely prevented, but it was significantly constrained, while the Danish declaration of neutrality created a pressure point for Britain if any perception should develop that the Germans were receiving favored treatment. Von Tirpitz himself later regretted the restrictions on the Germans' use of these passages and the "respect" shown Denmark.[1]

Before the British entered the war, the Russians were in daily expectation of a German attack. Further minelaying was conducted to reinforce the main fields of the Central Position and to close off the passages between the islands around Finland. Von Essen had his ships on patrol in the Gulf of Finland and used the daylight hours to work them up, while the available submarines maintained a watch outside the minefields. At night the fleet returned to Helsingfors (modern Helsinki). The operations were not incident free. The battleship *Andrei Pervozvanny* ran aground on 1 August and was severely damaged. Von Essen was unhappy with the restrictions, but the Sixth Army Command was still concerned with the potential for the Germans to land forces to attack Saint Petersburg and would not permit ventures into the Baltic. The Baltic Fleet would have to remain on the defensive.

As for the Germans, their operational situation improved daily as reserve units were activated and the conversions of minelayers and other auxiliary craft completed. An aviation unit at Holtenau began operations on 3 August; its handful of primitive machines meant that flying was effectively confined to the approaches to Kiel Bay. The limitations of both the aircraft and their inexperienced crews were brought sharply into focus with a crash on 4 August. The tiny air arm would need more work before it could become a reliable provider of reconnaissance, even at relatively short distances. The arrival of the small nonrigid airship PL6, formerly in civil use as an advertising platform, did not help much as her capabilities proved limited.[2]

There were other problems, due to a combination of inexperience and shortages. The torpedo boat *S143* suffered a boiler explosion and sank under tow on 4 August. On 11 August the armored cruiser *Freya* was badly damaged in collision and would need at least a month for repairs. Prince Heinrich had already sought reinforcements in the form of *Blücher* and permanent assignment of the Fourth Squadron of the older battleships, but this was initially refused by the Admiralstab because of the threat in the North Sea. For the moment, the prince would have to make do, although he continued to press for a higher priority. With early Russian advances on land and an apparent lack of activity on the part of the British fleet in the North Sea, by 7 August, however, Admiral von Pohl's attitude changed and he pressed for "energetic action" in the Baltic.[3]

By this time there was a little more material to hand. Three reasonably modern torpedo boats were available in the form of *V186*, *V25*, and *V26*. On 9 August a reconnaissance in strength under Rear Admiral Mischke began with the deployment of *Augsburg* and two torpedo boats from Kiel, and *Magdeburg* and the third unit from Swinemünde, now activated as a forward base. The little force ventured into the eastern Baltic. There was at least one night encounter with Russian patrol forces, but the Germans were acutely aware of their vulnerability in the absence of any covering units and withdrew. Over the next few days short bombardments were conducted of the lighthouse at Dagerort, and of Russian positions close to the frontier. Interrogation of neutral merchant ships confirmed that the Russian approach was essentially defensive and confined to the Gulf of Finland.

This judgment brought about a plan to close one of the most likely exit routes for Russian forces from the Gulf of Finland. Mischke was directed to escort the auxiliary minelayer *Deutschland*. The admiral had misgivings about the ability for a relatively slow minelayer to conduct a covert deployment without being intercepted. The Russians clearly had forward patrols deployed, and penetrating these without detection would be extremely difficult. The existence of such patrols was confirmed through further exchanges with merchantmen while en route to the Gulf of Finland. The approach to the Gulf on the afternoon of 17 August was therefore made with caution, particularly as visibility was good and many hours of daylight remained. The Germans were soon detected, something confirmed for them by the heavy Russian wireless traffic that followed. Mischke now recast his plan and ordered *Deutschland* to be ready to lay her mines off the entrance to the Gulf, rather than well inside.

Late in the afternoon, as they approached Odensholm Island, the Germans encountered the Russian cruisers *Gromoboi*, *Admiral Makarov*, *Pallada*, and *Bayan*, accompanied by light forces. Mischke immediately deployed his cruisers and torpedo boats to mask *Deutschland* and ordered the latter to begin her lay. His tactics were successful. Rear Admiral Kolomeitsov in *Gromoboi* was confused and initially believed that he was facing the armored cruisers *Roon* and *Prinz Heinrich,* with the possibility of greater German strength in their rear. It was here that the sheer foolhardiness of the German sortie paid dividends, because Kolomeitsov would not risk closing the little force that opposed him. He was conscious of his highly restrictive orders and his staff navigator suggested that the German intent was to lure the cruisers onto a minefield. As soon as *Deutschland* had done her work, Mischke ordered a withdrawal. He was not followed.

Mischke knew that he had to maintain the pressure. After a conference with his captains, the admiral decided to return to the Gulf of Finland the following day in an attempt to draw the Russian heavy units onto the minefield. Critically, he believed that its deployment had not been observed and, now that *Deutschland* had been detached, his remaining units had the speed to outrun the Russians. The three torpedo boats bombarded Dagerort lighthouse and trailed their coats off Odensholm, again encountering Russian cruisers and destroyers. The Russian cruisers engaged the German craft, but the latter quickly withdrew under a smoke-screen. Once more, the Russians did not follow, even when they realized that their adversaries of the previous day had almost certainly not been armored cruisers.

Mischke came in for a great deal of largely undeserved criticism on his return to port. Prince Heinrich felt that the minefield had been laid too far west to be of use, but the fact was that the sixteen-knot (at best—she may have been having trouble with her coal) *Deutschland,* in a curious parallel to *Königin Luise,* should never have been employed on an offensive operation that carried such risks. Mischke had been wise to change his orders and remarkably successful in concealing *Deutschland*'s presence. The minefield itself, however, was soon discovered after neutral sinkings on 20 August. Noting the general location, the Russians did not attempt to sweep it up. Once its boundaries were known, they incorporated the field into their own defensive scheme, allowing them to shorten their own patrol lines.

Despite his efforts, Mischke had lost the confidence of his C-in-C and new arrangements were made. Mischke remained in command of the Coast Defence Division with responsibility for the western Baltic, while Rear Admiral Ehler Behring, an experienced torpedo boat commander invalided from the navy just before the outbreak of the war, was restored to the active list as detached admiral in the Baltic. By contrast with the load placed on Hipper in the North Sea, Behring was deliberately kept free of administrative responsibilities and allocated tactical command only of the ships actually available for offensive operations in the eastern Baltic. In practice, this meant the best of the light cruisers and torpedo boats, as well as U-boats when they came available. He hoisted his flag in *Augsburg* on 23 August.

A new sortie was soon in train: another attempt to penetrate the Gulf of Finland. The caution that the Russian heavy ships had displayed suggested that there was the opportunity to isolate some of the light craft in the outer patrol areas. The problem for the Germans was that the uncertainty of the positioning of their first minefield required that the approach to the Gulf be biased to the north, departing from a landfall on the Aaland Islands in order to have a sufficiently accurate navigational solution. Behring, however, chose to rely on a combination of astronavigation and dead reckoning. It might have been enough, but for thick fog. This did not stop the German operation, because it created the possibility of a surprise torpedo attack on the Russian cruisers, but did result in *Magdeburg* losing contact with her flagship at 2100 on 25 August. *Augsburg* continued on her preplanned track, southeast to the vicinity of Odensholm Island. *Magdeburg* made her own way as best she could, basing her course changes on wireless updates from *Augsburg*. Very early on 26 August she went heavily aground on Odensholm, close by the lighthouse. Every effort to lighten the ship and drive her off the rocks failed. By dawn it was clear that *Magdeburg* was caught fast. Odensholm lighthouse and signal station were bombarded at short range and were soon in ruins, but the Germans realized that the Russian Fleet Command was almost certainly aware of *Magdeburg*'s predicament. The arrival of their heavy units could not be long delayed.

Bogatyr, Pallada, and a division of destroyers were already on their way. Alerted by the increasingly heavy Russian radio traffic, *Magdeburg*'s captain decided to blow up the ship. Demolition charges were set and *V26* came alongside to take off the crew just as the Russians approached. In the melee that followed, *V26* was able to recover the majority of personnel, leaving the captain and a handful on board *Magdeburg*. Only the forward charges exploded, devastating the ship forward of her second funnel. This ensured that *Magdeburg* could herself be of no military value to the Russians, but there were omissions in the evacuation and demolitions that would cost the Germans dearly.

V26, burdened by *Magdeburg*'s survivors, escaped into the mists, despite a hail of Russian fire and at least one direct hit by a 6-inch shell, which knocked out a turbine. Yet again, the Russians did not pursue and *V26* was able to withdraw successfully and rendezvous with *Augsburg*. The Russians had their own muddles to deal with. As soon as *Magdeburg*'s grounding was confirmed, the destroyers *Lieutenant Burakov* and *Ryvany* had left Reval with Captain Nepenin, chief of the communications service, embarked. In the fog, *Burakov* mistook *Bogatyr* for *Roon* and fired a torpedo, which fortunately missed.

This confusion resolved, *Burakov* dispatched a boarding party to the wreck. There they captured *Magdeburg*'s captain and six companions and began the recovery of material from the ship, while forty-five German personnel ashore on the island were secured. The Russians were quick to realize that they had gained access to a veritable treasure trove of information—not only multiple copies of a major code book (the *Signalbuch der Kaiserlichen Marine* [SKM]), but also material from the radio room that confirmed the procedures in use, as well as German handbooks and tactical publications. There would be another result from the discovery of the *Magdeburg* material. Reconstruction of the events of 17 August from the documents confirmed the weakness of the German forces and the opportunity lost to the Russians. As a result, Admiral Kolomeitsov and his navigator, Sakelari, were relieved of their posts.[4]

When news of *Magdeburg*'s grounding reached Germany, the various commands immediately sought to assemble reinforcements in order to provide cover while the ship was refloated. The disjointed command and control arrangements meant that the collection of forces was piecemeal, Prince Heinrich dispatching armored cruisers and the newly active Fourth Squadron, while the C-in-C of the High Sea Fleet hurriedly arranged to transfer torpedo boats and light cruisers from the North Sea. The difficulty was that the latter units could not be at Kiel for almost a full day, and this forced the sailing of the old and slow armored ships of the Fourth Squadron with only a handful of almost as elderly torpedo boats as escort. Confirmation that *Magdeburg* could not be salvaged brought the sensible decision to recall them.

Behring was in no mood to retreat. He made a rendezvous with the cruiser *Amazone,* which had the submarine *U3* in tow, and exchanged the survivors and the damaged *V26* for *U3. Augsburg* then turned back to the east with the submarine in company. Despite the U-boat's very primitive equipment, Behring had in mind to use her as a trap. The encounter with the Russian cruiser squadron that followed was very nearly successful. Behring turned away and was initially chased by the Russians. The latter approached *U3* but, as they came within firing range, the submarine broke surface and revealed her position. The old submarine was at her limits of capability in such circumstances and could do no more once the Russians withdrew. Although disappointed by the results, Behring realized the potential of submarines in the eastern Baltic and began to press for reinforcements.

The kaiser took the news of *Magdeburg* calmly, remarking to von Pohl, "Chips have to fall in such times."[5] For his part, Behring was undismayed and soon had *Augsburg* back in the eastern Baltic, supported by the torpedo boats and some of the older light cruisers. The latter had to be carefully managed, being too slow and weakly armed to face up to the Russians. With losses in the North Sea on 28 August further reducing the Germans' overall cruiser strength, Behring knew that he also had to be extremely careful with *Augsburg* herself.

This did not stop him pushing his patrol line north from Gotland, which meant inevitable interaction with the Russians, now operating their ships just outside the Gulf of Finland as confidence increased that the Germans were not out in strength. Von Essen gathered a force consisting of *Rurik,* three of the older armored cruisers, and the destroyer *Novik* and sailed on 1 September. Late that night *Augsburg* sighted the Russian cruiser squadron and then came in contact with *Novik,* the individual unit perhaps most feared by the Germans, who were well aware of her capabilities. *Novik* chased *Augsburg* and eventually launched four torpedoes at long range. They were easily evaded and the two units lost sight of each other in the darkness. In firing so early, *Novik* was clearly suffering her own first night nerves, but managed to avoid engaging *Bogatyr* and her sisters by mistake before she was recalled to join *Rurik* for an officer to brief von Essen on events.[6] There was another encounter the following morning, but *Augsburg* was able to evade *Bogatyr* and *Oleg* and withdraw. Although it had been von Essen's intention to push his reconnaissance as far west as Danzig, bad weather prevented him bringing any flotilla craft other than *Novik.* This significantly increased the risk for the heavy ships as they approached German waters and was probably the key factor in von Essen's return to Russia on 3 September.

Von Essen followed his sortie with the issue of a new operational concept. This moved the active patrols out to the meridian of Dagerort Island and ordered the bases on the Baltic coast to be reactivated in preparation for their use by light craft. The Gulf of Riga itself, initially left out of the defensive system of the Central Position, was also to be made defensible. Von Essen was convinced that the farther forward the Russians were positioned, the greater the ability to mount the offensive mining operations and other incursions into the western Baltic that he had in mind when the nights grew longer. An important associated point was that the restored bases, being on the Baltic Sea itself, were less likely to become ice bound than those inside the Gulf of Finland and could thus remain effective for most of the winter months.

The Russian activity he encountered outside the Gulf had the immediate effect of forcing Admiral Behring back to the vicinity of Gotland, since he was well aware of the weakness of his own forces. In Kiel, Prince Heinrich continued to agitate for reinforcements, supported, unbeknownst to him, by von Tirpitz, who urged the transfer of *Blücher* to the Baltic as a logical counterweight to a Russian offensive led by *Rurik*. The news that the Russians had moved out of the Gulf provided the Baltic commander's plea for reinforcements with further support; the temporary allocation of *Blücher* and supporting units was finally allowed, together with permission for the Fourth Squadron to deploy from Kiel.

Between 4 and 9 September, Prince Heinrich, with his flag in *Blücher*, led a demonstration into the eastern Baltic. Its material effects were few—the sinking of a Russian merchant steamer in the Gulf of Bothnia and the destruction of some Russian shore stations. However, there was an encounter at the entrance to the Gulf of Finland between the Germans and *Bayan* and *Pallada*. *Blücher* opened fire at just under 16,500 yards but had to stop after five salvoes when the range reached 18,500 yards, since the Russians were behind their minefields and opening to the east. *Blücher* could not follow them.[7]

The affair served to confirm both the advantages and limitations of the Russian Central Position concept. Von Essen himself did not emerge because the sortie caught *Rurik* and other major units coaling at Helsingfors. Although the Germans later believed that their radio activity would have alerted the Russians to the size of their operation, this does not seem to have been the case until contact was made between the two cruiser forces. Von Essen argued that the German failure to penetrate the Gulf indicated how secure the Russian defenses had been made and that the enemy would not attempt offensive operations against the Central Position. With such a strong position on which to fall back, this suggested that the Russian fleet could assume a more active role and he continued to press for greater freedom of action.

The Germans felt that their sustained presence, the shock of their interference with the transport artery of the Gulf of Bothnia, and demonstration of their ability to operate so close to the Russian coast restored their moral advantage. However, the sortie showed up many deficiencies, notably the very limited endurance of the torpedo craft, while the threat of submarine attack was not yet taken seriously. The big ships frequently hove-to in order to coal the torpedo craft, which would have presented an easy target to an enterprising submarine.

From the evidence of the sortie, Prince Heinrich felt that he had overestimated the Russians and wanted to do more.[8] To his disappointment, the fear that a new British operation was under way in the North Sea meant the immediate withdrawal of *Blücher* and her escorts from the Baltic. The Fourth Squadron was also detached, but, in the curious way in which the dispositions were being managed in the confused command environment, remained in Kiel. Given that the handful of remaining units fit for employment in the eastern Baltic required maintenance, it was inevitable that a lull should follow, with only a few of the older light cruisers at sea as scouts in the central Baltic. Heinrich was comforted by the arrival of limited reinforcements of large torpedo boats, as well as three submarines that were unsuitable for the long-range operations now becoming the norm for the North Sea–based U-boats, while the armored cruiser *Friedrich Carl* was promised as a new flagship for Behring.

The lull was quickly ended with a demand from the German army for support on the seaward flank of the Russian army's retreat along the coast, but the forces available could do little to help and Behring's attention soon shifted to training his new arrivals and developing a plan for operations in the eastern Baltic. The needs of the army, however, were thrown into prominence again with a request from the Army High Command for an amphibious demonstration against the Russian coast at Windau (modern Ventspils), in order to prevent the expected transfer of Russian troops from Poland to Galicia. Von Pohl passed the request on, but was soon informed that at least fourteen days would be required to prepare.[9] The Germans were paying the price for a lack of attention to combined operations before the war. There were no plans in place for the conversion of ships to serve as troop transports and no equipment for amphibious operations. Any thoughts on the part of the German General Staff that an actual landing might be possible were rapidly abandoned, but even the idea of a brigade being embarked for the demonstration had to be dispensed with, since the time taken to prepare the transports would be much longer than the operational deadline.

As a result, although some colliers and mine breakers accompanied the hastily assembled force, the only troops on board were a reserve battalion embarked in Danzig at the last minute. Prince Heinrich had little confidence in such a small number of partly trained soldiers with no experience of amphibious operations. The demonstrations that were conducted were a combination of surveying parties in small boats from the torpedo craft that could safely close the shallow coast, and the prince's own inspection of Windau as he led the old armored ships past the town and harbor. The lively response to the would-be depth sounders and the casualties incurred through fire from the shore indicated that the Russian army was present in some strength, while Heinrich's assessment was that the partly blocked harbor with its long but narrow moles was unsuitable for an assault in the face of any opposition.

Matters were complicated for the demonstration by reports that British forces were about to penetrate the Belts and enter the Baltic. These ranged from lurid descriptions of the main British fleet to sightings of submarines. From the eastern Baltic, Prince Heinrich did the best he could to coordinate a response while contemplating a return to Kiel. Transfers were organized from the North Sea, the remaining forces in the western Baltic were hastily deployed, and additional minefields laid. The scare died only when aerial reconnaissance and close questioning of merchant ships that had been using the Belts confirmed that there was little of substance to the intelligence. Confirming that all was well took time, however, and an uncertain Prince Heinrich decided to cut the deployment short and bring his ships back from the east.

The incident was an uncomfortable reminder that the passages from the Kattegat, controlled as they were to allow commercial traffic vital to all the littoral states, could still permit the covert transit of British submarines. The difficulty was that an undetected entry into the Baltic could not be ascribed to any one passage and thus to the failure of a particular neutral nation. Denmark could claim that the transit had been through Swedish waters, while Sweden could assert that a Danish channel had been employed. The Germans decided to increase their own patrols at the approaches, but they were conscious that they remained vulnerable.

Prince Heinrich's early withdrawal meant that the destroyers dispatched by the Russians when they became aware of the demonstration found nothing. Von Essen sailed in *Rurik* and spent three days in the eastern Baltic, encountering increasingly foul weather but not the enemy. It is clear that von Essen considered the fast and powerful *Rurik* his key asset for offensive operations, while his insistence on personally leading such sorties reflected his recognition of the need for active leadership in maintaining morale and encouraging an aggressive outlook in his subordinate commanders.

Admiral Behring was finally able to resume his training of the newly arrived submarines at the end of September. He remained convinced of the potential of the cruiser-submarine combination and exercised his forces with this scenario in mind. The success of the U-boats in the North Sea gave new confidence, and Behring sailed on 8 October with a large force designed to convey the impression that an assault was being planned on the Russian coast, in order to entice the Russians into a submarine trap outside the Gulf of Finland. Despite mechanical troubles forcing *U25* to withdraw, the Germans were able to deploy *U23* and *U26* west of the Central Position in the early hours of 10 October. With daylight came the first opportunity of an attack when *U26* sighted the cruiser *Admiral Makarov* en route to her patrol station. The Russians had taken some precautions, but they were yet to have their "*Aboukir, Hogue,* and *Cressy* moment" and it is significant that *Admiral Makarov's* formation was on its way to search a suspicious merchant ship. The submarine fired two torpedoes at 1,300 yards range—too much as it proved, for both missed the zigzagging cruiser, which turned shortly after they were fired. *U26* did not at first realize that her attack had been detected and an emergency report broadcast by the Russian cruiser.

Light forces were immediately dispatched to hunt for the intruder and *U26* spent the afternoon keeping well out of the way. Despite the clear evidence that German submarines were now in the northeastern Baltic, the pattern of Russian heavy ship operations did not change. Late on the morning of 11 October, *U26* encountered *Pallada* and *Bayan* accompanied by destroyers. In the first-ever successful submarine attack on an escorted force, she fired a single torpedo at *Pallada,* which detonated the forward magazine. *Pallada* blew up and sank with all hands within two minutes; the German official history noted wryly that the only item found from the ship was her icon.[10]

The Russians now understood the submarine threat much better. There were renewed efforts to provide effective antisubmarine defenses to the fleet's major bases, tight restrictions were applied to the movement of neutral traffic in areas that might reveal the pattern of naval operations, while the use of heavy ships as patrol forces stopped. The geography of the region was utilized, with a protected secret passage east–west through the Finnish skerries set up to allow the transit of surface forces unexposed to submarines. In the continuing debate with the Sixth Army and the Supreme Command, the loss of *Pallada* also forced von Essen to reconsider some of the elements of the form that his offensive strategy should take.

The Germans were confident that the destruction of the armored cruiser would create a new restraint on the Russians and, to a degree, they were correct. The key to their own future offensive efforts would be a combination of submarines and mines, but two or more could play at this game. The German Baltic forces had yet to experience the reality of the underwater threat, however deep their concern over the possibility of the passages from the Kattegat being penetrated. This situation was shortly to change. The British were coming—and so were the Russians.

HELIGOLAND BIGHT

9

THE IDEA WAS KEYES' IN THE FIRST PLACE. IT WAS NOT ENOUGH TO WAIT for the Germans: the British must enter the Bight to have any chance of dealing a blow (map 9.1). Keyes had confirmed that German torpedo boats were patrolling at high speeds during daylight hours—too high for submarines to attack. In the late afternoon these units were relieved by other torpedo craft that, supported by light cruisers, stood out to sea before returning at dawn. Many had been observed overnight in an area forty miles off Heligoland and Keyes proposed to intercept them. He wrote to Rear Admiral Leveson, "[I]t is not by such incidents [the failure to pursue *Stralsund*] that we shall get the right atmosphere—for ourselves absolute confidence and a certain knowledge that 'when the enemy come out we shall fall on them and smash them,' and, on the other side, 'When we go out those damned Englanders will fall on us and smash us. . . .' We must both prepare for 'The Day' by creating the correct atmosphere on both sides . . . the loss of a few light craft will surely be a small price to pay."[1]

Keyes wanted Tyrwhitt's flotillas to close the coast and, at dawn, turn and drive what he hoped would be a confused huddle of the German day and night patrols into the North Sea. Keyes' nine available submarines would be in two groups—half occupying the attention of the German torpedo boats, thus keeping them away from the coast, and half close inshore where they could intercept emerging heavy units. To seaward would be British covering forces sufficient to deal with any German cruisers that might appear. Keyes intended that the Grand Fleet operate as distant cover and he envisaged Goodenough's six light cruisers being in close support, while battle cruisers patrolled outside the Bight. The plan relied on two assumptions. First, that Tyrwhitt would not meet heavier metal to seaward of him, for this would trap him within the Bight. Second, that the operation was conducted at utmost speed; any delay would permit warning to get through to the capital ships thought to lie at immediate readiness in the Jade. While Tyrwhitt returned to sea, Keyes went to the Admiralty on 23 August, where he "found the Staff too fully occupied . . . to give the matter much attention."[2] Infuriated, Keyes sought an interview with the First Lord. Churchill summoned

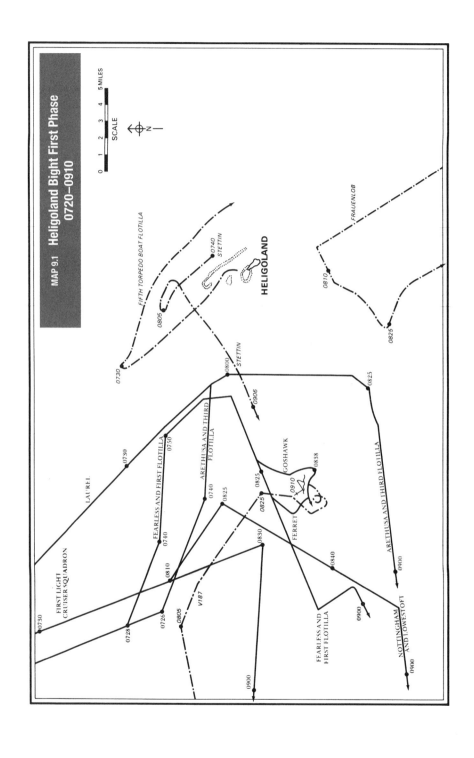

MAP 9.1   Heligoland Bight First Phase
0720–0910

Tyrwhitt (who had to return posthaste to port) and the War Group to meet the following afternoon. Delayed by Commodore (T)'s late arrival, the meeting accepted the proposal, but with critical alterations.

Despite the plea for the entire Grand Fleet, particularly the battle cruisers, Sturdee would approve use of only Cruiser Forces C, with the five antiquated *Bacchantes*, and K, with *Invincible* and *New Zealand*. The sweep's direction was also changed. It would now begin inshore at 0400, when the Harwich Force would steam south for four hours, before altering course to the west. Sturdee did not believe that the Harwich Force should risk an engagement with both the German night and day patrols. With this revision he calculated that, by the time any forces met, the night units would be in harbor and the stand-by ships expecting a peaceful day ahead. Keyes was to sail on 26 August and the remaining ships on the twenty-seventh, the sweep starting on the morning of Friday the twenty-eighth.

Fairly pleased with the decision, Keyes and Tyrwhitt returned to Harwich. Incredibly, however, Jellicoe was not informed until two days later. This was an inexcusable omission by the War Staff. Even with the poor excuse of the separation of the Southern Force from the Grand Fleet, Force K was still the C-in-C's direct responsibility. What was worse, when the Admiralty did eventually tell Jellicoe, the message gave no more than the barest outline: "A destroyer sweep of First and Third Flotillas with submarines suitably placed is in orders for Friday from east to west, commencing between Horn Reef and Heligoland, with battle cruisers in support."[3]

Jellicoe was both alarmed and confused by this bald declaration. Realizing that there was danger of the light forces and their inadequate support becoming entangled with superior German forces, he replied, "Propose to cooperate with sweep on Friday [28 August], moving Grand Fleet Cruisers and Destroyers to suitable positions with Battle Fleet near. Request that I may be given full details of proposed operations by wire tonight. I am leaving at 6 a.m. tomorrow."

After the message had been transmitted, Jellicoe's concerns increased. He telegraphed again, somewhat plaintively: "Until I know the plan of operations I am unable to suggest the best method of co-operation, but the breadth of sweep appears to be very great for two flotillas. I could send a third flotilla, holding a fourth in reserve, and can support by light cruisers. What officers will be in command of operations and in what ships, so that I can communicate with them? What is the direction of the sweep and [the] northern limits, and what ships take part."

Even these messages did not have the desired effect on the Admiralty that, in the words of the postwar naval staff analysis, "seems to have been preoccupied at the time with the prospect of the Germans gaining Calais and Dunkirk."[4] Sturdee informed Jellicoe that the battle fleet was not needed, but the battle cruisers could provide support "if required." Having failed to keep the C-in-C within the decision-making process from the start, Sturdee was compounding the error by ambiguous instructions. Although Jellicoe acted swiftly, dispatching Beatty and Goodenough at 0500 on 27 August and following with the battle squadrons shortly after, neither he nor his subordinates knew precisely what was happening. The Admiralty had yet to send them detailed information. Beatty summed up this curious situation when he signaled his force at 0800: "Imagine 7th cruiser squadron and various odds and ends will also take part, but know very little. Shall hope to learn more as we go along."

Keyes and Tyrwhitt had already sailed. Not until 1310 on 27 August did the Admiralty attempt to send them word of the reinforcements. There was some excuse for the delay, since the Admiralty needed to find out what Beatty and Goodenough were planning, but the light forces should have been told as soon as possible that these forces were at sea. As it was, the delay was such that the message failed to get through. It was sent on the destroyer wavelength, on which the small ships were not capable of reliably receiving messages at long range. This was a near-fatal omission. The units originally involved, notably the submarines, had been instructed that the *only* British ships above destroyer size in the Bight would be Tyrwhitt's two light cruisers, *Arethusa* and *Fearless*. All other major units were to be attacked on sight. There was another problem: *Arethusa* was brand new. The commodore received his flagship only on 26 August and Tyrwhitt's enthusiasm had overtaken his judgment. Although an impressive jump in capability, the new cruiser was in no way an efficient fighting unit and should not have deployed. She was not worked up and had fired her guns only once.

Jellicoe sailed with the Second and Fourth Battle Squadrons on 27 August. The First and Third were already exercising at sea and the C-in-C planned to rendezvous next day. Beatty, with his three battle cruisers, decided to join Moore at a position ninety miles northwest of Heligoland. Jellicoe, off the Orkneys, would still be too far away to support the operation directly, but he had restored some chance of success to a very doubtful venture. It remained, however, for Tyrwhitt and Keyes to be told. This was urgent as Goodenough was on a course that would bring him into contact with the Harwich Force by 0800 on 28 August. That morning, as Tyrwhitt's ships moved into position, they sighted the indistinct shapes of three warships. Tyrwhitt made the challenge and, to his surprise, received the correct reply. Confused, he signaled, "Are you taking part in the operations?," and Goodenough replied, "Yes, I know your courses and will support you. Beatty is behind us."

The Harwich Force began the sweep, steaming east-northeast at twenty knots. *Arethusa* was in the lead, with the Third Flotilla disposed in four divisions of four ships, two on each beam of the light cruiser, while *Fearless* and the sixteen destroyers of the First Flotilla were similarly positioned two miles astern. Eight miles farther back were the six ships of the First Light Cruiser Squadron. Beatty's five battle cruisers were thirty miles to the west of Tyrwhitt, loitering as they waited upon events.

On the morning of 28 August, which dawned calm and misty, the German patrols were particularly weak. Outer and inner lines were being maintained, the outer consisting of nine modern torpedo boats of the First Torpedo Boat Flotilla and the inner of nine old converted torpedo boats of the Third Minesweeping Division. This was in order, but the stand-by cruisers left much to be desired. Of the vessels in the vicinity of Heligoland, one, *Hela*, was an 1896 museum piece that would be outgunned by a British *L*-class destroyer. Two of the other three, *Ariadne* and *Frauenlob*, were efficient enough, but would stand little chance against a British *Town* class. Only the fourth, *Stettin,* could be considered modern, and she was at anchor east of Heligoland with steam up in just eight of her eleven boilers. It would take time before she could make her designed speed of twenty-four knots. *Mainz* was lying off the Ems to the south, but all seven of the other assigned light cruisers were in Wilhelmshaven or Brunsbuttel.

There was an even more fundamental problem, which left the patrols terribly exposed. The capital ships lying in the Jade could not get out. On the morning of 28 August low water was at 0933, leaving a depth of only twenty-five feet of water over the outer bar. This meant that it was impassable by the battle cruisers between 0700 and 1200.[5] The problem had not been properly thought through by the High Sea Fleet staff. One observer later suggested that the possibility was not considered because the assumption was that the patrol lines could simply retire under cover of the defenses on Heligoland.[6] This might have worked in clear weather, but the fog produced a very different result.

The first incident occurred at dawn, when the torpedo boat *G194* sighted the periscope of *E9*. *G194* turned to ram, but *E9* hurriedly went deep, firing a single torpedo, which missed. *G194* reported this encounter and the Fifth Torpedo Boat Flotilla and aircraft were ordered out to search. The first surface contact was made just before 0700, when the British Third Flotilla sighted *G194* to the southeast. *Laurel* and her three sisters in the Fourth Division took up the chase as *G194* fled in the same direction, the ships exchanging scattered fire. A few minutes later, when *G194* was able to confirm them as British despite the haze, she signaled to her consorts and to Rear Admiral Maass in *Cöln,* "G194 attacked by enemy cruisers. Enemy is in 54 degrees 22 minutes N., 7 degrees 35 minutes E., steering south." The signal was not read by higher authority for twenty minutes, but *G196,* which had picked it up, herself transmitted at 0706, while she steamed toward the sound of gunfire, "*G194* is being chased by enemy cruisers."

As the reports came in, Hipper was convinced that the torpedo boats were being attacked only by British light craft and that no armored ships would dare enter the Bight. He had no idea that Beatty was so near. He and other senior German officers also did not realize how bad the visibility was off Heligoland. Inshore, the day was clear and bright. Their ignorance, not remedied for hours, meant that they assumed that the forces were more than adequate to deal with the reported light craft. As a result, Hipper merely ordered *Stettin* and *Frauenlob* to "hunt destroyers," while he directed the remainder of the light cruisers to raise steam. No orders were issued to the heavy ships.

Tyrwhitt was concerned that *Laurel* and her sisters should not become separated, but his recall signal was not received. At 0726 he turned to follow the Fourth Division, just as other German vessels were beginning to appear in the mist. These were the units coming out in expectation of a submarine chase. Only *G9,* their leader and better manned to monitor radio traffic, realized from the start that the gunfire was from a surface action. Despite the obvious risk, Lieutenant Commander Anschutz in *G9* continued to run northwest until he could ascertain whether the ships ahead were British. *Laurel* and the other three *Ls* fired on sight, and Anschutz immediately hauled his flotilla around to return to Heligoland. Even now the other boats thought that the shell splashes erupting around *G9* were from her own guns, firing at a submarine. Only when they finally saw the British ships did they grasp the situation.

Arethusa and her remaining twelve destroyers chased the German torpedo boats at maximum speed, and this continued until 0740 when Tyrwhitt altered course to east from east-southeast and came down to twenty-six knots. The ships were spread out in an elongated line abreast, maneuvering by divisions so as to get their guns to bear. The British fire, though steady, was ineffective. The German torpedo boats later reported that many of the British 4-inch shells failed to explode. However, *Arethusa*'s forward 6-inch began to get the range, the shell splash creeping closer to the Germans with every shot. *Fearless* and her brood were paralleling the Third Flotilla's movements four miles to the northwest, in sight of the Germans but not within effective range, although one division briefly opened fire. To the northwest, *Laurel*'s division had not been distracted by *G9* and continued to chase *G196* and *G194* as the two raced for the shelter of Heligoland. By default, as they pursued their course southeast, the four destroyers were accomplishing the return to the fold that Tyrwhitt wanted.

The German Fifth Flotilla was in trouble. Expecting only operations against submarines and worn down by the previous weeks, several boats were unprepared for high-speed steaming. The situation was particularly grave in *V1* and *S13:* their speed had dropped to twenty knots. While *V1*, lagging behind, was smothered in British shell splashes, *G9* signaled urgently for cruiser support and covering fire from the gun batteries on Heligoland, which were well within range. Unfortunately, the battleground was still shrouded in mist. Although the gunners strained to see through the murk, they could not discern the British ships and did not open fire. *V1* was struck first at 0750, a 4-inch shell exploding in the after stoke-hold. It killed one man and wounded two. A few minutes later, a second shell struck under the bridge. This disabled a turbine and wrecked the steering controls.

The inner patrol, meanwhile, had not picked up any of the enemy reports and thought that the gunfire came from an unscheduled gunnery practice. *D8* was soon disabused when she came in sight of *Arethusa* and the Third Flotilla. They poured a hail of fire into her. Struck by five shells in quick succession—captain and first lieutenant dead, seventeen men wounded, and her speed much reduced—*D8* could take little more punishment. Her four sisters were still hidden from the British, but there was no doubt as to their fate if they could not get back to Heligoland. Their only hope lay in immediate intervention.

It came. In accordance with Hipper's instructions, *Frauenlob* left her anchorage, working up speed to twenty-one knots. *Stettin*'s captain, Karl Nerger, decided that the situation demanded his presence and sailed without waiting for the remaining boilers to be flashed up. Steaming at less than twenty knots, *Stettin* appeared out of the mists to the east at 0757, the leading British ships sighting her at the same time as they discerned *Frauenlob* coming up from the south-southeast. The German cruisers put a very different complexion on events, and the British forces immediately broke off their actions and altered away. *Arethusa* fired a few salvoes at *Stettin* as she turned south, but the shells went nowhere near their target and *Stettin* was not even aware *Arethusa* was firing.

The efficient *Fearless* opened fire on *Stettin* and soon found the range. By 0805 this had dropped to seven thousand yards. *Fearless* scored one hit, knocking out one of *Stettin*'s starboard side guns and causing several casualties. *Stettin* turned away. Her first duty was done and the embattled torpedo boats were safe under the guns of Heligoland. The minesweepers were still at sea, but *Stettin*'s speed had dropped to fifteen knots, and the cautious Nerger decided to take the opportunity to raise steam in all boilers. *Fearless,* in accordance with the orders to continue the sweep, did not follow, but turned to follow Commodore (T) (map 9.2).

As *Frauenlob* came up from the south-southeast, *Arethusa* moved to engage her. The German cruiser had the edge. Despite her destroyers' support, *Arethusa* was soon in trouble. Two of her port side 4-inch guns jammed. There was some warning of this during gunnery practice the previous day, but it had been shaken off as there was little that could be done. A third was knocked out by a shell that started a major cordite fire, extinguished only through the bravery of the gun captain. The cruiser's wireless was damaged and searchlights destroyed. Even more critical, a shell penetrated the main feed tank and the engine room began to flood. This had a cumulative effect disastrous for *Arethusa*'s speed. Tyrwhitt later wrote, "I was surprised that so many projectiles could fall all round one and burst in all directions and yet so few people killed. We lost eleven killed, including poor Wesmacott who was killed at my side on the bridge, and about sixteen wounded. . . . We had fifteen direct hits on the side and waterline and many inboard, besides hundreds of shrapnel holes."[7]

Frauenlob continued to have the advantage as the range dropped, but not everything went her way. *Arethusa* scored ten hits, mainly with her forward 6-inch, and there were heavy casualties at *Frauenlob*'s guns and control positions.

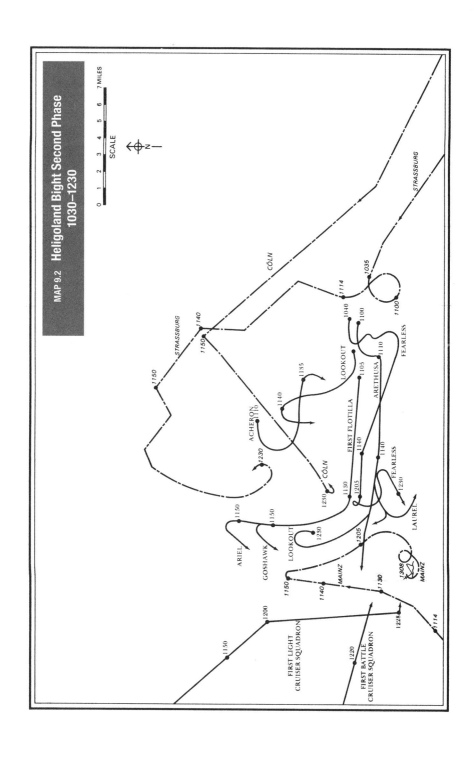

MAP 9.2 Heligoland Bight Second Phase
1030–1230

SCALE

0 1 2 3 4 5 6 7 MILES

N

At 0820 *Arethusa* began altering course slowly to starboard, and by 0830 was heading almost due west. She scored one spectacular, albeit ineffective, hit under the German's bridge just before turning away. Despite *Arethusa*'s obvious damage, *Frauenlob* would not follow and instead turned east. The patrols had been saved from disaster and *Frauenlob*'s captain, Commander Konrad Mommsen, decided to leave any retribution to the reinforcements he expected. *Arethusa* and her flotilla had already attempted to torpedo his cruiser and *Frauenlob* alone would stand little chance in a melee with the numerous British destroyers. With the Harwich Force steering west-southwest at twenty knots, the First Flotilla with divisions in line abreast of *Fearless,* the Third Flotilla in a very rough line ahead formation about *Arethusa* and *Frauenlob* withdrawing to the southeast, it seemed the battle had ended. There were, however, other actors in the wings.

To the northwest Commodore Keyes, with his pair of destroyers, began to glimpse four funneled cruisers through gaps in the mist. Still ignorant of Goodenough's presence, he thought these vessels must be hostile and reported their presence to Tyrwhitt. But Keyes did not attack, for, if they were hostile, they would be able to cut down his two little ships before they got within effective torpedo range. And, Keyes reasoned, perhaps they were not the enemy. Why had they not opened fire? Keyes' urge to caution was serving him well.

Eight miles northwest, Goodenough was receiving Tyrwhitt's action reports. He detached *Nottingham* and *Lowestoft* to assist the Harwich Force. The two altered east, but Captain C. B. Miller of *Nottingham* decided that the action must be farther to the south and accordingly turned in that direction. He thus unwittingly sealed the fate of the German torpedo boat *V187.* Although the other outer patrol units had got clear and were making for the Jade, *V187,* with her flotilla's senior officer, Commander Wallis, embarked, was running to Heligoland. At 0820 *Fearless* and her consorts sighted the lone German six thousand yards ahead. Captain Blunt at first detached *Goshawk*'s division to chase, but then had doubts as to *V187*'s identity, fearing she might be Keyes' *Lurcher.* He attempted to recall *Goshawk,* but to Commander Meade it was obvious that *V187* was hostile. He continued the chase.

V187 at first tried to head for the Jade to the south-southeast, but the four British destroyers started to overhaul her. *V187*'s captain, Lieutenant Commander Lechler, turned her southwest. Exchanging fire with her pursuers, *V187* began to have some hope of escaping in the mists and the increasing pall of smoke. This was dispelled when *Nottingham* and *Lowestoft* came upon the pursuit from the northwest. They immediately opened fire at a range of four thousand yards. *V187*'s captain determined on a last-ditch attempt to save his ship. It nearly succeeded, as *V187* suddenly hauled around to the northeast and sped past *Goshawk* and her consorts. They reacted a little late and it seemed for a moment as though *V187* might get away.

There remained the rest of the First Flotilla. Its divisions were now well spread, and they formed a wall through which the unfortunate torpedo boat could not break. The Third Division opened fire as it came into range. Within a few minutes *V187* was being smothered by shells from two directions as the Fifth Division turned, came north, and joined in. All but her after gun were knocked out of action and *V187* was brought to a standstill. The forecastle a mass of flames, the ship "one mass of black smoke" and Lechler wounded, Commander Wallis ordered scuttling charges to be exploded as the British closed around, calling on him to surrender.[8] At 0910 *V187* sank. *Defender* and others of the Third Division stopped engines and lowered boats to rescue the survivors. They were joined by the Fifth Division, but operations were suddenly interrupted.

Stettin had just got her boilers on line when signals came in reporting the continuing British attacks. Working up to full power she turned west and came upon the scene at 0906. Nerger, later to distinguish himself as captain of the raider *Wolf,* signaled Hipper, "Am in action with a flotilla."[9] *Stettin* immediately opened fire. The first salvo appeared to straddle and the Germans believed that they were making hits. Most of their targets scattered rapidly, but two remained stopped, suggesting early and severe damage. The two destroyers were in fact desperately trying to get their boats back with the German survivors. *Stettin*'s fire was not very accurate, but heavy enough to force *Defender* to leave two whalers and ten of her own people to shift for themselves. *Lizard* was able to get her crew back on board before she "cleared out as fast as our engines would let us."[10] *Stettin* never saw the boats in the water and did not realize that rescue operations were in progress, contrary to accusations afterward levelled at her captain. The cruiser also scored no serious damage on the destroyers and was herself struck three times, suffering eleven casualties in the brief engagement. *Ferret* fired a torpedo, which missed, before breaking off the action.

Stettin did not follow. Her wireless was temporarily inoperative and Nerger, who had on board Feldmann, the Second U-Boat Flotilla's commander, decided to remain near Heligoland, making repairs and issuing orders to the handful of U-boats at sea. It was not until 1100 that *Stettin* resumed a cautious advance. *Defender*'s boats were later picked up by *E4*, which surfaced alongside and took on board the ten British personnel, as well as a German officer, petty officer, and rating as a sample. The remainder were given provisions and a compass and the direction of Heligoland, but this kindness proved unnecessary, for they were picked up at noon by the minesweepers *G9* and *G11*.

To the north the British were being confused by Keyes' continuing reports of enemy cruisers. Goodenough found it difficult to reconcile *Lurcher*'s reported positions with the location at which he thought Commodore (S) should be; it may have crossed his mind that this was a case of mistaken identity. In any event he delayed until 0830 before altering to the west, at which time he would certainly have turned had the sweep met with no opposition at all. *Falmouth* sighted Keyes' two destroyers at 0820, but they went unrecognized. The poor visibility was proving a bane for both sides, but at this moment it was worse for the British as their forces groped about. Goodenough's alteration had the effect of convincing Keyes that "enemy" cruisers were chasing him and he hastily turned to where he thought Moore would be waiting. He was, however, still unsure that his contacts were hostile. At 0910 Keyes signaled Tyrwhitt, "Have our light cruisers come into our area?" Because of the damage to *Arethusa's* wireless, he got no reply.

Fearless rejoined the crippled *Arethusa* at 0855. They continued a slow movement west-southwest as Tyrwhitt's flagship attempted to repair her damage and waited for the dispersed destroyer divisions to reassemble. The results of the sweep had been barely satisfactory, although Tyrwhitt was well aware that more German cruisers and torpedo craft would soon be emerging. If the Germans did not know of Beatty's presence, and if the British forces could coordinate their activities, a substantial success might still be possible. On board *Arethusa,* engineers and other personnel worked frantically to make repairs, although the wireless and feed tank defects were defying all effort expended on them.

The German light cruisers were moving at last. *Hela,* smallest and weakest of those on patrol, was coming down from her station. By providence, since the little ship would not have lasted five minutes in a general engagement, a signal from *Stettin* reporting that the enemy had withdrawn stopped her advance. *Hela* returned to the north and took no further part in the battle. *Ariadne* was also approaching, but the gunfire died away as she neared the scene. Fearing that he would only cause further confusion by groping about in the fog, her captain decided to take *Ariadne* back to her previous billet. Meanwhile, *Cöln* and *Strassburg* were emerging from Wilhelmshaven. They passed the Outer Jade Light at 0934. Maass was unsure of what to expect and did not know whether the action was still in progress. Determined to solve the puzzle, he steamed into the Bight, hoping that he might pick off some British stragglers. *Mainz,* for her part, got under way from the Ems well before 0900, but her progress was impeded by heavy fog, which also foiled a seaplane from Borkum's attempt to scout for the cruiser.

The battle cruisers were already raising steam when, at 0850, Hipper requested permission from von Ingenohl to send *Moltke* and *Von der Tann* out under Rear Admiral Tapken. The C-in-C approved, but the force could not leave the Jade until at least 1200. Worse still, these two battle cruisers were the only ones immediately available. *Blücher* was coaling inside Wilhelmshaven and *Seydlitz*, Hipper's flagship, was suffering condenser trouble. For the time being, the Germans would be able to make no reply to Beatty or even to Goodenough's 6-inch-gunned light cruisers. The U-boats were also not deployed to give any chance of success, since none was to seaward of Heligoland. The Germans still expected that the British heavy ships, if they came at all, would be rash enough to venture into the inner

Bight, to attack German units as they emerged. Such an operational concept had long been rejected by the British planners and the U-boats were wasted defending against it.

Away from the battleground, Beatty's five battle cruisers were waiting, with the armored cruisers farther out still. Beatty was determined not to use the *Bacchantes* if he could avoid it. As the battle cruisers circled about, the admiral tried to make sense of the signal traffic. Unable to guess more than that the Harwich Force appeared to be moving west, at 0930 Beatty began to steam west-southwest. At just the same time, the submarine *E6* attempted to attack Goodenough's light cruisers, mistaking them for the *Strassburg* class. Realizing at the last moment that the ships were British, she went deep as *Southampton*, thinking she was being attacked by a U-boat, attempted to ram. Goodenough added a laconic note in his own hand to his later report to Beatty, "Fortunately I missed her."[11] Lieutenant Commander C. P. Talbot in *E6* called it "a very severe trial of my self-restraint."[12]

At 0945 Keyes signaled to Moore, "Am being chased by four light cruisers; am leading them in your direction." Both Beatty and Tyrwhitt, the latter's radio just restored to service, received this signal. Beatty decided to let Keyes lead these "hostile" vessels on. Accordingly, he reduced speed and began loitering again in order that Keyes might find the battle cruisers (albeit in greater strength) roughly where he expected them. Tyrwhitt hastily turned back to the east. *Arethusa*'s speed was down to ten knots but Tyrwhitt was determined to aid his colleague. At 0948 he signaled to Goodenough, "Please chase eastward. Commodore (S) is being chased by 4 light cruisers." A few minutes later, he made to Keyes, "I am fast coming to your assistance." Tyrwhitt's position was complicated by a side-action that occurred when *Stettin,* which had again emerged from the inner Bight, suddenly came in sight. *Fearless* attempted to engage, but was thrown into confusion when she had to go astern to avoid one of her own flotilla. Only a few shots had been exchanged when *Stettin* disappeared yet again.

The problem of Commodore (S) was at last resolved. The mists around *Lurcher* and *Firedrake* were finally clearing. Keyes issued the challenge at 0950—and received the correct reply. As he closed Goodenough, Keyes signaled to the battle cruisers, "Cruisers are our cruisers whose presence in the area I was not informed [*sic*]." Confirmed in his decision to remain outside the Bight, at 1000 Beatty signaled, "S.O. 1st Light Cruiser Squadron and all destroyers, especially *Lurcher*. My position 54deg. 26'N, 6deg. 14'E, remaining here." He was not needed yet. Meanwhile, *Lurcher* and *Southampton* were communicating. Keyes, at first relieved by his discovery, was alarmed at the risk to the cruisers from his own submarines. He signaled, "I was not informed you were coming into this area: you run great risk from our submarines. Position of Commander [*sic*] T at 0945 should read 45 miles west. Please give me present position. Your unexpected appearance has upset all our plans. There are submarines off Ems."

This raised eyebrows in *Southampton* and Goodenough replied, "I came under detailed orders. I am astonished that you were not told. I have signaled to *Lion* that we should withdraw. *Nottingham* and *Lowestoft* are somewhere in the vicinity."

Keyes had neglected the Harwich Force in his relief at discovering the cruisers' identity, but Blunt and Tyrwhitt were by now almost certain that Keyes had been laboring under a misapprehension. Tyrwhitt asked Blunt, "Is *Firedrake* and *Lurcher* among you?" and, receiving a "No," was certain of the mistake. *Fearless* came close alongside *Arethusa* at 1017 and the two senior officers exchanged information by semaphore, the Third Flotilla being sent on ahead. As they conversed, *Arethusa's* engineers completed the repairs necessary to bring her speed back up to twenty knots. When this was done, Tyrwhitt decided to withdraw. Keyes had obviously solved his problem and it was dangerous to linger near Heligoland when the enemy must be coming out in strength. At 1039 movement west was resumed. *Arethusa* worked up to twenty knots, while *Fearless* went to rejoin her flotilla with instructions to keep *Arethusa* in sight, in case the repairs did not stand up to the strain.

As Goodenough and Keyes were also steaming west, it seemed as if the action had come to a close. This reckoned without the German reinforcements emerging from the inner Bight. *Strassburg, Cöln,* and *Mainz* were closing in on the Harwich Force from different directions. Maass was so eager to pursue the raiders that he did not delay to concentrate his forces. Such tactics were reasonable if, as he must have thought, the enemy consisted of only a few small cruisers and destroyers, but they were to bring disaster when the Germans came into contact with Goodenough and Beatty.

Approaching from the southwest, *Strassburg* was the first in sight. Tyrwhitt had been half expecting this and hurriedly altered course to bring *Arethusa's* reduced broadside into play. *Fearless*, too, altered to close with *Strassburg*. Blunt instructed the destroyers to disregard his movements and continue west, but Commander Arthur Dutton of *Lookout* immediately turned the Third Flotilla back toward the fray. As it was soon apparent to Tyrwhitt that *Arethusa* was outgunned, he ordered the First Flotilla to make a torpedo attack on *Strassburg*. Three divisions joined *Fearless* and began to maneuver to launch their weapons. Faced with two cruisers and so many destroyers intent on attacking, *Strassburg* turned away into the mist, Retzmann, her commander, unwilling to engage single-handed. *Fearless* and the destroyers would have followed her, but Tyrwhitt was anxious to make as much ground westward as possible and did not want them embroiled with heavier ships. He ordered the First Flotilla to rejoin.

Blunt obeyed and turned his ships west, but as he did so *Cöln* appeared from the southeast. The British moved to engage (photo 9.1). Tyrwhitt, mistaking *Cöln* for a *Roon*-class armored cruiser, sent two urgent signals in rapid succession to Beatty: "Am attacked by large cruiser," and "Respectfully request that I

PHOTO 9.1   SMS *Cöln*   *Bibliothek fur Zeitgeschichte*

---

may be supported. Am hard pressed." Beatty responded immediately by instructing Goodenough to detach two cruisers, but Goodenough took matters into his
own hands and brought his entire squadron in at twenty-five knots. The decision
remained as to what the battle cruisers should do. It would not be an easy one.

Cöln, too, could not face the massed ranks of the Harwich Force, so turned
away and disappeared. This afforded Tyrwhitt's vessels a respite and they again
started to head west. Despite his reputation as a tactician, Maass still did not
attempt to concentrate his forces. Once again, *Strassburg* appeared and resumed
her duel with *Arethusa.* Tyrwhitt wrote, "We were receiving a very severe and
almost accurate fire from this cruiser; salvo after salvo was falling between 10 and
30 yards short, but not a single shell struck."[13] *Strassburg* was steering northwest
and the Harwich Force turned to open their gun arcs. As *Strassburg's* shells fell,
Blunt added his pleas to those of Tyrwhitt, sending to Beatty and Goodenough,
"Assistance urgently required." Chatfield, Beatty's flag captain, described what
happened: "The Bight was not a pleasant spot into which to take great ships; it
was unknown whether mines had been laid there, submarines were sure to be on
patrol, and to move into this area so near to the great German base at Wilhelmshaven was risky. Visibility was low and to be surprised by a superior force of
capital ships was not unlikely. They would have had plenty of time to leave harbor
since Tyrwhitt's presence had first been known."

The assumption about the big ships reflected a failure of British planning.
The information about the Jade Outer Bar was available in the *North Sea Pilot.*[14]
Unless the Germans kept large numbers of units constantly outside the protected
anchorages—not only difficult in terms of fuel, but also risky in itself—the element

of surprise meant, at worst, that only detachments of the High Sea Fleet would be available for the next few hours. Chatfield recalled, "Beatty . . . said to me, 'What do you think we should do? I ought to go and support Tyrwhitt, but if I lose one of these valuable ships the country will not forgive me.' Unburdened by responsibility, and eager for excitement, I said, 'Surely we must go.'"[15]

At 1135 Beatty turned southeast, increasing speed to twenty-six knots. Ten minutes later he altered east-southeast, forming his ships into line ahead and increasing speed again to twenty-seven knots. He signaled, "Am proceeding to your support."

The action between *Strassburg* and the Harwich Force continued. At 1135 Tyrwhitt ordered a general attack with torpedoes and the First and Third Divisions of the Third Flotilla immediately moved to close. The First Division of the First Flotilla turned back and delivered an attack at the same time. Two more divisions of the Third Flotilla that had been on *Arethusa*'s disengaged side crossed astern of her in an attempt to get at *Strassburg*, but failed to achieve a firing position. *Strassburg*'s captain had feared such an attack and kept his distance. When the twelve destroyers launched their torpedoes, the cruiser swerved away, one torpedo passing to port and another close astern. Two torpedoes were fired by *Strassburg* at *Arethusa* in return as she was swallowed up by the mist, but they ran short and no British ships were hit. Clearly outmatched by the mass of the Harwich Force, *Strassburg* steamed northwest for a short period before turning south to look for *Mainz*.

This had been another small victory for the British, but the units of the First Flotilla in advance of the main body were not in such a happy position. At 1130 they sighted *Mainz* moving north ahead of them (photo 9.2). The three divisions, eleven boats in all, hastily turned into line and paralleled *Mainz*'s course to get their broadsides into action and prepare to launch torpedoes. Both sides were soon moving north-northwest and *Mainz* had the better of it, repeatedly straddling the destroyers, but sustaining no damage in return. The lack of developed tactics for flotilla craft facing more heavily armed scouts showed up. The destroyers were at a disadvantage, "with no one to look where the shot falls, except perhaps the Captain, who has a lot of other things to attend to. We have no spare personnel and no range finder and no masts to look down from."[16] Torpedoes were launched, but to no avail, and Commander Moir in *Ariel* edged away to open the range and reduce the accuracy of *Mainz*'s fire. By 1145 the action had developed into a chase and it could not be long before *Mainz* disabled one of the destroyers. Then at 1150 Goodenough appeared from the northwest. *Mainz* spotted the British cruisers first and hastily reversed course. A few minutes later the destroyers, to their great relief, saw what had happened. Immediately, the three divisions turned 16 points about, the First positioning itself in the van, with the other two falling in astern of Goodenough's light cruisers.

PHOTO 9.2   SMS *Mainz*   *Bibliothek fur Zeitgeschichte*

Mainz was fleeing for her life. *Southampton* opened fire and began scoring hits. The German was soon in trouble: "[T]he first hit cut the supply to the steam siren and the air was filled with its hissing."[17] Disappearing into a bank of mist and cramming on speed, *Mainz* began to leave her pursuers behind. By 1155 only the flash of the British guns could be seen. Transmitting, "Am chased by enemy armored cruiser," *Mainz* hoped to escape, but it was not to be. Her run brought her into the path of the Harwich Force. To the east appeared successively *Fearless,* the First and Second Divisions of the Third Flotilla, and, after a few minutes, *Arethusa* and the other destroyers. *Fearless* immediately opened fire, damaging *Mainz*'s rudder so that the ship began circling slowly to starboard. The divisions of the Third Flotilla opened out, the First and Second following *Arethusa* to the northwest, while the Third and Fourth closed *Mainz.*

Three guns out of action, her rudder damaged, and fires burning amidships, *Mainz* was in a sorry state but continued to fight. Her remaining gun crews concentrated on the destroyers of the Fourth Division, which had closed to fire torpedoes at a range of less than four thousand yards. They suffered badly. *Laurel* launched two torpedoes but, as she turned away, three shells smashed into her. The first exploded in the engine room, killing four men. The second struck the forecastle, knocking the forward mount out of action and killing three. The third exploded on the amidships gun mounting and detonated the ready use ammunition. All of the gun's crew were killed or wounded and the after-funnel was knocked over the side. *Laurel* crawled away, shrouded in a pall of smoke and steam and with her captain unconscious.

Liberty was next into the hail of fire. She, too, had launched her torpedoes when a shell struck the bridge, killing the captain and bringing down foremast and searchlight. Her first lieutenant took command and, zigzagging to throw off *Mainz*'s gun-layers, *Liberty* continued in action. The third destroyer of the division, *Lysander,* hauled out of line to avoid the damaged *Laurel* and by doing so escaped unscathed. The fourth, *Laertes,* received four hits from *Mainz's* closely grouped salvoes. Her captain "was watching the *Mainz . . .* saw her broadside flash out—and knew what was coming."[18] One shell burst inside a boiler, another destroyed the center-funnel, and a third exploded in No. 2 Boiler Room and cut the supply of feed water to the boilers. The ship stopped dead. Their work, however, was not in vain. One torpedo struck *Mainz,* fired by *Lydiard* of the Third Division. Lieutenant Johannsen, leading the repair parties, reported, "[*Mainz*] . . . reared, bent perceptibly from end to end and continued to pitch for a considerable time. The emergency lights went out. Every bit of glass that had remained intact was now shattered, . . . we had nothing left but electric pocket lamps."[19]

Crippled, and with her rudder still jammed to starboard, *Mainz* was trapped. Goodenough's light cruisers were now less than six thousand yards away and pouring fire into her. Behind the cruisers came *Lurcher, Firedrake,* and the Second and Third Divisions of the First Flotilla, adding to the cannonade. To the east were *Fearless* and the battered destroyers of the Third Flotilla's Fourth Division. Circling to the north were *Arethusa* and the other destroyers. *Mainz's* captain ordered that the ship be scuttled, but he was killed immediately afterward and the order was not passed to all parts of the ship. The remaining guns continued to be fought. Stephen King-Hall, in *Southampton,* wrote, "We closed down on her, hitting with every salvo. She was a mass of yellow flame and smoke as the lyddite detonated along her length. Her two after funnels melted away and collapsed. Red glows, indicating internal fires, showed through gaping wounds in her sides."[20]

One of *Mainz's* gun captains, Petty Officer Willi Klein, testified, "The condition of the *Mainz* was indescribable. Our W/T [wireless telegraphy] room was a heap of ruins, and was burning fiercely, two of the funnels had been brought down. . . . Guns crews, voice-pipe men and ammunition supply parties were literally blown apart. The upper deck was a chaos of ruin, flames, scorching heat and corpses, and everything was streaked with green and yellow residue of explosive shells that emitted suffocating gases."[21]

The view from *Birmingham* was just as appalling, "The carnage was horrible to look at. All round the guns were heaps of dismembered bodies. . . . The wreckage amidships was indescribable, funnels, guns, etc., all heaped in a smoldering mass."[22] After *Mainz's* last gun was finally silenced, at 1225 Goodenough ordered "cease fire."

Liverpool, Firedrake, and *Lurcher* closed in to rescue survivors. The latter won the race and, with consummate seamanship, Commander Wilfred Tomkinson placed *Lurcher* alongside *Mainz's* quarter. The ship had not yet taken on a list and there was time to transship the bulk of the survivors, most of the remainder being cut off from the stern by fires amidships. Keyes observed an officer who had been superintending transfer of the wounded standing motionless on *Mainz's* quarterdeck. Keyes guessed what was in the young man's mind and shouted that he had

PHOTO 9.3   HMS *Liverpool*   *Imperial War Museum*

done splendidly and should jump on board the destroyer. "He drew himself up stiffly, saluted and said 'Thank you, no.'"[23] *Lurcher* barely escaped being impaled on *Mainz*'s propeller as the cruiser heeled over to port, hung for about ten minutes and then, at 1310, capsized and sank. *Firedrake* and boats from *Liverpool* picked up the few left in the water, including the young officer who had refused Keyes' offer of rescue as well as the son of Grand Admiral von Tirpitz (photo 9.3).

While Goodenough's ships dealt with *Mainz,* a new engagement erupted. At 1225 *Cöln* and *Strassburg* came into sight to the north. As they bore down, the situation again seemed critical for the Harwich Force. It looked as if Tyrwhitt would not be able to withdraw without suffering heavy losses. *Arethusa*'s speed had dropped again. The destroyers had expended many of their torpedoes and were widely scattered, with three of the *Ls* badly damaged. *Fearless* and the destroyers *Goshawk, Lizard,* and *Phoenix* steered boldly to engage the two Germans, even though they were outgunned.

Beatty's timing was perfect, for even "five minutes' delay in his intervention would have had serious consequences."[24] His battle cruisers appeared out of the mist, passing between the First Light Cruiser Squadron to the south and *Arethusa* to the north. The two German cruisers could only flee. *Strassburg,* farther north than her consort, immediately turned away in that direction and was swallowed up by the fog. *Cöln* was less fortunate. She delayed too long and the seven minutes spent in clear sight were enough for the battle cruisers to open fire, find the range, and begin to score hits. Though *Cöln* was becoming indistinct in the haze, it appeared as though she had but a few minutes of life remaining. The sudden appearance of another German cruiser won her a reprieve.

Ariadne, older and slower, had been following *Cöln* to the battlefield (photo 9.4). Not knowing the weight of the opposition, she steered for the sound of the

PHOTO 9.4   **SMS** *Ariadne*   *Bibliothek fur Zeitgeschichte*

guns, confused as to the progress of events. The only hostile unit she had seen to this point was *E4* and the submarine had immediately dived and made an unsuccessful attack. Just before 1300 *Lion* came in sight. At a range already less than six thousand yards and rapidly dropping, *Ariadne* had no chance. She immediately came around to the southeast, but *Lion* shifted target and opened fire: "The first salvo fell about 300 meters short, but the second dropped so close to the bow that the towering columns of water collapsed over it and flooded the forecastle."[25]

Lion's next two salvoes struck home. As other battle cruisers joined the attack, *Ariadne* staggered away, badly damaged. The entire aftercastle burst into flames. Forward, shells pierced the armored deck and exploded, wrecking the fire mains, dressing station, and torpedo room, and killing most of the damage control team. The heat was tremendous as fires raged forward and aft. Although the hull was still intact, the forward magazine was flooded and several boilers were out of action. The upper deck amidships was relatively untouched, which saved many lives, but internally *Ariadne* was a mass of flames and smoke. The little cruiser was no longer a worthwhile target and, at 1310, Beatty altered away, signaling to all British forces in the area to retire before he turned west at sixteen knots at 1315. As the battle cruisers disappeared from sight, *Ariadne*'s commander, Captain Seebohm, decided that the fires and exploding ready-use ammunition made it too dangerous to continue efforts to save the ship. He mustered the crew on the forecastle, where they began to sing patriotic songs.[26] The cruiser *Danzig* had come out of the Jade at 1130 and searched desperately for her own forces, guided, like the others, only by the sound of gunfire. She had just encountered *Stettin* when she saw *Ariadne*. In answer to the sinking cruiser's signal "Assistance urgently required," *Danzig* approached and began rescue operations as *Ariadne*'s crew abandoned ship.

Meanwhile, the other cruisers were playing a macabre game of blindman's buff with Beatty and Goodenough's ships. *Stralsund*, fresh from Wilhelmshaven, had also been blundering about in the fog, unable to make contact with her own side, when at 1306 she sighted the units of the First Light Cruiser Squadron still with Goodenough, moving away from the sinking *Mainz*. At a range of eight thousand yards, *Stralsund* paralleled the British cruisers' track as they steered to join Beatty. The engagement was brisk; a succession of hits, one of which temporarily knocked out the ship's wireless, convinced *Stralsund*'s captain that it was a futile battle. He turned away to the southeast and stayed on this course until 1330, when he hoped that he was clear of the British. Goodenough did not pursue. He had received the order to retire and was aware that he could well be drawn south into the arms of superior forces (map 9.3).

Strassburg caught sight of the British cruisers to the south at a range of eight thousand yards at 1308, just after *Stralsund*, but Retzmann did not attempt to get involved. The cruiser began to circle to the northeast, hoping to make contact with other German units. At 1330 she sighted Beatty's battle cruisers to the southeast at eight thousand yards. By this time, visibility was changing minute by minute as ships moved in and out of fog banks. Retzmann knew that his one chance was for the four-funneled *Strassburg* to be mistaken for a British *Town*-class cruiser. Accordingly, he held his course. The ploy succeeded. The British battle cruisers had just resighted *Cöln* and were preoccupied with their engagement of the crippled ship. At the sight of *Stralsund* they hesitated and issued the challenge. At that minute, *Stralsund* was swallowed up by the fog. Retzmann, realizing the implications of his encounter, hurriedly radioed, "First Battle Cruiser Squadron of the enemy in 117e" before he began a wide circle to the south. Even as this signal was being received, Hipper, now conscious that things were badly amiss, signaled, "All light cruisers retire on *Moltke* and *Von der Tann*."

This did not save *Cöln*. Maass had continued northeast. Thinking that the ship was clear of the British but, too early, *Cöln* came around at 1300 to a new course southeast. At 1325, at a range of four thousand yards, *Cöln* and *Lion* sighted each other. The battle cruisers immediately altered course southwest and opened fire. *Lion*'s opening salvoes dealt the death blow. Within seconds, *Cöln*'s steering gear was wrecked, the engines disabled and the boilers riddled, one exploding and tearing the side out of the ship. A shell pierced the armored conning tower and killed every man inside. *Cöln*'s sole survivor later reported that "so many shells were tearing and bursting inside the hull that at any minute I expected the ship would explode." *Cöln* had become a wreck: "The deck was torn in many places and resembled a desert strewn with debris. There was a tangled mess of boat parts,

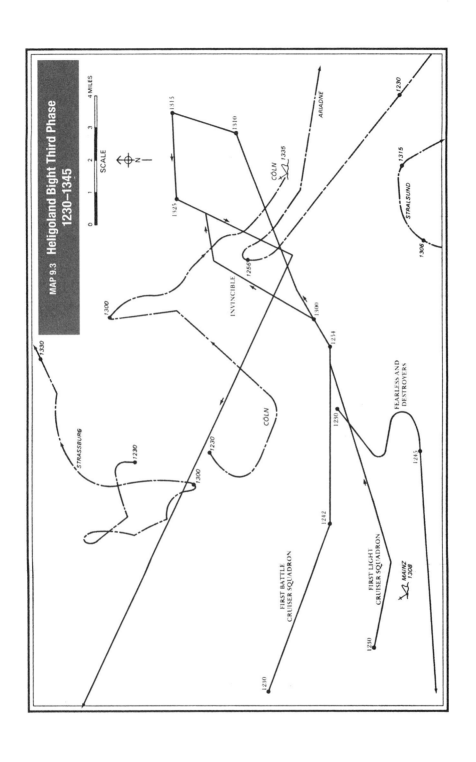

MAP 9.3 Heligoland Bight Third Phase
1230–1345

SCALE

0 1 2 3 4 MILES

N

ARIADNE

CÖLN 1335

STRALSUND 1315

1306

INVINCIBLE

1256

1300

1315

1310

1325

1254

1300

STRASSBURG

1330

1230

1300

CÖLN

1230

1230

FEARLESS AND
DESTROYERS

1245

FIRST BATTLE
CRUISER SQUADRON

1242

FIRST LIGHT
CRUISER SQUADRON

MAINZ
1308

1230

1230

davits, cleats, ladders, shrouds, charred lifejackets, antennae, signal lines, ammunition and splinters. The funnels were riddled with shot. The bridge was completely destroyed. . . . Giant holes gaped in the sides of the ship."[27]

In spite of the onslaught, *Cöln*'s gunners were able to get away some two hundred rounds at her huge adversaries. They scored five hits on *Lion*, which, however,
did no damage beyond "breaking a few electrical circuits. . . . One felt the tiny four
inch shells spatter against the conning tower, and the pieces 'sizz' over it."[28]

The survivors of the crew mustered on the quarterdeck, gave three cheers, and
sang the "Flag Song" before they were ordered to abandon ship. *Cöln* was settling
fast but, to speed the end, the last remaining engineer officer set scuttling charges.
Barely ten minutes after the firing had begun the unfortunate cruiser disappeared.
Beatty ordered destroyers to search the area, but they found nothing. In the poor
visibility, they may have searched the wrong spot. Two days later German torpedo
boats rescued a single man, Stoker Adolf Neumann, who told a harrying story of a
handful of survivors progressively succumbing to exhaustion and cold. The Germans regarded their being left in the water by the British with some bitterness, but
it appears that the fog of the Bight combined with the fog of war.[29]

Beatty's concern now was to get away without loss. He need not have worried. The German light cruisers that had evaded him were still trying to make
contact with each other, and it would be more than an hour before their battle
cruisers arrived in the outer Bight. *Stralsund, Danzig,* and *Kolberg,* which last had,
by reason of her slow speed, come to the fray too late, were attempting to save the
stricken *Ariadne. Kolberg* was patrolling to the northwest to give warning should
Beatty reappear, while *Stralsund* and *Danzig* took survivors on board. As the fires
died away, it looked as though *Ariadne* might be saved and her captain began
to make plans for *Stralsund* to take her in tow. However, at 1510 *Ariadne* heeled
over to port, capsized, and sank. Her casualties included fifty-nine dead and forty-
three wounded.

Moltke and *Von der Tann* came in sight at 1425. All German decisions were
characterized by extreme caution. Their movements had been restricted both by
von Ingenohl, who signaled, "The large cruisers are not to become engaged with
the enemy armored cruiser squadron," and Hipper, an hour astern in *Seydlitz.*[30]
The latter told Tapken to wait for his arrival. Intercepted signals had made it clear
that, of the cruisers still afloat, only *Ariadne* required assistance. Hipper did not
want to risk the two battle cruisers without *Seydlitz* (or himself) being present.
As Tapken came up to *Ariadne,* he detached the Sixteenth Torpedo Boat Half-
Flotilla to assist *Kolberg*'s patrol, but could do little else save watch *Ariadne*'s end.
When Hipper arrived at 1510 he began a reconnaissance to the north-northwest
with *Kolberg, Stralsund,* and *Strassburg* spread out ahead of the three battle cruis-
ers. The search for the missing light cruisers was not pressed far because of von
Ingenohl's restrictions. In any case, Hipper was convinced that both had sunk and

that the British had rescued any survivors. Had the sweep advanced four miles more to the location of *Cöln*'s sinking, it may have found men in the water. Joined by *Blücher* at 1600, the First Scouting Group turned for home to make the Jade before dark. With the ten torpedo boats of the Eighth Flotilla, minesweepers from Heligoland, and the cruisers *Kolberg, Hela,* and *München*, the night patrols were set. After darkness had fallen, *Seydlitz* anchored in Wilhelmshaven Roads and Rear Admiral Hipper went across to the flagship *Friedrich der Grosse* to make his report. It had been a black day.

The Harwich Force nursed its cripples home. *Lapwing* attempted to take *Laertes* in tow, but her first wire parted and she was just starting a second attempt when *Fearless* came up. Captain Blunt ordered *Lapwing* off and took *Fearless* alongside to set up the tow. This was accomplished in short order and the little group got under way for the west. In their wake came *Laurel*. Herculean efforts by the ship's engine room staff had managed to bring her speed up to ten knots. *Arethusa,* reduced to six knots, gathered the other destroyers about her and headed west once more. Beatty and Goodenough continued to maneuver at high speed. Beatty, still worried by the possibility of a German counterattack, was keen to get Tyrwhitt's ships away as quickly as possible.

There were repeated scares as ships believed they could discern German torpedo boats in the mist. When darkness fell, however, the Harwich Force was clear of the Bight and hopeful of getting all its cripples home. At this point *Arethusa*'s battered machinery finally gave out. Darkness and *Arethusa*'s relative bulk made it too difficult for a destroyer to attempt the tow, so the ship wallowed helplessly while Tyrwhitt waited for the armored cruisers, which Beatty had ordered in. *Hogue* closed *Arethusa* and her captain, Wilmot Nicholson, an old friend of Tyrwhitt's, hailed him, "Is that you, Reggie?" As Tyrwhitt later wrote, "I never was so glad to see him before."[31] *Hogue* took *Arethusa* in tow. The other armored cruisers met with *Fearless*' more advanced group before sunset, *Cressy* embarking the wounded and the attached scout *Amethyst* taking *Laurel* in tow. Rear Admiral Christian detached ten destroyers and, with the three remaining cruisers, reestablished the Terschelling patrol.

The other ships went on at ten knots. *Hogue, Arethusa,* the damaged destroyers, and a small escort headed for Sheerness, while the remainder returned to Harwich. The next day Beatty and Goodenough parted from the Harwich Force and began their voyage back to Scapa. A combination of great good luck, courage, and individual foresight had brought a considerable success, even if it had been a very near-run thing. As *Hogue* and *Arethusa* approached Sheerness, the two ships were met by an excursion steamer. There was a hush as the ship passed the battered *Arethusa*, but cheers erupted from the passengers as she came alongside *Hogue*. "Tyrwhitt signaled to Nicholson, 'They evidently think you have a prize in tow,' to which his friend replied, 'And so I have, but not the sort they think.'"[32] The news of the battle swept the country. Tyrwhitt and his men found that they had become heroes, although there was a little resentment that the first credit was assigned to the big ships and not the flotillas.[33] The victory went to Britain's head; in the gloom of the retreat in France, it was badly needed. Patriotic postcards, cartoons, and verses were made up, eulogizing Tyrwhitt and Beatty.

The admiral knew little of this as he led the First Battle Cruiser Squadron north, while Moore took his two into the Firth of Forth until a decision was made about the Humber's mining. Not until late on 30 August did Beatty's battle cruisers enter Scapa Flow, faced with the wearisome task of coaling. Waiting for them was the battle cruiser *Inflexible,* a long-desired reinforcement. Twelve hours later, as the Third Battle Squadron left Scapa for another of the already tedious succession of sweeps, Jellicoe brought in the remainder of the Grand Fleet. *Iron Duke's* anchor had barely taken ground before Beatty came on board to report. There was little to be said. Both knew the value of the victory and both understood the risks taken to gain it. They had cause to be relieved. *Invincible*, for example, was convinced that torpedoes had twice been fired at her by submarines. Beatty summed up their joint opinion when he declared years later to the Conservative politician, Arthur Balfour, "The end justified the means, but if I had lost a Battle Cruiser I should have been hanged, drawn and quartered. Yet it was necessary to run the risk to save two of our light cruisers and a large force of destroyers which otherwise would most certainly have been lost."[34]

Keyes wrote to Goodenough,

> I think an absurd fuss was made over that small affair. . . . It makes me sick and disgusted to think what a complete success it might have been but for, I won't say dual, but—multiple control. We begged for light cruisers to support us and to deal with the Enemy's light cruisers which we knew would come out. Destroyer's short range guns are no match for light cruiser's guns—but we were told none were available. If you had only known what we were aiming at, had had an opportunity of discussing it with Tyrwhitt and me, and had been inshore with *Fearless* and *Arethusa* we might have sunk at least 6 cruisers and had a "scoop" indeed.[35]

Jellicoe's confidence in the Admiralty was shaken. He protested and received the assurance that he would be informed at all times in the future of the Admiralty's intentions. Goodenough, for his part, was so disturbed by the encounter between *Southampton* and *E6* that he complained to the Second Sea Lord about the incompetent staff work involved.[36] Rear Admiral Duff summed up the feeling of many when he noted, "The more one hears of that affair the more one realizes that it was a case of good luck + bad management."[37]

Quick to draw lessons, Jellicoe laid down the necessity for tighter tactical control. Not only the War Staff, but also Goodenough, Keyes, and Tyrwhitt were criticized for letting events get out of hand. All this was due to poor communications, as well as failures of process. Atmospheric conditions were unfavorable for radio (they often are, in fog) and signals failed to get through. But there was as yet neither a sufficiently coherent system of giving and receiving tactical orders, nor of creating the picture of events necessary not only to exercise command, but also to make intelligent and useful reports. The destroyers were neither manned nor equipped for such work—Tennant was not surprised to find by 1400 that "no one, needless to say, had the slightest idea where we were" or at 1500 that his reckoning was out by twenty-five miles. Like Frewen, he confirmed that, in action, just conning the ship and directing her weapons absorbed the complete attention of all concerned.[38] The light cruisers were not much better off. There was still no concept by which an action plot was maintained in addition to the individual ship's navigational track, and not every ship had yet designated an officer specifically for signals' duties at action stations—if they had one available. When the commanders remembered their wireless (and it worked), they failed to give either their own or the enemy's course, speed, and position. Although he himself had yet to comprehend all the problems involved, Jellicoe was now all the more conscious that personnel from stokers to flag officers required exhaustive training.

But the victory was a godsend for Britain, as everyone had to admit and Churchill trumpeted when he visited *Arethusa* and "fairly slobbered" over Tyrwhitt. As the cruiser would require repairs, Churchill extravagantly promised the best unit he could find to substitute as Commodore (T)'s flagship. The First Lord was as good as his word and the Admiralty ordered Goodenough to detach his newest light cruiser, *Lowestoft*. This was not quite what Tyrwhitt had wanted, as she was "a size larger than the *Arethusa* but slower and rather too big."[39] Since Goodenough was not pleased by the transaction, it was a lesson to Tyrwhitt to be wary of talking to politicians, particularly when they were the First Lord.

Churchill went somewhat too far when he wrote in *The World Crisis*, "Henceforward the weight of British naval prestige lay heavy across all German sea enterprise," but there was some truth in the effect on the German outlook.[40] Every doubt as to the Imperial German Navy's ability to face up to its older and heavier opponent had resurfaced. Only in the behavior of the crews of the sunken or damaged ships was there reason to be satisfied. This had been exemplary. In command and control, tactics and material, there were many failures. "Hipper felt the results of this action very keenly. He repeatedly went into the question of responsibility and could reach no other conclusion than that the system adopted by the naval command dealing as it did in half measures, was to blame."[41]

The kaiser, still jealous but also nervous of the Royal Navy, was badly frightened by the loss of the three cruisers and *V187*, following as they did hard on the heels of the grounding of *Magdeburg* in the Baltic. He announced that the restrictions on the fleet must be tightened. Von Pohl and von Müller acquiesced, but it caused a confrontation between the kaiser and von Tirpitz. Thinking that a beloved son had been killed, the grand admiral was desolated by the initial reports, but appalled that the heavy ships had been trapped inside the Jade by the tide. In his view there was a fundamental flaw in the dispositions and only "two correct commands: either everything immediately available out or in!"[42] In this von Tirpitz was right. By devising patrols to seaward of Heligoland, the Germans had fallen into the trap that the British avoided when they abandoned ideas of close blockades. Since the patrols had to have some sort of system, which could be closely studied by submarines and had to be based on the average of available forces, not their maximum strength, it was always open to defeat in detail at a selected moment.[43] Furthermore, while there was some justification in a measured response to the initial reports, Hipper and von Ingenohl should have been aware of the implications of the tide in the Jade and got heavy units out early in the morning.

The problems over half measures went further. Von Ingenohl, in an ambiguous position as C-in-C, whereby he could be dictated to by the kaiser or von Pohl—and heavily influenced by von Tirpitz—at times interfered with Hipper's dispositions. At the beginning of the war, Hipper planned to have a battle cruiser available in the inner Bight, but had been overruled. Von Ingenohl agreed to the patrol system but objected to battle cruisers lying in anchorages that he considered vulnerable. He feared the British submarines too much. Hipper's staff officer, Raeder, later acknowledged the difficulty of maintaining a battle cruiser presence, but was critical of von Ingenohl's micromanagement.[44]

The German naval command was forced to realize that a plan for the defense of the Bight that did not drain the navy's fighting strength was of as much importance as protection of the inner anchorages and bases. The obvious solution was careful seeding of mines in the approaches. Unfortunately, von Ingenohl overreacted. The reorganization after the battle not only included a new minefield off the Norderney Gat, and the allocation of trawlers and roving groups of torpedo boats to replace the "three-tier" system, but also almost every available U-boat. The absence of the submarines on 28 August had been a major deficiency, but it was clearly unwise to allocate practically the entire force to coastal defense. The submariners protested bitterly, although it was several weeks before von Ingenohl was brought to see sense.

Meanwhile, von Tirpitz was not prepared to let matters rest. Although news soon arrived that his son survived (at which the old admiral broke out the champagne),[45] it is likely he never forgave Hipper for the defeat. He continued to intrigue against the Scouting Groups commander, who was protected by von Müller and the collective opinion of the senior officers, who thought he had made the best of a bad job.[46] He also assailed the kaiser about the restrictions on the fleet. Increasingly conscious that the navy's political position was slipping, von Tirpitz favored a more aggressive approach and made his point in repeated audiences. They "had no success, but on the contrary there sprang up . . . an estrangement between the Emperor and myself, which steadily increased."[47] The kaiser moderated his language somewhat, but the restrictions stood.

The Imperial German Navy had other things to think about. The light cruisers' tactical performance was poor. Their dispersal and the way in which semi-independent operations had become the norm meant that they failed to concentrate from the start. This was inexcusable: several times potentially weaker British forces were able to repel isolated advances. A coordinated attack would have ensured far better results and might have saved one or more of the cruisers lost when Beatty came out of the mist. It would almost certainly have saved *Mainz*. Poor wireless conditions did not help, but the German reporting performance was not much better than the British. Their system made locating reports simpler and faster, but there were failures to inform at critical moments, as well as omissions of vital information. All this contributed significantly to false conclusions and uncertainty among the commanders and units still inshore.

Zeppelin L3's performance was disappointing. Ordered out by Hipper when news of the attack was received, she observed both the fleeing German torpedo boats and their pursuers, but soon developed defects, which forced her return to base. L3's only enemy report was of a single British light cruiser. The failure to continue flying meant that she did not detect the British battle cruiser force, although communications difficulties suggest that any warning the zeppelin could have given would have come too late.[48] To be fair, L3 had conducted useful reconnaissance sorties in preceding weeks. The zeppelins were an important new capability, but it was clear their crews had much to learn and that weather represented a significant limitation. On 29 August Rear Admiral Otto Philipp was appointed Chief of the Naval Air Forces, relieving Hipper of direct responsibility for their operations. This would not, however, result in a consistent approach to the airships' employment. Rear Admiral Behncke was beginning to urge that the zeppelins attack Britain itself.

The torpedo boats were deficient in offensive powers. German units were too small and, with their lighter gun armament and lower speed, vulnerable. British destroyers were half as large again and threw, albeit not very accurately, three times the weight of broadside. The Germans did not even have the consistent advantage of a heavier torpedo armament. Although the German 50-cm weapon was every bit as good as the British 21-inch, the Royal Navy's newest destroyers had an edge with their two twin mountings. The cruisers, too, were underarmed. The 10.5-cm gun was an excellent weapon, but did not have the weight of shell required to stop large numbers of destroyers. *Mainz* demonstrated the problem. Although her fire was rapid and accurate, the British destroyers were nevertheless able to get their torpedoes away before suffering any major damage. What was more, not one of the German cruisers could match a *Town* armed with 6-inch guns. The arrival of one 100-pound shell was far more devastating than that of two 38 pounders—and the rate of fire of the 10.5-cm was hardly twice that of the 6-inch. This was a bitter pill to swallow, but the dose was to be repeated in the months to come.

Enter the Submarines

FOLLOWING THE HELIGOLAND BIGHT ACTION, THE ADMIRALTY PREPARED plans for a second sweep. Churchill wanted to know whether the Germans had ships at sea about the Skagerrak. He proposed that the Grand Fleet's light cruisers and destroyers, covered by the battle squadrons, traverse the area and destroy whatever was to be found. Jellicoe agreed. Discovery of the east coast minefields put him in favor of any measure that might end the German mining campaign. He suggested, however, certain modifications. The Grand Fleet would position as proposed, but the Harwich Force, again supported by Cruiser Forces C and K, would approach from the southwest and meet the Grand Fleet flotillas off the Horns Reef, trapping any German ships at sea.

The operation would have been fruitless, since there were no German units so far north, but it never took place. On 31 August the Admiralty received intelligence that four cruisers and six submarines had left the Baltic with the mission of crossing the North Sea to attack any battleships they encountered. Jellicoe immediately sent Beatty and the available cruiser squadrons to the Skagerrak, while he swept east of the Orkneys in the hope of cutting off these ships. The report was a false alarm. Although the British had many human sources around the Baltic entrances, as well as merchant ship reports, they were subject to rumor and mistaken identities.

Keyes and Tyrwhitt pressed hard for another Bight operation. Even Jellicoe was in favor, provided there was proper planning. Questioning prisoners taken on 28 August had revealed that the First Scouting Group would have come out of the Jade as soon as the tide permitted. Had the action continued, it might well have been followed by any heavy ships that were ready for sea. On 3 September the Admiralty (with wording that suggested Churchill himself) telegraphed to Jellicoe: "We must therefore be prepared to meet not only battle cruisers, but perhaps a division of the High Sea Fleet or the whole fleet. You should therefore be in a position with the Grand Fleet to take full advantage of so fortunate a chance."[1]

The new operation was initially set for 10 September, but was delayed a day to give Jellicoe's heavy ships an opportunity to rest. The strain was beginning to tell. The Channel Fleet would patrol to the south, covering the transportation to France of the Sixth Division, and the Grand Fleet to the north. Beatty's First Battle Cruiser Squadron (reinforced by the exchange with Force K of *Inflexible* for the faster *New Zealand*) and the other Grand Fleet cruiser squadrons and flotillas would be north and northwest of the Bight. Moore's two battle cruisers and a small escort would be to the west. Tyrwhitt in *Lowestoft*, accompanied by the Third Flotilla, would move into the Bight near Heligoland and start sweeping westward from the island before 0400. Farther south, off the Ems, Blunt was to begin his sweep with the First Flotilla an hour later, covered to seaward by the dubious protection of the *Bacchantes*. Keyes managed to scrape together five submarines. *D8* would operate off the Ems and *E4* to the north of Heligoland, while the other three were to conduct a surfaced sweep from west to east in the outer Bight, the two attached destroyers scouting ahead. To his chagrin, Keyes would not be present. The First Sea Lord (Keyes blamed Sturdee) had forbidden his going to sea again in a destroyer and his request for a light cruiser had been refused.

The operation started on schedule and achieved nothing. The Germans had intelligence that there would be a raid between 8 and 11 September. Unfortunately, von Ingenohl had allowed the battle cruisers to begin urgent machinery repairs. Only *Seydlitz* was in fighting trim and she was limited to twenty knots. Even so, Hipper had his flagship and two armored cruisers, *Roon* and *Prinz Adalbert,* lying outside the minefields at immediate notice for sea. The C-in-C kept the battle squadrons at two hours' notice during daylight. A single row of 689 mines had been laid twenty miles to the west-southwest of Heligoland, stretching past the Norderney lightship. By some miracle, the British Third Flotilla missed the field. Had it gone any farther south, losses would have been heavy, since the mines were set shallow enough for destroyers to detonate.

The conditions repeated those of 28 August, with the entire Bight shrouded in mist. Under the Germans' new system of patrols, the U-boats and torpedo craft did not take up their stations until dawn. By that time the British were out of sight. One German torpedo boat, *S129,* spotted the Third Flotilla as it moved west, but was not herself observed and there were no other encounters between surface vessels. The only British craft that saw German units were the submarines *E4* and *D8.* The latter spent an uncomfortable seventy minutes dived after attempting to torpedo *U28.* Seeing the torpedo coming, the German boat hastily submerged. As the British staff history remarked, "[S]talemate was practically inevitable for neither boat knew what to do with the other; and after an hour and a quarter, during which the two boats simultaneously rose and simultaneously dived again, the German retired out of the area."[2] *E4* tried to attack other U-boats and was equally unsuccessful. A small and maneuverable submarine made an extremely difficult target, but this worked both ways. Although hunted by several German units, *E4* also escaped unscathed.

The Germans finally received indication of the British presence from seaplane No.29's dawn reconnaissance from Borkum. The aircraft sighted both the *Bacchantes* and the Third Flotilla as the latter headed west, but, when its report after landing reached the Fleet Command, the staff was unable to understand the British intent. When a further air reconnaissance at 0700 revealed that the Bight was clear of British ships, the mystery deepened. The patrols were alerted, but, in these circumstances, von Ingenohl would not send out any ships.

Jellicoe's sweep to the north drew a similar blank. Apart from the now customary alarms (the pre-dreadnought *Zealandia* believed she had rammed a submarine, despite there being none in the area), nothing was seen. By dusk the sweep was over. Still unhappy about Scapa Flow's lack of defenses, Jellicoe decided to use a temporary anchorage at Loch Ewe, which he hoped was out of U-boat range. It is likely that Jellicoe wanted to stir the Admiralty into action, since it was tantamount to admitting that the British had lost control of the North Sea. Although von Ingenohl was yet to release the U-boats from coast defense, a few were available for offensive missions and it was now, at the beginning of September, that they really began to have an effect on British operations. Two incidents had convinced Jellicoe that putting to sea at any alarm was not enough.

The Grand Fleet's routine was having a bad effect on the ships' machinery and their crews, since insufficient opportunity existed to make repairs, or to relax and sleep (photo 10.1). Breakdowns were mounting, particularly in the most modern battleships. *Orion* was in the midst of a series of unsuccessful efforts to repair her condensers, which involved replacing some 8,500 tubes by hand.[3] It was the last straw when, at 1830 on 1 September, *Falmouth* thought she saw a periscope inside the Flow and opened fire. The cruiser believed she had sunk the U-boat, reporting bubbles and the smell of petrol, but every ship in the anchorage hurriedly raised steam. All storing, ammunitioning, and coaling halted, and the Grand Fleet sailed in darkness. Inside the Flow, the situation was chaotic: "Destroyers, trawlers, light cruisers & steam boats chasing in every direction."[4] The battle squadrons cleared

| PHOTO 10.1 | The Grand Fleet at Scapa Flow | *Imperial War Museum* |

Scapa, encountering thick fog in Pentland Firth, and leaving behind the Second Destroyer Flotilla. The destroyers found nothing, and one observer commented—accurately—"very probably seals come to the surface," but it was a warning.[5] On 2 September there was another submarine alarm, this time in the Firth of Forth. Force K, there after the mining of the Humber, sent boat patrols away. Although the report was not believed, it highlighted that the Forth was as poorly protected as Scapa, with no nets and only two sets of gun batteries.

Then, on 5 September, came the first real shock. The Admiralstab deduced from newspaper reports that the British were using the Forth as a base and *U20* and *U21* were ordered there. *U20* got to below the Forth Bridge but, not knowing that two battle cruisers lay just above it, withdrew on finding nothing in the outer anchorage. *U21* had just begun her attempt when she sighted a patrolling cruiser. This was *Pathfinder,* leader of the Eighth Destroyer Flotilla. *U21* fired a single torpedo at a range of fifteen hundred yards. It struck the forward magazine, which blew up, breaking *Pathfinder*'s back. She sank within ten minutes, barely ten miles from May Island. The Eighth Flotilla's destroyers came on the scene only more than an hour later. By this time many of the survivors had slipped off the debris left afloat and drowned.[6] When her wounded captain was picked up and explained that *Pathfinder* had been torpedoed, a hunt began and continued until dusk. *U21* nevertheless escaped, having claimed the first sinking by a submarine. The news was received as a "ray of light" by an excited kaiser.[7]

German joy was soon confined. Just after von Ingenohl had steeled himself to allow the High Sea Fleet to exercise in the Heligoland Bight, a British submarine struck back. On 13 September *E9,* under Lieutenant Commander Max Horton, intercepted the tiny and elderly cruiser *Hela* off the Jade and put a torpedo into her. *Hela*'s bulkheads gave way and she sank within twenty-five minutes. The aggressive Horton made his own escape difficult by staying to confirm the kill and was hunted for some hours before darkness allowed *E9* to surface and withdraw.

The military value of *Hela* was much less than *Pathfinder,* but her sinking renewed von Ingenohl's concerns at the risks the High Sea Fleet would run emerging into the Heligoland Bight. The C-in-C believed that any British demonstration would involve a submarine trap and he had little confidence in the precursor efforts of light craft. Von Ingenohl declared that he was prepared to accept such hazards if the operational situation justified, but the Bight could not be considered a suitable exercise area. The western Baltic would have to be utilized instead, battle squadron by battle squadron, paralleling Jellicoe's use of Loch Ewe. The problem was that a squadron required two days to transit the Kiel Canal. This could not practicably be less, since it involved ships reducing their draft. With eight to ten days needed for a comprehensive gunnery and tactical exercise program, the fleet would be too weak to risk an operational deployment into the North Sea for up to a fortnight at a time.[8]

The British took new precautions. Fifteen *C*-class submarines were organized to "search for, stalk and, if possible, attack enemy submarines."[9] Jellicoe assessed that all the southern anchorages were now too dangerous for such important vessels and ordered Moore to bring Force K from Rosyth and rejoin Beatty. This nearly saved *Aboukir, Hogue,* and *Cressy*. Cruiser Force K had been organized to support the forces based on Harwich, especially the old armored cruisers. With its departure, they were now open to attack. Tyrwhitt and Keyes had long been agitating for their removal. Keyes wrote to Leveson on 21 August: "Think of the tale two or three well-trained German cruisers will tell if they fall in with those *Bacchantes*. . . . [T]he Germans must know they are about, and if they send out a suitable force, God help them."[10]

At the Admiralty, Captain Philip Dumas wrote on 14 September, "[V]ery worried about Brian [Egerton, his brother-in-law] who is in the *Euryalus* cruising up+ down the Broad Fourteens with the *Cressy, Hogue, Aboukir* &c + there must be a disaster before long. Everyone in the Admiralty except the staff realizes this but no one will listen."[11]

His tone was even more desperate two days later, "*Everyone* but the War Staff expects that fleet to be sunk daily + it must happen."[12] However, although it was later asserted (in the junior ranks) that the operations "the cruisers had been employed on had been . . . asking for an attack by submarines, on which I think everyone of us had remarked," this was not reflected in the official debate.[13] Not even Keyes made the submarine argument. The critics focused instead on the risk of the *Bacchantes* being set upon by superior heavy forces or surface torpedo craft.[14] The commander of the Southern Force, Christian, was himself worried by the threat posed by a "strong [German] cruiser squadron."[15] The very sobriquet "live bait" had the inference that surface forces would be drawn out to attack the old cruisers. Ironically, the Germans did not know that the patrols existed.

On 12 September two of the *Bacchantes* were sent to the Swarte Bank to watch for cruisers suspected to be coming out of Emden, while the remainder stayed with the destroyers on the Broad Fourteens. This divided patrol continued, for Sturdee decided that German heavy units making for the Channel might well slip past if the *Bacchantes* were concentrated. Although engine repairs generally kept one or two in harbor, the cruisers were meant to stay at sea, going in only to coal, while the destroyer half-flotilla was relieved every two or three days. This joint patrol was supposed to be interrupted only by operations such as those of 28 August and 10 September. In truth, the destroyer presence was spasmodic. The little ships already had to run for shelter several times and the equinoctial gales were beginning. The cruisers were meant to patrol at fifteen knots, but this proved impossible. The ships' aged machinery suffered frequent breakdowns and they were voracious coal eaters over thirteen knots. As a result, the maximum sustained speed was twelve knots—often closer to nine. Zigzagging was neglected, largely because there had not yet been a single confirmed submarine sighting by any of the ships. None had yet been able to work up to full fighting efficiency. All were paper tigers.

Debate over the *Bacchantes* came to a head at a conference held on board *Iron Duke* in Loch Ewe on 17 September. Churchill and Sturdee, accompanied by Oliver and Hood, left London on 15 September. With them went Tyrwhitt and Keyes, largely at the First Lord's instigation. During their trip, the commodores gave Churchill their views on a wide range of subjects. Indeed, at this point the two were a large part of the First Lord's "many and various sources of information."[16] The conference itself confirmed the operational policies in force since the outbreak. An attack on Heligoland was rejected outright, as was any surface venture into the Baltic. One by submarines did receive approval, although further assessment would be needed. Continued fleet sweeps into the North Sea were endorsed and, for this reason, mining the Heligoland Bight was also rejected so as not to reduce the sea room available.[17]

Keyes and Tyrwhitt raised their objections to the *Bacchantes*' routine and found Jellicoe in agreement. Churchill, "instantly arrested" by the expression "live bait squadron," needed little convincing.[18] The problem was Sturdee, who had responded to Keyes' earlier pleas with, "My dear fellow, you don't know your history. We've always maintained a squadron on the Broad Fourteens."[19] However, the gathering broke up with the resolution to discontinue the patrol. The next day Churchill wrote to the First Sea Lord: "The *Bacchantes* ought not to continue on this beat. The risk to such ships is not justified by any services they can render. The narrow seas, being the nearest point to the enemy, should be kept by a small number of good, modern ships."[20]

Battenberg agreed. For much the same reasons as Keyes, he had never been happy with the *Bacchantes*' situation. Sturdee, however, did not. Obsessed by the need to watch for a German thrust into the Channel, he persuaded Battenberg that recent weather proved the destroyers could not maintain the patrol, which the *Bacchantes* should continue until more light cruisers became available. The First Sea Lord gave way. On 19 September Sturdee ordered Christian to concentrate on the Broad Fourteens. *Euryalus, Aboukir, Hogue,* and *Cressy* assembled off the Maass lightship in the early hours of 20 September. The weather was still bad and, although a division of destroyers briefly appeared, Christian sent them home.[21]

The patrol was soon reduced to three. Christian's flagship, *Euryalus,* needed coaling and repairs: her radio aerial had been damaged in the gale. Forced to return with his ship to Harwich because the seas were too steep to transfer to another unit, Christian handed over command to Captain J. E. Drummond in *Aboukir.* This was unusual. Campbell, whose flagship was *Bacchante,* was in command of the cruiser squadron itself and *Euryalus* had been on patrol only to keep up the numbers. Christian, commanding the Southern Force, had other concerns. While he could hardly do anything else on 20 September than remain with *Euryalus*, his error—and Campbell's—was permitting the latter to remain in *Bacchante* in harbor while the squadron was at sea. Campbell's presence probably would have made little difference, but he should have been there.

All through 20 and 21 September the cruisers continued their patrol, wallowing in the short, steep seas characteristic of the area. The cruisers' broadside 6-inch gun muzzles dipped under water as they rolled; that they were unworkable in such conditions was well known.[22] Christian's signaled instructions were ambiguous, typical of those in force over the six weeks of war: "When patrolling and squadron is spread it is left to captains to carry out alterations of course to guard against submarine attack. Suspicious vessels should be boarded if weather permits. . . . No destroyers will be out on patrol at present."[23]

Christian did not mention destroyer support to Drummond in his handover and this bald signal was the only reference made to it. Consequently, Drummond did not realize that he was responsible for ordering out destroyers if the weather eased. His ignorance would be fatal. At sunset on 21 September, when conditions began to moderate, Drummond did nothing beyond radioing to Harwich, "Still rather rough, but going down." By midnight the wind eased away completely. In the west, however, it still appeared unsuitable to send out small ships. Not until 0500 did Tyrwhitt sail from Harwich with *Lowestoft* and eight destroyers of the Third Flotilla. They made their course for the Broad Fourteens, but they were four hours too late.

With the German General Staff beginning to regret the presence of the BEF in France and their interest in interdiction of its supplies rapidly increasing, the navy's focus shifted to the Channel. A first sortie earlier in September, consisting of *U24* and *U8,* was cut short by the same heavy weather that hindered the British. The storm reached hurricane strength in the southeast and destroyed the seaplane base at Borkum, but the submarines' success in riding it out increased confidence in their seagoing capabilities. This promised well for the winter to come. Afterward, on 20 September, *U9,* now the only U-boat available, sailed from Heligoland (photo 10.2). She had a difficult transit in seas so rough that they disabled her gyro compass. This forced her captain, Lieutenant Commander Otto Weddigen, to navigate through a combination of depth sounding and making landfall at intervals.

Nevertheless, *U9* succeeded in her passage. At the same hour Commodore (T) was leaving Harwich, Weddigen sighted the three armored cruisers steering north-northeast at ten knots. He assumed that they were the advanced screen of a major fleet, but soon realized that there were no other ships and made preparations to attack. *Cressy, Aboukir,* and *Hogue* were steaming at two-mile intervals on a line of bearing abaft *Cressy*'s beam. None was zigzagging. With their slow speed and steady course, they could not have presented better targets as Weddigen approached *Aboukir* from fine on her port bow (map 10.1).

PHOTO 10.2   **German U-boat *U9***   *Imperial War Museum*

U9 fired one torpedo, which struck the cruiser amidships on her port side. This single hit was enough. Crippled, *Aboukir* lost way. Within minutes, heavy flooding brought a list 20 degrees to port. All that could be done was to load the wounded into the one available boat and fall in the crew on the upper deck before abandoning ship. At first thinking *Aboukir* had been mined, Captain Drummond had the mine warning hoisted and ordered the other two cruisers to close. Minutes later he realized that the explosion was from a torpedo and ordered his consorts away.

Hogue and *Cressy* kept coming. Nicholson in *Hogue* assessed that if he remained on the side away from the submarine's original attack, his ship would be safe. Losing way to launch her boats, *Hogue* came to a stop a little more than a mile from the stricken *Aboukir*. Contrary to Nicholson's expectations, Weddigen brought *U9* around to the east, only three hundred yards off *Hogue's* port beam. He could hardly miss. At 0655, just as *Aboukir* gave a final lurch, heeled over, and sank, two torpedoes struck *Hogue* amidships and immediately flooded the engine rooms. With the ship's watertight doors still partially open, there was little to stop the ingress. One of the very young cadets who survived the sinking said, "I saw *Hogue* slowly turn over on her side, pause for a moment and then disappear under the waves. I didn't feel the slightest bit of suction, but saw large fountains of water coming out of her scuttles, forced up, I suppose, by air being compressed in the compartments below."[24]

By 0705 the second cruiser had gone.

Despite the danger, Johnson in *Cressy* lingered, his ship having barely steerage way as she picked up *Hogue's* survivors. A periscope was reported and *Cressy*

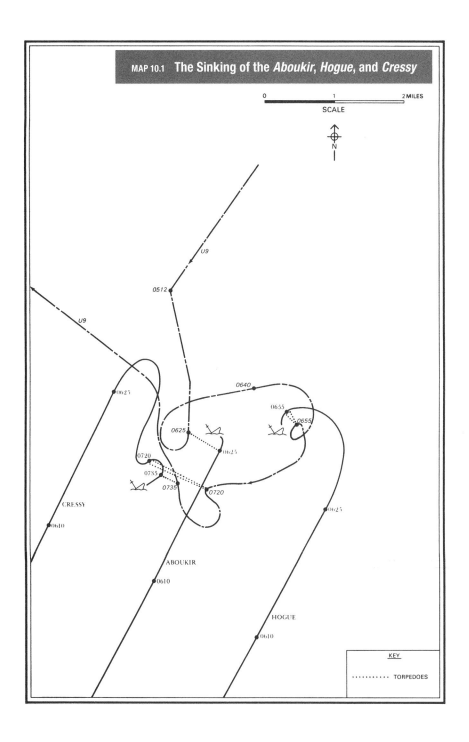

MAP 10.1 The Sinking of the *Aboukir*, *Hogue*, and *Cressy*

SCALE

0   1   2 MILES

N

hurriedly got under way. In his concern for the men in the water, Johnson still did not leave the area, transmitting wireless requests for help and keeping guns' crews at the ready as the boats came alongside with men from the sunken ships. Johnson's precautions were not enough. *U9* approached and, at 0720, fired two torpedoes, one of which struck *Cressy* on her starboard side forward. The damage was negligible and, for a few minutes, it seemed as if the cruiser might escape. Weddigen, however, was a determined man. He brought *U9* within five hundred yards before firing a last torpedo. This did the job.

Tyrwhitt received the radio message, "*Aboukir* and *Hogue* sunk" at 0707: "I dashed off at full speed and a few minutes later we received their position from the *Cressy* and part of a signal which ended abruptly and then was no more. . . . I could not think of 2100 men drowning without giving them all the assistance in my power."[25]

The nine ships arrived at the scene at 1030. The sinkings had been observed by other vessels. Despite the danger of mines, most very gallantly came to the rescue. The Dutch merchantman *Flora* picked up 286 men, but did not wait as there were many seriously wounded whom she took into Ymuiden. The Dutch later returned the survivors, although they would have been within their rights to intern them. The Dutch vessel *Titan* and two British trawlers, *Coriander* and *J. G. C.*, were picking up more men when Tyrwhitt arrived. He wrote, "We first went up to a small English trawler which was loaded with men. They looked just like rows and rows of swallows on telegraph lines, all huddled together to keep themselves warm; they were all naked or nearly so . . . and were very cold."[26]

Lowestoft and half the destroyers began to transship the survivors while the remainder steamed around as an antisubmarine patrol. The operation was fraught with difficulty as many of the survivors were paralyzed with cold. The process was also punctuated by submarine alarms that did little for morale. The sightings were false. Having expended all her torpedoes, *U9* was heading for home. The nine warships collected 581 men before they could find no more. In all, 60 officers and 777 ratings were saved, while 62 officers and 1,397 ratings died. What made the tragedy especially poignant was that the ships were crewed substantially by the Royal Fleet Reserve of former permanent service ratings, middle-aged men with families to support. All had been manned from the Chatham depot. A naval doctor wrote, "[T]he crowds of wailing women strove around the steps of Chatham Town Hall in order to read the list of casualties. . . . I had to shut the hospital windows in order to keep the sound of them from my patients' ears."[27]

Furthermore, in each gunroom were cadets mobilized from the Royal Naval College, Dartmouth. Nicknamed the "war babies," most were no older than fifteen. Many died. Keyes wrote, "[A]t 2 A.M. my secretary woke me up to give me a letter from the Admiralty which he thought might be important. It was from the Director of Mobilization, saying that he would carry out my suggestion to exchange young men from the depot ships, with the pensioners and reservists in Cruiser Force 'C.' . . . So that was satisfactory. [But] at about 7 A.M. I was awakened by a signalman, with an intercepted signal from the *Cressy*."[28]

On his own authority, Keyes, "feeling very bloody minded," ordered the First Destroyer Flotilla to raise steam. Since his two destroyers were at sea, he went on board *Fearless* to see Captain Blunt and wonder as to the cause of the cruisers' loss. "I could only wait, simply boiling with rage that my last effort on their behalf had been acted on just too late." As soon as Keyes learned that that the assailant was a U-boat, he persuaded Blunt to sail under his command, rang the Admiralty to tell them where he was going, and headed for Terschelling in an attempt to cut off the submarine's escape, ordering *Lurcher* and *Firedrake* to join him. Thirsting for revenge, Keyes convinced Blunt that they should raid German patrols as "some salve to the wounded feelings of the country."[29] Keyes signaled to Jellicoe, "Propose to attack light patrol off Ems River at dawn with First Destroyer Flotilla." Jellicoe approved and moved to organize a covering force, but Sturdee was enraged by Keyes' cavalier announcement, which also contravened the direction that he was not to go to sea on operations. At 1900 Keyes "was most peremptorily ordered back to Harwich and told to present myself at the Admiralty." There Keyes received a dressing-down, but was "forgiven," probably because Sturdee must have known that his own position was very weak and that the blame might well be laid at the War Staff's door.[30]

There were immediate consequences. *Bacchante* and *Euryalus* were not allowed back into the narrow seas. Instructions went out that armored ships in submarine waters were to zigzag, steaming at least thirteen knots. No heavy ship was to be used for boarding operations in home waters, an order long overdue after a period that saw super-dreadnoughts heave-to simply to interrogate trawlers, and any other operation that required major units to stop was to be avoided.[31] The Admiralty declared, "[I]f one ship is torpedoed by submarine or strikes mine, disabled ship must be left to her fate, and other large ships clear out of dangerous area calling up minor vessels to render assistance."[32]

With the advantage of hindsight, Christian wrote to Jellicoe, "I cannot tell you how much I have felt this tragic disaster. . . . *Cressy* need not have been sacrificed and probably not *Hogue* if they had only dashed up within say a mile to windward, out all boats and away again. . . . A court of enquiry assembles here [Chatham] today on the loss of the cruisers. I am extremely glad of such an opportunity to clear my professional reputation as I feel nothing I could have done could have averted the disaster."[33]

The court soon focused on the submarine threat and the unsuitability of a permanent patrol in such an area. Its real views were reflected not so much in the findings as in its questions and the answers of witnesses. Christian, the court's members apparently felt, erred in countenancing the vague system of command at Harwich. Campbell's absence was viewed with particular concern, not helped by his poor performance as a witness and apparent failure to subject his situation to any critical assessment. The court made sensible recommendations for better watertight integrity and damage control procedures, including more auxiliary lighting, as well as life jackets for all personnel. The inquiry also put to rest lurid stories of multiple submarines (witnesses reported up to five) coordinated by a trawler flying a Dutch flag, which also attacked men in the water. Many of these claims came from older personnel, further evidence that officers and ratings were suffering stress from the new threats that they faced.[34] Captain Drummond was formally criticized for having neither zigzagged nor called for destroyers when the weather moderated. The court was careful to note that it was not privy to the operational concerns of the War Staff. Nevertheless, its unambiguous judgment that the cruisers' stationing was due to Admiralty direction clearly suggested where the real blame lay.[35]

Despite private acknowledgment that the Admiralty had erred, Battenberg was not prepared to accept such criticism from junior officers and appended a scathing memorandum. Churchill took a different view. He had been conducting his own inquisition to discover why his direction to remove the cruisers had not been carried out. The First Lord refused to let Battenberg reprove the members of the court for their *lèse majesté*.[36] Sturdee defended himself by emphasizing that Christian and Tyrwhitt had been given wide discretion, including the authority to recall the cruisers (as well as light craft) "for weather."[37] His explanation was less than convincing, although matters were let rest. Fisher, from retirement, showed his anger when he wrote, "It was *pure murder* sending those big armored ships in the North Sea! and H. H. Campbell (like the damned sneak he is)[38] staying in harbor when he ought to have hoisted his flag in one of the other ships of his Squadron. . . . [H]e, Campbell, is the culprit who should have been tried had he been in his proper place."[39]

Ramsay, flag lieutenant to Gamble in the Fourth Battle Squadron, recorded the developing frustrations of more thoughtful officers:

> From what we can gather yesterday morning one ship was sunk by a submarine & the other stupid ships went to her assistance & simply asking to sink too [sic]. It does seem childish to think that it should be so but the evidence is rather strong. It just shows how utterly without imagination of war the majority of our senior naval officers are. About a month ago I remarked at lunch that I supposed it was recognized that if a ship of the fleet got hit by a submarine that she could expect no assistance from the other ships & the V. A. [vice admiral] said that really I was too bloodthirsty & pessimistic for anything and why should I always be thinking of the worst side of things.[40]

Captain Dumas expressed the outlook of many when he wrote, "Very strong feeling everywhere about the loss of our cruisers + I consider the staff should be called upon for clear reasons as to their employment in such a place."[41] Churchill took much of the public blame, although this was one occasion when his "interference" should have had free rein.[42] It was politically convenient for many to ascribe the obvious muddle to the mercurial First Lord, but confidence in the Admiralty as a whole was diminishing.

Euryalus and *Bacchante* were sent to Gibraltar on convoy duty, after which *Euryalus* was dispatched to join Wemyss. Christian and Campbell were ordered to haul down their flags, although both were eventually reemployed. (Campbell received "hearty cheers" from *Bacchante*'s crew when he disembarked, suggesting he had made a mark somewhere.)[43] Tyrwhitt and Keyes were once more placed under Jellicoe's operational control, which they viewed as a more satisfactory state of affairs—for the moment. With the Channel Fleet well to the south and the Grand Fleet sheltering in Loch Ewe, however, the Harwich Force now had no heavy support. Apart from a handful of pre-dreadnoughts, the east coast lay open to German attack.

Germany was delighted by *U9*'s success and Weddigen and his crew received a heroes' welcome. Following hard on their own loss of *Hela*, the incident convinced the Fleet Command and Admiralstab as much as their British opponents of the submarine's offensive potential. For the first time it appeared as if the campaign of attrition might have a chance of success. The immediate effect, ironically, was to blight an operation against the northern patrols that Hipper had been planning with his battle cruisers. This proposal had been the subject of increasingly bitter debate. Von Ingenohl, supported by Behncke and the Admiralstab in Berlin, was initially prepared to deploy the battle cruisers with *Kaiser*-class battleships in support and the remainder of the Fleet close to the Bight, but this was opposed by von Pohl and von Müller, as well as von Ingenohl's own chief of staff, Eckermann. Von Ingenohl tried to bring the matter to a head with a submission to the Admiralstab on 25 September, which included a request to reopen the Danish passages to the Kattegat. When the kaiser became aware of the arguments, he confirmed the restrictions on the battle squadrons in terms that von Ingenohl felt left him no chance to deploy the High Sea Fleet to seize even the most favorable opportunity. The idea of the battle cruisers going alone was eventually adopted, but Jellicoe's policy of staying at sea as much as possible prevented its execution for fear of the First Scouting Group running into the British fleet. The Germans were receiving many reports from neutral merchant ships of warships operating in the higher latitudes of the North Sea and these made von Ingenohl unwilling to allow the battle cruisers out. After *U9*'s achievement, the sortie was postponed indefinitely, although a foray by two auxiliary minelayers, *Berlin* and *Kaiser,* continued. This was not a success. Neither ship succeeded in reaching their planned laying positions off the east coast and Moray Firth. They soon returned, relieved that they had not been intercepted and, in the case of *Kaiser*, believing that she had narrowly avoided being torpedoed as she approached German waters.

At von Müller's behest, von Pohl travelled to Wilhelmshaven to discuss the situation and the kaiser's guidance with von Ingenohl; the meeting took place on board *Friedrich der Grosse* on 3 October. Although the conference included the fleet's key flag officers, an invitation was not extended to Behncke, who suspected that von Pohl did not welcome his activist outlook and his support for von Ingenohl's tentative ambitions. As it was, Behncke came on his own initiative. He arrived too late to contribute to the discussion, in which von Ingenohl found himself opposed not only by the Chief of the Admiralstab, but also by his own chief of staff and squadron commanders. The *Kleinkrieg* would remain the priority.

Another submarine thrust was made at the Channel, this time by *U18*. She unsuccessfully attacked the light cruiser *Attentive*. So close was *U18* when she fired that *Attentive,* which had sighted her and was turning, nearly ran her down. The submarine's presence was enough to stop movements across the Channel for twelve hours and the Admiralty placed an outright ban on daytime sailings. The umbilical cord to the western front, the Channel passage was both vital and vulnerable. It was becoming increasingly clear that better means had to be found to combat the U-boats.

Farther north, preoccupation with the Firth of Forth caused the German Fleet Command to organize near-continuous U-boat surveillance of its approaches. They found no big ships, but their encounters with light forces demonstrated to the British the chronic inability of surface vessels, even destroyers, to counter well-handled submarines. *U19* hit British torpedo boat *No.33* with a single torpedo, which failed to explode, while *U22* unsuccessfully attacked the destroyer *Vigilant.* The idea that they might be targets shocked the flotillas and forced fundamental changes. Owen in *Stour* complained, "This new move is a distinct jar, as it was thought they'd not waste their torpedoes on small fry like ourselves." The next day he wrote, "[I]nstead of just trolling backwards + forwards . . . at about 6 knots, as I generally do, I've been steaming continuously at 10 to 12 knots altering course 3 or 4 points every quarter of an hour! This a great bother, is far less comfortable + makes navigation more trouble, but it is the only way to flummox submarines if they are about as you can't see the brutes, except just by luck, the only common sense thing to do is to act all the time as if you knew they were in the vicinity."[44]

This greatly increased the strain on crews, particularly in coal burners like *Stour* (about which Owen had moaned that she "looks about as clean as a bankrupt fishing boat!!!"), as well as wear and tear on machinery.[45] It was a problem for all his ships, of which Jellicoe was becoming acutely aware. Nevertheless, he continued to stay at sea as much as he could, well north of latitude 54, since the unprotected Loch Ewe could be only temporary refuge. When U-boats were reported in its locality, the C-in-C returned to Scapa Flow, playing a naval form of the shell game. He pleaded with the Admiralty for destroyers, minesweepers, and antisubmarine vessels, as well as armed merchant cruisers to supplement the Northern Patrol.

There remained fundamental problems of training and material, although the Admiralty was trying hard. Rear Admiral Edward Charlton was appointed Admiral East Coast Minesweepers on 13 September. Large numbers of civil craft were being requisitioned and converted for patrol and minesweeping duties. Payments were arranged for merchant ships and fishing vessels that reported sightings of mines or submarines, although it was often difficult to sort out fact from imagination. The anchorages required for the North Sea campaign all demanded considerable resources to create the fixed defenses, such as booms and nets, needed against submarines. The old solution of allocating obsolete battleships and light craft for coast defense was no longer sufficient. Scapa Flow in particular would need much work to block its navigable entrances. It would be months before all the North Sea bases were fully secure.

The Royal Navy was paying the price for unbalanced development before the war. This soon became apparent with minelaying. The Channel demanded new solutions for its protection. G. A. Ballard, now promoted rear admiral, had an extensive, albeit largely theoretical, background in mine warfare from work over many years on war plans. As Admiral of Patrols, he suggested that submerged U-boats could be prevented from entering the Channel by defensive minefields across its northern approaches. Deploying mines in what were partially international waters was a new step for the British, but one that the Germans had already taken. It could be justified as a defensive measure and would be another move toward controlling shipping in the North Sea, since declared fields forced merchant ships into mine-free areas.

Churchill (perhaps influenced by Fisher) and the War Staff approved, despite their earlier reluctance to undertake mine warfare. This had been partly because of worries about neutral opinion, and also because of a belief that minefields would not only constrain British operations, but also reduce the likelihood of the Germans venturing out. The Admiralty issued a public declaration on 2 October, announcing a danger area in the northern approaches to the English Channel that effectively closed all but the swept channel immediately off the British coast.[46] Significantly, Dumas, assistant Director of Ordnance and Torpedoes and responsible for mine procurement, was "staggered" to be told by Churchill on the day of the first operation that mines were to be laid in the Channel, commenting, "As all our mining was dropped & our mines, sinkers & mooring ropes are worthless the results must be a failure."[47] Given that Cabinet had been briefed on the plan a few days before, Dumas' ignorance was stark demonstration that the operational and material elements of the Admiralty were not talking to each other.

Four of the old converted cruiser-minelayers, *Apollo, Andromache, Iphigenia,* and *Intrepid*, were assembled. The first lay took place on 2 October, further fields going between 3 and 10 October. They were not a success. During the first sortie, a mine blew up under *Intrepid*'s stern, causing superficial damage. *Andromache* suffered similarly. On return to harbor, the arming pistols on the mines were hurriedly changed before the ships went out again. By 3 October Dumas had heard rumors of the trouble and been ordered to obtain 15,000 mines of a new design to add to the 4,000 in stock.[48] Bereft of expert advice, he was forced to make the selection of a new model himself.

As Dumas predicted, there were other defects in the existing weapons. The remaining operations were completed without mishap, but within a few days (or hours) mines began to break their mooring cables and drift. Passage across the Channel became hazardous, punctuated by rifle shots at passing "drifters" and occasional explosions. It would take longer to appreciate that mines that did not break their cables were dragging their moorings. Betrayed by bad design and poor construction, the British weapons were as much a liability as an asset. Their problems would not be completely solved until much later, largely due to failures on the part of the experimental authorities in HMS *Vernon*. This was as much the result of outlook as resources once the war started, but the lack of rigor in testing and analysis had roots in the financial austerity that had restricted development.

October was a grey month for the Grand Fleet as it shifted base again and again. The Northern Patrol had begun to attract German attention and U-boats were dispatched to the area. Many British units were committed to surveillance because several German liners, including *Brandenburg* and *Prinz Friedrich Wilhelm*, were sheltering in Norwegian ports and there were fears of an imminent breakout. As a result, every available cruiser was pressed into service to assist de Chair. On 9 October the armored cruiser *Antrim* was attacked by *U16* and escaped only through the timely action of her navigating officer. This was a warning of the risks being run, for *Antrim* had been zigzagging at high speed, but the patrols had to continue. The Canadian Divisions were crossing the Atlantic and a successful attack on their convoy would have had disastrous consequences for empire unity. Although Jellicoe thought it improbable, the Admiralty feared a sortie by the German battle cruisers and the escort was eventually reinforced by the old battleship *Majestic* and, in great secrecy, the battle cruiser *Princess Royal*.

On 15 October Otto Weddigen in *U9* repeated his success by sinking the cruiser *Hawke* off Aberdeen. Incredibly, only half an hour before the torpedo struck, *Hawke* stopped for fifteen minutes to take on mails from the *Endymion* (which did a round-robin of transfers with the remainder of de Chair's units). Some were focused on the threat. *Endymion* herself "took unusual precautions . . . only slowing down enough to drop the boat, then steaming around at about 10 knots. . . . [W]e joked together about these excessive anti-submarine precautions."[49] With the ships spread out of sight, the sinking was discovered only after *U17*'s unsuccessful attack on *Theseus*. *Hawke* was struck amidships and capsized and sank within ten minutes. Dark rumors circulated among her consorts as to *Hawke*'s serviceability and maximum speed, and some personnel were becoming overwrought.[50] The destroyer leader *Swift* and the Norwegian steamer *Modesta* found seventy-one survivors the next day, but some five hundred men were lost. *Swift* herself stood into danger, but her high speed prevented *U17* making an attack. The rescue was a harrowing introduction to the reality of war. Wintour of *Swift* wrote, "May I never see another sight like the sea where the poor old 'Hawke' sank. Floating bodies in life-belts . . . all in a ghastly area through which we charged backwards + forwards at high speed. . . . [After the funeral service] . . . I had the strongest tot of whisky I've ever drunk . . . + then I made Vaughan take the gramophone up on deck + play music-hall tunes to the men—for they'd had just about as much as they could stand."[51]

Jellicoe was out on a sweep north of Scotland. On learning of *Hawke*'s loss he ordered yet another change of anchorage. The fleet would move in two divisions to Loch na Keal and Lough Swilly. The former was farther south on the west coast of Scotland than Loch Ewe, while Lough Swilly was on the north coast of Ireland. Jellicoe hoped that they would be far enough away from the German bases to ensure his ships' safety, but his move was undermined from the start.

The real threat to the Canadian convoy was under water. The German General Staff had pressed hard for something to be done to prevent its arrival. Despite concerns about the danger from mines, *U8* and *U20* were dispatched to the Channel. The Germans expected that the troops would be deposited immediately in France. The Canadians' state of training and equipment, however, meant that they required preparation in Britain. Wisely, their disembarkation was shifted from Southampton to Plymouth, as far down threat from the U-boats as possible.

Neither boat had any success in the eastern Channel, *U8* having a periscope damaged in an encounter with the destroyer *Ferret*. *U20*, however, made the most ambitious German submarine deployment to date, circumnavigating the British Isles. Passing Plymouth, she missed the Canadian convoy by a few hours, to the latter's good fortune. Its escort commander, Wemyss, was under few illusions as to the target presented by the "long line of huge transports stretching from Plymouth Breakwater to the Eddystone, awaiting their turn to be taken up harbor."[52] Continuing her passage west-about, *U20* encountered part of the Second Battle Squadron north of the Hebrides. The battleships were not escorted, something noted by *U20*'s surprised captain, Otto Dröscher, although they were steaming at seventeen knots. *U20* was unable to attack, but made a safe return to Germany on 20 October.

The German command could not confirm from *U20*'s report which alternative anchorages the Grand Fleet was employing, but it was clear that major units were operating west of Scotland. Moves were already in train to ensure that the British would not find the area a safe haven. While Jellicoe was completing his new dispositions by moving the various cruiser patrols farther north, the German mining campaign had got under way again. Three minelayers set out on 16 October. Two, the *Kolberg* and *Nautilus,* attempted to mine the Firth of Forth, but turned back halfway after they saw smoke on the horizon, then intercepted heavy wireless traffic that convinced them that substantial British forces were in their vicinity.

The third, the converted passenger liner *Berlin,* was more enterprising. Ordered to mine the southern approaches to the Clyde on the west of Scotland, she successfully made her way out into the Atlantic. Wireless traffic convinced *Berlin's* captain, Hans Pfundheller, he could not penetrate the Irish Sea unobserved. Furthermore, Pfundheller discovered that the coast lights that he had planned to fix on were all either dimmed or extinguished. This made the nighttime deployment of a field close to the coast highly problematic. He decided not to attack the Clyde, but lay his mines off Tory Island, northwest of Lough Swilly. Much of the wireless had clearly been from warships, but Pfundheller had no idea that the Grand Fleet was in the vicinity. He determined the location because it was on the nearest major shipping lane, and he hoped its discovery would result in "general dismay, especially in trade and shipping circles."[53]

On the night of 22–23 October, *Berlin* laid two hundred mines in a long "V" pattern. Evading nearby patrols, the minelayer escaped into the Atlantic and rounded Iceland before turning east again. Intent on intercepting merchant traffic to Russia, *Berlin* lingered off the northern Norwegian coast, but found nothing. On 16 November, her coal running low and machinery needing repair, *Berlin* entered Trondheim to be interned. Her field had long since done its work. On 26 October the British merchant ship *Manchester Commerce* struck a mine, but it was not until two days later that survivors were brought into Fleetwood with news of her sinking. By this time the Grand Fleet had suffered a heavy loss.

Vice Admiral Warrender took the Second Battle Squadron out of Loch na Keal for firing practice on 27 October. At 0805, in the middle of a turn on to the range, *Audacious* struck a mine aft on her port side. *Berlin* had set the mines deep to avoid their being struck by light craft and this reaped a double reward. The weapon exploded precisely where the battleship's underwater protection was least satisfactory. With the ship still turning, the port engine room flooded within seconds. *Audacious* began to list and settle by the stern. Thinking the ship had been struck by a torpedo, her captain had the submarine warning hoisted and *Audacious'* consorts sheered away (photo 10.3). Captain C. F. Dampier turned the *Audacious* south for Lough Swilly. Although the ship was barely manageable, she could still make nine knots on her starboard engine. Dampier hoped to get the stricken ship twenty-five miles to land and beach her before she sank. While

PHOTO 10.3   HMS *Audacious* mined and sinking   *Imperial War Museum*

the other battleships steamed away, the cruiser *Liverpool* stood by the crippled *Audacious,* which was steadily broadcasting signals (largely en clair) reporting her plight. In response, Jellicoe sent every available destroyer and tug to assist her. The C-in-C did not dare dispatch a battleship to tow *Audacious* in, because of the submarine menace, but he ordered several auxiliaries out to see what they could do. Meanwhile, the liner *Olympic* (sister to the ill-fated *Titanic*) arrived, having intercepted *Audacious'* radio messages. Her captain, Commodore H. J. Haddock, was also an officer in the Royal Naval Reserve.

For two hours *Audacious* struggled on, covering fifteen miles as the seas rose. Flooding worsened in the remaining engine room and, at 1050, the ship stopped. Dampier feared that *Audacious* might capsize and he brought her head to sea to disembark personnel. All but 250 were removed in the ships' boats, aided by several from *Liverpool* and *Olympic* (photo 10.4). The remainder stayed, for Captain Dampier thought that there was still a chance of saving the ship. *Audacious* continued to settle by the stern, but her list did not increase. At 1330 Haddock suggested that *Olympic* try a tow. The fleet auxiliaries had not yet appeared, so Dampier readily agreed. The attempt was made half an hour later, the line being passed with great skill by the destroyer *Fury.* However, while Haddock managed to get the two ships under way, *Audacious* quickly became unmanageable, sheering into the wind and straining the towing hawser so much that it parted.

Liverpool and the newly arrived collier *Thornhill* tried in their turn, again assisted by *Fury,* but they too failed. It was rapidly becoming clear that the ship was doomed, but Dampier and Vice Admiral Bayly, just arrived in the boarding vessel *Cambria,* had not given up all hope. By now aware that *Audacious* had been mined, not torpedoed, Jellicoe sent the pre-dreadnought *Exmouth* to attempt another tow. She had not joined when Bayly ordered *Audacious* to be abandoned as darkness fell. The ship sank deeper. Just as *Exmouth* came up to the little group, *Audacious* gave a sudden lurch, hung for a moment and capsized. Shortly

PHOTO 10.4   HMS *Liverpool (in wartime)*   *Imperial War Museum*

afterward she blew up, scattering debris and causing the sole casualty, when a piece of armor plating struck a petty officer on the deck of *Liverpool*, some eight hundred yards off. Several miles away "the explosion was bright enough to recognize most people on our upper deck."[54]

The ships returned to Lough Swilly, taking with them *Olympic*, which was not allowed to resume her voyage until the Admiralty had decided what to do. Jellicoe was desperately concerned that the Germans should not know of the disaster. Although the Grand Fleet still had an advantage in numbers, the C-in-C reasoned that the Germans' other capabilities made the balance so delicate that the sinking tipped it in their favor. Jellicoe considered his own forces were only half-trained and felt that German expertise with the torpedo and mine combined to make the result of any general engagement doubtful. The heavier guns of the British superdreadnoughts were, Jellicoe believed, the only clear advantage that the Grand Fleet possessed and the loss of *Audacious* too heavy a blow to be admitted.

There were other problems. In mid-October Beatty noted, "[W]e have no place to lay our heads. . . . We have been running now hard since the 28th July; small defects are creeping up which we haven't time to take in hand."[55] Several of the fleet's battleships had machinery troubles brought on by continual high-speed steaming. "Wrapperitis," the leaking of feed water from the tube ends of water tube boilers, a problem resulting from design decisions a decade before, and "condensiritis," the leaking of coolant sea water into the tubes containing the condensing "used" steam, were chronic.[56] "Condensiritis" particularly affected some of the most modern dreadnoughts and was a source of acute anxiety.[57] *Orion*'s embattled engineers refitted the condensers several times before her problems were fixed, and other ships were not much better off. The truth was that the fleet was wearing out, subject to an operational regime that had never been tried in peacetime. As one officer noted, "We were finding out every day that theory is often very much different from actual practice."[58]

Coaling was a festering sore. The shock was not that it had to be done and at great speed, but that it happened so often. It was no surprise that *Princess Royal* had to coal four times between 27 July and 8 August 1914, the battleship *St. Vincent* four times between 27 July and 13 August and *Southampton* four times between 27 July and 11 August.[59] What burdened personnel was that coaling continued "with disagreeable frequency."[60] It was "a burning topic that was always in our minds."[61] By 18 October *Orion* had coaled ten times since the outbreak, at an average interval of little more than seven days.[62] Cleaning up took a long time and was of limited effectiveness. Apart from the coal dust that remained on the person, "it took at least two days hard work thoroughly to clean the ship from the coal-dust that penetrates everywhere."[63] It was arguable that "coal burning ships were, in fact, never really clean during the war" and this was certainly the case during the unremitting sea time of 1914.[64] Wintour of *Swift* commented, "I went on board *Active*—I have something to be thankful for in having an oil-ship + not coal. The *Active* has to coal every 3rd day—the men are dog-tired and the state of the dirt + coal dust simply filthy—no time to wash down. The Captain's cabin was like an empty coal hole."[65]

It was true that reinforcements were joining. These included some powerful ships such as *Benbow* and *Emperor of India* and the battle cruiser *Tiger* (photo 10.5), as well as the "Turks," the 13.5-inch-gunned *Erin* and the seven-turreted 12-inch-gunned *Agincourt*. All, however, had somewhat scratch crews (*Agincourt's* combined men from the Royal Yachts with veterans of detention cells, while *Tiger* had seventy-three returned deserters) and their completion had been rushed, which made achievement of fighting efficiency difficult.[66] Even an apparently small matter, such as absence of the final internal clean by the builder before handover, created significant problems. Dockyard workers customarily used the lower compartments as latrines during fitting out, to the point that some spaces "could only be entered wearing sea boots and oilskins, which had to be discarded and cleansed as soon as the compartment was left."[67] Their remaining filthy when the new units sailed to join the fleet created immediate problems for the health of raw and barely organized crews, particularly with winter approaching and in ships shut down with little external ventilation.

Jellicoe knew it would be weeks, if not months, before he could rely on the new arrivals. He proposed that the sinking be kept secret and the Admiralty agreed. There was a recent precedent, of which Jellicoe and others may have been aware, since the historian Julian Corbett was working at the Admiralty and had recently completed a secret staff history of the Russo-Japanese war. The Japanese had successfully concealed the loss of a battleship, *Yashima,* at a critical point in 1904.[68] Cabinet also consented. The government was concerned with the effect on Turkey,

PHOTO 10.5   HMS *Tiger*   *Imperial War Museum*

whose neutrality hung in the balance. Furthermore, the situation in France was tense, the outcome seeming to rest on the battle for Ypres, then raging. Censorship was set in motion immediately. While news was given out that the ship had been damaged, her crew was distributed around other ships. Up to the end of the war, *Audacious'* name was retained on all lists of ships' movements and activities.

Concealment was reasonable enough for a week or two, but grew ludicrous as time passed. Many of *Olympic's* passengers were Americans and it was impossible to stop them talking. Some had taken photographs. American newspapers soon began to scent that something had happened. On 14 November a photograph of the disabled *Audacious* was published that left in no doubt that the ship had been in extremis.[69] Although it was not until 19 November that *Audacious'* destruction was accepted in Germany, Britain should have admitted the loss before this. Soon every neutral country took the sinking as fact. By February 1915 a very junior pay-master officer who had not been in the Grand Fleet at the time was writing home with "the *true* story of the *Audacious*"—in a letter that may well have passed by a censor.[70] To be fair, Churchill planned to admit the loss when the chance came (the prime minister was at him on the subject in early December), but his intent to do this in the wake of the victory of the Falkland Islands at the end of 1914 was stymied by Fisher. The latter "cajoled and threatened and browbeat him to such an extent that he (the First Lord) allowed himself to be turned away from his intended course."[71] Continued silence only convinced the world and many in Britain itself that the government was unreliable. This had disastrous repercussions after the Battle of Jutland in 1916.

Though the Grand Fleet's dispiriting pilgrimage continued throughout October, to the south Tyrwhitt and Keyes were not idle. Their principal concern became cooperation with the army, as the Race for the Sea began. With Allied and German armies reaching stalemate at many points along the western front, both sides were attempting a breakthrough by striking along the coast. All the forces that Britain could muster were being prepared for crossing to link up with the embattled Belgian army. Dunkirk and Ostend became important ports, for they were the most accessible to the threatened areas. Because they were also closer to Germany, protection of the passage was all the more critical. Apart from the largely unsuccessful minelaying, Tyrwhitt and Ballard began a new system to deal with the threat of German submarines and light forces. Keyes pointed out that after the loss of the three armored cruisers, "the main difficulty of a submarine was to find target ships, and that her opportunities would be few and far between, if regular and well defined patrols were avoided."[72] From now on, they were. Although at least a half-flotilla of the Harwich Force was at sea at all times, the ships avoided instituting a beat such as *Cressys* employed. This system had just started when a second change was made in the transport route across the Channel.

The situation in Belgium was deteriorating. Antwerp was being encircled by the Germans and the Belgian government decided to withdraw their field army and link up with the French and British forces farther south. While this was a valid military decision, it left the Channel ports undefended. The Admiralty considered that a German naval presence in those ports would make the Channel untenable. Churchill believed that Antwerp was the key and had to be held, at least until the retreating Belgian army had completed its junction with the Allied field forces. After an emergency Cabinet meeting on 3 October, Churchill volunteered to go and see what he could do. Taking matters into his own hands, he ordered in the Royal Naval Division to assist with the defense. The Royal Marine brigade was already in France and soon moved to Antwerp, but the two naval manned brigades were at Deal and could not arrive until 5 October. Brave and well-meaning but hardly trained, ill-armed, and badly equipped, these six thousand men (and their leaders) had little or no experience of land warfare. Captain Richmond wrote with a grain of truth when he called them a "rabble."[73]

Although Churchill stiffened the resistance for a few days, the division could not prevent Antwerp's fall. Churchill was recalled by Cabinet on 7 October, after his request to stay in the field had been refused. Antwerp surrendered two days later. Despite the criticism heaped on Churchill for his behavior, the arrival of a British cabinet minister did encourage the Belgians to hold on for a time, and the Royal Naval Division's gallant, albeit disorganized, stand enabled the Allied armies to consolidate a defensive line to the coast. The division's casualties were, however, heavy—over 25 percent, including many interned in the Netherlands after they escaped over the border.

Two divisions were promised to aid the Belgians and French. The original plan was to land the formations at Ostend and Dunkirk, but the War Office decided that Zeebrugge was a better destination. The Admiralty agreed to the change, even though it would place a heavy strain on shipping. Tyrwhitt and Keyes were horrified because the minefields already laid were intended to protect the approaches to Dunkirk. The route from Dover to Zeebrugge lay directly over the first of the fields—which meant it would have to be swept. The commodores rose to the situation. Tyrwhitt ordered every ship that he could find to mount patrols off the Dutch coast for the three crucial days from 6 to 8 October. Rough weather made conditions extremely unpleasant at the start but eventually moderated. The calm was "quite a change" but brought unpleasant results for "the dead from the sunken cruisers have now come up again + need no description."[74] The surveillance nevertheless achieved its objective as the divisions got across without loss.

Keyes' role was more pugnacious. He had been afraid that the Germans might attempt to bombard the disembarkation from the sea. With the Admiralty's grudging consent, he took his two destroyers and two E-class submarines to lie off Zeebrugge and himself went into the port. Stunned by the scale of the Belgian facilities, he stayed at Zeebrugge for two days, watching the troops entrain and taking down details of the harbor. He wrote, "I proposed to destroy the latter [the locks and gates] when Antwerp fell, and we realised that the place must be abandoned . . . but everyone was optimistic in those days, and the army hoped to be using Zeebrugge again before too long, so this was not approved."[75]

Keyes left Zeebrugge on 8 October and returned to Harwich to be greeted with the welcome news that Horton in the E9 had sunk the torpedo boat S116 after a very difficult attack on 6 October. Horton described his success: "She went up beautifully and when I had a chance of a good look around about five minutes afterwards, all that was to be seen was about fifteen feet of bow sticking up vertically out of the water."[76] Although it provided a useful lift, Horton's achievement reinforced Keyes' growing conviction that the North Sea was not worth the attentions of the entire Overseas Flotilla. German heavy ships avoided the Bight and von Ingenohl's ban on exercises there continued. Thus, the only targets for submarines were the elusive torpedo boats—Horton spent three hours stalking S116 and admitted that he got her in the end only by luck—or the German submarines themselves. The idea of a Baltic Enterprise had already been canvassed on 17 September and Keyes pressed the concept on the Admiralty. E-class submarines would be dispatched to harry the Germans in their own backyard. Despite concerns over the potential infringements of Scandinavian neutrality, consent was finally given. The operations were to be very successful, but the detachments reduced the British submarine presence in the Bight until new construction became available.

The week after the fall of Antwerp was quiet. Tyrwhitt concentrated his patrols in the eastern North Sea to prevent the Germans sending any units to use the newly captured Belgian ports. By now the Harwich Force had been reinforced by the arrival of the brand new light cruisers *Aurora* and *Undaunted*, the latter under the command of Fox, formerly of the mined *Amphion*. Fox also took over the Third Flotilla from Tyrwhitt, which made the commodore's overall control of his force much easier. Divisions of the First and Third Flotillas meanwhile rotated, each spending two days on patrol, two days in stand-down, and three days as required. There was disquiet among the small ships as to the value of the work they were doing. William Tennant summed it up: "[I]t seems to be the idea that the Germans will try and get their submarines through—we are to stop them! How? No destroyer yet has succeeded in doing any harm to a submarine. Whereas I am afraid the converse does not hold good. However 'orders is orders'!"[77] The need for new sensors, new weapons, and new techniques was increasingly clear.

With the German occupation of the Belgian coast, the Admiralty decided to create a separate Dover Command, reducing the Admiral of Patrols' concern to the east coast. Protection of the Channel was ever more critical, with men and stores pouring into France and a stream of refugees coming back to Britain. Its defense would be harder when the Germans began operating out of Zeebrugge and Ostend. Churchill and Battenberg had little difficulty in selecting the man for the job and Rear Admiral Hood handed over as naval secretary to Oliver and hoisted his flag on 11 October. Hood had been pining for sea service and was better placed there than in the Admiralty. Beatty, who thought highly of him, put the problem in a nutshell (and expressed the opinion of many) when he wrote, "I am glad to hear that Bertie [Hood's nickname] has gone to sea for his own sake. I don't think he was able to control Winston or he wd never have permitted him to make such a damned fool of himself over Antwerp."[78] It remained to be seen how well the laconic Oliver could "control" the First Lord.

Hood's command included responsibility for operations supporting the army on the Belgian coast, although the four light cruisers, twenty-four small destroy-ers, fourteen elderly submarines, and the auxiliary patrol vessels under his flag would need reinforcement. One addition proved immediately useful. Three river monitors building for Brazil had been requisitioned on completion. Renamed *Humber, Mersey,* and *Severn*, their two 6-inch guns and 4.7-inch howitzers could lay down a bombardment several miles inland. At this stage almost invulnerable as far as the German army was concerned, they were worth many gun batteries ashore. Their shallow draught proved its value in other ways. An attack by *U8* on *Mersey* failed when the torpedoes passed harmlessly underneath.

The Germans had already occupied Zeebrugge and Ostend, but the Belgians were making a stand in front of Nieuport and Hood's ships would be critical to the outcome. This was recognized when, a few days after the monitors went into action, the battleship *Venerable* was ordered to assist them. Although hampered by her draught, her 12-inch guns were a useful addition. She was part of a surprise supplement to the Dover Command. Hood was concerned about the monitors being exposed to surface attack if they went without support and despatched large numbers of escorts, but he had been anticipated by Sturdee. The latter initially planned to send the battleships *Queen* and *Implacable* to Dover, but mindful of the danger of Tyrwhitt's forces going without heavy cover, diverted them to Harwich and ordered up two more, *Irresistible* and *Venerable.* The main reason for the diversion was the fear that heavy units of the High Sea Fleet would sortie to support a wholesale transfer of torpedo boats and submarines to the Belgian ports. Sturdee instructed Hood that the battleships could be used for the defense of Dunkirk, but only as a last resort, given their value and vulnerability. It did not take Hood long to convince himself that the position was grave enough to justify the risk.

Meanwhile, French and British minelayers were setting offensive fields in an attempt to close off Ostend and Zeebrugge, but there had already been a surface encounter that suggested the Germans were on the move. With the Belgian ports in German hands, von Ingenohl at last felt able to act against British forces in the Channel. He had refused before to allow torpedo boats to sortie south because he believed it would be too easy to cut them off from their bases. Now that the ports stood ready as refuges, an attack should have a much greater chance of success. Four torpedo boats, *S119, S115, S117,* and *S118,* under Lieutenant Commander August Thiele, were selected to undertake a minelaying operation on the Downs or, failing that, at the mouth of the Thames. The primary targets were the British monitors, already proving a thorn in the side of the army. The little ships were stripped of superfluous equipment and each loaded with a dozen mines. They left the Ems at 0330 on 17 October. After an abortive encounter with the submarine *E8,* the unfortunate Germans ran straight into the Harwich Force's Terschelling patrol at 1340 that afternoon. Five ships, including the light cruiser *Undaunted* and the Third Flotilla's First Division, consisting of *Lance, Lennox, Legion,* and *Loyal,* were under the command of Captain Fox. *Undaunted* sighted smoke bearing north-northeast and, as the British ships closed to investigate, they made out the four German torpedo boats, steaming in line abreast. On sighting *Undaunted* and her consorts, Thiele immediately turned his half-flotilla around and made for home.

There could only be one end. The British ships rapidly began to overhaul their quarry. The top speed of the torpedo boats when built was only twenty-six knots; now they could barely make twenty. At 1405 *Undaunted* opened fire at eight thousand yards, but scored no hits before she paused to allow the range to close. The Germans did their best to evade the British, laying smoke and zigzagging, while ditching their mines in order to clear their torpedo tubes. By 1500 the range was down to 1,500 yards and the destroyers and *Undaunted* opened fire. Although British shooting was more rapid than accurate, *Lennox* and *Lance* left *S115* dead in the water and half awash within minutes. The other destroyers dealt with *S117* in the same fashion before all concentrated on the remaining pair of Germans.

S118 began to suffer badly. On fire, with her machinery damaged and unable to make an effective reply with her own popgun four pounders (which had a range of barely two thousand yards), she turned toward *Undaunted* in a gallant attempt to torpedo her. Thiele in *S119* followed, but in a close quarters action in which the range dropped to a few hundred yards, the two boats were smothered in British fire. By 1517 *S118* had sunk and she was followed at 1530 by *S119*, ablaze from stem to stern before her own scuttling charges put her under. It took more time to finish off the other two torpedo boats, crippled and burning as they were. Not until 1630, after the expenditure of much more ammunition, did *S115* finally slip below the surface. Only thirty-six officers and men were saved out of 270—thirty-four by the British and two the next day by a Dutch fishing vessel. *Undaunted* and the four destroyers returned in triumph to Harwich. It was a useful little victory and Tyrwhitt was delighted, although chagrined at not being present, writing, "Just my luck! . . . The very day [Fox] takes on he gets a delightful show!"[79] In spite of his success, Cecil Fox may well have been an early victim of traumatic stress. He left *Undaunted* little more than a week later and was never employed at sea again.[80]

The British did not discern the real reason for the sortie. Although they suspected the survivors' explanation that they had been conducting a reconnaissance, they did not realize that the torpedo boats were modified for minelaying. Curiously, despite the abiding concern that mines would be deployed tactically, particularly in a chase, the Germans' desperate efforts to ditch their weapons had passed unseen. The Admiralty, however, could not believe that the enemy would not attempt something against Hood's forces and assessed that a cruiser sortie was in train. Tyrwhitt was ordered out to sweep to the Dutch coast, supported by *Queen* and *Implacable* to the west.

Tyrwhitt's force met no warships, but there was an encounter that indicated how ruthless the conflict was becoming. After the loss of the torpedo boats, the Germans dispatched hospital ships to search for survivors, as they had done following the sinking of *S116*. While there was a lively debate in Royal Navy circles about the need for such vessels, the British viewed the German units with suspicion, believing that they operated as scouts.[81] *Ophelia* was boarded, assessed to be in breach of the relevant conventions, and sent into Lowestoft. Her arrest and later condemnation by a prize court were deeply resented by the Germans and, at least for this war, effectively closed off the use of rescue ships.[82]

It had been a successful few days for the British, although the accuracy of shooting should have been cause for concern. The Overseas Submarine Flotilla, however, suffered a heavy blow when *E3* was reported overdue. Keyes suspected that she had been stalked and sunk by submarines and seaplanes working together and was not far off the mark. *E3* was conducting a surfaced watch on the Ems when attacked by a submerged *U27* on 18 October. She went down with all hands, the first time one submarine had been sunk by another. Though the British did not confirm the circumstances until after the war, her disappearance rammed home the risks being run off the German coast.

For the Germans' part, the loss of the torpedo craft caused considerable debate, but this did not resolve the anomalies in their strategy. There were obvious problems in dispatching such slow and ill-armed craft when more modern units were available. The boats had been something of a suicide squad and regarded themselves as such.[83] The lack of heavy support, not provided even when it became clear that the half-flotilla was under attack, reflected von Ingenohl's own overly cautious approach as much as the formal restrictions under which the High Sea Fleet suffered. But von Ingenohl had some justification. Many of the most modern German battleships and battle cruisers were suffering problems with both condensers and boilers. German design practice, notably in adopting small tube boilers, was in some ways more advanced than the British, but engineering reliability was proving to be poor.[84]

Keyes and Tyrwhitt began to agitate once again for an offensive operation into Heligoland Bight. Tyrwhitt went up to the Admiralty on 22 October. "I arrived at 5 p.m. and was at once taken to the Holy of Holy rooms, where Prince Louis, Winston and Sturdee were, and a long discussion followed. I produced my little plan (or rather, Roger Keyes' little plan) and got it through right away.... Well they kept me a long time."[85]

The Admiralty had reason to do so. It had been burdened, partly through Churchill's enthusiasm, with responsibility for the aerial defense of Britain. The First Lord's great worry was the threat of the growing zeppelin force; he wanted to attack its principal base. The location was unknown, but was thought to be at Cuxhaven. Despite the lack of hard intelligence, Churchill felt something had to be done. The converted cross-Channel steamers *Engadine* and *Riviera* each carried three seaplanes. While their conversion was makeshift and both carriers and aircraft had a long way to go before they were fully efficient, Churchill pushed the Admiralty to employ the new capability.[86] The commodores' scheme could be incorporated into an attack. Covered to the north by Moore's battle cruisers, Tyrwhitt was ordered to escort the two ships into the Bight and stand by while the seaplanes were launched, made their raid, and returned. As a diversion, farther south, Blunt and the First Flotilla would conduct the sweep off the Ems that Tyrwhitt and Keyes had originally proposed.

The operation was a failure. Although the force sailed into calm seas on 24 October, heavy rain set in. It continued to pour all the way across the North Sea. When, at dawn on 25 October, the seaplanes were put into the water and tried to take off, "four of the machines failed to rise from the water; one flew 12 miles but had two engine failures due to the rain, and returned; and the sixth, after slipping its 100lb bomb, managed to rise and fly 20 miles, but returned owing to the remote chance of finding the objective and the uselessness of endangering the force for no result."[87]

Blunt's ships sighted no surface vessels and just one aircraft, seaplane No.21. The only incident to enliven proceedings occurred when the destroyer *Badger* rammed, but did not sink, *U19*. The destroyer's captain mistakenly slowed before he hit the U-boat and the German was able to go deep with only superficial damage. Seaplane No.21 landed at Norderney and made a reasonably accurate report, but the information reached the Fleet Command too late for anything to be done. Zeppelin L4 was also up, but saw nothing in the poor visibility. Tyrwhitt was irritated and inclined to blame the aviators "for his having been made a fool of," but he got "considerable butter" at the Admiralty. Churchill had more practical understanding of aviation than Commodore (T) and regarded the failure as a temporary setback. The First Lord knew that the aviators were working hard to improve their performance and soon revived Tyrwhitt's enthusiasm to the extent that "we are going to try again and I can't help thinking we shall succeed this time."[88]

Meanwhile, the Germans began to suspect that their security was compromised. Although the British had not yet started systematic radio interception and decryption and the encounter with the torpedo boats was pure coincidence, the size and position of the British force seemed so apt that they had to be deliberate.[89] A hunt for spies found nothing, although the Germans were inclined to suspect their mail system. In later months the telephone network also came into question, given that the dispersal of senior officers between Berlin, Wilhelmshaven, and GHQ required its continual use. In the meantime, the C-in-C decided against any further surface raids, but ordered out five submarines to attack Hood's forces. They sailed between 22 and 26 October. While *U19* was forced to return for repairs after her encounter with *Badger*, by 23 October the remainder began arriving in the Channel. They soon made their presence felt with a series of attacks. In response, all the larger Allied units not actually conducting bombardments were hurriedly sent into harbor.

The U-boats managed to avoid the destroyers and submarines sent to hunt for them. Navigation proved more of a challenge, *U21* grounding on a sandbank when British forces were in close proximity. She was able to extricate herself, but this confirmed that local conditions could be difficult. The U-boats had no success until 26 October, when *U24* under Lieutenant Commander Rudolf Schneider torpedoed the steamer *Amiral Ganteaume*, crowded with Belgian refugees. Forty were killed. Because the ship was under escort and could not be boarded, the attack was legitimate. Nevertheless, this proved another false move by Germany, since the Belgians' plight was already arousing considerable concern in neutral countries.

Then, on 31 October, the old cruiser *Hermes* was sighted by *U27*. She was ferrying aircraft to reinforce the naval air squadrons in France. Although there was a general ban on ships crossing the Channel in daylight, her captain, Charles Lambe, apparently decided that *Hermes'* duties were too important. In any case, the cruiser was zigzagging at thirteen knots when the submarine fired a single torpedo from a range of three hundred yards. *Hermes* immediately turned away, but the weapon struck aft and exploded. She was beginning to settle by the stern when *U27* fired a second torpedo. This also hit and *Hermes* sank within a few minutes. The bulk of the crew was picked up by destroyers and the steamer *Invicta*.

The Admiralty hastily clamped even more restrictions on Channel operations and *Venerable* was ordered back to Sheerness. In daylight, "no vessel larger than a destroyer or, in exceptional cases, a scout, was to cross the Channel east of the meridian of Greenwich." In response to his pleas for support, Hood was promised that the antique battleship *Revenge*, resurrected from the disposal list, would be sent if the need arose. But the Admiralty pointed out that the loss of a battleship would be a grave blow; it preferred to avoid the risk until practical antisubmarine measures could be devised.

Thus, October in the North Sea closed with the Germans having enjoyed more substantial success than the British. Much had been learned, but both sides were experiencing the strain of the unexpected. Among the British, opinion was growing that something was fundamentally wrong at the Admiralty. It is difficult, a hundred years after, to comprehend the British attitude to the Royal Navy. Since the end of the Napoleonic Wars, the reality of that struggle, the years of blockade, and the frequent invasion scares punctuated only occasionally by glorious success, had been largely forgotten. The aura of invincibility remained. Many had expected that the Grand Fleet would steam into Heligoland Bight and annihilate its opponent. Months after the start of hostilities, nothing of the sort had happened. Some minor successes had been gained, but against the record of the Harwich Force and Keyes' submarines had to be set the loss of several cruisers and the rumored destruction of *Audacious*. In foreign waters, not one raiding cruiser had been caught. *Emden* was taking a huge toll of shipping in the Indian Ocean, seemingly unchecked. *Königsberg* had sunk the old cruiser *Pegasus* at Zanzibar, while Vice Admiral Maximilian Graf von Spee's *Scharnhorst, Gneisnau,* and their consorts had disappeared into the Pacific.

The fault was at least partly Sturdee's. The Chief of the War Staff was not alone on his underestimation of the submarine threat, but his assumption that the newly commissioned Third Fleet cruisers could automatically be considered efficient fighting machines was culpable. It would soon exact an even heavier price at Coronel. Most of the criticism, however, was of Churchill and Battenberg. Churchill had displayed such interest in the navy before hostilities and spent so much time in the fleet (in a blaze of publicity) that, now war had begun, popular opinion was inclined to credit him with playing an even greater part in supervising operations than he did. All the apparent inconsistencies in Admiralty policy were laid at his door because he was known to be hot-headed, a view only reinforced by his behavior at Antwerp. Churchill was feared and distrusted by the Conservatives, his former party, and not much liked by the Liberals, being too brash and self-assertive for many of his colleagues. He had the same effect on admirals. Keyes and Tyrwhitt, who knew more than most and were of his generation, were probably his only champions. Even Beatty, to some degree a confidante, would have preferred his departure. But Churchill had the support of the prime minister, Herbert Asquith, and Chancellor of the Exchequer David Lloyd George. With their backing, he remained in a relatively strong position. Neither Asquith nor Lloyd George, however, had the same confidence in Churchill's naval colleagues.

Their quarry was Prince Louis, ostensibly because of the erosion of popular confidence over his German origins. Rumors flew that the First Sea Lord had been dealing with the Germans, that he had deliberately engineered the loss of the armored cruisers, and that he had even been imprisoned in the Tower.[90] Despite the iniquity of these allegations, Battenberg was ripe for removal. There was growing agreement within the inner Cabinet that he had neither proved strong enough to manage Churchill and direct the War Staff, nor sufficiently active in his own right. Dumas in the Admiralty noted the "rumors that PL is going + really it's just as well."[91] By late October Battenberg's morale and health were deteriorating and Asquith, urged on by senior ministers, was pressing Churchill to get rid of him. The loss of *Audacious* came hours after the First Lord's finally consenting to push Battenberg aside and must have confirmed the prime minister's judgment. If he delayed much further, he himself would have been increasingly vulnerable. Churchill was by no means a willing party. Whoever came in Battenberg's place, it was unlikely that a new First Sea Lord would be so amenable to the First Lord's methods.[92]

Churchill and Battenberg had a "most delicate + painful interview," followed by a formal exchange of letters in which face was saved by Battenberg resigning because, "at this juncture my birth and parentage have the effect of impairing in some respects my usefulness on the Board of Admiralty."[93] Battenberg later wrote that he "had no choice from the moment it was made clear . . . that the Government did not feel themselves strong enough to support me by some public pronouncement."[94] Sorry as the politicians were for Prince Louis, his departure acted as a sop for rising dissent against the government and temporarily stilled the more vocal elements among the Conservatives and in the press. Nonetheless, although Churchill had already decided on the new First Sea Lord and had Asquith's agreement, the question of who was to succeed Battenberg was by no means settled.

The situation in Germany was not as dramatic, but there were increasing tensions. The kaiser was alternately elevated and depressed by the news from the sea. Von Tirpitz remained unhappy and used the loss of the torpedo boats to attack von Ingenohl's methods.[95] A visit to the C-in-C on 24 October was not a success and von Tirpitz came away unimpressed. He had a point about von Ingenohl's judgment and the emperor knew enough of the limitations of the units involved to share his concern at their selection for the minelaying operation. Von Pohl was equally puzzled.[96] Nevertheless, von Müller was right to be concerned about von Tirpitz's activities.

There were new possibilities. Von Ingenohl was considering a raid on the east coast, while the stabilization of the Flanders front and the increasing certainty that Zeebrugge and Ostend would remain in German hands opened them to permanent use by U-boats and light craft. The Marinekorps Flandern was beginning to take up its duties. Preliminary minesweeping to clear the entrance of Zeebrugge had already begun, but neither port could be fully utilized until coastal batteries had been installed to keep the British ships away. This work was soon in hand.

11

The Return of Fisher

P REPARING FOR BATTENBERG'S DEPARTURE, CHURCHILL WARNED THE KING, who had long detested Fisher, that he proposed to nominate him as First Sea Lord. George V was horrified by the prospect. He searched for alternatives but, as Churchill knew quite well and the king was forced to admit, the higher ranks were largely devoid of men with the talents required. Jellicoe could not be spared from the fleet and Callaghan was thought too old (or Churchill knew how formidable a colleague he would make). Hedworth Meux was not up to date. Some of the vice admirals, notably Sir Stanley Colville, might have been a success, but the First Lord could not raise a junior officer to the navy's supreme professional position without arousing a storm of dissent—and Churchill disliked Colville anyway.[1] Beatty's advancement had caused enough trouble. Moreover, Churchill would have been vulnerable to the accusation that he was installing a cipher to keep control in his own hands.

Alternatives exhausted, the king finally acquiesced on 29 October. The popular response was enthusiastic, naval opinion more doubtful. The new First Sea Lord would bring much needed energy, but, apart from legacies of old feuds, there was concern over the combination of Fisher and Churchill. Captain Dumas commented, "I am very glad, but I don't give him [Fisher] any time before trouble arises with Winston."[2] A vastly junior—but well-connected—observer reflected the fleet's judgment: "Fisher is a strong man though unpleasant and rather a cad; he won't be bossed by Winston as Prince Louis was."[3] Beatty summed it up: "They will quarrel before long."[4]

It was just as well that the new spirit so publicly entered the Admiralty. On 3 November came another setback. On the other side of the North Sea, new moves had been in train for a raid. After the failure of the minelaying attack on the Forth, the Admiralstab proposed to catch the British off guard by mining sections of the east coast, rather than harbors, since the local surveillance systems seemed too efficient. The Second Scouting Group was ordered to mine an area off Lowestoft to destroy passing traffic and fisheries, which the Admiralstab thought were particularly active off the Norfolk and Suffolk coasts. As a diversion, Hipper, as he had long recommended, was to bombard east coast ports. From the start, Hipper took a different view from the Admiralstab and developed War Plan 19 with bombardment of Great Yarmouth as the prime activity.

Use of the First Scouting Group was approved only after considerable debate. Von Ingenohl was anxious to improve morale in the increasingly dissatisfied High Sea Fleet, but did not want the battle cruisers exposed. Nevertheless, he was under pressure, not least from von Tirpitz. On 25 October the grand admiral wrote to urge a sortie, "not so much as a matter of battle as for prestige after the war."[5] Von Ingenohl telegraphed a request for the operation to von Pohl on 29 October. Its wording was deliberately vague, with minelaying the priority, noting only that the Scouting Groups would be "in support." The proposal was strongly backed by Behncke, clearly anxious that von Pohl should overcome the kaiser's fears. In fact, the Chief of the Admiralstab obtained the necessary approval, subject to "reconnaissance of every kind, including airship and seaplane reconnaissance, [being] carried out . . . to prevent the retreat being cut off."[6]

At dusk on 2 November Hipper led *Seydlitz, Moltke, Von der Tann,* and *Blücher* out of the Jade. They were accompanied only by *Stralsund* (which was to lay the mines), *Strassburg, Graudenz,* and *Kolberg.* The torpedo boats were left behind as the weather was deteriorating and Hipper did not think that they could keep up. Since he had concerns over integrating even the light cruisers with the battle cruisers, it is likely Hipper took a bleak, but realistic view of the flotillas' training for offshore night operations and their capacity for accurate navigation.[7] The raiding force was followed out by the First and Third Squadrons with a heavy escort. These ships were to go only to the edge of the Bight, with a screen of submarines to seaward. Von Ingenohl would venture no farther unless absolutely necessary.

It was the perfect time for a raid. British forces around Yarmouth were very weak. Since the removal of the surviving armored cruisers, no heavy ships had been allowed into the area other than the old pre-dreadnoughts from Sheerness. All Jellicoe's forces were so far away that not even the battle cruisers could reach the southern North Sea in time to make contact. There were at least patrols on the Broad Fourteens and farther east. Tyrwhitt had planned to attack German minesweepers off the Ems, but bad weather forced him to cancel the operation. Instead, *Aurora* and four destroyers were sent to scour the Broad Fourteens for submarines, while Captain F. G. St. John, the new Captain (D) of the Third Flotilla, took *Undaunted* and three destroyers to patrol off Terschelling. Ordered to rendezvous at 0800 on 3 November, the two formations spent much of their time sinking drifting mines.

Hipper's force passed through the British rendezvous at midnight, when the Germans altered to the west and worked up to eighteen knots. By this time St. John's ships, which were to the northwest, had turned south. For three hours the German and British forces converged. At 0300 *Undaunted* and her consorts passed within ten miles of the First Scouting Group. In the darkness they missed the Germans completely, indicative of the significant limitations of night operations in the absence of knowledge of an adversary's location and movement. The Harwich Force ships therefore spent an uneventful night while the Germans approached the English coast. The Scouting Groups repeatedly encountered groups of fishing vessels. Despite Hipper's best efforts to avoid them, some were always in sight. He could do nothing to confirm his suspicions that they were reporting his movements.

The Admiralty's policy of removing navigational aids and dousing lights reaped its reward. The Germans were not sure of their position within ten miles and had real concerns for safety in relation to both minefields and sandbanks. Although he had been instructed to begin the lay near Smith's Knoll at 0530, *Stralsund*'s captain decided to drop the mines at greater intervals than had been planned. His judgment proved correct. At 0630 *Seydlitz* ran almost right over a buoy marked "Smith's Knoll Watch." The ships were an hour behind in their reckoning, having accumulated an error nearly twice as much as their estimate. Relying on depth soundings, the Scouting Groups began to work their way south to the Cross Sand lightship to begin the attack on Yarmouth. From here they would steer for the Corton lightship, laying down the bombardment as they went south.

But Hipper was deflected by the smallest of adversaries. Only six elderly destroyers and the antiquated minesweeping gunboat *Halcyon* permanently operated in the area. Plans were afoot to make Yarmouth a major escort base, with a full destroyer flotilla and a dozen minesweeping trawlers, but little had been done. There were no land defenses. Before the war there had been a mobile battery of 6-inch guns, of little use against heavy warships. Keyes pointed out that their presence technically made Yarmouth liable to attack, but they been removed for the campaign in France.

Halcyon sailed from Yarmouth at dawn to search for drifting mines. She was followed out a few minutes after by the first of three destroyers, *Lively, Leopard,* and *Success,* for the day patrol. It was a relatively calm but misty morning. *Halcyon* was approaching Cross Sand when *Strassburg* and *Graudenz* appeared five miles away and immediately opened fire. Fearing mines, Hipper ordered them back and directed *Seydlitz* alone to engage the little *Halcyon,* but the British ship escaped unscathed. At their first sight of an enemy vessel since the outbreak, overeager gunnery teams misinterpreted the admiral's order and two other units opened fire, their shell splashes smothering the target and rendering spotting impossible. In the few minutes that it took to sort out the muddle, *Lively* came up to the fleeing *Halcyon.* Her captain, Lieutenant Commander H. T. Baillie-Grohman, handled *Lively* expertly, laying a smokescreen to hide *Halcyon,* while he dodged in and out of the smoke to draw fire, altering course radically, whenever he "saw a ripple of flame from the enemy salvoes."[8] Hipper soon realized that the action was a waste of resources and turned east. The operation was already an hour late and a run south would take the force into mined waters. As they withdrew, the battle cruisers conducted a sporadic bombardment, but none of their shells got nearer Yarmouth than the beach.

Lively and *Leopard*, which had just joined, turned to follow. *Halcyon* broadcast a warning of the German presence, but she had been anticipated by *Leopard*, senior officer of the destroyers, which signaled, "Two battle cruisers and two armored cruisers open fire on *Lively* and myself."[9] British forces now began to move. By chance, lying in Yarmouth were the submarines *E10, D5,* and *D3*. Hearing gunfire, they prepared to get under way. Harwich had been alerted by *Leopard*'s signal and Captain A. K. Waistell, commanding in Keyes' absence, felt the submarines would have a better chance if they went straight to the Bight. He ordered them to sail immediately. *Success* joined the other destroyers as they followed Hipper east. The three "off duty" destroyers, which had put into Lowestoft, were raising steam as fast as they could, but would play no part. Tyrwhitt in Harwich was rousing his flotillas, while out to sea *Aurora, Undaunted,* and their divisions were alerted.

The Admiralty was puzzled to understand the raid's intent and this uncertainty was reflected in its silence. The problem was that no attempt was made to inform the operational and local commanders of what had passed. They were left to their own devices in the apparent expectation that all would have received *Leopard*'s en clair message. Tyrwhitt, on receiving *Halcyon*'s signal reporting the German withdrawal at 0800, immediately appreciated that the only forces capable of intercepting the Scouting Groups were the units already at sea. Accordingly, he ordered *Undaunted* and *Aurora* to move west and make contact. Meanwhile, as the Germans turned for home, the senior officer of the three small destroyers pursuing Hipper's force decided that his old ships had done all they could. He ordered them back to Yarmouth. Not until *Halcyon* got into Lowestoft and the Admiralty received her full report by land line did the War Staff act, despite the fact that the German strength was already known from interception of a signal from *Halcyon* to Tyrwhitt an hour before. At 0955 the Admiralty finally began to issue instructions, summoning Beatty south and ordering the Grand Fleet to sail from Lough Swilly, while the Channel Fleet was to assemble at Spithead. Jellicoe was returning from London and the Grand Fleet's orders were therefore sent to Warrender.

By this time, however, Hipper was already fifty miles into the North Sea and contact had been made between his ships and the Harwich Force. *Undaunted* and her division steamed southwest after Tyrwhitt's orders came through. When by 0840 they had seen nothing, St. John reversed course, hoping to cross the Germans' path. Over the next hour he was repeatedly seen by the First Scouting Group but had only one brief glimpse of them. The two forces were in fact converging slowly, and by 0950 Hipper's heavy ships were in view. Thinking that Hipper would chase him, St. John circled around and then, in an elaborate attempt to shake off the supposed pursuit, steamed directly away. But the British had only been in sight for a matter of minutes. In any case, Hipper, intent on getting home without loss, did not pursue. He had enough concerns. The Scouting Groups had been steaming at speeds up to twenty-three knots since *Strassburg* began to lay her mines and defects were emerging. Notably, *Von der Tann* was suffering the effects of "bad coal," a problem that would dog the German battle cruisers whenever sustained high speed was required.[10]

Von Ingenohl turned for home before 0800, believing that, unless any of Hipper's ships had been disabled, no heavy British forces could cut them off. He was correct, yet made this assessment with little evidence, and risked leaving the Scouting Groups without support. By nightfall all the German ships were inside the inner Bight. There was, however, another scene to play. Fog shrouded the coast and von Ingenohl ordered his ships to remain in the Schillig Roads overnight. The armored cruiser *Yorck* had developed severe machinery defects and received permission to go straight into Wilhelmshaven. In the gloom, she passed to the wrong side of the vessel marking the swept channel between the defensive minefields. Within minutes she exploded two mines and sank with heavy loss of life.

The raid had not been a success, even if doing something was infinitely preferable to the inactivity of the preceding weeks. Intercepted mine warnings confirmed that *Stralsund*'s field was already discovered. Three unfortunate fishing vessels went down within twelve hours, but no major units fell victim. The breakdown of fire control procedures had ensured that not a single British ship was sunk, a source of particular irritation for Hipper.[11] On the other hand, he and his staff had not thought through the use of ammunition against shore targets. The bombardment was a dismal failure. The battle cruisers were forced to fire armor-piercing rounds, since no high explosive shells were available, which would have limited their effect even if they had found real targets. Hipper came in for a great deal of criticism, but the recriminations were short lived. None of this had been practiced before and many of the challenges involved did not become clear until reality intervened. The experience showed how future operations should be managed, at least tactically. What was not thought through was whether the military and morale benefits of an attack on a largely civilian target outweighed the propaganda value the British would derive from such an event.

At the same time, the Royal Navy had much to consider. The fleet's location so far north meant that the east coast was particularly vulnerable. A redistribution was required, despite the admirals' concerns about the security of anchorages. The War Staff had not distinguished itself, partly because the system could not move signals quickly enough within the organization to allow effective intervention. Even if the information initially received was insufficient to make new dispositions, the failure to broadcast what was known until 0900 demonstrated that processes needed to improve. *Leopard* gave an accurate description of the German force at 0720, confirmed by *Halcyon*'s report of "four armored ships" sent out as a general signal at 0735. Decision making also needed to be faster. Not for more than an hour after the signals were to hand did the Admiralty act. Preoccupied with the Channel and the difficult overseas situation as the Admiralty was, the heavy units should have been ordered out earlier. While it is possible to argue that caution prevailed, the final orders, which included sailing the Grand Fleet in daylight, directly contravening the policy introduced to avoid submarine attack, seem to belie this. If, as Churchill has claimed, some major thrust in concert with the raid was expected, then sailing the pre-dreadnoughts from the Nore and Dover was a dubious move, contrary to the principle of concentration.[12]

The absence of submarines in the Bight was a major deficiency, since the High Sea Fleet might have provided an opportunity for successful torpedo attacks. As it was, *D5* was struck by a drifting mine as she emerged from Yarmouth and sank with heavy loss of life. Neither of the other boats saw anything as they could not get across the North Sea in time. Keyes needed more submarines to be able to maintain patrols in German waters and support the Harwich Force's offensive operations. The Baltic venture was worthwhile, but new construction had not yet made up the numbers and there was no margin for wear and tear.

The tactics of the Harwich Force were not ideal. *Undaunted* and her destroyers were the only units to achieve contact. *Aurora* and her division stood too far to the north. It was only good luck that later kept the cruiser away from the Germans' mine-strewn track. Indeed, one of the destroyers, *Lark*, passed right over it. *Arethusa*, with Tyrwhitt on board, also only just missed running into the field with an entire flotilla. Coordinating the three formations provided stark demonstration of the difficulties involved with scattered units and increasing pools of error. Tyrwhitt had to resort to steaming to the usual rendezvous for the patrols and staying there until he had all his subordinates in sight. It was 1530 before he managed this.

The observer must wonder whether the senior officer of the old destroyers could have been more enterprising and hung on to the Scouting Groups for as long as possible. Equally doubtful was the outlook demonstrated by the Captain (D) in the *Undaunted*. A daylight torpedo attack was out of the question, but St. John overreacted to his sighting. He had the heels of the Scouting Groups and could have shadowed them for several hours, with relatively little risk. Something might have been achieved later, particularly if other units joined. St. John's caution was arguably part of a pattern of behavior. As with Blunt's hesitation in August and the notorious incident in the Mediterranean in which a British force failed to engage the battle cruiser *Goeben*, there was an assumption among many that the heavier gun would always prevail. This was true enough for single ship-to-ship encounters, but when multiple units (particularly small, fast ones) were involved, the equation was much more complex. Something must be left to chance.

The difficulty of balancing caution and aggression was faced directly by Jellicoe. On 30 October he had dispatched to the Admiralty a letter containing his intentions for the conduct of the Grand Fleet. There were to be repercussions on the whole war at sea from this document. No history would be complete without it.

> The experience gained of German methods since the commencement of the war make it possible and very desirable to consider the manner in which these methods are likely to be made use of tactically in a fleet action.
>
> 2.   The Germans have shewn [*sic*] that they rely to a very great extent on submarines, mines and torpedoes, and there can be no doubt whatever that they will endeavour to make the fullest use of these weapons in a fleet action, especially since they possess an actual superiority over us in these particular directions.
>
> 3.   It, therefore, becomes necessary to consider our own tactical methods in relation to these forms of attack.
>
> 4.   In the first place, it is evident that the Germans cannot rely with certainty upon having their full complement of submarines and minelayers present in a fleet action, unless the battle is fought in waters selected by them and in the southern part of the North Sea. Aircraft, also, could only be brought into action in this locality.
>
> 5.   My object will therefore be to fight the fleet action in the Northern portion of the North Sea, which position is incidentally nearer our own bases, giving our wounded ships a chance of reaching them, whilst it ensures the final destruction or capture of enemy wounded vessels, and greatly handicaps a night destroyer attack before or after a fleet action. The Northern area is also favorable to a concentration of our cruisers and torpedo craft with the battlefleet; such a concentration on the part of the enemy being always possible, since he will choose a time for coming out when all his ships are coaled and ready in all respects to fight.
>
> 6.   Owing to the necessity that exists for keeping our cruisers at sea, it is probable that many will be short of coal when the opportunity for a fleet action arises and that they might be unable to move far to the Southward for this reason.

7. The presence of a large force of cruisers is most necessary, for observation and for screening the battlefleet, so that the latter may be maneuvered into any desired position behind the cruiser screen. This is a strong additional reason for fighting in the Northern area.

8. Secondly, it is necessary to consider what may be termed the tactics of the actual battlefield. The German submarines, if worked as is expected with the battlefleet, can be used in one of two ways:
   (a) With the cruisers, or possibly with destroyers.
   (b) With the battlefleet.

   In the first case the submarines would probably be led by the cruisers to a position favorable for attacking our battlefleet as it advanced to deploy, and in the second case they might be in a position in rear, or to the flank, of the enemy's battlefleet, which would move in the direction required to draw our own Fleet into contact with the submarines.

9. The first move at (a) should be defeated by our own cruisers, provided we have a sufficient number present as they should be able to force the enemy's cruisers to action at a speed which would interfere with submarine tactics.

   The cruisers must, however, have destroyers in company to assist in dealing with the submarines, and should be well in advance of the battle fleet; hence the necessity for numbers.

10. The second move at (b) can be countered by judicious handling of our battlefleet, but may, and probably will involve a refusal to comply with the enemy's tactics by moving in the invited direction If, for instance, the enemy's battlefleet were to turn away from an advancing Fleet, I should assume the intention was to lead us over mines and submarines and should decline to be so drawn. [underlined in original]

11. I desire particularly to draw the attention of Their Lordships to this point, since it may be deemed a refusal of battle, and, indeed, might possibly end in failure to bring the enemy to action as soon as is expected and hoped.

12. Such a result would be absolutely repugnant to the feelings of all British Naval Officers and men, but with new and

untried methods of warfare new tactics must be devised to meet them.

I feel that such tactics, if not understood, may bring odium upon me, but so long as I have the confidence of Their Lordships I intend to pursue what is, in my considered opinion, the proper course to defeat and annihilate the enemy's battlefleet, without regard to uninstructed opinion or criticism.

13. The situation is a difficult one. It is quite within the bounds of possibility that half our battlefleet might be disabled by under-water attack before the guns opened fire at all, if a false move is made, and I feel that I must constantly bear in mind the great probability of such an attack and be prepared tactically to prevent its success.

14. The safeguard against submarines will consist in moving the battlefleet at very high speed to a flank before deployment takes place or the gun action commences.

This will take us off the ground on which the enemy desires to fight, but it may, of course, result in his refusal to follow me.

If the battlefleets remain within sight of one another, though not near the original area, the limited submerged radius of action and speed of the submarines will prevent the submarines from following without coming to the surface, and I should feel that after an interval of high speed manoeuvring I could safely close.

15. The object of this letter is to place my views before Their Lordships, and to direct their attention to the alterations in pre-conceived ideas of battle tactics which are forced upon us by the anticipated appearance in a fleet action of submarines and minelayers.[13]

This attempt to commit the Admiralty irrevocably showed the C-in-C had no intention of becoming a scapegoat like the unfortunate Admiral Byng in 1757. Sturdee and Wilson did not think that a fleet action in the north of the North Sea was likely. Wilson, who had a more realistic view than Jellicoe of the problems that the Germans would face in operating U-boats with the High Sea Fleet, suggested that the prospect of a decisive battle could be considered as "only a dream." Nevertheless, Fisher insisted that the Admiralty's "confidence and approval" be conveyed both personally and in writing.[14] When Jellicoe received a formal response that Their Lordships approved "your views as stated . . . and desire to assure you of their full confidence in your stated conduct of the fleet in action," he knew what to do. A special messenger was dispatched to lodge a sealed envelope containing the original with the manager of the National Provincial Bank at Piccadilly.[15] If Jellicoe went down, he would take the Admiralty with him.

Jellicoe had been on his own journey of understanding. The Grand Fleet was a much larger formation than he (or, arguably, any other admiral) had ever commanded before, while tactical development since he had left the Home Fleets in 1912 had been at the same time frenetic but ambiguous in its results. The new open sea capabilities of submarines were one factor, as was the increased range of the torpedo. Integrating the destroyer flotillas into the main fleet had proved extremely difficult. The evolution of the Grand Fleet's battle orders reflected Jellicoe's struggle to develop effective control. Their general thrust was toward centralization and the tone markedly more cautious than the orders that he had issued to the Second Division two years before. But they were dealing with a much more complex and dangerous environment than one in which "the approach and the fleet speed will be slightly less than that obtained at 3/5th power by the slowest ship in the line."[16]

Jellicoe was almost certainly right to be so cautious on the information available in late 1914. He had to be prepared to encounter the High Sea Fleet at any time with his average strength, while the Germans had the potential to sortie with their maximum strength. The British did not know of the Germans' difficulties in finding safe sea room in which to train or of their machinery problems. Jellicoe also had legitimate concerns over the preparedness of his own ships, while the operational regime revealed many problems of propulsion and hull design. He needed time to train, and "long[ed]" for a secure base at Scapa.[17] Perhaps most of all, Jellicoe still had to master commanding the Grand Fleet himself.

Before Jellicoe could expect a reply, he was called for a conference with the prime minister in London on 2 November. This was Fisher's initiative to address fundamental strategic and operational matters.[18] Whatever long-term plans the new First Sea Lord was developing to intervene in the Baltic, he was determined to close the North Sea to the Germans, as well as control the flow of material and goods into Germany through the Netherlands and Scandinavia.[19] He also needed to manage Churchill's continuing desire for a forward operating base.

Jellicoe had strong views about the dangers of shipping being allowed into the areas where the Grand Fleet operated. The same problem worried the War Staff, which suspected that the Germans were disguising minelayers as neutral merchant ships. These were additional reasons for a radical stroke, one endorsed at the meeting. Fisher's motivation was to free the British to adopt an offensive minelaying campaign and seal the Germans within the Heligoland Bight. The North Sea was declared a "military area" with effect from 5 November, when "[A]ll ships passing through a line drawn from the northern point of the Hebrides, through the Faroe Islands to Iceland[, would] do so at their own peril."[20]

Apart from allotted channels along the British coast, and the passage between minefields for shipping to the Netherlands, the Admiralty assumed belligerent rights over the entire North Sea. Preparations were also made to change navigation markers in the major shipping routes. Special exceptions to use the northern passages were made for certain companies, but the reaction of the neutral countries would have been much more serious had the Admiralty's announcements of *Berlin*'s minefield across a major trans-Atlantic shipping lane, and *Strassburg*'s off Smith's Knoll, not been made almost simultaneously. They gave some credibility to British justifications, heavily larded with allegations as to German breaches of international law. Many were untrue, but the fields having been laid without warning (except for the declaration shortly after the outbreak) weakened the German position.

The difficulty, as Fisher was discovering, was that the tools did not exist to conduct a mining offensive. In the meantime, the First Sea Lord suggested to Jellicoe that he end his sweeps into the North Sea. The latter had a more realistic view of the threat to heavily escorted ships zigzagging at speed and did not alter his policy. On the other hand, Jellicoe approved of anything that allowed stronger enforcement of the blockade. He was well aware of the dissatisfaction among the blockade forces at the number of detained vessels being released after Foreign Office intervention. His immediate interest, however, was in the Admiralty discussions that followed. The various departments were directed to allocate him everything he wanted, including fifty trawlers and armed yachts, an extra flotilla of destroyers, hastened work on harbor defenses, armed boarding vessels, extra minesweepers and a seaplane carrier. As Fisher wrote the next day, "[M]ind like Oliver Twist you *'ask for more.'*"[21] There could be too much of this, as Oliver discovered: "Fisher wrote private letters to Jellicoe and he replied every day and they were a hell of a nuisance to me as soon as I got a new sloop to hunt submarines Jellicoe would want it, and Fisher would tell me to do it to keep Jellicoe in a good temper."[22]

Greater problems soon preoccupied the Admiralty. On 1 November a weak cruiser squadron was overwhelmed by von Spee's superbly trained force at Coronel off the west coast of South America. News of the disaster did not reach London until the fourth and full details not until the seventh. Fisher was furious, believing that the War Staff had violated almost every canon he held dear. The First Sea Lord immediately determined on a bold stroke, reflecting his original conception of battle cruisers as the oceanic nemesis of cruiser commerce raiders. He directed that *Invincible* and *Inflexible* be prepared for service in the South Atlantic, the likely route for von Spee's return to Germany. Ignoring every plea for time, the First Sea Lord ordered that the ships depart on 11 November and sail they did.

Fisher rapidly made changes in the Admiralty. He detested Sturdee, in earlier years associated with his arch-enemy, Lord Charles Beresford, and was convinced that the Chief of the War Staff bore responsibility for the disaster. Churchill knew that Sturdee could not remain, yet was unwilling to sack him, perhaps because the latter had made at least one attempt to divert a battle cruiser to join operations against von Spee, but was overruled. Since the ship concerned was sent back to the Dardanelles, the First Lord may have had an uneasy conscience.[23] Fisher compromised, declaring that, since Sturdee had caused the mess, he should sort it out. Oliver was appointed Chief of the War Staff as an acting vice admiral, while Sturdee was dispatched to deal with von Spee.

Oliver was in some ways a good selection. While prone to overcentralize, he was skilled in managing both Churchill and Fisher. Oliver could out-argue neither, but developed the technique of listening quietly and then doing as he thought best. He was rarely challenged, perhaps because a further complication was introduced by Admiral of the Fleet Sir Arthur Wilson, who joined the Admiralty as an unpaid assistant. Churchill had offered Wilson Sturdee's job, but the old admiral refused, ostensibly because he preferred not to take sides between Fisher and the First Lord. In reality, he provided a mobile majority. As Oliver later observed, with only some exaggeration, "[T]wo out of the 3 were always violently opposed to the plan of the third under discussion."[24]

Leveson, Director of the Operations Division, was also a marked man. He took loyally Oliver's going over his head, but Fisher mistrusted him for his connections with Beresford and Sir William May, another *bête noire*. Leveson was sent to join the Grand Fleet in January and knew perfectly well who was really responsible for "turning him out and refusing him any reason for summary eviction."[25] In the months ahead the combination of Churchill, Fisher, and Wilson, supported by Oliver, nicknamed the Cabal, effectively constituted the naval staff, largely independent of outside advice. The other Sea Lords were busy with their administrative and technical duties and it would have been a brave junior officer who crossed swords with Churchill or either of the admirals of the fleet.

The South Atlantic provided for, Fisher turned to the possibility that von Spee might pass through the newly opened Panama Canal, join the light cruiser *Karlsruhe*, still believed to be at large (her loss by internal explosion was not discovered until well into 1915), and harass Atlantic shipping. Acting on his long-held view that "one armadillo can lick up millions of ants, and the bigger the ant the more placid the digestive smile," Fisher ordered *Princess Royal* to the western Atlantic.[26] This strained relations with Jellicoe. The C-in-C took advantage of a gale to delay *Princess Royal*'s departure and signaled, "Is *Princess Royal* to go? . . . Strongly urge *New Zealand* instead." This was too much for Fisher in his present mood and he replied, "*Princess Royal* should have proceeded at once on Admiralty orders." Jellicoe was forced to comply, but could not remain silent and replied, "I am quite certain that the Germans, if they send battle cruisers into the Atlantic Ocean, will not send one, but all." Jellicoe had reason to feel dismayed by Fisher's dictatorial behavior, particularly, as he wrote to the First Sea Lord, "In your letter of 7/11 you say: I'm sure you'll AT ONCE telegraph to me personally in cypher *if you want anything or wish anything altered or doubt the wisdom of any orders you get* [emphasis in original]."[27] The Admiralty asserted on 13 November that "since war began you have gained two Dreadnoughts on balance, and will have by 20th, 27 superior units to 20," but the position was not nearly so rosy. Jellicoe had little knowledge of the German situation, but his "27 superior units" included, as he signaled, "three ships, two of which have never fired a gun, and the third is only partially trained."

The super-dreadnoughts were still having condenser trouble and the ex-Turkish *Agincourt* was an odd number of dubious value, whose poor bunker layout limited her operational radius. *Benbow* and *Emperor of India* had been commissioned for a matter of weeks, while *Erin* (a 13.5-inch gun unit much more aligned to Royal Navy practice than *Agincourt*) was also not yet worked up. The battle line was thus only just superior to that of the High Sea Fleet. Furthermore, as Jellicoe pointed out, the recent detachment of the Third Battle Squadron to reinforce the Channel Fleet had been agreed on the understanding that *King Edward VIIs* would be able to rejoin the Grand Fleet when necessary. Jellicoe did not believe this could be achieved, but had thought he was strong enough to bear the loss. It was not so now. The situation was especially critical for the battle cruisers. The detachments reduced Beatty's ships to three. Although Beatty's three 13.5-inch gunned ships and *New Zealand* could be considered superior, if barely so, to Hipper's four battle cruisers—which now included the newly completed *Derfflinger* (thought to carry 35-cm guns)—removal of the efficient *Princess Royal* would make a great difference. To compensate, Fisher ordered the brand new *Tiger* to cut short her practice firings and join the First Battle Cruiser Squadron posthaste. *Tiger* would be of little value until she was worked up, but Fisher comforted himself that her presence would at least balance that of *Blücher*. Beatty did not agree and complained to Fisher, "*Tiger* is not yet fit to fight. Three out of four of her dynamoes are out of action . . . and her training is impeded by bad weather. . . . [A]t present she is quite unprepared."[28]

This harsh judgment was confirmed by the ship's officers. Captain Pelly commented, "We had had only nine days, during which my officers had worked their hardest to train this [largely untrained] ship's company. . . . Nine days and we were 'Ready for Action'??"[29] One officer wrote later, "We commissioned in a really nasty state and rushed through all our trials in a hopeless way, finally joining up with the Grand Fleet exhausted and inefficient."[30] Jellicoe pointed out, "[S]he would simply be a present for the Germans."[31] Churchill's later complaint, that Jellicoe "always credited them [the Germans] with several ships more than we now know they had, or were then likely to have," perhaps true later, was unfair now.[32] What justifiably annoyed Jellicoe was that "*Princess Royal*'s coal expenditure for the distance is not far from *double* that of *New Zealand*."[33] Fisher had to concede that the older ship was better suited to such a deployment: "Certainly I would have sent *New Zealand* had I known all you tell me. . . . It won't happen again. Just then I was sore pressed."[34]

The Admiralty tried to compensate. *Indomitable* was recalled from the Mediterranean, although it would be weeks before she could join. This was followed by the recall of *Warrior* and *Black Prince,* two of the most modern armored cruisers also in the Mediterranean. They would be useful, but could not make up for the battle cruisers. The Third Battle Squadron was moved again. The Admiralty proposed that the "Wobbly Eight" go to Rosyth, covering the coast southward. Jellicoe demurred, complaining that the squadron would be too far away from the main fleet to allow proper support by destroyers. He suggested Cromarty, base of the Fourth Destroyer Flotilla and only a hundred miles from Scapa. Churchill and Fisher overruled him and the ships were sent to Rosyth. They telegraphed, "The coast has been so denuded of destroyers for the sake of strengthening the force with you . . . that there is only a skeleton force of patrol vessels available . . . we are reluctantly compelled to decide on the *King Edwards* and the 3rd Cruiser Squadron going to Rosyth and you should detach half a flotilla of the 71 destroyers at Scapa Flow, to act with them."

The tone of the message appeared sterner than it was, since the following day the Admiralty ordered a half-flotilla home from the Mediterranean "as soon as possible." Nevertheless, for all the compensation, at this point the Grand Fleet was at its weakest in relation to its opponent. It will be seen what use the Imperial German Navy made of this opportunity.

In November the War Office became preoccupied with the threat of invasion. This represented at least in part reversal of the army's earlier priority of France, which had seen it urge the dispatch of divisions that Cabinet was unwilling to commit. New respect for the mobility and efficiency of the German army may have combined with realization of the implications of the loss of the Belgian ports. The Admiralty did not believe invasion possible because of the difficulties involved in transporting 250,000 troops (the number the Imperial General Staff thought the Germans could have available), their equipment, and supplies, even apart from the fact that seasoned British divisions could return from France. It was true that the naval arrangements were insufficient to stop a surprise descent by a smaller force. Coastal submarines had once seemed the answer, but, as Keyes reported, he "had an insufficient force of submarines to meet invasion in every possible locality."[35] Nor were the depleted destroyer patrols in any better position, while Burney reported that he could not get the Channel Fleet to the east coast inside twenty-four hours, the time needed to achieve a landing uninterrupted.

Jellicoe also reminded the Admiralty that it was impossible to keep a sustained watch on the Germans because of the dangers that surface scouts off their coast faced from U-boats. He proposed that an "anti-invasion" force be created on land, with pre-dreadnoughts stationed at each of the major ports. He further suggested that preparations be made to destroy the facilities at any port under threat, to prevent the Germans gaining control of an all-weather disembarkation point. Fisher and Wilson pointed out, however, that demolitions could be triggered by over-zealous personnel were the Germans to attempt even a simple bombardment. The problem was partially solved by the movement of the Third Battle Squadron to Rosyth, but the defenses on the east coast were reinforced by additional *Majestic*-class battleships.

The invasion threat was a chimera. The Germans might have been able to land two or three divisions, but no more, in a surprise descent, but they would have been devoid of artillery or cavalry support. Considerable material damage could have been caused in Britain, but the German losses would have been terrible, since it is unlikely that a single transport or warship of the covering force would have escaped the combination of the Grand Fleet coming south and the Channel Fleet and Harwich Force moving north. In any case, the Germans never seriously considered the possibility. Events in the Baltic showed they had made no preparations for amphibious work before August 1914. The German army had little enthusiasm for combined operations at this stage of the war, while such an attempt would have inevitably forced a showdown between the High Sea Fleet and the British forces.

At the start of November the British added a priceless intelligence weapon to their armory. With little fanfare, the Admiralty had obtained copies of two out of three of the major German codes and shortly secured the third. The merchant ship, U-boat, small ship, and zeppelin code—*Handelsverkehrbuch* (HVB)—was captured on 9 August when the Royal Australian Navy took possession of a German steamer. Already being exploited by the Australians in the hunt for von Spee in the Pacific, copies arrived in London in late October. In the same month, the cruiser *Theseus* returned to Scapa Flow carrying the major unit code, the SKM, which the Russians made available after capturing the wrecked cruiser *Magdeburg*. Russian officers accompanied the material and it is likely that they explained their own progress with signals intelligence. The third and final code, *Verkehrsbuch* (VB), came into the Admiralty in November. In what was described as "the miraculous draught of fishes," a trawler working the Broad Fourteens, scene of the torpedo boats' sinking on 17 October, brought up a chest containing cypher material.[36] This included VB, the code employed between Germany and its embassies and consulates, as well as by warships in foreign waters. Consequently, the British possessed the key to all levels of German maritime radio communications. For North Sea operations, HVB was the most significant capture. In Patrick Beesly's words, "[A] mass of seemingly routine and unimportant messages disclosed information of great value." "[I]t was often the HVB signals which gave warning of the sorties of the Hoch See Flotte."[37]

The Germans were slow to realize the vulnerability of their system, which employed wireless for routine fleet administration. With an extremely well-organized communications network, the convenience of radio when ships were in dispersed anchorages was undeniable. Yet it was exposed not only to decryption, but also to traffic analysis and direction finding. As the British noted, the Germans consistently underestimated the range of their local low-power transmissions and thus the likelihood of their being monitored.[38] The British practice of flagships and depot ships lying at buoys with specially provided telegraph and (later) telephone lines was much more secure, particularly since visual means or hand messages were used to convey instructions to other ships. Given the weaknesses of British cyphers, it was well for the Royal Navy that the Germans were slower to begin systematic analysis of radio signals and that British use of wireless overall was relatively much less.

The germ of an organization already existed. Oliver had initially enlisted the services of the Director of Naval Education, Sir Alfred Ewing, to conduct counterintelligence work against suspected spies thought to be dispatching encoded information to Germany, as well as to examine some of the messages that the Germans were sending overseas through their high-power transmitters. Ewing recruited academics fluent in German and capable of dealing with the mathematics involved. He soon enlisted a wealth of talent. If the members of what was designated Room 40 lacked direct experience of cyphers and cryptography, they would soon make up for it by hard work.

The new body had a serious fault at the outset. Room 40 was not given enough experienced naval personnel to assess the content of deciphered messages. This was a crippling defect, for the means by which information is obtained from signals analysis is to build up such a comprehensive knowledge of the enemy's procedures and routines that any transmission out of the ordinary becomes immediately apparent. This naturally calls for a body of experts with a deep knowledge of naval operations. Room 40 would have matured much more quickly if more regular naval personnel had been brought in from the start. That they were not was primarily the fault of Oliver, who had a (not wholly unjustified) mania for secrecy and insisted that the War Group be the sole recipient of all deciphered material. When he became Chief of the War Staff, Oliver continued to dominate Room 40 and excluded the Naval Intelligence Division almost completely. The DNI should have been Room 40's controller, but this did not happen until 1917.

Since Churchill and Fisher were occupied with other matters, Oliver and Wilson were at first almost the only analysts. The two could not possibly cope with the mass of deciphered material and inevitably made mistakes. In his own insistence on security, Churchill compounded the error in directives of 8 and 29 November by opening up the decrypts only to the War Group, the Director of Operations, and the DNI. As for officers outside the Admiralty, only Jellicoe and Madden,

Beatty, Keyes, Tyrwhitt, and Hood were aware of Room 40's activities and they were permitted access to only such material as the Admiralty saw fit. Seeing the potential tactical advantage of being able to decipher the High Sea Fleet's transmissions at sea, Jellicoe asked for a copy of the SKM. Apparently, after Oliver's intervention, this was refused.

The concern for secrecy was understandable, but as early as October 1914 it was apparently common knowledge in the Grand Fleet that *Theseus* had brought home "confidential books and papers" from *Magdeburg*.[39] Sub Lieutenant Philip Bowyer-Smith noted in his diary, "We have their code—the Russians collared it some time ago from a ship that went ashore and of course gave it to us."[40] An intelligence coup would have been confirmed by the wealth of translated documents on German tactics and procedures issued to the fleet in the following months.[41] The appointment of Commander H. W. W. Hope as liaison officer was a step in the right direction, but Oliver's peculiar organization limited his utility as just one man, although his knowledge of German procedures was soon formidable.[42] Hope himself was not allowed to deal directly with Room 40 until Fisher intervened personally. This had not helped Hope with his early assessments, which meant that Oliver "got prejudiced . . . both against my work and myself; it took a long time to break down this prejudice."[43] Matters improved when Fleet Paymaster Rotter, who should have been involved from the start, was allowed access.

November in the Channel was a month of largely inconclusive activity. The first signals deciphered were of little operational value but, on 5 November Room 40 broke several messages announcing the departure of U-boats to attack the forces off the Belgian coast. The German Fleet Command had sent *U29* and *U12* to deal with Hood's bombardment units, which were continuing to be a thorn in the side of the German armies on the coast. Hood was ordered to withdraw all but the smallest gun-vessels to form an anti-invasion flotilla, while the now operational *Revenge* remained at Dover as a reserve for the "last eventuality" on the Belgian coast. Transport sailings across the Channel were hastily reorganized and ships forbidden to sail except at night and, if possible, under protection. The British escort forces still in the area were, however, not strong, amounting only to Hood's ships, as well as some elderly torpedo gunboats and six destroyers out of Portsmouth. Much of the work had to be done by French forces.

Tyrwhitt ordered *Fearless* and a half-flotilla to sail in an attempt to intercept the submarines as they passed down the Dutch coast. He sent *Undaunted, Aurora,* and seven destroyers out to reinforce them two days later. Although the British ships must have come very close to the U-boats, no one saw anything as heavy fog covered the area. Commodore (T) joined *Fearless'* half-flotilla to continue the patrol while he sent the other light cruisers and destroyers back to Harwich. On 9 November Tyrwhitt received a message that delighted him. Room 40 had interpreted a German signal to read that a torpedo boat flotilla would be patrolling off the Gabbard for thirty-six hours from the evening of 10 November. Units rushed to the area but, after three days' wait in steadily worsening weather, had seen nothing. The signal group that represented "Heligoland" in a routine order to the patrol flotilla at the island had been misread as "Gabbard." The frequency of this sort of mistake would lessen as Room 40's personnel became used to German procedures, but it did not raise their credibility in the eyes of either Tyrwhitt or the War Staff.

The two U-boats had limited success, only *U12* claiming a victim when she sank *Niger* in the Downs on 11 November. The torpedo gunboat was employed on examination duties but, her machinery too unreliable for continuous patrolling, spent most of the time riding at anchor with steam up. It was thus that *U12* found her. The submarine fired a single torpedo from two thousand yards. *Niger*'s captain saw its track and attempted to pivot the ship around her anchor, but to no avail. The torpedo struck amidships, sinking the old gunboat within twenty minutes. The really ominous note, had the British realized it, was not *U12*'s destruction of *Niger*, but the submarine's stand-off in Zeebrugge before she returned to Germany.

Further submarine scares plagued Jellicoe for the next few weeks, disrupting exercise programs, burdening already overworked destroyers, and once more throwing doubt on the security of the bases. The scares were largely imaginary. Typical of this sort of sighting was one that roused Keyes out to defend the Nore: "At daylight I motored round the coast interviewing all the people who claimed to have seen submarines. Five more were sighted by natives while I was in the neighborhood; one had been seen to chase, at a speed of quite 20 knots, one of the destroyers which had been seen to hunt for the enemy! The supposed submarines were flights of wild geese or other wild fowl skimming the surface. A wild goose chase indeed!"[44]

The civilians were not alone. "Submarinitis" still reigned in the fleet, although observers were beginning to exercise more discrimination. After a sighting by *Ajax* off the Butt of Lewis, at which the captain of *Orion* admitted "[W]e all fled," order was restored when *King George V* reported that her officers had seen "some black fish" in the same place.[45] The German Fleet Command had sent only *U22*, which escaped patrols off Scapa. Ironically, with Loch Ewe's use now known to the Germans, *U22* was ordered to examine the area and went there, despite sighting cruisers operating around the Flow. On 20 November light nets were laid at the entrances to Scapa and twenty trawlers arrived to take over harbor defense duties. With this protection, Jellicoe could at last begin to give his heavy ships time to do essential maintenance and grant engineering staff some rest. This immediately proved a benefit, as machinery troubles steadily reduced. The new enemy, at sea and in Scapa Flow's exposed anchorage, would be the weather. Winter was coming.

The C-in-C continued to be preoccupied with the weakness of the Grand Fleet. He had no high opinion of British security and feared the absence of the three battle cruisers would become known to the Germans. If the time was ever right for the High Sea Fleet to emerge, it was now. Within a few months the battle cruisers would have returned, the new battleships worked up to full efficiency, and the first of the 15-inch gun units joined. Within a year the Grand Fleet's battle line would be overwhelming, but, for the rest of 1914, Jellicoe knew that the outcome would be doubtful, particularly if it took place on German terms. In fact, Jellicoe did not yet need to worry about the battle cruisers' absence. The general roundup of known spies at the beginning of the war had largely destroyed the German network.[46]

The Admiralty was also apprehensive. Early on 17 November Room 40 deciphered a signal directing three half-flotillas of torpedo boats to assemble off Heligoland the next day. This was actually a signal ordering a heavier patrol, as Hipper was worried about a repetition of the 28 August action, but the Admiralty warned Jellicoe and placed the Channel Fleet and the vessels assigned to coastal defense on immediate notice for sea. Jellicoe sent Beatty and all the cruiser squadrons to patrol off the Shetlands, while the battleships prepared to sail. Oliver and others at the Admiralty believed from the intercepted traffic that the Germans would strike south, while Jellicoe remained concerned by the possibility that German battle cruisers might break out into the North Atlantic. Tyrwhitt was ordered to take *Aurora* and *Undaunted* to scout the Bight, and obeyed with alacrity. The two ships spent several hours in the area, but saw nothing, not even patrolling German torpedo boats.

It had been a false alarm, but the Admiralty's attention now turned to a different approach. Elements within the War Staff argued that, while it was unwise for the Grand Fleet to accept battle in all circumstances, a properly set trap, with a lure sufficient to entice out the German battle squadrons could ensure that the British fought at maximum advantage. The factor that ensured Jellicoe's cooperation was that submarine activity in the north and in the Channel seemed to indicate that there would be few U-boats in the North Sea over the next few days. Thus, the risk would be minimal for a venture south.

The "bait" would be a second attack on the zeppelin sheds. Jellicoe had not been impressed by the initial effort and did not believe that the aircraft were yet reliable enough to be used in such a way, but the Admiralty had intelligence that German ships were assembling in the Jade and the C-in-C was overruled. Tyrwhitt was to lead a coat-trailing operation, escorting the carriers *Engadine* and *Riviera*. Their seaplanes would be launched against Cuxhaven while Tyrwhitt's ships made their presence known. Jellicoe would bring his units within 110 miles of Heligoland, while, forty miles nearer, Beatty lay with his battle cruisers. In close support, only forty miles from the island, would be the Second Cruiser Squadron and two light cruisers.

The Admiralty decided this operation could be combined with one farther south. The threat of submarines using Zeebrugge was of deep concern because of the vulnerability of the transport lines across the Channel. The difficulty was that the Germans had already created strong defenses and any attempt to block the entrance would be difficult and costly. A bombardment by heavy ships seemed the only alternative. Four *Duncan*-class battleships were now based at Dover as an anti-invasion force. Their commander, Rear Admiral Stuart Nicholson, was ordered to take two, together with a half-flotilla of the Harwich Force and eight minesweepers, to attack Zeebrugge. Spotting of the fall of shot was to be provided by two newly commissioned airships, *Astra Torres* and *Parseval*. The principal object was to destroy the locks to the inner harbors, preventing their use.

The bombardment took place on 23 November. Despite considerable difficulties with minesweeping, several submarine warnings and the failure of the airships to fly due to weather, *Russell* and *Exmouth* fired more than four hundred rounds before Nicholson broke off the action. The attack had little effect; the locks and pumping stations remained largely unhurt, despite lurid press reports in the Netherlands of great destruction and "submarines reduced to scrap iron."[47] The destroyers made valiant efforts to spot for the battleships, but were less than successful. There were obvious problems in tackling shore installations with flat trajectory naval guns and shells containing little high explosive; the massive works at Zeebrugge were not ideal targets. Nicholson recommended against any further operations.

Farther north the attack on Cuxhaven proved equally abortive. Tyrwhitt left Harwich at 0500 on 23 November, having been delayed by the need to complete repairs to *Arethusa*. With his flagship were *Engadine* and *Riviera,* two more light cruisers, and eight *L*-class destroyers. The weather was easing when the force sailed and Tyrwhitt was confident that the seaplanes would be able to make the attack. However, four hours out he received a signal ordering the carriers back to harbor. Room 40 had deciphered messages indicating that a force of German armored cruisers would be directly in the path of the British sortie. This obviously made the seaplane raid impossible, although Tyrwhitt was "very disappointed as the morning was perfect."[48] In reality, it was *Derfflinger* completing her work-up with a small escort, but the Admiralty feared that the entire First Scouting Group might be out. Tyrwhitt sent the carriers back with his destroyers, keeping only the light cruisers. In the early morning darkness, however, *Lennox* became detached from her sisters and wound up back with Tyrwhitt, "like a lost pup looking for companionship."[49] Jellicoe, informed of the abandonment of the seaplane attack, now altered his plans. Tyrwhitt was ordered to reconnoiter within fifteen miles of Heligoland. If he made contact with any German ships, he was to attempt to lure them toward the Second Cruiser Squadron, which in turn would draw them onto the battle cruisers.

The venture into the Bight began early on 24 November, preceded by confusion on the lines of 28 August. Tyrwhitt discovered at 0715 that he had been chasing the two light cruisers attached to the Second Cruiser Squadron for half an hour, mistaking them for *Strassburg*-class ships. He then spent the morning in company with Gough Calthorpe's squadron, but saw nothing apart from a few torpedo boats and a submarine lying under the guns of Heligoland. As Commodore (T) wrote, "[W]e reconnoitred Heligoland [and the garrison] got very excited. They fired a lot of stuff . . . at us but no one of them came within miles of us. . . . We pirouetted about for an hour admiring the view. . . . [A]s no one appeared anxious to come out after us I retired."[50]

The German Fleet Command knew from radio interceptions that the British were out in force, but von Ingenohl still feared a submarine attack on his ships. He directed that the torpedo boat flotillas be reinforced, but ordered them to keep well clear of the enemy. The lone submarine, *U5,* could not get into an attack position. Two seaplanes and an airship were ordered out to investigate, but only one came near the British ships. This aircraft dropped five hand bombs on *Liverpool.* Tyrwhitt commented, "[T]hey missed. I wish she had come my way, as I was dying to try my aerial guns, but she was never in range."[51] The aircraft was identified as German only after she attacked and *Liverpool* was caught by surprise, her three-pounder antiaircraft gun secured and the crew fallen out on the captain's direction. This left her gunnery officer to comment that the bombs "made a grey smoke of some size, about a 30' diameter. And that's how I feel."[52] The delay in identification was partly due to a warning not to confuse British with German aircraft. This incident indicated the importance of ensuring situational awareness in subordinate formations. Confirmation that none of the seaplane carriers would conduct flight operations would have made it clear that any aircraft in the Bight was hostile, whether or not it "had the appearance of a Sopwith biplane."[53]

As the British withdrew, there was a scare that the German torpedo boats might come out after them. Von Ingenohl had been considering a sortie by light craft, but cancelled it when news came through that the cruisers had withdrawn. He was still ignorant of the Grand Fleet's presence only 110 miles away. By 25 November Tyrwhitt was back in harbor and "furious" at the Admiralty's decision: "They waited until I was well in the danger zone and then told me by wireless that a large force was patrolling in the area I was going to operate in. I had then to do a sort of disappearing trick with about half my force without making signals, etc.—a very difficult operation on a pitch-black night."[54]

Tyrwhitt had a point, although being able to achieve such a "trick" suggested improving standards in night operations, at least within the Harwich Force. Room 40 had again made a mistake in deciphering, and yet again this resulted in considerable disruption. The key question was whether matters should have been left to the judgment of the commander on the spot. The seaplane carriers were certainly vulnerable, but there was a strong argument that some risk had to be accepted if the Germans were ever to be drawn out.

When the Grand Fleet returned to Scapa Flow on 27 November, it was greeted with the welcome news that *U18* had been sunk and her crew captured. What gave Jellicoe pause was that she had reached the entrance to the Flow, to find, to the crew's chagrin, "The nest was empty!"[55] *U18*'s captain, Heinz von Hennig, would have attempted to penetrate the net defenses, which he thought were too light and shallow to be effective, had there been worthwhile targets.[56] *U18* achieved much in managing the navigational challenges for as long as she did. She was rammed by the destroyer *Garry*, which bent her periscope, ran aground in Hoxa Sound but got off, was rammed again by a trawler, and suffered a series of increasingly serious defects. It was only after the submarine almost broke in half on the Pentland Skerries that her captain finally came to the surface and scuttled her.

The attempt was part of an effort involving five submarines against the Shetlands and Scapa Flow. *U16* entered Lerwick harbor undetected, but found no warships. The other boats sighted patrolling forces, but conducted no attacks and, although they were convinced that the Grand Fleet was operating from Scapa Flow, made no contact with the main body. Battered and exhausted by the increasingly poor weather and heavy seas, all took the direct line between the Orkneys and the Ems River for their return. They missed the Grand Fleet, which Jellicoe wisely kept to the eastern side of the North Sea, hugging the Norwegian coast until the battle squadrons turned west.

The last days of November marked a lull in operations, but two unfortunate incidents occurred. *D2,* commanded by Lieutenant Commander C. G. W. Head, was one of two submarines ordered into Heligoland Bight on 26 November to investigate German activity. The other boat, *E15,* found nothing and withdrew in the teeth of a rising gale. *D2* disappeared. The British guessed that she had been sunk in Heligoland Bight, but the Germans have no record of any encounter. In these circumstances, the postwar judgment that the submarine struck a drifting mine is probably correct. *D2* was the first of the Overseas Flotilla to be sunk without out trace.

Another, heavier loss had already been suffered. The Channel Fleet was lying at its moorings at Sheerness on 26 November when the pre-dreadnought *Bulwark* blew up. Yeoman of Signals Charles Luff, in *Prince of Wales,* was looking at *Bulwark* when he "suddenly saw a bright golden flame with white and black smoke just before the after turret—after flame appeared, he heard a long rumbling noise." Boy First Class Illman on *Prince of Wales'* forecastle reported that *Bulwark*, "seemed to heave amidships about half way along the waist, [her] stern coming out of [the] water, and smoke and debris flying up." When the smoke cleared, Luff declared, the ship "had completely disappeared."[57]

Despite a desperate search, there were only a dozen badly injured survivors out of a crew of 750. Yet again, a note of hysteria sounded as personnel, by now "in a fine set of nerves," reacted to the disaster.[58] John Price, *Agamemnon*'s boatswain, was convinced that he had encountered a periscope in his cutter, sighting it not once, but three times.[59] He was initially supported in his assertions by his crew, but on dubious grounds: "[M]y mate 'e saw it and I saw the ripple myself, but blest if she hadn't dived when I looked round."[60] Others were more restrained: "[M]ost of us were greatly relieved to find that it was only a floating spar."[61]

The board of inquiry discovered that the temperature in the ammunition passages in a sister ship, *London,* often rose to a much as "142 degrees in the conditions then obtaining."[62] Heat from adjacent boiler rooms and unprotected cordite inside a shut-down ship were a lethal combination, and this seemed sufficient explanation for the loss. Despite hasty revision of ammunition arrangements, the Royal Navy was to be plagued by a succession of such disasters, notably the loss of the armored cruiser *Natal* in 1915 and the battleship *Vanguard* in 1917. A lively exchange also followed with the local coroner, who sought testimony. The Admiralty had to explain the need for operational security. The coroner made an important point, however, that casualties from *Bulwark* lacked identification and that better arrangements were needed for identity tags. The loss meant little on the material scale, since the Fifth Battle Squadron to which she belonged still had eleven units.

The British cruiser forces were undergoing reorganization. Destruction of *Emden* and the blockade of *Königsberg* in the Rufiji River meant that the need for extensive patrols in the Indian Ocean had ended. The Admiralty was also hopeful that von Spee would be eliminated before very long. It was not to be disappointed and, with the removal of the other raiders, this meant that the cruisers on foreign stations could return home. The powerful armored cruiser *Minotaur* had already been ordered back from the Far East. The Grand Fleet was cheered on 26 November by the arrival of *Warrior* and *Black Prince.* They and the older *Leviathan* were formed into the First Cruiser Squadron and Rear Admiral Moore, whose previous command had been reduced to one ship by *Invincible* and *Inflexible*'s departure, transferred to *Leviathan* to lead them.

The elderly cruisers of the northern patrol were to be paid off. Antiquated to begin with, they suffered greatly as the weather worsened and they faced conditions for which they had not been designed. Matters came to a head in what was known as the great gale of 11 November. Rear Admiral de Chair said of his flagship, *Crescent,* that "we really did not think the old ship would weather it."[63] *Crescent*'s fore-bridge was smashed and a deck house and ventilating cowls carried away, as were her boats, forecastle breakwater, and guardrails. The ship lost internal lighting and power. So fierce was the storm that, despite steaming head to sea and wind at eight knots, *Crescent* was rolling 30 degrees either way and was pushed to leeward (effectively backwards) at a knot. It was indeed a "sensational night."[64] The changed nature of operations by comparison with peacetime is implicit in de Chair's associated comment that it was "quite the most appalling gale I ever experienced in all my years at sea."[65] His Majesty's Ships had rarely operated so far north at this time of year and even admirals had much to learn about the effects of weather.

The Tenth Cruiser Squadron could not continue this way. De Chair had already sent three ships south to refit and he informed Jellicoe and the Admiralty that similar treatment was needed for the remainder. Conversely, the handful of armed merchant cruisers already in commission had proved much better able to keep the seas in heavy weather. A new patrol system was approved, consisting of twenty-four armed merchant cruisers, supplemented by slightly smaller and slower boarding vessels, manned by a combination of the crews of the *Edgars* and reservists. Withdrawal of the old cruisers began on 20 November. De Chair and many of *Crescent*'s crew transferred to *Alsatian,* which became the new flagship of the patrol. The damage to the old cruisers was part of a wider issue. The ability of even the most modern ships to cope with rough seas had proved less than ideal. Beatty noted of the huge and weatherly *Lion,* "[T]he decks leak like a sieve and it's like living under a perpetual shower bath." Personnel were simply not used to driving ships into heavy weather and did not like the results.[66]

On 5 December Tyrwhitt was informed that he was to be advanced from commodore second class to commodore first class. The appointment seemed reasonable on the surface, since Tyrwhitt's force was expanding all the time. It meant that he would no longer have to command his own ship, which freed Tyrwhitt from the minutiae of running a light cruiser in favor of his responsibilities to the Harwich Force as a whole. But the matter was not quite so simple. Lord Fisher probably meant the appointment as much as a slight on Keyes. While the latter always thought that Fisher's animus was largely due to confusion with Fleet Paymaster J. A. Keys, once Beresford's secretary and firmly in the anti-Fisher camp, Fisher believed that the submarine service had stagnated since 1910 and that it was largely the fault of the supervising captains and commodores. Keyes was a marked man. Matters were not improved by early exchanges between Fisher and Keyes over new construction, and the First Sea Lord began his campaign by importing Captain S. S. Hall, an old associate in submarine development, to take over the material side. He had intended more than this, but Churchill would not allow Keyes' removal. The First Lord apparently managed to calm Fisher down because, on 8 November, the latter wrote to Keyes, saying, "*On no* account imagine that I have any designs on you. If I had any such designs you would certainly have been told—but, like many other things, I have not yet mastered on what basis our submarines harm the enemy more than ourselves!"[67]

Keyes responded enthusiastically, but by the end of November Fisher was again intent on Keyes' removal. It was thus that Tyrwhitt's new appointment came as a heavy blow. Keyes was four years senior to Tyrwhitt as a captain, but remained a commodore second class. Although Keyes would reach flag rank much earlier, it was an obvious slight and could imply only that the Admiralty considered Tyrwhitt to be in charge of all operations from Harwich. Their relationship suffered accordingly. They had an argument and Tyrwhitt was "horribly hurt at [Keyes'] attitude."[68] It was several days before things were patched up. Tyrwhitt took some time to get used to not being in command of his own ship, and would have preferred to remain "Second Class" rather than "some sort of freak."[69] The benefit, however, was that his position as Commodore (T) was much stronger, a commodore first class being in all but name a rear admiral.

12

THE SCARBOROUGH RAID

THE START OF DECEMBER WAS QUIET. FOR THE BRITISH, THERE WERE THE now regular submarine scares, but work on protecting the anchorages proceeded steadily. New appointments and the whirlwind entry of Lord Fisher galvanized activity, and Jellicoe now thought that the Grand Fleet would have enough secure harbors before the end of the year, which would ease the strain of having no certainty of safety in port.

Despite this prospect, Jellicoe still believed that the situation was very dangerous. He was convinced that Germans had to be aware of the absence of at least *Invincible* and *Inflexible* and would be planning a sortie. He pinpointed 8 December as the most likely date for a raid, when there would be no moon and favorable tides. The C-in-C proposed sending the battle cruisers south to cut off the German retreat, while the Grand Fleet operated to the north. The Admiralty, gaining increasing confidence in Room 40, assessed there were no signs of German activity and that it was unnecessary to risk the battle cruisers. Jellicoe took the hint and cancelled the operation.

The Germans were indeed planning another attack, but issues of strategy and of personality were proving difficult to resolve. Following the Yarmouth raid, there were increasing concerns that the *Kleinkrieg* was not enough. With von Spee at large and the oceanic war retaining promise, Hipper even took up a proposal by one of his captains for the longer-range battle cruisers to attack British shipping in the Atlantic. The problem was endurance. The battle cruisers could be modified to carry additional coal supplies, but this would not be enough. Hipper suggested that resupply could be managed by a combination of anchorages in Iceland, using colliers that had run the blockade, and a descent on an Allied port. There were huge risks, not least of which was the battle cruisers' engineering reliability, but this was at least an attempt to break free of the impasse.[1]

The proposal did not sit well with either von Ingenohl or von Pohl, and Hipper's scheme was shelved. Thinking within both the Fleet Command and Admiralstab was focused on the emerging potential of the U-boats. German attitudes to the blockade were hardening. While global trade was reviving and the European neutrals provided many alternative avenues for raw materials and goods from the United States in particular, Britain's long-term position still appeared stronger than Germany's. The U-boat could provide a way of striking at Britain's supply lines while the High Sea Fleet remained in being.[2]

There were other forces at work. Von Tirpitz made a determined effort to push Ingenohl aside and install von Pohl as his replacement. Von Müller saw this for what it was, a ploy by von Tirpitz to take charge of naval operations, and refused to recommend any change to the kaiser. Von Müller took soundings in the fleet that confirmed that von Ingenohl was still considered the best man for the job—he had been preferred to von Pohl in 1913 at least partly because of the squadron com-manders' collective view, as well as the previous C-in-C (von Holtzendorff).[3] Von Tirpitz's political position was not strong enough to override von Müller. The fall of Tsingtau in China to an Anglo-Japanese siege temporarily discredited him, as he had long championed the colony's development, despite doubts as to its ability to survive attack. Furthermore, as von Müller and others were well aware, he had endorsed the *Kleinkrieg* strategy at the outbreak. Nevertheless, it was clear that the grand admiral would resume his personal offensive as soon as the opportunity offered. Matters within the naval command were not improved by the increasing divergence in thinking between von Pohl, isolated at GHQ, and Behncke and the Berlin Admiralstab. Von Müller himself did not help. His methods encouraged the more outspoken and well-connected subordinate commanders to take part in the intrigues, which did little for their loyalty.

Hipper became interested in attacking shipping in the Skagerrak, but von Ingenohl, who now knew that British capital ships had been sent to hunt down von Spee, inclined to bombardment of a defended port. The problem, as the C-in-C saw it, was the uncertainty over which ships the British had detached, one or two battle cruisers being the usual estimate. The absence of *Princess Royal* was not even suspected. Furthermore, both Fleet Command and Admiralstab were still preoccupied with security. Von Ingenohl in particular worried that any operation might be compromised from its inception. Finally, continuing bad weather made submarine reconnaissance of targets on the east coast almost impossible.

In mid-November von Ingenohl decided on a raid on Hartlepool and Scar-borough if he could obtain the kaiser's consent. He wanted to force the British to base units farther south, exposing them more frequently to submarine and mine attack. Flushed with the victory at Coronel, Wilhelm was willing to agree to almost anything and detailed planning began. The Admiralstab, however, ordained that every ship in the First Scouting Group must be available. This meant a delay until mid-December when *Von der Tann* would be back from the dockyard after suffer-ing serious machinery troubles. As planning progressed, mention was made of the possibility that the wireless codes had been broken, but the focus remained on the alleged activities of spies and the compromise of land lines.

Von Ingenohl began to waver, but his resolve stiffened when news arrived of the near annihilation of von Spee's force off the Falkland Islands on 8 December. At one stroke the British had regained much prestige, as well as their moral advantage. Von Ingenohl felt that a swift counterstroke was necessary to show that the German navy had not become impotent. The clinching factor was that at least two British battle cruisers were definitely away from the North Sea. Von Ingenohl decided to act before they could return. He would take the entire High Sea Fleet as far as the Dogger Bank. This decision he kept from the kaiser, who was severely depressed by von Spee's demise, as such a movement would certainly risk a fleet action.

Precautions were taken. At Scheer's suggestion the oldest pre-dreadnoughts stayed in the Baltic, rather than operating as coast defense units in the North Sea. This avoided a potentially attention-arousing movement through the Kiel Canal. With a lull in the weather, *U27* was sent to report on the target areas and returned with the welcome news, confirmed by a second reconnaissance, that the defenses were weak and minefields nonexistent. Despite these arrangements, fleet wireless traffic continued in liberal fashion as the raid moved toward execution. This was enough for Room 40 to deduce the major part of what was to happen. The Admiralty informed Jellicoe in Churchillian tones on 11 December, "They can never again have such a good opportunity for successful offensive operations as at present, and you will no doubt consider how best to conserve and prepare your forces in the interval, so as to have the maximum number possible always ready and fresh. For the present the patrols to prevent contraband passing are of small importance."[4]

The cryptographers did not predict everything. The signals intercepted gave an accurate picture of the forces assigned to Hipper, but did not mention that the entire High Sea Fleet would deploy to the Dogger Bank. It was a key omission. The Admiralty was convinced that only detachments would be necessary to entrap Hipper's ships. Consequently, it ordered Jellicoe to detail off Beatty and seven destroyers of the Fourth Flotilla, out of Cromarty, Pakenham with the Third Cruiser Squadron from Rosyth, Warrender with six battleships of the Second Battle Squadron out of Scapa, and Tyrwhitt from the south. The various formations were ordered to be in position on the morning of 16 December, so as to cut the Germans off when they began their withdrawal. This meant that the First Scouting Group would bombard Hartlepool and Scarborough almost unopposed, but the Admiralty was prepared to exchange this for destruction of the German battle cruisers.

Jellicoe was unhappy about the division of his battle squadrons and events proved him right. As before, the Admiralty confused the achievement of relative superiority with the overwhelming strength that was more likely to produce a decisive result and that was also immune to defeat in detail. The Grand Fleet's ascendancy depended on its concentration. Warrender's six battleships were precisely the force that the Germans dreamed of being able to isolate and destroy and thereby attain the superiority in numbers that they so fervently desired.

There were other problems for the British. Command and control arrangements were fragmented. In particular, there was no coherent guidance as to the flagships' responsibilities for keeping their higher commands apprised of events if the War Room, with its other sources of information, was to be effective. This equally applied to the C-in-C on board *Iron Duke*.

At 0200 on 15 December Hipper sailed from the Jade. The First Scouting Group was at full strength, with *Seydlitz, Derfflinger, Moltke, Von der Tann,* and *Blücher* present (photo 12.1). They were escorted by four light cruisers of the Second Scouting Group and two flotillas of the best torpedo boats. One of the light cruisers, *Kolberg,* was designated to lay a minefield in conjunction with the bombardment, and had one hundred mines embarked. Von Ingenohl followed his subordinate out in the afternoon. He set course for the eastern edge of the Dogger Bank, where he planned to hold the High Sea Fleet at daylight the next morning. This position was still too far to the east to properly cover the bombardment and withdrawal, but von Ingenohl felt that he could not venture any farther.

Warrender sailed from Scapa at 0530 the same day, his ships suffering badly in the tidal race in Pentland Firth. The British had not yet developed full understanding of local conditions, in spite of the guidance given in Admiralty publications such as the *North Sea Pilot.* Things started badly with a departure in darkness that saw collisions, luckily superficial, between the battleship *Monarch* and a collier, *Monarch* and *Emperor of India,* and *Ajax* and a trawler. Matters did not improve outside the Flow. A few hours either way would have avoided the particular combination of wind and tide that created a sea state that was "the worst . . . we have ever had."[5] The seas swept three men overboard from *Conqueror* and so badly damaged the cruisers *Boadicea* and *Blanche* they had to be

PHOTO 12.1   **SMS** *Seydlitz*   *Bibliothek fur Zeitgeschichte*

sent home.[6] Beatty sailed at 0600, the destroyers of the Fourth Flotilla following independently because of the heavy seas. Warrender and Beatty met off the Moray Firth at 1100. By 1500 all Pakenham's cruisers and the destroyers were in sight and the rendezvous was complete. Warrender himself was unconvinced that Hartlepool or Scarborough were the targets. He signaled Beatty that he considered the Germans could just as easily strike against Harwich or the Humber. Meanwhile, he disposed his forces for the night. The orders were for the ships to be in position 54 degrees 10'N, 3 degrees E at 0730 the next morning, ready to cut Hipper off. This was a bare thirty miles south of von Ingenohl's intended position.

Tyrwhitt was detailed off by the Admiralty to watch Hipper's movements and sailed at 1400 on 15 December, with four light cruisers and two flotillas. He was ordered to be off Yarmouth by daylight, with selected fast destroyers spread out on observation lines farther to the north and south. Warrender requested the Admiralty—in a view shared by Jellicoe—that Tyrwhitt join him to protect against German torpedo craft. This was refused and Commodore (T)'s orders confirmed. The Harwich Force had problems on departure; the destroyer *Lark* became entangled in a navigation buoy and was left behind. Keyes was also out with eight submarines. They were sent to Terschelling, supported by *Lurcher* and *Firedrake*, intending to be in position by late on 16 December to cut off the enemy's retreat.

The Germans sailed in calm, if murky, weather, taking a wide northward sweep past Heligoland. The weather worsened as the day drew on, and the force began to pick up British wireless activity. This raised the possibility that they had been reported, either by a submarine or by supposed spy-trawlers, but Hipper decided to keep going. At 1700 the Scouting Groups passed the Dogger Bank and set a course west-southwest at fifteen knots, heading almost directly for Warrender. Hipper crossed ahead of the British forces at 0015, passing only fifteen miles away from Beatty and ten miles from Goodenough's light cruisers, which were spread to the west. In the darkness and rough seas, neither force discovered the other, despite the activities of German torpedo boat *S33*. Perhaps because she had a temporary captain, Lieutenant Hartmut Buddecke, this vessel suffered the experience that all flotilla craft feared at night and became separated from her consorts. *S33* called up *Strassburg*, asking, "Have lost touch; course please." The cruiser immediately replied, "Stop wireless," and an enraged Hipper complained, "Doesn't the ship know where we're heading for! Can't they get into touch again at daylight? The fools will give us away yet!"[7]

He had a point, but no British unit detected the exchange and *S33* was not the only unit to break radio silence—*Moltke* signaled her position at 0334.[8] At 0200 *S33* turned back for Germany, her captain deciding that it would be impossible to regain contact. Then, at 0400, the torpedo boat ran almost straight into four of Warrender's destroyers. *S33* hastily turned to parallel their course, in the hope of being mistaken for a consort. Although the distance, in Buddecke's estimate, was less than two hundred yards, the ruse succeeded and *S33* was able to edge away, signaling, "Four destroyers 54deg 55'N, 2deg 15'E." The report, in which the lost *S33* put the British fifteen miles too far west, was relayed by *Strassburg* and added another dimension to the problem that Hipper had to solve.

The weather was steadily getting worse. *V29* had already been sent back with condenser trouble and Hipper did not think the remaining light craft could continue into the teeth of the rising gale. Now came news that there were British forces behind the Scouting Groups. It was the fact that von Ingenohl was at sea that convinced Hipper to continue. However, despite his concerns as to their sea keeping, *S33*'s report meant that he dared not risk sending the torpedo boats back unaccompanied.

The High Sea Fleet remained near the Dogger Bank. The British destroyers that *S33* had encountered, led by *Lynx*, were steaming southeast ten miles to the northeast of Warrender's battleships, followed at some distance by the remaining three in the force. At 0515 they sighted *V155* on their port bow. The High Sea Fleet was steaming west-northwest with the three battle squadrons in line ahead, five light cruisers to starboard, the light cruiser *Rostock* and the Fifth and Seventh Flotillas to port, the Second and Eighth Flotillas astern, and the armored cruisers *Roon* and *Prinz Heinrich* and the Sixth Flotilla ahead.

V155 had been detached from the Sixth Flotilla to investigate a Dutch merchant ship when she sighted the British. Both sides were uncertain and issued the challenge before they exchanged fire, signaling as they did so. There remained a key difference in the quality of the reports. *V155*'s second signal included her position; not one of *Lynx*'s did. Furthermore, despite the British superiority in numbers and fire power, they suffered in the engagement. *Lynx* was hit twice by shells that caused flooding forward, pierced an oil tank, and jammed her rudder to port. As *Lynx* went involuntarily hard over, the others followed her around. *V155* put a shell into *Ambuscade*, which caused a bad fire, before she turned away. The British destroyers were in some confusion. *Ambuscade* hauled out of line to the west and *Lynx* and *Unity* to the southeast as the other four destroyers came around to a south-southwest course.

The light cruiser *Hamburg* and two attached torpedo boats turned to close when they received *V155*'s enemy report. At 0553 *Hamburg* sighted *Hardy*, which was leading the other three so far undamaged destroyers. *Hardy* and *Shark* opened fire at eight hundred yards, while the cruiser illuminated them with searchlights and replied in kind. In another confused, close-quarters action, *Hamburg* concentrated on *Hardy*. The cruiser took some damage, but quickly reduced *Hardy* to a shambles. The British destroyer suffered seventeen casualties, had her steering gear and forward 4-inch wrecked, and was on fire amidships when *Hamburg* turned away to avoid torpedoes. To the relief of the British, she did not reappear.

It was now 0603 and the sky was lightening. The British destroyers were in a sorry state, scattered in three groups with several badly damaged. *Ambuscade* was struggling northwest to get clear of the action, while *Unity* and *Lynx* were still to the east of the other destroyers. *Hardy* had also hauled out of the line as she tried to repair her steering gear. They were in no condition to fight another engagement against more-powerful forces.

The situation was greatly in the Germans' favor, but did not seem so to their anxious C-in-C, who put a very different complexion on it. He had earlier considered *S33*'s report of four destroyers, which, because the position was so far to the east (despite its error), he found very difficult to believe. He was, however, desperately concerned by the possibility of a massed torpedo attack by the Grand Fleet flotillas. Dawn was little more than two hours away, but von Ingenohl's fears increased with the arrival at 0520 of *V155*'s report of destroyers to the west.

Incredibly, the C-in-C ordered the fleet to turn away to the southeast. This was a completely mistaken decision. At the moment that von Ingenohl determined upon a retreat, Warrender's and Beatty's ships were barely ten miles south-southwest of the armored cruiser *Prinz Heinrich*, deployed ahead on the port wing of the High Sea Fleet. With the imperial dictum preying on his mind, von Ingenohl convinced himself that the destroyers to his west and northwest were the screen of the entire Grand Fleet (map 12.1). The reality was otherwise: "Here at last were the conditions for which the Germans had been striving since the beginning of the war. A few miles away on the port bow of the High Sea Fleet, isolated and several hours steaming from home, was the most powerful homogenous battle squadron of the Grand Fleet, the destruction of which would at one blow have completed the process of attrition and placed the British and German fleets on a precisely even footing as regards numerical [dreadnought] strength."[9]

Von Ingenohl, as he later argued, had no idea that there was a major formation behind the destroyers, but his strategic situation required him to be tactically aggressive—and tactically inquisitive.[10] Never again would such an opportunity to redress the balance present itself. Furthermore, the withdrawal conflicted with the internal logic of the operation by which the covering force would not turn for home until the Scouting Groups had withdrawn from the English coast. Von Ingenohl did not inform Hipper of his decision, something that would add to the bitterness felt in the Scouting Groups in the aftermath.

Despite considerable wireless interference, the turn was executed at 0542. As the battle squadrons wheeled around to the southeast, the cruisers and torpedo boats followed suit, falling in behind the main body as they did so. The armored cruiser *Roon* and her escorts, which had all been directly ahead of the battleships, thus at first turned toward the northeast to assume their new positions. At 0616 *Roon* came in sight of *Lynx* and *Unity*, now heading south-southeast. At first unsure of their identity, *Roon* challenged them. Commander Parry in *Lynx*

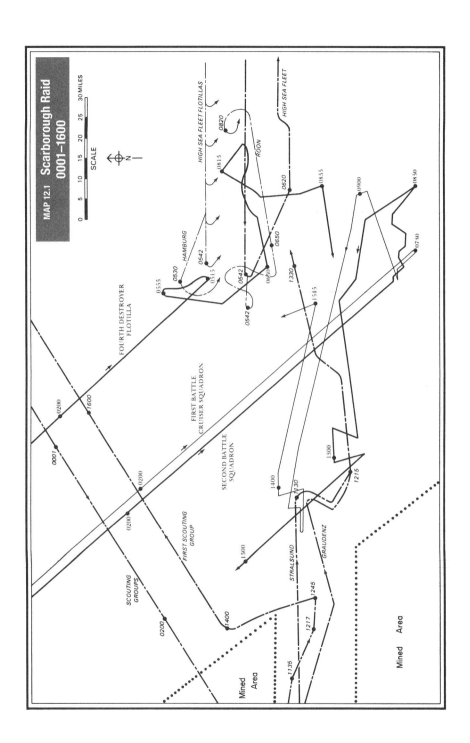

MAP 12.1 Scarborough Raid
0001–1600

SCALE

0 5 10 15 20 25 30 MILES

N

HIGH SEA FLEET FLOTILLAS

0820

0815

ROON

0620

0650

0855

HIGH SEA FLEET

0900

0850

0740

0530

HAMBURG

0542

0515

0542

0650

1330

1545

0555

FOURTH DESTROYER
FLOTILLA

0542

FIRST BATTLE
CRUISER SQUADRON

SECOND BATTLE
SQUADRON

0200

1600

0001

0200

0200

1400

1300

1215

1400

1130

1500

STRALSUND

1245

1217

1135

GRAUDENZ

SCOUTING
GROUPS

FIRST SCOUTING
GROUP

0200

Mined
Area

Mined   Area

remembered the signal that *V155* had used and replied with four white and five green lights. "This appeared to satisfy the enemy and he disappeared to the eastward."[11] In fact the captain of *Roon* was so worried about torpedoes that he turned away to prevent an attack rather than opening fire immediately. By the time he felt the range was enough to permit opening *Roon*'s broadside, *Lynx* and *Unity* were out of sight. The cruiser and her consorts therefore turned to follow the main body. For his part, Parry, who had also lost sight of his opponent in the continuing gloom, decided to resume his previous course until full daylight. Farther north, *Hardy* managed to repair her steering gear. At 0620 Commander Loftus Jones in *Shark* ordered the four destroyers to follow him, a few minutes later altering course south-southeast to follow Warrender's planned track. For the time they could see nothing, since the British battleships were more than twenty miles away, but Jones decided to stick to the course in the hope of sighting the Germans again.

Warrender and Beatty were both wondering what was afoot. The difficulty was that the reporting system was failing. Although as early as 0540 *Lynx* had informed them that she was chasing German torpedo boats, all her succeeding signals lacked position, or course, or both. Consequently, although Warrender had largely been able to piece together the course of events, he was in the dark as to where the engagements had taken place. Since it was at least clear that the large ship sighted had been of cruiser size, which meant that the German ships could either be alone or part of a formation as large as the High Sea Fleet itself, Warrender decided to continue for the morning rendezvous. If German ships were actually to the northeast, it would be better to let them get as far west as possible before the Second Battle Squadron turned north to cut them off. All this was fair enough, but Warrender did not update Jellicoe or the Admiralty, which among other things prevented any additional warning going out to the coastal patrols or the Harwich Force.

By 0710 Goodenough was in sight and, a few minutes later, Beatty and the other two commanders turned their squadrons in toward Warrender before taking up their daylight stations. At 0650 Loftus Jones' destroyers had sighted smoke to the southeast and gone to investigate. They soon made out five torpedo boats— *Roon*'s half-flotilla. The British destroyers immediately worked up to full speed and, at 0708, at a range of four thousand yards, opened fire. Visibility was still poor and it was not for some minutes that Jones realized that a large cruiser was steaming behind the torpedo boats. He correctly surmised that this could only be *Roon*. Altering northeast, he signaled to Beatty: "My position is lat 54deg 22'N, long 3deg 20'; am keeping touch with large cruiser *Roon* and five destroyers steaming east."

This was a better report, but it fell victim to the limitations of the existing technology and expertise. *Shark* was out in her navigational reckoning and this signaled estimate put her a good fifteen miles farther south than she actually was.

This made Warrender think that the Germans were only fifteen miles away from his 0730 position. There was further confusion at the receiving end. *Shark* had difficulty getting the signal away because of German interference—perhaps due as much to their own attempts to communicate as deliberate jamming—but it was finally sent at 0725. Two of the battleships received the message and passed it on to their flagship. *New Zealand*, the destroyer wave guard for the battle cruisers, took in the report but failed to pass it to *Lion*, which left Beatty in ignorance.

At the time he received the signal in *King George V*, Warrender's battleships were steaming east, while Beatty's battle cruisers were moving north to cross behind them and take up their screening position. It appeared to Warrender as though Beatty was heading toward the position that *Shark* had given and it was not until 0736 that he realized something was amiss and radioed, "Have you received messages . . . from *Lynx* [*sic*]?" *Lion* did not receive this signal. When Beatty turned the battle cruisers to take up their screen position and so away from the enemy, Warrender was certain. At 0755 he flashed by light, "Are you going after *Roon*?"

Beatty was astonished and replied, "Have heard nothing of *Roon*." Warrender then passed on the signals. Just as *Lion* was taking these in, *New Zealand*, after a delay of half an hour, finally chose to relay the key 0725 signal from *Shark*. Immediately Beatty turned the battle cruisers about and worked up speed to twenty-two knots. Ordering Goodenough to spread his light cruisers to the north and Pakenham to remain and screen Warrender to the west with his three armored cruisers, Beatty headed for the position given by *Shark*.

Jones was continuing to shadow *Roon* and the torpedo boats as they moved east at a speed of twenty knots, closing the armored cruiser after 0740, when mist lowered visibility still further. When, ten minutes later, the mist suddenly cleared, Jones discovered that he was facing not one, but three cruisers, *Roon* having been joined by *Stuttgart* and *Hamburg*. With the range closing rapidly, Jones hastily turned northwest and worked up to thirty knots to get clear, signaling to Beatty as he did so, "I am being chased to westward by light cruisers; my position lat 54deg 34'N, long 3deg, 48'E." The position was still a misestimate, placing *Shark* at least ten miles farther south-southeast than she actually was.

The British destroyers drew away, despite the battered *Hardy*'s speed dropping to twenty-six knots. So quickly did they get out of range that, at 0802, *Roon* ordered her consorts to break off the chase and turn southeast. This was the last engagement involving the High Sea Fleet itself, for submarine alarms from ships in the main body convinced von Ingenohl to continue the withdrawal. By sunset the precious battle squadrons would be safe within Heligoland Bight.

Jones thought the Germans had turned to open their gun arcs and moved to parallel them. In the haze not one of the British destroyers realized that the Germans had withdrawn. This confusion at least had the benefit that the four destroyers were now approaching Beatty and Goodenough rapidly, so fast that it largely wiped out discrepancies between *Shark's* and the flagships' reckoning. At 0850 *Shark* caught sight of Goodenough's light cruisers. But Warrender, Beatty, and Goodenough were no longer concerned with pursuit of *Roon*. Between 0841 and 0900 reports began to trickle in of the bombardment of the east coast. At 0850, still concerned for the *Humber*, Warrender turned the Second Battle Squadron north-northwest, but Beatty understood immediately that Scarborough had been the enemy's main objective and, at 0900, ordered his force west-northwest. A few minutes later Warrender reached the same conclusion, although he maintained his course to let Beatty and Goodenough get ahead of the battleships. Commander Jones caused momentary confusion after he had come up to the main force when he signaled to Beatty, "Am being chased by light cruisers." Beatty assessed that Goodenough, at least, must be able to see such an enemy and directed the commodore to engage them. Goodenough, whose northern horizon was empty, held his course. If, as the commanders separately estimated, the Germans had bombarded Scarborough only an hour before, then they would soon be in sight.

The hours before dawn were anxious ones for Hipper. After his decision to continue, the weather steadily worsened. At 0600 Commander Retzmann, scouting ahead with *Strassburg* and the Ninth Flotilla, reported that he had sighted neither land nor any lights, and that, in the heavy seas and wind, the torpedo boats could not keep their course. Hipper decided on a change of plan. At 0632 he ordered all the torpedo boats and light cruisers, except *Kolberg*, to turn back and make for the 0600 rendezvous of the High Sea Fleet (photo 12.2). By 0640, after

PHOTO 12.2   **SMS** *Kolberg*   *Bibliothek fur Zeitgeschichte*

sighting the coast and with the help of depth soundings, Hipper was finally sure of his position. The First Scouting Group divided in two. *Von der Tann, Derfflinger,* and *Kolberg,* under Rear Admiral Tapken, were to head south for Scarborough and Whitby, while Hipper took *Seydlitz, Moltke,* and *Blücher* north to Hartlepool.

The patrol forces were very weak that morning. This was partly due to the Admiralty's failure to provide a full assessment to Ballard, Admiral of Patrols, who did not necessarily receive the signals addressed to the main seagoing forces. His instructions were not particularly specific: "All patrol flotillas should be specially alert tomorrow, Wednesday morning. Weather permitting, they are to be under way off their harbors before daylight, in such positions that they can be communicated with quickly."

This was not the first such signal that Ballard had received and the serviceability of the aging patrol forces was of increasing concern to the admiral and his local commanders. Critically, there had been an exchange the month before, when warning was given of a possible attack on *Humber.* Ballard asked whether the local destroyers that were boiler cleaning should raise steam in readiness, but the Admiralty responded that this "was not advisable . . . as the destroyers must be kept efficient."[12] In the absence of further information, and after many false alarms—with the Admiralty's caveat of "weather permitting"—it was reasonable that the Admiral of Patrols left the dispositions to the Captain (D) on the spot. It was regrettable that the latter, Captain A. C. Bruce, kept his light cruisers, *Patrol* and *Forward*, and the small submarine *C9*, in harbor. The latter's absence would be crucial.

At 0745 *Seydlitz* was challenged by Hartlepool's war signal station. Ten minutes later the destroyers *Doon, Waveney, Test,* and *Moy* sighted the Germans to the southeast at a range of nine thousand yards. Lieutenant Commander H. M. Fraser in *Doon* led his consorts to investigate. The three big ships immediately opened fire. Amidst the hail of shell, all the destroyers but *Doon* turned away to the north. The latter attempted to launch a torpedo, but at five thousand yards the range was too much for her 18-inch weapons and German fire too heavy to have any chance of success. Fraser turned *Doon* away, the destroyer riddled with splinters and with eleven casualties.

Hipper did not follow, for his priority was Hartlepool. At 0803 the Germans began their bombardment. *Blücher* circled to the south while *Seydlitz* and *Moltke* steamed up and down on a line to the northeast of the town. Their gunfire was devastating, but far more hurt was done to civilians than to military installations. Eighty-six were killed and 424 wounded during the half hour attack, although Hartlepool's 6-inch gun batteries made some reply. They hit *Blücher* four times, damaging a 21-cm turret, knocking two 88-mm guns out of action, and causing eleven casualties. Both *Seydlitz* and *Moltke* were also hit, the former three times and the latter once, but their damage was minimal. The accuracy of both sides' fire was hampered by a very heavy mist (which contributed to initial confusion ashore as to the ships' nationality). The British were probably more favored, since it partly sheltered their ships from the consequences of the inept patrol arrangements.

Patrol and *C9* got under way immediately the alert was sounded, but had little luck. *C9* dived to avoid the Germans' fire. In doing so, she grounded on the bar at the entrance to Hartlepool harbor. In the mist and confusion, *Patrol* might have been able to do something. As she passed the breakwater, however, the light cruiser was struck by three heavy shells that caused so much damage that Captain Bruce was forced to put her aground. *Patrol* was out of action for the remainder of the engagement. *C9* took so long to extricate herself that by the time she was clear the Germans had disappeared. *Forward* was not even able to raise steam in time. When she finally emerged, it was to discover that Hipper had disappeared.

The bombardment of Scarborough and Whitby went entirely unopposed. The three ships in Tapken's force approached the coast from northeast of Whitby and ran south to Scarborough before they opened fire. Both ports were undefended, so the battle cruisers were uninterrupted. At 0806, they opened fire at a range of less than one thousand yards with their secondary armament. At 0816 the two heavy ships reversed course, heading north to attack Whitby. By the time this first stage of their bombardment ceased at 0835, they had killed eighteen and wounded ninety-one civilians and destroyed or damaged more than two hundred buildings. Meanwhile, *Kolberg* continued south and began to lay her mines at 0814, from the coast to ten miles offshore. By 0841 the job was finished. The British war channel blocked, *Kolberg* turned to rejoin the First Scouting Group. *Von der Tann* and *Derfflinger* began their second bombardment at 0906. It lasted only seven minutes. Although the battle cruisers fired nearly two hundred shells into Whitby and caused severe damage, there were, happily, only five casualties. By 0930 the First Scouting Group and *Kolberg* were reunited and Hipper was shaping course for Germany, signaling to von Ingenohl, "Have carried out operation. . . . Course south-south-east, 23 knots."

The Admiralty was making arrangements to meet the situation. From 0818 it began to intercept signals from the ships off Hartlepool. By 0840 it was clear from both Scarborough and Hartlepool that the expected attack was under way, involving at least two, and probably four heavy ships. In rapid succession, orders were sent to Warrender and Tyrwhitt to join and search for the bombarding forces. The Third Battle Squadron was ordered out of Rosyth to join Warrender. Jellicoe, however, who had at last been ordered to sea (his ships were already at short notice), directed Bradford to rendezvous with the Grand Fleet off Berwick. The C-in-C was concerned that the Germans might strike north and he was determined to have the Grand Fleet concentrated to prevent this.

As Warrender and Beatty turned west, Tyrwhitt led his forces out from behind the shallows off Yarmouth where they had been sheltering. As soon as the Harwich

Force got into the open sea, the commodore realized that his destroyers could not take being pushed into the teeth of the gale, and sent them back to Yarmouth Roads. He had little choice. As Tennant noted, "I have never seen water come over a destroyer the way it did then."[13] Tyrwhitt pressed on with the light cruisers. He ordered twenty-five knots, but conditions were so bad that his ships could barely make fifteen as they battered into the short, steep sea. Weather damage began to mount. Tyrwhitt wrote later, "*Undaunted* had 3 scuttles banged in by the sea. I have trod the plank for 33 years but never saw a scuttle bashed in before. Our bridge rails were bent aft + I thought the 6" gun forward would go over the side."[14]

Warrender's problem was not an easy one. He had the advantage of good local weather and visibility of some ten miles, but this would not necessarily last. Jellicoe had earlier ordered that the ships of the Grand Fleet were not to pass west of a line drawn northwest/southeast off the east coast because of the existence of German minefields. Although the vice admiral was now steering for Scarborough, the Germans could emerge from any point along a hundred-mile stretch of the forbidden area. To find Hipper, he would have at least to send in the light cruisers. Therefore, as the cruisers deployed in front of the heavy ships, Warrender signaled "Light cruisers must go in through minefield to locate enemy." This, perhaps not surprisingly, made the outlook of those in Goodenough's squadron "rather murky" and a few minutes later a doubtful Warrender asked the Admiralty, "Is it safe to go across mine fields?"[15] On board *Iron Duke* Jellicoe had been studying the charts and something became clear to him that Warrender had missed. Although the C-in-C had bidden his ships not go west of the line described, the actual danger areas did not extend the entire length of the coast; there was a gap due east of Whitby and Scarborough. At 1004 Jellicoe signaled to Warrender and Beatty, "Gap in minefield between parallel lat 54deg 40' and 54deg 20' and [W] as far as 20 E long. Enemy will in all probability come out there."

Jellicoe's assessment was correct. Hipper's ships emerged from almost exactly the middle of the gap, although avoiding mines was little of Hipper's concern. He wanted to gain as much easterly ground as possible to link up with the High Sea Fleet. Had he steamed straight for Germany, his ships would have passed at least twenty miles south of the British and avoided making contact at all.

The Second Scouting Group and the torpedo flotillas suffered as they made their way east, bringing the bad weather with them. The seas on their quarter, several torpedo boats rolled their masts out. With ready-use ammunition and other gear being carried away as the ships broached-to, one by one each cruiser had to order her attendant half-flotilla to turn into the wind to connect their auxiliary bow rudders. British signal traffic was intercepted to the east and the anxious senior officer ordered each group to proceed independently at maximum speed. Nevertheless, their progress was erratic and Hipper, with his four more weatherly big ships and *Kolberg*, was beginning to catch up to his light forces.

By 1025 the British forces had largely taken up formation. Warrender was steaming west, with Pakenham's three armored cruisers to the south-southwest. Ten miles north, Beatty and Goodenough were also about to turn west, with the light cruisers spread ahead at two mile intervals in line abeam. The battle cruisers, in close order, were following *Southampton*, the southernmost ship in the line, while farther north still the remaining destroyers attached themselves to *Falmouth*. Until 1100 conditions were good, but squalls then set in and visibility became patchy, frequently dropping to less than two miles. The light cruisers were forced to close in to maintain visual communication. Even then, *Nottingham* and *Birmingham* lost touch and caused confusion when *Nottingham* suddenly sighted her consort and reported her as an enemy. This muddle was only just sorted out when, at 1125, *Southampton* sighted real adversaries.

Three miles ahead of the British cruiser, and steaming straight toward her, were *Stralsund* and the torpedo boats of the Eleventh Half-Flotilla. Turning hard to starboard to open his broadside, Goodenough ordered the other light cruisers to concentrate on *Southampton* and signaled Beatty, "Am engaging a cruiser and destroyers." At the same time, *Stralsund* sighted *Southampton* and herself turned hard to starboard. Both cruisers opened fire, but their shooting was wild and they scored no hits. *Birmingham* soon joined and found accurate gunnery just as difficult, since "the seas were now coming over us absolutely green."[16] When he sighted the second British cruiser, *Stralsund*'s captain, Harder, ordered the torpedo boats to lay a smoke screen. *Strassburg* and *Graudenz* were fast nearing *Stralsund* because of the latter's turn south. As they approached her, both ships and their supporting half-flotillas also turned in that direction.

As *Nottingham* and *Falmouth*, which had yet to sight the Germans, turned southwest to support Goodenough, the commodore realized that there were two more light cruisers and even more torpedo boats behind *Stralsund*, but failed to report this. Farther east, Beatty thought that *Southampton* and *Birmingham* were engaging only one light cruiser. He was preoccupied by the need to make contact with Hipper. On the information to hand, the German heavy ships could be anywhere within a wide semicircle to the north, south, or west. Had Goodenough now informed him about the other light cruisers and torpedo boats, it would have been obvious to Beatty (as it should to Goodenough) that his scouts had encountered the entire Second Scouting Group, and that the First Scouting Group must logically be some distance astern, to the west.

But Goodenough did not report. To the northwest, Beatty sighted *Falmouth* and *Nottingham* moving to support *Southampton* and *Birmingham*. The vice admiral, wanting to keep as much horizon under observation as possible for the first sign of the enemy's heavy ships, and thinking that Goodenough had more than enough strength to deal with *Stralsund*, made a light signal to the two light cruisers: "Resume your position for lookout duties. Take station ahead five miles."

It was here that another error crept in. Seymour, Beatty's flag lieutenant, did not address the message specifically to *Falmouth* and *Nottingham*, but rather to the light cruiser squadron as a whole.

Astern of *Southampton*, *Birmingham* took in the signal and passed it to the flagship, as did *Nottingham*. Goodenough then made his next mistake. He still had not reported the additional German ships, and it should have been clear to him that this information would have radically changed Beatty's picture of the tactical situation. Nevertheless, at 1155 the commodore broke off the engagement and turned his ships 16 points about to rejoin *Lion*. Goodenough later justified his decision by pointing out that, when he turned away, the Germans were steering south, directly toward the Second Battle Squadron and the Third Cruiser Squadron. Despite this, it was a serious error, particularly as visibility was worsening, dropping to less than half a mile when the ships were enveloped in squalls.

As his cruisers headed away, Goodenough temporarily resighted *Stralsund* to the south. She had become separated from her sisters and the British mistook her for yet another German cruiser. At this, Goodenough finally made a new report: "Enemy's cruisers bearing south by east," but Beatty had only just received this message when, to his astonishment, he realized that *Southampton* was making for *Lion*, apparently out of contact with the enemy. At 1212 the vice admiral signaled, tartly, "What have you done with enemy light cruisers?" Goodenough replied, "They disappeared south when I received your signal to resume station." An acid exchange followed.

BEATTY: Engage the enemy.

GOODENOUGH: There is no enemy in sight now.

BEATTY: When and where was the enemy last seen? When you sight enemy, engage him. Signal to resume previous station was made to *Nottingham*. *I cannot understand why, under any circumstances, you did not pursue enemy* [emphasis added].

Strong words for an operational signal.

While the British engaged in recriminations, Harder's cruisers and torpedo boats drew away. They were now fast approaching Warrender and, at 1210, *Stralsund* caught sight of the Second Battle Squadron through a gap in the mists. Harder hastily turned east and, attempting to deceive, flashed the recognition signal that he had seen the British use. Warrender did not at first see the Germans but, a few hundred yards away, the squadron's second division, under Rear Admiral Arbuthnot in *Orion*, had a clear view. *Orion* reported, "Enemy in sight," to *King George V*, but did nothing else. Her captain, Frederic Dreyer, one of the gunnery experts of the day, was frantic. Ordering the main armament laid on the leading light cruiser, he begged for permission to shoot. But Arbuthnot was adamant, and replied, "No, not until the Vice Admiral signals 'open fire.'" Warrender, however, did not give such an order when he sighted the Germans himself three minutes later but directed Pakenham to take his armored cruisers and chase, while he informed Beatty of what had been seen. Dreyer later wrote of Arbuthnot, "He never spoke to me about it . . . but I am certain . . . that he was mortified to realize that he had been too punctilious. If we had fired, the other five battleships would have done so too. . . . One of the German light cruisers challenged the *Orion* by flashing 'B.O.X.' at us with a searchlight. He would have had a thick ear for that, if we had fired!"[17]

Dreyer may have exaggerated when he declared that "our golden moment had been missed."[18] It was only twenty minutes before the German ships, which hauled rapidly away from the Third Cruiser Squadron, finally disappeared into yet another squall. Gunnery in 1914 was not well adapted to firing at long range at small vessels in heavy seas and poor visibility. Although part of the fire control solution was relatively simple, since range changed slowly in a chase, pitch and roll in such a sea state made keeping guns on the target a very difficult matter. What was more critical to the outcome was the effect of Warrender's signal on Beatty's movements. At 1203 the battle cruisers turned west. It was Beatty's intention to head for the gap between the minefields and, at 1230, to turn south to begin patrolling along a north-south line. Had he remained here, he would almost certainly have sighted Hipper at around 1300.

The First Scouting Group was steaming almost due east when, at 1139, Hipper received from *Stralsund*, "Enemy main body in [square] beta 093 [54 degrees 30'N, 2 degrees 16'E]. Am being chased SW by S." He immediately turned the battle cruisers southeast and then south-southeast at twenty-three knots. The signals that Hipper received from his light cruisers were confusing, as they variously reported the enemy's course as being south-east by south, south-easterly, and westerly. Then at 1213 came a signal from *Stralsund*: "5 enemy battleships in beta 5, 089 [54 degrees 15'N, 2 degrees 7'E]."[19] Despite the muddle, it was clear these ships were at least twenty miles south of those reported earlier and that Hipper was faced by not one, but two separate battle squadrons. Nevertheless, he realized his light cruisers needed support and that he had to risk the First Scouting Group in what he described as "certain action."[20] By this time Hipper was aware that the High Sea Fleet was running for home, information that produced sulphurous language and that did not bode well for his relationship with von Ingenohl.[21] He was on his own. At 1217 Hipper altered course to east by south and held on. By this time the First Scouting Group was steaming straight through the middle of the gap—directly toward Beatty's intended patrol line.

But the British missed this chance. As soon as Beatty received Warrender's signal, he turned his ships back to the east. At 1240 Beatty received, "Enemy's course east—no battle cruisers seen yet," and at 1257 another message: "Second

Battle Squadron have resumed original position." Warrender failed in this signal to inform Beatty that he had lost contact with the German cruisers and torpedo boats, but the latter realized that this must be the case. It was now evident that Hipper must have been well astern of his light forces and was thus still to the west. To Beatty it was apparent that Hipper would turn north, avoiding the shallowest areas of the Dogger Bank and the battleships reported nearby.

This was precisely what Hipper had done. Knowing that at least two concentrations of heavy ships were to the east of him and that he would have to chance encountering one or both in supporting the Second Scouting Group and the flotillas, Hipper's relief must have been intense when, at 1244, he received from *Stralsund*, "Enemy out of sight." Harder could be left to get home, as he had a clear run. Only a minute afterward Hipper turned the First Scouting Group north, hoping to clear the danger area as fast as possible, while he sought confirmation that all was well, signaling "Are you in danger?" At 1305 *Seydlitz* received a bald, but cheering, "No" from *Stralsund*. With his light forces clear of the enemy and steering east-northeast, Hipper continued north. In the prevailing poor visibility, Hipper had a growing confidence that his forces would escape the British. After his latest alteration, he had good reason. When Hipper turned at 1245 his heavy ships were little more than twelve miles away from the First Battle Cruiser Squadron.

At 1315 Beatty turned north and, nine minutes later, Warrender decided that Hipper's ships must have evaded him in the mist. He turned northwest. Room 40 now began to release to the Admiralty a stream of deciphered signals, some within an hour of their original transmission. The first of these was one that Hipper had sent to von Ingenohl at 1215, giving his position and course. This information was dispatched to the ships at sea at 1325. Over the next few hours, Beatty and Warrender tried to interpret the German movements. The problem in these circumstances, despite Room 40's facility, was that time taken for the ships to receive the information was too much to do more than confuse the tactical picture.

The first signal caused Beatty, who was doubtful, but had little else to go on, to turn east at 1355 and so lose whatever chance remained to catch the First Scouting Group. Warrender for his part decided to continue north, conscious that if the Germans crossed the Dogger Bank from the position given they would be well to the east of his ships and effectively out of reach. At all events, by doing so he came closest to Hipper. *Kolberg*, which had been lagging behind, her decks and superstructure swept by the seas into which she was plowing, sighted funnel smoke just after the First Scouting Group turned northeast at 1245. With the sea now on her beam, *Kolberg* was able to work up speed rapidly and rejoin Hipper, leaving the smoke behind. Neither Pakenham's armored cruisers nor Warrender's battleships saw anything.

Hipper's captains were still worried and both von Reuter in *Derfflinger* and von Levetzow in *Moltke* proposed a diversion to the Baltic to return to Germany through the Little Belt. Hipper, more confident than his subordinates, rejected the suggestion.[22] He was correct and all the Scouting Groups enjoyed a clear run home, all the easier because the weather moderated rapidly. The exchange suggested, however, that the senior captains were not entirely confident in their admiral's judgment or that of his staff, a view partly justified for von Levetzow at least by Hipper having earlier confided his worries to him.[23] This issue would have further play in the coming weeks. In the meantime, navigation was a bigger problem and the First Scouting Group had to feel its way toward the coast by depth soundings alone.

Another intercepted signal, this time from *Friedrich der Grosse* to *Stralsund*, at last gave the Admiralty to understand that the High Sea Fleet was or had been at sea. It hastily warned Warrender not to go too far east. Yet another decrypted German signal gave Hipper's position when he turned at 1245. When this signal was sent to Warrender and Beatty at 1450 and taken in, it became obvious that they had missed Hipper. At 1547 Warrender ordered Beatty to "Relinquish chase—rejoin me tomorrow."

In the Admiralty, despite bitter disappointment, there was no intent to accept the failure as final. Warrender was advised, "Twenty destroyers of the First and Third Flotillas are waiting off Gorleston. If you think it advisable you may direct Commodore (T) to take them to the vicinity of Heligoland to attack enemy ships returning in dark hours." It would have been a vain effort, as the flotillas could not possibly have got across the North Sea in time. Both Warrender and Jellicoe, who had intercepted the signal, decried the idea. Warrender replied, "Certainly not advisable, as there is a strong NW wind and nasty sea." Jellicoe simply signaled to Warrender, "It's too late." By sunset all British forces were moving north. Jellicoe ordered Tyrwhitt to join the Grand Fleet the next day.

There remained just one chance of inflicting any damage on the Germans. It was now Keyes on whom Churchill had his remaining hopes pinned, although Fisher was less sanguine. Keyes was anxiously waiting on events near Terschelling when, at 1034, *Lurcher* intercepted a signal from *Monarch* to the destroyer *Ambuscade*, warning that the Germans were off Scarborough. Commodore (S)'s reaction was prompt. He immediately dispatched *Firedrake* to get within wireless range of the tender *Adamant*, lying at Harwich with a telephone link to the Admiralty. *Firedrake* was to inform the Admiralty that Keyes was gathering his submarines and would await instructions. Meanwhile, *Lurcher* steamed up and down the patrol line, attempting to collect the boats. In the poor visibility, it was a difficult job. During the bad weather on passage out several submarines had separated from the main body and hardly knew their position within thirty miles. Keyes wrote, "I had a most trying day endeavoring to collect the submarines. . . . [T]hey had to dive the moment they sighted a vessel . . . and once submerged, it was very difficult to get them on the surface again."[24]

At 1410 the Admiralty signaled, "High Sea Fleet is at sea, and at 12.30 p.m. was at lat. 54deg 38'N, long. 5deg 55'E. They may return after dawn tomorrow, so proceed to Heligoland and intercept them. They probably pass five miles west of Heligoland, steering south for Weser Light."

When this signal arrived at 1535, Keyes had managed to gather only four submarines, the *French Archimede, E10, E11,* and *E15.* These he dispatched to Heligoland but, faced with the Admiralty's signal, Keyes was uncertain as to what to do himself. There was a critical error in the text. The estimate of the High Sea Fleet's movements was twelve hours too slow. Von Ingenohl would actually have the battle squadrons in harbor that night. Keyes naturally thought they would still be at sea at dawn the next day and that there was enough time for him to muster the other submarines—assuming that he found them—and send them into the Bight. He toyed with taking his two destroyers in, but knowing little or nothing of other British movements and ignorant of the weather on the other side of the North Sea, he assumed that Tyrwhitt must be following the High Sea Fleet, ready for a night torpedo attack. Keyes knew that his appearance without warning could cause untold, perhaps fatal confusion. Having been accused of "bush-thwacking [*sic*]" even by the impetuous Churchill, he could not risk further criticism.[25] Finally, if the Germans were still going to be at sea the next morning, it was clearly his job as a submarine commander to reassemble the missing four boats and send them into the Bight. They would have a much better chance of attacking the Germans than his destroyers. Keyes decided not to go in. Already too late to intercept von Ingenohl, he might have been able to attack Hipper, whose battered forces were steaming home in scattered groups, had the Admiralty's next signal at 2012 been passed correctly: "We think Heligoland and Amrum lights will be lit when ships are going in. Your destroyers might get a chance to attack about 2.0 a.m., or later, on the line given you."

This signal should have reached Keyes within an hour. But it was not until after 0120 that an enraged Commodore (S) held the message in his hand. The problem with operating from a destroyer was that the destroyer wavelength had a reliable range of little more than sixty nautical miles. While *Lurcher* and *Firedrake* could transmit only on this wavelength, which was the reason for Keyes' detaching *Firedrake* to act as a relay, they could receive messages at much longer distances on the big ship wavelength. Keyes specifically requested the Admiralty that it pass all messages via *Adamant,* which would transmit them on the big ship band. But this signal was instead relayed via Ipswich to the depot ship *Woolwich,* which spent three hours trying to raise Keyes on the destroyer band, a practical impossibility. Not until 2238 did the Admiralty learn that the message had not been sent, and not until 0023 was it correctly transmitted. Keyes had good cause to be annoyed. For, at 2000, having found no more submarines, he reluctantly turned for the rendezvous arranged for any unit that had not been able to make contact.

Keyes received the signal a good two hundred miles away from Heligoland. As he later wrote, "Words fail me, even now, after more than nineteen years, to express my feelings when I received this belated message."[26]

The submarines had little better luck. Hipper, with great difficulty, managed to enter the Jade in darkness through the unwatched eastern passage and was not seen by any of the four sentinels. Only *E11*, under Nasmith, got a chance. The First Squadron had been sent into the Elbe the previous night and von Ingenohl ordered it to the Jade at dawn. *E11* observed the transit and launched a single torpedo at the battleship *Posen* from four hundred yards. This probably ran too deep and passed under *Posen*'s keel. Nasmith tried again at another, but this battleship zigzagged toward *E11*, forcing the submarine deep so suddenly that Nasmith lost control. *E11* shot to the surface, broaching-to before her crew could get her back under command. The Germans scattered at high speed. Nasmith attempted to attack the rear ship in the formation, but she also eluded him and *E11* was forced to return home empty-handed.

Of the other submarines, *Archimede*, a steam-driven boat, had her funnel bent in the heavy seas. She could not dive and had to crawl across the North Sea with most of the crew desperately baling out the water that flooded through the funnel. She arrived at Harwich late on 19 December, followed at intervals by the other submarines. The British staff history rather maliciously understated the attitude of *Archimede*'s captain, reporting that he was "considerably impressed by the weather and conditions of winter service in the Bight."[27] *Archimede* had another narrow escape when she was challenged on approaching the coast by the destroyer *Stour*. The Admiral of Patrols had not been informed that a French boat was operating with the British and sighting her was the first thing *Stour* knew about it.[28] *Archimede* was not deployed into the North Sea again.

Jellicoe wrote to Fisher, telling him how "intensely unhappy" he was and that the "business requires explanation."[29] It certainly did. British forces had repeatedly been offered the opportunity to make contact with the Scouting Groups and missed their chances. The sea commanders returned to harbor to face a veritable inquisition, which included calling in many of the records of the ships concerned.[30] Given the Admiralty's part in the debacle, it was not necessarily a sufficiently introspective investigation. Even Tyrwhitt was under pressure, since the Admiralty did not understand how bad the weather was in his vicinity. He commented to Wintour of the Fourth Flotilla, "I recd very decided criticisms as to my action but I shd do the same tomorrow under similar circs. I very nearly received the order of the Sack between ourselves. Sure to get it next time!"[31]

Beatty escaped without censure. He had generally exercised good judgment, the validity of which had been set at naught by his flag lieutenant's error, Goodenough's failure, and the poor information he had received. Of the three, the questionable element was his choice of Seymour. The latter was not a qualified signals officer and, although personally congenial, was arguably not up to the job. This was not to be his last error in battle and Seymour was to pay a heavy price, committing suicide after the war. Jellicoe summed up the official view when he penciled, "There never was such bad luck."[32] Fisher replied, "How unkind was the heavenly mist!"[33]

Warrender survived, despite his mediocre performance. He had been poorly served by some of his subordinates and by the Admiralty, but, as Fisher commented, "A. K. Wilson says that very few Admirals from his experience have the 'mooring board' mind! They steer for where the enemy is, not where he will be."[34] Warrender had been hampered by the heavy weather and poor visibility, all the more critical as factors because of navigational discrepancies and inadequate contact reporting, but his own lack of reporting had been a serious failure in itself. He certainly had too few destroyers and no fast light cruisers to hand, but had been less than enterprising in his use of Pakenham's cruisers, a point taken up by Fisher, who complained of "Warrender . . . covering so little space when he ought to have spread like a fan."[35] Indeed, as more information came to light, there were times when it appeared to analysts that it was Beatty exercising local command, not Warrender. Beatty, as the senior cruiser admiral, had responsibility for direction of all the scouting forces of the Grand Fleet (the reason for his acting promotion to vice admiral), but at key times Pakenham was operating in direct support of Warrender and should have been ordered accordingly. It would have been dubious practice for Warrender to have scattered his battleships, but the Third Cruiser Squadron had little opportunity to act as a proper scouting force. Separated, they might have been vulnerable to Hipper's battle cruisers, but the risk should have been accepted. In the event, Jellicoe had Warrender relieved in late 1915 because of failing health. Warrender may already not have been completely fit (he died in January 1917) and Alexander Duff described him in January 1915 as "deafer + more absent minded than ever."[36] A letter from Stephen King-Hall to his father, Admiral Sir George King-Hall, appears to talk of Warrender: "If what you say about Sir What's-his-name is true, everyone thoroughly agrees in the mess. He is defined as follows: 'He never spoke in peace because he was deaf; everyone thought he must be thinking a lot. When War came, everyone said, good gracious, what on earth was he doing the whole time?' "[37]

There was a painful interview between Beatty and a mortified Goodenough. Despite the signal error, of which Jellicoe later noted, "Beatty [is] very severe on Goodenough but forgets that it was his own badly worded signal to the cruisers that led to the Germans being lost out of touch," the commodore's actions were inexcusable.[38] Beatty wrote, "[T]ime after time I have impressed upon Goodenough the necessity of always using his own initiative and discretion—that my orders are expressions of intentions and that they are not to be taken too literally. The Man on the Spot is the only one who can judge certain situations."[39]

Jellicoe made the point to Fisher: "The Commodore had reported the presence of the light cruiser and destroyers and knew that the V. A. [vice admiral] was aware of their being in sight; there is therefore every justification for his obeying the signal from this point of view, but he had not reported the sighting of the three [*sic*] other cruisers and in my opinion, he should certainly have disobeyed the signal on this account, and kept touch with them until he had informed the V. A."[40]

In short, Goodenough had been, as Fisher succinctly remarked, "a fool."[41] Fisher wanted him relieved, but Churchill would not hear of it. Beatty was tempted by a change, but on reflection neither he nor Jellicoe wanted one. Beatty did go so far as to suggest a possible relief (Lionel Halsey, captain of *New Zealand*).[42] However, as his flag commander Plunkett wrote after Beatty's death of the interview with Goodenough, "He [patiently] explained his views, but, as he said afterwards, 'I never blamed him, and we parted friends.'"[43] Beatty and Plunkett had an exchange after the latter submitted a paper summarizing the lessons of 16 December. Plunkett wrote, "I earnestly submit that it would be of value if some of these lessons could be impressed on Flag Officers, Commodores and Commanding Officers who may be detached. Also the urgent importance of using initiative so as not always to 'wait for instructions' when in doubt, and not always to be tied by the letter of an order when it is obviously unsuitable."

Beatty responded waspishly, "Quite agree but [it is] so obvious that if they do not understand [?] them they are not fit for command and should be removed. It is too late to begin to impress obvious truths such as this on flag officers at this stage who no doubt think that they already comprehend their duties."[44]

Notwithstanding the truth of his observation, in this case Beatty was partly wrong and Plunkett partly right. If officers were to be sacked for a single failure, however egregious, it raised the prospect of their being afraid to take any risks at all. This was something of which Churchill was aware and of which Jellicoe and Beatty were both conscious. The latter made the point that Goodenough would either have to be relieved—and quickly—or else have the matter closed without delay. Further recrimination would only serve to damage his judgment. Jellicoe agreed and, despite Fisher's fury, Goodenough retained his command.

Although the mercy shown paid dividends in this case—Goodenough's activities in later actions were to be models of scouting and concise reporting—there was a problem that needed addressing and Plunkett put a finger on at least part of it. If two officers with such reputations for aggressiveness and eagerness for responsibility as William Goodenough and Robert Arbuthnot could act as they did, one breaking off action on the authority of a signal patently made without the benefit of critical information, and the other failing to open fire without direction under conditions in which contact might be lost at any minute, something was very wrong. The cult of the senior officer present reigned.

Matters had not been helped by the communications system. Commanders at every level had still to understand that they had responsibilities for what would now be called information management in reporting up the chain—and down. Also fundamental to effective reporting was that all units be within the same frame of reference, even if they moved out of sight of each other. The solution of promulgating a reference position by the flagship and transmitting an update at regular intervals out from the center of the force to the dispersed units had yet to be devised, although there was hard thinking going on about the problem in *Iron Duke*. A small start was made within a few days with a memorandum promulgating reference points.[45] Even when such a system had been created, however, it would not answer the problem of aligning the positions of units that sailed from separate bases and had never been in company.

Wireless needed as much work. The Germans had appreciated the problem of remote reporting better than the British and their reports almost always included a position—conveyed by the simpler but less accurate predesignated squares. This eased the task at every point in the draft/transmit/receive/read chain, particularly for light craft with basic equipment and overstretched personnel. The British had yet to grasp that, in the variable conditions of the North Sea, every unit had to consider itself potentially a scout. The destroyers in particular did not think in such a way, unless they were divisional leaders (and not always then). This was partly the result of attempts to ensure that the limited capacity of wireless was not swamped, but it meant critical information was not made available to senior command. The series of signals from the destroyer *Lynx* (which *was* a divisional commander) during the encounter before dawn on 16 December is typical. First: "Am chasing enemy's destroyers in north-west direction." Then: "Am being chased by enemy's cruiser; am steering south-south-west." Followed, nearly an hour later, by: "Have reason to believe one destroyer sunk. *Ambuscade* damaged, *Unity* standing by her." Only *Lion*'s interception of signals passing between the destroyers (which suggests that the flagship began to monitor the destroyer wavelength, rather than relying on the tardy *New Zealand*) enabled Beatty to have some idea of what was taking place. A sighting report should contain four elements: what, where, whither, and when. The Germans had grasped the importance of the second element, the British had not. Jellicoe tried to make the point, as had been done before: "Officers commanding squadrons or captains of single vessels should be most careful to give full information to the nearest flag or senior officer as to any enemy vessels sighted. Attention is once again directed to the absolute necessity for indicating the position of the reporting ship and of the enemy."[46]

It would not be enough. Not until late 1915 was a signal format for contact reporting finally promulgated, and even then many units still did not grasp their responsibilities.

The relationship among Room 40, the War Staff, and the fleet required further work. Messages from Room 40 had taken too long to get to the commanders at sea; the latter generally failed to keep the War Room in the picture. Fisher's criticism that Warrender failed to interpret correctly the signals that he received was valid, but the admiral's task would have been greatly eased had he either been sent the signals earlier, or the Admiralty had attached its appreciation to the decrypt. Either would have been practicable. The fundamental importance of timeliness in an operational headquarters was not yet fully understood.

There were other repercussions. The Admiral of Patrols and the senior naval officer at Hartlepool received a sharp, but not wholly deserved, reprimand over the failure to have C9 at sea. Oliver had a poor opinion of Ballard (whom he described as "useless") and claimed in later years that he "took bits of his command away at the north and south ends till there was nothing left," but this was an exaggeration and Ballard remained on the east coast for another year.[47] Keyes came in for blame about C9, largely the result of Fisher's continuing dissatisfaction with the alleged lack of progress in the prewar submarine service. All Fisher's concerns erupted again and Ballard had a stormy interview with him. As the latter reported to Keyes, with more than a hint that the First Sea Lord held Commodore (S) to account as much as the Admiral of Patrols, Fisher's tirade included claims that "submarines didn't require a harbor as they could always lie quite comfortably on the bottom [and] that the 12 submarines under my orders should make it impossible for a German ship to show herself anywhere from St. Abb to Harwich if I knew how to use them." Ballard had discovered the hard way that submarines with their very limited submerged mobility were not necessarily the most effective defensive units for a long coastline. He was quite justified when he remarked, "[T]he sooner somebody makes clear to him what submarines can do and cannot do the better."[48] Churchill had to calm the First Sea Lord, if only because he himself had a share of responsibility for the state of the submarine service. He wrote to Fisher, saying, "Keyes is a brilliant officer, with more knowledge of and feeling for war than almost any naval officer I have met. I think the work and efficiency of our submarines are wonderful."[49]

One major change in the Grand Fleet's dispositions reflected the Admiralty's increasing resolve to control operations via the War Room, as well as its concern for the east coast. The defenses at Rosyth were now complete and there was space above the Forth Bridge for Beatty's forces, as well as for the Third Battle Squadron and the Third Cruiser Squadron that were already based there. On 21 December the First Battle Cruiser Squadron and the First Light Cruiser Squadron left Cromarty for Rosyth. The Firth of Forth was to be the battle cruisers' base for the remainder of the war. The battle cruisers were on their way to becoming a separate fleet, albeit never as independent of the Grand Fleet as some came to believe. When renamed the Battle Cruiser Force, Beatty's command was roughly analogous to that of the Channel Fleet, subordinate to the C-in-C Grand Fleet, but effectively autonomous until within range to allow tactical combination. The First Light Cruiser Squadron and the First Destroyer Flotilla were also now permanently under Beatty. Furthermore, although Beatty was junior to Vice Admiral Bradford, the latter received instructions that he was not to interfere with Beatty's command. The Admiralty emphasized to Jellicoe that both the Harwich Force and the Overseas Submarine Flotilla would be under central control. But one lesson had been learned at last: "[I]n the event of our getting information of another raid, your whole fleet should be sent to sea, in which case you would assume complete charge of the whole operations."[50]

In the aftermath, Beatty received a useful reinforcement. The battle cruiser *Indomitable*, refitting in the south after returning from the Mediterranean, was ordered to join at Rosyth. Her arrival brought the strength of the battle cruisers up to five, a number that Beatty considered was the minimum he needed to operate with confidence against the First Scouting Group.

Apart from the shift of the battle cruisers' base, the policy stood of keeping the Grand Fleet in the north, despite the popular furor in the wake of the bombardments. The realization that the Germans could apparently attack ports with impunity and cause massive damage and civilian casualties came as a shock to many. Lieutenant Charles Daniel's foreboding was all too correct that "we shall probably be as mud in the eyes of the British public."[51] "Where was the navy?" was the public cry and opposition newspapers did not hesitate to use the affair as a stick with which to beat the government, and the First Lord in particular. Churchill felt the pressure, particularly as the nature of the near miss could not be made public.[52] However, other elements came out in support and students of naval strategy hastened to point out the dangers inherent in dividing the Grand Fleet merely to protect the east coast.

If the British public was dissatisfied with the Admiralty and the admirals at sea, there was little joy in Germany. The Scouting Groups were deeply unhappy over the premature withdrawal of the High Sea Fleet and Hipper's confidence in his superior was badly shaken. The fact that the British Second Battle Squadron had been "quite alone" was soon apparent and von Ingenohl's caution all the more a source of frustration within the fleet.[53] The C-in-C came under severe criticism from the kaiser himself, as well as from the Admiralstab. Rear Admiral Behncke pointed out in his assessment, "The C-in-C takes the modifying explanations of the War Order as a guiding line and feels so much tied down by them that there is little hope of favorable opportunities being seized in an energetic manner."[54]

Debate as to von Ingenohl's future intensified. Von Tirpitz's frustration redoubled, but his personal influence with the kaiser remained weak and neither von Pohl nor von Müller were yet prepared to propose the C-in-C's relief. Von Pohl was aware that he was the most likely alternative candidate, but he was willing to take the post only if directly ordered and thought, given the difficulties that he faced, von Ingenohl had done quite well.[55] The C-in-C would stay where he was—for the moment. There were other intrigues afoot. In January von Levetzow of *Moltke* fired the first shot in a campaign to have Hipper relieved by writing to the retired, but still highly influential, Admiral von Holtzendorff.[56] Von Levetzow's target was as much the staff as the admiral, which suggested continuing problems within the First Scouting Group.

The Germans also found themselves somewhat wrong-footed in the propaganda war. Hartlepool had clearly been a legitimate target, but the other ports lacked protective gun batteries. There was ambiguity as to their status because of the presence of local military encampments, but the bombardment was represented by the British as a breach of the Hague Convention, to which Germany was a signatory. While the navy could comfort itself with the blow that had been struck to British prestige, the reality was that the venture further damaged Germany's moral position. The sobriquet "baby killer" conferred on Hitler illustrated the dilemmas that Germany faced in responding to the British blockade. The latter could and did have lethal effects on the German nation, but did not actually spill civilian blood, particularly neutral blood, whereas practically every response involved violent death. This was a conundrum the Germans never resolved.

13

MINES AND ICE

D ESPITE THE SETBACK OF *PALLADA*, VON ESSEN'S PLANS FOR A MORE offensive approach continued to mature. To gain Sixth Army approval, he suggested that operations in the southern Baltic would help protect the army's seaward flank, while he made a second point that Russia needed to interrupt Germany's seaborne trade with Sweden. The Sixth Army Commander, however, remained fixated on the vulnerability of the approaches to Petrograd. Protecting the western shores of Russian territory had a much lower priority and interrupting supplies to the German economy one lower still.

This was too important an issue to be kept at a regional level and von Essen submitted his proposals to the Supreme Command, albeit with the Sixth Army Commander's comments attached. The response was mixed. The efforts already in train to include the Gulf of Riga and the entire Gulf of Finland in the defensive system were approved, but strict limits were retained on the fleet as a whole. The loophole that von Essen was able to exploit, and may well have aligned with his own inclination, resulted from the Russian leadership's preoccupation with preservation of the new dreadnoughts. Although approval was required for the battleships' deployment, there was allowance within the Supreme Command's new directive for limited operations by other units in "favorable" conditions.[1] What constituted "favorable" conditions the fleet commander felt himself fully qualified to judge. Von Essen was no von Ingenohl.

Given that the battleships were the focus of the operational restrictions, von Essen ordered that the faster cruisers, including *Rurik,* be modified as minelayers. However, the start of the campaign would have to rely on light forces alone. He planned a series of minelaying sorties, employing *Novik* and other destroyers, to lay fields across the major shipping lanes in the southern Baltic, as well as at the approaches to Germany's eastern naval bases. The fields placed near them would reduce the risk of attack by German forces on operations undertaken farther to the west. The latter would also be conducted later in the year, when the hours of daylight were near their minimum. The fact that the minelayers would not be accompanied by heavy units placed a premium on their remaining covert.

Preparations continued during October, with forward facilities being reestablished in Moon Sound to provide an advanced base for the minelayers. The Russians recognized that a weakness lay in their inability to conduct effective surveillance of the southern Baltic, creating the possibility that the minelayers could run straight into the arms of a superior enemy force. The only alternative to physical reconnaissance was increased exploitation of signals intelligence, something made possible not only by the material from *Magdeburg,* but also by establishment of a series of interception and direction-finding stations. Even at this early stage of the war it had become clear that the Germans were active users of wireless; there was considerable intelligence to be gained from traffic analysis and radio direction finding, as well as from the decryption effort now possible.

Von Essen's plans were complicated by the British decision to send submarines into the Baltic. The idea of such a venture had first been formally debated at the meeting on board HMS *Iron Duke* on 17 September, as part of more general discussions over the deployment of British forces. The consensus was that submarines were probably the only practical means the British possessed for putting pressure on the Germans in the Baltic and more detailed planning was put in hand for such a venture. Sensibly, the preparations included a reconnaissance by submarines *E1* and *E5* into the Kattegat to get a better idea of local conditions. Less sensibly, while the First Lord had made a general declaration of intent for Baltic operations in a letter to Russian authorities in August, planning did not include giving any details to the Russian naval attaché in London—or to the British naval attaché in Petrograd. Despite the cooperation shown over *Magdeburg,* the British were not well informed as to the status of operations in the theater and did not realize that the Russians had withdrawn from Libau and the other Baltic coast ports.

After delays due to machinery defects, *E1* and *E9* finally left for the Baltic on 15 October. *E11* was held back by further engineering trouble and did not sail until some hours after. *E1* was the first out of the Sound late on the evening of 17 October. Her passage, accomplished largely on the surface, but trimmed down to present the minimum silhouette, was relatively straightforward, with only one or two close encounters with merchant ships and patrol craft in the darkness, but it was still a strain. Her first lieutenant described the night of 17 October as "the longest of my life."[2] The Germans were already receiving reports that there were submarines in the area, but *E1*'s attack on the old cruiser *Viktoria Luise* on 18 October came as a shock. The first of two torpedoes missed close astern and a rapid alteration of course saw the cruiser run parallel to the second weapon for several minutes. *Viktoria Luise* did not remain in the area and *E1*'s later efforts to pursue other German forces were also unsuccessful. But the message was clear. German heavy ships exercising in Kiel Bay, including the new battle cruiser *Derfflinger,* were hastily withdrawn into harbor, while additional patrols were instituted. This included aerial surveillance by the small airship PL19. The old cruisers of the Coast Defence Division remained at sea—the Germans had yet to experience their submarine attack moment—but with strict orders to remain under way.

Lieutenant Commander Max Horton in *E9* had been more cautious than his colleague in *E1,* Noel Laurence, and emerged from the Sound some twenty-four hours later to find a veritable hornets' nest. The possibility of a successful attack on a major unit rapidly disappeared as Horton found his progress continually interrupted by patrolling light craft. Whether *E9* was observed or not remains unclear, but it is certain that the German Baltic forces were suffering from submarinitis as much as any units in the North Sea. The Seventeenth Half-Flotilla conducted a spirited action with two phantom submarines on 19 October and came away convinced that it had sighted and engaged both "units."

The two British boats soon began to head east. The third unit, *E11,* under Lieutenant Commander Martin Nasmith, did not make it into the Baltic. She arrived at the northern entrance of the Sound late on the afternoon of 18 October and found that the patrols in the area were much more intense. It is likely that some were Swedish units demonstrating their neutrality, but Nasmith was forced to withdraw to charge *E11*'s batteries before making a second attempt the next day. It was while setting up for this that *E11* detected another submarine on the surface outside neutral territorial waters. The vessel resembled one of the oldest U-boats, but apparently carried no distinguishing markings or flag. *E11* fired two torpedoes. Fortunately, both missed, because the submarine was the Danish *Havmanden.* The Danes later accepted the British government's apology, given the difficulties of the operational situation, particularly since *Havmanden* had recently been modified in a way that made her resemble *U3.* As for *E11,* her later efforts to transit the Sound were no more successful. Although Nasmith seems to have mistaken other traffic for hunting patrols, he made little progress and had difficulty in keeping his battery topped up, a vital concern, given the environment. He finally withdrew on 22 October and returned to Harwich.

E9 made for Danzig Bay, but a motor defect prevented Horton from the close examination of the approaches to Danzig that he had intended. Meanwhile, to the Russians' astonishment, *E1* arrived at Libau on 21 October. Laurence discovered to his horror that he had come straight over a German minefield, while Libau itself was no longer capable of serving as a base. Similarly fortunate with the minefield, *E9* arrived the following morning and the two boats began their own repairs while they awaited *E11* and new orders. Although Admiral von Essen was quick to see the potential of the capable British submarines, he was justifiably irritated by the lack of warning. The British attaché reported that von Essen "would have been even more pleased had he received timely notice of their coming, or been informed as to whose orders they were intended to be subordinate."[3] The fact that *E11* was possibly still at sea forced the delay of the first of the Russians' offensive minelaying sorties, while von Essen now had to consider where best to station the British boats and determine what help they would need. He demonstrated his personal support by assigning his son Otto to *E9* as a liaison officer. By 24 October, when it was clear that *E11* had not made it, orders were sent to the other two submarines to proceed to Lapvik. *E1* and *E9* sailed the next day, with the immediate objective of a reconnaissance of Danzig Bay.

Life was now much more complicated for the Germans. Their challenge was to develop effective countermeasures against the submarines, while continuing offensive operations in the eastern Baltic. Pressure was hastily put on Sweden to restrict the passage through the Sound. The Swedes obliged by removing some of their navigational markers, but insisted that the passage had to remain open for commercial traffic, forcing the Germans to continue their watch on the southern entrance. After hearing of the sinking of *E3* in the North Sea, Prince Heinrich decided to substitute submarine patrols for the torpedo boats in Kiel Bay. Surface vessels were cleared from the area and the older U-boats were given free run to seaward of Kiel until 27 October. Their inability to search large areas was compensated for in part by seaplane and airship patrols. In the short term, this was an imaginative response to the submarine problem, but, although releasing surface craft to keep a watch on the Sound and the Belts for additional British submarines, it represented only a local solution to a seawide threat and a partial one at that. The Imperial German Navy's safest exercise areas were no longer inviolate. The issue of protecting merchant shipping had yet to be addressed at all.

The Germans gave the Allies more credit for cooperation than they deserved and Rear Admiral Behring was warned to be ready for a Russian sortie. The latter's declarations of closures of northern Baltic areas to merchant shipping had created suspicions that they were intending to embark on a program of minelaying and the Germans were anxious to get a better idea of the activity in the region. In addition to his submarines, Behring now had the armored cruiser *Friedrich Carl* as his flagship, supported by two of Rear Admiral Jasper's cruisers, while two seaplanes were embarked in *Friedrich Carl* to assist with reconnaissance. The real combat capability of the force was represented by the three U-boats, and Behring's main use for his elderly ships was as bait to entice the Russians into a submarine trap. He began a new operation with this intent on 24 October, but it soon became clear, after the loss of *Pallada*, that the Russians had no intention of risking their heavy units outside the Gulf in such a way again.

Behring was frequently reminded of the threat in his rear. Repeated reports of submarines all around the Baltic also confirmed the view that the old training cruisers were of little military value. Growing manpower shortages sealed their fate and they were recalled to Kiel to be paid off. If Behring wanted to retain freedom of movement, the British units had to be his priority. The Germans initially had intelligence that the boats were using Libau as their base and Behring decided to position *U23, U25,* and *U26* as a blockade force, with the hope of intercepting *E1* and *E9* as they entered or left harbor. Only *U25* and *U26* were contacted in time to allow their immediate reassignment, but Behring soon realized that the watch would be a drawn out affair. *U23*'s early return to Danzig meant that she was available to relieve the other two units and extend the patrol until 9 November, being reinforced by the newly acquired *UA*, a boat originally ordered for Norway, on 6 November.

They were in the wrong place, as the Germans began to realize. After their sortie into Danzig Bay, the two British submarines made a rendezvous with a Russian destroyer on 30 October and were escorted into Lapvik, where they had a warm welcome and were provided with an old steam corvette as their depot ship. *E1* and *E9* soon transferred with their new mother unit to Reval, where the maintenance facilities were much better. This was an important advantage. The early *E*-class submarines were the best in the world when commissioned, but the two boats were operating at their limits and mechanical problems were all too frequent. Although an engineer officer had been brought with *E1,* the problems of a long-term deployment to the Baltic had not been thought through—if indeed that had been the original intention, since a supply of spare parts and torpedoes had yet to be arranged. If the boats were to remain operational, much improvisation would be required. The coming winter did provide one benefit in that the operational season would soon be over, which would allow repair work and a supply link with Britain to be organized before the spring.

Sure of the location of the British boats, von Essen was at last able to set in train a minelaying sortie in the southern Baltic (map 13.1). This centered on using the fast *Novik* to deploy the fields in the locations of high risk to the west, while a destroyer division sowed mines in offshore positions. The latter would have another division as a close escort, with a third as a stand-by farther astern. *Novik*'s first field would be across the shipping lane between Danzig and the west; the other destroyers would work off Memel. The ships sailed on 30 October. The field off Memel, designated 1D, was successfully deployed, but poor weather created significant difficulties. The destroyers took so much water that some of the mine safety devices switched off as a result of saltwater contact and they were fortunate to get their 105 mines away without accident. *Novik,* which had farther to go, followed the destroyer groups until the time came to head west. She had barely turned to the new course when the weather worsened even further. Despite reducing speed, the conditions were too much. *Novik* "was rolling 36 degrees either way. . . . [S]he went so far over that at times we thought she would capsize."[4] Desperate efforts were required to secure mines that repeatedly broke adrift. It was soon clear that the operation could not go ahead. With some difficulty in the steep seas, *Novik* turned and made for home. Conditions improved rapidly as she steamed north, but the minelayer had no alternative target location. After making

Mine barrier number	Date of laying	Number of mines
1	31 Oct 1914	105
2	5 Nov 1914	140
3	5 Nov 1914	50
4	19 Nov 1914	240
5	20 Nov 1914	105
6	24 Nov 1914	50
7	27 Nov 1914	50
8	14 Dec 1914	64
9	14 Dec 1914	120
10	15 Dec 1914	240
11	13 Jan 1915	196
12	14 Jan 1915	98
13	14 Feb 1915	70
14	14 Feb 1915	70

MAP 13.1   Russian Minefields in the Southern Baltic, 1914

contact with the other units, *Novik* spent the night in Moon Sound and then sailed for Helsingfors to refuel. While en route, she encountered the British submarines and their escort. *Novik*'s crew gave them some "resounding cheers."[5]

Despite the failure of *Novik*'s lay, von Essen was reasonably encouraged by the results of this first sortie and overruled his mine forces commander, who wanted to wait for even longer nights. This was taking counsel of fears, since in early November daylight was already down to less than eight hours, and von Essen directed that further operations were to be conducted as soon as possible. His priority was to get enough fields laid to ensure that no direct approach could be made toward the Russian coast from the west, with the remaining fields filled in later.

There were a number of lessons. The first was the need to consider the weather. While the other destroyers had some trouble, *Novik*'s experience was a reminder of the extreme conditions that could develop very rapidly. The Russians set up a reporting system around the areas of the coast that they still held to provide better warning of weather events. Provision for alternative targets was included within each operation, although it was made clear to commanders that deploying their mines close to the coast was the priority, it being more important to know exactly where they were laid than that they be in a particular position.

A second mission went ahead on 5 November and this was more successful, with fields laid across the Danzig-Memel shipping lane and off Pillau. The four destroyers conducting the Danzig-Memel lay encountered the old light cruiser *Thetis,* which was on passage from Memel to Danzig. *Thetis* spotted two ships in darkness just before 2300, but mistook them for cruisers. The old ship was no match for any Russian cruiser in the Baltic and her captain turned away. Curiously, *Thetis* made no sighting report at this stage. Two hours later *Thetis* encountered *Novik*, which had completed her lay and was heading home at twenty-four knots. *Thetis* challenged, illuminated *Novik* with searchlights, and opened fire. The fifteen rounds fired before she lost sight of the Russian in the darkness were fairly accurate, but she scored no hits as *Novik* cleared the area at thirty-two knots, twice the speed of which *Thetis* was capable. The German cruiser reported this action, but had no alternative except to resume her passage for Danzig. *Thetis'* captain, Commander Paul Nippe, was heavily criticized, both for his failure to make an initial report and for not adopting more aggressive tactics in the first encounter with ships that were clearly not eager to fight, and that were much more likely to have been destroyers than cruisers. Nippe was relieved on the grounds of poor eyesight—he admitted that he had to rely on his subordinates' reports. Admiral Behring's concern was that the enemy units might have been minelayers, which it was "absolutely essential to reconnoiter and sink."[6] He had a point. There were soon other indications that Russian forces had been active in the southern Baltic, with possible sightings by *UA* and *Augsburg* of the minelayers withdrawing to the north. Unfortunately for the Germans, there was no clear evidence as to where mines had been laid and, in any case, there were no minesweepers capable of operating offshore.

Prince Heinrich had meanwhile decided to block Libau and render it unable to support any Russian naval activity. Although the Germans were aware of the sinking of ships in the fairway, it was clear that Russian light forces were still able to use the port, something confirmed by the arrival of the British submarines. The prince's motive was not only to remove the base as a source of concern, but also to keep the Russians off balance. As the nights drew in, he knew that his weak forces were particularly vulnerable to raids, a threat only increased by the evidence that the British were now willing to attempt the passage into the Baltic.

Behring's relatively small force of cruisers, destroyers, and block ships was at first assigned an unexpected reinforcement. The High Sea Fleet's Second Squadron was released from the gunnery training that it had been conducting off Kiel and assigned to the Baltic Command. Aware of the increasing restlessness within the battle squadrons, von Ingenohl was eager to give the battleships a chance to blood themselves. However, the Second Squadron and the Fourth Scouting Group had barely left Kiel on 9 November when they received an order from the kaiser himself forbidding their participation. This was on von Pohl's advice, although his primary concern was submarines rather than mines.[7]

Behring was undismayed and continued with plans for an attack on Libau. He deployed his two available submarines outside the Gulf of Finland to intercept any Russian surface forces, while he planned on using block ships to complete the closure of Libau and his cruisers to bombard its facilities. After poor weather the operation finally got under way on 15 November. It met with disaster. Very early on 17 November, on passage to Memel, Behring's flagship, *Friedrich Carl,* struck a mine. Believing that she had been torpedoed, the armored cruiser turned west to clear the area. Although the ship's damage control parties responded as best they could, it soon became apparent that *Friedrich Carl* was in danger of sinking. With her speed dropping, the best course seemed to be toward Memel, little more than thirty miles away, where the ship could be beached. This decision sealed the armored cruiser's fate because it took her back into the minefield laid on 5 November. Just after she turned east, *Friedrich Carl* struck a second mine. This caused extensive flooding aft and disabled one engine. Shortly afterward, the rudder jammed, leaving *Friedrich Carl* describing a circle at slow speed. A power failure and damage to her radio equipment meant that the cruiser could not at first call for help, but arrangements were eventually jury-rigged and other German units alerted to the flagship's peril.

Augsburg was soon on her way, with *Amazone* some hours behind. The force designated to block Libau also picked up the distress calls, but decided that the operation should continue, given *Augsburg*'s availability to support *Friedrich Carl*. However, the steamer *Elbing* and harbor craft sailed from Memel to see what they could do. *Augsburg* arrived on scene at 0600 and, with great skill, Commander Johannes Horn immediately took his ship alongside *Friedrich Carl* and began embarking her crew. *Augsburg* "had not come a moment too soon"; shortly after she pulled away, *Friedrich Carl* capsized and sank.[8] *Augsburg* at first steered for Memel, detaching the newly arrived *Amazone* to join *Lubeck* off Libau. The Germans were increasingly sure that *Friedrich Carl* had been mined, not torpedoed. This was confirmed when the approaching *Elbing* blew up and sank on the minefield which had been laid close to Memel. Burdened by survivors, it was clear that the risk of attempting an entry to Memel was too great and *Augsburg* turned away for Danzig.

The operation against Libau had started early on 17 November. The sinking of the block ships to complete the closure of the port met with almost no resistance, but was not completely successful. One broke adrift before her scuttling charges had done their work and this left a passage wide enough for light craft. The bombardment by *Lubeck* that followed after dawn was of also little practical use. The cruiser's 10.5-cm shells were too small to achieve mass effects, despite maintaining deliberate fire on the town for several hours. *Amazone* and some torpedo craft took part in the final stages of the attack, but the Germans later had to admit that no substantial damage had been caused.

Although *U23* and *U25* remained on station off the Gulf of Finland for several more days, the surface forces all returned to Danzig before 2359 on 17 November. The Germans had much to ponder. Reconstruction of the previous few weeks made it clear that the Russians had embarked on an offensive mining campaign, creating new risks in areas hitherto thought safe. As a first measure, the forward operating base for Behring's surface units was shifted west to Swinemünde. The British submarines were a further complication, and Prince Heinrich declared that he regarded the destruction of one "as important as that of a Russian armored cruiser."[9] While additional minesweepers would need to be organized, the German lead for offensive action had now to go to the submarines, which would continue to operate from Danzig. For the older officers, recognition of the situation was not easy. Behring complained to Prince Heinrich that, "the advent of submarines, torpedoes and mines has shorn naval warfare of its poetry. But that cannot be helped and one must make up one's mind to it."[10]

Von Essen's mining campaign had only just begun. It took a new form on 19 November with the first offensive lay by the minelayer *Amur*, escorted by *Rurik*, *Oleg*, and *Bogatyr* under Vice Admiral Ludwig Kerber, von Essen's chief of staff. This field of 240 mines, designated 9N, was much farther west than any previous field and lay north of the Shtolpe Bank across one of the shipping lanes from the western ports. Meanwhile, another minefield was laid on the Memel-Danzig route by destroyers. Both sorties went undetected, as did the attack conducted by *E9* on the light cruiser *Gazelle*. Despite firing two torpedoes, both missed and the cruiser's routine maneuvering prevented Horton getting another shot. *Amur's* sortie began the pattern of operations for the coming weeks. Further Russian missions increased the number of fields near Memel and *Novik* completed the work begun with Field 9N by laying a second, 4N, south of the Shtolpe Bank. This meant that both the usual east-west shipping lanes in the southern Baltic were blocked.

The Germans did not remain passive. The navy was under increasing pressure from the German General Staff over the supplies passing through Sweden and across the Gulf of Bothnia to sustain the Russian war effort. While there was concern that Sweden had to be handled with care, mining the Finnish ports and providing some warning to the Swedes about the danger to their shipping seemed a reasonable compromise. *Deutschland* was dispatched on 3 December. The ship was provided with some distant cover in the form of Behring's light cruisers and a half-flotilla of torpedo boats, but these units remained outside the Gulf of Bothnia. The sixteen-knot *Deutschland* was on her own. Despite considerable navigational difficulty, *Deutschland* was able to lay fields close off Rauma and Bjorneborg, on the Finnish southwest coast, on 6 December and withdraw without detection. Her employment indicated the German poverty in fast minelayers, partly as a result of their heavy losses of cruisers, but the minefields were immediately effective. Two merchant ships sank the same day and a third on 7 December. All were Swedish. Although traffic was temporarily interrupted between Sweden and Finland, however, the mines were soon swept.

The diplomatic pressure that Germany experienced as a result of the sinkings highlighted the need for access to the Gulf of Bothnia and the anomalous situation of the Aaland Islands. These Russian possessions lay between Sweden and Finland. Their fortification had been forbidden in the 1856 Treaty of Paris, but the Germans had indications of Russian military activity. The latter were indeed setting up observation posts and listening stations, which did not technically qualify as fortifications. The Germans were increasingly aware that the islands were key to controlling the Gulf of Bothnia and the Russian lifeline to Sweden, but their assault and occupation were propositions too formidable to consider at this stage of the war.

Meanwhile, the Russian mining sorties continued to push into the western Baltic. Von Essen sent *E1* and *E9* out ahead of the operation to the west of Bornholm on 11 December, with instructions to both submarines to ensure that the Germans became aware of their presence. The Russian submarine *Akula* was intended for similar employment, but was delayed by weather. The British units had little more luck; *E1* snapped a shaft shortly after a failed attack on a German torpedo boat and then was herself unsuccessfully attacked by *U25* as she returned to base on 16 December. *E9*'s patrol was a little quieter, but the loss of a propeller blade brought about her return on 17 December.

The mining operation went ahead successfully. The armored cruiser *Bayan* suffered machinery problems and was forced to turn home, but *Rurik* and *Admiral Makarov* and the minelayer *Enisei* deployed more than 420 mines in additional fields across the shipping lanes from the west to Memel and Danzig. All the ships returned safely by 16 December and the Russians immediately began to prepare for another sortie, given the limited time before the winter ice took hold. This new venture was even more ambitious. Covered by *Rurik, Bayan,* and *Admiral Makarov,* two separate operations were conducted. The cruiser *Rossiya* ventured west of Bornholm, farther than any Russian unit since the start of the war, and laid a field north of Rügen Island off Cape Arkona on 14 January. At the same time, *Oleg* and *Bogatyr* set mines to the east of Bornholm. The Russians were able to withdraw undetected, despite *Rossiya* encountering *Undine* at night as she steamed to rejoin the covering force. *Rossiya* carried considerably more powerful armament than the elderly German light cruiser, but her captain did not initiate contact in order to avoid giving any indication of the minefield's presence.

Weather and defects prevented any German sorties until late January. Admiral Behring was finally able to sail from Swinemünde on 22 January with the intention of reconnoitering the Swedish coast for shipping and combining this with a bombardment of Libau. His intent remained to keep the Russians off balance, something that was becoming even more important, given the increasing strength of their Baltic Fleet. Although there was evidence that the Russians were no longer using Libau at all, Behring felt that an attack on the port would confirm German local dominance. He decided to minimize the mine danger by approaching along the coast from the south, with torpedo boats sweeping ahead of *Prinz Adalbert* and an additional unit prepositioned to provide a navigational reference. Both elements failed. The sweep wires repeatedly parted and the marker, *G132,* was late getting into position. The latter brought the armored cruiser undone and she grounded heavily early on 24 January. Had the torpedo boats been fitted with sounding gear, they may have been able to warn *Prinz Adalbert* soon enough of the rapidly reducing depth. As it was, the reports of their hand leadsmen were too late to help. The ship's captain did all he could to lighten the ship and drive her off, but it was only after he organized the torpedo craft to steam by at close range and generated an artificial swell that he was able to lift *Prinz Adalbert* clear and refloat her. This was fortunate, since the presence of the ship had already been discovered by the Russians. *E9* was at sea and the Russian Fleet Command redirected her to the scene. Horton arrived early the same afternoon, but by this time the German force had got away.

The operation aborted, Behring returned with the armored cruiser and her escorts to Swinemünde, but there were more disasters in store. *Augsburg* and her half-flotilla conducted a reconnaissance aimed at intercepting contraband traffic west of Gotland, but found nothing. In the early hours of 25 January, during the return to Swinemünde, *Augsburg* hit one of the mines laid to the east of Bornholm by *Oleg* and *Bogatyr.* Struck amidships, the cruiser suffered severe flooding and the loss of a boiler room. The crew were able to control the flooding, but contamination of feedwater eventually brought *Augsburg* to a halt and she was taken under tow by a torpedo boat.

The news got worse. That same afternoon, the light cruiser *Gazelle* struck one of *Rossiya's* mines while on patrol off Cape Arkona. The cruiser was badly damaged, but misjudged the source of the attack. Convinced that they had been torpedoed, the crew conducted a battle with two phantom submarines that they thought that they detected shortly after the explosion. Like *Augsburg,* Behring was able to get the cruiser towed into Swinemünde, where examination soon confirmed that both cruisers had been mined. The elderly *Gazelle* was not worth repairing for seagoing service and was decommissioned. *Augsburg* and *Prinz Adalbert* both had to go into dockyard hands for major repairs. Neither would emerge until well into March.

One final blow remained. An ill-judged sortie by the airship PL19 against Libau resulted in its loss. The airship did not have the same operational capabilities as the zeppelins and had been finding the weather conditions in the Baltic increasingly difficult, even in the western Baltic. The dispatch of such a unit, not equipped with radio, on a sortie at the limits of its operational endurance at this time of year had not been wise. The Russians claimed to have shot the airship down and certainly captured its crew.

These heavy losses, the onset of winter, and the need to deal with the mines in the western Baltic forced the termination of German offensive efforts until the spring. The weather alone made this inevitable, but the Germans had much to consider. The Russian minefields had begun to take a heavy toll of Baltic merchant shipping. The technique of offshore mining was proving itself a difficult weapon to counter. Not only were the fields hard to locate, but the minesweepers also required cover if they were not to be vulnerable to Russian raids. Prince Heinrich initially set his face against the protection of what he considered was commerce, but he was eventually convinced that this represented one of Germany's supply life lines. It was becoming increasingly apparent that the Baltic minesweeping effort needed to be strengthened for both offshore and coastal work.

The Russians had one more card to play before the freeze. The start of the winter in the Gulf of Finland proved relatively mild, keeping the major bases open for longer than expected. A final major mine operation was put in hand on 12 February. Although the *E*-class boats had already found the winter conditions extremely difficult, Laurence agreed to take *E1* out on 8 February. Icing had proved more manageable than expected during the previous patrols, Horton in *E9* having hit on the solution of diving at intervals to free the boat of ice. This was practicable provided that the hatches were kept clear. Nevertheless, the new patrol was at the edge of practicality. This was confirmed when *E1* became caught fast in ice after suffering machinery troubles. Fortunately, although she had had problems with her radio, her faint signal for help was finally heard by a unit in Reval and the icebreaker *Petr Velikiy* sent to bring the submarine home. Visibility was very poor and *E1*'s crew reduced to shouting in unison to attract the icebreaker's attention. Their chorus was eventually successful and *E1* was discovered and towed back to Reval. Her first lieutenant commented, "Since this episode I have had no desire to become an arctic explorer."[11]

The Russian sortie did not fare as well as its predecessors. In thick fog, destroyers laid two more fields in the shipping lanes offshore of Danzig, but the simultaneous effort in the west came to an ignominious end. Four cruisers left Reval in thick weather on 12 February. Their plan to pass down the coast of Gotland was dependent on making an accurate landfall on its northeastern corner, marked by the Farö lighthouse. In the poor visibility and uncertain currents, soundings and dead reckoning were not enough to keep the force safe and, on 13 February *Rurik* struck an isolated rock at sixteen knots. This ripped her hull open and flooded a boiler room. The operation was perforce abandoned and *Admiral Makarov, Oleg,* and *Bogatyr* escorted *Rurik* back to Reval for what proved to be lengthy repairs. There would be no more such operations until the spring thaw and the curtain thus rang down on the first act of the Baltic War.

14

TRYING THE OFFENSE

IN LATE DECEMBER TYRWHITT AND KEYES RECEIVED PERMISSION FOR ANOTHER attack on the zeppelin sheds at Cuxhaven. The threat of air raids preoccupied the Admiralty and the British public, particularly in the capital. Although the defenses needed were obvious—coordinated searchlights and gun batteries, combined with fighter aircraft—they were not yet in place. The only option available was to attack the zeppelins at their bases. Intelligence as to their location remained vague, but much more was known than had been on the first attempt.

A report that the High Sea Fleet might sortie again caused the Admiralty to order a delay until Christmas Day. At 0500 on Christmas Eve, *Arethusa* and *Undaunted*, six destroyers, and the seaplane carriers *Engadine, Riviera,* and *Empress* sailed from Harwich. This was only a small formation, since Tyrwhitt believed that it would be easier for a limited number of ships to penetrate Heligoland Bight undetected. He arranged, however, that *Fearless* and a half-flotilla of destroyers would follow and support the withdrawal. Keyes sent ten submarines into the Bight, stationing some around the planned launch and recovery positions and the remainder inshore. The Grand Fleet would be at sea but, despite the obvious weakness of Commodore (T)'s forces, would not venture south unless the Germans came out in strength.

The Germans believed the British were planning a sortie, but focused on the possibility of a massed attack by two hundred block ships. This derived from garbled reports of the dozen old merchant ships refitted as dummy capital ships in Belfast, but it alarmed the Fleet Command. Minefields were reinforced, U-boats deployed as pickets and torpedo boats dispatched daily to scout to the Horns Reef, while the available zeppelins conducted local reconnaissance. Late on Christmas Eve, the Fleet Command received information that an attack could be expected the next day. Prevented by thick cloud from operating on 24 December, zeppelins L5 and L6 were ordered to survey the Bight early on Christmas morning, while seaplane sorties were also organized.

What saved Tyrwhitt was the German expectation of penetration on a massive scale. This played to all the old ideas about a British assault on German harbors, which meant a return to dispositions exercised before the war, the major units remaining inshore. Given the expected enemy strength, fear of a repetition of 28 August also restricted the use of light forces. This meant that the zeppelins, seaplanes, and U-boats would do all the work. However, it would take more than their reports to convince von Ingenohl that Tyrwhitt's ships were not the vanguard of a British armada. Furthermore, there was an additional weakness. Despite the expectation that attack was imminent, only two U-boats were deployed that day.

As Tyrwhitt's ships sailed, the weather seemed perfect. It was bitterly cold, but calm with not a hint of fog. At 1000 *Fearless* led out her half-flotilla. Conditions held and the British crossed the North Sea without incident. At 0430 on Christmas Day, when Tyrwhitt's ships were thirty-five miles northwest of Heligoland, they passed four vessels trawling with lights up. Commodore (T) decided to ignore them, but a few minutes after they had dropped out of sight, *Arethusa* intercepted German wireless traffic that suggested a small ship's installation. The "telefunken" was not from any trawler, but rather from *U6*. Within half an hour the ether was filled with signals, particularly from Heligoland, many prefixed by the recognizable group for "urgent." Still three hours from the launch position, Tyrwhitt debated what to do. If the ships went on, they risked being cut off before the seaplanes could be recovered. With a practical maximum of only eighteen knots (much less than their advertised twenty-one), the seaplane carriers were not fast enough to outrun German light cruisers. If these ships were already at sea—and the British believed they patrolled the inner Bight—there would be ample time to intercept. But Tyrwhitt decided to continue, taking as his inspiration the appearance of Venus, "magnificent" on the horizon.[1] Believing it a good omen, he pressed on.[2]

U6 turned to follow the Harwich Force, hoping to attack, as well as to ascertain the enemy's strength. The British steamed southeast until, half an hour before dawn, the three seaplane carriers hove-to. Each hoisted out three seaplanes. Despite the perfect conditions, two aircraft failed to take off and four more also had trouble. Thus, after some delay, only seven made their way southeast toward Cuxhaven. The lack of wind itself caused difficulties, since the seaplanes were forced to make a long take-off run, consuming fuel desperately needed for the sortie. The half-hour evolution gave *U6* a chance to approach, but the submarine was foiled when, at 0820, Tyrwhitt turned his ships southwest toward the recovery position. By this time there were other distractions. Zeppelin *L6*, alerted by *U6*'s warnings, had been crisscrossing the northern Bight before her captain decided to examine the area west of Heligoland. He was rewarded when he came upon Tyrwhitt's ships. The British, having sighted *L6*, were waiting apprehensively to see just what the much-vaunted zeppelins could do (photo 14.1).

Lagging behind because of poor coal was the carrier *Empress*. She was an attractive target, isolated from her more heavily armed consorts, and *L6* made

PHOTO 14.1   **Zeppelin L6**   *Bibliothek fur Zeitgeschichte*

straight for her, in an attempt to begin history's first real air-sea action. The zeppelin was beaten to it by a pair of seaplanes. The first dropped six small bombs very inaccurately, but the second had two larger weapons and straddled *Empress* with them, "shaking the ship severely."[3] Once they were clear, L6 tried to come in from directly astern of *Empress,* presenting a difficult target to the riflemen who were the ship's only defenses. From three miles ahead the two cruisers attempted to cover *Empress* with their new antiaircraft guns, but had to check fire frequently to avoid hitting her. Despite these problems, the carrier's captain, Lieutenant F. W. Bowhill, soon observed that the airship could not put her bows through the wind when altering course, but had to wear right around.[4] He took immediate advantage: "My method of defence was to watch [the zeppelin] carefully as she maneuvered into position directly overhead. I then went hard over. I could see her rudders put over to follow me, I put my helm over the other way."[5]

By turning 8 points each time the airship came overhead, *Empress* avoided the bombs dropped around her, although there were several near misses. L6's captain, Lieutenant Horst Baron von Buttlar, stated that he dropped only a single 110-pound bomb on *Empress*, later jettisoning the remainder as ballast, but this does not accord with surface witnesses.[6] Bowhill bemoaned the absence of an antiaircraft gun, since the airship appeared to be extremely vulnerable. Von Buttlar clearly shared his view and took L6 away, with nine bullet holes in her gas bags. Frewen in *Lookout* recorded, "The sailors, delighted at the Christmas entertainment, clapped the conclusion of each 'turn.'"[7]

This was not the only air-sea action as a seaplane attacked *Fearless'* group, but was driven away by the cruiser's gunfire. The destroyers felt that their leader fired too early, preventing them putting up a much more intense barrage at close range.[8] There was then a respite from air attacks and the Harwich Force steered for the recovery position. Arriving at 0930, there was nothing to be seen and Tyrwhitt ordered his ships to spread and search for the aviators. Shortly after, *Fearless* and her destroyers joined him and were sent to the west, extending the search line to six miles. For nearly an hour the force continued south, but found only two seaplanes. Keyes in *Lurcher*, stationed farther west, picked up the crew of a third, but Tyrwhitt realized that the other four were half an hour over their endurance and had to be considered lost.

The search was confused by the appearance of L5, commanded by Lieutenant Klaus Hirsch, and more seaplanes. By now *Empress* had closed up with the force, but the German aircraft still made for the carriers as the best targets. In the action that followed, seaplanes and airship again proved less than effective. No bombs hit and L5 had great difficulty in making an accurate approach over Tyrwhitt's zigzagging ships. The seaplanes did a little better, spattering one of the cruisers with splinters, but their hand bombs threatened only exposed personnel. Commodore (T) assessed that "given ordinary sea room, our ships have nothing to fear." He wrote to his sister, "Zeppelins are not to be thought of as regards ships. Stupid great things, but very beautiful. It seemed a pity to shoot at them."[9] However confident his assertions, Tyrwhitt's judgment was based directly on the technology then available to the aviators and would need constant review. It was already clear that antiaircraft armament required improvement. The Germans did not succeed in hitting the British, but the British had not done much harm to their airborne opponents; only one machine was damaged beyond repair (this was seaplane No.25, which took at least two hits).[10] As the last attack died away, Commodore (T) signaled, "I wish all ships a Merry Christmas."[11] At 1100, on a more somber note, having reconnoitered to the Norderney Gat without finding the seaplanes, Tyrwhitt ordered his ships to return to Harwich, which they did without further interference.

There were incidents that suggested that the balance between readiness and relaxation required attention, although it was being found by some. Later that day, as the force continued its withdrawal, *Ferret* was ordered to investigate a Dutch trawler. The boarding officer found that his boat's crew—and the deck teams—had dined not wisely, but too well in recognition of the holiday. The examination was completed successfully and the boat eventually recovered, but Tennant complained, "I could have found a crew on Margate beach in July who would have hooked the boat on as quickly."[12] The ratings' mid-day tot of rum with their meal was strong enough by itself; things got complicated on special occasions, when illegal hoards were sampled. There were other approaches to the festival. On board *Southampton*, a covering unit, Stephen King-Hall enlivened a dull day at action stations by installing a gramophone in the after control position. He then placed

PHOTO 14.2   **HMS** *Southampton* **at Scapa Flow**   *Imperial War Museum*

every telephone handset and flexible voice pipe in the vicinity into the gramophone horn and broadcast music around *Southampton*. "The idea worked beautifully, as delighted messages from various parts of the ship testified."[13] Many things
had changed since August (photo 14.2).

Happily, Keyes' submarines rescued the crews of three of the four missing
aircraft. *E11*, under Nasmith, was off Norderney when seaplane No.120 sighted her
and landed alongside, having run out of fuel. *E11* attempted to tow the seaplane to
the rendezvous, but, just as the two got under way, progress was rudely interrupted
by the sudden appearance of L5, as well as two more British seaplanes, No.814 and
No.815, also out of fuel. To add to Nasmith's worries, a submarine appeared on the
surface, heading directly toward his little group. It was *D6*, well out of position,
that had observed the seaplanes and was coming to see if she could help. Thinking
her a U-boat, and with L5 barely a mile away and losing height rapidly in what was
clearly an attack run, Nasmith hastily embarked the three crews. He machine-
gunned the seaplanes' floats and dived just as L5 dropped two bombs. Although
they fell nearby, *E11* was undamaged and slipped away without further trouble.
D6, however, had a narrow escape. She also dived as L5 approached. Trying to
ensure the seaplanes were not captured by the Germans, Lieutenant Commander
Halahan surfaced his boat too early and found L5 directly above the submarine—
at barely fifty feet! Halahan hastily submerged again amidst a hail of machine-gun
fire. Fortunately, the submarine suffered no damage and she, too, made for home.

During the day, the other submarines traversed the German minefields, the
latest of which Tyrwhitt had, unknowingly, narrowly avoided. *E10*, mistaking
Lurcher for a German, was about to attack when her captain recognized Keyes'
flagship. *D7* was spotted by L5, fresh from her encounter with *E11* and *D6*. The

airship forced the submarine under and waited overhead. It was dark before *D7* was able to shake L5 off. She finally got home just as she was being given up for lost. Despite the zeppelins, mines, and U-boats, all the British submarines returned from the Bight. In fact, not a man was lost in the operation, for the pilot of the seventh aircraft was picked up by a Dutch trawler and returned as a "shipwrecked mariner." The consensus in the Harwich Force was that Flight Commander Hewlett's "experiences were none too rosy, for the trawler after rescuing him continued to fish for five days before they landed him!"[14]

Of the seven seaplanes, only one or two got to the airship base. Apart from having to nurse their primitive aircraft, the crews found things very different from the clear conditions to seaward as they approached the coast. Thick fog was moving over from inland. It disoriented the aviators and disguised many of the landmarks they intended to use for navigation. The result was a confusion of individual adventures.[15] One aircraft may have dropped bombs near the zeppelin shed, but not as a deliberate attack on it. Another bombed sheds on the island of Langeoog, thinking that they were for aircraft, while a third dropped a bomb on a passing U-boat before a fractured fuel pump forced her down.

Of the remainder, No.811 attacked the light cruiser *Graudenz* and achieved one relatively near miss (two hundred yards), while No.136 had the most interesting career. Engine misfiring, her pilot turned back, passing over the Schillig Roads in an attempt to achieve the mission's secondary aim and reconnoiter the High Sea Fleet's dispositions. No.136 carried not only Flight Commander C. F. Kilner, but also the only "expert" tactical observer, Lieutenant Erskine Childers, Royal Naval Volunteer Reserve. Childers was indeed knowledgeable about the German coast, having spent many summers sailing the estuaries and basing his best-selling invasion novel, the *Riddle of the Sands,* on that experience. His commissioning had been intended for just this purpose and the two officers were able to bring back valuable information. Childers' reputation helped, but it was clear, once his report and those of the other aviators were analyzed, that aircraft possessed great potential value for reconnaissance and, in the longer term, strike. The raid had failed to destroy any zeppelins, but the promise was there and, as Tyrwhitt discovered on visiting the Admiralty, something of a morale boost. "I was really surprised at everybody's pleasure and delight. They want more."[16]

The seaplanes caused the Germans considerable anxiety. Ships and shore installations put up heavy and fairly effective fire, which damaged several machines, notwithstanding Childers' sang froid comment, "[O]ne could take one's notes undisturbed."[17] Discipline was poor, however, and the Germans were lucky not to suffer casualties from stray shells. The use of wireless was no better controlled, making it difficult to develop a clear picture and hindering efforts to respond to the surface incursion into the Bight. It was also apparent that the zeppelin facilities needed antiaircraft defenses and camouflage.

These were not excuses for this new failure of the Germans' defensive schemes. Von Ingenohl was so preoccupied with the possibility that the Harwich Force would be followed in by a British fleet, with submarines waiting off the estuaries, he refused to allow out any surface ships. The Scouting Group commanders pleaded to be sent into the Bight but, despite proposing to take every available torpedo boat, this was denied. Ironically, all four battle cruisers were at high readiness in the outer anchorages, as were large numbers of torpedo craft. Such a combination could have easily caught up with Tyrwhitt and annihilated his relatively weak force. The situation was not improved by having only two U-boats on patrol—von Ingenohl later admitted that this was insufficient. Efforts to get more submarines to sea reflected well on their commanders, but were too late. Seaplanes and zeppelins were not enough, despite the aviators' cheerful reports that they had sunk at least two submarines and damaged a seaplane carrier. Yet, apart from agreeing to send out all available submarines when the next such warning came, the C-in-C would allow no alteration to his plans. Von Ingenohl's unmasterly inactivity had a further depressing effect on the fleet. Influential flag officers and captains began openly to discuss the possibility of a new C-in-C. The lack of confidence in von Ingenohl was now such that it would take a major success for such dissent to be stilled—and success would have to come soon.

Although the British were relieved to discover zeppelins were not the menace they had feared, not all had gone well. Despite several submarine alarms, Jellicoe's covering force pursued its sweep in peace. However, when the Grand Fleet returned to Scapa Flow, there was a serious collision between the super-dreadnoughts *Monarch* and *Conqueror*. This was partly the result of the battle squadrons' inexperience in approaching the anchorage's fixed defenses, since the formations were too close together. In a following wind of Force 8 and visibility reduced almost to nothing by thick funnel smoke, efforts to avoid an unexpected encounter with one of the gate vessels ended with *Monarch* being impaled by *Conqueror*. Both had to be sent south to refit. Once again, the incident was chalked up to experience, but patrol craft were warned, in future, the battleships would simply run them down.[18]

It was a heavy blow; at a stroke, two of Jellicoe's best ships were out of action. Had the incident occurred earlier, the position might have been precarious, but the C-in-C could reflect that all four *Iron Duke* class and the two ex-Turkish ships were now worked up. Furthermore, his cruiser strength had been vastly increased. If the detached battle cruisers had not rejoined, they were at least on their way home. Despite the defects that continued to crop up under war conditions, the fleet was much more efficient than it had been in August—and Jellicoe arguably a more proficient commander.

While Jellicoe was considering his position at Scapa Flow, other affairs were in progress in the south. On 17 December Bayly and Burney exchanged commands. This event reflected a temporary coincidence of views within the higher command. Neither admiral had been happy. Bayly chafed for more active employment. The First Battle Squadron gave him little outlet as his duties were largely administrative. He continued to bombard his chief with suggestions for attacks against the German coast. Burney's attitude to such ventures was otherwise and he fretted over the Channel Fleet's exposed situation. He believed that his big ships were vulnerable to torpedo craft, particularly as the only support formally allocated was the Harwich Force. Achieving a combination with Commodore (T) had already proved problematic and Burney pressed for light forces to be permanently assigned to him.[19] Matters came to a head as part of the effort to find a more effective strategy against the Germans. Fisher, more than ever determined that the Grand Fleet not be risked in the southern North Sea, was interested in attacking the enemy's Belgian coast bases to prevent their use by submarines and light craft. The bombardment of Zeebrugge, however limited its results, was the first indication of this new focus, although Fisher recognized that further action would require cooperation with the army.

Wilson still wanted to attack Heligoland, although he did have its occupation in mind as the precursor to closing off the German passages to the open sea by mines and light craft. Churchill, on the other hand, remained wedded to the capture of Borkum for an advanced base, an idea that Fisher never supported and that was opposed by most officers.[20] Arguably, the only real proponent other than the First Lord was Bayly himself. This made his presence in the Channel Fleet particularly attractive to Churchill, who told the Prime Minister that "Burney belongs to the 'No' & Bayly to the 'Yes' School."[21] Since Burney also did not support operations on the Belgian coast, he was regarded by Fisher as "dismal."[22] For his part, Jellicoe viewed Burney as a more congenial subordinate than Bayly and jumped at an exchange.

Bayly had Borkum in mind when he hoisted his flag in *Lord Nelson*. Fisher commented shortly afterward that the Channel Fleet's commander wanted "to attack Borkum tomorrow!"[23] This was to be a preliminary bombardment of the island, something that Bayly intended to shake down his new command, but wiser counsels prevailed, ostensibly because gunnery efficiency needed improvement before such a venture. Burney had done his best to work up the ships, but the lack of facilities and escorts for practices at sea restricted progress. The solution was to dispatch Bayly and the Fifth Battle Squadron to Portland, still considered relatively safe from submarines, while the Sixth Battle Squadron took the Fifth's place at Sheerness. In order to give the Sixth the chance for their own gunnery practice, the movement was delayed until 30 December.

The submarine situation had been quiet, with no firm reports of U-boats for several weeks. But one, *U24*, was at sea when Bayly sailed from the Nore. *U24* should have been detected by the Channel patrols, but heavy weather and recurrent defects had sapped the strength of Hood's forces and all eight designated patrol areas could rarely be occupied at once. The destroyers were being worn down by the monotonous routine, lack of rest in an exposed harbor, and the now pervasive cold and damp. The French Channel patrols were in no better condition. *U24* arrived in the Strait of Dover on 28 December and was able to wait for a major target. Meanwhile, Bayly was preparing to move. Notable for ignoring the submarine threat before the war, nothing suggested that he now took it more seriously. Since there were no submarine warnings extant in the Channel, he did not believe an escort necessary, but the Admiralty insisted on destroyers for the passage to Folkestone.

On 29 December Bayly ordered Tyrwhitt to make the necessary arrangements. Folkestone was the normal western limit of German submarine activity, and Bayly seems to have been confident that it was safe to operate unescorted past this point. It is fair to note that the Admiralty itself ordered an escort for the reciprocal movement of the Sixth Battle Squadron only from Folkestone to the Nore—and not before. The Fifth Battle Squadron sailed from Sheerness into calm seas at 1000 on 30 December. Bayly had eight battleships and two light cruisers in company and deployed them in single line ahead (arguably the formation most vulnerable to submarine attack), Bayly leading in *Lord Nelson,* with the cruisers fallen in astern. While they were in company, three destroyers from Harwich were deployed on either bow. Bayly informed the Admiralty before he sailed that the force would be steaming at fifteen knots. For no reason that was explained, on leaving harbor he ordered only eight knots. At no time did he zigzag. Thus it was that the battleships came down the Channel. Two hours later the Sixth Battle Squadron passed on its way to the Nore. Once through the Strait of Dover, Bayly dismissed the destroyers and began tactical exercises.

By dawn on 31 December the force was thirteen miles south of Portland Bill. The weather worsening, the battleships began to prepare for heavy seas. All that day, Bayly exercised his command in slow time. The greatest speed ordered was twelve knots. These were methods of the past. Even when the second in command, Rear Admiral Currey, drew attention to a Norwegian flagged tramp that was acting suspiciously, Bayly did not change his arrangements.[24] As dusk fell, he turned down Channel. Things might have been better for the British had the very heavy seas that came up after 0100 risen earlier. Conditions were ideal for a night torpedo attack. There was a full moon, and the night was cloudy but clear, with visibility of some three miles. A fresh breeze was blowing, the sea was choppy and a swell running, but not sufficient to drive light craft into shelter. The battleships were still in line ahead, at intervals of two cables, steaming at only ten knots. *Topaze* and *Diamond* were a mile behind. The Fifth Battle Squadron presented a target that was a submariner's dream.

U24 was in the Channel. She had sighted both squadrons the previous day, but failed to get into a firing position. Her captain, Lieutenant Commander Rudolf

Schneider, eventually withdrew to charge *U24*'s batteries. He had largely given up hope after his last sight of the battleships steering east, apparently for Portsmouth. When the charge was complete, Schneider turned *U24* toward Start Point, running on the surface. At 0008 on New Year's Day he sighted three large ships to starboard. Immediately recognizing them, he fired a single torpedo at the third unit, *Queen*. The weapon missed astern.

Schneider now observed the other five battleships, which were separated from the leaders of the column, and turned toward them. Crossing astern of the last in line, he turned again and launched two torpedoes. One struck. Schneider's target was the pre-dreadnought *Formidable* (photo 14.3). The torpedo exploded under the forward funnel. Assessing that his ship had been badly damaged, *Formidable*'s captain, A. N. Loxley, hauled her out of line and turned head to wind. The seas were rising rapidly as, with great difficulty, the ship's boats were hoisted out. Loxley held few hopes that *Formidable* could be saved and ordered personnel up from below. In the surf around the ship, one of the cutters capsized and was smashed against the side, while several other boats were damaged. *Formidable*'s remaining personnel began to heave wooden mess tables and other gear over the side to support men in the water (map 14.1).

Only *London* of the battleships saw *Formidable* leave the line. She reported this to Bayly, not knowing the reason for it. The two light cruisers had seen the incident, however, and *Topaze* immediately closed the stricken ship and began to

PHOTO 14.3   **HMS *Formidable***   *Imperial War Museum*

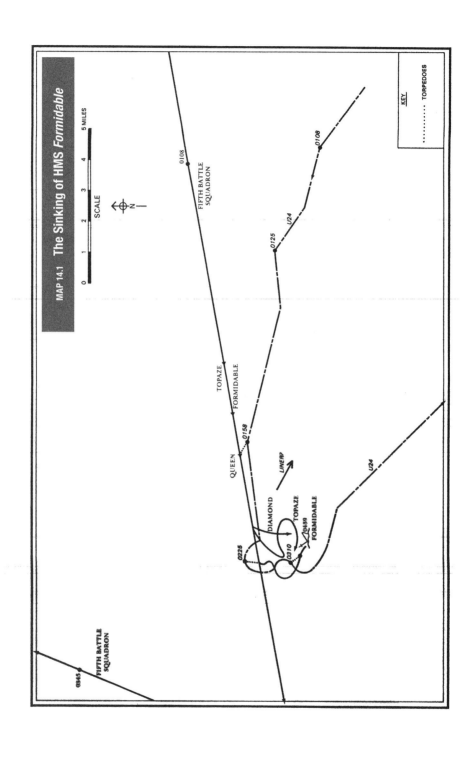

MAP 14.1 The Sinking of HMS *Formidable*

SCALE

0 1 2 3 4 5 MILES

N

FIFTH BATTLE
SQUADRON

0108

0125

U24

TOPAZE

FORMIDABLE

0158

QUEEN

LINER?

DIAMOND

TOPAZE

0349

FORMIDABLE

0310

0225

FIFTH BATTLE
SQUADRON

0845

0108

U24

KEY

·········· TORPEDOES

pick up survivors. A passing liner was asked to assist, but she refused and continued on her way. *Diamond* was more worried about the continuing threat, but she also eventually closed *Formidable* and joined the rescue. At 0310, just as *Diamond* approached, *U24* fired another torpedo into the battleship. Schneider had been following progress and decided that *Formidable* was not sinking fast enough. The weapon struck amidships on the port side. The resultant flooding immediately brought *Formidable* back to an even keel, but she was settling fast. Satisfied with his work, Schneider took *U24* away to the southeast. *Topaze* saw the periscope, but dared not open fire with so many men in the water and *Diamond* fouling the range.

At 0300, just as he turned toward Portland, Bayly received a signal from *Topaze* reporting the damage to *Formidable* and the progress of operations. As he increased to eighteen knots, the old battleships' practical maximum, Bayly could see *Formidable*'s distress signals to the east. With the strict Admiralty instructions as to submarines, Bayly had to content himself with ordering out light craft. Directing the cruisers to stay with the stricken ship, he turned the squadron north-northeast to get well clear of the danger area. All thought of exercises forgotten, Bayly's purpose was now to reach harbor without loss.

The seas were becoming steadily rougher. *Diamond* and *Topaze* were almost unmanageable as they struggled to pull men from the water. Torpedo boats and other craft sent out from Portland and Devonport found conditions so bad they had to turn back. At 0439 *Formidable* closed matters by quietly going under, bows first. The two cruisers remained on scene until daylight and did the best they could to save life. However, many of the boats had capsized or been crushed, and human beings did not last long in a mid-winter Channel storm. By 0900 it was clear that no more could have survived and *Diamond* and *Topaze* reluctantly turned for Portland, carrying altogether only 114 out of *Formidable*'s complement of 780. Four destroyers were sent out from Portsmouth, but found just five more survivors. Yet others still lived. *Formidable*'s launch, although badly holed, managed to get away from the ship but was not found by the cruisers. The seventy-three on board were picked up at noon by the Brixham-sailing trawler *Provident,* having survived some of the heaviest seas in living memory. One more boat, the pinnace, stayed afloat and put into Lyme Regis close to midnight with six of the fifty-five on board dead from exposure and three more dying. In all, only 233 men survived. They did not include Captain Loxley.

U24 arrived in port to find Germany ringing with her exploit. Announcement of *Formidable*'s sinking was the first British admission that the policy of attrition was having any result. The success had a considerable tonic effect on both the German nation and its navy. For Britain, the news came as a heavy blow. *Audacious'* loss was rumored, that of *Bulwark* and numerous cruisers known. The sinking also came hard on the failure to intercept the raid on Scarborough. Yet again, popular and political opinion was doubtful as to the state of the Royal Navy.

The Admiralty finally recognized that the submarine threat was all-pervasive within home waters. Destroyers were hastily dispatched to escort any capital ships on passage around the British Isles. No heavy ship was allowed to sail unprotected and the brand new 15-inch gunned battleship *Queen Elizabeth* was sent to Gibraltar to conduct her firings in a safe area. Yet even now the operational response was not quite complete. The battleship *Commonwealth* had been sent west-about from Rosyth to refit at Chatham. Unescorted, she was off the Start exactly twenty-four hours after the sinking of *Formidable*. Had *U24* remained on station, she might well have claimed *Commonwealth* with her last two torpedoes, for it was not until the afternoon of 2 January that the battleship was met by destroyers.

Bayly's initial defense was that the Admiralty gave no warning that submarines could be found so far west, that there had been no protest when he declared that he intended to dismiss his escort off Folkestone, and that precisely the same arrangements had been made for the Sixth Battle Squadron. *Cornwallis'* captain pointed out to Dewar of *Prince of Wales,* "The Admiralty gave Admiral Bayly written orders to moor targets off Portland and practice the Fifth Battle Squadron at bombarding a buoyed area with two ships anchored in the vicinity for marking purposes. On the face of that they had the impertinence to ask him if he did not know the Channel was infested with submarines, to which Bayly replied that if it were so, why was he not informed."[25]

Despite the Admiralty's culpability, Bayly lacked common sense. Reflecting a personal failure of imagination, he admitted to his staff, "[N]othing that had occurred in the war had developed on the lines that he had expected."[26] As Fisher wrote of Bayly's first attempt at an explanation, "It is pressing to send following telegram to Admiral Bayly, 'Remain at your present anchorage at Portland pending further orders,' for the reason that his letter indicates no sense on his part of the dangers of submarine attack and of necessary precautions, and until this telegram is sent we may have another calamity put upon us by a pig-headed officer."[27]

Bayly might have survived had he not been so obtuse. As another admiral observed, Bayly replied to Jellicoe's message of condolence "in the best hot air style breathing vengeance."[28] It did not sound well. On board *Marlborough,* Burney was grieved by the death of his son-in-law, Charles Ballard, *Formidable's* executive officer, and believed the loss would not have happened under his command.[29] Churchill finally agreed to Bayly's removal and he was relieved on 16 January. The Admiralty judged in its letter of 11 January that his behavior "was marked by a want of prudence and good seamanship in the avoidance of un-necessary risks inexplicable in an officer holding high and responsible command."[30]

Bayly spent just half a page on the affair in his memoirs, remarking that "he had asked for a court-martial, but was refused—I have never known why. It sounds like a fairy story . . . and presumably was done to encourage other admirals."[31] Bayly was quite right; it was, but Churchill still cherished some regard and dispatched him to the Royal Naval College at Greenwich to replace Sir Alexander Bethell, his relief in the Channel Fleet. Bayly continued to protest that he had done nothing wrong, but Currey, second in command on the night, closed his commentary on the affair with a chart of the Fifth Battle Squadron's movements pasted into his journal, which, he noted, "speaks for itself."[32] It does.

With Bayly's undignified exit, ambitious plans to use the pre-dreadnoughts died a sudden, if temporary, death. Bethell was a more subtle man than Bayly, held in high regard by Fisher. His experience in intelligence and war staff work meant that he was well grounded in many of the operational issues being faced. Even Wilson seems to have accepted that battleships could not be dispatched into enemy waters without comprehensive protection, although he continued to work at plans to seal the U-boats in within their bases, as the best approach to dealing with the menace they constituted.[33] A lot more thinking was needed.

The Admiralty searched for ways to break the stalemate. Churchill and Fisher remained fundamentally at odds and the First Lord was making no progress with his Borkum project. In any case, the coming winter meant a landing on Borkum—or anywhere else around the North Sea—would not be practicable for several months. His frustration was one of the factors behind an increasing interest in an assault on the Dardanelles. In the circumstances, Churchill's desire to do *something* meant that he was now prepared to allow offensive mining, although he still doubted its value in the open sea. Fisher would brook no opposition from other quarters, but faced resistance from Keyes, who wanted the Bight to remain clear for submarine operations. The boats were developing an understanding of German operating patterns and Keyes believed that they should be allowed to monitor the most likely routes, rather than having to cope with the changes that would inevitably follow discovery of British mines. Although Fisher worked hard to enlist Jellicoe's support, the latter was not enthusiastic, preferring to focus on the potential for tactical mining during and after a fleet action. Recognition of the problems with the British mines may have been an element of this preference for short-term use. Evidence of their deficiencies was mounting and it was now known that some from the early fields in the Channel had dragged their moorings fifteen miles in a single month.

Oliver shared many of the same concerns, while there was a general acknowledgment that the old minelayers were not up to offensive missions. Nevertheless, since the elderly ships were all that were available, the First Sea Lord's imperative prevailed. Orders were cut for a raid. Keyes' argument was accepted as valid to a degree, but locating the fields in the area around the Amrum Bank, north of the Bight, was intended primarily for targets other than the High Sea Fleet. The latter did not normally use the passage, which was not on a direct line between its bases and the British coast, but submarines and, more importantly, merchantmen moving up and down the Jutland coast did. In fact, the route was the formally declared access to the German North Sea ports. The Chief of the War Staff also suggested a potential follow-on, perhaps comforting in prospect to Churchill and certainly attractive to Commodore (T). Given that the fields would reveal their presence when the first drifters broke their moorings, whether they claimed any victims or not it stood to reason that the Germans would dispatch forces to clear them. This could provide an opportunity for a sweep targeted against the minesweepers and any covering forces.

Orders for Operation OQ were issued on 5 January. Escorted by Harwich Force destroyers, four minelayers, including *Naiad* as senior ship, *Apollo, Iphigenia,* and *Latona,* were to sail from the Nore at daylight on 7 January. The destroyers were to continue only until *Aurora* and *Undaunted* met the force outside Harwich at dusk. The two light cruisers would then convoy them to a point thirty miles west of Amrum Bank and wait until the minelayers returned. Tyrwhitt himself did not go, since *Arethusa* was undergoing repairs, and Nicholson in *Aurora* was the senior officer. The minelayers and destroyers left Sheerness in relatively high visibility and smooth seas. As is often the case in a North Sea winter, a fog descended so thick that the minelayers' commander, Captain M. H. Cobbe, had to anchor the force for two hours. Later in the afternoon they met *Aurora* and *Undaunted,* which had been similarly delayed. The Admiralty learned of the fog and telegraphed to postpone proceedings for twenty-four hours. Tyrwhitt, who guessed that the cruisers and minelayers would successfully meet and go on their way, did nothing of the sort, although he was fretting somewhat himself. "It was the first sizeable operation that had taken place without his presence," as he had reminded the Admiralty.[34] The point was not disputed and the order simple, "Let plan continue."[35]

The operation went as intended, but not without problems. Security was taken too far. The destroyers had no idea of the operation plan and attributed their detachment to a "rare flash of generosity" on the part of the senior officer.[36] Mine-catchers had been fitted on the bows of the minelayers in an attempt to protect them from any unexpected fields and these broke adrift, with resultant chaos. Fortunately, there were no German patrols near the Amrum Bank on the night of 8 January and conditions were perfect. Hidden by darkness and frequent heavy rain squalls, the minelayers completed their work and withdrew to rejoin *Aurora* and *Undaunted.* The force returned to harbor on 10 January and Cobbe and his crews received the Admiralty's well-deserved appreciation. The old *Apollos* were floating death traps for any further operations—Fisher had previously predicted that they would "be butchered if they go out."[37] A single mission was worth the risk, but the Germans would soon realize that a mining campaign was in progress, greatly increasing the chance of interception. Further sorties would need to wait on fast merchant ship conversions and the modification of destroyers.

On 11 January the plan for the attack on the expected German minesweeping effort was issued, designated Operation OR. Tyrwhitt was to take two cruisers and sixteen destroyers into the Bight and, dividing the latter into two groups, have them fall simultaneously on the Germans from north and south at dawn on 13 January, while the cruisers waited to the west. The Admiralty insisted on one condition, with which Tyrwhitt could not argue. If the weather was so bad that the destroyers would not be able to run away from any German light cruisers encountered, the operation was to be cancelled. Commodore (T) had barely left harbor when he realized that the seas were too heavy. Bitterly disappointed, he turned back. In spite of Tyrwhitt's frustration, it was not an entirely gloomy homecoming. Keyes was already immersed in plans for yet another seaplane raid against the zeppelin sheds, or, if the bad weather continued, a simple probe of the German patrols around Heligoland.

The Amrum Bank minefields had effects unlooked for by the Admiralty. Their existence was discovered within twenty-four hours, betrayed first by drifting mines and then by the destruction of a Norwegian merchant ship, *Castor*. As well as halting much of the commercial traffic to and from the north, they upset preparations for another raid on the east coast. Emboldened by the success against Hartlepool and Scarborough, the C-in-C had decided that the venture should be repeated. Hipper was particularly enthusiastic and von Ingenohl consented to bring out the entire High Sea Fleet and, this time, keep it within supporting distance of the Scouting Groups.

The target was the Humber, and the main objective the laying of a minefield outside its approaches, for the Germans believed at least six heavy ships were based there. The attack was due for dawn on 13 January, but discovery of the Amrum fields changed everything. Von Ingenohl was concerned that the High Sea Fleet might be cut off from its bases and suspected the fields were the beginning of a bigger British scheme to seal off the Bight. The C-in-C refused to take the battle squadrons into the North Sea until the passage beside the Amrum Bank was clear.

Sweeping the fields would take at least ten days, longer if the weather was bad, but the operation would only have been delayed, had it not been for reemergence of the obsession with a possible British attempt to block the entrances to the various rivers. Vastly exaggerated reports poured in of the dummy warships the British had fitted out. Tied with other information, including reports of the Admiralty's continuing push to control North Sea merchant traffic, opinion grew that the minefields were the signal that such an attack was imminent. Consequently, von Ingenohl's decision was confirmed: the heavy ships would stay in their anchorages.

This did not prohibit the use of light forces and a minefield off the Humber was seen as useful in one of the most likely locations for assembling block ships. On 14 January, Hipper directed Captain Harder of *Stralsund* to take his ship and *Strassburg* to the Humber. Accompanied by the Fourth Torpedo Boat Flotilla, they sailed at 1600 and emerged from the Bight into a heavy head sea. The torpedo boats suffered badly, decks swept clear and equipment smashed or lost overboard. After *V25* and *V26* collided, luckily with only superficial damage, the flotilla's commander, Herzbruch, decided to turn back. As with the British, this was now standard procedure if conditions deteriorated to the point at which the smaller ships could make less speed than their bigger consorts.

The weather moderated enough to let *Strassburg* lay her 120 mines early on the morning of 15 January and the rest of the operation passed without trouble, *Stralsund* and *Strassburg* getting home after dusk the same night. Hipper was relieved to see them return. Sending such ships into enemy waters was dangerous, all the more so since cruiser strength had been grievously depleted. Future raids, he believed, should have the support of the First Scouting Group, if not the entire fleet. The battle cruisers would at least be able to fight anything from which they could not run, more than could be said for light cruisers on their own. The mine-field, however, had been laid south of the Humber near the Indefatigable Banks and well away from any British swept channels. It was thus of little use, claiming only one unfortunate trawler and remaining undiscovered for six months.

As for the British, Keyes and Tyrwhitt were ready for a new seaplane raid in the first fine weather. The plan for Operation Z1 was more sophisticated than earlier ventures. Keyes intended to keep two submarines with each of his destroy-ers, setting the remainder outside the various entrances to the major German anchorages. Commodore (S) fervently hoped that this time events would not run away from him. Tyrwhitt decided on one major change to his own dispositions: Keeping all three carriers and their escorts together had proved cumbersome and possibly made them vulnerable to repeated air or submarine attack. Each carrier would now operate independently, accompanied by a single division of destroyers as she launched, awaited, and recovered her aircraft. Seven miles east, up threat to take the brunt of any attack, would be Tyrwhitt with three light cruisers and a fourth division of destroyers.

Careful as the arrangements were, all depended on the Heligoland Bight being calm. In the dismal weather of mid-January there seemed little possibility of this, as the War Staff appreciated. On 14 January, when the two had barely got back to Harwich from a previous session, Keyes and Tyrwhitt were recalled to the Admiralty. In the discussions that followed, Plan Z1 was postponed. They had just returned to their ships when word came that they were wanted again in Whitehall. A tired Tyrwhitt complained understandably that "they must have all gone off their onions."[38]

The recall was justified. Room 40 now had indication that the Germans were increasingly concerned by the prospect of a British attack and were taking pre-cautions. This assessment was correct: there were preparations in hand to deploy response forces around the anchorages. The conclusion that the Admiralty drew, reasonably, was that the Heligoland Bight would be thick with German torpedo boat patrols. In reality, the Germans were not taking such an approach, but holding their forces back—sensible if a massed block ship attack was intended, but also reflecting the inshore mindset of previous years.

Tyrwhitt was ordered to make a sweep northeast from Borkum toward the Horns Reef, to gather up patrols believed to operate along that line, while Keyes was directed to send three submarines to lie off Heligoland and the Ems. As cover, Beatty's battle cruisers were to remain outside the Bight until the Harwich Force had withdrawn. Tyrwhitt sailed at 1430 on 18 January, straight into a blizzard. Conditions inside the Bight had been predicted clear, but this was not the case when the Harwich Force arrived at the sweep's start point at 0630 on 20 January. The weather was foul and all that was seen among the snowstorms and choppy seas was a single seaplane, No.80 and, somewhat later, zeppelin L5. Beatty ordered a general withdrawal at 1000, and the disappointed British forces turned for home.

The only units the Germans had sent into the Bight were seven U-boats, but air reconnaissance had been organized for the morning. Despite the high winds, to the aviators' credit all the aircraft and L5 got up. To the west U8 and U17 sighted Beatty's battle cruisers soon after dawn. They made desperate efforts to raise the shore radio stations to report their sightings, but failed to get through, although U17 was eventually able to communicate with L5. Seaplane No.80 spotted Tyrwhitt's force through a break in the clouds but, having no wireless, her pilot immediately turned back for base, thinking that there were at least one hundred ships within the Bight. He was too eager; had he waited to make a more precise count, he would probably have realized that there were far fewer ships in sight, and no heavy units among them.

As it was, No.80's report aligned with the Fleet Command's preconceptions. Von Ingenohl alerted the coast defenses, ordered the High Sea Fleet to raise steam and confirmed that there were no German surface forces at sea. When additional aircraft were sent out, they saw nothing, since the British were withdrawing. Only a glimpse from L5 of Beatty, a fleeting encounter with the battle cruisers by another aircraft, and the eventual reports of the U-boats confirmed that the young pilot of No.80 did not have an overactive imagination. Some hopes were entertained that the submarines outside the Bight and elsewhere in the North Sea might achieve something, but these were dashed when only six returned, with the unenviable score of a single merchant ship and, as U22 confessed, U7, which had been en route to Flanders. U22 mistook her for an enemy boat. To make matters worse, U31 was never heard of again. Probably lost to a mine with all hands, the Germans came to believe in later months that her hulk had drifted into Yarmouth, her crew dead from gas poisoning.[39] U31's fate remains unknown, but the report of her capture helped conceal the real sources of British information on the German fleet's activities. The British came to have the same false ideas about German salvage of the sunken E3, but they put them to better use by replacing a number of cyphers.

For the British, the raid was also a disappointment, only confirming that the Germans did not have patrols out as a matter of course and that aerial reconnaissance was becoming an important element in their surveillance scheme. "Repel Aerial Attack" was by now a customary bugle call, but neither ships nor aircraft had been able to hit each other. No material success had been achieved, while on the debit side two destroyers had collided during the return. On 21 January British spirits were further depressed when it was realized that *E10* had been lost without trace. Even the usual morale boost after venturing into German waters was absent, for the weather was so bad that the entire sortie was a sodden misery for all concerned. The only cheerful members of the Harwich Force were those whose ships had *not* been able to take part. They were relieved not to have missed out on anything: "Selfish?—Yes! but we *were* pleased."⁴⁰

For both sides it seemed as though some new move was needed to restore morale and confidence, even if captains such as Tomkinson of *Lurcher* made the best of the terrible weather by organizing snow fights ashore as an alternative to physical training.⁴¹ The Germans, encouraged by the first zeppelin raids on England, were prepared to wait until a protracted lull in the weather had set in, but Tyrwhitt and Keyes were already pressing for another raid on the airship bases. A plan against Cuxhaven was devised and this was added to the existing one for Emden. They were designated Operations Z2 and Z1. On 21 January Tyrwhitt began to hope that the weather would ease. If it did, he could go ahead. The attacks were all the more important now because of the popular clamor over the zeppelins. There seemed little that could be done against them except an attack at source. However, despite the enthusiasm of the Admiralty and the Harwich Force for the project, yet again the venture was overtaken by events. The Germans were on the move.

THE BATTLE OF THE DOGGER BANK

THE GERMANS WERE TRYING TO UNDERSTAND HOW THEIR OPERATIONS were being compromised with such consistency. One school of thought held that Berlin and the naval dockyards were rife with spies and that the British had penetrated to the highest levels. From the limited evidence available as to British prewar sources, there was some justification for this belief. However, repeated spy hunts discovered little and later inaccurate assessments of German shipbuilding suggest that sources active before August 1914 were no longer available to the British.[1]

A second body of opinion was in the High Sea Fleet, centered on the chief of staff, Eckermann. He and many commanders, including Hipper, were still convinced that among the fishing vessels that littered the North Sea were wireless-equipped observation units, masquerading as neutrals. Furthermore, Hipper was concerned at what this might lead to—perhaps spy trawlers launching a torpedo attack or deploying mines in the path of a German force. It was true that every time that the Germans had been in the North Sea they passed boats apparently fishing. To link them with the British habit of being uncomfortably prompt in reply to any major sortie was not, in the circumstances, unreasonable, even if no such disguised vessels had yet been found.

Eckermann and Hipper agreed that if spy trawlers did exist, their best station was the Dogger Bank. This was one of the finest fishing grounds in the North Sea, but also straddled the direct route between the Jade and the east coast, a route that Hipper's ships had already taken to bombard the English ports. A wireless message from the Bank and a prompt response would, the Fleet staff believed, allow the British to be in position by the time that the First Scouting Group began its withdrawal. Furthermore, the Germans now believed that British scouting forces were operating around the Bank without the support of their own heavy units, providing a chance to avenge the debacle of 28 August. Plans for executing this scheme had so far been frustrated by heavy weather. Eager to achieve a greater success, Hipper proposed a mining raid on the Firth of Forth combined with the thrust to the Dogger Bank. The operations would be covered by the First Scouting

Group, supported to the east by the battle squadrons. Success in both missions would neutralize Beatty and any British information gatherers at one blow.

The weather did not improve and the Germans resigned themselves to an idle January. Then, quite suddenly, on 22 January the sky cleared, promising calm days. Eckermann felt that the opportunity should not be wasted and persuaded von Ingenohl to allow the First Scouting Group out, despite the fact that much of the High Sea Fleet was unavailable. The Third Squadron, including the new *König* class, had transferred to the Baltic to conduct tactical exercises and practice firings. This was the *Königs'* first chance since commissioning and they badly needed training. The Scouting Groups were also under strength. Hipper himself had not expected to venture out until at least 7 February, as *Von der Tann* was yet again undergoing machinery repairs.[2] Several of the light cruisers and torpedo boats were also refitting. Winter had proved hard on the small ships, and inexperience had resulted in unnecessary damage.

Nevertheless, the Dogger Bank plan went ahead, although the C-in-C refused to deploy the High Sea Fleet. To von Ingenohl's mind, this would be inviting trouble. He also felt that any sign of the battleships preparing for sea would somehow be detected by the British and prejudice the chances of achieving surprise. Worried by the prospect of going without support, notwithstanding his intention to run for home at the first suspicion of British heavy units, Hipper was nonetheless pleased when von Ingenohl finally gave him a verbal order to "reconnoiter Dogger Bank."[3] This was confirmed at 1010 on 23 January, when the C-in-C signaled, "1st and 2nd Scouting Groups, S.O. Destroyers and 2 flotillas to be selected by S.O. Scouting Forces are to reconnoiter Dogger Bank. Sail this evening after dark, return tomorrow evening after dark."[4]

On the other side of the North Sea the listening British stations intercepted the message and passed it to Room 40.

Hipper included the armored cruiser *Blücher* in his force (photo 15.1). This was the subject of criticism afterward, but the ship was relatively fast, despite her reciprocating machinery, and very efficient. *Blücher* had been the gunnery training ship, with a core of expert staff closely involved in the latest experimental firings, while her 21-cm guns, though too light to be really effective against capital ships, were the longest-range weapons in the force. Compared with the battle cruisers' engineering problems, *Blücher's* trouble-free performance in previous sorties reinforced Hipper's confidence in the ship. Where he may have erred, given the need to withdraw in the face of a stronger enemy, was putting her at the rear, the most vulnerable position in any chase.[5]

Hipper's ships left the Jade at 1745 on 23 January. There was a little apprehension as to how successful British intelligence might be on this occasion, but, in the words of Hipper's first biographer, "No one on board had any idea that the plan was known to the enemy and that every movement and disposition was

PHOTO 15.1   SMS *Blücher*   *Bibliothek fur Zeitgeschichte*

followed . . . as accurately as if the British themselves were directing them."[6] The Germans steamed into the North Sea.

The British watched the clearing weather and wondered what it might portend. The bulk of the Grand Fleet was in its anchorages, but the Harwich Force and the submarines were on the move. On 22 January Tyrwhitt and Keyes received permission to proceed with Operations Z1 and Z2. Commodore (S) sailed at 1300 the next day, escorting eight submarines with his two destroyers, *Lurcher* and *Firedrake*. A few minutes later he was recalled, but the difficulty of communicating with the submarines in the confusion that inevitably accompanies countermanded orders meant that Keyes did not return to Harwich until 1600. In the meantime, the Admiralty was well roused. The day started quietly with Fisher in bed with influenza. Churchill, never an early riser, went across to the First Sea Lord's residence in mid-morning and had a long discussion. He later wrote, "It was nearly noon when I regained my room in the Admiralty. I had hardly sat down when the door opened quickly and in marched Sir Arthur Wilson unannounced. . . . Behind him came Oliver with charts and compasses. 'First Lord, those fellows are coming out again.' 'When?' 'Tonight. We have just got time to get Beatty there.'"[7]

At noon Tyrwhitt was instructed, "Negative Plan Z. All your light cruisers and destroyers will be wanted tonight."[8]

Twenty-five minutes later the Admiralty ordered Beatty, "Get ready to sail at once with all battle cruisers and light cruisers and sea-going destroyers. Further orders follow."

No one was expecting this: "Sunday, January 23rd, found us with the impression that nothing would ever happen again and we were fixed in the Firth of Forth forever."[9]

Ships began raising steam immediately. They had little time to wait before the Admiralty made the dispositions. These were decided personally by Wilson and

Oliver, although it was the latter's calculations that prevailed, he being "sure that a German admiral would steer N45W and not merely to the north westwards . . . laid off his course accordingly and fixed a rendezvous on it." This was not the position that Wilson proposed, but Oliver side-stepped an argument and waited until the old admiral was clear before telegraphing his instructions.[10] In the afternoon they took the plan to Fisher, still in bed. To the latter's later regret, he did not suggest that the rendezvous be moved farther east to be "*behind* the enemy."[11]

The plan was simple. Beatty and Tyrwhitt were to rendezvous at dawn on 24 January near the Dogger Bank with the hope that they would make contact with the German force to the west at that time. Bradford, with the Third Battle Squadron, and Pakenham with the three ships of the Third Cruiser Squadron would rendezvous forty-five miles to the northwest, "to intercept the enemy if they are headed off by our battle cruisers and attempt to escape north." Jellicoe was to be farther north, against the event that the German battle squadrons were at sea. Keyes was ordered to take four submarines to act against any German units leaving or entering the Jade and send four more to close off the other channels to the German anchorages, just in case the enemy force stayed out longer than expected. However, as these submarines could not possibly be in position before the morning of 25 January, they were to play no part in events. The dispositions were inevitably flawed in that only three of the four sides of the trap were secure. The British could only trust to luck to ensure the closure of the most important fourth side—the east.

The ships at Rosyth were the first to move: "[T]here was no doubt about it this time. There was a frantic commotion at the slipway where the steam boats were waiting and much panic on the part of individual officers lest their respective boats should depart without them. In half an hour the pier was empty."[12]

New Zealand had a distinguished visitor, Prince Louis of Battenberg, come to visit his son, Prince George. Battenberg yearned to go with the force, but insisted that he be put ashore. Both the admiral and ship's captain pleaded with him to stay, but Battenberg felt that it would create trouble for Moore and Halsey.[13] Given Prince Louis' very strong views on previous failures to engage the enemy aggressively (notably the *Goeben* incident), his presence might well have influenced for the better what followed.[14]

The battle cruisers sailed at 1800, working up to eighteen knots as the force pushed down the Forth. At 2030 Bradford's "Wobbly Eight" (reduced to seven with the absence of *Commonwealth*) weighed anchor. Beatty proceeded more slowly than Oliver had assumed he would—eighteen knots had become something of a standard speed for him. Beatty was probably wise to husband both stokers and fuel, but as a result the battle cruisers had to cut a corner, passing over a suspected minefield near Saint Abb's Head. The Admiralty came in for a great deal of abuse over this, but it was clearly a matter for Beatty's judgment.[15] This reflected in a small way the continuing need to evolve the relationship between the operating forces and the War Room. In retrospect, the deployment orders were set at the right level—indicating the rendezvous to be achieved, but leaving it to commanders at sea how they got there.

The First, Second, and Fourth Battle Squadrons left Scapa in independent formations between 1830 and 2030. A wholesale exit of the Grand Fleet was difficult, even under ideal conditions, and rarely attempted. Jellicoe would concentrate in the morning, 150 miles north-northwest of the battle cruisers' 0730 rendezvous. Tyrwhitt sailed at 1730. His intention to keep his ships together was defeated by fog that came down just as he took *Arethusa* and the *M*-class destroyers out of port. The fog delayed the sailing of the remainder of the Harwich Force, but Tyrwhitt decided to press on, leaving *Aurora, Undaunted,* and the other destroyers to follow when they could. They eventually sailed some forty minutes late.

Spirits rose among the British. Whatever the suspicions as to its source, there was growing appreciation of the quality of the intelligence. The fleet was at sea and there had to be a good reason. Filson Young commented, "[W]e were confident on this occasion, in a way we had never been before, that we should meet the enemy on the morrow. No one had any doubt about it and there was an air of suppressed excitement which was very exhilarating."[16]

The Scouting Groups were not as confident; there remained the fear of a trap. They had few illusions as to their fate if they came in contact with the Grand Fleet. Hipper was well aware of the implications of von Ingenohl's decision not to bring the High Sea Fleet out. If he encountered the enemy in any strength, the only option was to turn for home. He could not afford to be cut off.

As the winter night drew to its close, the various forces were approaching conjunction. Hipper was steering toward the British coast with his heavy ships in column and the destroyer flotillas disposed ahead of them. The light cruisers *Stralsund* and *Graudenz* were in the van, a few miles ahead, while *Kolberg* and *Rostock* were steaming ten miles out on each flank. Hipper remained apprehensive, particularly as the day gave ample indication that the weather would be clear. There was no chance that rain and mist would hide the Scouting Groups as they had done during the Scarborough raid.

Beatty, meanwhile, was steering south-southeast with his five battle cruisers. His fervent hope was that the Germans would be found to the west of his own units, in which case they would be caught with a superior force between themselves and their base. Tyrwhitt was moving north, with *Arethusa* and the seven *M* class still ahead of the remainder of the Harwich Force. At 0630 Beatty signaled to Commodore (T), ordering him to deploy his ships west of the battle cruisers, Goodenough's light cruisers being to the east. Tyrwhitt was to lament the rendezvous that the Admiralty had ordained. Had the whole force assembled later, he felt, the Germans would have passed to the west and been isolated.[17]

At 0705, as the first glimmerings of dawn appeared, *Aurora* sighted *Kolberg* and four torpedo boats four miles to the east. In the gloom it appeared to Captain Nicholson that the three-funneled cruiser might be *Arethusa* and he issued the challenge by light. *Kolberg* noted down the code group and flashed a single letter in reply before opening fire. She immediately signaled to Hipper. *Stralsund* had already reported columns of smoke to the north-northwest and the Germans began to intercept British radio traffic. *Kolberg*'s gunnery was uncomfortably accurate and she scored three hits on *Aurora,* which caused minor damage. The British cruiser took longer to settle down, but eventually hit *Kolberg* twice. The first shell struck below the waterline and the second under the bridge. The damage was not great, but two ratings were killed. Realizing the weight of metal he was facing as the advantage of the British 6-inch told, *Kolberg*'s captain turned away to the northeast.

The situation was ambiguous. Hipper thought he was facing only light forces. Beatty in *Lion* saw the gun flashes to the south and immediately turned in that direction, ordering Goodenough to do the same. *Aurora* signaled a report, but it was unhelpful in the extreme, being merely, "Am in action with the German Fleet." The pretension of this statement caused some amusement in the flagship, but it gave little useful information to Beatty. He ordered Tyrwhitt to take station ahead of *Lion* and continued his run south. *Undaunted, Aurora,* and their flotillas meanwhile altered course northeast to parallel the movements of *Kolberg.*

At 0730 Goodenough made simultaneous sightings of cruisers to the south and east. Visibility was rapidly increasing to about ten miles and the Germans to the east were silhouetted against the dawn. Goodenough challenged both. Receiving the correct response only from *Aurora* and the Harwich Force units to the south, he began to haul around to the southeast to pursue the other contacts, *Stralsund* and *Graudenz.* By now *Aurora* had sighted the German battle cruisers, assisted by their vast pall of smoke. She communicated her news to *Southampton.*

Goodenough immediately informed his vice admiral that enemy heavy units had been sighted steering north. To David Beatty the golden moment seemed at hand. He continued south and started to increase speed. If the two forces maintained their relative courses and speeds for a few more minutes, the Germans would be cut off. If, on the other hand, the Scouting Groups turned, forcing a stern chase, British possession of the lee gauge in the prevailing northeasterly wind would ensure that they had the advantage of visibility unimpeded by their own funnel smoke. While Beatty and his staff awaited events on *Lion*'s bridge, morale in the British ships reached tremendous heights. It was their first real chance to get at the German big ships since the war began (photo 15.2).

On board *Seydlitz,* Hipper was worried. *Kolberg* and *Stralsund* had reported seeing smoke clouds—reliable indication of the presence of heavy units—in different positions. As *Stralsund* pressed home her reconnaissance she reported

PHOTO 15.2   HMS *Lion*   *Imperial War Museum*

eight enemy heavy ships to the north-northwest. Hipper and his staff were in an agony of indecision. They knew from intelligence that Beatty had no more than five battle cruisers.[18] Yet the volume of wireless traffic that they were intercepting indicated that numerous units were at sea. If this was one of the battle squadrons (and radio analysis suggested that it was, once again, the Second Battle Squadron), where was Beatty?[19] And why were the British units *here* and *now*?

Hipper appreciated his relative weakness and the danger of being drawn into a trap. Every minute that his ships continued to steam northwest increased the risk. *Kolberg*'s meeting with light forces and her report of smoke to the south-southwest meant that he could already be cut off. Hipper ordered his ships to reverse course, "in order to get a view of the whole situation" as he later reported.[20] At the same time that his big ships were altering course in succession, Hipper recalled the detached light cruisers and torpedo boats. In the event of a chase, it was important that they not be strung out astern. Their lack of protection made them vulnerable to British heavy guns and any disabled unit would have to be left behind. This was sound reasoning on Hipper's part, but should have been applied to *Blücher*. Hipper signaled to the C-in-C the sketchy information that he had been able to gather: "7.45 a.m. position left center of square delta 053 (54deg 57'N 3deg 30'E), Course S.E. 20 knots. 8 large ships, one light cruiser and 12 destroyers in sight."

Within a few minutes Ingenohl was ordering the Second Squadron, the only battleships then in the North Sea anchorages, the Fourth Scouting Group, and all available light craft to assemble in Schillig Roads, but it would be at least three hours before this could be completed. Hipper's forces were quite alone.

The situation was beginning to clear for *Lion*. Signaled reports were still individually often incomplete, although Goodenough's were comprehensive and timely. Together they said enough for Beatty to figure things out. At 0735 *Aurora*, *Undaunted*, and their destroyers altered course to the east to follow the German cruisers, the First Scouting Group now just in sight on the horizon. *Southampton* and her squadron had wheeled to the east-southeast and were in line with the Harwich Force vessels, the whole being spread on a rough north-south line. *Arethusa* was to the west of these ships, heading to the south of where Tyrwhitt, who could not yet see them, surmised the German battle cruisers to be (map 15.1).

As Beatty gained a grasp of the situation, he increased speed still further. At 0743 he turned southeast and then, refining his estimate, turned successively south-southeast and then east-southeast as the First Scouting Group appeared temporarily to be heading northeast in the midst of their wheel. When the German movements started to become clear, Beatty turned farther to the east, waiting for precise resolution of Hipper's course.

Both sides' scouting units were moving into battle order. The Germans had a fairly clear-cut defensive problem to resolve, but the British one was complex. The cruisers and destroyers had to position themselves so that they did not mask their own heavy ships' guns or impede their fire control with their funnel smoke. They also had to be ready to repel torpedo attacks and launch their own if the enemy turned suddenly. Finally, they had also to remember their role as scouts. In view of their small speed advantage, decisions had to be made quickly. Goodenough determined to place his four light cruisers on the Germans' port quarter. This would give him a clear view, free of smoke, and keep him in a favorable tactical position. Accordingly, at 0753 he began maneuvering and within a few minutes was settled on a course of south-southeast, putting him what he thought was a comfortable 17,000 yards from *Blücher*.

By 0750 Beatty had Hipper's battle cruisers in sight to the east at what he underestimated was a range of 20,000 yards. The pall of smoke between the German ships and his own force made precise identification difficult, although the accuracy of Goodenough's earlier reports helped greatly. For his part, Hipper began to discern the five clouds of smoke that marked the path of the British battle cruisers. To his relief he realized that he was facing only one force instead of the two reported. Since the battle cruisers were logically the out-runners of the Grand Fleet, it was unlikely that any other force was interposed between the Scouting Groups and the Jade. Giving Hipper, von Egidy, and Raeder concern was the nature of their meeting with the British, who had clearly been in the midst of a rendezvous. The implications were alarming that this should have been timed for dawn directly on the intended position of the Scouting Groups.

The ships of the Harwich Force were taking up station to port and ahead of the battle cruisers. *Aurora* and *Undaunted* were still abreast, about seven thousand yards apart, with their flotillas strung out astern. *Arethusa* was moving into a position nearly ahead of *Lion* with the *M*-class destroyers accompanying her. Tyrwhitt, however, gave the Tenth Flotilla leader in *Meteor* a free hand, in view of his new destroyers' far superior speed.

At 0807 Hipper turned sharply to port to allow his laboring torpedo boats and light cruisers to assume their stations around his heavy ships. Observing this,

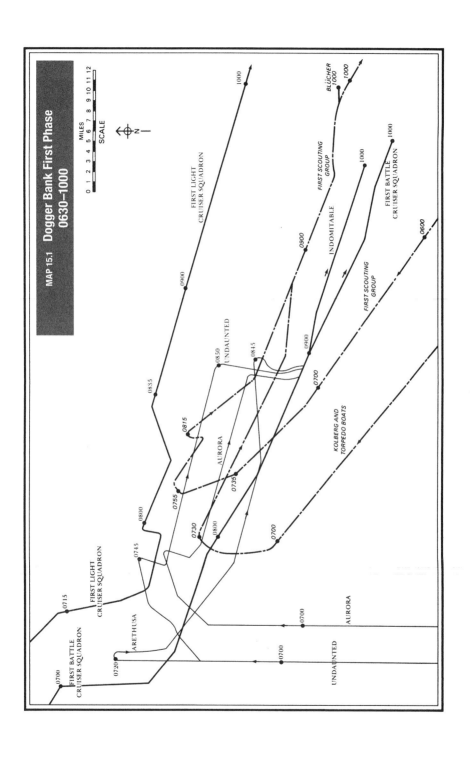

MAP 15.1 Dogger Bank First Phase 0630–1000

SCALE
MILES
0 1 2 3 4 5 6 7 8 9 10 11 12

N

FIRST LIGHT
CRUISER SQUADRON

1000

BLÜCHER
1000

1000

FIRST SCOUTING
GROUP

INDOMITABLE

0900

1000

FIRST BATTLE
CRUISER SQUADRON

1000

FIRST SCOUTING
GROUP

0600

0900

0900

UNDAUNTED

0850

0815

AURORA

0835

0755

0815

0800

0735

0730

0800

0700

KOLBERG AND
TORPEDO BOATS

0700

0700

FIRST LIGHT
CRUISER SQUADRON

0745

0715

FIRST BATTLE
CRUISER SQUADRON

0700

ARETHUSA

0720

AURORA

0700

UNDAUNTED

0700

Goodenough hastily turned his squadron east to avoid closing the distance and coming under fire. He informed Beatty and Jellicoe, but did not turn his ships any farther away, as he guessed the nature of the movement and did not think that the Germans would hold their new course for very long. He was correct. Within a few minutes Hipper hauled round to the south-southeast to gain as much southing as possible before Beatty's ships came in range. The British battle cruisers' speed was steadily rising. Beatty ordered twenty-five knots at 0816 and then, at 0823, twenty-six knots. Although some of his staff (as well as those in the older ships) were dubious as to the practicality—*Indomitable* was thought capable of twenty-five knots at best—Beatty believed that it would be a target to aim at for the engineers and the stokers in particular. Indeed, enthusiasm spread, especially when it became clear that the two oldest battle cruisers were keeping up.

The range dropped slowly. At 0814 the distance from *Lion* to *Blücher* was estimated at 25,000 yards, only 3,000 more than the maximum effective range of the 13.5-inch gun. At 0816 Beatty ordered his battle cruisers to form a line of bearing on *Lion*'s port quarter. This had the dual intent of facilitating visual signals and clearing the arcs of fire of the units astern. The chase was settling down. The speed limits of the *Blücher* have always been thought why Hipper never ordered more than twenty-three knots, but in reality *Seydlitz, Moltke,* and *Derfflinger* were just as hard pressed. The lack of experience in sustained high-speed steaming and the poor-quality coal both told. Hipper's hopes of escaping dimmed as the British ships loomed on the horizon. As he later commented, "The pace at which the enemy was closing in was quite unexpected. The enemy battle cruisers must have been doing 26 knots."[21] For the next half hour, both sides settled to the pursuit. Muffled in greatcoats and scarves, admirals, staffs and commanding officers stood on windswept compass platforms and signal bridges. And waited.

Dawn on 24 January had found Commodore (S)'s little force well to the south of Beatty and Tyrwhitt. Keyes decided to alter the Admiralty's dispositions. Realizing from intercepted signal traffic that a major engagement was under way, he attempted to get across the German line of retreat, detaching only *E11* to proceed as previously planned to the swept channel at Norderney Gat. Not until 1055 did the Admiralty think to inform him directly of the action and order him, "Send submarines to Heligoland Bight." Here the five hours lost by the return to Harwich came into fatal play. Keyes could not leave the three submarines behind as they were his only real offensive capability. An unsupported attack by the two destroyers on the heavily escorted German force would be suicidal. The E-class submarines were the best the Royal Navy had, but their utmost surface speed was only fifteen knots. This was not enough.

Beatty's light forces, closest to the enemy, had the clearest view. *Arethusa* signaled at 0817 that Hipper's torpedo boats were stationed on the First Scouting Group's starboard bow. This was vital knowledge for Beatty if he were to maintain the pursuit with security. Fear that the German light craft would stage a massed torpedo attack was one factor, and their potential to drop mines across the path of the oncoming battle cruisers the other. And Hipper himself could turn back to create a wholly new tactical situation—a possibility the subject of considerable debate before the war.[22] At 0823 Goodenough, remembering his responsibilities to the C-in-C, signaled to Jellicoe, "Position 55deg 02' north, 4deg 4' east. Enemy in sight consisting of four battle cruisers, steering between east and south-east."

More could have been said, but this was the kind of information that Jellicoe needed.

As the British ships began to draw dangerously close, Hipper altered to the southeast. When this became apparent to Beatty at 0830 he steered the same course. At 0834 he ordered twenty-seven knots—more than *New Zealand*'s designed speed. The ground Hipper had gained to the south put the Harwich Force close behind and to the north of *Blücher*. *Arethusa* and the *M*-class destroyers were steadily closing the armored cruiser. Hipper's signals in this period were few. His dispositions made, he could only wait on events. He could move no faster without risking a break-up of the formation. He considered ordering his light forces to drop back and attack, but rejected the idea, since it would have been difficult, if not impossible for them to catch up again. If he were to initiate a melee, it would be better within the Heligoland Bight. By this time, Beatty would inevitably have outrun any supporting units and the positions could be reversed, with the British turning to flee and having their stragglers picked off one by one. In the meantime, *Blücher* would have to rely on her own defenses.

Meteor and her six sisters approached too close to *Blücher*. She opened fire at a range of seven thousand yards. No hits were scored, but Beatty decided that it was futile to hope for a stern attack by torpedo craft at this speed, particularly as the Germans gave no sign of turning back. He ordered the destroyers to take station astern and soon followed this with directions to the remainder of the Harwich Force to station on his beam. The light cruisers and destroyers turned southwest to close the battle cruisers. Hipper signaled, "*Seydlitz* position 0830 delta 083 (54deg 50'N 3deg 55'E) S.E. 21 [*sic*] knots. Am being followed by 7 [*sic*] enemy light cruisers and 26 destroyers, more columns of smoke in the rear. Intend not to attack until reaching inner Ger. Bight."

The range was dropping farther. Reconstruction indicates that at this point the speed of the leading British battle cruisers was something over three knots more than their quarry. Beatty had by now ordered twenty-eight knots, more than either *Indomitable* or *New Zealand* could possibly reach. Gaps began to open between the three "Splendid Cats" and the two astern; *Indomitable* began to fall back from *New Zealand*.[23]

At 0852 *Lion*'s rangefinder informed the gunnery officer, Lieutenant Commander Geoffrey Longhurst, that the range was down to 22,000 yards. Longhurst reported this to Captain Chatfield and a sighting round was ordered. The short length of the rangefinders meant that accuracy dropped off sharply over 15,000 yards and practically disappeared after 20,000 (20,200 was formally designated as the maximum as this was the greatest range on the 13.5-inch sight settings).[24] Salvo firing would be an almost certain waste of shell. Amidships, one gun of "Q" turret elevated and fired the first shot in the first engagement between dreadnoughts. It fell short.

At 0854 Beatty signaled twenty-nine knots and, a minute later, "Well steamed, *Indomitable*." The effort being made in the big ships on both sides was incredible. Vice Admiral B. B. Schofield, midshipman in *Indomitable,* wrote of the ship at full power:

> Anyone brought up in the oil fuel age can have no idea of the physical effort required of the stokers of a coal-burning ship steaming at high speed. With the fans supplying air to the boilers whirring at full speed the furnaces devoured coal just about as fast as a man could feed them. Black, begrimed and sweating men working in the bunkers in the ship's side dug the coal out and loaded it into skids which were then dragged along the steel deck and emptied on to the floorplates in front of each boiler in turn. . . . If the ship rolled or pitched there was always a risk that a loaded skid might take charge with resultant danger to life and limb. Looking down from the iron catwalk above, the scene had all the appearance of one from Dante's *Inferno*, "For flames I saw and wailings smote mine ears." Watching the pressure gauges for any fall in the steam pressure, the Chief Stoker walked to and fro encouraging his men. Now and then the telegraph from the engineroom would clang and the finger on the dial move round to the section marked "MORE STEAM." The Chief would press the reply gong with an oath. "What do the bastards think we're doing," he would exclaim, "Come on boys, shake it up, get going," and the sweating men would redouble their efforts, throw open the furnace doors and shovel still more coal into the blazing inferno.[25]

The firing of "deliberate" shots continued as the shell splashes crept closer to their target. At 0900 *Tiger* started firing sighting rounds. By 0905 *Lion* assessed she had *Blücher's* range and Beatty signaled, "Open fire and engage the enemy." *Lion* and *Tiger* at once began to fire full salvoes. At about 0907 *Princess Royal,* five hundred yards behind *Tiger,* began her own series of sighting shots. Farther astern, *New Zealand* and *Indomitable* remained silent. Their 12-inch main armament could not hope to span the distance.

Hipper made another signal at 0903, distinguished by its brevity: "Am in action with 1st battle cruiser squadron, delta 109 (145 miles WNW of Heligoland). Steering S.E." In the Jade, von Ingenohl noted the signal and continued his preparations, but, farther north of Hipper, it was taken in by another unit. The zeppelin L5 was flying a reconnaissance patrol and her captain, Hirsch, immediately turned south.

At 0911 the Germans opened fire at what they estimated was 20,000 yards. Aiming was abominably difficult because the funnel smoke pouring out to leeward frequently masked the British ships. There was much to learn about the practical problems created by battle conditions. The Germans were astonished by the range at which the British were firing. It required a response—and arguably their long-range performance proved better—but they began to believe that the British wanted to maintain the distance for their own advantage. This was not the case, since Beatty was desperately trying to close the range while remaining well clear of the German track. The gunnery problem was simple in some ways, since the range was dropping only slowly, but was confused by the extreme distance, funnel smoke, the limitations of the ranging systems, and the fact that a significant error (known as "cross-roll") was introduced by the roll of the ships in the swell as they fired along a line so close to their bows or sterns. The Germans' tight salvo groups impressed the British. The very close near misses of *Blücher*'s shells on the disengaged side of her targets also suggested much higher gun elevation (the ship's 28-cm were capable of 30 degrees) than the British could manage. They came to think that the German battle cruisers were similarly equipped.

It appeared to observers in *Lion* that at this time she made her first hits on *Blücher*. This seems so, although the early hits made on the armored cruiser's quarterdeck did not affect her fighting efficiency. The estimates need, however, to be treated with caution. Notwithstanding Filson Young's declaration, "There was no mistaking the difference between the bright, sharp stab of white flame that marked the firing of the enemy's guns and this dull, glowing and fading glare which signified the bursting of one of our own shells," this clear distinction was not the case.[26] There was often confusion between the firing of salvoes and shells striking home.

Beatty had second thoughts about his light forces. The risk of Hipper attempting to redress the balance with a torpedo attack increased as the Heligoland Bight drew nearer. At 0930 he ordered the Harwich Force to take station ahead, at "utmost speed." Although this would put some of the older destroyers into difficulties, Beatty knew he had *Arethusas* and the seven *M* class as outriders, whatever his battle cruisers' speed. By this time *Aurora* was stationed to starboard, *Arethusa* and *Undaunted* to port of her, with their flotillas astern and the *M*-class destroyers ahead and to starboard.

As the range dropped, *Lion* shifted her fire to *Moltke*, but not before observing another hit on *Blücher*. *Derfflinger* and *Seydlitz* were also starting to become

clear to the control teams. In her turn, *Lion* was being straddled by German salvoes: "[M]ost of them burst and sent vicious fragments flying over and round us."[27]
Lion was to be the main target for the First Scouting Group throughout the battle.
This was not only because the leading ship was the logical target, but also because
the Germans were finding the lesser range of their weapons an infuriating limitation. At about this time *Blücher* struck *Lion* on "A" turret with a 21-cm shell. It did
not pierce the armor, but the concussion was severe and knocked out the left gun
for two hours. Two wing compartments had already been flooded by detonations
below water level. The question arises as to what would have happened to *Lion* had
she been subjected earlier to 28-cm and 30.5-cm rounds.

At 0933 Beatty altered course east-southeast and, at 0935, signaled "Engage
the corresponding ship in the enemy's line." *New Zealand's* better shells and slight
margin of speed put her in range of *Blücher,* but *Indomitable* was well behind.
Chatfield took this into account when he suggested the distribution of fire. Each
ship was to engage her opposite number: *Lion* to take *Seydlitz, Tiger* to take *Moltke*,
Princess Royal to take *Derfflinger,* and *New Zealand* to take *Blücher.* Inexperience,
however, took charge in *Tiger. Tiger* had been shooting badly and disappointment
might have contributed to Captain Henry Pelly's mistake, although it seemed to
him "that my right target was the leading ship."[28] He chose to engage *Seydlitz* and
leave *Moltke* alone. He afterward justified his decision on the basis of one of the
Grand Fleet Battle Orders on gunnery: when the enemy's ships were in lesser number than the British, the two leading British ships should engage the first of the
enemy. The process was to be continued down the line until the numbers were
equalized and the latter ships were engaging each other one-for-one.[29] Were all
five battle cruisers in action, this would have been correct, but *Indomitable* was
clearly not firing.

The mistake was aggravated by the fact that *Tiger's* gunnery officer, Lieutenant Commander Bruce-Gardyne, took the shell splashes that marked the fall of
Lion's shot as *Tiger's.* Within three minutes the acute Goodenough signaled from
his vantage point, "Salvoes of three, apparently from *Tiger,* falling consistently
over," but, although *Lion* took this signal in, there is some doubt that *Tiger* did
so. It was not recorded in either ship's signal log.[30] Bruce-Gardyne did not order a
range decrease at the time. Yet *Tiger* did score a hit—a 13.5-inch shell struck the
forecastle of *Seydlitz* and caused minor damage. By a fluke, the correction ordered
from *Lion's* salvoes resulted in *Tiger* getting *Seydlitz's* range at least temporarily.
Unfortunately, *Tiger's* error resulted in *Moltke* being able to concentrate undisturbed on her leading opponents. Her efficiency in gunnery would ensure that she
made the most of the opportunity.

In every heavy ship senior officers were finding their conning towers less than
useful. Chatfield of *Lion* went unwillingly to his, "noisy and wet from spray and
from steaming at high speed through the vast columns of water, which somehow

incredibly forced its way through the lens threads of my Ross binoculars."[31] The situation was just as bad in other positions. Having the lee gauge brought vast amounts of spray inboard. Prince George of Battenberg, turret officer in *New Zealand,* wrote, "By this time my range-finder was useless; I was soaked through to the skin by the spray coming in through the slit in my [turret] hood, hitting me in the face and then trickling down outside and inside my clothes, and I was frozen by the wind which came in with the spray. My eyes were extremely sore, and I was blinking all the time."[32]

By 0943 the range from *Lion* to *Seydlitz* was under 17,000 yards, and *Lion* was straddling *Seydlitz* with every salvo. *Princess Royal* was engaging *Derfflinger,* which was suffering the effects of underwater concussions from near misses, while *New Zealand* was engaging *Blücher.* Hipper was becoming increasingly concerned for his weakest ship. *Blücher* had not the armor to stand up to even the oldest British battle cruiser and was beginning to show signs of wear. But the first crippling blow would be to *Seydlitz* herself. The flagship had already been struck by one 13.5-inch shell, which caused little damage, when a 13.5-inch armor-piercing round from *Lion* hit her aft. In Admiral Scheer's words,

> The . . . shell had a terrible effect. It pierced right through the upper deck in the ship's stern and through the barbette armor of the [after] turret, where it exploded. All parts of the stern . . . near where the explosion took place were totally wrecked. In the reloading chamber, where the shell penetrated, part of the charge in readiness for loading was set on fire. The flames rose high up into the turret and down into the munition chamber, and thence through a connecting door usually kept shut, by which the men from the munition chamber tried to escape into the fore turret. The flames thus made their way through to the other munition chamber, and thence again up to the second turret, and from this cause the entire guns crews of both turrets perished almost instantly. The flames rose high as a house above the turrets.[33]

Filson Young, in the fore-top of *Lion,* wrote, "Well do I remember seeing those flames and wondering what kind of horrors they signified."[34] On board *Moltke,* von Levetzow turned to his bridge team and said, "Have a good last look at the *Seydlitz* before she goes."[35] *Seydlitz* was in great danger. Were the flash to penetrate to the magazines, they would explode, break the battle cruiser's back, and send her to the bottom within seconds. She was saved by three men, led by the executive officer Lieutenant Commander Hagedom, who worked their way to the magazines' flooding station. In later years Pumpmaster Wilhelm Heidkamp was given special credit for braving toxic fumes and blistering heat to admit the six hundred tons of water involved.[36] *Seydlitz* was still afloat. Her after turrets were useless, but her speed was unimpaired. In spite of the impact, engines, boilers, and propeller shafts were still sound. She was badly down by the stern, but remained a fighting unit. All this time Hipper stood impassive, the sole indication of strain being his chain smoking. Captain von Egidy's reaction was to order rapid salvoes to do as much damage as possible to the enemy before the ship was lost. *Seydlitz* was now firing faster than she ever had before, with right and left gun salvoes every thirty seconds. The rapidity of German gunfire was something that had impressed the British already and this only confirmed it.

Seydlitz's damage dramatically altered the balance, since one of Hipper's three battle cruisers had now lost almost half her fighting power. He signaled von Ingenohl, "[A]m in urgent need of support"; another hit of that kind and the First Scouting Group would be lost. Von Ingenohl received the signal within a few minutes, but it was already too late. Even though U-boats were on their way, getting the main body into the Bight would take at least two hours. The High Sea Fleet could not possibly be in a position to support Hipper until 1430, even if the battle continued its course.

The German torpedo boats were also cause for worry. Disposed on the starboard bow of the First Scouting Group, abreast and ahead of the light cruisers, some were having trouble maintaining their station, even with the relatively calm seas and the battle cruisers' speed of little more than twenty-three knots. They began to drop astern and passed from starboard to port behind *Blücher*, their courses erratic as they tried desperately to avoid fouling the heavy ships' range. Beatty could not be sure what they were doing. The movements lacked the cohesion of a torpedo attack but it seemed possible, given that fewer than four thousand yards lay between the German's track and his own intended course, that the light craft would attempt to drop floating mines across his path. Beatty started to haul around to the southeast to increase the lateral distance between the two forces and prevent such a ploy.

The British battle cruisers were separating beyond mutual support. At this stage, *Lion* was probably making just over twenty-eight knots, slightly less than Beatty estimated, but not the 29.5 knots that triumphant engineers later claimed. *Tiger* was keeping up, a feat possibly due to the fact that Beatty's squadron engineer, Captain C. G. Taylor, was on board and had devoted much time to the new ship. All the other battle cruisers were falling astern, including the foul-bottomed *Princess Royal*, which had not dry-docked after her return from the West Indies. *New Zealand* was doing extraordinarily well—twenty-seven knots by her own calculations and something like 26.5 knots over the ground, but it was not enough. At 0952 Beatty signaled a reduction to twenty-four knots. This would close his big ships up and permit the slower units of the Harwich Force to regain a forward position for defense against attack by the enemy flotillas. As German waters approached, such precautions were more important. At the same time, still unable to ascertain *Tiger*'s fall of shot, Pelly shifted target to *Blücher,* whose much closer position would allow even the raw *Tiger* to hit consistently. This was probably wise, but it left the problem of *Moltke* unresolved.

Knowing the extent of *Seydlitz*'s damage, and with *Blücher* in mind, Hipper bore away to the east-northeast, attempting to confuse the British gunnery in the pall of smoke that now hung between the adversaries. Hipper was also watching the First Light Cruiser Squadron, which appeared to be closing slowly, perhaps intent on isolating *Blücher*. A feint would force them off. Sixteen thousand yards north, Goodenough saw the maneuver. Discretion was the better part of valor and he turned away until he was sure what Hipper intended. When he had increased the distance to 20,000 yards, beyond the Germans' main and secondary armament ranges, Goodenough brought his ships back to the southeast. The turn away was only just in time, for *Blücher* opened a heavy and accurate fire with her 15-cm guns. Stephen King-Hall in *Southampton* had a curious feeling "that the *Blücher* was behaving rather badly by firing at us, and that we were not so much participants in the battle as interested and harmless spectators."[37]

With the guns of *Seydlitz* and *Moltke* concentrated on her, *Lion* began to suffer. At 1001 she was struck by a shell from *Moltke*. This pierced the side-armor and flooded the engineers' workshop, passing through the 4-inch magazine trunk. It failed to explode, but the flooding had serious consequences. The water reached the main switchboard and short-circuited two of the three ships' dynamos. The loss of power disabled the after main fire control and secondary armament control circuits, while flooding caused *Lion* to take on a list to port. Despite the damage, she maintained her speed (map 15.2).

As the movements were carried out, the leading units temporarily lost contact. The German ships were almost invisible in the mass of smoke that continued to obstruct their own view of their opponents. On the British side, *Lion* and *Princess Royal* were forced to check fire at frequent intervals. In such conditions the Germans had the advantage of stereoscopic rangefinders, which provided a relatively accurate result even when the target was indistinct. The unfortunate *Blücher*, however, was still in clear sight. Both *New Zealand* and *Tiger* were straddling her. She was not yet crippled, but had little hope of survival if this kept up.

To Beatty it appeared that Hipper was turning to use the smoke to hide his ships, while they set up for a mass torpedo attack. At 1010 Beatty ordered the Harwich Force to "attack enemy destroyers." This signal had no immediate results as Hipper's light craft were not attempting to drop back and all the British destroyers and light cruisers were already straining to pass the battle cruisers. Since *Princess Royal* and *New Zealand* had regained station, Beatty ordered twenty-six knots and, to prevent the range opening farther, altered course east-southeast. *Seydlitz* now had only *Moltke* in line astern, *Derfflinger* and *Blücher* being strung out to

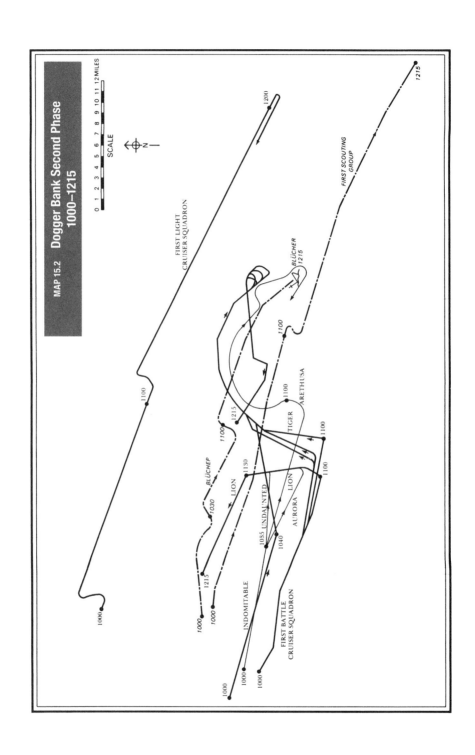

MAP 15.2 Dogger Bank Second Phase 1000–1215

SCALE

0 1 2 3 4 5 6 7 8 9 10 11 12 MILES

FIRST LIGHT
CRUISER SQUADRON

FIRST SCOUTING
GROUP

BLÜCHER
1215

1200

1215

1100

1100

1100

1100

1100

ARETHUSA

TIGER

1215

BLÜCHER

1030

LION

1150

1035 UNDAUNTED

AURORA

LION

1040

1215

INDOMITABLE

FIRST BATTLE
CRUISER SQUADRON

1000

1000

1000

1000

1000

1000

1000

the north. Hipper began to resume his former course. The British battle cruisers had not followed him north. As a result, the German position was worse, a wedge being driven farther between his ships and the safety of the Bight. As the battle began to settle down again, *Lion* discovered that she was firing over by more than two thousand yards, another lesson in long-range gunnery. The elevation was stepped down and *Lion* began to straddle *Seydlitz* once again.

From the north appeared zeppelin L5. Hirsch turned his airship on a reciprocal course to that of the First Scouting Group and cruised down the battle cruisers' disengaged side. Understandably, the First Light Cruiser Squadron was concerned by L5 looming nearby and opened fire with 6-inch shrapnel at maximum elevation. They were surprisingly accurate and an alarmed Hirsch forced L5 up into the protection of the clouds. He decided to remain north and look for any forces coming from that direction. This was a surprisingly limited approach, since a reconnaissance to the west would have confirmed there were no other British forces close behind. As it was, the airship created apprehension among the British that it might be the harbinger of the approaching High Sea Fleet. The Bight was nearing.

Lion suffered critical damage at 1018. Two 28-cm shells from *Seydlitz* struck her. In the fore-top, "we thought that she had been torpedoed, and the mast, to which the fore-top was secured, rocked and waved like a tree in a storm, and the ship seemed to be shaking herself to bits. We looked at one another prepared to alight from our small cage into whatever part of the sea destiny might send us, but nothing happened, and the old *Lion* seemed to pick herself up and go on again."[38]

One shell hit the waterline forward, penetrated the armor belt and exploded in a wing compartment. Within a few minutes extensive flooding up to the main deck had occurred. The capstan compartment was among those flooded. A splinter also pierced the exhaust pipe from the capstan engine, permitting saltwater to pass into the secondary condenser. Within hours the resultant contamination of the boilers would stop the ship. The second shell struck below the waterline and drove in two 6-inch armor plates, shattering the backing. Coal bunkers forward were flooded and the inner and outer bottoms were bulged in over a large area of hull.

Blücher was dropping behind. Her fighting capacity was largely unimpaired, but she was well astern of *Derfflinger*. Hipper, however, did not attempt to bring his squadron back into close formation. Given the British gunnery, it was better for the four ships to be well spread and steering erratic courses. Beatty himself was becoming anxious. After nearly ninety minutes, despite the damage to *Seydlitz*, no decisive blow had been struck. Every mile worsened his tactical position and improved Hipper's. At 1027 Beatty signaled, "Form on a compass line of bearing NNW and proceed at your utmost speed." It was all out now.

The signal system was breaking down. Never before had such a strain been placed on visual signaling. The battle cruisers were steaming at between twenty-four and twenty-eight knots. The wind's force made standing up in the fore-top of *Lion* almost impossible. The signal flags streamed out almost dead astern and were extremely difficult to read. Beatty had understood this when he ordered a line of bearing, but the angle gave only marginal improvement. Nor was visibility good. The funnels were emitting thick black smoke, while each unit was enveloped by cordite fumes every time a salvo was fired. *Lion*'s bridge was visible from the fore-top only at irregular intervals, and the situation was no better in looking for the next astern, especially as the cordite smoke was driven directly back onto the signal bridges. The exposed positions were continually swept by spray and splinters, while there were also the concussive effects of guns fired and of hits and near misses. Lieutenant Blagrove, turret officer in *Tiger*, complained that he "was knocked out of my sighting hood 3 times by wind of projectiles passing close."[39] Even Beatty was forced to shelter temporarily in the conning tower. It is not surprising that errors crept in.

Tiger and *Princess Royal* received the signal and repeated it correctly. *New Zealand* and *Indomitable* did not. Both mistook "Form line of bearing" for "course." *Indomitable* did not even see the second half, although fortunately it was of little importance to her. Rear Admiral Moore and Captain Halsey in *New Zealand* were mystified. What was wanted with a north-northwesterly course? Something had to be wrong. When *Lion* hauled down her pennants as the executive signal, Moore decided to hold his course. He was confirmed in that decision by *Lion* not altering. Light dawned when *Princess Royal* and *Tiger* sheered out of the previous formation and *New Zealand* quietly followed suit. In such a situation subordinates had to exercise initiative.

On board *Indomitable*, Captain Kennedy was doing just that. It was plain that some mistake had been made, but he was not sure whether Beatty intended to close regardless of the danger posed by torpedo craft. When the executive was made, Kennedy hauled out and bore away nearly due east. This was a good decision, since it cut the distance between *Indomitable* and the German ships and made her that much more useful to Beatty. Kennedy knew the risks involved, but the value of *Indomitable*'s broadside would be enormous. He stood on. *Indomitable* was not masking any of her consorts' fire and was well within supporting distance. Frewen in *Lookout* wrote, "The *Indomitable* gave up chasing her consorts & struck out . . . coming right through the Flotillas & firing when she got a chance to see clear of our smoke, over our heads. . . . [I]t speaks magnificently for her stokers that she should actually have picked up on us now, at the 3rd hour."[40] Beatty appreciated Kennedy's decision. Although the German torpedo boats seemed dangerously close to his planned track, he signaled at 1035, "Turn together 1 point to port." All received this signal except *Indomitable*, but as she had anticipated the move, it did not matter—this time. The crisis of the battle was at hand.

Derfflinger received a hit at 1040. It failed to penetrate and burst outside, causing superficial damage. For *Blücher*, however, time ran out. Two shells struck amidships. They pierced her armored deck and exploded in the amidships ammunition gangways, setting fire to the ready-use propellant that lay stacked all around. The flash penetrated to two 21-cm wing turrets on the port side. It wrecked both and killed every man inside them. The concussion also had a serious effect on the ship's machinery. All *Blücher*'s engines were either temporarily or permanently disabled and her steering gear jammed. *Blücher* began to sheer away to port as other shells struck, one forward that started yet another fire and knocked out "Anna" turret. She sent to Hipper, "All engines out of action." It was the signal he dreaded, forcing the choice of turning back in support or leaving the unfortunate ship to her fate.

The British, it seemed, had finally cracked the German nut. Beatty moved to deal with the "loose end" of *Blücher* and ordered *Indomitable* to deal with "the enemy breaking away to the north," thus allotting the force required. At 1045 Beatty again signaled a turn 1 point to port. At 1047 he threw caution to the winds and ordered, "Close the enemy as rapidly as possible consistent with keeping all guns bearing." Beatty was confident that he was moving in for the kill, but he also knew that any delay increased his own danger. Two things told against him. First, none correctly received the signal. *Princess Royal, New Zealand,* and *Indomitable* did not even see it, while *Tiger* only got "Close the enemy." In the short term, this failure was of little importance, since the course already steered was near the optimum possible. In the longer term, however, it was a disaster. Had Moore read this signal, he would have had a much clearer idea of Beatty's intentions.

Second, feed water contamination was beginning to tell; *Lion* was losing speed, so much that *Tiger* was now abreast the flagship. Any successive turn to port Beatty might have had in mind was impossible. A 28-cm shell burst against the armor of "A" barbette. This caused a small fire in the turret lobby. It was extinguished with little difficulty, but a message went to the bridge that there was danger of a magazine explosion. The order was passed to flood the magazine. There were two feet of water in the compartment before the alarm was realized to be false. Between 1049 and 1051 *Lion* was hit repeatedly. The effect of one shell was catastrophic. It burst on the armor belt amidships and forced a nine-inch plate two feet inward. The port feed tank was opened up and this overflowed into the reserve tanks. Only the fact that the valves to the port engine room were shut saved that compartment from serious flooding. The port engine itself had to be stopped and the ship's speed dropped to fifteen knots. Although the port engine room was temporarily safe, flooding in other compartments increased the ship's list to 10 degrees. This had the disastrous effect of shorting the single remaining dynamo. All light and power gone, *Lion* was in a sorry state, with three thousand tons of water on board, "A" turret and the main fire control out of action, and all but two signal halliards shot away.[41]

Tiger thrust ahead of the flagship and headed after the Germans, but she too began to suffer, with three hits in rapid succession. The tight German salvo groups paid a dividend. The first struck the roof of "Q" turret amidships. It did not pierce the armor, but the turret's left gun was disabled, two men killed, and several wounded. A second shell exploded in the forward superstructure, destroying the intelligence office and signal distribution station and killing eight, including Engineer Captain Taylor. The third round struck amidships. This exploded among the boat stowage, igniting the petrol tank that was a fuel store for the motor boats. Flames shot funnel high. *Tiger* looked like a torch, the entire ship aft of the bridge being hidden in a mass of smoke and fire. Although the ship's fighting abilities were unaffected, observers in *Moltke* thought the blaze was *Tiger*'s funeral pyre and jubilantly claimed her sunk. But, aided by the fact that little remained to burn, repair parties had the fire under control within fifteen minutes. The damage done, however, was not just to *Tiger* and her crew. Beatty wrote in his *Report of Proceedings,* "At 10.54 a.m. submarines were reported on the starboard bow and I personally observed the wash of a periscope, 2 points on our starboard bow [1059]. I immediately [1100] signaled 'Turn 8 points to port together.'"

This was the most controversial of Beatty's decisions in the battle, not just because of the dubious tactical thinking involved, but because of the signal itself. Pelly of *Tiger* wrote,

> *Lion* hoisted the signal, "Alter course 8 points to port." Whilst this signal was still flying I observed the flagship developing a big list. She was evidently badly damaged. She began to drop back. . . . *Tiger* steered to pass between her and the enemy, and the German's fire was concentrated on her. For nearly five minutes this alter course signal remained flying and giving us all plenty of time to comment on it.
>
> I remember asking my navigator if he could explain the meaning of it, for to my mind it seemed to mean breaking off the action, He replied, "I have no idea, unless the *Lion* has better knowledge of minefields about than we have."[42]

There was confusion on the bridge of *Lion*. Beatty not only made the sighting himself, but also ordered the turn *without* giving the reason why. The signal was thus hoisted without the submarine warning. The flag commander, Plunkett, astonished by the order, recorded a few days later that his first reaction was to say, "Good heavens Sir, you're surely not going to break off the engagement?"[43] There were only two signal halliards remaining and no power to the signal lamps, but Beatty should have realized the confusion that the bald signal must inevitably cause.

As his battle cruisers thundered off, Beatty tried to regain control. In this attempt the final confusion set in. Beatty first ordered "Course North East" in order to resume the pursuit. By themselves, the "Compass" pennant and the letter flag "B" meant just what was intended—"Course North East." For Beatty, however, this was not enough. Time was slipping away and the quarry was escaping. Plunkett, who was not a signals specialist, suggested, "Attack the rear of the enemy."[44] Beatty agreed and here a critical ambiguity developed. The signals were hoisted nearly simultaneously on the two halliards left—which happened to be adjacent. When *Lion* put up "Compass B" on one and "A F" on the other, what was intended as "Course North East. Attack the enemy's rear" could be read as "Attack the rear of the enemy, bearing North East." Once more, Seymour did not serve his admiral well. He made two mistakes. The first was permitting both signals' display and their being hauled down together so that they looked like the one order. The second was in allowing Plunkett's suggestion to go without independent assessment—which he as flag lieutenant had a duty to provide, even with the most hurried look at the well-laid-out (and easy-to-read) 1906 Fleet Signal Book. Two entries above "A F" was the group "A D": "Attack the van of the enemy." Two pages on was an even clearer direction: "A U": "Pass the Sternmost Ships of the Enemy and endeavour to destroy, or disable, the Headmost Ships."[45] This would have made obvious the admiral's intent; the flags as hoisted did not.[46] The accumulation of missed signals, scares, inexperience, and snap decisions now brought about British failure.

Not one of Beatty's captains, still less Moore, was sure what the vice admiral intended by his signals. What had he meant by his 8-point turn? What was "the rear of the enemy"? In *New Zealand* Moore must have reflected on the anomaly between his commander's character and his apparent actions. And, as Andrew Gordon has pointed out, there was a section in battle cruiser battle orders that directed that fire be concentrated on ships that had been damaged and reduced in speed.[47] It was not like Beatty to give up the chase while there was still a chance of complete victory, yet what else could be meant? The tragedy of the decision Moore reached in the few minutes given to him lay in the signal halliards of *Lion*. Had the flagship been untouched here, or had *all* the halliards been shot away, matters might have turned out differently.

But Beatty was hoist not only with the petard of the senior officer present, but also with his own formidable command style. The vice admiral, Moore reasoned, must have had some good purpose in mind. What was the enemy's rear? *Blücher*. What did *Blücher* bear? Northeast. What did the signal read? "Attack the rear of the enemy bearing North East." Yet there was still one chance. Were *Tiger* to steer for the enemy main body, Moore would follow. All, however, was not well with the ship now in the lead. Blast from the shell that destroyed *Tiger*'s intelligence office had gone up through the conning tower and the gun control tower above it and "rattled us all . . . very considerably." Pelly found most of his internal communications severed. He also thought that the director and the main gunnery control systems were out of action. "There was a good deal of chaos and eventually

I decided more or less to complete the turn which appeared to be in accordance with the other ships' movements."[48] In reality, since *Tiger* was leading, it she who was calling the tune. *Princess Royal* had to follow suit or be run down. Her captain knew something was amiss but was unable to control the runaway events, since *Princess Royal* was effectively hemmed in.

Blücher now bore less than eight thousand yards to the east of *Tiger* and the battle cruisers were starting to work into line. The vice admiral and his staff, not understanding how their signals had been read, could not believe what was happening. Beatty tried again to restore sanity to proceedings. Plunkett said to Beatty, "What we need now is Nelson's signal, 'Engage the enemy more closely.'" Struck by the suggestion, Beatty replied, "Yes, certainly. Hoist it." Seymour looked at the signal book and discovered that the signal no longer existed. He hoisted instead, "Keep nearer the enemy," but this less specific command had no effect.[49] Only the accompanying "Repeat the signal the admiral is now making" was seen, and that only by *Princess Royal* and *Indomitable*.

Hipper and his officers were mystified. Hipper could only surmise that the British had suffered more than he had hoped. As he watched the battle cruisers approach *Blücher*, Hipper proposed a move southwest to support the stricken ship. The three heavy ships were turned to the new course and the light forces ordered to prepare for a torpedo attack; within a few minutes the latter directive was cancelled, since Hipper preferred to keep his ships together. The British, it seemed, were getting another chance, but, to a man, Hipper's staff were against the foray. Von Egidy declared that *Seydlitz* was unfit for battle and had barely two hundred rounds of 28-cm ammunition left. Raeder suggested, tentatively, that Hipper might be giving way to sentiment in seeking action with the four, possibly little-touched, British ships. At this, Hipper pulled himself together, ordered a course southeast, and "dismissed any further thought of supporting the *Blücher*."[50] Hipper's own postaction reflections indicated that he believed he would have been overwhelmed by the British—with the "near certainty of losing my remaining battle cruisers without justification."[51] The return to a southeasterly course soon put the German ships out of range and *Seydlitz* ceased fire at 1114. As they drew away, all eyes were on *Blücher*, which, at Hipper's last sight, "was still firing vigorously with all her guns."[52] A young officer serving in *G9* backed his admiral's judgment, noting of the torpedo craft that "their attack, having regard to the wide intervals between the British ships, could only have been against a single ship, and at the same time the [torpedo boats] would merely have run under the guns of enemy light cruisers and destroyers. . . . [T]he turn of the [German] battle cruisers was of great assistance to individual ships . . . and gave them an opportunity to join up again."[53]

Tyrwhitt was ordered by Beatty to detach units to form a screen around the crippled battle cruiser. Commodore (T) left *Undaunted, Aurora,* and all their destroyers, save *Lookout*'s division, to stay with *Lion*. The seven *M*-class destroyers were closing *Blücher*. With the three *Ls* working their way north to support the First Light Cruiser Squadron, it was time to administer the coup de grace. Screening arrangements made, Tyrwhitt took *Arethusa* to be in on the kill.

Lion, her escort falling into place, turned for home. Beatty longed to regain control and decided to shift his flag. The destroyer *Attack*, commanded by Lieutenant Commander C. V. Callaghan, son of Sir George, was called alongside at 1120. In spite of Callaghan's seamanship, the process of transfer to the destroyer occupied another precious twenty minutes. Beatty was sped on his way by a cheerful stoker, on deck for a breather, who clapped him on the back and roared, "Well done, David!" Seymour wrote later to his mother, "The men came up from below to see the Admiral leave, and the sight of him seemed to send them off their heads. . . . *Lion* was one huge grandstand of cheering men, but she looked rather a sad sight heeled over to port with a good many holes in her side."[54]

Blücher was still fighting valiantly, despite a heavy list to port and a fraction of her armament still in action. So effective was her fire that at 1105 Goodenough's cruisers were forced into a hurried turn away together to throw *Blücher*'s gunners off. It was a tribute to her crew's training that, with their ship badly damaged, they were able to straddle fast-moving light cruisers at over 12,000 yards. Only when the distance had opened to 16,000 yards did the commodore feel confident enough to bring his ships back to their former course.

At 1120 Commander Meade led *Meteor* and three other destroyers in to attack with torpedoes. *Blücher* still had some sting left and hit *Meteor* in the forward boiler room. The shell itself did not explode, but passed right through the hull. A boiler's collapse killed four stokers, as "the most remarkable cloud of steam + smoke shot hundreds of feet into the air, until the whole destroyer was blotted out by it. . . . [A]bout half a minute later the *Meteor* appeared again . . . apparently none the worse."[55] She and her division managed to get their weapons away, scoring what they estimated were five hits. However many actually struck, they destroyed most of what was left of *Blücher*'s capacity, but she still managed to launch a torpedo at *Arethusa*. This missed and *Arethusa* now closed to within 2,500 yards, "a very dashing + somewhat risky attack considering that *Blücher* was still firing."[56] The armored cruiser did not have long to live. Her guns began to fall silent and the list increased. Conditions on board were appalling:

> [T]he shells came thick and fast with a terrible droning hum . . . they tore holes in the ship's side. . . . They bore their way even to the stoke-hold. The coal in the bunkers was set on fire. . . . In the engine room a shell licked up the oil and sprayed it around in flames of blue and green, scarring its victims and blazing where it fell.
>
> The terrific air pressure resulting from explosion in a confined space left a deep impression on the minds of the men of

the *Blücher*. The air . . . roars through every opening and tears its way through every weak spot. . . . As one poor wretch was passing through a [hatch] a shell burst near him. He was exactly halfway through. The [hatch] closed with a terrific snap. . . . [M]en were picked up by that terrible *luftdruck* [air pressure] . . . and tossed to a horrible death amidst the machinery.[57]

Arethusa launched two torpedoes and both struck—one under the fore turret and one in the engine room. All light and power failed, although even now a few guns spoke. At 1145 Tyrwhitt signaled to Moore, "Enemy has struck." *Blücher* "was in a pitiable condition—all her upper works wrecked, and fires could be seen raging through enormous shot holes in her side."[58] Men were emerging from all over the ship and hundreds clustered on her starboard side and torpedo net shelves. They raised a defiant cheer as *Arethusa* came close in to begin rescue operations. Then *Blücher* herself took a hand. As she wallowed, her list to port had increased steadily. Quite suddenly the ship gave a heave and turned turtle. She floated bottom up for a few minutes and then sank. When *Arethusa* and the destroyers began to pick up survivors, one note of comedy sounded. As a sailor was being hauled in by a rather stout stoker named Clarke, he looked up at his rescuer and said, "Hello, Nobby [the naval nickname for anyone named Clark or Clarke], fancy meeting you here!" The two had been neighbors in prewar Hull.[59]

Arethusa picked up eleven officers and 110 sailors, but the effort was cut brutally short. Thinking only to find out what was going on, Hirsch brought L5 over the sinking. He kept his airship high and would probably have been little noticed had it not been for one of the more futile incidents of the sea war. Seaplane No.83, sent from the German carrier *Santa Elena* off Borkum, suddenly appeared, raining hand bombs down on stopped British ships. The crew probably mistook *Blücher* for a British unit because of her tripod mast, unique in the German navy, and did not see boats in the water until after their attack. Damaged by shrapnel, the seaplane was little more than a nuisance, but the same could not be said of the zeppelin and heads craned anxiously at the droning shape above.

Goodenough ordered an immediate withdrawal. Tyrwhitt's *Arethusa* engaged the seaplane and kept the rescue going as long as possible, while individual units such as *Lookout* delayed as much longer as they could.[60] In consequence, all but a few were picked up before the Harwich Force turned for home. The tragedy lay in the fact that if there were any casualties from the bombing, it was men in the water. In the end, out of a complement of 1,026—and at least 1,200 were actually on board, the balance made up by temporary drafts from *Von der Tann*—only 234 survived.

Content while the action was in progress to follow *Tiger's* movements, Moore bestirred himself when Tyrwhitt signaled, "Enemy has struck." Most of the battle cruisers ceased fire immediately and Moore had to decide whether to resume the pursuit of Hipper. The German battle cruisers were already nearly 30,000 yards away and it would take at least two or three hours to get back into range, by which time the force would be dangerously near Heligoland. He was also influenced by a signal from the Admiralty to Commodore (S) that *New Zealand* intercepted: "Send submarines to Heligoland Bight. High Sea Fleet are coming out." *New Zealand's* signals staff unfortunately transposed the sender and recipient. Moore was told it was Keyes who had provided the critical information that the German fleet had sailed. Admiralty intelligence could be taken with a grain of salt; information from a man on the spot could not. The last real chance of the chase continuing crumbled away, for Moore now thought that the High Sea Fleet must be at least two hours farther advanced than it actually was.

Moore realized that there was no immediate danger from German surface forces; on the other hand, a few hours more to the southeast. . . . He was also becoming worried about *Lion*. The battle cruisers had last seen her rapidly losing way, with a heavy list to port. Since then, there had been no word. Moore resolved to withdraw. At 1152 he signaled, "Form single line ahead in sequence of 4,3,2,5 [*New Zealand, Princess Royal, Tiger, Indomitable*] course west." A few minutes later he informed the Admiralty, reporting, "Commodore(S) reports High Sea Fleet coming out. Am retiring." At the same time, Goodenough, operations against *Blücher* complete, signaled Moore, "Lost touch with the enemy. What are your course and speed?" He was directed to "Retire north-west."

Beatty came up to the battle cruisers at noon. There was no time for recrimination and he immediately turned the big ships back to the southeast. Callaghan brought *Attack* alongside *Princess Royal,* and Beatty "clambered with great agility over the torpedo net" as he embarked.[61] By 1227 he had hoisted his flag again. Given time to think, Beatty realized that the chase was hopeless. The First Scouting Group could not be overtaken before it reached the German coast. The British commanders all believed that the High Sea Fleet was coming out. Although Jellicoe was moving in from the northwest, the battle cruisers were in no condition to tangle with the German battle line. Furthermore, Beatty had the crippled *Lion* to consider, while there was always the threat of submarine attack. At 1245 he ordered the battle cruisers to close *Lion*. Jellicoe knew that the battle cruisers' engagement was over, but had to consider the potential of a foray by the High Sea Fleet. Concerned that Beatty's and Bradford's squadrons should not go unsupported, he continued south at nineteen knots.

Meanwhile, the Scouting Groups made their way unmolested toward the Bight. Hipper pondered on sending his torpedo boats back for a night attack, but they were short of fuel. The High Sea Fleet flotillas were not far enough into the North Sea to do the job, given the likely requirement to overhaul the withdrawing British. Here Hipper was not well served by L5. Probably through inexperience, Hirsch decided that his duty lay in covering the retreat, rather than venturing west to develop a better overall picture. This meant that he failed to observe the crippled *Lion*, onto which he could have homed German forces. Furthermore, because he had not seen *Lion* fall out of line, Hirsch's response of "four" to Hipper's query as to the number of enemy battle cruisers contributed to the misapprehension that *Tiger* had blown up. This belief in partial success may have reduced the imperative to salvage something more from the situation. Any chance of a further sally disappeared with another contribution from L5. Asked specifically by the C-in-C as to whether any reduction in the enemy's speed had been seen, the airship replied, "Enemy forces disappeared out of sight. . . . No reduction in speed observed."[62] On the basis of this assessment, von Ingenohl finally ruled out an attack by light forces.

U-boats were dispatched toward the Humber, but none achieved anything significant. It was soon appreciated that the British were taking a more northerly course, but subsequent efforts to redirect them failed, while several units became confused as to the continuing need for their mission after they had observed the Scouting Groups' safe return. The only serious interaction was with Keyes' little force. Attacks were made by both by *U32* and *U17*. The former's single torpedo was not even noticed (although *U32* reported that she had to go deep when one of the destroyers turned to ram), while *U17* did not even get a weapon away before *Lurcher* forced her down.

British submarines were no more successful. Thinking that Tyrwhitt's light forces would be following the Germans as they retreated, Keyes at first intended to proceed to the vicinity of Norderney Gat, but when he learned from intercepted signals that all the destroyers and light cruisers were escorting *Lion* home, he made a sweep to the northeast. By 1800 Keyes was close to Heligoland, while *E7* and *E4* had just been detached to take up stations to the south of Heligoland and at the mouth of the Weser River. At 2030 *E8* assumed her billet north of Heligoland. The remaining boat, *E11,* was off Norderney. At 1900 Keyes came round to a southwesterly course, hoping to make contact with any German units coming in or out of the various channels.

He was too late. The High Sea Fleet was out before Keyes could span the passages. After the rendezvous with Hipper, the main body returned via Norderney Gat just as dusk was falling. By the time that Keyes had turned and sped down to the western corner of the German triangle, they were through the channels and home. Once into the Jade, there was nothing even Keyes could do. It was his faint hope that the Germans might have been delayed by cripples, but he knew by midnight that this was vain. Commodore (S) stayed in the vicinity of the Ems for a few more hours before turning his two destroyers for Harwich. Unlike the submarines, it would be foolhardy for them to linger in an area frequented by strong German patrols.

The submarines, even *E11,* saw nothing but trawlers as they patrolled on the surface during the dark hours. *E11* had arrived off Norderney Gat just too late, but in any case the primitive nature of submarine night warfare would have made an attempt against the Germans doubtful, even had the High Sea Fleet been later in entering the channel. The next day, *E8* spotted three flotillas of torpedo boats near Heligoland and unsuccessfully attacked *T92* on their return to port. At sunset on 26 January, all the British submarines began to withdraw. They were in Harwich twenty-four hours later.

The First and the Second Scouting Groups went into the Jade River after dark on the night of 24 January. They anchored there until the morning, when *Seydlitz, Derfflinger,* and *Kolberg* left to have their battle damage repaired in Wilhelmshaven. *Derfflinger* and *Kolberg* were able to berth almost immediately, but *Seydlitz* had to pump out six hundred tons of water from her after magazines before her draft was reduced enough to get her into the locks.

Meanwhile, the British were caring for *Lion*. Her very efficient executive officer, Commander C. A. Fountaine, soon had collision mats rigged and suspect bulkheads shored, flooding being largely stopped. The engine rooms, however, were cause for concern. The only thing preventing the wholesale flooding of the huge port engine room was a badly crushed 12-inch diameter, 0.25-inch thick copper suction pipe. The port engine was completely out of action and Engineer Commander E. C. Green soon realized that the contamination of feed water was such that all the boilers and thus the starboard engine would have to be shut down as well. For only a few hours more could *Lion* make even ten knots.

Beatty now had as his primary object *Lion*'s safe return. A strong destroyer screen was disposed around her and the battle cruisers and Goodenough detailed off to act as a covering force. The Third Cruiser Squadron came in sight at 1345, but Bradford recalled them and turned to conform to Beatty's course, remaining twenty miles clear. He also placed the Second Light Cruiser Squadron under Beatty's orders to assist in screening *Lion*. At 1530 Jellicoe met Bradford and ordered his ships to join the Grand Fleet. An hour later Jellicoe came in sight of Beatty and, in his turn, hauled his force around to the same course. He then detached the light cruiser *Galatea* and seventeen destroyers of the Second Flotilla and *Caroline* and eighteen of the Fourth Flotilla to strengthen the screen. Jellicoe had just received an urgent signal from the Admiralty: "Germans are preparing a night attack by destroyers, but the two flotillas which were out with their battle cruisers last night have not enough fuel to take part. Our destroyers should protect damaged ships."

The advice was gratuitous, but a night attack was a serious threat. Destruction of *Lion* would more than redress the loss of *Blücher*. The British could not afford the possibility of the victory being further sullied. With confirmation from the Admiralty that the German heavy units were on their way home, *Lion* and the crippled *Meteor* now had an escort of four battle cruisers, thirteen light cruisers, and sixty-seven destroyers, most of the Royal Navy's frontline strength.

At 1500 Commander Green informed Chatfield that the engines were unlikely to remain operational during the night. Beatty decided to have *Lion* taken in tow and selected *Indomitable* for the job. The operation was ticklish at the best of times, but *Lion's* condition made it particularly difficult. Although Green had managed to reduce the list by counter-flooding, the ship was virtually helpless as both capstans were out of action—one blown away by the hit on the forecastle and the other disabled by a fractured steam pipe. The operation took nearly two hours, everything being done by hand in *Lion*. A 5.5-inch wire hawser was passed and successfully secured, but the wire parted when the strain of *Lion's* nearly 30,000 tons came on too quickly. On the second attempt, a 6.5-inch hawser held. By nightfall *Indomitable* was working up to ten knots. Aware of the vulnerability of his charges to underwater attack, Tyrwhitt signaled to his forces, "Keep a good look-out for submarines at dawn. If seen, shoot and ram them regardless of your neighbors." The night passed quietly as internal order was restored to *Lion*: "[T]he silence of the ship was the strangest element of all. . . . [T]he echo of voices . . . [and] the strange gurgling of water where no water should be. Most of us had headaches, all of us had black faces, torn clothes and jangled nerves. The ship was as cold as ice. . . . [T]he sickbay was a mass of blood and dirt, feebly lighted by oil lamps."[63]

Filson Young was not exaggerating about the difficulties in the sickbay, which had no power or running water. *Lion* was lucky to have relatively few casualties, but her damage made their treatment very difficult. In such conditions, infection of the wounds was almost inevitable. There was much to learn in the treatment of casualties during and after battle.[64]

By dawn the threat of a surface attack had disappeared and Jellicoe decided to take his battle squadrons north before reentering Scapa Flow. He detached Bradford's pre-dreadnoughts and the Third Cruiser Squadron to return to Rosyth. Their entry did not go without incident. The Third Battle Squadron entered the Forth in thick fog and was set much farther to port by the current than expected. A late sighting of Inchkeith light just prevented the flagship, *Dominion*, going ashore, but in the confusion *Britannia* went aground.

All day Beatty's ships crept across the North Sea, the destroyers maintaining a close watch for U-boats. Just after midnight, they finally arrived off May Island. *Indomitable* transferred the tow to waiting tugs and Beatty detached the ships additional to his command. The British were lucky to avoid a serious collision, given the number of ships in close proximity in almost zero visibility. *Lookout* had to go "full speed astern & avoided ramming a scout by an acid drop [*sic*] . . . a hospital yacht, a destroyer [and] a huge ship with about 3 steaming lights."[65] In the continuing fog, at least one destroyer went straight through the boom off Oxcars, luckily without damage.[66] As the transfer was made, Beatty came on board, accompanied by Tyrwhitt, and remained on the bridge for the passage to Rosyth. Early on the morning of 26 January 1915, *Lion* was brought safely to anchor.

16

Seeking New Solutions

THE GERMANS SUFFERED HEAVY CASUALTIES AT THE DOGGER BANK. Among those lost in *Blücher* and *Seydlitz*, the First Scouting Group had almost a thousand killed, with about three hundred more wounded or taken prisoner. The material damage was less dramatic. *Kolberg* and *Derfflinger* needed only a few weeks to repair. Although the German official history recorded only one hit on *Derfflinger,* this was overrigorous application of the word "hit." At least two very near misses opened up the underwater hull and misaligned the outer starboard propeller shaft.[1] Another reason for the restriction came from not including shell hits that did not pass through plating of 20-mm or less thickness.[2] Eyewitness testimony that *Derfflinger* was hit aft therefore cannot be ignored.[3] There were problems realigning the shaft, but *Derfflinger* was operational by 17 February. *Seydlitz* took longer to repair. Her entire after-battery and a large section of forecastle were rebuilt, and the work was not complete until 1 April.

Despite surprise over the range at which the action was fought, the First Scouting Group had reason to be satisfied with its gunnery. In difficult conditions, the Germans had crippled *Lion* and, they thought, sunk *Tiger*. The hit rate, taken in comparison with the British hits on *Derfflinger, Seydlitz,* and long-range successes against *Blücher,* must have been far greater than their opponents'. Ammunition expenditure was a shock. In *Seydlitz* a wing turret that maintained continuous fire had twenty-five rounds remaining. Both the rate of fire and the number of rounds expended were much greater than anticipated. Increased magazine capacity, however, required extensive redesign and the Germans were in no hurry to extemporize ammunition handling. *Seydlitz*'s near loss meant antiflash precautions were drastically improved. In contrast to the British, the amounts of ready use ammunition and prepositioned propellant charges were reduced. These measures effectively dealt with the weakness. Although battle cruisers suffered similar hits at Jutland, there was never any real danger of the ships being lost this way. The same improvements were applied to the battleships and armored cruisers, although the older units' layout meant that they remained vulnerable.

The advantage of the British heavier armament was clear to the Germans, even if there were obvious problems with their shells. The 28-cm and 30.5-cm were at the limits of development; their value fell off sharply at very long ranges because of problems with accuracy, barrel wear, and penetration. Although 38-cm gunned battleships were building, the Germans faced the dismal prospect of at least ten 15-inch gun vessels joining the British fleet within the next two years, while they would muster only a few at the end of that time.

At least something could be done about the cruisers. *Arethusa* and *Kolberg*'s duel came as final confirmation that the 10.5-cm gun was inadequate. By the end of 1915 some bow and stern weapons had been replaced by single 15-cm guns, paralleling the earlier British light cruisers. As the heavier weapon became available, more modern ships had their remaining 10.5-cm removed, receiving a homogenous armament of 15-cm. All new construction units would emerge with 15-cm guns. The first ship so armed, the ex-Russian *Pillau*, had just commissioned as a very welcome addition to the scouting forces.

The dockyards at Wilhelmshaven and Kiel were under strain. *Seydlitz*'s long tenancy of Wilhelmshaven's floating dock disrupted the refit program. *Yorck*'s capsize and sinking cast doubt on the stability of many of the older armored ships, forcing extensive alterations. The poor steaming performance of the torpedo boats and their inadequate endurance meant revision of their boilers and fuel arrangements. Finally, although the work was largely done by ships' staff, the capital ships required modifications to their fire control arrangements to cope with very long-range actions. All this maintenance meant that the High Sea Fleet could not emerge in strength until at least the spring.

The Scouting Groups were well aware of the mistakes made at the Dogger Bank. The battle squadrons should have been at sea, allowing the battle cruisers to fall back on them and convert retreat into triumph. The action also rammed home the necessity for selecting the moment of greatest strength. The Germans could pick their time, even if it required much more careful management of refit and training programs than they understood. The force should never have sailed without *Von der Tann*. As Hipper implicitly admitted in his report, *Blücher* should also not have been included. Although he never acknowledged this, she should not have been last in line. He had been particularly struck by the British speeds and aggrieved at the German failure to achieve similar performance. Hipper's conclusions were concise:

1. It is again possible for us to damage the English fleet by U-boats in the North Sea.

2. All operations have to be planned so that a reserve formation is available for timely support of advanced forces . . . in the future the fleet will [have to] stand to with its full strength . . . in a state of readiness to support such operations.[4]

He stressed that a future fleet action had to be conducted in the "most favorable circumstances possible," no farther than seventy miles from Heligoland with U-boats positioned to attack British forces during their approach and withdrawal. He was particularly concerned that the torpedo forces be better integrated.[5] The light forces in the engagement were too few and individually weak, so outmatched that an assault on the First Battle Cruiser Squadron could well have resulted in a massacre. Despite the need for numbers, the Schichau-built vessels of the Fifteenth Half-Flotilla should not have accompanied the sortie. With their coal burning, reciprocating engines they could not keep up, or keep their funnels clear of the smoke that did so much to impede gunnery. Had they been forced to engage the enemy with their popgun four pounders, they would have been more of a liability than an asset. They needed rearmament as much as did the light cruisers.

There remained the problem of command. There were fears that Hipper might be blamed for *Blücher's* loss, but von Ingenohl had the moral courage to approve his actions. This was enough to protect Hipper from von Tirpitz's continuing enmity in particular. The C-in-C, however, was much more vulnerable and expected to be made a scapegoat.[6] Captain Hans Zenker, von Pohl's chief of staff, laid the blame for the fiasco squarely on von Ingenohl's shoulders, suggesting that the belief that the Grand Fleet was out of the North Sea was no assurance that the Scouting Groups would not encounter a superior force. The British had been alerted by the previous raids and had already displayed an uncomfortable foreknowledge of German sorties, something only confirmed by 24 January. He went on to say,

> The lack of foresight and prudence . . . is all the more astonishing and regrettable, because the disaster of 28th August was due to the same cause and because it was pure chance that the two raids on the English coast had no serious consequences for our ships. Neither from these experiences, nor from naval history has the Fleet Command learnt the doctrine that a dissipation of forces is always disastrous, particularly for the weaker side, whose only hope of success lies in a systematic and strict concentration of all its whole strength. . . . After all these misfortunes, which can be traced so clearly to the faults of the Fleet Command, the confidence of the officers in their leader, which is essential if victories are to be won, must be sorely shaken.[7]

Other influential figures had the same concerns and it was clear that von Ingenohl had to go. His relief, however, was an unpleasant surprise to "the front," who wanted Scheer, now commanding the Third Squadron, and adoption of the combined arms approach against the British. Determined, however, not to give von Tirpitz any additional authority, the kaiser was equally insistent that the

C-in-C could be trusted not to hazard the fleet. This made von Pohl the inevitable selection, despite Hipper's comment that "a more unlikely choice could not have been made."[8] On 2 February von Ingenohl was ordered to take over as Chief of the Baltic Station from Vice Admiral Bachmann, who in turn relieved von Pohl in the Admiralstab.

Although the reaction to the new C-in-C in the higher ranks of the navy was unfavorable, it was very different among the sailors and public. They remembered von Pohl's prewar reputation as a seaman and tactician. Furthermore, the declaration of unrestricted submarine warfare would shortly label him the most aggressive of the German leaders. Indeed, the appointment had the temporary effect of convincing many on both sides that a massive thrust by the High Sea Fleet was at hand.

This was not so. Von Pohl was committed to the *Kleinkrieg*, albeit with a new focus, the attack on shipping, or *Handelskrieg* (trade war). Pressure had been building with repeated proposals from the U-boat flotilla commanders, supported by Scheer. There was also increasing public and semi-official complaint as the Allied blockade began to take effect. Von Pohl was convinced there had to be some reply. He argued that a declaration that gave fourteen days' notice would deprive the neutrals of any good reason for complaint. On 1 February a conference with the chancellor, the foreign secretary, and the Chief of the German General Staff approved the initiation of commerce warfare. Von Pohl's last act in the Admiralstab was to sign the proclamation issued on 4 February:

1. The waters around Great Britain and Ireland, including the entire English Channel, are hereby declared a military area. From February 18 every hostile merchant ship found in these waters will be destroyed, even if it is not always possible to avoid thereby the dangers which threaten the crews and passengers.

2. Neutral ships also incur danger in the military area, because in view of the misuse of neutral flags ordered by the British Government on January 31 and the accidents of naval warfare, it cannot always be avoided that attacks intended to be made on enemy ships may also involve neutral ships.

3. Traffic northwards around the Shetland Isles, in the east part of the North Sea, and a strip of at least 30 miles in breadth along the coast of Holland, is not endangered.[9]

But the new campaign had not been thought through. The U-boat force was not big enough. Forty-nine submarines had been ordered since August, of which thirty-two were coastal types for use from the bases on the Belgian coast.

Fifty-four more would be ordered shortly. The total force available at the beginning of February was thirty-four boats, which included those in the Baltic as well as the units soon sent to the Mediterranean. Despite the belief that these numbers were enough to strike a heavy blow, it could not be heavy enough, however much the enemy mishandled the new challenge. Furthermore, submarines were a hazardous trade. Seven had already been destroyed; of those operational in early 1915, fourteen would be lost that year. Contrary to von Pohl's assessment about warning time, the impact on neutral opinion of ship losses and civilian casualties was profound, further confirmation that the human toll of this form of warfare cast it in a different light than the British blockade, however terrible the latter's indirect results.[10] Given the leakage, if not flood, of goods and material—including British products—through neutral countries, it is also arguable that the Germans were scoring an additional own goal. Many cargoes sunk were actually intended for Germany.[11]

There was another issue. The policy remained to attempt to cut off a detachment of the Grand Fleet, but von Pohl was not sanguine as to its chances. Allocating submarines to commerce warfare reduced the numbers that could operate in conjunction with the fleet and restricted progress in the combined arms warfare intended to overcome Britain's superiority. Von Pohl may already have had the seeds of the cancer that killed him in early 1916 eroding his capacity for action, but he was firm in his determination that the fleet should not be hazarded. This remained so after the kaiser's restrictions were partially lifted on 30 March 1915, since the new C-in-C never extended his forays into areas where contact with units of the Grand Fleet became a serious possibility.

Some of von Pohl's more reasonable concerns contributed to inactivity. One was that the fleet needed extensive training, particularly difficult in the depth of winter. He also refused to deploy unless all capital ships were available. This adherence to the principal of concentration partly arose from the wish to avoid von Ingenohl's failures, but the way it was managed meant that the dockyards could not maintain a stable workload because no coherent plan for specific periods of availability or nonavailability was devised. As a result, many repairs were skimped or deferred. This was bearable in the short term, but created increasing problems—as von Pohl discovered in July 1915 when he could not proceed with a sortie because of machinery defects.[12]

Ennui began to set in and the ground was laid for the mutinies of 1917 and 1918. The High Sea Fleet's record in 1915 was monotonous and dispiriting, perhaps in keeping with the mood of the ailing C-in-C. It made several sorties in early 1915, but these were rigidly confined by von Pohl's determination only to risk operating in waters where he could achieve an absolute superiority in light craft and had precisely sited minefields—in other words, close to Heligoland Bight. These operations seemed in the nature of rats emerging from their holes only to scuttle back at the slightest smell of danger and had an unsettling effect. The reservists gave the most trouble. Many were mature and successful men in the outside world, who had mobilized with the intention of coming to grips with the British. They were eager to serve, but unwilling to endure inactivity, particularly when it compared so unfavorably to the sacrifices of the army. It all became too much when combined with poor food and harsh treatment. The burgeoning submarine fleet, aviation arm, and Flanders forces were draining off many of the most reliable senior personnel and the best junior officers and young sailors. The division between officers and men, already marked, became even deeper as supervisors of less understanding and poor quality replaced those who had gone. As early as June 1915 there were disturbances in *Derfflinger* and Stumpf was recording the hatred of officers beginning to fester on the lower deck.[13]

The British faced their own problems, although their personnel losses at the Dogger Bank were small compared with the Germans. *Tiger* had one officer and three men killed and a total of eleven wounded. *Meteor* suffered four killed and one wounded, while *Lion* got off extremely lightly with only one man killed and twenty wounded.

It remained to deal with the damage. *Lion* lay at anchor off Rosyth, still listing and almost helpless. Commodore A. H. F. Young of the Salvage Corps organized salvage vessels to pump out the water. Jellicoe ordered the fleet repair ship *Assistance* down from Scapa, there being no heavy repair facilities available ashore. Damaged sections of the armor belt were enclosed by wooden cofferdams and concrete poured into the affected compartments. This temporary work was completed in a few days and *Lion* made ready to proceed south. At this point Fisher intervened. With his poor opinion of dockyard security, he felt that news leaking of the ship being dry-docked would negate the efforts made to convince the Germans and neutrals that little damage had been suffered (something greatly helped by small casualty lists). Despite the lack of a large enough dry dock, Fisher ordered that *Lion* undergo repairs in the Tyne.

Beatty and Chatfield cursed the decision. Had the ship been docked in Devonport, the work would have taken a few weeks. As it was, the job proved difficult and time consuming for Armstrong's Elswick yard. *Lion* had to be lightened and heeled over to expose the damaged areas of plate. Larger wooden cofferdams were installed to keep the damage clear of the water and, piece by piece, the armor plate was removed, repaired, and replaced. The concrete sealing the hull proved impossible to remove by hand or machinery. Armstrong had to resort to small charges of dynamite to break it up. However hard and well the contractors worked, they could not make up for the lack of a dry dock, and *Lion* did not emerge for several months. *Tiger*'s stay in the Tyne was more successful. A new armored roof was soon fitted to her damaged turret and she was operational within a fortnight.

As to the commanders, Beatty could feel the trembling of his throne as questions were asked about the German escape, but Fisher and Churchill both thought highly of him. Fisher, in his explosive manner, wrote at intervals, concluding on 31 January with, "I've quite made up my mind. Your conduct was glorious! Beatty beatus!"[14] Churchill had particular reason to be grateful because it greatly strengthened his political position.[15] The action reassured the British public that the Grand Fleet was not entirely passive. Neither Admiralty nor press was thus disposed to make anything of Beatty other than the disappointed hero. Indeed, while Beatty's conduct of the action had been far from perfect, most in the navy thought he had done well and would have been more successful had he been better served. Jellicoe wrote, "The more I hear of the fight the greater is my sympathy with you that you were knocked out in the *Lion* as it seems certain that otherwise you would have had one if not two battle cruisers to your credit in addition to *Blücher*."[16]

Truth to say, Jellicoe was puzzled by aspects of the engagement, particularly the gunnery, and read the reports with care. Much Grand Fleet guidance was revised in the following months on the basis of that information and intelligence gained from the survivors of *Blücher*. In the meantime, however, Fisher was out for blood. The letters praising Beatty expressed severe displeasure at Moore's performance, which he labelled "*despicable*," as well as *Tiger*'s captain ("*a poltroon*").[17] His comments on the reports were equally lurid: "No signals (so often unintentionally ambiguous in the heat of action) can ever justify the abandonment of a certain victory such as offered itself here."[18]

Although "in a disturbed frame of mind," according to Beatty, Churchill was more cautious.[19] Moore had supported him at a critical time over introduction of the 15-inch gun as Director of Naval Ordnance and Torpedoes, and then Controller. There were other factors at work. Rear Admiral Troubridge's court martial for failing to engage the battle cruiser *Goeben* had been conducted only two months before. Although in camera, Troubridge's acquittal was well known and the reaction had not been good, while much of the evidence directed blame at the Admiralty. Moore's case would be even less clear-cut and proceedings so drawn out that any salutary effect from a conviction (if achieved) would be lost.

Beatty disliked Moore and must bear considerable blame for not creating a better understanding with his subordinate, a problem that was to recur at Jutland.[20] He had clearly indulged his animosity, writing to Keyes in September, "I must pick up 'that other' cur [?] as you call him. He's a stinker but I've got his measure now. Halsey on the subject is as good as a play."[21] Beatty was more restrained when he commented later to Jellicoe, "Well frankly between you and I he is not of the right sort of temperament for a B.C.S [Battle Cruiser Squadron]," but there remains the question what Moore would have done had he been fully in Beatty's confidence.[22] Churchill was disposed to let the admiral off lightly and maintained this view, writing of Moore in *The World Crisis* that "fortune presented herself to him in mocking and dubious guise." He went on to make a lucid exposition of the difficulties of command at sea, concluding, "There are a hundred ways of explaining a defeat on land and of obscuring the consequences of a mistake. Of these, the simplest is to continue the attack next day in a different direction or under different conditions. But on the sea no chance returns. The enemy disappears for months and the battle is over."[23]

Churchill had his way. Moore was "kicked sideways" on 8 February to Cruiser Force I with his flag in the elderly *Europa*. Operating among the Canary Islands, this was, as Churchill delicately put it, "an appointment of a more suitable character."[24] Concealed within a wider reorganization, Moore's departure passed with little comment. It was left to Jellicoe to close the matter. Having read the reports and signal logs, together with Moore's additional letter of explanation, he wrote to the Admiralty:

> [I]t is to be observed that [Moore's] interpretation of the signal made by the Vice Admiral is borne out by an examination of the signal logs of the other ships engaged, and according to his reading of the signal he carried out what he conceived to be the intentions of the Vice-Admiral. . . .
>
> The Vice-Admiral in his report . . . does not say to what extent it was apparent that the enemy's ships other than the *Blücher* had suffered, although he mentions the fact of fires on board. Further . . . he makes no comment on the failure to follow up the retreating enemy. In these circumstances it is difficult for one who was not conversant with the conditions prevailing at the time to give a definite opinion on the correctness or otherwise of the Rear-Admiral's procedure.
>
> If as has since been stated two of the enemy's battle cruisers were very severely damaged <u>and the fact was apparent at the time</u> [underlined in original], there is no doubt whatever that the Rear Admiral should have continued the action.[25]

Jellicoe was himself on the point of calling Beatty back when he received Moore's withdrawal signal.[26] The distance to Germany was diminishing and he believed there were submarines deployed to attack the British as they approached the Bight. The view that the battle cruisers could have done something more, but only for a short period, was also expressed by Kennedy of *Indomitable*, a man who held no brief for Moore.[27]

Pelly, in an even more precarious position, stayed in *Tiger*. Beatty pointed out to Jellicoe that "the shell that landed under the conning tower . . . knocked those in the conning tower out temporarily although he won't say so, but for a time *Tiger* was all over the shop. . . . Pelly has done very well up to then, he has had difficulties to contend with. . . . I am all against changes; it is upsetting and inclined to destroy confidence."[28]

Pelly admitted the "good deal of chaos" in his memoirs and his real error lay in his decision about distribution of fire.[29] There were strong feelings in *Lion* that ascribed being put out of action to *Moltke* being able to shoot undisturbed. Chatfield declared it "a fatal mistake," although he erased the comment before submitting his formal report.[30] Matters for *Tiger* were not helped by the impression that her gunnery was poor —largely on the basis of *Southampton*'s and other reports of salvoes "apparently from *Tiger*" falling well over their target.[31] As a result, her gunnery officer, Bruce-Gardyne, was relieved. *Tiger*'s ship's company resented the accusation bitterly and always believed that they had hit other ships than *Blücher*.[32] They had—one on *Seydlitz* and another on *Derfflinger*.[33] Bruce-Gardyne might have had deficiencies as a control officer, but he had done a great deal to train the *Tiger*'s gunnery teams in very difficult circumstances. His career was not ended and he finished the war as executive officer of *Lion* herself. Perhaps he gained most satisfaction from the fact that *Tiger*'s crew spontaneously manned the side and cheered him as he left the ship.

Beatty did his best to improve relations between his flagship and *Tiger* by mustering both ships' companies on the dock at Rosyth and declaring, "You have won the first round so now keep on keeping on." He capped this by quoting Fisher's paraphrase of a Gilbert and Sullivan song, "There is a terrific outpouring, When the *Lion* starts a-roaring, And the *Tiger* starts a-lashing of her tail."[34] Beatty clearly had two audiences in mind. The verse appealed to his sailors, but he also knew how pleased the First Sea Lord would be with its use.

There remained Ralph Seymour, Beatty's "little round flag lieutenant."[35] With most admirals his accumulation of mistakes would have ensured his removal. It must be emphasized, however, that the notorious signal to turn away was not originated by Seymour, if Plunkett is to be believed, while the latter dominated the abortive attempts to retrieve the situation.[36] Beatty himself did not think that Seymour had done badly and clearly liked having him about. There would soon be an assistant flag lieutenant to help but (as Andrew Gordon has suggested) in view of the events at Jutland in 1916 Beatty should have sent Seymour to command a destroyer, which would have been no disgrace, and got the very best signals specialist whom he could find to interpret his orders unambiguously.[37]

Filson Young wrote of the Dogger Bank's aftermath, "Discussions and conferences were held among experts in the various technical branches involved, and a mass of very valuable material, which would have furnished food for a real staff for months was collected and forwarded to the Admiralty. But it soon became apparent that technical interest in these matters was pretty well confined to our own force. The Admiralty, having acknowledged receipt of the masses of material presented to it, made no further sign."[38]

This was not completely true. There were many recommendations made, but the majority required attention by squadron and fleet staffs while those that were the Admiralty's responsibility often related to long-term matters, such as new construction. The Controller's department paid close attention to postaction reports in order to embody war experience into the new ships.[39] Both Grand and Battle Cruiser Fleets developed many new instructions and modified procedures as a result of the Dogger Bank. These in turn were often promulgated to the wider navy in *Admiralty Weekly Orders* as well as more highly classified directives. Not all the changes proved right. What was lacking, particularly in tactical development, were organizations that could conduct dispassionate analysis of the evidence from first principles, rather than as immediate responses to individual, but potentially linked problems. These were not to emerge until much later.

The fixation with fast shooting typified the problem. Chatfield, responsible to Beatty for the battle cruisers' gunnery, came to believe that "a mistake was made in firing too slowly during the earlier stages of the Action. . . . That *rapidity of fire* is essential. . . . The main object when opening fire must not be the straddle but to obtain a *big volume of fire* short and then work it up by *small* 'ups' until hitting commences."[40] As a result, achieving a high volume of fire became a key requirement. This was not necessarily a bad thing, but it encouraged dangerous practices. To maintain rates of fire, large amounts of propellant were kept in the working chambers, already a widespread practice for antitorpedo craft armament. The near loss of the cruiser *Kent* from a cordite fire at the Falklands caused the Admiralty to issue a warning, but this was largely ignored.

Chatfield's ideas were supported (to a degree) by Jellicoe and became part of the Grand Fleet's gunnery doctrine, but proved fatal for the battle cruisers. Rosyth was not a good location for gunnery practice, particularly compared with Scapa Flow. Evidence mounted during 1915 that there were problems with the battle cruisers' shooting, but remedial measures started only in 1916 and proved too late for Jutland. Beatty's Splendid Cats would be more distinguished by the speed of their shooting than their accuracy. A second problem was even more serious. The battle cruisers' weak protection meant their turrets could be penetrated by German shells. In consequence, a serious hit would become catastrophic when masses of stand-by charges ignited in the handling areas.[41] Ironically, *Lion*, the ship that led the rapid fire push, was saved by its newly joined master gunner, Alexander Grant, who insisted on strict enforcement of magazine regulations and limits on the amount of propellant in the system. He had his way, probably only because he trained the crews so that, despite the restrictions, "the supply was faster than the guns could take it."[42] The unanswered question will always be why these rules were not imposed on the other battle cruisers.

Communications remained a weak area. Perhaps the greatest improvement was in radio security. The Admiralty noted comments by German survivors that the earlier raids into the Heligoland Bight had been compromised by wireless traffic. Oliver complained that there had been "little success" in persuading the fleet to keep quiet, but radio silence became a priority and was more successfully enforced in the months ahead.[43] However, neither the mechanics of signaling nor its culture was properly addressed. The new and improved signal book, whose issue had been delayed by the start of the war, remained unpublished. It already included many signal groups that recognized the potential exigencies of modern sea warfare, but additions to the existing book were issued instead. Richmond, at Plunkett's behest, "called the attention of the Powers that be to the omission of 'Engage the enemy more closely'" and ensured that this and four other groups, which covered disablement of the flagship and transfer of command, were issued by 27 February.[44] The Signal Book would be the subject of comprehensive reexamination, but one that focused on the construction of signal groups, not the problem of communicating in action. Arguably, this would never be properly addressed while Jellicoe was C-in-C because his concerns over the vulnerability of the fleet manifested themselves in a determination to maintain tight control over the whole formation, particularly the battle line. Given the limitations of gunnery technology and of situational awareness, there may have been no alternative in 1915, but Jellicoe's methods did too little to encourage his subordinates to think for themselves. He would pay a heavy price for this at Jutland.

The most obvious change in organization, although it reflected the Admiralty's existing desire to have a striking force closer to the southern North Sea, was creation of the Battle Cruiser Fleet, with three separate squadrons. The detached battle cruisers were steadily returning to home waters. Within weeks all but *Inflexible*, whose homecoming would be delayed by her mining in the Dardanelles, were concentrated at Rosyth. *Lion* was fleet flagship, while the battle cruiser squadrons consisted of the First, *Princess Royal* (flag), *Queen Mary,* and *Tiger*; the Second, HMAS *Australia* (flag), *New Zealand,* and *Indefatigable*; and the Third, *Invincible* (flag) and *Indomitable*, to which last was eventually attached *Inflexible*.

Sorting out the flag officers proved complicated. That Sir George Patey, who came with *Australia,* was senior to Beatty was initially dealt with by granting Beatty seniority as a vice admiral for the purpose of command "while holding his present appointment during the period of hostilities" of 3 August 1914.[45] Jellicoe observed that "never was promotion better deserved," but this was unfair on Patey who had performed well in the Pacific as commander of the Australian Fleet.[46] Probably to the relief of all concerned, he was soon reappointed to the North America and West Indies Station as C-in-C. Pakenham was posted in his stead, while Osmond Brock was appointed commodore in the First Battle Cruiser Squadron, a temporary solution until his promotion to rear admiral. As Brock had to remain in *Princess Royal* while Beatty used her as his temporary flagship as well, the new captain, Walter Cowan, had a thin time of it, "wandering about the ship like a lost soul for a few days."[47]

Since there would be a delay before all the older battle cruisers joined, the Third Battle Cruiser Squadron was temporarily combined with the Second. No admiral had yet been found (even Pakenham's appointment had been the subject of debate). The officer would have to be both an experienced cruiser commander and someone acceptable to Beatty—there were few who satisfied both criteria. Not until May, by a combination of circumstances, would the choice fall on Hood. Beatty also got an additional light cruiser squadron, the new formation being the First, of brand new fast light cruisers under Commodore E. S. Alexander-Sinclair, while Goodenough retained the older, but more powerful, *Town* class in the Second.

Churchill and Fisher pleaded with Jellicoe to bring the Grand Fleet down to the Firth of Forth and move the battle cruisers to the Humber. Both he and Beatty were set against it. The latter was unhappy enough with Rosyth because of its distance to the open sea and vulnerability to mines. It took so long to sweep the channel that, as he complained to Churchill, he sometimes had to sail without any sweeping being done. Beatty would have preferred Cromarty, as a clearer and safer anchorage, but Fisher asserted, "It's 150 miles too far off."[48] When Churchill raised the possibility of the Humber, with the Grand Fleet at Rosyth, the vice admiral reported to Jellicoe that he was able to dispose of the idea without difficulty:

> I made it plain that I did not agree with putting the battle cruisers at the Humber. First of all and lastly it is impossible, as there is insufficient water. When I say impossible I mean as a base which one can leave or enter at any time of the tide; this we cannot do for three hours each side of low water, i.e. for 6 hours; that I think puts the hat on it. I also think that it would be a mistake to move the battle fleet to Rosyth. It no doubt could be made safe with extra craft and extra vigilance, but it seems to me it would be playing into the enemy hands to bring within nearer reach our capital ships, and in a position where going in or out (no matter what precautions we take) they would be far more vulnerable to submarine attack than at Scapa, also destroyer attack if they ever develop it, and most certainly mine-laying, and take them away from a place where they can enjoy some measure of opportunity for gunnery practices.[49]

The words might have been written by Jellicoe himself. Both he and the commander of the new Battle Cruiser Fleet were settling in for a long war. Beatty did suggest that the lesser draft battleships of the Third Battle Squadron go to the Humber instead, since they could sail at all stages of tide. This proposition was eventually taken up, but for the rest the First Lord "seemed to concur" and nothing more was said.[50] The other dispositions, all of which were to hold for the Battle of Jutland, stood.

The new arrangements meant that Beatty now had a very powerful force at his disposal. He had every right to be confident about meeting the First Scouting

Group, but there were dangers in separation from the Grand Fleet. In March 1915 Jellicoe wrote a very carefully phrased letter to Beatty:

> I should imagine that the Germans will sooner or later try to entrap you by using their battle cruisers as a decoy. They must know that I am—where I am—and that you are—where you are, and they may well argue that the position is one that lends itself into a trap to bring you into the High Sea Fleet, with the battle cruisers as a bait. They know that if they can get you in a chase, the odds are that you will be 100 miles away from me, and they can under such conditions draw you well down into the Heligoland Bight without my being in effective support. It is quite all right if you keep your speed, of course, but it is the reverse if you have some ships with their speed badly reduced in the fight with the battle cruisers, or by submarines. . . . [O]ne must concern oneself very seriously with the result to the country of a piece of real bad luck culminating in a serious decrease in *relative* strength. Of course the whole thing is a question of the game being worth the candle and only the man on the spot can decide.[51]

There was one more important personnel change. Churchill, Oliver, and Keyes agreed that the position of Commodore (S) was untenable. Matters came to a head when Fisher read Moore's signal to Jellicoe indicating he was withdrawing and that "Commodore (S) reports High Sea Fleet coming out."[52] He immediately placed the blame on Keyes. The latter was able to deny making any such signal, but, in discussions afterward, Keyes declared that it would be better if he were out of Fisher's reach. As Keyes wrote, "It was a great relief to me to get this off my mind and I think that the First Lord was relieved too, for he had expended a good deal of time and energy fighting my battles, which was all wrong."[53]

Matters had not been improved by a second falling-out between Keyes and Tyrwhitt just before the Dogger Bank. It developed from Keyes at last getting a promise from the Admiralty of a light cruiser, which meant one fewer for the Harwich Force. Tyrwhitt was extremely annoyed, and the issue of their relative seniorities boiled up again. Keyes wrote bitterly to his wife that Tyrwhitt "thought I might be in his way one day" and it is likely that this was so.[54] The operational relationship was basically unstable and, although the two were reconciled, it was well for both that Keyes was going. Ordered to the Mediterranean on 8 February as chief of staff of the force assembled for the attack on the Dardanelles, Keyes was out of England within hours, his colleagues envious at his chance of action. Fisher's protégé, S. S. Hall, was appointed as Commodore (S), now a purely administrative job, while Waistell, as commander of the Overseas Submarine Flotilla, took charge of its operations.

Keyes' translation was a metaphor for what was going on at the Admiralty in January and February 1915. The division between the First Lord and the First Sea Lord increased day by day. Fisher remained intent on closing off the North Sea with mines and tightening the blockade as the essential precursors to any more ambitious projects. Churchill's frustrations at not having a forward operating base at Borkum, or—as Wilson wanted—at Heligoland, and the increasingly desperate desire of the government to break free of the apparent stalemate meant that the proposed attack on the Dardanelles was assuming ever more importance. It also consumed increasing amounts of the First Lord's and the Admiralty's time. The transfer of many of the pre-dreadnoughts to the Mediterranean was beginning and with them, to Fisher's dismay, much more modern units that had been intended for the Grand Fleet.

The Dardanelles would eventually cause the downfall of both Churchill and Fisher and the installation of an Admiralty regime with very different methods. The shift of attention to the eastern Mediterranean was already having an important effect in making the C-in-C of the Grand Fleet more influential over policy in home waters. Although undesirable in principle, this perhaps provided stability hitherto absent in much of the planning. Whatever flaws he possessed as a commander, Jellicoe's constancy of strategic vision cannot be denied. He understood the importance of the war of supply as well as any and the relationship between its successful prosecution and the maintenance of the Grand Fleet as guarantor of the strategy. The weaknesses of the blockade were becoming clearer to him as the weeks passed and he determined to do what he could to fix them. To the slowly increasing fleet staff on board *Iron Duke*, Jellicoe quietly added his own trade and economic unit, at first taking advantage of the presence of expert volunteers such as Edward Hilton Young, transferred from *Cyclops* ostensibly to assist with cypher duties, but soon employed as an economics adviser, lecturing the C-in-C and his staff.[55] This consciousness-raising exercise was only the prelude to an effort to push the British government toward more resolute enforcement of the blockade.[56] In the meantime, the Grand Fleet at last secure in its bases, he would wait to see what the Germans would do. It would be a long watch.

17

Summa

A T THE POINT THIS WORK CONCLUDES, NEARLY FOUR YEARS OF GLOBAL war lay ahead. There were unpleasant surprises in store for the protagonists and the capabilities of the emerging technologies were minuscule by comparison with those of late 1918. The greatest naval battle had yet to be fought, and so did its most important campaign. Yet enough had happened that the six months described here can be called the true beginning of modern naval warfare. Between the outbreak and *Blücher*'s sinking, practically every element of the new technology was employed, albeit with varying success. Submarines came into their own as weapon systems; aircraft began to play an important role; open sea minelaying was commonplace; and surface actions were fought at long range and high speed, in poor weather and influenced by signals intelligence. Two questions may therefore be asked: How well prepared were the navies for war?, and How did they respond to war's challenges?

Answers must recognize context. All the navies were hamstrung by incoherent national strategies. They must take responsibility for some, but by no means all, of the failures involved. The mechanisms for effective joint planning either did not exist or, in the British situation, were not forced to work properly. There was rarely effective guidance from governments. All suffered from divisions between navies and armies and the operation of parallel and often uncoordinated plans. The mechanisms of alliance management were also inadequate. Most significant for the naval war, the direct relationship between the effectiveness of the British blockade and any effort by Russia to hinder trade between Scandinavia and Germany was not explored and therefore could not be systematically exploited. This failure to make all the necessary links between operations and conduct of the war of supply was at the root of the deficiencies in much British thinking on concepts such as the Baltic Project, and even Churchill's desperate efforts to initiate the capture of a base for forward operations in the North Sea.

It should now be clear just how experimental practically every aspect of naval warfare was in 1914 and how unexplored were so many of the operational problems that the protagonists faced. The differences between the fleets of 1909 and those of 1914 are arguably the greatest of any five-year period in peacetime history; they rival in scale developments between 1914 and 1918 and 1939 and 1945. The best, most intelligent, and relatively most experienced had still to understand what their jobs were and spent the war's opening months learning exactly that. This is most apparent with the submarine and aviation forces. Few submarine commanders in August 1914 could successfully attack a surface ship. Most aviators, whether in fixed wing or lighter-than-air machines, were doing well if they managed to take off and land safely, let alone conduct a mission. These were extremes, but there was much the same requirement for a learning curve within every fighting arm.

Yet, to an observer in 2014, although so much had still to be worked out, the key issues were those of planning and command. Both had systemic and cultural elements. None of the navies possessed really effective staffs. The deficiencies rested not only in the strategic and operational planning systems, although there were fundamental problems there, but also in the wider arrangements required to conduct what would now be described as raise, train, and sustain activities. The relationships between these elements and the campaign planners were, in 1914, weak, at least partly because there were too few expert people in too few established appointments to do the work needed. However imperfect the Admiralty machine might still have been in November 1918, it was vastly more sophisticated and powerful, capable of dealing with problems that were far more complex than little more than four years earlier. The multitude of *Technical Histories* and *Naval Staff Monographs (Historical)* and other studies produced within the Admiralty following the war is indicative both of that sophistication and of the processes by which it had been achieved. Perhaps most important, an effective relationship with science had come into being, even if it needed further development.

There was equivalent progress within the fleet's organization. The machinery that supervised the Grand Fleet evolved significantly and created a construct by which the major formations of the Royal Navy would be managed for the next half century. It was not perfect. The fleet may have ended up with too much centralization *into* the C-in-C's staff, as well as *within* it, problems that dogged the Royal Navy for the remainder of the twentieth century (and arguably still do). But it met a vast range of requirements—doctrinal, material, and human—for large numbers of ships and other units of varying capabilities in a way never before possible. Particularly notable was the logistic achievement in sustaining the battle fleet so far from the existing network of dockyards, as well as from the normal sources of supply. This was as much the Admiralty's achievement as that of the fleet staff, but it required constant planning and coordination by those on the spot. By February 1915 the development of such systems was well under way, even if much was still to be learned.

It would take longer to create the more effective operational planning that had been identified as lacking by observers during prewar Grand Maneuvers, something amply confirmed during the first months of the war. This not only required the assembly of the necessary staff, but also the evolution of procedures that made the distinction between essential detail and micromanagement. Jellicoe's fixation on centralized command of the Grand Fleet limited progress in some ways, but there is no doubt that the operational orders issued in the future by both Admiralty and fleet commanders would have a coherency largely absent in August 1914.

One problem remained unresolved at sea that was not cultural, but rather one of understanding. It would require much more thinking to solve. Plotting and reporting procedures that allowed dispersed ships and formations to operate within a common frame of reference were yet to be developed, with mechanisms by which relative errors could be removed or at least reduced to the point where the pool of those errors did not become so large that it invalidated the tactical picture. The very first steps were being taken, but much more was needed. The blindfolds were starting to come off, but all concerned were still in a darkened room.

At least for the Royal Navy the First World War was thus the period in which the organization of the service caught up with the second and third generations of industrialization taking place in the ships themselves. The analogy of the tiny brain and huge body has been employed by other critics, but more valid is its extension that it was also the navy's central nervous system that was insufficient for the task. The Royal Navy as a single entity was probably the most sophisticated organization in the world in 1914, whether considered in industrial, social, administrative, or warfighting terms. Yet, just adequate for the peace—and still evolving—it was not enough to meet the challenges of global war without much greater change.

In these pre-late industrial arrangements, what is noticeable, particularly by comparison with the British performance in the Second World War, is the importance of individuals, but it was a disruptive rather than creative importance. The Admiralty would have been a different place without Churchill, but the question is open as to whether it benefitted from his energy more than it suffered from his ignorance. Even with the role played by the kaiser and the intrigues of von Tirpitz, it is clear that a stronger man than von Ingenohl could have implemented a much more active policy for the High Sea Fleet and taken the German navy down more productive paths.

That there were cultural problems is undeniable. The Royal Navy was bedeviled by the cult of the senior officer present. This resulted not simply in failures to act when the assumption was made that authority must somehow know more than the man on the spot. It also stifled independent thought. The absence of working through possibilities and developing different potential courses of action by many at each level of command is something that strikes the critical observer a century later. There was a deficiency of what would now be described as operational art.

This was both partly caused by and contributed to the common assumption that a major conflict would necessarily be short, but there was a clear inability to align ends, means, and ways. There were problems of method and understanding. Personnel did not have the information that they needed, but often did not realize that they needed the information in the first place.

Much has been made of the Royal Navy's lack of staff training: this certainly contributed to the problem as much as did the culture itself, because the more comprehensive the training and the wider its spread, the greater the likelihood of key problems being identified. One result was that the War Staff was ill equipped to cope with Churchill's enthusiasms, particularly his passion for detailed lists of ships and equipment in drafting operational instructions (a passion for lists that puts the reader in mind of Churchill's fictional contemporary, the Water Rat of *The Wind in the Willows*). The manning and methods used by all the services between 1939 and 1945 to overcome Churchill's sillier ideas—and explore his more interesting ones—by careful preparation of studies and plans did not exist in 1914.

Where culture and personality did come together and not necessarily with good results was in Jellicoe's management of tactical development, something that also said much about his leadership. In a time of such profound technical change, maintaining a balance between innovation and a clear collective understanding of the C-in-C's intent and the part that each formation and unit had to play would always be difficult. In many aspects of his command of the Grand Fleet, Jellicoe rose to the challenge in a way that few could have done. The success of the organization that supported him was largely due to his careful management, but in tactical doctrine, he failed. The roots of that failure can be seen in the correspondence in later months between Jellicoe and Sturdee, after the latter joined the Grand Fleet and sought to examine what Jellicoe viewed as much riskier divided tactics and battle fleet turns together.[1] That Jellicoe should have rejected Sturdee's ideas is not so much the problem. Indeed, given the difficulties of fire control and maintaining situational awareness, it is arguable that there was no practical alternative to the C-in-C's concepts between 1914 and 1916. It was rather the way Jellicoe forbade further discussion—as though the debate itself might undermine his command of the fleet. This says something about Jellicoe's self-confidence, but when such an approach combined with the culture of the senior officer present, the results could not be good.

It is encouraging to see the seeds of an operational renaissance in the way that junior and middle-rank officers expressed their personal dissatisfaction in their diaries and correspondence. That the Royal Navy embarked on a successful campaign of cultural change after 1918, however informal its methods, is undeniable, and the fruits were evident at the River Plate in 1939 and around Norway in 1940. Many who would distinguish themselves in the Second World War watched the events of 1914–15 and did not like what they saw. One can make too much of the influence of the new fighting arms of the navy on the culture of the whole, but many who were influential during the next global conflict and the years leading up to it were, if not very close to the center of events on board the flagships, serving in destroyers or submarines. Their combination of perspectives would create a momentum for change that proved unstoppable. For the leadership, it was achieved in three ways.[2] The first was through new organizations such as the tactical school, which allowed the dispassionate examination of tactics and the exploration of new ideas; the second was realistic training in which risks were taken, with the acceptance of "broken eggs to make the omelet."[3] The third, visible in the performance reports and selections for flag rank of the 1920s and 1930s, was choosing the right people, particularly for seagoing command. Drive and a willingness to take the initiative were key factors. That this was so is perhaps best demonstrated by the removal of Admiral Sir Dudley North from his command at Gibraltar in 1940. The real grounds for his dismissal by the First Sea Lord— whom we have met as executive officer of *Colossus*—were not that he had made the wrong decision: they were that he had failed to make any decision at all, but instead looked to higher authority when time did not permit.[4] Pound's judgment almost certainly had its origin in the events of 1914.[5]

German problems were more subtle. Perhaps the difficulties of recovering the situation in a navy conceived to fight the wrong opponent, at the wrong place and in the wrong way, were too great ever to be overcome. But the absence of consideration of ends/means/ways was even more the case for the Imperial German Navy than it was for the Royal Navy. There was a tendency to place too much weight on supposed moral and psychological factors rather than on practicalities, and with this tendency came an expectation that something had only to be desired for it to come true. Both the zeppelin air raids and the inception of the first unrestricted submarine campaign demonstrate a complete mismatch between the result wanted and the capacity of the force at hand to achieve it. This attitude also affected the understanding of German vital interests and supply flows, resulting in the failure to comprehend that there was a relationship between the U-boat assault on international trade and Germany's access, albeit indirect and covert, to the world economy.

The diversion of the aviation and submarine arms to their grand campaigns had other effects. Directly, they impeded the development of combined arms tactics and operational concepts to the degree that the High Sea Fleet lost any chance of entangling British forces in unfavorable situations and thereby achieving significant attrition early in the war. There would be a second effect, more difficult to prove, but apparent to the thoughtful observer. The Imperial German Navy's pool of talent was not deep. It had expanded too fast and the body of expertise was too small for it to manage easily the transfer of so many of the more enterprising and dynamic to the emerging submarine and aviation arms, as well as to the naval forces ashore in Flanders. Too much of the Fleet Command and Admiralstab's limited planning capacity was consumed, in the same way that the Dardanelles came to take up the British leadership's time, but for a much longer period. Such distractions were bad enough for the British; they were disastrous for the Germans, if only because the latter, in moving from what had been effectively a coast defense construct to a more flexible, offshore approach, had even more to think through than their adversaries.

There was another aspect to this problem. The need to look after the lower deck may have been clearer to the Grand Fleet in its remote anchorages than it was to the home-ported High Sea Fleet. Efforts to provide for welfare and entertainment were still primitive in the Royal Navy in 1914–15, but they were already more sophisticated than those of the Imperial German Navy, and advanced much further in the years ahead. The British effort may have been only just enough, but that of the Germans was inadequate to a degree that would have a profound influence on the events of 1918. To be fair, an equivalent revolt of the coal face to that of the Royal Navy and a parallel process of cultural change occurred within the postwar German navy. However dubious their political outlook, there was a determination to improve the relationship between the lower deck and officers that made the navy of 1919 and after a very different place to the navy of the Great War.

It would be too easy to regard the Russians as the poor cousins in any assessment of capability and performance, but this was not the case. Just as navies in general represent one of the most sophisticated, and thus most revealing, manifestations of national intent and practice, so the Imperial Russian Navy can be considered a microcosm of the flawed entity that was the Russian Empire. Too much depended on one man, and this became clear after von Essen's untimely death in early 1915. But the navy possessed formidable capabilities and, had von Essen had more freedom to use them—perhaps with some tempering of his judgment by higher authority (whether or not he would have proceeded with a coup de main against the Swedish fleet had he been allowed remains uncertain)—the Russians may well have made the German position in the southern Baltic unmanageable even in 1914. The destruction of *Pallada* aside, what one can observe in von Essen's operational concepts is a better relative understanding of his navy's capabilities and limitations than was apparent among many of his professional equivalents. In this he was not alone, and von Essen was supported by some talented officers with a flair for lateral thinking, as demonstrated by the development of signals intelligence and weather reporting. But there were not enough such leaders and the overall quality of the Russian sea officer corps was insufficient to overcome the host of factors driving the Baltic Fleet toward its part in the revolutions of 1917.

The more one comprehends what happened at sea in 1914 and early 1915, the more that the events of Jutland, the Dardanelles, and of 1917–18 become understandable, if not inevitable. For the professional naval officer of 2014, the problems of the time should evoke both sympathy and a certain discomfort in the present capacity to cope with the effects of technological and social change in a fighting service. It seems fitting to close with a remark made by Rear Admiral Hood. He once commented that when he saw another ship or officer in trouble as a result of their own decisions, his first response was to say, "There but for the grace of God goes Horace Hood."[6] Thinking about 1914, as one who has commanded at sea himself, the author cannot escape the same feeling. If there is a lesson, it is that technology, organization, and culture matter, and navies need to get all of them right.

NOTES

ABBREVIATIONS IN NOTES

ADM	Admiralty
CCA	Churchill College Archives
HMSO	His Majesty's Stationery Office
IWM	Imperial War Museum
NHB	Naval Historical Branch
NMM	UK National Maritime Museum
RN	Royal Navy
RNM	Royal Naval Museum
TNA	UK National Archives

INTRODUCTION

1. Copies are available in the UK National Archives, the RN's Historical Branch at Portsmouth, and in the Royal Australian Navy's Sea Power Centre in Canberra.
2. Re: "historically informed fiction," the absence of high-quality fictional treatments of 1914–18 at sea by comparison with 1793–1815 and 1939–45 is striking—let alone treatments of the war on land. Where such fiction does exist, it is by contemporary writers such as "Taffrail" (Captain H. Taprell Dorling) and "Bartimeus" (Paymaster Lewis Ricci). While giving color and some insight, their writing does not display the depth of works such as Nicholas Monsarrat's classic of the Battle of the Atlantic, *The Cruel Sea* or Herman Wouk's *The Caine Mutiny*.
3. Admiralty, *Narrative of the Battle of Jutland* (London: HMSO, 1924), 3.

CHAPTER 1. THE BEGINNING

1. "Opening of the North Sea and Baltic Canal," *Times of London,* 21 June 1895.
2. "Etienne" (Stephen King-Hall), *A Naval Lieutenant 1914–1918* (London: Methuen, 1919), 7.
3. Captain Otto Groos, *Der Krieg zur See: Der Krieg in Der Nordsee: Nordsee,* vol. 1, trans. British Admiralty Naval Historical Branch (NHB) (Berlin: Mittler, 1920), 7. Pagination for this reference and other volumes in the series will be from the NHB translation.

4. "Better for dancing on," Midshipman Colin Buist, *HMS Princess Royal*, midshipman's journal entry, dated week ending 27 June 1914, Buist Papers, CCA; "supper hall," Stephen Roskill, *Admiral of the Fleet Earl Beatty: The Last Naval Hero: An Intimate Biography* (London: Collins, 1980), 73.

5. Captain Wilfred Henderson, naval attaché Berlin, Report No. 26/14, dated 3 July 1914, Matthew S. Seligmann, ed., *Naval Intelligence from Germany: The Reports of the British Naval Attaches in Berlin 1906–1914* (Aldershot, UK: Ashgate and Navy Records Society, 2007), 542–43.

6. Admiral Sir William Goodenough, *A Rough Record* (London: Hutchinson, 1943), 86.

7. Georg von Hase, *Kiel and Jutland* (London: Skeffington, 1921), 39.

8. To make clear the distinction between the British Admiralty and its German equivalent, Admiralstab will be used for the latter throughout.

9. Groos, *Der Krieg zur See: Nordsee,* vol. 1, 11.

10. Admiralstab to SMS *Eber*, Telegram No. 11, 7 July 1914 (later decrypted by the British Admiralty), TNA ADM 137/4065. See also Groos, *Der Krieg zur See: Nordsee,* vol. 1, 8–9. The captain seems to have ignored this direction, but managed to get his repairs done and get clear in time, to the later fury of the absent British naval commander-in-chief (C-in-C). See Admiral Sir Herbert King-Hall, *Naval Memories and Traditions* (London: Hutchinson, 1926), 245.

11. "We might have to," Stephen King-Hall, *My Naval Life 1906–1929* (London: Faber & Faber, 1952), 87.

12. Admiral J. H. Godfrey, *Naval Memoirs*, vol. 1, *1902–1915,* 92, GDFY 1/1, Godfrey Papers, CCA.

13. Major General Sir Charles Fergusson to Captain J. Fergusson, RN, letter, dated 25 March 1914, in *The Army and the Curragh Incident*, ed. Ian F. W. Beckett (London: Army Records Society, 1986), 340. See also Ian F. W. Beckett and Keith Jeffery, "The Royal Navy and the Curragh Incident," *Historical Research*, 62, no. 147 (1989): 54–69.

14. First Lord, minute, dated 22 October 1913, TNA ADM 116/1309.

15. Godfrey, *Naval Memoirs,* vol. 1, 95.

16. Air Chief Marshal Sir Arthur Longmore, "Naval Flying 1913/14," *Naval Review* 55, no. 2 (April 1968): 138. See also Longmore, *From Sea to Sky 1910–1945* (London: Geoffrey Bles, 1946), 36.

17. Groos, *Der Krieg zur See: Nordsee,* vol. 1, 17.

18. Admiralstab Telegrams Nos. 13, 15 and 6 to East Asiatic Squadron, SMS *Eber* and SMS *Konigsberg,* dated 25–26 July 1914, intercepts collated in TNA ADM 137/4065.

19. Groos, *Der Krieg zur See: Nordsee,* vol. 1, 18–19.

20. Admiralty to C-in-C Home Fleets 24 July 1914. Unless otherwise indicated, all British signals and Admiralty official statements in this chapter are taken

from Appen. A to *Naval Staff Monograph (Historical),* vol. 3, Monograph 6, *Passage of the BEF* [British Expeditionary Force], *August 1914,* 24 et seq.

21. Lieutenant B. W. L. Owen, HMS *Stour,* diary entries, dated 24–31 July 1914, BWO1/3, Owen Papers, IWM.

22. Richard Hough, *Louis and Victoria: The Family History of the Mountbattens* (London: Weidenfeld and Nicholson, 1984), 261.

23. Lieutenant A. B. Downes, HMS *Birmingham,* diary entry, dated 28 July 1914, Downes Papers, RNM Library.

24. Lieutenant Bertram Ramsay, HMS *Dreadnought,* diary entry, dated 19 July 1914, Ramsay Papers, NMM.

25. Captain Lionel Dawson, *Flotillas: A Hard Lying Story* (London: Rich & Cowan, 1929), 129.

26. Groos, *Der Krieg zur See: Nordsee,* vol. 1, 56.

27. Captain Albert Hopman, diary entry, dated 30 July 1914, Michael Epkenhans, ed., *Das ereignisreiche Leben eines "Wilhelminers": Tagebücher, Briefe, Auzfeichnungen 1901 bis 1920* (Munich: Oldenbourg Verlag, 2004), 405.

28. Admiralty to C-in-C Home Fleets, Telegram No. 285, dated 31 July 1914, Backhouse Papers, NHB.

29. George M. Nekrasov, *Expendable Glory: Russian Battleship in the Baltic 1915–1917* (New York: Columbia University Press, 2004), 35.

30. "Movements were wholly free," Groos, *Der Krieg zur See: Nordsee,* vol. 1, 33.

31. Despite the earlier ceremonial reopening, the first big ship trial transit had not occurred until 25 July with the battleship *Kaiserin.* Groos, *Der Krieg zur See: Nordsee,* vol. 1, 31, 34.

32. Groos, *Der Krieg zur See: Nordsee,* vol. 1, 39.

33. Lieutenant B. W. L. Owen, HMS *Stour,* diary entry, dated 2 August 1914, Owen Papers, IWM.

34. Captain C. J. Wintour, HMS *Swift,* diary entry, dated 1 August 1914, Wintour Papers, IWM.

35. Cipher telegram to British ambassador in Paris, 2 August 1914, sent 1650, *Passage of the BEF,* August 1914, 27.

36. Admiralty signal, intercepted 2120, 2 August 1914, sent 2120, recorded in signal log kept for Rear Admiral Bernard Currey in HMS *Prince of Wales,* Currey Papers, Liddell Hart Centre for Military Archives, King's College, London.

Chapter 2. The British

1. Jon Tetsuro Sumida, "Challenging Parkinson's Law," Seminar on World War I, Robert McCormick Tribune Foundation/United States Naval Institute, August 1993, *Naval History* no. 8 (November–December 1994).

2. Nicholas A. Lambert, "Strategic Command and Control for Maneuver War-fare: Creation of the Royal Navy's 'War Room' System, 1905–1915," *Journal of Military History* 69, no. 2 (April 2005), 380.

3. "Had no staff," Admiral Sir Dudley de Chair, *The Sea Is Strong* (London: Harrap, 1961), 144.

4. "Eighteen civil personnel," Nicholas Black, *The British Naval Staff in the First World War* (Woodbridge, UK: Boydell, 2009), 58. Black's work gives a com-prehensive analysis of the organization and activities of the naval staff within the Admiralty in this period.

5. Admiralty, *The Navy List,* July 1908, HMSO, London, shows twenty-eight officers assigned to the NID, five of whom are notated "temporary" and another who was lent away.

6. General Sir David Fraser, "Alanbrooke," in John Keegan, ed., *Churchill's Generals* (London: Warner, 1992), 91.

7. The best summary of this relationship is contained in Black, *The British Naval Staff,* 60–74.

8. Jellicoe to Captain F. C. Dreyer, RN, letter, dated 28 May 1914, DRYR 3/2, Dreyer Papers, CCA.

9. King-Hall, *My Naval Life,* 76.

10. "Personal Staff Officer," Roskill, *Admiral of the Fleet Earl Beatty,* 54; "Hood was largely confined," Admiral of the Fleet Sir Henry Oliver, unpublished *Memoirs,* vol. 2, 115, Oliver Papers, NMM.

11. "As the keeper," de Chair, *The Sea Is Strong,* 140.

12. Air Chief Marshal Sir Arthur Longmore, speech at the opening of the Jubilee of Naval Aviation exhibition at the NMM, quoted in Captain A. W. Clarke (writing as "Onlooker"), "The Fleet Air Arm—Another Fiftieth Anniver-sary," *Naval Review* 52, no. 4 (October 1964), 366.

13. Hough, *Louis and Victoria,* 185.

14. Battenberg to Captain P. T. Beamish, RN letter, dated 16 May 1915, BEAM2/10, Beamish Papers, CCA.

15. "Lambert was an early enthusiast," Vice Admiral Sir Peter Gretton, *Former Naval Person: Winston Churchill and the Royal Navy* (London: Cassell, 1968), 124.

16. "Refused to agree," Nicholas A. Lambert, *Sir John Fisher's Naval Revolution* (Columbia: University of South Carolina Press, 1999), 289; "Battenberg's preference," Admiral of the Fleet Sir Doveton Sturdee, "Some Reminiscences of the War," 1, SDEE 1/18, Sturdee Papers, CCA.

17. "An early and sensible priority," Sturdee, "Some Reminiscences of the War," 2–3.

18. Oliver, *Memoirs,* vol. 2, 99.

19. Captain Herbert Richmond, diary entry, dated 14 August 1914, RIC1/9, Richmond Papers, NMM.

20. Rear Admiral C. G. Brodie (writing as "Sea Gee"), "Women Aboard," *Naval Review* 49, no. 4 (October 1961): 389.

21. Martin Gilbert, *Winston S. Churchill*, vol. 3, *1914–1916: The Challenge of War* (Boston: Houghton Mifflin, 1971), 185.

22. Black, *The British Naval Staff*, 76.

23. "Often went in," Sturdee, "My Service Connections with Lord Fisher," Sturdee Papers, CCA.

24. These calculations are by comparison of the strength of the Mediterranean and China Fleets listed in the Admiralty's *Navy List* of July 1904 and July 1914, based on established complements in each ship.

25. "More than 55 percent," Jon Tetsuro Sumida, *In Defence of Naval Supremacy: Finance, Technology and British Naval Policy 1889–1914* (Boston: Unwin Hyman, 1989), Table 3 "British Naval Expenditure, 1889–90 to 1914–15." The figures used for this calculation are the 1900–1902 estimates of 33,206,918 pounds and the last peacetime year 1913–14 at 51,609,402 pounds.

26. Sumida, *In Defence of Naval Supremacy*, Table 8 "Expenditures on Warship Construction by General Category, 1888–89 to 1913–14 [not including cost of armament]" and Table 10 "Expenditures on Flotilla Construction by Type, 1889–90 to 1913–14 [not including cost of armament]."

27. Sumida, *In Defence of Naval Supremacy*, Table 12 "Expenditure on Active Naval Personnel System, 1889–90 to 1913–14."

28. Admiral Sir John Fisher to the Earl of Selborne, letter, dated 24 December 1901, in *Fear God and Dread Nought: The Correspondence of Admiral of the Fleet Lord Fisher of Kilverstone*, ed. Arthur J. Marder, vol. 1, *The Making of an Admiral 1854–1904* (London: Jonathan Cape, 1952), 220.

29. Nicholas A. Lambert, "On Standards: A Reply to Christopher Bell," *War in History*, vol. 19, no. 2 (2012), 234.

30. Captain John Wells, *The Royal Navy: An Illustrated Social History, 1870–1982* (Stroud, UK: Sutton, 1994), 61–62. For a deeper study, see Elinor Romans, "Selection and Early Career Education of Officers in the Royal Navy, c 1902–1939," unpublished PhD thesis, University of Exeter, UK, 2013.

31. It is still used, at least in the Royal Australian Navy.

32. Naval Staff, Admiralty, "Anti-Submarine Development and Experiments prior to December 1916," CB 1515(40), September 1920, NHB. See also papers of Admiral Bernard Currey relating to antisubmarine warfare 1913–15, Liddell Hart Centre.

33. Willem Hackmann, *Seek and Strike: Sonar, Anti-Submarine Warfare and the Royal Navy 1914–1954* (London: HMSO, 1984), 9–10.

34. Norman Friedman, *Network-Centric Warfare: How Navies Learned to Fight Smarter through Three World Wars* (Annapolis, MD: Naval Institute Press, 2009), 264, fn23. See also TNA ADM 116/1214.

35. List compiled by Admiral Philip Dumas, "The *Britannia* Term. July 1881," *Naval Review* 16, no. 4 (November 1928): 784.

36. List compiled by Vice Admiral A. W. Craig Waller provided by his son, the late Commander A. L. Craig Waller.

37. List compiled by Rear Admiral D. T. Norris, "A *Britannia* Term. Autumn 1889," *Naval Review* 16, no. 2 (May 1928): 352.

38. "Selection process in 1886," Robert L. Davison, *The Challenges of Command: The Royal Navy's Executive Branch Officers, 1880–1919* (Farnham, UK: Ashgate, 2011), 62. This book gives an excellent survey of issues facing the officer corps.

39. "By Andrew Gordon," Andrew Gordon, *The Rules of the Game: Jutland and British Naval Command* (London: John Murray, 1996).

40. Lambert, "Strategic Command and Control," 398.

41. Vice Admiral Lord Nelson, Memorandum before the Battle of Trafalgar dated 9 October 1805, in *The Despatches and Letters of Vice Admiral Lord Viscount Nelson with Notes by Sir Nicholas Harris Nicolas,* vol. 7 (London: Colburn, 1845), 90. The clearest near-contemporary statement of this view is in Admiral Sir Barry Domvile's memoir, *By and Large* (London: Hutchinson, 1936), 52–72.

42. I am indebted to Dr. Jon Tetsuro Sumida for this insight.

43. Vice Admiral Richard Bell Davies, *Sailor in the Air: The Memoirs of the World's First Carrier Pilot* (Barnsley, UK: Seaforth, 2008), 88.

44. "Although this was starting to change," *Admiralty Weekly Order,* no. 138/1914, dated 17 July 1914, "Commissions &c.—Length of," NHB.

45. For excellent analyses of the issues facing the Royal Navy at this time, see Brian Lavery, *Able Seamen: The Lower Deck of the Royal Navy 1850–1939* (London: Conway, 2011), esp. 168–70; and Anthony Carew, *The Lower Deck of the Royal Navy 1900–39: The Invergordon Mutiny in Perspective* (Manchester, UK: Manchester University Press, 1981).

46. "An enthusiast," minute by Captain A. Gordon Smith RN, Second Naval Member Australian Commonwealth Naval Board, dated 14 May 1914, Australian Archives File MP 1042: 40/14/4962; "would take any," Bell Davies, *Sailor in the Air,* 13.

47. As in the battle cruiser HMAS *Australia.*

48. Vice Admiral Harold Hickling, *Sailor at Sea* (London: William Kimber, 1965), 105.

49. Cited in Christopher McKee, *Sober Men and True: Sailor Lives in the Royal Navy 1900–1945* (Cambridge, MA: Harvard University Press, 2002), 122. This book provides an important window into the lower deck.

50. Chaplain G. H. Hewetson (writing anonymously), "A Contribution to the Study of Naval Discipline," *Naval Review* 1, no. 3 (1913): 160.

Chapter 3. The Germans

1. Grand Admiral Alfred von Tirpitz, *My Memoirs* (London: Hurst & Blackett, 1919), vol. 1, 159.

2. Michael Epkenhans, *Tirpitz: Architect of the German High Seas Fleet* (Washington, DC: Potomac, 2008), 40.

3. Von Hase, *Kiel and Jutland*, 30.

4. Captain Herbert Heath, British naval attaché, Germany Report 27/10, 6 August 1910, Seligmann, *Naval Intelligence from Germany*, 263. See also Terrell D. Gottschall, *By Order of the Kaiser: Otto von Diederichs and the Rise of the Imperial German Navy* (Annapolis, MD: Naval Institute Press, 2003), 242–56, for an early example.

5. "Even his protégés," Carl-Axel Gemzell, *Organization, Conflict and Innovation: A Study of German Naval Strategic Planning, 1888–1940* (Lund, Germany: Esselte Studium, 1973), 122–23.

6. "Not impressed his personality," in *The Private War of Seaman Stumpf: The Unique Diaries of a Young German in the Great War,* ed. Daniel Horn (London: Leslie Frewin, 1969), 31.

7. Hopman, diary entry, dated 2 October 1914, Epkenhans, *Das ereignisreiche Leben eines "Wilhelminers,"* 450.

8. Epkenhans, *Tirpitz*, 51.

9. Walter Gorlitz, ed., *The Kaiser and His Court: The Diaries, Notebooks and Letters of Admiral Georg Alexander von Müller, Chief of the Naval Cabinet, 1914–1918* (London: Macdonald, 1961), 15.

10. Walter Hubatsch, *Der Admiralstab und die obersten—Marine behörden in Deutschland, 1848–1945* (Frankfurt, Germany: Wehrwesen Bernard und Graefe, 1965), 166.

11. Admiral Hugo von Pohl diary entry, dated 11 August 1914, Ella von Pohl, ed., *Aus Aufzeichnungen und Briefen während der Kriegszeit* (Berlin: Karl Siegismund, 1920), 10.

12. Admiral Hopman, *Das Logbuch eines Deutschen Seeoffiziers* (Berlin: August Scherl, 1924), 401.

13. See Gerhard Granier, *Magnus von Levetzow: Seeoffizier, Monarchist und Webereiter Hitlers* (Boppard, Germany: Boldt, 1982), 6–12.

14. For excellent analysis in English of these issues, see Holger Herwig, *The German Naval Officer Corps: A Political and Social History* (Oxford, UK: Oxford University Press, 1973); and Herwig, *Luxury Fleet: The Imperial German Navy 1888–1918* (London: Allen & Unwin, 1980).

15. "More comfortable in office work," Heath, British naval attaché, Germany Report no. 27/10, 6 August 1910, in Seligmann, *Naval Intelligence from Germany*, 264; Captain H. R. D. Watson, British naval attaché, Germany Report

no. 75/12, "Report on the German Naval Manoeuvres in the North Sea, September 1912," c. late 1912, Backhouse Papers, NHB.

16. Watson, British naval attaché, Germany Report no. 51/12, 1 July 1912, Seligmann, *Naval Intelligence from Germany*, 442.

17. Gary E. Weir, *Building the Kaiser's Navy: The Imperial Naval Office and German Industry in the von Tirpitz Era, 1880–1919* (Annapolis, MD: Naval Institute Press, 1992), 83–84, 132.

18. Fritz Fisher, *War of Illusions: German Policies from 1911 to 1914*, trans. Marion Jackson (London: Chatto & Windus, 1975), 162.

19. Groos, *Der Krieg zur See: Nordsee,* vol. 1, 69.

20. Von Tirpitz, *My Memoirs*, vol. 1, 137.

21. "As soon as sea-going boats," von Tirpitz, *My Memoirs*, vol. 1, 138–39.

22. Tobias R. Philbin, *Admiral von Hipper: The Inconvenient Hero* (Amsterdam: Gruner, 1982), 20–21.

23. Erich Gröner, rev. and expanded by Dieter Jung and Martin Maass, *German Warships 1815–1945,* vol. 1, *Major Surface Vessels* (Annapolis, MD: Naval Institute Press, 1990), 176.

Chapter 4. The Russians

1. Gene C. Stevenson, "Russian 'Lake' Type Submarines and the Baltic War 1914–1916," in *Warship 1990*, ed. Robert Gardiner (London: Conway, 1990), 80.

2. "And in the civil bureaucracy," Nekrasov, *Expendable Glory,* 7–8.

3. Sergei E. Vinogradov, "Battleship Development in Russia from 1905 to 1917," part 1, *Warship International* 35, no. 3 (1998): 269.

4. George Nekrasov, *North of Gallipoli: The Black Sea Fleet at War 1914–1917* (New York: Columbia University Press, 1992), 7–8.

5. David R. Jones, "Imperial Russia's Forces at War," in *Military Effectiveness,* vol. 1, *The First World War,* ed. Allan R. Millett and Williamson Murray (Boston: Unwin Hyman, 1988), 256.

6. John Leyland, "Foreign Navies," *The Naval Annual 1914,* ed. Viscount Hythe and John Leyland (London: Clowes, 1914), 49.

7. "With their own devices," Norman Friedman, *Naval Firepower: Battleship Guns and Gunnery in the Dreadnought Era* (Barnsley, UK: Seaforth, 2008), 272–77.

8. Norman Friedman, *Naval Weapons of World War One* (Barnsley, UK: Seaforth, 2011), 348.

9. "British firm of Vickers," Leyland, "Foreign Navies," 48.

10. "Train all year round," Canfield F. Smith, "Essen, Nikolai Ottovich," in *The Modern Encyclopedia of Russian and Soviet History,* vol. 10 *Do to Es*, ed.

Joseph L. Wieczynski (Gulf Breeze, FL: Academic International Press, 1979), 241.

11. "Not available to the Baltic Fleet," R. D. Layman, *Before the Aircraft Carrier: The Development of Aviation Vessels 1849–1922* (London: Conway, 1989), 96.

12. Stephen Mclaughlin, "Russia: Rossiiskii imperatorskii flot," in *To Crown the Waves: The Great Navies of the First World War,* ed. Vincent P. O'Hara, W. David Dickson, and Richard Worth (Annapolis, MD: Naval Institute Press, 2013), 231.

13. Captain R. W. Blacklock, RN, "Personal Reminiscences of World War 1, 1914–1919," Blacklock Papers, Liddell Archive, University of Leeds, UK, 56.

14. Blacklock, "Personal Reminiscences," 56.

15. Friedman, *Naval Weapons of World War One,* 382–83.

16. N. B. Pavlovich, *The Fleet in the First World War,* vol. 1, *Operations of the Russian Fleet* (New Delhi: Amerind, 1979), 62.

Chapter 5. Operational Challenges

1. "Airy navies grappling," Alfred Tennyson, "Locksley Hall" (Oxford, UK: Clarendon Press, 1947; poem originally published 1842).

2. Lambert, *Sir John Fisher's Naval Revolution*, 284–91 summarizes many of the issues.

3. The analysis of the climatic conditions has been drawn from Admiralty, *North Sea Pilots* and *Baltic Pilots,* of the period or in the decades immediately after; the latter have the advantage of basing their own summaries on observations that include the 1914–18 period.

4. Admiralty, *Baltic Pilot,* vol. 3, *Comprising the Gulfs of Finland and Bothnia and the Aland Islands* (London: HMSO, 1937), 21.

5. A point made to me by Dr. Norman Friedman.

6. *Admiralty Weekly Order* No. 915/14 established a Gyro Compass Log due to the "necessity of obtaining reliable data on its general behaviour in the present state of development." NHB.

7. Commander L. J. Pitcairn-Jones, "Navigation in War of 1914–1918," Lecture to the RN Staff College 1938, NHB.

8. See also the Admiralty's 1909 edition of *Manual of Seamanship*, vol. 2 (London: HMSO, 1909), 314–38.

9. See *Admiralty Weekly Order* no. 959/14, "Errors in Manoeuvring Compass of H.M.S. *Neptune*," NHB.

10. Admiralty, *North Sea Pilot,* part 3 (London: HMSO, 1933), xxiii.

11. Admiral Sir William James, *A Great Seaman: The Life of Admiral of the Fleet Sir Henry Oliver* (London: Witherby, 1956), 95–96.

12. Vice Admiral Gordon Campbell, *Number Thirteen* (London: Hodder & Stoughton, 1932), 77–78.

13. Dawson, *Flotillas*, 75.

14. Rudolph Firle, *Der Krieg zur See: Der Krieg in Der Ostsee*, vol. 1 (Berlin: Mittler, 1922–28), British Admiralty NHB, with translations available at NHB, 267.

15. Pitcairn-Jones, "Navigation in War of 1914–1918," 12.

16. Lieutenant G. F. Hyde, Royal Naval Reserve (later Royal Australian Navy), "Essay on Lessons to be Learned by the British Empire and More Particularly by the British Navy as regards: (1) Organisation and training for war. (2) Conduct of war, and especially as regards Naval Strategy and Tactics," winning essay, C-in-C Channel Fleet, Essay Competition, September (?) 1904, Australian War Memorial MSS 1494.

17. See Vice Admiral Sir Archibald Day, *The Admiralty Hydrographic Service 1795–1919* (London: HMSO, 1967), 206–87 for a narrative of the activities of the Royal Navy's Hydrographic Service during the period and on which much of this discussion is based.

18. Lieutenant the Hon. R. Plunkett, *The Modern Officer of the Watch,* 4th ed. (Portsmouth, UK: Griffin, 1910), 48.

19. Groos, *Der Krieg zur See: Nordsee,* vol. 1, 124.

20. Vice Admiral B. B. Schofield, *Navigation and Direction: The Story of HMS Dryad* (Havant, UK: Kenneth Mason, 1977), 20–31.

21. "Naval Manoeuvres 1913: North Sea Strategy," C-in-C Home Fleets, letter 1266/ Home Fleet 7 S, 28 August 1913, TNA ADM 116/3130.

22. C-in-C Home Fleets, letter, 0269 of March 1913 "Instructions for the Conduct of a Fleet in Action," Backhouse Papers, NHB.

23. Home Fleets Memorandum no. 0015, dated 22 December 1914, reproduced in *Naval Staff Monograph (Historical)*, vol. 3, *Monograph 12: The Action of Dogger Bank, January 24th 1915*, 225.

24. There is an interesting example in a handwritten record of such war games in 1913–14 from the German cruiser *Magdeburg*. It is contained in TNA ADM 137/4714.

25. A. H. Pollen "Memoranda and Instruction Introductory to the use of Pollen's Tactical Instrument," May 1909, in *The Pollen Papers: The Privately Circulated Printed Works of Arthur Hungerford Pollen, 1901–1916*, ed. Jon Tetsuro Sumida (London: George Allen & Unwin for The Navy Records Society, 1984), 237–42. I am indebted to Professor Sumida for pointing out this reference.

26. Captain F. C. Dreyer, letter, to Vice Admiral Commanding Second Battle Squadron, dated 4 May 1914, Backhouse Papers, NHB.

27. Filson Young, *With the Battle Cruisers*, intro. and notes by James Goldrick (Annapolis, MD: Naval Institute Press, 1986), 66.

28. Lambert, "Strategic Command and Control," 390.

29. Lambert, "Strategic Command and Control," gives the details of how this evolved.

30. See "German W/T Regulations (1913)," a translation made by the Admiralty in 1916 and promulgated as CB 0233 (July 1916), TNA ADM 137/4323. The German original is held in TNA ADM 137/4358. Also see Admiralty, "Wireless Instructions 1915," CB 0121, TNA ADM 186/682; and "Grand Fleet W/T General Orders," dated 19 December 1914, TNA ADM 137/290.

31. Home Fleets Memorandum no. 0306, 10 July 1913, "Naval Manoeuvres 1913: Blue Fleet Wireless Orders: General Instructions," Backhouse Papers, NHB.

32. "Remarks on the Conduct of a Fleet in Action Based on the Experience Gained during the Manoeuvres and Exercises of the Home Fleets during the year 1913," Home Fleets Memorandum no. 0235, dated 5 December 1913, Backhouse Papers, NHB; italics added.

33. See Gordon, *The Rules of the Game.*

34. "Russians were farther ahead," Thomas R. Hammant, "Russian and Soviet Cryptology I—Some Communications Intelligence in Tsarist Russia," *Cryptologia* 24, no. 3 (July 2000): 241–44.

35. Heinz Bonatz, *Die Deutsch Marine-Funkaufklärung 1914–1945* (Darmstadt, Germany: Wehr und Wissen, 1969), 17.

36. See note "Enemy Wireless," in papers of Admiral Sir Reginald Plunkett-Ernle-Erle-Drax (henceforth cited as Drax Papers), DRAX 1/45, Drax Papers, CCA, probably dated early September 1914, referring to German wavelength changes: "This was reported during German manoeuvres last year."

37. For example, there were two intercepts of signals in May 1914, later decrypted when the German code books became available. TNA ADM 137/4065.

38. J. C. Randel, "Information for Economic Warfare: British Intelligence and the Blockade, 1914–1918," PhD thesis, University of North Carolina, Chapel Hill, 1993, 123–24. That such attempts were possible and that the British had at least one spy in place to collect classified material is apparent from the document detailing the High Sea Fleet's winter organization for 1913–14 which is in the Backhouse papers at the NHB and, it is important to point out, had come into British hands before October 1913. See also Oliver, *Memoirs,* vol. 2, 102.

39. Home Fleets Memorandum No. 0306, 10 July 1913, "Naval Manoeuvres 1913: General Scheme, Rules: Errata and Corrigenda," Backhouse Papers, NHB.

40. Although they had the benefit of a copy of the German *VB* code, the officers of the British light cruiser *Glasgow* were able to crack the associated key and confirm the location of the German *Dresden* at Juan Fernandez in early 1915. See Hickling, *Sailor at Sea,* 103.

41. "Manoeuvres 1913: Miscellaneous Remarks." Probably drafted by Plunkett as flag commander for Rear Admiral Beatty as commander of the First Battle Cruiser Squadron. DRAX 4/1 Drax Papers, CCA.

42. Norman Friedman, *British Destroyers: From Earliest Days to the Second World War* (Annapolis, MD: Naval Institute Press, 2009), 94.

43. Captain S. S. Hall, RN (writing anonymously), "The Influence of the Submarine on Naval Policy—I," *Naval Review* 1, no. 3 (1913): 149.

44. "Abandoned the idea," Black, *The British Naval Staff*, 155–56; "Germans continued," Michael Wilson, *Baltic Assignment: British Submariners in Russia 1914–1919* (London: Leo Cooper, 1985), 69.

45. "From twelve knots," Ruddock F. Mackay, *Fisher of Kilverstone* (Oxford: Clarendon, 1973), 235; "while the turbine," John Wingate, *HMS Dreadnought: Battleship 1906–1920,* Profile Warship 1 (Windsor, UK: Profile, 1970), 17.

46. This is confirmed, among other sources, by the diary of Sub Lieutenant (later Admiral Sir) Charles Daniel, who was serving in the battleship *Orion* in the Second Battle Squadron. See the diary entries for 4, 5 and 6 August, when the Grand Fleet steamed at seven knots for lengthy periods. Daniel Papers, CCA.

47. "The German practice," Admiral Scheer, *Germany's High Sea Fleet in the World War* (London: Cassell, 1920), 16.

48. Captain S. D. Spicer (writing as "S. D. S."), "The Fuel of the Future?" *Naval Review* 23, no. 2 (May 1935): 333.

49. W. M. Brown, "The Royal Navy's Fuel Supplies 1898–1939: The Transition from Coal to Oil," unpublished PhD thesis, King's College, London, 2003, 21.

50. Such as HMS *Agincourt,* whose A and B boiler rooms were effectively inaccessible from many of her bunkers. She was fitted with additional oil fuel tanks in her double bottoms to compensate.

51. Gröner, *German Warships,* vol. 1, 177. The torpedo boats *V1–V6* had a range of 1,190 miles at seventeen knots, *S13–S24* had 1,050 miles at seventeen knots.

52. Groos, *Der Krieg zur See: Nordsee,* vol. 1, 130.

53. Captain A. W. Clarke (writing as "Onlooker"), "H. M. Navigation School 1903–1968," *Naval Review* 56, no. 3 (July 1968): 258.

54. Admiral Mark Kerr, *Prince Louis of Battenberg, Admiral of the Fleet* (London: Longmans, 1934), 147–48.

55. John Leyland, "Naval Manoeuvres," in *The Naval Annual 1909,* ed. T. A. Brassey (London: Griffin, 1909), 145.

56. "Customary for extended," King-Hall, *Naval Memories and Traditions,* 204.

57. "Raising the big ships' complement," C-in-C Home Fleets letter to Admiralty, 5 August 1912, TNA ADM 1/8269, cited in Nicholas A. Lambert, *The Submarine Service 1900–1918* (Aldershot, UK: Navy Records Society [Ashgate], 2001), 185.

58. Groos, *Der Krieg zur See: Nordsee,* vol. 1, 43. See also Scheer, *Germany's High Sea Fleet,* 16.

59. First Lord to First Sea Lord and Second Sea Lord, minute, dated 16 August 1914, Gilbert, *Winston S. Churchill,* Vol. 3 Companion, Part 1 *Documents,* 39.

60. Daniel, HMS *Orion,* diary entry, dated 20 August 1914, Daniel Papers, CCA.

61. "Created immediate concern," Richmond, diary entry, dated 20 August 1914, RIC1/9, Richmond Papers, NMM; "who complained bitterly," Beatty to his wife, letter, 6 November 1914, in B. McL. Ranft, *The Beatty Papers: Selections from the Private and Official Correspondence of Admiral of the Fleet Earl Beatty*, vol. 1, *1902–1918* (Aldershot, UK: Scolar Press for The Navy Records Society, 1989), 156.

62. Mark D. Karau, *"Wielding the Dagger": The Marinekorps Flandern and the German War Effort, 1914–1918* (Westport, CT: Praeger, 2003), 9–13.

63. "Until the outbreak." This remains the subject of investigation and I am very grateful to Dr. Michael Epkenhans for his searches of the German archives, so far silent on this matter. In the author's opinion, the circumstantial evidence, notably the trouble experienced by German big ships with their coal during practically every high-speed sortie of the High Sea Fleet, is that in peacetime full power trials of the larger units had been conducted with Welsh coal and that it was issued to the small ships as "torpedo boat" coal. There is evidence from a British decryption of a 26 July 1914 signal from Norddeich to Swinemünde referring to German naval holdings of Welsh and Scottish coal. TNA ADM 137/4065.

64. "Problems for their battle cruisers," Philbin, *Admiral von Hipper*, 56–57.

65. Friedman, *Naval Firepower*, 85.

66. See Jon Tetsuro Sumida, "Expectation, Adaptation and Resignation: British Battle Fleet Tactical Planning, August 1914–April 1916," *Naval War College Review* 60, no. 3 (Summer 2007): 102–22. This develops ideas presented in Sumida, "A Matter of Timing: The Royal Navy and the Tactics of Decisive Battle, 1912–1916," *Journal of Military History* 67 (January 2003): 85–136.

67. Lambert, *Sir John Fisher's Naval Revolution*, 284–91, summarizes the issues.

68. "Not trialed until 1910," Commanding Officer HMS *Forth*, letter to the Inspecting Captain Submarines, dated 24 July 1910, TNA ADM 116/1361.

69. C-in-C Home Fleets, letter 0235, dated 28 November 1913, "Fleet Exercises in North Sea, 6th—10th October 1913," papers of Vice Admiral D. W. Trevylyan Napier, TN/1/6, IWM.

70. "No more than thirty miles," Home Fleets Memorandum No. 0306, 10 July 1913. Note added by C. J. B. (?), dated 7 April 1911, to minute "Fitting Wireless Telegraphy to Submarines," TNA ADM 116/1361.

71. Home Fleets Memorandum No. 0306, 10 July 1913, "Naval Manoeuvres 1913: Blue Fleet Wireless Order: Corrigenda," Backhouse Papers, NHB.

72. Admiral of Patrols, "Naval Manoeuvre Order no. 26 of 18th July 1914," Backhouse Papers, NHB.

73. "Given opportunity," "For a first attempt," C-in-C Home Fleets, letter, HF 0235, dated 28 November 1913, "Fleet Exercises in North Sea, 6th—10th October 1913," in Trevylyan Napier Papers, TN/1/6, IWM.

74. "Perhaps above all other flag officers," Keyes, *The Naval Memoirs of Admiral of the Fleet Sir Roger Keyes,* vol. 1, *The Narrow Seas to the Dardanelles 1910–1915* (London: Thornton Butterworth, 1934), 69.

75. "Attack on his heavy ships," Philbin, *Admiral von Hipper*, 184.

76. Rear Admiral First Battle Cruiser Squadron, undated (prob. c. September 1913), "Manoeuvres 1913: Strategical Lessons," Backhouse Papers, NHB.

77. Douglas H. Robinson, *The Zeppelin in Combat: A History of the German Naval Airship Division, 1912–1918* (London: Foulis, 1966), 18–31.

78. Kapitanleutnant Johannes Mohl, cited in Peter Kilduff, *Germany's First Air Force 1914–1918* (London: Arms & Armour, 1991), 85.

79. Eric Grove, "Seamen or Airmen? The Early Days of British Naval Flying," in *British Naval Aviation: The First 100 Years,* ed. Tim Benbow (Farnham, UK: Ashgate, 2011), 23.

80. Groos, *Der Krieg zur See: Nordsee,* vol. 1, 86.

81. "Naval Manoeuvres 1913: General Scheme," 12, Backhouse Papers, NHB.

82. "Blue Fleet Orders—XVII," Home Fleets Memorandum No. 0306, 10 July 1913, Backhouse Papers, NHB.

83. Patrick Abbott, *The British Airship at War, 1914–1918* (Lavenham, UK: Terence Dalton, 1989), 19–20.

84. Oswald Frewen, *Sailor's Soliloquy,* ed. G. P. Griggs (London: Hutchinson, 1961), 157–77.

85. "Did not expect to lose," Admiral Sir Lewis Bayly, *Pull Together!* (London: Harrap, 1939), 121.

86. "Not justified in incurring," "Naval Manoeuvres 1913: General Scheme," 9, Backhouse Papers, NHB.

87. "Translation of *Taktische Befehle der Hochseeflotte 1914,*" 22, TNA ADM 137/2346.

88. Three of the German boats, *S42, S76,* and *S178,* were salvaged and returned to service.

89. Dawson, *Flotillas,* 63–79, 86–123.

90. Oscar Parkes, *British Battleships* (London: Seeley Service, 1960) gives summaries of ship histories.

91. Bell Davies, *Sailor in the Air,* 27–30, 58–60.

92. Admiral Sir Reginald Tupper, *Reminiscences* (London: Jarrolds, 1929), 198. The submarine commanding officer was not Horton, as Tupper alleges, but Lieutenant B. V. Layard who later was awarded a Distinguished Service Order.

93. Rear Admiral C. G. Brodie (writing as "Sea Gee"), "Some Early Submariners I & II," *Naval Review* 62, no. 4 (November 1963): 483; and *Naval Review* 64, no. 1 (January 1965): 86.

94. "During the 1912 Grand Maneuvers," W. S. Chalmers, *Max Horton and the Western Approaches* (London: Hodder and Stoughton, 1954), 17; "*actual*

capabilities," C-in-C Home Fleets, letter, no. 1266 Home Fleets 7 S of 28 August 1913 "Naval Manoeuvres 1913: Remarks on North Sea Strategy," TNA ADM 116/3130, italics added.

95. Pavlovich, *The Fleet in the First World War,* 65.

96. See, e.g., First Fleet Temporary Memorandum No. 241, dated 27 June 1914, "Economy of Fuel, and Time Under Way for Training," Backhouse Papers, NHB.

97. "23 percent in 1911–12," Sumida, table titled "Expenditure of Fuel &c, 1889–90 to 1913–14," in *In Defence of Naval Supremacy,* 353; "except for basic familiarization," First Fleet Temporary Memorandum No. 131, dated 16 April 1914, "Burning of Oil Fuel for Instructional Purposes," Backhouse Papers, NHB.

98. "Translation of *Taktische Befehle der Hochseeflotte 1914*": Battle Exercise 5, dated 17 April 1914, 3, TNA ADM 137/2346.

99. First Battle Cruiser Squadron Memorandum no. 0142, dated 4 June 1913; and "Remarks on High Speed Exercises of 5th June," dated 11 June 1913, in DRAX 1/2, Drax Papers, CCA.

100. TNA ADM 116/3151. I am indebted to Dr. Nicholas A. Lambert for this information based on his research.

101. "A 12-inch armor-piercing shell," Nicholas A. Lambert, "Admiral Sir Arthur Kynvet-Wilson V. C.," *The First Sea Lords: From Fisher to Mountbatten,* ed. Malcolm Murfett (Westport, CT: Praeger, 1995), 51, fn50.

102. I. D. 973, *Results of German Firing Practices 1912–1913,* December 1914, transl. of German original, TNA ADM 137/4799.

103. "First Battle Squadron Memorandum no. 419 dated 31st March 1914: VIII Special Orders for Day Group Firing; XI: Special Orders for Squadron Night Firing," Backhouse Papers, NHB.

104. "First and Second Battle Squadrons First Fleet: Gunnery and Torpedo Practices Carried Out during Present Commission up to 1st July 1914," Backhouse Papers, NHB.

105. "Results of the Firing Practices of Ships and Coastal Artillery in the Year 1912–13," No. 69 *Official Document of the Imperial German Navy* (Berlin, 1914), Admiralty War Staff Intelligence Division Translation, I. D. No 973, December 1914, TNA ADM 137/4799.

106. Edgar J. March, *British Destroyers, 1892–1953* (London: Seeley Service, 1966), 353.

107. "Naval Manoeuvres 1913, General Scheme, Rules &c: Instructions for Destroyers and Torpedo Boats," Backhouse Papers, NHB.

108. Admiral Sir Hugh Tweedie, *The Story of a Naval Life* (London: Rich & Cowan, 1939), 100.

109. For a comprehensive treatment of this tangled story, see Richard Dunley, "The Offensive Mining Service: Mine Warfare and Strategic Development in

the Royal Navy 1900–1914," unpublished PhD thesis, King's College London, 2013.

110. "Mooring wires, sinkers, and pistols," Captain Philip Dumas, diary entries, dated 2 and 4 October 1914, Dumas Papers, IWM.

111. "Naval Manoeuvres 1913: Orders for Ships of Blue Fleet Operating in Western Area: Part IV: Orders for the Malin Head Patrol," dated 5 July 1913, Backhouse Papers, NHB.

112. "Blue Fleet Operations Order Bo. 5: Instructions for Vice-Admiral Sir Frederick Hamilton KCB, CVO," dated July 1913 (?), Backhouse Papers, NHB.

113. C-in-C Home Fleets, letter, No. 1266 Home Fleets 7 S of 28 August 1913, "Naval Manoeuvres 1913—Remarks on North Sea Strategy," TNA ADM 116/3130.

Chapter 6. War Plans

1. The development of British naval war planning before the First World War is an extremely complex topic and one subject to scholarly disagreement. Sources for this chapter include Nicholas A. Lambert, *Planning Armageddon: British Economic Warfare and the First World War* (Cambridge, MA: Harvard University Press, 2012); and Black, *The British Naval Staff*. See also Greg Kennedy, "Strategy and Power: The Royal Navy, the Foreign Office and the Blockade, 1914–1917," *Defence Studies* 8, no. 2 (2008); and Kennedy, "Intelligence and the Blockade, 1914–1917: A Study in Administration, Friction and Command," *Intelligence and National Security* 22, no. 5 (October 2007); Christopher Martin, "The Declaration of London: A Matter of Operational Capability," *Historical Research* 82, no. 218 (2009); and Martin, "The 1907 Naval War Plans and the Second Hague Peace Conference: A Case of Propaganda," *Journal of Strategic Studies* 28, no. 5 (2005). Other sources include Christopher M. Bell, *Churchill and Sea Power* (London: Oxford University Press, 2012); Shawn T. Grimes, *Strategy and War Planning in the British Navy, 1887–1918* (Woodbridge, UK: Boydell Press, 2012); and Matthew S. Seligmann, *The Royal Navy and the German Threat, 1901–1914: Admiralty Plans to Protect British Trade in a War against Germany* (London: Oxford University Press, 1912).

2. "War College Lectures 1914"—"War and Food Supplies," by D. Owen is among the lectures listed in the War College papers of Vice Admiral D. W. Trevelyan Napier, TN/1/7, IWM. Later Sir Douglas Owen, KBE, and chair of the State War Risks Office Advisory Committee, he was a lecturer at the London School of Economics and honorary secretary and treasurer of the Society for Nautical Research. There were other lecturers of equivalent standing.

3. Avner Offer, "Morality and Admiralty: 'Jacky' Fisher, Economic Warfare and the Laws of War," *Journal of Contemporary History* 23, no. 1 (January 1988): 99–119.

4. First Lord to First Sea Lord, note dated 17 February 1913, TNA ADM 116/3412.

5. Re: "even as war started": ADM 137/452 gives details of the plans presented by Vice Admiral Bayly in June 1913, together with the debate that ensued after 30 July 1914; "marvelous," Domvile, *By and Large,* 50.

6. Sturdee, "My Service Connections with Lord Fisher," SDEE1/17, Sturdee Papers, CCA.

7. Goodenough, *Rough Record,* 90.

8. Winston S. Churchill, *The World Crisis,* vol. 1 (Sydney: Australasian Publishing, 1925), 217.

9. "What its contents were," Paymaster Rear Admiral Sir Hamnet Share, *Under Great Bear and Southern Cross: Forty Years Afloat and Ashore* (London: Jarrolds, 1932), 209.

10. The exchange is covered in detail in John Winton, *Jellicoe* (London: Michael Joseph, 1981), 141–42.

11. Winton, *Jellicoe,* 142.

12. Share, *Under Great Bear and Southern Cross,* 210.

13. Wintour, HMS *Swift,* diary entry, dated 4 August 1914, Wintour Papers, IWM.

14. Ramsay, HMS *Dreadnought,* diary entry, dated 4 August 1914, Ramsay Papers, NMM.

15. The Nore is the sandbank in the center of the estuary of the Thames River; it gave its name to the naval command embracing the entrance to the Thames and the adjacent coast.

16. Jellicoe to Beatty letter, of (undated) January 1915, Jellicoe Papers, Add. MS 49008, British Library. See also Winton, *Jellicoe,* 161.

17. The diaries of Admiral Sir George King-Hall for 1909–11 are particularly revealing in the pressure that half-pay placed on a senior officer who relied solely on his pay in keeping up appearances and educating his children. The financial difference was the result not only of the reduction in salary, but also in the absence of allowances such as so-called table money, which increased effective pay considerably. See the family diaries at https://sites.google.com/site/kinghallconnections/Home.

18. For which see both the Backhouse and Drax Papers.

19. Keyes, *The Naval Memoirs,* vol. 1, 69.

20. Fisher to Viscount Esher, letter, 20 September 1912, in Arthur J. Marder, *Fear God and Dread Nought,* vol. 2, *Years of Power 1904–1914* (London: Jonathan Cape, 1956), 479.

21. Captain S. S. Hall, letter to Lord Fisher, undated July 1913, Lambert, *The Submarine Service*, 193.

22. De Chair, *The Sea Is Strong*, 150–52.

23. "Job," de Chair, *The Sea Is Strong*, 143.

24. "Beatty's indignation," Beatty to Lady Beatty, letter, dated 1 August 1914, BTY17/28, Beatty Papers, NMM.

25. Midshipman C. H. Drage, HMS *London,* diary entry, dated 24 August 1914, Drage Papers, Liddell Collection.

26. "Principal Theatre of War," Admiralstab, "Draft Order of Battle for the Naval Forces for the Mobilisation Year 1913–1914 (Winter Period)," dated 1 September 1913, copy translated from photo original received by the British, dated 8 October 1913, Backhouse Papers, NHB.

27. Re: "the battle turn": Ships did not turn immediately when the order was executed, but as soon as it was clear that their next astern had begun to turn. This reduced the danger of collision if a particular ship had missed the initial signal and failed to turn.

28. The best English language analysis of the German naval planning effort is Ivo Nikolai Lambi, *The Navy and German Power Politics 1862–1914* (Boston: Allen & Unwin, 1984). See also Gamzell, *Organization, Conflict and Innovation*. An excellent recent summary of the dilemmas the Germans faced is Michael Epkenhans, "Die Kaiserliche Marine 1914/15," in *Skagerrakschlacht: Vorgeschichte—Ereignis—Verarbeitung*, ed. Michael Epkenhans, Jörg Hillmann, and Frank Nägler (Munich: R. Oldenbourg Verlag, 2009).

29. This was increased to twenty-nine feet in November 1914.

30. Groos, *Der Krieg zur See: Nordsee*, vol. 2, 347; and Firle, *Der Krieg zur See: Ostsee,* vol. 1, 193.

31. Watson, Germany Report no. 78, 21 October 1912, Backhouse Papers, NHB.

32. Hopman, *Das Logbuch*, 393.

33. Cited in Epkenhans, *Das ereignisreiche Leben eines "Wilhelminers,"* 369, fn60.

34. Cited in Epkenhans, "Die Kaiserliche Marine 1914/15," 116.

35. Cited in Groos, *Der Krieg zur See: Nordsee*, vol. 1, 79.

36. Admiral Friedrich von Ingenohl, "Die Flottenführung im ersten Kriegshalbjahr und des Seekriegswerk," *Marine Rundschau* 1 (January 1923): 1–2.

37. Von Müller, diary entry, dated 6 August 1914, Gorlitz, *The Kaiser and His Court*, 17. See also Gemzell, *Organization, Conflict and Innovation*, 178.

38. Gary E. Weir, "Reinhard Scheer: Intuition under Fire, 1863–1928," in *The Great Admirals: Command at Sea, 1587–1945*, ed. Jack Sweetman (Annapolis, MD: Naval Institute Press, 1997), 392.

39. Erich Raeder, *Grand Admiral* (Cambridge, MA: Da Capo, 2001), 21.

40. The following discussion is based substantially on Pavlovich, *The Fleet in the First World War*, vol. 1; and Rene Greger, *The Russian Fleet 1914–1917,*

trans. Jill Gearing (London: Ian Allan, 1972), as well as the perspectives of *Der Krieg zur See.*

41. Rear Admiral First Battle Cruiser Squadron, letter, to C-in-C Home Fleets, 20 November 1913 (referring to a report on the Russian Baltic squadron), DRAX 4/2, Drax Papers, CCA.

42. Re: "succession of commanders": General Alexander Blagoveshchenskiy until the end of August 1914, then General Konstantin Fan der Flit until June 1915.

Chapter 7. First Blood in the North Sea

1. "Angst for the signalmen," William Guy Carr, *By Guess and by God* (London: Hutchinson, 1930), 88; "desks and library cupboards," "The Royal Navy of Lieutenant Commander W. E. V. Woods, RN," in S. Morley, ed., *99 Years of Navy* (London: Cpg, 1995), 40.

2. Lieutenant William Tennant, HMS *Lizard,* diary entry, dated 4 August 1914, Tennant Papers, NMM.

3. King-Hall, *My Naval Life*, 91.

4. Vice Admiral K. G. B. Dewar, *The Navy from Within* (London: Gollancz, 1939), 161.

5. Daniel, HMS *Orion,* diary entry, dated 4 August 1914, Daniel Papers, CCA.

6. Eric Bush, *Bless Our Ship* (London: Allen & Unwin, 1958), 25.

7. "better off than the British," von Hase, *Kiel and Jutland,* 18, 21.

8. Scheer, *Germany's High Sea Fleet,* 64.

9. "Old Packs" Beatty to Lady Beatty, letter, dated 5 August 1914, BTY 17/28, Beatty Papers, NMM.

10. "'Blinker' Hall's *Queen Mary*," Beatty to Lady Beatty, letter, dated 5 August 1914, BTY 17/28, Beatty Papers, NMM.

11. Ramsay, HMS *Dreadnought,* diary entry, dated 4 August 1914, Ramsay Papers, NMM.

12. "A howl of joy," Admiral Lord Mountevans *Adventurous Life* (London: Hutchinson, 1946), 85; "At midnight," Owen, HMS *Stour,* diary entry, dated 4 August 1914, BWO1/3 Owen Papers, IWM.

13. Jonathan Reed Winkler, *Nexus: Strategic Communications and American Security in World War I* (Cambridge, MA: Harvard University Press, 2008), 5–6.

14. "Recent British practice," *Admiralty Weekly Order* no. 785, dated 9 January 1914, "Merchant Vessels Armed for Self-Defence," NHB. See also Naval Staff Admiralty, *Technical History: Defensive Armament of Merchant Ships* CB 1515(13), NHB; "carried armament in peacetime," Seligmann, *The Royal Navy and the German Threat,* 41–43.

15. Midshipman Alexander Scrimgeour, HMS *Crescent,* diary entries, dated 3 and 4 August 1914, in *Scrimgeour's Small Scribbling Diary 1914–1916,* ed. Richard Hallam and Mark Beynon (London: Conway, 2008), 32.

16. Keyes, *The Naval Memoirs,* vol. 1, 62.

17. "Had every appearance," Captain C. H. Fox, RN, "The Destruction of the *Königin Luise* and the Sinking of the *Amphion,*" *Naval Review* 5 (1917): 132.

18. Groos, *Der Krieg zur See: Nordsee,* vol. 1, 96.

19. Fox, "The Destruction of the *Königin Luise,*" 133.

20. Fox, "The Destruction of the *Königin Luise,*" 133.

21. "If we did go," "It was little thought," Fox, "The Destruction of the *Königin Luise,*" 134.

22. Len Barnett, "A 'Well Known' Incident Reassessed: The German Attempted Mining of the Thames in August 1914," *Mariner's Mirror* 89, no. 2 (May 2003): 189–90, gives considerable detail of the uncertainties over the position of the minefield.

23. Fox, "The Destruction of the *Königin Luise,*" 137.

24. "Automatically opened," "seeing red," Fox, "The Destruction of the *Königin Luise,*" 139.

25. *Naval Staff Monograph (Historical),* vol. 10 *Home Waters,* Part 1, *From the Outbreak of War to 27 August 1914,* 43.

26. *Naval Staff Monograph (Historical),* vol. 3, no. 7, *The Patrol Flotillas at the Commencement of the War,* 83.

27. "Disappointment at its inactivity," Seaman Richard Stumpf, diary entry, dated 5 August 1914, cited in Horn, *The Private War,* 27.

28. Alan Coles, *Three before Breakfast* (Havant, UK: Kenneth Mason, 1979), 27.

29. HMS *Monarch* signal to Rear Admiral Second Battle Squadron, sent 1700 8 August 1914, received 1729, log of Captain F. C. Dreyer, Dreyer Papers, CCA.

30. Commander A. D. P. R. Pound, HMS *Colossus,* diary entry, dated 9 August 1914; Paul G. Halpern, ed., "Dudley Pound in the Grand Fleet 1914–15," *The Naval Miscellany,* vol. 6, ed. Michael Duffy (Aldershot, UK: Navy Records Society/Ashgate, 2003), 393.

31. Daniel, HMS *Orion,* diary entry, dated 8 August 1914, DANL 1, Daniel Papers, CCA.

32. The diaries of Captain Frederic Dreyer and Lieutenants Charles Daniel, both on board *Orion,* and Bertram Ramsay, on board *Dreadnought,* for 8–10 August 1914, provide summaries of the incidents.

33. Grand Fleet Narrative, dated 9 August 1914, TNA ADM 137/414.

34. Erich Gröner, *German Warships 1815–1945,* vol. 2 *U-Boats and Mine Warfare Vessels* (Annapolis, MD: Naval Institute Press, 1991), 6.

35. *Naval Staff Monograph (Historical),* vol. 10, *Home Waters,* Part 1, 68.

36. Wintour, HMS *Swift,* diary entry, dated 10 August 1914, Wintour Papers, IWM.

37. Groos, *Der Krieg zur See: Nordsee,* vol. 1, 122.

38. Tennant, HMS *Lizard,* diary entry, dated 19 August 1914, Tennant Papers, NMM.

39. Tennant, HMS *Lizard,* diary entry, dated 18 August 1914, Tennant Papers, NMM.

40. Tennant, HMS *Lizard,* diary entry, dated 18 August 1914, Tennant Papers, NMM.

41. Lieutenant Oswald Frewen, HMS *Lookout,* diary entry, dated 21 (?) August 1914, Frewen Papers (no longer accessible).

42. "Somewhat inglorious venture," *Naval Staff Monograph (Historical),* vol. 10, *Home Waters,* Part 1, 96.

43. Keyes, *The Naval Memoirs,* vol. 1, 79.

44. *Naval Staff Monograph (Historical),* vol. 10, *Home Waters,* Part 1, 107.

Chapter 8. The Baltic Begins

1. Firle, *Der Krieg zur See: Ostsee,* vol. 1, 177. See also von Tirpitz, *My Memoirs,* vol. 2 (London: Hurst & Blackett, 1919), 373, fn1.

2. Robinson, *The Zeppelin in Combat,* 37.

3. Firle, *Der Krieg zur See: Ostsee,* vol. 1, 70.

4. V. Yankovich, "The Origins of Communications Intelligence," trans. Thomas R. Hammant, *Cryptologia,* 8, no. 3 (July 1984): 199.

5. Admiral Hugo von Pohl diary entry, dated 27 August 1914, in von Pohl, *Aus Aufzeichnungen und Briefen,* 33.

6. H. Graf, *La Marine Russe dans la Guerre et dans la Revolution 1914–1918* (Paris: Payot, 1928), 24.

7. Grand Admiral Prince Heinrich of Prussia, "Der Vorstöß S. M. S. *Blücher* vor dem finnischen Meerbusen am 6. September 1914," in *Auf See unbesiegt: Erlebnisse im Seekrieg erzhält von Mitkämpfern,* vol. 1, ed. Eberhard von Mantey (Munich: Lehmanns Verlag, 1922), 36.

8. Prince Heinrich, "Der Vorstöß S. M. S. *Blücher,*" 37.

9. Von Pohl, diary entry, dated 19 September 1914, in von Pohl, *Aus Aufzeichnungen und Briefen,* 68.

10. Firle, *Der Krieg zur See: Ostsee,* vol. 1, 219.

Chapter 9. Heligoland Bight

1. Keyes, *The Naval Memoirs,* vol. 1, 76.

2. Keyes, *The Naval Memoirs,* vol. 1, 80.

3. Admiralty to C-in-C Grand Fleet, 26 August 1914, sent 1305. Unless otherwise indicated, all British signals are taken from Appendix A to *Naval Staff*

Monograph (Historical), vol. 3, Monograph 11, *The Battle of the Heligoland Bight, August 28th, 1914,* 149 et seq.

4. *Naval Staff Monograph (Historical),* vol. 3, no. 11, 113.

5. *Naval Staff Monograph (Historical),* vol. 3, no. 11, 142. See also Groos, *Der Krieg zur See: Nordsee,* vol. 1, 210.

6. Commander John Creswell, "The Battle of the Heligoland Bight, 28th August 1914," lecture delivered to the Royal Naval Staff College, 2 May 1932, in Creswell Papers, CCA.

7. Commodore Reginald Tyrwhitt to his wife, letter, dated 29 August 1914, in A. Temple Patterson, *Tyrwhitt of the Harwich Force: The Life of Admiral of the Fleet Sir Reginald Tyrwhitt* (London: MacDonald, 1973), 62.

8. "One mass of black smoke," Lieutenant J. StE. Cardew, HMS *Lizard,* journal entry, dated 28 August 1914, Cardew Papers, RNM Library.

9. Groos, *Der Krieg zur See: Nordsee,* vol. 1, 244.

10. Tennant, HMS *Lizard,* diary entry, dated 28 August 1914, "Heligoland," Tennant Papers, NMM.

11. "Commodore 1st Light Cruiser Squadron Report of Proceedings 27th–28th August 1914," No C037H, dated 29 August 1914, DRAX 1/46, Drax Papers, CCA.

12. Lieutenant Commander C. P. Talbot, diary entry, dated 28 August 1914, cited in Julian Thompson, *The Imperial War Museum Book of the War at Sea 1914–1918* (London: Sidgwick & Jackson, 2005), 70.

13. *Naval Staff Monograph (Historical),* vol. 3, no. 11, 129.

14. *Naval Staff Monograph (Historical),* vol. 3, no. 11, 142. See fn4, that document, for the comment about the information available in the *Pilot.*

15. Admiral of the Fleet Lord Chatfield, *The Navy and Defence* (London: Heinemann, 1942), 124–25.

16. Lieutenant Oswald Frewen to Moreton Frewen, letter, published in *Morning Post* (London), 3 September 1914.

17. Kapitanleutnant Wolfgang von Tirpitz, "Der Untergang der *Mainz* am 28 August 1914," in *Auf See unbesiegt,* ed. Eberhard von Mantey, vol. 2, 21.

18. Lieutenant Commander M. L. Goldsmith, letter, to his father, dated 6 September 1914, Goldsmith Papers, Liddell Hart Centre.

19. Groos, *Der Krieg zur See: Nordsee,* vol. 1, 264.

20. Stephen King-Hall, quoted in Lady L. King-Hall, *Sea Saga* (London: Gollancz, 1935), 382.

21. Groos, *Der Krieg zur See: Nordsee,* vol. 1, 263.

22. Lieutenant A. B. Downes, HMS *Birmingham,* diary entry, dated 28 August 1914, Downes Papers, RNM Library.

23. Keyes, *The Naval Memoirs,* vol. 1, 88.

24. Tennant, HMS *Lizard,* diary entry, dated 28 August 1914, "Heligoland," Tennant Papers, NMM.

25. Kontreadmiral Hans Seebohm, "Der Endkampf S.M.S. *Ariadne*," in von Mantey, *Auf See unbesiegt,* vol. 2, 149.

26. Seebohm, "Der Endkampf S. M. S. *Ariadne,*" 154; and Groos, *Der Krieg zur See: Nordsee,* vol. 1, 273.

27. Stoker Adolf Neumann, account cited in Lieutenant Commander Fritz Otto Busch, "Die Hochseeflotte im Kriege," in *Unsere Marine im Weltkrieg,* ed. Fritz Otto Busch and Georg Gunther von Forstner (Berlin: Brunnen-Verlag, 1934), 78.

28. Chatfield, *The Navy and Defence*, 125.

29. Groos, *Der Krieg zur See: Nordsee,* vol. 1, 318–19.

30. Groos, *Der Krieg zur See: Nordsee,* vol. 1, 284.

31. Temple Patterson, *Tyrwhitt of the Harwich Force*, 61.

32. Temple Patterson, *Tyrwhitt of the Harwich Force*, 62.

33. Tennant, HMS *Lizard,* diary entry, dated 29 August 1914, Tennant Papers, NMM.

34. Beatty to Arthur Balfour, letter, dated 21 June 1916, quoted in Arthur J. Marder, *From the Dreadnought to Scapa Flow*, vol. 2, *The War Years: To the Eve of Jutland 1914–1916* (London: Oxford University Press, 1965), 52.

35. Keyes to Goodenough, letter, dated 5 September 1914, Paul G. Halpern, *The Keyes Papers: Selections from the Private and Official Correspondence of Admiral of the Fleet Baron Keyes of Zeebrugge,* vol. 1, *1914–1918* (London: Navy Records Society, 1972), 19.

36. Goodenough to Keyes, letter, dated 14 September 1914, Halpern, *The Keyes Papers,* vol. 1, 20.

37. Duff, HMS *Emperor of India,* diary entry, dated 14 January 1915, Duff Papers, NMM.

38. Tennant, HMS *Lizard,* diary entry, dated 28 August 1914, Tennant Papers, NMM.

39. "Fairly slobbered," "a size larger," Tyrwhitt to his sister, letter, dated 10 September 1914, Temple Patterson, *Tyrwhitt of the Harwich Force*, 65.

40. "Henceforward the weight," Churchill, *The World Crisis,* vol. 1, 309.

41. Captain H. von Waldeyer-Hartz, *Admiral von Hipper* (London: Rich & Cowan, 1933), 114.

42. Admiral Hopman, *Das Kriegstagebuch einers deutschen Seeoffizieres* (Berlin: August Scherl, 1925), 37.

43. Groos, *Der Krieg zur See: Nordsee,* vol. 1, 311.

44. Raeder, *Grand Admiral*, 46–47.

45. By a personal courtesy of Churchill's.

46. Philbin, *Admiral von Hipper,* 74–77, for details on von Tirpitz's relations with Hipper. It is notable that Hipper was one of the very few in the senior leadership who had not worked with von Tirpitz as state secretary.

47. Von Tirpitz, *My Memoirs*, vol. 2, 358. See also pp. 456–58 for extracts from his letters of the time.

48. "The British battle cruiser force," Robinson, *The Zeppelin in Combat*, 42.

CHAPTER 10. ENTER THE SUBMARINES

1. Admiralty to C-in-C Grand Fleet, 3 September 1914, sent 1945. Unless otherwise indicated, all British signals in this chapter are taken from *Naval Staff Monograph (Historical)*, vol. 11, *Home Waters*, Part 2, *September and October 1914*, 154 et seq.

2. *Naval Staff Monograph (Historical)*, vol. 11, *Home Waters*, Part 2, 37.

3. Dreyer, HMS *Orion*, diary entry, dated 1 September 1914, Dreyer Papers, CCA.

4. Ramsay, HMS *Dreadnought*, diary entry, dated 1 September 1914, Ramsay Papers, NMM.

5. "Very probably seals," Downes, HMS *Birmingham*, diary entry, dated 1 September 1914, Downes Papers, RNM Library.

6. See Downes, HMS *Birmingham*, diary entry, dated 7 September 1914, Downes Papers, RNM Library, for an account by a surviving officer. It does not tally with the official record, but appears credible.

7. Von Müller, diary entry, dated 8 September 1914, in Gorlitz, *The Kaiser and His Court*, 29.

8. Groos, *Der Krieg zur See: Nordsee*, vol. 2, 30–33.

9. *Naval Staff Monograph (Historical)*, vol. 11, *Home Waters*, Part 2, 45.

10. Keyes, *The Naval Memoirs*, vol. 1, 76–77.

11. Dumas, diary entry, dated 14 September 1914, Dumas Papers, IWM.

12. Dumas, diary entry, dated 16 September 1914, Dumas Papers, IWM.

13. "The cruisers had been employed," Tennant, HMS *Lizard*, diary entry, dated 22 September 1914, Tennant Papers, NMM.

14. "Set upon by superior heavy forces," "Appreciation by the Naval General Staff, Berlin, 13th September 1914," Red team analysis by Plunkett, DRAX1/7, Drax Papers, CCA.

15. Rear Admiral *Euryalus*, letter, to Admiralty, 14/028, dated 19 September 1914, TNA ADM 137/47.

16. Churchill, *The World Crisis*, vol. 1, 323.

17. C-in-C Grand Fleet to secretary of the Admiralty, letter, Home Fleets 0022, dated 24 September 1914, TNA ADM 137/995.

18. Churchill, *The World Crisis*, vol. 1, 323.

19. Marder, *From the Dreadnought to Scapa Flow*, vol. 2, 57, fn27 sources this quotation of Sturdee from a letter from Admiral Sir William James passing on a story given to him by Keyes.

20. Churchill, *The World Crisis,* vol. 1, 324.

21. "Rear Admiral *Euryalus* Statement to Court of Enquiry," dated 29 September 1914, TNA ADM 137/47.

22. Rear Admiral *Euryalus,* letter, to Admiralty 14/028, dated 19 September 1914, TNA ADM 137/47.

23. Flag *Euryalus* to General Signal, 20 September 1914, sent 1504, *Naval Staff Monograph (Historical)* vol. 11, *Home Waters,* Part 2, 52.

24. Testimony of Midshipman Hereward Hook, Bush, *Bless Our Ship,* 32.

25. Tyrwhitt to his sister, letter, dated 30 September 1914, Temple Patterson, *Tyrwhitt of the Harwich Force,* 73.

26. Tyrwhitt to his sister, letter, dated 30 September 1914, Temple Patterson, *Tyrwhitt of the Harwich Force,* 73.

27. Surgeon Rear-Admiral J. R. Muir, *Years of Endurance* (London: Philip Allan, 1936), 51.

28. Keyes, *The Naval Memoirs,* vol. 1, 106.

29. "Feeling very," "I could only wait," "some salve to," Keyes, *The Naval Memoirs,* vol. 1, 106.

30. "Was most peremptorily," "forgiven," Keyes to Rear Admiral John de Robeck, letter, dated 29 September 1914, Halpern, *The Keyes Papers,* vol. 1, 33.

31. "To interrogate trawlers," Dreyer, diary photo placed on entry, dated 1 September 1914. Both trawler and the battleship *Orion* are clearly stationary and the note on the photo reads, "Standing by to board a trawler but did not do so and hailing was satisfactory." Dreyer Papers, CCA.

32. Admiralty to General Signal, dated 22 September 1914, sent 2200, *Naval Staff Monograph (Historical),* vol. 11, *Home Waters,* Part 2, 59. This was initialled by both First Sea Lord and First Lord. See TNA ADM 137/47.

33. Christian to Jellicoe, letter, dated 29 September 1914, A. Temple Patterson, *The Jellicoe Papers: Selections from the Private and Official Correspondence of Admiral of the Fleet Earl Jellicoe of Scapa,* vol. 1, *1893–1916* (London: Navy Records Society, 1966), 70–71.

34. See the testimony of Lieutenant Commander J. S. Parker, TNA ADM 137/47.

35. "Report of Court of Enquiry into the Sinking of HM Ships *Aboukir, Hogue* and *Cressy,*" dated 5 October 1914, TNA ADM 137/47.

36. See TNA ADM 137/47 ff. 381–86 for the exchange of comments.

37. Chief of Staff, note in response to First Lord, dated 3 October 1914, TNA ADM 137/47.

38. Campbell had been an associate of Lord Charles Beresford and equerry to King George V and was a bête noire of Fisher's because of his alleged influence on both of these old opponents of the former First Sea Lord.

39. Fisher to Mrs. Reginald McKenna, letter, dated c. early October 1914, Marder, *Fear God and Dread Nought,* vol. 3, *Restoration, Abdication and Last Years 1914–1920* (London: Jonathan Cape, 1959), 61.

40. Ramsay, HMS *Dreadnought,* diary entry, dated 23 September 1914, Ramsay Papers, NMM.
41. Dumas, diary entry, dated 23 September 1914, Dumas Papers, IWM.
42. "Interference," Churchill, *The World Crisis,* vol. 1, 326.
43. "Hearty cheers," Able Seaman W. Chesterton, HMS *Bacchante,* journal entry, dated 7 October 1914, Chesterton Papers, RNM Library.
44. Owen, HMS *Stour,* diary entries, dated 25 and 26 September 1914, Owen Papers, IWM.
45. "Looks about as clean," Owen, HMS *Stour,* diary entry, dated 26 August 1914, Owen Papers, IWM.
46. *Naval Staff Monograph (Historical),* vol. 11, *Home Waters*, Part 2, 71. This was a press announcement. Admiralty Notice to Mariners No. 1626/1914 was issued on the same subject on 9 October; NHB.
47. Dumas, diary entry, dated 2 October 1914, Dumas Papers, IWM.
48. See Dumas, diary entry, dated 3 October 1914, Dumas Papers, IWM ; and Friedman, *Naval Weapons of World War One*, 364.
49. Midshipman G. C. Harper, HMS *Endymion,* diary entry, dated 15 October 1914, Harper Papers, CCA.
50. "Serviceability and maximum speed," Scrimgeour, HMS *Crescent,* diary entry, dated 18 October 1914, Hallam and Beynon, *Scrimgeour's Small Scribbling Diary*, 81–82; re: "becoming overwrought," see the entry of Alexander Scrimgeour for 18 October, which provides a lurid story of an "encounter" between HMS *Crescent* and no fewer than three "submarines." Scrimgeour, diary cntry, dated 18 October 1914, Hallam and Beynon, *Scrimgeour's Small Scribbling Diary*, 79–81.
51. Wintour, HMS *Swift,* diary entry, dated 15 October 1914, Wintour Papers, IWM.
52. Wemyss "Memoirs," cited in Lady Wester Wemyss, *The Life and Letters of Lord Wester Wemyss* (London: Eyre and Spottiswoode, 1935), 181.
53. Konteradmiral Hans Pfundheller, "Der Durchbruch des Hilfkreuzers *Berlin*," von Mantey, *Auf See unbesiegt,* vol. 2, 273.
54. Sub Lieutenant A. E. Thomson, HMS *Circe,* quoted in "Taffrail" (Captain Taprell Dorling), *Swept Channels* (London: Hodder & Stoughton, 1935), 54.
55. Beatty to Churchill, letter, dated 17 October 1914, Ranft, *The Beatty Papers,* vol. 1, 141.
56. "Wrapperitis," David K. Brown, *The Grand Fleet: Warship Design and Development 1906–1922* (London: Chatham, 1999), 94; "condensiritis," Vice Admiral Sir Louis Le Bailly, *From Fisher to the Falklands* (London: Institute of Marine Engineers, 1991), 23. See also Commander P. M. Rippon, *Evolution of Engineering in the Royal Navy,* vol. 1, *1827–1939* (Tunbridge Wells, UK: Spellmount, 1988), 134, 147.

57. "Most modern dreadnoughts," Admiral Sir Frederic Dreyer, *The Sea Heritage: A Study of Maritime Warfare* (London: Museum Press, 1955), 89; "acute anxiety," Admiral of the Fleet Viscount Jellicoe, *The Grand Fleet 1914–16: Its Creation, Development and Work* (London: Cassell, 1919), 153.

58. William Guy Carr, *Brass Hats and Bell Bottomed Trousers: Unforgettable and Splendid Feats of the Harwich Patrol* (London: Hutchinson, 1939), 83.

59. "*Princess Royal*," Morley, "The Royal Navy of Lieutenant Commander W. E. V. Woods, RN," 26–33; "*St. Vincent*," Halpern, "Dudley Pound in the Grand Fleet, 1914–15," 386–95; "*Southampton*," King-Hall, *A Naval Lieutenant*, 12–15, 25–33.

60. Commander Barry Bingham, *Falklands, Jutland and the Bight* (London: John Murray, 1919), 41.

61. Victor Hayward, *HMS Tiger at Bay: A Sailor's Memoir 1914–18* (London: William Kimber, 1977), 81.

62. See Daniel, HMS *Orion,* diary entries, August–October 1914, Daniel Papers, CCA.

63. Bingham, *Falklands, Jutland and the Bight,* 41.

64. "Coal burning ships were," Admiral Sir Ragnar Colvin, *Memoirs of Admiral Sir Ragnar Colvin 1882–1954* (Durley, UK: Wintershill, 1992), 38.

65. Wintour, HMS *Swift,* diary entry, dated 14 August 1914, Wintour Papers, IWM.

66. "Veterans of detention cells," Richard Hough, *The Big Battleship: The Curious Career of HMS Agincourt* (London: Michael Joseph, 1966), 148–52; "returned deserters," Beatty to Hamilton, letter, dated 21 February 1915, Ranft, *The Beatty Papers,* vol. 1, 260–61.

67. Muir, *Years of Endurance,* 64–65. This describes the state of HMS *Tiger* on commissioning.

68. Julian S. Corbett (with an introduction by John B. Hattendorf and Donald M. Schurman), *Maritime Operations in the Russo-Japanese War 1904–05* (Annapolis, MD: Naval Institute and Naval War College, 1994), 241.

69. Gilbert, *Winston S. Churchill,* vol. 3, 142.

70. Assistant Paymaster Guy Ward-Smith, letter, to his mother, dated 28 February 1915. He had picked up the story at the admiral's office in Queenstown on returning from Canadian waters. The envelope with the letter is stamped "Passed by Censor," but the date mark is not clear and it is possible that it is one of a different date mixed up with others when Ward-Smith reviewed the material in later years. Ward-Smith Papers, RNM Library.

71. Rear Admiral Sir Douglas Brownrigg, *Indiscretions of the Naval Censor* (London: Cassell, 1920), 32.

72. Keyes, *The Naval Memoirs,* vol. 1, 110.

73. Richmond, diary entry, dated 4 October 1914, RIC1/10, Richmond Papers, NMM.

74. Tennant, HMS *Lizard,* diary entry, dated 8 October 1914, Tennant Papers, NMM.

75. Keyes, *The Naval Memoirs*, vol. 1, 113.

76. Chalmers, *Max Horton and the Western Approaches*, 20.

77. Tennant, HMS *Lizard,* diary entry, dated 11 October 1914, Tennant Papers, NMM.

78. Beatty to his wife, letter, dated 18 October 1914, BTY17/30, Beatty Papers, NMM.

79. Tyrwhitt to his wife, letter, dated 17 October 1914, Temple Patterson, *Tyrwhitt of the Harwich Force*, 79.

80. *The Navy List* of January 1915 shows Captain F. G. St. John in "temporary" command with effect from 26 October 1914. That became permanent some time early in 1915.

81. "While there was a lively," Richmond, diary entry, dated 16 October 1914, RIC1/10, Richmond Papers, NMM.

82. "Her arrest and later condemnation," Groos, *Der Krieg zur See: Nordsee*, vol. 2, 255–57.

83. Groos, *Der Krieg zur See: Nordsee*, vol. 2, 242–43. See also Kapitanleutnant Franz Guilleaume, "Die Todesfahrt der VII. Torpedoboots-Halbflottille (Thiele)," von Mantey, *Auf See unbesiegt,* vol. 2, esp. 96–101.

84. Von Ingenohl, "Die Flottenführung im ersten Kriegshalbjahr und des Seekriegswerk," 7.

85. Tyrwhitt to his wife, letter, dated 23 October 1914, Temple Patterson, *Tyrwhitt of the Harwich Force*, 81.

86. "While their conversion was makeshift," see the diary of newly commissioned Lieutenant Erskine Childers, Royal Naval Volunteer Reserve (RNVR), in HMS *Engadine*, Childers Papers, IWM.

87. *Naval Staff Monograph (Historical),* vol. 11, *Home Waters*, Part 2, 139.

88. Tyrwhitt to his wife, letters, dated 24 and 27 October 1914, Temple Patterson, *Tyrwhitt of the Harwich Force*, 82–83. "For his having" and "considerable butter," 24 October letter, 82; "we are going," 27 October letter, 83.

89. Re: "Although the British had not," this is contrary to the suggestion in Sir Julian Corbett's *Naval Operations,* vol. 1, *To the Battle of the Falklands December 1914* (London: Longmans Green, 1920), 217: "Information had been coming in of a certain activity of the German flotillas in the Bight." This is denied by the later Admiralty naval staff study, although the Germans took it at face value in *Der Krieg zur See.*

90. Hough, *Louis and Victoria*, 302–5.

91. Dumas, diary entry, dated 24 October 1914, Dumas Papers, IWM.

92. The best accounts of the machinations behind Battenberg's removal are Lambert, *Planning Armageddon,* 279–92; John B. Hattendorf, "Admiral

Prince Louis of Battenberg (1912–1914)," *The First Sea Lords: From Fisher to Mountbatten,* ed. Malcolm H. Murfett (Westport, CT: Praeger, 1995), 84–88; and Gilbert, *Winston S. Churchill*, vol. 3, 145–51.

93. "Most delicate," Herbert Asquith to Venetia Stanley, letter, dated 28 October 1914, cited in Gilbert, *Winston S. Churchill*, vol. 3, 149; "at this juncture," Churchill, *The World Crisis,* vol. 1, 400–401.

94. Battenberg to Hood, letter, dated 13 November 1914, HOOD6/2, Hood Papers, CCA.

95. Hopman, diary entry, dated 19 October 1914, Epkenhans, *Das ereignisreiche Leben eines "Wilhelminers,"* 468.

96. Von Pohl, *Aus Aufzeichnungen und Briefen*, 80–81.

Chapter 11. The Return of Fisher

1. Jellicoe to Hamilton, letter, dated 29 January 1915, Temple Patterson, *The Jellicoe Papers,* vol. 1, 131.

2. Dumas, diary entry, dated 30 October 1914, Dumas Papers, IWM.

3. Scrimgeour, HMS *Crescent,* diary entry, dated 31 October 1914, Hallam and Beynon, *Scrimgeour's Small Scribbling Diary*, 89.

4. Beatty to his wife, letter, dated 30 October 1914, BTY17/30, Beatty Papers, NMM.

5. Von Tirpitz to von Ingenohl, letter, dated 25 October 1914, cited in Epkenhans, *Das ereignisreiche Leben eines "Wilhelminers,"* 487.

6. Groos, *Der Krieg zur See: Nordsee*, vol. 2, 326.

7. "Since he had concerns," Philbin, *Admiral von Hipper,* 89.

8. "Saw a ripple," Vice Admiral H.T. Baillie-Grohman *Flashlight on the Past* vol. 1, 133, unpublished memoirs, Baillie-Grohman Papers, NMM.

9. HMS *Leopard* Signal 3 November 1914. Unless otherwise indicated, all British signals and telegrams are taken from *Naval Staff Monograph (Historical),* vol. 12, *Home Waters,* part 3, *From November 1914 to the end of January 1915,* 214 et seq.

10. "Bad coal," Groos, *Der Krieg zur See: Nordsee*, vol. 2, 343.

11. Philbin, *Admiral von Hipper,* 90.

12. "If, as Churchill," Churchill, *The World Crisis,* vol. 1, 441.

13. C-in-C Grand Fleet letter Home Fleets 0034, dated 30 October 1914, TNA ADM 137/995. Also cited in Marder, *From the Dreadnought to Scapa Flow,* vol. 2, 75–76; Temple Patterson, *The Jellicoe Papers*, vol. 1, 75–77; Dreyer, *The Sea Heritage*, 82–84.

14. Chief of the War Staff memorandum dated 31 October 1914 (which suggests that the original letter got to the Admiralty very quickly and was actioned instantly). "Only a dream," Admiral of the Fleet Sir Arthur Wilson

memorandum, dated 22 November 1914; "confidence and approval," First Sea Lord minute, dated 1 November 1914, TNA ADM137/995.

15. Secretary of the Admiralty to Jellicoe, letter, dated 7 November 1914, and holograph note re: lodgment, Jellicoe Papers, Add. MS 49012, British Library.

16. Second Division Home Fleets Battle Orders 1912, Jellicoe Papers, Add. MS 49012, British Library. There are other extracts in Temple Patterson, *The Jellicoe Papers*, vol. 1, 1, 23–25.

17. Jellicoe to Churchill, letter, dated 30 September 1914, Jellicoe Papers, Add. MS 49012, British Library.

18. Lambert, *Planning Armageddon,* 296–303.

19. "Whatever long-term plans," see Andrew Lambert, "Looking for an Offensive Opportunity: The Royal Navy's War from the July Crisis to the Eve of Jutland," published in German as "'The Possibility of Ultimate Action in the Baltic': Die Royal Navy im Krieg, 1914–1916," Michael Epkenhans, Jörg Hillmann, and Frank Nägler, *Skagerrakschlacht: Vorgeschichte—Ereignis—Verarbeitung* (Munich: Oldenbourg, 2009), 73–112.

20. *Naval Staff Monograph (Historical),* vol. 12, *Home Waters,* part 3, 22.

21. Fisher to Jellicoe, letter, dated 3 November 1914, Marder, *Fear God and Dread Nought,* vol. 3, 65.

22. Oliver, *Memoirs,* vol. 2, 125–26, Oliver Papers, NMM.

23. Admiral Sir Edmond Slade to Sturdee, letter, dated 11 December 1914, Sturdee Papers, CCA.

24. Oliver, *Memoirs,* vol. 2, 122, Oliver Papers, NMM.

25. Duff, HMS *Emperor of India,* diary entry, dated 19 January 1915, Duff Papers, NMM.

26. "One armadillo can lick," Fisher to Beatty, letter, dated 19 November 1914, Marder, *Fear God and Dread Nought,* vol. 3, 77.

27. Jellicoe to Fisher, letter, dated 11 November 1914, Marder, *Fear God and Dread Nought,* vol. 3, 69.

28. Beatty to Fisher, letter, dated 15 November 1914, Marder, *Fear God and Dread Nought,* vol. 3, 171.

29. Admiral Sir Henry Pelly, *300,000 Sea Miles* (London: Chatto & Windus, 1938), 136.

30. Lieutenant H. E. C. Blagrove, letter, to Lieutenant Oswald Frewen, dated 6 March 1915, SLGF3, Shane Leslie Papers, CCA.

31. Jellicoe to Fisher, letter, dated 10 November 1914, Marder, *Fear God and Dread Nought,* vol. 3, 68.

32. "Always credited them," Churchill, *The World Crisis,* vol. 1, 443.

33. Jellicoe to Fisher, letter, dated 11 November 1914, Marder, *Fear God and Dread Nought,* vol. 3, 69.

34. Fisher to Jellicoe, letter, dated 16 November 1914, Marder, *Fear God and Dread Nought,* vol. 3, 72.

35. Keyes, *The Naval Memoirs*, vol. 1, 137.

36. "The miraculous draught," Patrick Beesly, "Cryptanalysis and Its Influence on the War at Sea 1914–1918," Fifth Naval History Symposium, Annapolis, MD, 1981, 4.

37. Beesly, "Cryptoanalysis," "A mass of," 5; "[I]t was often," 7.

38. W. F. Clarke and F. Birch, *A Contribution to the History of German Naval Warfare 1914–1918,* vol. 1, *The Fleet in Action,* unpublished, held by NHB, chap. 2, 27–28.

39. Harper, HMS *Endymion,* diary entry, dated 24 October 1914, Harper Papers, CCA.

40. Sub Lieutenant P. W. Bowyer-Smyth, HMS *Superb,* diary entry, dated 24 November 1914, cited in Thompson, *The Imperial War Museum Book*, 85.

41. See the TNA ADM 137 series files: 4313, 4323, 4325, and 4326 for such material.

42. Beesly, "Cryptoanalysis." See ADM 137/4168 for Hope's handwritten notes on the German sortie of December 1914 based on the decryptions made.

43. Admiral H. W. W. Hope, "Narrative of Captain Hope," dated c. 1948, CLKE 3, William Clarke Papers, CCA.

44. Keyes, *The Naval Memoirs*, vol. 1, 139.

45. Dreyer, HMS *Orion,* diary entry, dated 19 November, Dreyer Papers, CCA.

46. Christopher Andrew, *Defend the Realm: The Authorised History of M.I.5* (London: Allen Lane, 2009), 50–52.

47. *Naval Staff Monograph (Historical),* vol. 12, *Home Waters,* part 3, 69.

48. Tyrwhitt to Sturdee, letter, dated c. 14 December 1914, Sturdee Papers, CCA.

49. Temple Patterson, *Tyrwhitt of the Harwich Force*, 89.

50. Tyrwhitt to his wife, letter, dated 28 (?) November 1914, Temple Patterson, *Tyrwhitt of the Harwich Force*, 89.

51. Tyrwhitt to his wife, letter, dated 28 (?) November 1914, Temple Patterson, *Tyrwhitt of the Harwich Force*, 89.

52. Lieutenant R. G. Dinwiddy to Downes, letter, dated 14 January 1915, Downes Papers, RNM Library.

53. Lieutenant R. G. Dinwiddy to Downes, letter, dated 14 January 1915, Downes Papers, RNM Library.

54. Tyrwhitt to his wife, letter, dated 28 (?) November 1914, Temple Patterson, *Tyrwhitt of the Harwich Force*, 89.

55. Lieutenant Neuerburg, "My Cruise in U.18," 12, NID translation, TNA ADM 137/995.

56. Groos, *Der Krieg zur See: Nordsee*, vol. 3, 20.

57. "Suddenly saw," "seemed to heave," "had completely," "Testimony to Court of Inquiry into Loss of HMS *Bulwark*," TNA ADM 116/1370.

58. "In a fine set of nerves," Midshipman A. A. Fraser MacLiesh, HMS *Agamemnon,* diary entry, dated 26 November 1914, Papers of A. A. Fraser MacLiesh, CCA.

59. Boatswain J. A. Price, RN, Testimony to Court of Inquiry, TNA ADM 116/1370.

60. Midshipman H. W. Williams, letter, to his mother, dated (end?) November 1914, Thompson, *The Imperial War Museum Book*, 85.

61. MacLiesh, HMS *Agamemnon,* diary entry, dated 26 November 1914, Papers of A. A. Fraser MacLiesh, CCA.

62. *Naval Staff Monograph (Historical),* vol. 12, *Home Waters,* part 3, 79.

63. De Chair, *The Sea Is Strong,* 181.

64. Scrimgeour, HMS *Crescent,* diary entry, dated 11 November 1914, Hallam and Beynon, *Scrimgeour's Small Scribbling Diary,* 94–99; "sensational night," 99.

65. De Chair, *The Sea Is Strong,* 181. See also Peter H. Liddle, *The Sailor's War 1914–1918* (Poole, UK: Blandford, 1985), 90, for another witness' account of the storm.

66. "The decks leak," Beatty to his wife, letter, dated 29 September 1914, Ranft, *The Beatty Papers,* vol. 1, 137; "Personnel were simply," Beatty to his wife, letter, dated 23 October 1914, Ranft, *The Beatty Papers,* vol. 1, 146.

67. Keyes, *The Naval Memoirs,* vol. 1, 133.

68. Tyrwhitt to his wife, letter, dated 6th December 1914, Temple Patterson, *Tyrwhitt of the Harwich Force,* 91.

69. Tyrwhitt to Sturdee, letter, dated circa 14th December 1914, Sturdee Papers, CCA.

CHAPTER 12. THE SCARBOROUGH RAID

1. "There were huge risks," Philbin, *Admiral von Hipper,* 92–96.

2. Remaining "in being" is a very old term to describe the use of an inferior fleet which, by avoiding action, remains a threat to a superior fleet.

3. Gorlitz, *The Kaiser and His Court,* 43–45.

4. Admiralty to C-in-C Grand Fleet, Telegram No. 267, 11 December 1914, sent 0020. Unless otherwise indicated, all British signals and telegrams in this chapter are taken from *Naval Staff Monograph (Historical),* vol. 12, *Home Waters,* part 3, 214 et seq.

5. Daniel, HMS *Orion,* diary entry, dated 15 December 1914, Daniel Papers, CCA.

6. "Swept three men overboard," Dreyer, HMS *Orion,* diary entry, dated 15 December 1914, Dreyer Papers, CCA; "had to be sent home," Jellicoe, *The Grand Fleet,* 176.

7. Von Waldeyer-Hartz, *Admiral von Hipper,* 133.

8. Groos, *Der Krieg zur See: Nordsee,* vol. 3, appendix 1 lists German signal traffic during the raid.

9. *Naval Staff Monograph (Historical)*, vol. 12, *Home Waters*, part 3, 101.

10. Von Ingenohl, "Die Flottenführung im ersten Kriegshalbjahr und des See-kriegswerk," 15–16.

11. "HMS *Lynx* Report of Proceedings 16th December 1914," TNA ADM 137/295. See also *Naval Staff Monograph (Historical)*, vol. 12, part 3, 102.

12. Admiralty to Admiral of Patrols, Telegram No. 217, 13 November 1914, sent 2238, *Naval Staff Monograph (Historical)*, vol. 12, *Home Waters*, part 3, 193.

13. Tennant, HMS *Ferret*, diary entry, dated 16 December 1914, Tennant Papers, NMM.

14. Tyrwhitt to Wintour, letter, dated 26 December 1914, Wintour Papers, IWM.

15. King-Hall, *A Naval Lieutenant*, 64.

16. Downes, HMS *Birmingham*, diary entry, dated 16 December 1914, Downes Papers, RNM Library.

17. Dreyer, *The Sea Heritage*, 103–4. It should be noted that his contemporary journal does not include this story, although it is true that the document as a whole is generally devoid of criticism or analysis. Dreyer Papers, CCA.

18. Dreyer, *The Sea Heritage*, 104.

19. Interpretations of position are from the *Naval Staff Monograph (Historical)*, vol. 12, *Home Waters*, part 3.

20. Philbin, *Admiral von Hipper*, 99.

21. Von Waldeyer-Hartz, *Admiral von Hipper*, 136.

22. Groos, *Der Krieg zur See: Nordsee*, vol. 3, 137A.

23. Philbin, *Admiral von Hipper*, 101.

24. Keyes, *The Naval Memoirs*, vol. 1, 145.

25. "The impetuous Churchill," Keyes, *The Naval Memoirs*, vol. 1, 146.

26. Keyes, *The Naval Memoirs*, vol. 1, 147.

27. *Naval Staff Monograph (Historical)*, vol. 12, *Home Waters*, part 3, 124.

28. Rear Admiral George A. Ballard, letter, to Keyes, dated 20 December 1914, Halpern, *The Keyes Papers*, vol. 1, 62.

29. Jellicoe to Fisher, letter, dated 18 December 1914, Marder, *Fear God and Dread Nought*, vol. 3, 98.

30. The material is available in TNA ADM 137/295.

31. Tyrwhitt to Wintour, letter, dated 26 December 1914, Wintour Papers, IWM.

32. Jellicoe to Fisher, 18 December 1914, notation on memorandum on the affair, Temple Patterson, *The Jellicoe Papers*, vol. 1, 108.

33. Fisher to Jellicoe, letter, dated 20 December 1914, Marder, *Fear God and Dread Nought*, vol. 3, 100.

34. Fisher to Jellicoe, letter, dated 21 December 1914, Marder, *Fear God and Dread Nought*, vol. 3, 102.

35. Fisher to Jellicoe, letter, dated 20 December 1914, Marder, *Fear God and Dread Nought*, vol. 3, 100.

36. Duff, HMS *Emperor of India,* diary entry, dated 23 January 1915, Duff Papers, NMM.

37. King-Hall, *Sea Saga*, 420.

38. "Beatty [is] very severe," in note by Jellicoe on envelope containing Beatty to Jellicoe, letter, dated 20 December 1914, Jellicoe Papers, Add. MS 49008, British Library. This comment was almost certainly made *after* the war and in the light of the controversies and ill feeling over Jutland.

39. Beatty to Jellicoe, letter, dated 20 December 1914, Jellicoe Papers, Add. MS 49008, British Library.

40. C-in-C Grand Fleet to Admiralty, covering letter, forwarding "Reports of Proceedings of 16th December 1914," dated 23 December 1914, TNA ADM 137/295.

41. Fisher to Jellicoe, letter, dated 20 December 1914, Marder, *Fear God and Dread Nought,* vol. 3, 100.

42. Beatty to Jellicoe, letter, dated 20 December 1914, Jellicoe Papers, Add. MS 49008, British Library.

43. Admiral Sir Reginald Plunkett-Ernle-Erle-Drax, writing as "R. P. D," "D. B. II" obituary in *Naval Review* 24, no. 2 (May 1936), 215.

44. No date, DRAX 1/6, Drax Papers, CCA.

45. Home Fleets Memorandum No. 0015, 22 December 1914, reproduced in *Naval Staff Monograph (Historical)*, vol. 3, no. 12, 225.

46. "C-in-C Grand Fleet to Flag Officers and Commodores," memorandum, dated 30 December 1914, TNA ADM 137/295; italics added.

47. "Took bits of his command," Oliver, *Memoirs,* vol. 2, 118–119, Oliver Papers, NMM.

48. "Submarines didn't," "The sooner somebody," Rear Admiral George A. Ballard, letter, to Keyes, dated 20 December 1914, Halpern, *The Keyes Papers,* vol. 1, 63.

49. Churchill to Fisher, letter, dated 21 December 1914, Marder, *Fear God and Dread Nought,* vol. 3, 105.

50. Admiralty to C-in-C Grand Fleet, Telegram No. 509, 20 December 1914, sent 1720, *Naval Staff Monograph (Historical)*, vol. 12, *Home Waters,* part 3, 124; italics added.

51. Daniel, HMS *Orion,* diary entry, dated 16 December 1914, Daniel Papers, CCA.

52. Churchill, *The World Crisis,* vol. 1, 478.

53. "Quite alone," Groos, *Der Krieg zur See: Nordsee*, vol. 3, 143.

54. Groos, *Der Krieg zur See: Nordsee*, vol. 3, 140.

55. Von Pohl to his wife, letter, dated 25 December 1914, von Pohl, *Aus Aufzeichnungen und Briefen,* 95.

56. The letter is reproduced in Granier, *Magnus von Levetzow,* 204–9.

Chapter 13. Mines and Ice

1. Pavlovich, *The Fleet in the First World War*, vol. 1, 86.
2. Blacklock, "Personal Reminiscences," 49.
3. Naval attaché, letter, to British ambassador in Petrograd, dated 6 November 1914, TNA ADM 137/271.
4. Graf, *La Marine Russe*, 37.
5. Graf, *La Marine Russe*, 38.
6. Firle, *Der Krieg zur See: Ostsee,* vol. 1, 262.
7. Von Pohl, letter, to his wife, dated 17 November 1914, von Pohl, *Aus Aufzeichnungen und Briefen*, 88.
8. "Had not come," Korvettenkapitan Werner Grassmann, "Die brave alte *Augsburg,*"von Mantey, *Auf see Unbesiegt*, vol. 2, 199.
9. Firle, *Der Krieg zur See: Ostsee,* vol. 1, 277.
10. Firle, *Der Krieg zur See: Ostsee,* vol. 1, 280.
11. Blacklock "Personal Reminiscences," 57.

Chapter 14. Trying the Offense

1. "Magnificent," Tennant, HMS *Ferret,* diary entry, dated 25 December 1914, Tennant Papers, NMM.
2. Tyrwhitt to Ramsay, letter, undated but written early January 1915, Ramsay Papers, NMM.
3. "Report of HMS *Empress,*" dated 26 December 1914, contained in *Report on Seaplane Operations against Cuxhaven carried out on 25th December 1914,* Air Department, Admiralty, February 1915, TNA ADM 186/567.
4. "Lieutenant F. W. Bowhill," later Air Chief Marshal Sir Frederick Bowhill (1880–1960) of the Royal Air Force.
5. "Report of HMS *Empress,*" dated 26 December 1914, contained in *Report on Seaplane Operations against Cuxhaven.*
6. "A single 110-pound bomb," Robinson, *The Zeppelin in Combat,* 45.
7. Frewen, diary entry, dated 26 (?) December 1914, Frewen Papers (no longer accessible).
8. Tennant, HMS *Ferret,* diary entry, dated 25 December 1914, Tennant Papers, NMM.
9. Tyrwhitt, letter, to his sister, dated 31 December 1914, Temple Patterson, *Tyrwhitt of the Harwich Force*, 98.
10. Groos, *Der Krieg zur See: Nordsee*, vol. 3, 167.
11. Temple Patterson, *Tyrwhitt of the Harwich Force*, 98.
12. Tennant, HMS *Ferret,* diary entry dated 25 December 1914, Tennant Papers, NMM.

13. Etienne [King-Hall], *A Naval Lieutenant*, 72.

14. Tennant, HMS *Ferret*, undated insert to diary entry, dated 25 December 1914, Tennant Papers, NMM.

15. In addition to the report available in ADM 186/567, the best popular account of the operation is R. D. Layman, *The Cuxhaven Raid: The World's First Carrier Air Strike* (London: Conway, 1985), although it did not have the benefit of all the British archival sources.

16. Tyrwhitt to his wife, letter, dated 29 December 1914, Temple Patterson, *Tyrwhitt of the Harwich Force*, 98.

17. Lieutenant Erskine Childers, RNVR HMS *Engadine* and seaplane No.136, diary entry, dated 29 (?) December 1914, Childers Papers, IWM.

18. This does not seem to have occurred in the First World War, but in 1940 the battleship *Revenge* sank a small boom defense vessel at Halifax rather than risking collision with the boom itself.

19. Duff, HMS *Emperor of India*, diary entry, dated 8 January 1915, Duff Papers, NMM. This details a conversation between Duff and Burney on the subject. TNA ADM 137/995 contains further material on Burney's concerns over the weaknesses of the Channel Fleet.

20. A somewhat different but persuasive new interpretation of the debate going on within the Admiralty on these issues and the roles of Churchill and Wilson in particular will shortly be published. David Morgan-Owen, "Cooked Up in the Dinner Hour? Sir Arthur Wilson's War Plan, Reconsidered," *English Historical Review* (forthcoming).

21. H. H. Asquith to Venetia Stanley, letter, dated 24 December 1914, Gilbert, *Winston S. Churchill*, vol. 3, *Companion, Part I, Documents*, 333.

22. Fisher to Jellicoe, letter, dated 28 December 1914, Marder, *Fear God and Dread Nought*, vol. 3, 115.

23. Fisher to Jellicoe, letter, dated 28 December 1914, Marder, *Fear God and Dread Nought*, vol. 3, 115.

24. Dewar, HMS *Prince of Wales*, diary entry, dated c. 1 January 1915, Dewar Papers, NMM. See also Rear Admiral Bernard Currey, diary entry "Notes on Loss of *Formidable*," dated c. 1 January 1915, Currey Papers, Liddell Hart Centre.

25. Dewar, *The Navy from Within*, 169. There is a pencilled addition to his diary that seems to refer to this conversation. The date of the addition is unknown, the original entry was written before 5 January 1915. Dewar Papers, NMM.

26. Dewar, HMS *Prince of Wales*, diary entry, dated 5 January 1915, Dewar Papers, NMM.

27. First Sea Lord to the Chief of the War Staff and First Lord, minute, dated 6 January 1915, Marder, *Fear God and Dread Nought*, vol. 3, 126.

28. Duff, HMS *Emperor of India*, diary entry, dated 3 January 1915, Duff Papers, NMM.

29. Duff, HMS *Emperor of India*, diary entry, dated 8 January 1915, Duff Papers, NMM.

30. Marder, *From the Dreadnought to Scapa Flow*, vol. 2, 99. See also *Naval Staff Monograph (Historical)*, vol. 12, *Home Waters*, part 3, 153.

31. Bayly, *Pull Together!*, 76.

32. Rear Admiral Bernard Currey, "Notes on Loss of *Formidable*," diary entry, dated c. 1 January 1915, Currey Papers, Liddell Hart Centre.

33. Morgan-Owen's "Cooked Up in the Dinner Hour" gives a new interpretation of how Wilson and Churchill's ideas were coming together by the end of 1914.

34. Temple Patterson, *Tyrwhitt of the Harwich Force*, 101.

35. Temple Patterson, *Tyrwhitt of the Harwich Force*, 101.

36. Frewen, HMS *Lookout,* diary entry, dated 8 (?) January 1915, Frewen Papers (no longer accessible).

37. Fisher to Churchill, letter, dated 21 December 1914, Gilbert, *Winston S. Churchill,* vol. 3, *Companion,* Part I *Documents*, 322.

38. Tyrwhitt to his wife, letter, dated 17 January 1915, Temple Patterson, *Tyrwhitt of the Harwich Force*, 102.

39. Groos, *Der Krieg zur See: Nordsee*, vol. 3, 235.

40. Tennant, HMS *Ferret,* diary entry, dated 19 January 1915, Tennant Papers, NMM.

41. Commander Wilfred Tomkinson, HMS *Lurcher,* diary entry, dated 20 January 1915, Tomkinson Papers, CCA.

Chapter 15. The Battle of the Dogger Bank

1. Keith Jeffery, *MI6: The History of the Secret Intelligence Service, 1909–1949* (London: Bloomsbury, 2010), 84–85. See also Michael Smith, *Six: A History of Britain's Secret Intelligence Service,* Part I, *Murder and Mayhem 1909–1939* (London: Dialogue, 2010), 113–20.

2. Philbin, *Admiral von Hipper*, 104.

3. Von Waldeyer-Hartz, *Admiral von Hipper*, 147.

4. C-in-C High Sea Fleet to S. O. Scouting Forces. Sent 1010 23 January 1915. All German signals in this chapter are taken from Groos, *Der Krieg zur See: Nordsee*, vol. 3, appendix VIII, 1 et seq.

5. There is a discussion of the issues involved in Philbin, *Admiral von Hipper*, 110–11.

6. Von Waldeyer-Hartz, *Admiral von Hipper*, 148.

7. Winston S. Churchill, *The World Crisis,* vol. 2 (Sydney: Australasian Publishing, 1925), 129.

8. Admiralty to Commodore (T), Telegram No. 58, 23 January 1915, sent 1200. Unless otherwise indicated, all British signals in this chapter are taken from *Naval Staff Monograph (Historical)*, vol. 3, no. 12, 219 et seq.

9. Young, *With the Battle Cruisers*, 176.

10. Oliver, *Memoirs,* vol. 2, 144, Oliver Papers, NMM.

11. Fisher to Churchill, letter, dated 25 January 1915, Gilbert, *Winston S. Churchill,* vol. 3, *Companion,* Part I, *Documents,* 449.

12. Young, *With the Battle Cruisers*, 177.

13. Kerr, *Prince Louis of Battenberg*, 288–89.

14. Battenberg to Captain Percy Tufton Beamish, letter, dated 16 May 1915, BEAM 2/10, Beamish Papers, CCA.

15. "The Admiralty came in," Young, *With the Battle Cruisers*, 178.

16. Young, *With the Battle Cruisers*, 179.

17. Temple Patterson, *Tyrwhitt of the Harwich Force*, 104–5.

18. Von Waldeyer-Hartz, *Admiral von Hipper*, 151.

19. "And radio analysis suggested," S. O. Scouting Forces to C-in-C High Sea Fleet Signal, sent 0809, 24 January 1915, Groos, *Der Krieg zur See: Nordsee*, vol. 3, Appen. 8, 2.

20. Von Waldeyer-Hartz, *Admiral von Hipper*, 151.

21. Von Waldeyer-Hartz, *Admiral von Hipper*, 152.

22. "Tactics of Two Fleets Engaged on Opposite Courses," C-in-C Home Fleets Memorandum No. 0235, 20 April 1914 (enclosing a paper by Captain W. W. Fisher), Backhouse Papers, NHB.

23. "Splendid Cats" was a popular term for *Tiger* and the ships in the *Lion* class.

24. Buist HMS *Princess Royal,* journal entry, dated 30 January 1915, BUIS/5, Buist Papers, CCA. See also the battle reports of the 13.5-inch gun units in TNA ADM 137/305.

25. Vice Admiral B. B. Schofield, " 'Jacky' Fisher, HMS *Indomitable* and the Dogger Bank Action: A Personal Memoir," in *Naval Warfare in the Twentieth Century,* ed. Gerald Jordan (New York: Crane Russak, 1977), 68.

26. "There was no mistaking," Young, *With the Battle Cruisers*, 190.

27. Commander R. A. R. Plunkett, "First Rough Notes," DRAX 1/47, Drax Papers, CCA.

28. Pelly, *300,000 Sea Miles*, 147.

29. Commanding Officer HMS *Tiger,* letter, dated 26 February 1915, TNA ADM 137/305.

30. The radio and visual logs are available in TNA ADM 137/305. *Lion's* appears to be an amalgam of the two put together after the event. *Tiger's* look to be original.

31. Chatfield, *The Navy and Defence*, 133.

32. Lieutenant Prince George of Battenberg, "The Engagement of the Dogger Bank," *Naval Review* 5 (1917), 152.

33. Scheer, *Germany's High Sea Fleet*, 84.

34. Young, *With the Battle Cruisers*, 191.

35. Korvettenkapitan Richard Foerster, "Der 24. Januar 1915," von Mantey, *Auf See unbesiegt*, vol. 1, 76.

36. Epkenhans, Hillmann, and Frank, *Skaggerakschlacht*, 239, fn d.

37. Etienne [King-Hall], *A Naval Lieutenant*, 79.

38. Young, *With the Battle Cruisers*, 194.

39. Lieutenant H. E. C. Blagrove to His Father, letter, dated 28 January 1915, Blagrove Papers, IWM.

40. Frewen, HMS *Lookout,* diary entry, dated 27 (?) January 1915, Frewen Papers (no longer accessible).

41. "Out of action," N. J. M. Campbell, *Battlecruisers: The Design and Development of British and German Battlecruisers of the First World War Era* (London: Conway, 1978), 29–30; "all but two," Lady Seymour, *Commander Ralph Seymour, RN* (Glasgow: University Press, 1926), 70.

42. Pelly, *300,000 Sea Miles*, 148–49.

43. Plunkett, "First Rough Notes," DRAX 1/47, Drax Papers, CCA.

44. Plunkett "First Rough Notes," DRAX 1/47, Drax Papers, CCA.

45. Admiralty, *Fleet Signal Book* (1906), 29–31, TNA ADM 186/657.

46. See Rear Admiral Moore's *apologia* in Rear Admiral Second Battle Cruiser Squadron, letter, 2/17, dated 7 February 1915, TNA ADM 137/305.

47. Gordon, *The Rules of the Game*, 95. See also "Battle Orders for 1st B. C.S dated 17th July 1913," DRAX 1/2, Drax Papers, CCA.

48. "Rattled us all," "There was a good deal," Pelly, *300,000 Sea Miles*, 150.

49. See Marder, *From the Dreadnought to Scapa Flow*, vol. 2, 163. This cites a letter from Admiral Drax to Marder dated 7 February 1962.

50. Von Waldeyer-Hartz, *Admiral von Hipper*, 153.

51. Philbin, *Admiral von Hipper*, 112.

52. Von Waldeyer-Hartz, *Admiral von Hipper*, 154.

53. Von Waldeyer-Hartz, *Admiral von Hipper*, 155.

54. Lady Seymour, *Commander Ralph Seymour, RN*, 67.

55. Tennant, HMS *Ferret,* diary entry, dated 24 January 1915, Tennant Papers, NMM.

56. Tennant, HMS *Ferret,* diary entry, dated 24 January 1915, Tennant Papers, NMM.

57. Young, *With the Battle Cruisers*, 214–15.

58. Tyrwhitt to his wife, letter, dated 27 January 1915, Temple Patterson, *Tyrwhitt of the Harwich Force*, 107.

59. Commander Barry Domvile, HMS *Miranda,* diary entry, dated 28 January 1915, Domvile Papers, NMM. See also Paymaster H. Miller, HMS *Arethusa,* cited in Thompson, *The Imperial War Museum Book,* 85.

60. Frewen, HMS *Lookout,* diary entry, dated 27 (?) January 1915, Frewen Papers (no longer accessible).

61. Lieutenant G. F. Bowen, RNVR, diary entry, 25 (?) January 1915, cited in Gordon S. Maxwell, *The Naval Front* (London: Black, 1920), 55.

62. Groos, *Der Krieg zur See: Nordsee,* vol. 3, 295.

63. Young, *With the Battle Cruisers,* 210.

64. See Matthew Seligmann, "The Battle Cruisers *Lion* and *Tiger* at Dogger Bank: The View of the Ships' Medical Officers," in *Warship 2013,* ed. Stephen Dent & John Jordan (London: Conway, 2013), 67–77.

65. Frewen, HMS *Lookout,* diary entry, dated 27 (?) January 1915, Frewen Papers (no longer accessible).

66. Domvile, HMS *Miranda,* diary entry, dated 28 January 1915, Domvile Papers, NMM.

Chapter 16. Seeking New Solutions

1. Groos, *Der Krieg zur See: Nordsee,* vol. 3, 272.

2. I am indebted to the late Dr. N. J. M. Campbell for this information. He made the discovery during his extensive research into the German damage reports produced in the repair yards.

3. Horn, *The Private War,* 60.

4. Philbin, *Admiral von Hipper,* 114.

5. Philbin, *Admiral von Hipper,* 113–15; "most favorable circumstances," 113.

6. Von Ingenohl, "Die Flottenführung im ersten Kriegshalbjahr und des Seekriegswerk," 18.

7. Captain Hans Zenker Minute, dated 1 February 1915, cited in Groos, *Der Krieg zur See: Nordsee,* vol. 3, 311–12.

8. Philbin, *Admiral von Hipper,* 117.

9. *Naval Staff Monograph (Historical),* vol. 13, *Home Waters,* part 4, *From February to July 1915,* 29.

10. Epkenhans, "Die Kaiserliche Marine 1914/15," 122–23.

11. I am indebted to Dr. David Stevens for this point.

12. Von Pohl to his wife, letter, dated 17 July 1915, von Pohl, *Aus Aufzeichnungen und Briefen,* 137.

13. Horn, *The Private War,* 98–99.

14. Fisher to Beatty Letters, dated 25, 27, and 31 January, Marder, *Fear God and Dread Nought,* vol. 3, 146, 147, 150; "I've quite made up," 150.

15. Churchill, *The World Crisis,* vol. 2, 146–47.

16. Jellicoe to Beatty, letter, dated 7 February 1915, Temple Patterson, *The Jellicoe Papers*, vol. 1, 142.

17. Fisher to Beatty, letter, dated 31 January, Marder, *Fear God and Dread Nought,* vol. 3, 150.

18. First Sea Lord, note, dated 2 May 1915, on Vice Admiral 1st Battle Cruiser Squadron, "Report of Action on 24th January 1915," TNA ADM 137/305.

19. "In a disturbed," Beatty to Jellicoe, letter, dated 8 February 1915, Temple Patterson, *The Jellicoe Papers*, vol. 1, 144.

20. Gordon, *The Rules of the Game,* 54–58.

21. Beatty to Keyes, letter, dated 18 September 1914, Halpern, *The Keyes Papers,* vol. 1, 29. The person is not named, but the letter is dated just after *New Zealand* had rejoined the 1st Battle Cruiser Squadron from Force K and while Force K itself was being recalled from Rosyth to rejoin the 1st Battle Cruiser Squadron.

22. "Well frankly," Beatty to Jellicoe, letter, dated 8 February 1915, Temple Patterson, *The Jellicoe Papers*, vol. 1, 144.

23. Churchill, *The World Crisis,* vol. 2, 141.

24. First Lord, file note, dated 11 February 1914, TNA ADM 137/305, fn196.

25. Jellicoe to secretary of the Admiralty, letter No. 443 Home Fleets 0022A, 3 March 1915, TNA ADM 137/305.

26. Jellicoe to Beatty, letter, dated 26 January 1915, Temple Patterson, *The Jellicoe Papers*, vol. 1, 130.

27. Interviews by the author with Vice Admiral B. B. Schofield, dated 18 December 1979 and Captain F. H. Kennedy, dated 27 December 1979.

28. Beatty to Jellicoe, letter, dated 8th February 1915, Temple Patterson, *The Jellicoe Papers*, vol. 1, 144–45.

29. "Good deal of chaos," Pelly, *300,000 Sea Miles*, 151.

30. Commanding Officer, HMS *Lion,* letter, "Remarks on Action 24 January 1915," dated 2 February 1915, BTY4/2, Beatty Papers, NMM.

31. *Naval Staff Monograph (Historical)*, vol. 3, no. 12, 221.

32. Hayward, *HMS Tiger at Bay*, 80.

33. N. J. M. Campbell, *Battlecruisers,* 40, 44, 50.

34. Hayward, *HMS Tiger at Bay,* 70–71.

35. Rear Admiral W. S. Chalmers, *The Life and Letters of David Earl Beatty* (London: Hodder & Stoughton, 1951), 210.

36. For which see Plunkett, "First Rough Notes," DRAX 1/47, Drax Papers, CCA.

37. "As Andrew Gordon has suggested," Gordon, *The Rules of the Game,* 96.

38. Young, *With the Battle Cruisers*, 224–25.

39. Norman Friedman, *British Cruisers: Two World Wars and After* (Annapolis, MD: Naval Institute Press, 2010), 41 et seq. for some of the early responses to postaction reports from 1914–15.

348   Notes to Pages 294–303

40. Commanding Officer, HMS *Lion,* letter, "Remarks on Action 24th January 1915," dated 2 February 1915, BTY4/2, Beatty Papers, NMM.

41. For a detailed analysis of the ammunition arrangements, see Nicholas A. Lambert "'Our Bloody Ships' or 'Our Bloody System'? Jutland and the Loss of the Battle Cruisers, 1916," *Journal of Military History* 62, no. 1, January 1998, 29–55.

42. Eric Grove, ed., "The Autobiography of Chief Gunner Alexander Grant: HMS *Lion* at the Battle of Jutland, 1916," in *Naval Miscellany* vol. 7, vol. ed. Susan Rose (Aldershot, UK: Navy Records Society & Ashgate, 2008), 370–406, esp. 388–90.

43. "Little success," Chief of the War Staff, note, dated 5 March 1915, fn90 (reverse), TNA ADM 137/305.

44. "Called the attention," Richmond to Plunkett letter, dated 15 (?) February 1915, DRAX 1/48, Drax Papers, CCA.

45. *Admiralty Weekly Order* No. 200, dated 12 February 1915, NHB.

46. "Never was promotion" Jellicoe to Beatty, letter, dated 25 February 1915, Temple Patterson, *The Jellicoe Papers*, vol. 1, 146.

47. Young, *With the Battle Cruisers*, 234.

48. Fisher to Beatty, letter, dated 3 February 1915, Marder, *Fear God and Dread Nought,* vol. 3, 152.

49. Beatty to Jellicoe, letter, dated 8 February 1915, Temple Patterson, *The Jellicoe Papers*, vol. 1, 143–44.

50. Beatty to Jellicoe, letter, dated 8 February 1915, Temple Patterson, *The Jellicoe Papers*, vol. 1, 144.

51. Jellicoe to Beatty, letter, dated 23 March 1915, Temple Patterson, *The Jellicoe Papers*, vol. 1, 152.

52. *Naval Staff Monograph (Historical)*, vol. 3, no. 12, 222.

53. Keyes, *The Naval Memoirs,* vol. 1, 173.

54. "Thought I might be," Keyes to his wife, letter, dated 30 January 1915, Halpern, *The Keyes Papers,* vol. 1, 77.

55. Share, *Under Great Bear and Southern Cross*, 218.

56. Lambert, *Planning Armageddon*, 476–80.

Chapter 17. Summa

1. See the series of letters, culminating in Jellicoe to Sturdee, letter, dated 17 November 1915, Sturdee Papers, CCA.

2. "For the leadership," see Surgeon Rear Admiral Michael Farquharson-Roberts, "To the Nadir and Back: The Executive Branch of the Royal Navy 1918–1939," PhD thesis, University of Exeter, UK, 2011, for an analysis of what was achieved in the junior officers.

3. See S. W. C. Pack, *Cunningham the Commander* (London: Batsford, 1974), 61–66, for this at work in the Mediterranean Fleet destroyers 1935–36 under A. B. Cunningham; "broken eggs," 64.

4. See Robin Brodhurst, *Churchill's Anchor: Admiral of the Fleet Sir Dudley Pound GCB, OM, GCVO* (Barnsley, UK: Pen & Sword, 2000), for a biographical study which gives an excellent insight into this outlook.

5. N. A. M. Rodger touches on this subject in "The Royal Navy in the Era of the World Wars: Was It Fit for Purpose?" *Mariner's Mirror* 97, no. 1, 2011.

6. As told to the author in 1979 by the late Captain F. H. Kennedy, RN, son of the captain of the *Indomitable* in 1914–15. The story is one that seems to have been well known in the Royal Navy.

BIBLIOGRAPHY

Books

Abbott, Patrick. *The British Airship at War, 1914–1918*. Lavenham, UK: Terence Dalton, 1989.

Andrew, Christopher. *Defend the Realm: The Authorised History of M.I.5*. London: Allen Lane, 2009.

Aspinall-Oglander, Brigadier C. F. *Roger Keyes*. London: Hogarth Press, 1951.

Bacon, Admiral Sir Reginald. *The Life of John Rushworth, Earl Jellicoe*. London: Cassell, 1936.

———. *The Life of Lord Fisher of Kilverstone*. London: Hutchinson, 1929.

Bayly, Admiral Sir Lewis. *Pull Together!* London: Harrap, 1939.

Beatty, Charles. *Our Admiral: A Biography of Admiral of the Fleet Earl Beatty 1871–1936*. London: W. H. Allen, 1980.

Beckett, Ian F. W., ed. *The Army and the Curragh Incident*. London: Army Records Society, 1986.

Bell, Christopher M. *Churchill and Sea Power*. London: Oxford University Press, 2012.

Bell Davies, Vice Admiral Richard. *Sailor in the Air: The Memoirs of the World's First Carrier Pilot*. Barnsley, UK: Seaforth, 2008.

Bennett, Captain Geoffrey. *Naval Battles of the First World War*. London: Batsford, 1968.

Bingham, Commander Barry. *Falklands, Jutland and the Bight*. London: John Murray, 1919.

Bird, Keith W. *Eric Raeder: Admiral of the Third Reich*. Annapolis, MD: Naval Institute Press, 2006.

Black, Nicholas. *The British Naval Staff in the First World War*. Woodbridge, UK: Boydell, 2009.

Bonatz, Heinz. *Die Deutsch Marine-Funkaufklärung 1914–1945*. Darmstadt, Germany: Wehr und Wissen, 1969.

Bradford, Vice Admiral Sir Edward. *Life of Admiral of the Fleet Sir Arthur Kynvet Wilson*. London: Murray, 1923.

Brodhurst, Robin. *Churchill's Anchor: Admiral of the Fleet Sir Dudley Pound GCB, OM, GCVO*. Barnsley, UK: Pen & Sword, 2000.

Brooks, John. *Dreadnought Gunnery and the Battle of Jutland*. London: Frank Cass, 2005.

Brown, David K. *The Grand Fleet: Warship Design and Development 1906–1922*. London: Chatham, 1999.

Brownrigg, Rear Admiral Sir Douglas. *Indiscretions of the Naval Censor*. London: Cassell, 1920.

Burt, R. A. *British Battleships 1889–1904*. Annapolis, MD: Naval Institute Press, 1988.

Busch, Fritz Otto, and Georg Gunther von Forstner, eds. *Unsere Marine im Weltkrieg*. Berlin: Brunnen-Verlag, 1934.

Bush, Eric. *Bless Our Ship*. London: Allen & Unwin, 1958.

Buxton, Ian. *Big Gun Monitors: Design, Construction and Operation 1914–1945*. Barnsley, UK: Seaforth, 2008.

Bywater, Hector. *Cruisers in Battle: Naval Light Cavalry under Fire 1914–18*. London: Constable, 1939.

Campbell, N. J. M. *Battlecruisers: The Design and Development of British and German Battlecruisers of the First World War Era*. London: Conway, 1978.

Campbell, Vice Admiral Gordon. *Number Thirteen*. London: Hodder & Stoughton, 1932.

Carew, Anthony. *The Lower Deck of the Royal Navy 1900–39: The Invergordon Mutiny in Perspective*. Manchester, UK: Manchester University Press, 1981.

Carr, William Guy. *Brass Hats and Bell Bottomed Trousers: Unforgettable and Splendid Feats of the Harwich Patrol*. London: Hutchinson, 1939.

———. *By Guess and by God*. London: Hutchinson, 1930.

Chalmers, W. S. *Full Circle: The Biography of Admiral Sir Bertram Ramsay*. London: Hodder & Stoughton, 1959.

———. *The Life and Letters of David Earl Beatty*. London: Hodder & Stoughton, 1951.

———. *Max Horton and the Western Approaches*. London: Hodder & Stoughton, 1954.

Chatfield, Admiral of the Fleet Lord. *The Navy and Defence*. London: Heinemann, 1942.

Churchill, W. S. *The World Crisis*. Vol. 1, *1911–1914*. Sydney: Australasian Publishing, 1925.

———. *The World Crisis*. Vol. 2, *1915*. Sydney: Australasian Publishing, 1925.

Clarke, W. F., and F. Birch. *A Contribution to the History of German Naval Warfare 1914–1918*. Vol. 1, *The Fleet in Action*. Held by Naval Historical Branch (unpublished).

Coles, Alan. *Three before Breakfast*. Havant, UK: Kenneth Mason, 1979.

Colvin, Admiral Sir Ragnar. *Memoirs of Admiral Sir Ragnar Colvin 1882–1954*. Durley, UK: Wintershill, 1992.

Corbett, Sir Julian S. *Maritime Operations in the Russo-Japanese War 1904–05* (with an introduction by John B. Hattendorf and Donald M. Schurman). Annapolis, MD: Naval Institute and Naval War College, 1994.

———. *Naval Operations,* vol. 1, *To the Battle of the Falklands December 1914.* London: Longmans Green, 1920.

Corbett, Sir Julian, Sir Henry Newbolt, and Lieutenant Colonel E. Y. Daniel. *History of the Great War: Naval Operations.* 4 vols. London: Longmans Green, 1920–1931. Revised 1938 (Vol. 1) and 1940 (Vol. 3).

Cork and Orrery, Admiral of the Fleet the Earl of. *My Naval Life 1886–1941.* London: Hutchinson, 1942.

Cradock, Captain Christopher. *Whispers from the Fleet,* 2nd ed. Portsmouth, UK: Griffin, 1908.

Cunninghame-Graham, Admiral Sir Angus. *Random Naval Recollections.* Privately published, Dumbartonshire, UK, 1979.

D'Enno, Douglas. *Fishermen against the Kaiser.* Vol. 1, *Shockwaves of War 1914–15.* Barnsley, UK: Pen & Sword Maritime, 2010.

Davison, Robert L. *The Challenges of Command: The Royal Navy's Executive Branch Officers, 1880–1919.* Farnham, UK: Ashgate, 2011.

Dawson, Captain Lionel. *Flotillas: A Hard Lying Story.* London: Rich & Cowan, 1929.

———. *Sound of the Guns: Being an Account of the Wars and Service of Admiral Sir Walter Cowan.* Oxford, UK: Pen-in-Hand, 1949.

Day, Vice Admiral Sir Archibald. *The Admiralty Hydrographic Service 1795–1919.* London: HMSO, 1967.

de Chair, Admiral Sir Dudley. *The Sea Is Strong.* London: Harrap, 1961.

Dewar, Vice Admiral K. G. B. *The Navy from Within.* London: Gollancz, 1939.

Domvile, Admiral Sir Barry. *By and Large.* London: Hutchinson, 1936.

Dreyer, Admiral Sir Frederic C. *The Sea Heritage: A Study of Maritime Warfare.* London: Museum Press, 1955.

Epkenhans, Michael, ed. *Das ereignisreiche Leben eines "Wilhelminers": Tagebücher, Briefe, Auzfeichnungen 1901 bis 1920.* Munich: R. Oldenbourg Verlag, 2004.

———. *Tirpitz: Architect of the German High Seas Fleet.* Washington, DC: Potomac, 2008.

Epkenhans, Michael, Jörg Hillmann, and Nägler Frank, eds. *Skagerrakschlacht: Vorgeschichte—Ereignis—Verarbeitung.* Munich: R. Oldenbourg Verlag, 2009.

Etienne [Stephen King-Hall]. *A Naval Lieutenant 1914–1918.* London: Methuen, 1919.

Firle, Rudolph. *Der Krieg zur See: Der Krieg in Der Ostsee.* Vol. 1. Berlin: Mittler, 1922. Translation available at the NHB.

Fisher, Admiral of the Fleet Lord. *Memories.* London: Hodder & Stoughton, 1919.

———. *Records.* London: Hodder & Stoughton, 1919.

Fisher, Fritz. *War of Illusions: German Policies from 1911 to 1914.* Translated by Marion Jackson. London: Chatto & Windus, 1975.

Fremantle, Admiral Sir Sidney. *My Naval Career 1880–1928*. London: Hutchinson, 1949.

Frewen, Oswald. *Sailor's Soliloquy*. Edited by G. P. Griggs. London: Hutchinson, 1961.

Friedman, Norman. *British Carrier Aviation: The Evolution of the Ships and their Aircraft*. Annapolis, MD: Naval Institute Press, 1988.

———. *British Cruisers: Two World Wars and After*. Annapolis, MD: Naval Institute Press, 2010.

———. *British Destroyers: From Earliest Days to the Second World War*. Annapolis, MD: Naval Institute Press, 2009.

———. *Naval Firepower: Battleship Guns and Gunnery in the Dreadnought Era*. Barnsley, UK: Seaforth, 2008.

———. *Naval Weapons of World War One*. Barnsley, UK: Seaforth, 2011.

———. *Network-Centric Warfare: How Navies Learned to Fight Smarter through Three World Wars*. Annapolis, MD: Naval Institute Press, 2009.

Gemzell, Carl-Axel. *Organization, Conflict and Innovation: A Study of German Naval Strategic Planning, 1888–1940*. Lund, Germany: Esselte Studium, 1973.

Gibson, Langhorne, and Vice Admiral J. E. T. Harper. *The Riddle of Jutland*. London: Cassell, 1934.

Gibson, R. H., and Maurice Prendergast. *The German Submarine War 1914–1928*, 2nd ed. London: Constable, 1931.

Gilbert, Martin. *Winston S. Churchill*. Vol. 3, *1914–1916: The Challenge of War*. Boston: Houghton Mifflin, 1971.

Gladisch, Admiral Walter. *Der Krieg zur See: Der Krieg in Der Nordsee*. Vols. 6–7. Berlin: Mittler, 1937 (both). British Admiralty Naval Historical Branch (NHB) translations (except vol. 7) are available at the NHB.

Goodenough, Admiral Sir William. *A Rough Record*. London: Hutchinson, 1943.

Gordon, Andrew. *The Rules of the Game: Jutland and British Naval Command*. London: John Murray, 1996.

Gorlitz, Walter, ed. *The Kaiser and His Court: The Diaries, Notebooks and Letters of Admiral Georg Alexander von Müller, Chief of the Naval Cabinet, 1914–1918*. London: Macdonald, 1961.

Gottschall, Terrell D. *By Order of the Kaiser: Otto von Diederichs and the Rise of the Imperial German Navy*. Annapolis, MD: Naval Institute Press, 2003.

Graf, H. *La Marine Russe dans la Guerre et dans la Revolution 1914–1918*. Paris: Payot, 1928.

Grainger, John D. *The Maritime Blockade of Germany in the Great War: The Northern Patrol, 1914–1918*. Aldershot, UK: Ashgate for the Navy Records Society, 2003.

Granier, Gerhard. *Magnus von Levetzow: Seeoffizier, Monarchist und Webereiter Hitlers*. Boppard, Germany: Boldt, 1982.

Grant, R. M. *U-Boats Destroyed*. London: Putnam, 1964.

———. *U-Boat Intelligence*. London: Putnam, 1969.

Greger, Rene. *The Russian Fleet 1914–1917*. Translated by Jill Gearing. London: Ian Allan, 1972.

Gretton, Vice Admiral Sir Peter. *Former Naval Person: Winston Churchill and the Royal Navy*. London: Cassell, 1968.

Grimes, Shawn T. *Strategy and War Planning in the British Navy, 1887–1918*. Woodbridge, UK: Boydell Press, 2012.

Gröner, Erich. *German Warships 1815–1945*. Vol. 1, *Major Surface Vessels*. Revised and expanded by Dieter Jung and Martin Maass. Annapolis, MD: Naval Institute Press, 1990. (First publication in English)

———. *German Warships 1815–1945*. Vol. 2, *U-Boats and Mine Warfare Vessels*. Revised and expanded by Dieter Jung and Martin Maass. Annapolis, MD: Naval Institute Press, 1991.

Groos, Captain Otto. *Der Krieg zur See: Der Krieg in Der Nordsee*. Vols. 1–5. Berlin: Mittler, 1920, 1922, 1923, 1924, 1925. Translations are available at the NHB.

Hackmann, Willem. *Seek and Strike: Sonar, Anti-Submarine Warfare and the Royal Navy 1914–1954*. London: HMSO, 1984.

Hallam, Richard, and Mark Beynon, eds. *Scrimgeour's Small Scribbling Diary 1914–1916*. London: Conway, 2008.

Halpern, Paul G. *The Keyes Papers: Selections from the Private and Official Correspondence of Admiral of the Fleet Baron Keyes of Zeebrugge*. Vol. 1, *1914–1918*. London: Navy Records Society, 1972.

———. *A Naval History of World War I*. Annapolis, MD: Naval Institute Press, 1994.

Hamilton, C. I. *The Making of the Modern Admiralty: British Naval Policy-Making, 1805–1927*. Cambridge, UK: University Press, 2011.

Hampshire, A. Cecil. *The Blockaders*. London: William Kimber, 1980.

———. *The Phantom Fleet*. London: William Kimber, 1977.

Hayward, Victor. *HMS Tiger at Bay: A Sailor's Memoir 1914–18*. London: William Kimber, 1977.

Herwig, Holger. *The German Naval Officer Corps: A Political and Social History*. Oxford, UK: Oxford University Press, 1973.

———. *Luxury Fleet: The Imperial German Navy 1888–1918*. London: Allen & Unwin, 1980.

Hezlet, Vice Admiral Sir Arthur. *The Aircraft and Sea Power*. London: Peter Davies, 1971.

———. *The Electron and Sea Power*. London: Peter Davies, 1975.

———. *The Submarine and Sea Power*. London: Peter Davies, 1967.

Hickling, Vice Admiral Harold. *Sailor at Sea*. London: William Kimber, 1965.

Hopman, Admiral. *Das Kriegstagebuch einers deutschen Seeoffiziers*. Berlin: August Scherl, 1925.

———. *Das Logbuch eines deutschen Seeoffiziers*. Berlin: August Scherl, 1924.

Horn, Daniel, ed. *The Private War of Seaman Stumpf: The Unique Diaries of a Young German in the Great War*. London: Leslie Frewin, 1969.

Hough, Richard. *The Big Battleship: The Curious Career of HMS Agincourt*. London: Michael Joseph, 1966.

———. *First Sea Lord: An Authorised Biography of Admiral Lord Fisher*. London: Allen & Unwin, 1969.

———. *Louis and Victoria: The Family History of the Mountbattens*. London: Weidenfeld & Nicholson, 1984.

Hoy, H. C. *Room 40 O. B.* London: Hutchinson, 1932.

Hubatsch, Walter. *Der Admiralstab und die obersten—Marine behörden in Deutschland, 1848–1945*. Frankfurt, Germany: Wehrwesen Bernard und Graefe, 1965.

Hyatt, A. M. J., ed. *Dreadnought to Polaris: Maritime Strategy since Mahan*. Toronto: Copp Clark, 1973.

James, Admiral Sir William. *The Eyes of the Navy: A Biographical Study of Admiral Sir Reginald Hall*. London: Methuen, 1955.

———. *A Great Seaman: The Life of Admiral of the Fleet Sir Henry Oliver*. London: Witherby, 1956.

———. *The Sky Was Always Blue*. London: Methuen, 1951.

Jameson, Rear Admiral Sir William. *The Fleet that Jack Built: Nine Men Who Made a Modern Navy*. London: Hart-Davis, 1962.

———. *The Most Formidable Thing*. London: Hart-Davis, 1965.

Jeffery, Keith. *MI6: The History of the Secret Intelligence Service, 1909–1949*. London: Bloomsbury, 2010.

Jellicoe, Admiral of the Fleet Viscount. *The Grand Fleet 1914–16: Its Creation, Development and Work*. London: Cassell, 1919.

Karau, Mark D. *"Wielding the Dagger": The Marinekorps Flandern and the German War Effort, 1914–1918*. Westport, CT: Praeger, 2003.

Keegan, John, ed. *Churchill's Generals*. London: Warner, 1992.

Kerr, Admiral Mark. *Land, Sea and Air: The Reminiscences of Mark Kerr*. London: Longmans, 1927.

———. *Prince Louis of Battenberg, Admiral of the Fleet*. London: Longmans, 1934.

Keyes, Roger. *The Naval Memoirs of Admiral of the Fleet Sir Roger Keyes*. Vol. 1, *The Narrow Seas to the Dardanelles 1910–1915*. London: Thornton Butterworth, 1934.

Kilduff, Peter. *Germany's First Air Force 1914–1918*. London: Arms & Armour, 1991.

King-Hall, Admiral Sir Herbert. *Naval Memories and Traditions*. London: Hutchinson, 1926.

King-Hall, Lady L. *Sea Saga*. London: Gollancz, 1935.

King-Hall, Stephen. *My Naval Life 1906–1929*. London: Faber & Faber, 1952.

Lambert, Nicholas A. *Planning Armageddon: British Economic Warfare and the First World War*. Cambridge, MA: Harvard University Press, 2012.

——. *Sir John Fisher's Naval Revolution*. Columbia: University of South Carolina Press, 1999.

——. *The Submarine Service 1900–1918*. Aldershot, UK: Ashgate, Navy Records Society, 2001.

Lambi, Ivo Nikolai. *The Navy and German Power Politics 1862–1914*. Boston: Allen & Unwin, 1984.

Langmaid, Kenneth. *The Approaches Are Mined!* London: Jarrolds, 1965.

Lavery, Brian. *Able Seamen: The Lower Deck of the Royal Navy 1850–1939*. London: Conway, 2011.

Layman, R. D. *Before the Aircraft Carrier: The Development of Aviation Vessels 1849–1922*. London: Conway, 1989.

——. *The Cuxhaven Raid: The World's First Carrier Air Strike*. London: Conway, 1985.

Le Bailly, Vice Admiral Sir Louis. *From Fisher to the Falklands*. London: Institute of Marine Engineers, 1991.

Liddle, Peter H. *The Sailor's War 1914–1918*. Poole, UK: Blandford, 1985.

Longmore, Air Chief Marshal Sir Arthur. *From Sea to Sky 1910–1945*. London: Geoffrey Bles, 1946.

Lumby, E. W. R. *Policy and Operations in the Mediterranean 1912–1914*. London: Navy Records Society, 1970.

Mackay, Ruddock F. *Fisher of Kilverstone*. Oxford, UK: Clarendon, 1973.

March, Edgar J. *British Destroyers, 1892–1953*. London: Seeley Service, 1966.

Marder, Arthur J. *Fear God and Dread Nought: The Correspondence of Admiral of the Fleet Lord Fisher of Kilverstone*. Vol. 1, *The Making of an Admiral 1854–1904*. London: Jonathan Cape, 1952.

——. *Fear God and Dread Nought: The Correspondence of Admiral of the Fleet Lord Fisher of Kilverstone*. Vol. 2, *Years of Power 1904–1914*. London: Jonathan Cape, 1956.

——. *Fear God and Dread Nought: The Correspondence of Admiral of the Fleet Lord Fisher of Kilverstone*. Vol. 3, *Restoration, Abdication and Last Years 1914–1920*. London: Jonathan Cape, 1959.

——. *From the Dreadnought to Scapa Flow: The Royal Navy in the Fisher Era*. Vol. 1, *The Road to War 1904–1914*. London: Oxford University Press, 1961.

——. *From the Dreadnought to Scapa Flow: The Royal Navy in the Fisher Era*. Vol. 2, *The War Years: To the Eve of Jutland 1914–1916*. London: Oxford University Press, 1965.

——. *Portrait of an Admiral: The Life and Papers of Admiral Sir Herbert Richmond*. London: Jonathan Cape, 1952.

Maxwell, Gordon S. *The Naval Front.* London: Black, 1920.

McKee, Christopher. *Sober Men and True: Sailor Lives in the Royal Navy 1900–1945.* Cambridge, MA: Harvard University Press, 2002.

Millett, Allan R., and Williamson Murray. *Military Effectiveness.* Vol. 1, *The First World War.* Boston: Unwin Hyman, 1988.

Moore, Major W. Geoffrey. *Early Bird.* London: Putnam, 1963.

Mountevans, Admiral Lord. *Adventurous Life.* London: Hutchinson, 1946.

Muir, Surgeon Rear-Admiral J. R. *Years of Endurance.* London: Philip Allan, 1936.

Munro, Captain D. J. *Scapa Flow: A Naval Retrospect.* London: Sampson Low, 1932.

Murfett, Malcolm H., ed. *The First Sea Lords: From Fisher to Mountbatten.* Westport, CT: Praeger, 1995.

Nekrasov, George M. *Expendable Glory: Russian Battleship in the Baltic 1915–1917.* New York: Columbia University Press, 2004.

———. *North of Gallipoli: The Black Sea Fleet at War 1914–1917.* New York: Columbia University Press, 1992.

Offer, Avner. *The First World War: An Agrarian Interpretation.* Oxford: Oxford University, 1989.

O'Hara, Vincent P., W. David Dickson, and Richard Worth, eds. *To Crown the Waves: The Great Navies of the First World War.* Annapolis, MD: Naval Institute Press, 2013.

Onward HMS New Zealand. Devonport, UK: Swiss & Co. 1919.

Osborne, Eric W. *The Battle of Heligoland Bight.* Bloomington: Indiana University Press, 2006.

Pack, S. W. C. *Cunningham the Commander.* London: Batsford, 1974.

Parkes, Oscar. *British Battleships.* London: Seeley Service, 1960.

Pavlovich, N. B. *The Fleet in the First World War.* Vol. 1, *Operations of the Russian Fleet.* Translated by C. M. Rao. New Delhi: Amerind, 1979.

Pelly, Admiral Sir Henry. *300,000 Sea Miles.* London: Chatto & Windus, 1938.

Persius, L. *Der Seekrieg.* Charlottenburg, Germany: Wettlübine, 1919.

Philbin, Tobias R. *Admiral von Hipper: The Inconvenient Hero.* Amsterdam: Gruner, 1982.

———. *Battle of Dogger Bank: The First Dreadnought Engagement.* Bloomington: Indiana University Press, 2014.

Plunkett, Lieutenant the Honorable R. *The Modern Officer of the Watch*, 4th ed. Portsmouth, UK: Griffin & Co., 1910.

Raeder, Erich. *Grand Admiral.* Cambridge, MA: Da Capo, 2001.

Ramsay, David. *"Blinker" Hall Spymaster: The Man Who Brought America into World War I.* Stroud, UK: Spellmount, 2008.

Ranft, B. McL. *The Beatty Papers: Selections from the Private and Official Correspondence of Admiral of the Fleet Earl Beatty.* Vol. 1, *1902–1918.* Aldershot, UK: Scolar Press for The Navy Records Society, 1989.

Rippon, M. *The Evolution of Engineering in the Royal Navy*. Vol. 1, *1827–1939*. Tunbridge Wells, UK: Spellmount, 1988.

Robinson, Douglas H. *The Zeppelin in Combat: A History of the German Naval Airship Division, 1912–1918*. London: Foulis, 1966.

Rollman, Heinrich. *Der Krieg zur See: Der Krieg in Der Ostsee*. Vol. 2. Berlin: Mittler, 1929. Translation available at the NHB.

Roskill, Stephen. *Admiral of the Fleet Earl Beatty: The Last Naval Hero: An Intimate Biography*. London: Collins, 1980.

———. *Churchill and the Admirals*. London: Collins, 1977.

———. *Documents Relating to the Naval Air Service*. Vol. 1, *1908–1918*. London: Navy Records Society, 1969.

———. *Hankey—Man of Secrets*. Vol. 1, *1877–1918*. London: Collins, 1970.

Scheer, Admiral. *Germany's High Sea Fleet in the World War*. London: Cassell, 1920.

Schofield, Vice Admiral B. B. *Navigation and Direction: The Story of HMS Dryad*. Havant, UK: Kenneth Mason, 1977.

Seligmann, Matthew S., ed. *Naval Intelligence from Germany: The Reports of the British Naval Attaches in Berlin 1906–1914*. Aldershot, UK: Ashgate and Navy Records Society, 2007.

———. *The Royal Navy and the German Threat, 1901–1914: Admiralty Plans to Protect British Trade in a War against Germany*. London, Oxford University Press, 1912.

Seymour, Lady. *Commander Ralph Seymour, RN*. Glasgow: University Press, 1926.

Share, Rear Admiral Sir Hamnet. *Under Great Bear and Southern Cross: Forty Years Afloat and Ashore*. London: Jarrolds, 1932.

Smith, Michael. *Six: A History of Britain's Secret Intelligence Service*. Part I, *Murder and Mayhem 1909–1939*. London: Dialogue, 2010.

Spindler, Rear-Admiral Arno. *Der Krieg zur See: Der Handelskrieg mit U-Booten*. Vol. 1. Berlin: Mittler, 1932. Translation available at the NHB.

Staff, Gary. *Battle on the Seven Seas: German Cruiser Battles 1914–1918*. Barnsley, UK: Pen & Sword Maritime, 2011.

———. *German Battlecruisers 1914–18*. Osprey, Oxford, 2006.

———. *German Battleships 1914–18* (pt. 1). Osprey, Oxford, 2010.

———. *German Battleships 1914–18* (pt. 2). Osprey, Oxford, 2010.

Strachan, Hew. *The First World War*. Vol. 1, *To Arms*. Oxford, UK: Oxford University Press, 2001.

Sueter, Admiral Murray. *Airman or Noahs*. London: Pitman, 1928.

Sumida, Jon Tetsuro. *In Defence of Naval Supremacy: Finance, Technology and British Naval Policy 1889–1914*. Boston: Unwin Hyman, 1989.

———, ed. *The Pollen Papers: The Privately Circulated Printed Works of Arthur Hungerford Pollen, 1901–1916*. London: George Allen & Unwin for The Navy Records Society, 1984.

Sweetman, Jack, ed. *The Great Admirals: Command at Sea, 1587–1945*. Annapolis, MD: Naval Institute Press, 1997.

Taffrail [Captain Taprell Dorling]. *Endless Story*. London: Hodder & Stoughton, 1931.

———. *Swept Channels*. London: Hodder & Stoughton, 1935.

Taylor, Gordon. *London's Navy: A Story of the Royal Naval Volunteer Reserve*. London: Quiller, 1983.

Taylor, John C. *German Warships of World War I*. London: Ian Allan, 1969.

Temple Patterson, A. *Jellicoe: A Biography*. London: Macmillan, 1969.

———. *The Jellicoe Papers: Selections from the Private and Official Correspondence of Admiral of the Fleet Earl Jellicoe of Scapa*. Vol. 1, *1893–1916*. London: Navy Records Society, 1966.

———. *Tyrwhitt of the Harwich Force: The Life of Admiral of the Fleet Sir Reginald Tyrwhitt*. London: MacDonald, 1973.

Thompson, Julian. *The Imperial War Museum Book of the War at Sea 1914–1918*. London: Sidgwick & Jackson, 2005.

Tracy, Nicholas. *Sea Power and the Control of Trade: Belligerent Rights from the Russian War to the Beira Patrol, 1854–1970*. Aldershot, UK: Ashgate for the Navy Records Society, 2005.

Tupper, Admiral Sir Reginald. *Reminiscences*. London: Jarrolds, 1929.

Tweedie, Admiral Sir Hugh. *The Story of a Naval Life*. London: Rich & Cowan, 1939.

Usborne, Vice Admiral C. V. *Blast and Counterblast: A Naval Impression of the War*. London: Murray, 1935.

von Hase, Georg. *Kiel and Jutland*. London: Skeffington, 1921.

von Mantey, Eberhard, ed. *Auf See unbesiegt: Erlebnisse im Seekrieg erzählt von Mitkämpfern*. Vol. 1. Munich: Lehmanns Verlag, 1922.

———, ed. *Auf See unbesiegt: Erlebnisse im Seekrieg erzählt von Mitkämpfern*. Vol. 2. Munich: Lehmanns Verlag, 1922.

von Pohl, Ella, ed. *Aus Aufzeichnungen und Briefen während der Kriegzseit von Admiral Hugo von Pohl*. Berlin: Karl Siegismund, 1920.

von Tirpitz, Grand Admiral Alfred. *My Memoirs*. London: Hurst and Blackett, 1919.

von Waldeyer-Hartz, Captain H. *Admiral von Hipper*. London: Rich & Cowan, 1933.

Watts, A. J. *The Imperial Russian Navy*. London: Arms & Armour, 1990.

Weir, Gary E. *Building the Kaiser's Navy: The Imperial Naval Office and German Industry in the von Tirpitz Era, 1880–1919*. Annapolis, MD: Naval Institute Press, 1992.

Wells, Captain John. *The Royal Navy: An Illustrated Social History, 1870–1982*. Stroud, UK: Sutton, 1994.

Wester Wemyss, Lady. *The Life and Letters of Lord Wester Wemyss*. London: Eyre & Spottiswoode, 1935.

Wilson, Michael. *Baltic Assignment: British Submariners in Russia 1914–1919*. London: Leo Cooper, 1985.

Wingate, John. *HMS Dreadnought: Battleship 1906–1920*. Profile Warship 1. Windsor, UK: Profile, 1970.

Winkler, Jonathan Reed. *Nexus: Strategic Communications and American Security in World War I*. Cambridge, MA: Harvard University Press, 2008.

Winton, John. *Jellicoe*. London: Michael Joseph, 1981.

Wolters, Timothy S. *Information at Sea: Shipboard Command and Control in the U.S. Navy, from Mobile Bay to Okinawa*. Baltimore: Johns Hopkins University Press, 2013.

Woodward, E. L. *Great Britain and the German Navy*. London: Oxford University Press, 1935.

Woollard, Commander C. L. A. *With the Harwich Naval Forces 1914–1918*. Private printing, Antwerp, 1931.

Young, Desmond. *Rutland of Jutland*. London: Cassell, 1963.

Young, Filson. *With the Battle Cruisers*. Introduction and notes by James Goldrick. Annapolis, MD: Naval Institute Press, 1986.

JOURNAL ARTICLES AND CHAPTERS

Barnett, Len. "A 'Well Known' Incident Reassessed: The German Attempted Mining of the Thames in August 1914." *Mariner's Mirror* 89, no. 2 (May 2003).

Battenberg, Lieutenant Prince George of. "The Engagement of the Dogger Bank." *Naval Review* 5 (1917).

Beckett, Ian F. W., and Keith Jeffery. "The Royal Navy and the Curragh Incident." *Historical Research* 62, no. 147 (1989).

Beesly, Patrick. "Cryptoanalysis and Its Influence on the War at Sea 1914–1918." Fifth Naval History Symposium. Annapolis, MD, 1981.

Bell, Christopher M. "Sir John Fisher's Naval Revolution Reconsidered: Winston Churchill at the Admiralty, 1911–1914." *War in History* 18, no. 3 (2011).

———. "On Standards and Scholarship: A Response to Nicholas Lambert." *War in History* 20, no. 3 (2013).

Bird, Keith W. "The Origins and Role of German Naval History in the Inter-War Period, 1918–1939." *Naval War College Review* 32, no. 2 (March–April 1979).

Epkenhans, Michael. "Die Kaiserliche Marine 1914/15." In Epkenhans et al., *Skagerrakschlacht: Vorgeschichte*, 113–38.

Foerster, Korvettenkapitan Richard. "Der 24. Januar 1915." In von Mantey, *Auf See unbesiegt*, vol. 1, 74–83.

Fox, Captain C. H. "The Destruction of the *Königin Luise* and the Sinking of the *Amphion*." *Naval Review* 5 (1917).

Goldrick, James. "Coal and the Advent of the First World War at Sea." *War in History* 21, no. 3 (2014).

———. "The Impact of War: Matching Expectations with Reality in the Royal Navy in the First Months of the Great War at Sea." *War in History* 14, no. 1 (2007).

———. "John R. Jellicoe: Technology's Victim (1859–1935)." In Sweetman, *The Great Admirals*, 364–87.

Grassmann, Korvettenkapitan Werner. "Die brave alte *Augsburg*." In von Mantey, *Auf See unbesiegt*, vol. 2, 195–205.

Grove, Eric, ed. "The Autobiography of Chief Gunner Alexander Grant: HMS *Lion* at the Battle of Jutland, 1916." In *The Naval Miscellany*. Vol. 7. Edited by Susan Rose. Aldershot, UK: Navy Records Society & Ashgate, 2008.

———. "Seamen or Airmen? The Early Days of British Naval Flying." In *British Naval Aviation: The First 100 Years*, edited by Tim Benbow. Farnham, UK: Ashgate, 2011.

Guilleaume, Kapitanleutnant Franz. "Die Todesfahrt der VII. Torpedoboots-Halbflottille (Thiele)." In von Mantey, *Auf See unbesiegt*, vol. 2, 96–106.

Hall, Captain S. S. "The Influence of the Submarine on Naval Policy—I." *Naval Review* 1, no. 3 (1913).

Halpern, Paul G., ed. "Dudley Pound in the Grand Fleet 1914–15." In *The Naval Miscellany*, vol. 6, edited by Michael Duffy. Aldershot, UK: Navy Records Society/Ashgate, 2003.

Halvorsen, Peter. "The Royal Navy and Mine Warfare, 1868–1914." *Journal of Strategic Studies* 27, no. 4 (2004).

Hammant, Thomas R. "Russian and Soviet Cryptology I—Some Communications Intelligence in Tsarist Russia." *Cryptologia* 24, no. 3 (July 2000).

Hattendorf, John B. "Admiral Prince Louis of Battenberg (1912–1914)." In Murfett, *The First Sea Lords*, 75–90.

Heinrich, Grand Admiral Prince. "Der Vorstöß S. M. S. *Blücher* vor dem finnischen Meerbusen am 6. September 1914." In von Mantey, *Auf See unbesiegt*, vol. 1, 32–38.

Herrick, Claire E. J. "Casualty Care during the First World War: The Experience of the Royal Navy." *War in History* 7, no. 2 (2000).

Herwig, Holger H. "The German Reaction to the Dreadnought Revolution." *International History Review* 13, no. 2 (1991).

Hewetson, Chaplain G. H. "A Contribution to the Study of Naval Discipline." *Naval Review* 1, no. 3 (1913).

Hiley, Nicholas. "The Strategic Origins of Room 40." *Intelligence and National Security* 2, no. 2 (1987).

Hines, Jason. "Sins of Omission and Commission: A Reassessment of the Role of Intelligence in the Battle of Jutland." *Journal of Military History* 72, no. 4 (October 2008).

Jones, David R. "Imperial Russia's Forces at War." In Millett and Murray, *Military Effectiveness*, vol. 1, *The First World War*.

Kennedy, Greg. "Intelligence and the Blockade, 1914–1917: A Study in Administration, Friction and Command." *Intelligence and National Security* 22, no. 5 (October 2007).

———. "Strategy and Power: The Royal Navy, the Foreign Office and the Blockade, 1914–1917." *Defence Studies* 8, no. 2 (2008).

Lambert, Andrew. "Looking for an Offensive Opportunity: The Royal Navy's War from the July Crisis to the Eve of Jutland." Published in German as " 'The possibility of ultimate action in the Baltic': Die Royal Navy im Krieg, 1914–1916." In Epkenhans et al., *Skagerrakschlacht: Vorgeschichte*, 73–112.

Lambert, Nicholas A. "Admiral Sir Arthur Kynvet-Wilson V. C." In Murfett, *The First Sea Lords*, 35–54.

———. "On Standards: A Reply to Christopher Bell." *War in History* 19, no. 2, 2012.

———. " 'Our Bloody Ships' or 'Our Bloody System'? Jutland and the Loss of the Battle Cruisers, 1916." *Journal of Military History* 62, no. 1 (January 1998).

———. "Strategic Command and Control for Maneuver Warfare: Creation of the Royal Navy's 'War Room' System, 1905–1915." *Journal of Military History* 69, no. 2 (April 2005).

———. "Transformation and Technology in the Fisher Era: The Impact of the Communications Revolution." *Journal of Strategic Studies* 27, no. 2 (2004).

Leyland, John. "Foreign Navies." In *The Naval Annual 1914*, edited by Viscount Hythe and John Leyland. London: Clowes, 1914, 28–65.

———. "Naval Manoeuvres." In *The Naval Annual 1909*, edited by T. A. Brassey. London: Griffin, 1909, 134–46.

Longmore, Air Chief Marshal Sir Arthur. "Naval Flying 1913/14." *Naval Review* 56, no. 2 (April 1968).

Martin, Christopher. "The Declaration of London: A Matter of Operational Capability." *Historical Research* 82, no. 218 (2009).

———. "The 1907 Naval War Plans and the Second Hague Peace Conference: A Case of Propaganda." *Journal of Strategic Studies* 28, no. 5 (2005).

Mclaughlin, Stephen. "Russia: Rossiiskii imperatorskii flot." In O'Hara et al., *To Crown the Waves*.

Morgan-Owen, David. "An "Intermediate Blockade"? British North Sea Strategy, 1912–1914." *War in History* 21, no. 1, 2014.

———. "Cooked Up in the Dinner Hour? Sir Arthur Wilson's War Plan, Reconsidered." *English Historical Review* (forthcoming).

Morley, S. "The Royal Navy of Lieutenant Commander W. E. V. Woods, RN." In *99 Years of Navy*, edited by S. Morley. London: Cpg, 1995, 28–56.

Nägler, Frank. "Operative und strategische Vorstellungen der Kaiserlichen Marine vor dem Ersten Weltkrieg." In Epkenhans et al., *Skaggerakschlacht: Vorgeschichte*, 19–56.

Offer, Avner. "Morality and Admiralty: 'Jacky' Fisher, Economic Warfare and the Laws of War." *Journal of Contemporary History* 23, no. 1 (January 1988).

Onlooker [Captain A. W. Clarke]. "The Fleet Air Arm—Another Fiftieth Anniversary." *Naval Review* 52, no. 4 (October 1964).

———. "H. M. Navigation School 1903–1968." *Naval Review* 56, no. 3 (July 1968).

Pfundheller, Konteradmiral Hans. "Der Durchbruch des Hilfskreuzers *Berlin*." In von Mantey, *Auf See unbesiegt*, vol. 2, 262–76.

Pitcairn-Jones, Commander L. J. "Navigation in War of 1914–1918." Lecture to the Royal Naval Staff College 1938 Session (Naval Historical Branch).

[Plunkett, Commander R. A. R.]. "With the Grand Fleet (4th January 1915)." *Naval Review* 2, no. 1 (February 1915).

Rodger, N. A. M. "The Royal Navy in the Era of the World Wars: Was It Fit for Purpose?" *Mariner's Mirror* 97, no. 1 (2011).

R. P. D. [Admiral Sir Reginald Plunkett-Ernle-Erle-Drax]. "D. B. II." Obituary in *Naval Review* 24, no. 2 (May 1936).

S. D. S. [Captain S. D. Spicer]. "The Fuel of the Future?" *Naval Review* 23, no. 2 (May 1935).

Schofield, Vice Admiral B. B. "'Jacky' Fisher, HMS *Indomitable* and the Dogger Bank Action: A Personal Memoir." In *Naval Warfare in the Twentieth Century*, edited by Gerald Jordan. New York: Crane Russak, 1977.

Sea Gee [Rear Admiral C. G. Brodie]. "Some Early Submariners I & II." *Naval Review* 50, no. 4 (November 1962): 426; 51, no. 1 (January 1963): 82, 51, no. 2 (April 1963): 189.

———. "Women Aboard." *Naval Review* 49, no. 4, October 1961.

Seebohm, Kontreadmiral Hans. "Der Endkampf S.M.S. *Ariadne*." In von Mantey, *Auf See unbesiegt*, vol. 2, 146–55.

Seligmann, Matthew. "The Battle Cruisers *Lion* and *Tiger* at Dogger Bank: The View of the Ships' Medical Officers." In *Warship 2013*, edited by Stephen Dent and John Jordan. London: Conway, 2013, 67–77.

———. "A German Preference for a Medium-Range Battle? British Assumptions about German Naval Gunnery, 1914–1915." *War in History* 19, no. 1 (2012).

Smith, Canfield F. "Essen, Nikolai Ottovich." In *The Modern Encyclopedia of Russian and Soviet History*. Vol. 10, *Do to Es*. Edited by Joseph L. Wieczynski. Gulf Breeze, FL: Academic International Press, 1979, 239–41.

Stevenson, Gene C. "Russian 'Lake' Type Submarines and the Baltic War 1914–1916." In *Warship 1990*, edited by Robert Gardiner. London: Conway, 1990.

Sumida, Jon Tetsuro. "British Naval Operational Logistics, 1914–1918." *Journal of Military History* 57, no. 3 (July 1993).

———. "Challenging Parkinson's Law." Seminar on World War I, Robert McCormick Tribune Foundation/ United States Naval Institute, August 1993. *Naval History* no. 8 (November–December 1994).

———. "Expectation, Adaptation and Resignation: British Battle Fleet Tactical Planning, August 1914–April 1916." *Naval War College Review* 60, no. 3 (Summer 2007).

———. "Forging the Trident: British Naval Industrial Logistics, 1914–1918." In *Feeding Mars: Logistics in Western Warfare from the Middle Ages to the Present*, edited by John A. Lynn. Boulder, CO: Westview Press, 1993.

———. "Geography, Technology and British Naval Strategy in the Dreadnought Era." *Naval War College Review* 59, no. 3 (Summer 2006).

———. "A Matter of Timing: The Royal Navy and the Tactics of Decisive Battle, 1912–1916." *Journal of Military History* 67 (January 2003).

Vinogradov, Sergei E. "Battleship Development in Russia from 1905 to 1917." Part I. *Warship International* 35, no. 3 (1998).

von Ingenohl, Admiral Friedrich. "Die Flottenführung im ersten Kriegshalbjahr und des Seekriegswerk." *Marine Rundschau* 1 (January 1923).

von Tirpitz, Wolfgang. "Der Untergang der *Mainz* am 28 August 1914." In von Mantey, *Auf See unbesiegt*, vol. 2, 18–25.

Weir, Gary E. "Reinhard Scheer: Intuition under Fire, 1863–1928." In Sweetman, *The Great Admirals,* 388–404.

Yankovich, V. "The Origins of Communications Intelligence." Translated by Thomas R. Hammant. *Cryptologia* 8, no. 3 (July 1984).

Unpublished Theses and Dissertations

Brown, W. M. "The Royal Navy's Fuel Supplies 1898–1939; The Transition from Coal to Oil." PhD dissertation, King's College, London, 2003.

Dunley, Richard. "The Offensive Mining Service: Mine Warfare and Strategic Development in the Royal Navy 1900–1914." PhD dissertation, King's College London, 2013.

Farquharson-Roberts, Surgeon Rear Admiral Michael. "To the Nadir and Back: The Executive Branch of the Royal Navy 1918–1939." PhD dissertation, University of Exeter, UK, 2011.

Randel, J. C. "Information for Economic Warfare: British Intelligence and the Blockade, 1914–1918." PhD dissertation, University of North Carolina, Chapel Hill, 1993.

Romans, Elinor. "Selection and Early Career Education of Officers in the Royal Navy, c 1902–1939." PhD thesis, University of Exeter, UK, 2012.

———. "The Supply of Scapa Flow in World War One." MA thesis, University of Exeter, UK, 2005.

Official Documents

Admiralty. *Baltic Pilot*. London: HMSO.

Admiralty. *Manual of Seamanship*. London: HMSO, 1915 (vol. 1) and 1909 (vol. 2).

Admiralty. *Narrative of the Battle of Jutland*. London: HMSO, 1924.

Admiralty. *The Navy List*. London: HMSO (monthly)

Admiralty. *North Sea Pilot*. London: HMSO.

Director of Naval Construction. *Notes on Damage to Warships: 1914–1919* (Naval Historical Branch), 1920.

Naval Staff, Admiralty. *Naval Staff Monographs (Historical)*.

> Vol. 3, Monograph 6, *Passage of the BEF* [British Expeditionary Force], *August 1914*.

> Vol. 3, Monograph 7, *The Patrol Flotillas at the Commencement of the War*.

> Vol. 3, Monograph 8, *Naval Operations connected with the Raid on the North-East Coast, December 16th 1914*.

> Vol. 3, Monograph 11, *The Battle of the Heligoland Bight, August 28th, 1914*.

> Vol. 3, Monograph 12, *The Action of Dogger Bank, January 24th 1915*.

> Vol. 6, Monograph 18, *The Dover Command*, vol. 1.

> Vol. 7, Monograph 19, *Tenth Cruiser Squadron—I*.

> Vol. 7, Monograph 25, *The Baltic 1914*.

> Vol. 9, *The Atlantic Ocean, 1914–15, Including the Battles of Coronel and the Falkland Islands* (no monograph number given).

> Vol. 10, *Home Waters*, Part 1, *From the Outbreak of War to 27 August 1914* (no monograph number given).

> Vol. 11, *Home Waters*, Part 2, *September and October 1914* (no monograph number given).

> Vol. 12, *Home Waters*, Part 3, *From November 1914 to the End of January 1915* (no monograph number given).

> Vol. 13, *Home Waters*, Part 4, *From February to July 1915* (no monograph number given).

> *The Economic Blockade 1914–1919* (CB 1554).

> *Grand Fleet Gunnery and Torpedo Memoranda on Naval Actions 1914–1918* April 1922 (OU [official use] 5444).

> *The History of British Minefields*.

> *History of British Minesweeping in the War* (CB [confidential book] *1553*).

> *The Naval Staff of the Admiralty. Its Work and Development* (CB 3013).

> *Operations off the East Coast of Britain 1914–1918* (OU 6354(40)).

> *Progress in Naval Gunnery 1914 to 1918* (CB 902).

> *Review of German Cruiser Warfare 1914–1918* (OU 6337(40)).

Naval Staff, Admiralty. *Technical Histories* (CB 1515 series).
> *Ammunition for Naval Guns* CB 1515(29)
> *Anti-Submarine Development and Experiments prior to December 1916*
>   CB 1515(40)
> *Control of Merchantile Movements* Part 1 CB 1515(30)
> *Defensive Armament of Merchant Ships* CB 1515(13)
> *The Development of the Gyro-Compass prior to and during the War*
>   CB 1515(20)
> *Fire Control in H.M. Ships* CB 1515(23)

Personal Manuscripts

Backhouse, Admiral of the Fleet Sir Roger. Papers. (Naval Historical Branch)
Baillie-Grohman, Vice Admiral H. T. Papers. (National Maritime Museum)
Beamish, Rear Admiral Percy Tufton. Papers. (Churchill College Archives)
Beatty, Admiral of the Fleet Earl. Papers. (National Maritime Museum)
Bethell, Admiral Sir Alexander. Papers. (Liddell Hart Centre)
Bethell, Lieutenant Maurice. Papers. (Liddell Hart Centre)
Blacklock, Captain R. W. Personal Reminiscences. (Liddle Archive)
Blagrove, Rear Admiral H. E. C. Letters. (Imperial War Museum)
Buist, Commander Colin. Midshipman's Journal. (Churchill College Archives)
Cardew, Lieutenant J. St.E. Journal. (Royal Navy Museum Library)
Chesterton, Able Seaman. Journal HMS *Bacchante*. (Royal Navy Museum
      Library)
Childers, Lieutenant Erskine (Imperial War Museum)
Churchill, Captain C. F. H. Interview. (Liddle Archive)
Clarke, Captain Arthur. Midshipman's Journal and Diary. (Churchill College
      Archives)
Clarke, William. Papers. (Churchill College Archives)
Creswell, Captain John (Churchill College Archives)
Crooke, Admiral Sir Henry. Diaries. (Churchill College Archives)
Currey, Admiral Bernard. Papers. (Liddell Hart Centre)
Daniel, Admiral Sir Charles. Diary. (Churchill College Archives)
De Winton, Captain F. S. W. Memoirs. (Liddell Hart Centre)
Denniston, Alfred. Papers. (Churchill College Archives)
Dewar, Vice Admiral K. G. B. Papers. (National Maritime Museum)
Domvile, Admiral Sir Barry. Diaries. (National Maritime Museum)
Downes, Commander A. B. Journals. (Royal Navy Museum Library)
Drage, Commander C. H. Diaries. (Imperial War Museum and Liddle Archive)
Dreyer, Admiral Sir Frederic. Journals. (Churchill College Archives)
Duff, Admiral Sir Alexander. Diaries. (National Maritime Museum)

Dumas, Admiral Philip (Imperial War Museum)

Farquhar, Captain Malcolm. Papers. (Royal Navy Museum Library)

Fletcher, Chief Petty Officer Edwin. Diaries. (Royal Navy Museum Library)

Frewen, Captain Oswald. Diaries. (Formerly held by Mrs. Oswald Frewen)

Godfrey, Admiral J. H. Memoirs. (Churchill College Archives)

Goldsmith, Vice Admiral Lennon. Letters. (Liddell Hart Centre)

Haddy, Eng. Rear Admiral Frederick. Letters. (Royal Navy Museum Library)

Haldane, T. G. N. Diary. (Churchill College Archives)

Hamilton, Admiral Sir Frederick. Papers. (National Maritime Museum)

Harper, Lieutenant Commander G. C. Diary. (Churchill College Archives)

Heath, Lieutenant Commander J. M. Midshipman's Journal. (Liddle Archive)

Hood, Rear Admiral Horace. Papers. (Churchill College Archives)

Howson, Captain John. Papers. (Liddell Hart Centre)

Jellicoe, Admiral of the Fleet Earl (British Library)

Kennedy, Admiral Frances. Papers. (Liddell Hart Centre)

King-Harman, Captain R. D. Letters. (Imperial War Museum)

Leslie, Shane. Papers. (Churchill College Archives)

MacGregor, Lieutenant Commander Donald. Letters. (Royal Navy Museum
    Library)

MacLiesh, Commander Fraser. Diaries. (Churchill College Archives)

Napier, Admiral Trevylyan. Papers. (Imperial War Museum)

Nichols, Captain C. A. G. Memoirs. (Liddle Archive)

Noble, Admiral Sir Percy. Papers. (Liddell Hart Centre)

Oliver, Admiral of the Fleet Sir Henry. Memoirs. (National Maritime Museum)

Owen, Commander B. W. L. Journal. (Imperial War Museum)

Perry, Allan Cecil. Memoirs. (Liddle Archive)

Plunkett-Ernle-Erle-Drax, Admiral Sir Reginald. Papers. (Churchill College
    Archives)

Pound, Admiral of the Fleet Sir Dudley. Diary. (Imperial War Museum)

Ramsay, Admiral Sir Bertram. Diary. (National Maritime Museum)

Richmond, Admiral Sir Herbert. Papers. (National Maritime Museum)

Schofield, Vice Admiral B. B. Midshipman's Journal. (Imperial War Museum)

Shearer, G. Papers. (Royal Navy Museum Library)

Shearer, W. Papers. (Royal Navy Museum Library)

Somerville, Admiral of the Fleet Sir James. Diaries. (Churchill College Archives)

Sturdee, Admiral of the Fleet Sir Doveton. Papers. (Churchill College Archives)

Tennant, Admiral Sir William. Diaries. (National Maritime Museum)

Tomkinson, Vice Admiral Wilfred. Diaries. (Churchill College Archives)

Voysey, Sub Lieutenant T. A. Journals. (Royal Navy Museum Library)

Walters, Commander Jack. Diary. (Liddell Hart Centre)

Ward-Smith Paymaster Captain Guy. Papers. (Royal Navy Museum Library)

Wintour, Captain C. J. Diaries. (Imperial War Museum)

INDEX

ABOUT THE AUTHOR

JAMES GOLDRICK commanded HMA ships *Cessnock* and *Sydney* (twice), the multinational maritime interception force in the Persian Gulf, and the Australian Defence Force Academy during his service in the Royal Australian Navy. As a two-star rear admiral, he led Australia's Border Protection Command and then the Australian Defence College. His books include *No Easy Answers: The Development of the Navies of India, Pakistan, Bangladesh and Sri Lanka* and, with Jack McCaffrie, *Navies of South-East Asia: A Comparative Study.*

The Naval Institute Press is the book-publishing arm of the U.S. Naval Institute, a private, nonprofit, membership society for sea service professionals and others who share an interest in naval and maritime affairs. Established in 1873 at the U.S. Naval Academy in Annapolis, Maryland, where its offices remain today, the Naval Institute has members worldwide.

Members of the Naval Institute support the education programs of the society and receive the influential monthly magazine *Proceedings* or the colorful bimonthly magazine *Naval History* and discounts on fine nautical prints and on ship and aircraft photos. They also have access to the transcripts of the Institute's Oral History Program and get discounted admission to any of the Institute-sponsored seminars offered around the country.

The Naval Institute's book-publishing program, begun in 1898 with basic guides to naval practices, has broadened its scope to include books of more general interest. Now the Naval Institute Press publishes about seventy titles each year, ranging from how-to books on boating and navigation to battle histories, biographies, ship and aircraft guides, and novels. Institute members receive significant discounts on the Press's more than eight hundred books in print.

Full-time students are eligible for special half-price membership rates. Life memberships are also available.

For a free catalog describing Naval Institute Press books currently available, and for further information about joining the U.S. Naval Institute, please write to:

Member Services
U.S. Naval Institute
291 Wood Road
Annapolis, MD 21402-5034
Telephone: (800) 233-8764
Fax: (410) 571-1703
Web address: www.usni.org